Environmental Policy with Political and Economic Integration

NEW HORIZONS IN ENVIRONMENTAL ECONOMICS

General Editor: Wallace E. Oates, *Professor of Economics, University of Maryland*

This important new series is designed to make a significant contribution to the development of the principles and practices of environmental economics. It will include both theoretical and empirical work. International in scope, it will address issues of current and future concern in both East and West and in developed and developing countries.

The main purpose of the series is to create a forum for the publication of high quality work and to show how economic analysis can make a contribution to understanding and resolving the environmental problems confronting the world in the late 20th century.

Environmental Policy with Political and Economic Integration

The European Union and the United States

Edited by

John B. Braden
Professor of Agricultural Economics; Director, Water Resources Center and Head, Program on Environmental and Resource Economics, University of Illinois at Urbana-Champaign

Henk Folmer
Professor of Economics, Waginengen Agricultural University

Thomas S. Ulen
Professor of Law and Economics, University of Illinois at Urbana-Champaign

Edward Elgar
Cheltenham, UK • Brookfield, US

Published by
Edward Elgar Publishing Limited
8 Lansdown Place
Cheltenham
Glos GL50 2HU
UK

Edward Elgar Publishing Company
Old Post Road
Brookfield
Vermont 05036
US

British Library Cataloguing in Publication Data
Environmental Policy with Political and
Economic Integration: European Union and
the United States. – (New Horizons in
Environmental Economics Series)
  I. Braden, John B. II. Series
  333.7

Library of Congress Cataloguing in Publication Data
Environmental policy with political and economic integration : the
  European Union and the United States / edited by John B. Braden,
  Henk Folmer, Thomas S. Ulen.
    (New horizons in environmental economics)
    1. Environmental policy—European Union countries.
  2. Environmental policy—United States. 3. European Union
  countries—Economic policy. 4. United States—Economic
  policy—1993–   I. Braden, John B. II. Folmer, H. (Henk)
  III. Ulen, Thomas. IV. Series.
  GE190.E85E58   1995
  363.7'0094—dc20   94–45014
                                    CIP

ISBN 1 85898 217 0

Printed and bound in Great Britain by
Hartnolls Limited, Bodmin, Cornwall

Contents

v

Figures

Tables

Contributors

Lars Bergman
Professor of Economics, Stockholm School of Economics, Sweden

John B. Braden
Professor of Agricultural Economics; Director, Water Resources Center and Head, Program on Environmental and Resource Economics, University of Illinois at Urbana-Champaign, USA

Wim Brussaard
Professor of Agricultural Law, Physical Planning Law and Environmental Law, Department of Agrarian Law, Wageningen Agricultural University, the Netherlands

Kent Hughes Butts
Associate Professor of Political Military Strategy, Center for Strategic Leadership, US Army War College, USA

Simon Dalby
Assistant Professor, Department of Geography, Carleton University, Canada

Eric T. Freyfogle
Professor of Law, University of Illinois at Urbana-Champaign, USA

Henk Folmer
Professor of Economics, Waginengen Agricultural University, the Netherlands

Margaret Rosso Grossman
Professor of Agricultural Law, Department of Agricultural Economics, University of Illinois at Urbana-Champaign, USA; Visiting Professor (1993–94), Department of Agrarian Law, Wageningen Agricultural University, the Netherlands

Charles W. Howe
Professor of Economics and Director, Environment and Behaviour Program, Institute of Behaviroal Science, University of Colorado, USA

Charles D. Kolstad
Professor of Economics, Institute for Environmental Studies and Department of Economics, University of Illinois at Urbana-Champaign, USA

Rüdiger Pethig
Professor of Economics, University of Siegen, Germany

James E. Pfander
Associate Professor of Law, University of Illinois at Urbana-Champaign, USA

Stef Proost
Associate Professor of Economics and Research Fellow of the Belgian National Fund for Scientific Research, Catholic University of Leuven, Belgium

C. Ford Runge
Professor, Department of Agricultural and Applied Econcomics, Hubert H. Humphrey Institute of Public Affairs and Department of Forest Resources, Center for International Food and Agricultural Policy, University of Minnesota, USA

Kathleen Segerson
Associate Professor of Economics, University of Connecticut, USA

Perry Shapiro
Professor of Economics, University of California at Santa Barbara, USA, and Federalism Reseearch Center, Research School of Social Science, Australian National University, Australia.

James S. Shortle
Professor of Agricultural Economics, Pennsylvania State University, USA

Thomas S. Ulen
Professor of Law and of Economics, University of Illinois at Urbana-Champaign, USA

Alistair Ulph
Professor of Economics, University of Southampton, UK

1. Introduction

John B. Braden, Henk Folmer and Thomas S. Ulen

INTRODUCTION

Most scholars of environmental problems and policies base their analysis on the assumption that a unitary government implements policies by imposing constraints or conferring benefits on firms and consumers. But many jurisdictions of environmental policy do not have a unitary government; rather, they are federations or confederations. The United States is the most prominent example of a federation; the European Union, of a confederation.[1] Other examples of federations are Australia, Belgium, Canada, Germany, India, and Switzerland, while new confederations are on the verge of developing – notably those constructed to achieve market harmonization, such as the North American Free Trade Agreement (NAFTA) or the MERCOSUR in South America.

A basic feature of both federations and confederations is that the central, regional, and local governments share the power to impose policy. A notable difference is that in a federal system the central government has at least some direct power over citizens (e.g., to impose personal income taxes) while in a confederation only the constituent states may have direct powers over citizens. Moreover, in a federal system there are usually some areas that are the exclusive domain of the federal government, such as defense, monetary policy, and foreign policy while in a confederation the ultimate power is with the Member States.

Environmental policy in a federal or confederal system may deviate substantially from 'textbook environmental policy' in both theory and practice. Given the increase in environmental policy-making in (con)federal contexts and the fact that environmental scientists, including environmental economists, have paid relatively little attention to it, we believe that this issue should be on the research agenda. Several research problems present themselves, for example:

1. What is the most appropriate level of environmental policy-making in a (con)federal system? Of course, it may turn out that there is no unique optimal level for all problems, but that the optimal level varies along with

1

the problem at hand. Moreover, in some cases the optimum may consist of a combination of controls at different levels of government.

2. To further environmental goals, is there a need for harmonization of product norms, product standards and technical regulations by the federal or central government?

3. How does the level of government at which policy is made and implemented affect the choice of policy instruments?

The purpose of this volume is to develop some hypotheses with respect to these research problems by comparing various environmental policies and practices in the United States (US) and the European Union (EU).

FOUNDATIONS OF ENVIRONMENTAL POLICY AND OF FEDERAL AUTHORITY IN THE EU AND THE US

Part I of this book ('The economic and philosophical foundations of environmental policy') presents the basic framework for environmental policy in the EU and the US. The chapter by Charles W. Howe provides a comparative overview from an economist's point of view, and that by Eric Freyfogle presents and criticizes the fundamental moral and ethical justifications for environmental policy. There is a healthy tension between these two chapters. Professor Howe finds economics to be the principal guide to designing environmental policy in both Europe and the United States. By contrast, Professor Freyfogle finds much to criticize in the economic view of environmental policy and much to praise in a moral conception of the environment.

The papers in Part II ('The law and economics of authority in a federal system') by James E. Pfander and Perry Shapiro describe and contrast the federal institutions in the US and the EU. The usual distinction ascribed to the powers of the central government in a federation and a confederation – combined with the fact that the EU is a confederation and the US, a federation – would seem to suggest profound differences between the ability of the EU and the US to make coherent and consistent environmental policy. However, Professor Pfander finds that the distinctions between federal authority in the EU and the US are more apparent than real. Professor Shapiro uses economic analysis to discuss the most efficient division of responsibility for environmental policy in a federation.

A. The Institutional Framework for Environmental Policy

Many readers may not be familiar with the institutional framework within which environmental policy operates in the EU and the US. We, therefore, give this brief introduction.

1. The institutions of the European Union

The Treaty of Rome (1957), the legal cornerstone of an integrated Europe, divides central authority between the following four Community institutions:

- *The Commission of the European Community*, consisting of seventeen representatives chosen for four-year terms, performs both legislative and executive functions.[2] The Commission initiates legislative proposals, including directives and regulations. A directive requires each Member State to enact Community obligations into positive national law but leaves them with some implementation discretion. A regulation, on the other hand, is binding in its entirety and directly applicable in all Member States. In practice, the distinction between regulations and directives has eroded over time.
- *The Council of the European Union*, consisting of representatives of each of the twelve Member States, is the principal legislative body of the Union. It enacts Commission proposals into law. The members of the Council are Ministers from each Member State with full power to commit their national governments. The exact membership of the Council changes depending on the subject matter; for example, when agricultural policies are at issue, the Council may consist of the Ministers of Agriculture from each of the Member States.
- *The Court of Justice*, consisting of thirteen judges chosen for six-year terms, passes on the legality of legislation enacted by the Council and on the extent of Member State compliance.
- *The European Parliament*, consisting of 567 members directly elected (since 1979) by the 350 million people of the Member States, serves to supervise and advise the Commission and monitors Union policies by means of questions submitted to the Commission and the Council. Since the passage of the Single European Act and the Maastricht Treaty (1992), the Parliament has become more important in the adoption of directives and regulations.

Environmental policy at the level of the Community is rather new in the EU. Most observers trace it to the Paris Summit meeting of the heads of states in 1972. Since then the Council of the European Union has drafted a series of action programs that identify goals for environmental policy. Environmental policy initiatives take justification from Article 100 of the Treaty of Rome, which specifies that the Council shall issue directives.[3]

The division of authority in the Union locates a substantial measure of legislative power in the Commission by giving it control over the kinds of proposals that come before the Council for a vote. In practice, however, the legislative process has been characterized by intergovernmental bargaining. The reason is that the Council has institutionalized a process of Commission consultation with Council representatives.

The 1986 Single European Act (SEA) introduced some important changes in the framework of environmental policy-making. In particular, it provides an explicit legal basis for environmental policy at Community level. More specifically, it requires the environmental dimension to be an integral part of Community policies (Article 130r) and Commission proposals to give high priority to environmental protection (Article 130a).

After the Council adopts directives or regulations regarding environmental policy, the Member States must comply, either by conforming their own law to that of the Union or by enforcing the regulations adopted by the Council. Rather than creating a central enforcement agency, the Union relies upon Member States for monitoring and enforcement of environmental laws. If the members fail to comply, the Commission notifies them of their non-compliance and seeks to have the law enforced. If a settlement cannot be achieved between the Commission and the Member State, then the Commission may file an action against the member in the Court of Justice.[4]

It has gradually become clear that the Union's dependence on Member State-monitoring and enforcement is an important weakness of the control system. As a result, there have been various proposals for change. Among these are the strengthening of monitoring and enforcement powers of central institutions, such as a European Environmental Agency; a requirement that Member States report on the state of practical implementation along; a campaign to heighten public awareness of Member State non-compliance, designed to place more pressure for implementation on national governments; the authorization of the Court of Justice to impose penalty payments for non-compliance; the greater use of regulations, rather than directives; broadening of the doctrine of direct effect; and creating a greater political voice for environmental activists.

2. The institutions of the United States

The United States Constitution vests legislative power in a bicameral Congress, the executive power in the Presidency, which includes executive agencies, and the judicial power in one Supreme Court and such inferior courts as the Congress chooses to establish. Moreover, powers not delegated to the United States are reserved to the states or the people.

In a number of areas, notably interstate commerce and foreign affairs, the Constitution authorizes the national government to pass laws directly applicable to citizens of the US. Moreover, Congress's power over interstate commerce provides plenary authority over environmental regulation. However, Congress does not have the power to issue European-style directives to the states. When Congress decides to enter a field of environmental policy it has two options.

- It can establish national policies that preempt state enactments.
- It can utilize techniques of discretion or delegation that preserve state competence. In particular, it may develop a policy that leaves state law in place, or it may affirmatively delegate lawmaking competence to the states. Moreover, through positive or negative inducements, it can encourage states to cooperate with federal policies.

Congress has typically preferred the latter option. One of its advantages is that it permits the states to fashion innovative environmental policies and, indeed, to pursue more stringent policies than those of the Federal government. In contrast to European directives, however, the US statutes often leave the states a choice. The states can agree to adopt a policy or let the federal agency handle the problem.

With respect to enforcement, the executive agency in charge, the US Environmental Protection Agency (USEPA), must at first instance approve an enforcement plan for each state that elects to administer its own program to implement federal law. Moreover, the adequacy of the state's implementation and enforcement remains subject to ongoing oversight. If a state fails to meet federal standards, the EPA can take over enforcement responsibilities or impose sanctions. In some cases, however, the EPA fails to approve a state implementation plan or approves it in part, and this creates a legal twilight zone. In a departure from the European model the EPA can fill such a gap by supplying its own plan, although this may create other problems. A final source of enforcement authority appears in the citizen-suit provisions of US laws. Much like the doctrine of direct effect in the EU, these provisions authorize certain persons or groups with legal standing to institute a civil action to remedy alleged violations of federal environmental standards.

With respect to the federal–state relationship in pollution control, pleas for reform can be heard ranging from complete federal takeover to full devolution of responsibility to the states. The main argument in favor of the former is the inadequacy of state enforcement; of the latter, the notion that the Federal government has moved too far and too fast to impose uniform requirements on all states, without due regard for local circumstances. Nonetheless, the nature of the federal–state relationship is not likely to change dramatically in coming years. There is insufficient fiscal latitude at either level to afford a major shift in regulatory responsibilities; most states prefer to cooperate rather than compete with the federal agenda; and many environmental problems are regional or even global in scope and cannot be addressed state-by-state.

3. Comparing EU and US environmental institutions

In comparing the US and EU approaches to environmental governance, one of the major differences is the nature and use of directives. This difference has important consequences for the issues of instrument choice and the level of policy-making in environmental matters, and so it warrants closer attention, which it receives in the chapter by James Pfander.

Directives have the following clear advantages.

- They promote regulatory efficiency when the administrative schemes are already in place, as in the EU Member States.
- They offer greater regulatory flexibility relative to regulations. This is especially attractive in the context of cultural and legal heterogeneity.
- Economic inefficiency from inappropriate standards can be avoided.
- Member States retain control over their own environmental policy. In particular, they can adopt more restrictive requirements in certain areas and respond to pervasive desires for more local control of policy.

Despite these advantages, most European observers view the directive as too weak and hence recommend regulations as a more effective tool of environmental policy. Moreover, they seek to improve Member State enforcement of existing directives through an expanded enforcement and monitoring role for Union institutions, increased access to citizen suits, and broader sanctions for Member States in violation of Treaty obligations. In the US, on the other hand, the directive is viewed as too potent a tool – the fear is that, if the directive were available in the US, Congress would impose unfunded regulatory obligations. Moreover, there is also concern that the use of directives would drain state political processes of any content because state legislatures would be reduced to the role of merely adopting federally-specified standards into law.

In operation, environmental directives have accomplished less than might be expected. A major problem is that Europe has experienced non-compliance with directives that emerged unanimously from the Council. While the European Court of Justice has limited authority to declare the content of European law, it lacks the power to exercise direct appellate review of decisions of Member State courts. Under Article 169, the Court has jurisdiction over claims that a Member State has violated its obligations under the Treaty, and Article 171 grants authority to assess penalties for violation.

By comparison, in the US the courts have much stronger remedial powers. They can issue injunctions to state officials and award monetary judgments against states to compensate the claimants in civil suits.

In addition, directives have been weak because the EU lacks administrative and enforcement competence that might enable it to preempt Member States or induce them into action, as can the US government. The Commission cannot regulate directly, cannot threaten Member States with the partial preemption of their environmental programs, and lacks any sizeable environmental fund with which to induce Member State compliance with its decrees. Therefore, it has to rely on directives. By contrast, the US Congress can achieve its objectives through a broader array of mechanisms.

Arguably, the weakness of directives contributed to the adoption of a system of qualified majority voting in the Single European Act. This change has weakened Member State control over the final legislative product of the Community and increased the autonomy of the Commission.

INSTRUMENT CHOICE AND INTERNATIONAL TRADE

One of the most fundamental issues in a (con)federal context of environmental policy is how the decentralization that is desirable because of regionally different physical systems and social values can be reconciled with the existence of environmental externalities that imply the need for central environmental policy and enforcement. The preceding section showed that such a reconciliation is achieved, at least in part, through both European directives and American policies that leave state law in place or affirmatively delegate lawmaking to the states. In this section, and in Part III of the book, we examine some of the important economic forces affecting environmental governance.

In addition to directives and regulations, another structure provided by the Single European Act is the *subsidiarity principle*. It states that the primary responsibility and decision-making competence should rest with the lowest possible level of the political hierarchy capable of handling a particular problem. This principle implies that internal problems of the Member States, such as land use, should be handled at the national level, except when transnational interests are involved.

It follows that the need for harmonization of different environmental policies seems to be limited to those cases where transnational externalities exist. Moreover, the institutions for this kind of policy are in place. However, there are some caveats that relate to one of the most fundamental reasons for the establishment of (con)federations—the promotion of the free movement of goods.

Kathleen Segerson reviews both the positive and normative literature on the choice of policy instrument as it applies to environmental policy. She shows that, when environmental policy seeks to achieve goals other than static efficiency, there is no uniquely best policy instrument. Rather, it is better to use a combination of instruments, such as regulation, taxes, and civil liability. In practice, the actual instruments chosen reflect considerations of efficiency and other societal goals but also reflect, in a positive sense, political pressures from affected interest groups and geographical constituencies, and the like. When one adds the further complications that are likely to arise in coordinating policies between the central government and its constituent states in a federation, it becomes even more difficult to specify a single best environmental policy instrument. The implication is that in a federal setting environmental policy is a political art in which one attempts to do the best that one can do.

Rüdiger Pethig discusses how matters of strategic behavior are likely to affect plant location choice. In the case of mobile capital under perfect information, internationally-uncoordinated national environmental policies induce allocative distortions when countries are self-interested. It is not so much the weight of environmental regulations relative to the other location factors that matter, but rather the proportion that differences in abatement costs form in differences in fixed and variable costs as well as differences in profits between different locations. Moreover, with inter-industry linkages, environmental policies can trigger demand-side considerations that can amplify or dampen pressures to relocate. Finally, the endogeneity of market structure and the existence of scale economies have to be taken into account. Because in the strategic non-cooperative equilibrium at least one country may be worse off after market liberalization, there is scope for coordination of national environmental policies. The basic question, however, is how the supranational agency gets all the necessary information on national environmental damages and abatement costs and on the operation of the international capital market. The upshot is that harmonization of environmental policy in a (con)federal setting may be required not only for reasons of transboundary pollution but also because the individual Member States engage in inefficient strategic behavior in order to attract capital.

In Part IV, Alistair Ulph examines the linkages between trade and environmental policy. He argues that, in the absence of strategic behavior and in the case of a small country, liberalizing trade in a good with adverse, uncontrolled, localized environmental impacts improves a small country's welfare if, following liberalization, it imports the good. However, if it exports the good, the negative environmental effects must be subtracted from the gains from trade and the welfare effect is ambiguous. If optimal environmental policies are implemented in each country, trade liberalization will produce an unambiguous gain in per-capita income and national welfare through increased allocative efficiency, whether a small country is an importer or an exporter. However, economic growth usually also leads to sectoral restructuring. An improvement of the financial positions of firms and of the government debt and changes in the composition of output may trigger positive environmental impacts. For instance, better financial positions of firms and scale enlargement may allow environmentally friendly investments while growth in GDP in combination with a demand for environmental protection may lead to technological improvements. Without environmental policy, however, the pure trade benefits of liberalization would be even greater for the exporter. Efforts to put environmental protections in place must overcome this additional benefit of unrestricted trade. In particular, there would be incentives for governments to distort their environmental policies from the first-best rule of setting emission targets such that marginal damage costs equal marginal abatement costs. The extent of this ecological dumping depends on whether or not producers are also acting strategically and on the policy instrument chosen by the government. In this context, Ulph shows that emission taxes are dominant over other policy instruments.

The results presented by Ulph have been obtained under rather restrictive conditions and have not yet been empirically tested. But, under the assumption that the conditions are correct, these results raise doubts about whether environmental policies will converge across jurisdictions, in the sense that the marginal abatement costs equal marginal damage costs in the countries concerned. A related and largely unsolved problem concerns the intermeshing of trade obligations and international environmental agreements. This issue is brought into focus by C. Ford Runge, whose chapter in this book addresses the treatment of environmental regulations within international trade negotiations. The critical questions include the hierarchy of treaties, the treatment of parties and non-parties, the reach of extraterritorial actions to protect the environment and the issue of waiver for international environmental agreements. Finally, the linkage of environmental and non-environmental issues opens up ways to induce countries to cooperate. For instance, trade concessions may be employed to induce countries to cooperate with respect to transboundary environmental problems.

C. Ford Runge examines the general policy issues that arise at the intersection of environmental concerns and a liberal international trade regime. In both the North American Free Trade Agreement and the recently concluded Uruguay Round of the General Agreement on Tariffs and Trade there was a concern about two principal issues: first, that a more liberal trade regime would lead to environmental degradation, and second, that national measures designed to protect the environment might illegitimately become non-tariff barriers to trade. Runge reviews the very complex policy tradeoffs that exist in this area. As with many of the environmental policy issues that we have dealt with, there appears to be no easy or clear resolution of the conflicting claims of environmental protection and trade liberalization. Instead, policy-makers will have to steer a middle course that balances these legitimate societal interests.

CASE STUDIES

Part V of this book contains case studies that shed light on the research questions formulated in Section 1. Here, we summarize some of the highlights of these case studies.

A. Environmental Federalism in Agriculture: Pesticides and Nonpoint Source Pollution

The papers by Wim Brussaard and Margaret Rosso Grossman discuss the regulation of pesticides in the Netherlands and the US, respectively, and illustrate the similarities and differences between the EU and the US.

The first Dutch legislation on pesticides, the 1947 Pesticides and Fertilizers Act and its successors, the 1962 and 1975 Pesticides Acts preceded the 1991 EC Directive concerning the marketing of plant-protection products. The reason for this directive was market harmonization: the elimination of barriers to trade between the Member States. The directive contained the following provisions:

- prohibition of certain active substances in pesticides;
- the maximum levels of pesticide residues in and on fruits, vegetables and cereals;
- the classification packaging and labeling of pesticides; and
- the testing of pesticides according to principles of 'good laboratory practices'.

The directive orders the Member States to prescribe in their national legislation that plant-protection products may not be placed on the market and used in their territory unless they have authorized the product in accordance with the directive. In particular, only those products may be authorized whose active substances are included in a list of approved active substances. An important element in the directive is the *mutual recognition principle*. This case shows that a directive may be used to streamline existing national laws and not only to initiate national laws.

The case of the US shows close similarities to the situation in the EU. Pesticide regulation was the domain of state law until enactment of the 1910 Insecticide Act. The increased use of pesticides after World War II led to more comprehensive federal regulation in the form of the Federal Insecticide, Fungicide and Rodenticide Act of 1947. This Act was amended in 1972 and again in 1988. This and other relevant laws assign the leadership role to the USEPA but leave significant areas open to state regulation. As in the EU, the principle of mutual recognition applies. Another similarity between the US and the EU is that states have the option to regulate more stringently than the federal law. For instance, California has been particularly active in regulating pesticide use, imposing standards more stringent than under federal law. This case also shows that states may prohibit imports of products from other states that do not meet its standards, provided the standards are not hidden trade barriers.

It follows that in the area of pesticide regulation there are mostly similarities between the EU and the US. The main difference is in the issuance of (con)federal laws. While in the EU the directive is issued by the Council under unanimity or qualified majority voting, in the US it is Congress that acts under majority voting.

James Shortle considers how tensions in a federation are likely to affect the regulation of surface- and groundwater pollution from agriculture. He shows that a fully decentralized policy would have the advantage of optimal sensitivity to local costs and benefits but the disadvantage of ignoring cross-border spillovers. At the other extreme a fully centralized policy would optimally take account of the cross-border spillovers but would not adequately distinguish between different conditions in the constituent jurisdictions. He concludes that a mix of local and central control is optimal, and he finds that, by and large, the current regulatory scheme in the US for dealing with nonpoint pollution and groundwater policy comes close to this optimum. Shortle believes that there are some shortcomings – principally in the coordination of watershed management across borders – but that these can be relatively easily corrected by improved coordination among federal, state, and local authorities.

B. Global Warming

As a global and irreversible problem, warming of the earth's climate is widely perceived as potentially one of the most serious environmental problems. Policy responses at the global level (UNCED, 1992, for instance) as well as at various regional levels have been under debate for quite some time. In particular, possible responses by the EU and the US have been in discussion for several years.

Within the EU (and the rest of Europe, such as Sweden) individual Member States have been considering unilateral actions against substances thought to be responsible for warming. The main reason for this is that implementation of such policies at home might be instrumental in persuading other countries to follow suit. Unilateral policies, however, have been strongly opposed because it has been commonly believed that such actions in a small economy are both costly and ineffective. It has been postulated that the cost of domestic adjustment is high and international 'leakages' are considerable.

The chapter by Lars Bergman presents a computable general equilibrium (CGE) analysis of global warming policy that raises some doubts about these commonly held views. In particular, with a proper sectoral differentiation of carbon tax rates the cost in terms of full-employment national income might be small or even negative. Moreover, differentiation of domestic carbon taxes seems to be an almost perfect substitute for internationally-coordinated carbon taxes. Finally, when taken into account, some positive side effects of carbon taxation, such as a reduction of acid rain, increase the attractiveness of 'greenhouse gas' abatement policies at the national or regional level.

Bergman's analysis relates to a small open economy, and it is not clear to what extent the results hold for large economies like those of the US and the EU. The findings, however, indicate that similar analyses for large economies would be worthwhile. A particular problem within the EU for schemes suggested by Bergman's analysis is that tax harmonization, which is one of the key instruments for the completion of the Single European Market, may preclude differentiation of carbon taxes between countries.

The US approach to global warming is reflected in the chapter by Charles D. Kolstad. Kolstad emphasizes the uncertainty surrounding global warming and the costs and benefits of learning more about warming before taking costly action against greenhouse gases. The scientific evidence surrounding the hypothesized temperature change is mixed at best. Furthermore, the predictions of ecological and economic effects are largely conjecture. The policy question is whether to incur potentially high costs now to reduce the possibility of large environmental damages several decades in the future, or to wait until there is clearer evidence of need. This question is faced collectively by all nations and individually by any jurisdiction contemplating unilateral action.

Kolstad focuses on the process of resolving uncertainty through learning in the presence of irreversibilities. He posits two types of irreversibility: the effects of greenhouse gas emissions which, if they occur, will endure; and the consequences of investments in abatement capital which, if it occurs, will irretrievably displace other types of investment. In the presence of these irreversibilities, learning would suggest under-control for purposes of avoiding irreversible investments in abatement and over-control for purposes of irreversible climate change.

C. Tropospheric Ozone Pollution

Ground-level (tropospheric) ozone has long been recognized as an important respiratory irritant. Formed in the presence of sunlight by chemical reactions involving volatile organic compounds (VOC) and nitrous oxides (NO_x), hazardous levels of ozone occur in many parts of the EU and US. The NO_x precursors are especially associated with power generation and automotive traffic; VOCs are emitted by a wide range of activities employing solvents as well as by trucks and cars.

Ozone and its precursors are quite mobile. Elevated levels of ozone can occur up to several hundred kilometers downwind of the precursor sources. Thus, ozone problems routinely cross borders between states or nations. This transboundary aspect of ozone is a major challenge to governance structures. At the same time, ozone problems are not experienced everywhere – mainly in and downwind of urban or industrialized areas. Topographic features and more sunlight can exacerbate ozone problems, as is the case, for example, in the Los Angeles basin.

John B. Braden and Stef Proost compare in one chapter the governance of ozone pollution in the EU and US. The US has, for over two decades, taken a centralized approach. The European Council's unanimity requirements have thwarted centralized action, so the Member States have had to rely on decentralized policies. The different outcomes are striking.

In the US, the Federal government mandates minimum ozone air qualitystandards. It also sets emission limits for mobile sources (automobiles and trucks) and new industrial sources. States are responsible for enforcing these standards and regulating sources that existed prior to the passage of federal legislation. Where the air quality fails to meet federal standards, states must propose and enforce additional measures to reduce ozone precursors. They must be able to show progress towards meeting the federal air quality standards.

In Europe, however, action against ozone has largely followed a decentralized model. Community-wide action has been blocked by several westerly and southerly Member States. Oceans protect these nations from ozone intrusion, and their own emissions are either small or have their main impacts to the east and north, so there is little or no domestic advantage to be had from costly measures to reduce ground-level ozone. The only Union actions to date have been the acceptance of certain non-binding target ambient concentrations for ozone, the agreement to adopt uniform monitoring and reporting requirements, and, for purposes of harmonizing the internal market, the enactment of Union-wide emission control standards for new automobiles and for NO_x.

While binding action against ozone has been largely blocked, the Single European Act's provision for qualified majority voting has changed the prospects for ozone. The Council is more likely to pass discharge standards for VOCs and to make the ozone concentration standards binding.

Already several members of the Union voluntarily accept requirements more stringent than the Union norms. A few, with significant domestic consequences from ozone, have taken unilateral action. Wider acceptance has come about through a process of multilateral bargaining under the auspices of the Geneva Convention on Long-range Transboundary Air Pollution. All members of the EU except Ireland and Portugal, along with several non-Member European nations and the US and Canada, agreed to reduce discharges of VOC by 30 percent from levels in the late 1980s.

While the US and EU approaches to tropospheric ozone pollution are quite different, Braden and Proost argue that both reflect the central advantage of a federal structure: the capacity to neutralize destructive competition between jurisdictions while also allowing political autonomy. This has been accomplished in the US by allowing states to design their own implementation plans and by setting ambient quality standards as thresholds rather than specific requirements. It has been accomplished in the EU through a combination of Union-wide product standards justified by market harmonization and voluntary agreements to reduce discharges.

D. Environmental Dimensions of National and International Security

Concerns about environmental quality and about access to valuable natural resources have always been important in national defense and security decisions. But these concerns are growing. For example, the United States Department of Defense identifies 'environmental security' as one of the most important defense-related issues of the twenty-first century. The ways in which environmental and resource concerns can threaten national and international peace are numerous: transboundary pollution can be a continuing irritant in international relations; environmental degradation in a region may induce migration or a war of aggression against a neighbor to acquire access to valuable natural resources; land erosion, inadequate water and over-population could cause people to lose confidence in their leadership and give rise to a demagogue who exploits the situation to threaten international peace.

The chapters in this section of the book explore these defense-related issues. Simon Dalby gives an overview of the literature on environmental security. He finds that there is a very broad range of environmental issues that could spark international aggression, and he suggests that existing regional agreements, like the European Union, should be aware of these possibilities so as to be able to head off environmentally-related crises.

Kent Butts's paper focuses on the difficult security issues created for the European Union by the recently-liberalized countries of Eastern Europe and the former Soviet Union. Those developing countries paid very little attention to environmental quality during their decades of communist control. The result was some of the worst environmental and resource degradation in the world. Economic development in Eastern Europe and the former Soviet Union is likely to be hindered by the low quality of the environment and the low quantity of valuable natural resources. Moreover, if those countries were to impose environmental regulations like those in the US and the EU, their transition to market-based development would be severely handicapped. This set of circumstances is volatile. To deal with these potential problems for international peace, Butts strongly urges NATO to develop an awareness of environmental security issues and recommends the creation of certain institutions for managing those issues.

ACKNOWLEDGEMENTS

This volume is made possible by the generous financial support of the following organizations: the Council for European Studies, Deutscher Akademischer Austauchdienst, the Farm Foundation, University of Illinois (College of Agriculture, College of Law, Center for International Business Education and Research, Committee on European Studies, Institute for Environmental Studies, and Institute of Government and Public Affairs), the US Army Environmental Policy Institute, and the US Information Agency (University Affiliates Program). The papers were originally presented at a symposium sponsored by these organizations and held at the College of Law, University of Illinois at Urbana-Champaign, in September, 1993. We are grateful for their contributions.

In addition, Don Hodgman and Odelia Funke provided early and important inspiration and guidance. Karl-Goran Maler, Charles Kolstad, Rüiger Pethig, and Stef Proost helped with the initial planning. Edward Elgar Publishers gave our publication proposal an enthusiastic welcome. Wallace Oates, Editor of the Series 'New Horizons in Environmental Economics', was most supportive, and Dymphna Evans provided prompt and expert guidance through the publication process. Terry Iverson, Edna Spear, and Pola Triandis helped immensely in putting the conference together. We are especially indebted to Terri MacFarlane and Stephanie Spaulding for their proficiency and good cheer in helping with the organization of the conference and in working with the chapter authors and preparing the final manuscript.

NOTES

1. The distinction between a *federation* and a *confederation* is an important matter of degree as to the relative power between the central government and the constituent states. In a *confederation* the constituent states retain a greater degree of organization and sovereignty and yield a controlling power to the central government for a few limited purposes, such as external or diplomatic relations.
2. The terms become five years beginning in 1995.
3. Occasionally, Article 235 is invoked as a justification for environmental policy. That Article authorizes the issuance of such other forms of legislation as the regulation. Some environmental policies, such as the protection of habitat for endangered species, are not sufficiently tied to the aims of Article 100 (principally, harmonization of intra-community trade) to be justified under that Article. The papers by Professor Pfander, Professor Brussaard, and Professor Grossman discuss the use of directives and regulations in implementing environmental policy in the EU.
4. Another important instrument of enforcement is the doctrine of *direct effect*, developed by the Court of Justice. Under certain conditions, directives that create relatively specific rights for individuals may be asserted by them in national courts even when the Member State has failed to adopt the directive as national law.

REFERENCES

UNCED, (1992), 'The Global Partnership for Environment and Development. A Guide to Agenda 21', United Nations Conference on Environment and Development, UNCED, Geneva.

PART I

The Economic and Philosophical Foundations of
Environmental Policy

2. Making Environmental Policy in a Federation of States

Charles W. Howe

FORMS OF GOVERNMENT AND ENVIRONMENTAL POLICY FORMULATION

The institutional framework within which policies are formulated has a dominant effect on the forms of the policies that emerge. Which interests are represented, the degrees of freedom for policy variation from area to area, and the ability to control (or take into account) externalities among areas vary across forms of government. Naturally, each system has its unique history that continues to condition the relationships among sub-jurisdictions.

Political scientists distinguish among unitary, federal and confederal types of political systems, as pictured in Figure 2.1 below (taken from Greenberg and Page, 1991, p. 73).

In a *unitary* system, the central government retains all power and can change the constituent units and generally impose policy on them. Contemporary examples would include France and Japan (Greenberg and Page, 1991, p. 75).

In a *confederation*, the constituent units join together for the achievement of certain common purposes while retaining ultimate authority over other matters and holding veto power over confederation actions. Examples would be the European Union and the United Nations. Confederations are typically established by *treaties*. Confederation is generally a more limited form of government than federation, but, since the division of powers is specified in the treaties or in the constitution involved in each system, the division of central/local power usually depends on the issues involved.

Federalism divides powers between the central government and smaller units, with the division of powers being defined by a mutually agreed *constitution*. Federations tend to be geographically large, culturally diverse countries such as Canada, Germany, India, Switzerland and (formerly) the Soviet Union. The political history of the United States is, to an important extent, a description of the twisting path of definition of federal and state powers, a path that has generally gone in the direction of greater central Soviet Union. The political history of the United States is, to an important extent, a description of the twisting path of definition of federal and state powers, a path that has generally gone in the direction of greater central government power. The complexity of US federation is seen in the descriptors used in the literature: dual federalism, creative federalism, picket-fence federalism, fiscal federalism, permissive federalism, layer-cake and marble-cake federalism (Bradley and Ingram, 1986, p. 37)

In both the European Union and the United States, there exists a trend towards greater centralization of power in environmental programs. This is manifested in part in the central setting of standards and the oft-stated objective of cost minimization in reaching those standards. Centralized power involves the risk of several undesirable outcomes: (1) economic inefficiency from inadequately differentiated standards; (2) failure to incorporate local or regional economic, cultural or environmental aspirations in those standards; (3) failure to recognize the desire for more local control of policy and practice;

Figure 2.1:   Types of political systems

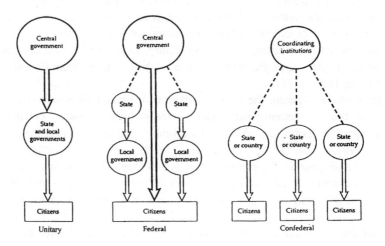

Source: Greenberg and Page, 1991, Figure 3.2, p. 73.

and (4) the possibility of widespread 'revolt' against the centralized environmental program apparatus – such as the 'Sagebrush Rebellion' in the United States in which western states tried to rally support in the Congress for greater local determination of policies regarding the use of federal lands.

The success of policies, especially environmental, will depend upon close collaboration among the levels of government and among the various functional agencies (e.g. environment, agriculture, public health, transport) at each level of government. As an example of this dependence in the United States, the federal Environmental Protection Agency (EPA) has initiated a program for management of asbestos, radon gas and lead in drinking water in public schools. Implementation has been given to the states. A recent study for EPA has shown that local school districts take more action when the relevant state agency has developed an active program with effective information dissemination and enforcement (rather than voluntary programs) (Fisher, et al., 1993). In the absence of effective collaboration between the Federal and state governments, local agencies are unlikely to conform to federal policies.

The *key issue* of environmental policy-making under any form of government is that of resolving the tradeoff between local freedom to adapt environmental standards and enforcement to local incomes, values and physical surroundings and the ability to deal with large-scale externalities. Basically, transboundary pollution remains the unsolved problem.

The 'EC Task Force Report on the Environment and the Internal Market, 1992: The Environmental Dimension' (EC, 1990) proposed five basic principles for environmental management in the Single Market: (1) prevention at the source; (2) the polluter pays principle (PPP); (3) the principle of subsidiarity; (4) economic efficiency/cost effectiveness; and (5) enforceability. While laudable, these policies are not internally consistent, leaving some important tradeoffs to be decided. In particular, subsidiarity (the relegation of policy-making and enforcement to the lowest level of authority consistent with the achievement of environmental goals) must be traded off against economic efficiency because of the existence of transboundary externalities.[1]

We thus turn to further discussion of subsidiarity, the need for some degree of central direction, and shortcomings of contemporary centrally-designed policies.

SUBSIDIARITY IN THE FACE OF EXTERNALITIES

The biggest unsolved issue is that of subsidiarity versus externalities. It is desirable to allow flexibility among states, countries and regions in the design of environmental policy. Yet each jurisdiction exerts environmental externalities on other jurisdictions – usually requiring some type of centralized policy-making or arbitration. This is particularly true in complex problems like Europe's acid deposition: characterized by many jurisdictions, different ecosystem vulnerabilities, and varied weather and climate systems.

The rationale for subsidiarity is to allow the preferences, population densities, and physical differences of different regions to be reflected in the ambient standards set for those regions and in the policies chosen to attain those standards. Environmental programs should be tailored to the preferences of local populations in the absence of significant external effects. The shift of policy design and enforcement to regional and local levels also shifts at least part of the budgetary burden to those levels.

There are other reasons favoring subsidiarity. By placing standard setting and enforcement at the local level, we better stimulate use of local knowledge of the physical environment, the economic base and political and social factors. We also incorporate the local social structure in the enforcement process. An example of growing importance in the US is *citizen enforcement*. Following the 1989 release by EPA of the Toxic Release Inventory, communities were often shocked to learn the volumes of pollutants being released by local industries. Many communities organized and protested both the industrial releases and local authorities' failure to act. Dozens of major companies have announced voluntary reductions (*Wall Street Journal*, February 1, 1991, p. 1).

A more diffuse factor but one of increasing importance is the desire for more local control – not just in environmental policies but in maintaining the economic base, constraining the powers of the market and 'foreign' ownership in shaping decisions important to local society. Examples are found in the (US) 'Sagebrush Rebellion', in the activities of groups like the Western Governors' Association which works to influence federal policies on natural resources and environment, and in the reluctance of France and Norway to let world markets displace existing agriculture and fisheries.

In spite of all the arguments favoring subsidiarity, externalities and other factors require some degree of central direction and/or mechanisms for conflict resolution. There are cases of genuine national–local value conflict over the use of natural resources, the resolution of which must give great weight to the national interest. In the western United States, electric power companies and the State of Utah wanted to build mine-mouth electric power stations on the Kaparowitz Plateau where huge coal deposits lie close to the Canyonlands and Grand Canyon National Parks. Strong national interests dictated the protection of these unique visual assets. The current controversy over protection of old growth forests in the northwestern US versus high timber harvest to maintain lumber industry jobs has approached a compromise solution only through federal direction.

When strong local business interests oppose environmental measures that are clearly justified on, say, public health grounds, the existence of central government standards and the threat of central enforcement can 'take the heat off' local authorities who recognize the need for control but are subject to local political pressure. On the other hand, central authority also may be needed to 'keep the heat on' local authorities who succumb to local pressures or refuse to take a broad, long-term view of the environment.

While it is clear that the existence of externalities requires some degree of central resolution, current centralized policies fall short in important ways, especially regarding equity among states or member countries.

For example, the US SO_2 trading program for large power plants established under the 1990 Clean Air Act has been promoted by economists for many years as a move towards greater use of economic motivation to lower costs. Indeed, the system as designed (1) holds the total SO_2 load constant over time; (2) provides motivation for polluters to seek technological improvements in reducing pollution; and (3) accommodates new sources of pollution through the sale of allowances. A major flaw, obvious from the beginning and apparently necessitated by regional political considerations, was the failure to distinguish among different locations of SO_2 sources in the vast region stretching from South Carolina to Minnesota. Since the key patterns of acid deposition are well known (from the Ohio Valley to northern New York State and southeastern Canada), trades of allowances among sources should be governed by 'exchange rates' reflecting relative contributions to the areas of most serious deposition. A problem has already arisen from Long Island Power Company's proposed sale of a large number of allowances to power companies in the Ohio River Valley. The State of New York is suing EPA to nullify the sale on the grounds that the sale will significantly increase damage to the State since Long Island pollution blows out to sea (perhaps to Europe) while Ohio pollution drifts back to New York.

The widely stated goal of minimizing the cost of achieving a predetermined set of ambient standards exhibits the same problem, namely that some areas under the minimum cost solution may actually be *worse off* in terms of the abatement costs they must incur and/or in terms of deposition experienced relative to pre-control conditions or relative to other strategies such as uniform percentage cutback. Table 2.1 below is taken from a study by Klaasen and Amann of SO_2 control in Europe, using the RAINS model (Klaasen and Amann, 1992). The deposition standards used in the study are those proposed for the new European sulphur protocol, increased by 40 percent.

The comparison shows the following: (1) the cost-minimization strategy costs less than half that of uniform percentage cutback; (2) total SO_2 emissions under cost minimization are nearly three times as great; (3) a much larger percentage of the total land area exceeds the 'critical loads' (the annual deposition rate at which significant ecosystem damage is judged to begin) of sulphur deposition under cost minimization than under uniform percentage cutback; (4) under uniform percentage cutback, no areas experience increased levels of deposition compared with 1980 levels, while under cost minimization, some areas experience increased deposition; (5) under cost minimization, 7 of the 36 countries in the model would incur higher abatement costs than currently (Klaasen and Amann, 1992, Table 7).

Table 2.1:   Comparison of scenario results from the RAINS model

	Scenario			
	1	2	3	4
	Cost-minimum	Uniform % cutback	Emission trading one-to-one	Emission trading exchange rate
Annual costs (Mio DM)	31200	63750	53267	44608
Annual costs (as % of uniform cutback)	49	100	84	70
Emissions (kt SO_2)	26524	11760	11760	19727
Exceedance of critical loads (% of land area)	23.0	10.4	10.1	12.6

Source: Klaasen and Amann, 1992, Table 7.

Thus, while cost minimization seems meritorious as a second-best criterion, it has some distinct drawbacks that may well be important politically. If individual countries can veto the SO_2 protocol, some sharing of costs and compensation for increased deposition will be needed if a cost-minimizing strategy is followed. The long-run implications of the much larger total SO_2 load also need to be considered further.

Oates, Portney and McGartland (1988) compared the net benefits from the current (CAC) control policy for total suspended particulates (TSP) in the Baltimore, MD region with net benefits from an incentive-based policy. They observed that the current CAC policy over-controls over much of the region. This over-control has some value and this value should be subtracted from the CAC costs before CAC costs are compared with those of a minimum-cost program. Table 2.2 exhibits the weighted average receptor TSP levels under the minimum cost and CAC policies for different (uniform) TSP standards.

Table 2.2: Population-weighted averages of receptor levels

Standard ($\mu G/M^3$)

	120	110	100	90
Policy				
Min. cost	77	73	69	63
CAC	71	68	64	60

The Oates team also calculated a measure of partial net benefits under the two policies: $45 million per year under minimum cost and $39 million per year under CAC. They thus conclude that a carefully designed CAC system[2] can compare favorably with a minimum-cost system when the added benefits of the former are counted.

INTEGRATING ENVIRONMENTAL POLICY INTO REGIONAL AND NATIONAL PLANNING

The Single European Act of 1987 sought the development of both economic and social cohesion of the member nations and to make environmental protection an integral part of EC policies. An interesting question raised by the existence of the Single Market is the extent to which member countries can maintain differentiated environmental policies in the face of a free market devoid of trade barriers. Folmer and Howe (1991) speculated that there is likely to be a convergence of national environmental policies because of arbitrage by consumers among the products of different countries and by firms in their selection of location. Completion of the market will produce greater interdependence and may give greater credibility to the higher standards adopted by the wealthier countries.

Whether standards are determined by individual member countries or imposed by the European Commission (by the EPA in the United States), it is important that environmental protection be built into policy-making at all levels. If environmental policy is not proactive, it will simply consist of trying to mitigate the environmental disasters left by the actions of other sectors.

During the 1970s in the US, acreage constraints were relaxed and income support programs enhanced to stimulate grain production for export. As a result, fragile grasslands were plowed and windbreaks of trees were eliminated, resulting in a large increase in erosion of soil and the siltation of streams.

Agricultural price supports, export subsidies and subsidized irrigation water continue to stimulate overexpansion of irrigated agriculture in the western United States. Irrigation has been extended to areas where soils are inappropriate, new irrigation creates water logging on existing acreage, and underlying soil layers contain toxic elements that poison drainage waters. The Kesterson National Wildlife Refuge case in the San Joaquin Valley of California is the most notorious of these situations, but similar problems exist at most major irrigation projects in the western US (National Research Council, 1989).

A large coal-fired generating plant was built in Arizona to provide power for pumping Colorado River water into the Central Arizona Project that provides highly subsidized water for agriculture and cities in central Arizona. That plant has been polluting the Grand Canyon and seriously reducing visibility. Ironically, this power plant replaced plans for two hydro-electric dams that would have flooded parts of the Grand Canyon and that were rejected on environmental grounds!

It is necessary to establish a *framework* within which consistent and well-defined environmental guidelines and constraints are built into the policy processes in *all* sectors of the economy, public and private: agriculture, industry, energy, transportation, etc. The United States attempted to provide such a framework by passing the National Environmental Policy Act (NEPA) of 1969. The most prominent result of NEPA has been the preparation of analyses required by the Act – the Environmental Impact Statement (EIS) required of nearly all projects in which the Federal government is directly or indirectly involved. An EIS must: (1) analyze and describe the environmental impacts of the proposed action; (2) describe any unavoidable adverse environmental effects of the action; (3) identify and analyze a range of alternatives to the proposed action, including the 'no action' alternative; (4) assess the consistency of the action with long-term sustainability of the environment; and (5) identify any irreversible and irretrievable commitments of resources implied by the action. The EIS was intended to be informational and no authority exists for vetoing a project on the basis of negative findings in the EIS. Several states require state EIS's for state actions.

The author of NEPA, Professor Lynton K. Caldwell of Indiana University, has written a critique of the 20 years experience with NEPA (1989). He notes that the intent of the Act was to establish *principles* that would be widely shared so the nation could fulfil its responsibilities toward succeeding generations, assure all Americans safe, healthful,... surroundings, and preserve important historic and cultural aspects of our natural heritage. Yet, he feels that the Act has been misinterpreted and perverted into a set of procedures:

Although NEPA is a policy act, it is widely interpreted by lawyers, judges, and journalists as essentially procedural because the legal profession is primarily concerned with the specific performance stipulated by the Act and open to challenge and litigation in the courts.

A frequent result of NEPA has been that when controversial projects are proposed, agency staff seek to construct an EIS that appears to support the project. This is exactly the fate that has befallen benefit–cost analysis in so many countries.

Yet, the EIS requirement, while costly and subject to perversion like benefit–cost analysis, has opened up the decision processes of government agencies at state and federal levels to public scrutiny and input. It has provided information on many dimensions of projects never covered by the traditional benefit–cost analyses. It is a practice that should be emulated, but in an environment where the resulting information will be used in an open decision process rather than as propaganda for a project.

SELECTED LESSONS FROM FEDERAL–STATE RELATIONS IN THE UNITED STATES

State–federal conflicts over natural resource and land issues go back to the earliest days of the Federation when different groups of states took quite different positions on incorporating the new western lands into the Federation. States that bordered the 'Northwest Territories' (the Midwest) wanted to extend their boundaries far to the west. Land-locked eastern states wanted these lands ceded to the central government to equalize state land holdings, as a source of central government revenue, and to build political solidarity among the states through possession of common lands (Bradley and Ingram, 1986). As the western land holdings expanded, eastern states were concerned about a shift of political power to the west, while the southern states worried about agricultural competition and support for slavery.

At the time of the Civil War, 75 percent of the land area between the Atlantic and Pacific was owned by the central government. By the turn of the century, 70 percent of these holdings had been transferred to state and private ownership. Federal land policy emerged from the balancing of many issues, from forestry and agriculture to the social issue of slavery. Many issues that were interpreted as conflicts between states and the central government were, in reality, the playing out of interstate conflicts through the mediation of central government.

The same tactics can be seen today in both the United States and the European Union as regional interests seek to influence central policies. The midwestern states managed to weaken the Clean Air Act of 1990 to avoid penalizing their use of high sulphur coal. The lower income EU countries have been able to secure large compensatory payments as a condition of their membership.

There is a presumption on the parts of many that the central government is 'more scientific' in its approach to policy-making than are the states. This impression got its start in the 'gospel of efficiency' (Hays, 1959) introduced by President Theodore Roosevelt and his close advisors, Gifford Pinchot and John Wesley Powell. The introduction of scientific forestry (Pinchot) and hydrology (Powell) from Europe led to the continuing impression that central government policies were based on scientific principles, while local governments were both uniformed and short-sighted.

In the environmental policy area, these impressions were largely correct until the mid-1970s when states came to realize that they needed scientific capabilities that would permit them to take part in the policy process. Naturally, many of the key issues in environmental policy-making are not scientific but relate to relative values and culture. Local governments are clearly more representative of these values than the central government.

In the environmental policy arena, there has been an ebb and flow of state and federal powers and responsibilities. Air and water legislation of the 1950s left standard-setting and enforcement to the states. Most states didn't have the expertise to design such systems, and nearly all states were reluctant to impose effective constraints for fear of losing industry. Thus, these state programs were largely ineffective (Kneese and Schultze, 1975). With the 1970 Clean Air Act Amendments and the 1972 Federal Water Pollution Control Act Amendments, Congress took primary authority away from the states. The new Environmental Protection Agency (EPA) was given standard-setting and permitting powers for air and water, although states could reassume these responsibilities if they presented acceptable plans. As will be seen, the states have again taken over much of the standard-setting and enforcement tasks.

The US environmental program has frequently been criticized for the high costs of its 'command and control' approach (Stewart, 1985; Tietenberg, 1985; Portney (ed.), 1990; US Congress, Office of Technology Assessment, 1984; Howe, 1993). How can such a high-cost program have persisted so long and why have economists' recommendations for the use of taxes and tradable permits been given so little weight? Some of the reasons are: (1) lawyers who are typically trained to believe in regulation write the rules; (2) legislators believe that regulations and enforcement are more reliable than economic motivation; (3) environmental groups have resisted treating the environment as an economic good; and (4) firms may have a cost advantage under regulation in comparison with taxes or permits (Stewart, 1985; Russell et al., 1986; Hahn, 1989).

Finally, federal powers have been limited by budget, by popular sentiments and by agency capture. The federal assumption of policy responsibility involves not only its own budgetary costs but also costs to the states in terms of a slower development of state policy capabilities and foreclosing of more flexible state policies.

State capabilities and motivation are improving as the states come to realize that a high quality environment has economic value and that they will lose influence over environmental policy unless they exhibit a willingness to accept these responsibilities. Portney ((ed.) 1990, pp. 282–6) notes that: (1) 40 states now handle all regulation (permitting and enforcement) under the Clean Water Act; (2) 40 states have assumed responsibility for issuing permits under the Clean Air Act; (3) 5 states have laws constraining acid deposition (acid rain) from state sources; and (4) 40 states have enacted their own 'superfund' legislation to expedite cleaning up old waste sites.

The states have a good deal of flexibility in designing their state water and air implementation plans. While they must meet federal minimum ambient air standards and must enforce federal water emission standards, they have latitude in the conditions imposed in air and water emission permits. The level of monitoring, the severity of 'compliance' conditions and the strictness of enforcement are allowed by EPA to vary considerably among states. It can be argued that this state-to-state variability makes up in part for the lack of regional differentiation in federal standards. It also is consistent with the subsidiarity principle.

The 'pollution havens' problem appears to have been more a fear than a reality in the US. In the Conservation Foundation's case studies (Netherlands Ministry of Housing, Physical Planning and Environment, 1990) concerning New Jersey (an industrial state with a very strict environmental program) and the siting decision for General Motors' Saturn automobile plant, no evidence or threat was found of businesses locating or relocating because of environmental standards. The US experience leaves no doubt, however, that industry frequently tries to sow fear of plant relocation and to exaggerate the costs of environmental controls. In a recent citizen lawsuit against pollution from Ashland Oil Inc's refinery in Catlettsburg, Kentucky, the company stated that the pollution was harmless and that further control would cause closure of the refinery (*Wall Street Journal*, Sept. 17, 1990, p. 1). Industry estimates of costs consistently exceed estimates by EPA and independent consultants by factors of two or more.

The Conservation Foundation study also found that the states have been of *substantial assistance to each other* in sharing experiences, success stories and technologies. The Western Governors' Association has been very active in promoting the sharing of experiences and the development of guidelines that fit the western US setting (WGA, 1993). The main unsolved problem is transboundary pollution. The state and Federal governments have not been able to design mutually agreeable programs for dealing simultaneously with intrastate standards and meeting desirable interstate ambient standards.

CONCLUSIONS

The major unresolved issue is dealing with externalities from member states to other member states, frequently in a very complex pattern of interactions. Yet, the powers of central government are limited – in part by treaty or constitution, but equally by budget limitations, information availability and public acceptance. There can be no broadly defined optimum distribution of authority among governments.

A facet of policy formulation mentioned earlier is that of *local control* – a growing desire of states, regions and nations to have more control over their destinies. This issue must be considered both by the US and Europe as environmental (and other) policies are formulated. The long-term welfare of the political union must be considered.

In a treatise on competing legal doctrines on the control of interstate waters, Albert E. Utton, distinguished legal scholar and Editor of the *Natural Resources Journal*, discussed the pros and cons of two contradictory legal philosophies incorporated in two decisions by the US Supreme Court in 1982:[3] the doctrine of 'equitable apportionment' of interstate waters between states and the 'commerce clause' doctrine that declares water to be an article of commerce (marketable commodity) and thereby subject to constitutional protections against interstate trade restraints (Utton, 1985). The former doctrine is concerned with equity between states that share a water source, while the latter doctrine asserts that market forces should be allowed to determine water allocation among states, subject to some welfare and police powers qualifications. Utton argues that there are issues beyond market efficiency that warrant the acceptance of the equity doctrine – 'to protect the balance within the federal union of states and to insure the stability necessary for state and regional water planning' (p. 986). He concludes:

> However, if there is merit to the idea of the founding fathers that it is desirable to maintain balance between member states, if there is merit to the idea that diversity contributes to a strong economy, and if there is value in the suggestion that viable constituent parts contribute to a stronger federation, then perhaps it is appropriate to design a doctrine of interstate water allocation which, while limiting the territorial sovereignty of individual states, recognizes the territorial integrity of member states and equitably balances their competing needs...

Perhaps we can substitute 'environmental policy' for 'interstate water allocation' and use Professor Utton's conclusion as a philosophy for environmental policy-making.

NOTES

1. To a lesser degree of importance, the PPP may not be consistent with the efficient resolution of transboundary pollution since the downstream receptor may have to 'bribe' the upstream polluter.
2. See the report for the exact procedures labeled CAC.
3. Colorado versus New Mexico, 459 US 176, 183 (1982), commonly known as the Vermejo River Case; and Sporhase versus Nebraska, 458 US 941 (1982).

REFERENCES

Bradley, Dorotha and Helen M. Ingram, (1986), 'How Federalism Matters in Natural Resources Policy', Chapter 2 in Maynard Silva (ed.) *Ocean Resources and US Intergovernmental Relations in 1980s*, Westview Press, Boulder and London.

Brubaker, S. (1984), *Rethinking the Federal Lands*, Resources for the Future, Inc., Washington, DC.

Caldwell, Lynton K. (1989), 'A Constitutional Law for the Environment: 20 Years with NEPA Indicates the Need', *Environment*, 31(10), December.

Clawson, Marion, (1983), *The Federal Lands Revisited*, Resources for the Future, Inc., Washington, DC.

European Economic Community, Council of Environmental Ministers, 'Task Force Report on the Environment and the Internal Market: 1992 – The Environmental Dimension', Economica Verlag, Bonn.

Fairfax, Sally, (1982), 'Old Recipes for New Federalism, *Environmental Law*, 12:945–80.

Fisher, Ann, Lauraine G. Chesnut, Ruth H. Chapman and Robert D. Rowe, (1993), 'Schools Respond to Risk Management Programs for Asbestos, Lead in Drinking Water and Radon', photocopy of 7/23, RCG/Hagler, Bailly, Inc., Boulder, CO.

Folmer, H. and C. Howe, (1991), 'Environmental Problems and Policy in the Single European Market', *Environmental and Resource Economics*, 1(1):17–42.

Foss, Phillip O., (1960), *Politics and Grass: The Administration of Grazing the Public Domain*, University of Washington Press, Seattle, WA.

Greenberg, Edward S. and Benjamin I. Page, (1991), *The Struggle for Democracy*, Harper Collins College Publishers, New York.

Hahn, Robert W., (1989), 'Economic Prescriptions for Environmental Problems', *Journal of Economic Perspectives*, 3(2).

Hays, Samuel P., (1959), *Conservation and the Gospel of Efficiency: The Progressive Conservation Movement, 1890–1920*, Harvard University Press, Cambridge, MA.

Howe, Charles W., (1993), 'The US Environmental Policy Experience: A Critique with Suggestions for the European Community', *Environmental and Resource Economics*, 3:1–21.

Klaasen, Ger and Markus Amann, (1992), 'Trading of Emission Reduction Commitments for Sulfur Dioxide in Europe', IIASA Status Report SR–92–03, May 18.

Kneese, Allen V. and Charles L. Schultze, (1975), *Pollution, Prices and Public Policy*, The Brookings Institution, Washington, DC.

National Research Council, (1989), *Irrigation-Induced Water Quality Problems*, National Academy Press, Washington, DC.

Netherlands Ministry of Housing, Physical Planning and Environment, (1990), *Environmen tal Policy in A Federal System: The United States and the European Community*, a report by the Conservation Foundation, DOP, postbus 20014, 2500 EA 's-Gravenhage, The Netherlands.

Oates, Wallace E., Paul R. Portney and Albert M. McGartland, (1988), 'The Net Benefits of Incentive-Based Regulations: The Case of Environmental Standard-Setting in the Real World', Discussion Paper CRM 89–03, Resources for the Future, Inc.

Portney, Paul R. (ed.), (1990), *Public Policies for Environmental Protection*, Resources for the Future, Inc., Washington, DC.

Russell, Clifford S., Winston Harrington and W.J. Vaughn, (1986), 'Enforcing Pollution Control Laws', Resources for the Future, Inc., Washington, DC.

South Coast Air Quality Management District, (1993), 'RECLAIM: The Regional Clean Air Incentives Market – A Market Incentive Air Pollution Reduction Program for NO_x and SO_x, Volume I, Development Report and Proposed Rules', Diamond Bar, CA, October.

Stewart, Richard B., (1985), 'Economics, Environment and the Limits of Legal Control', *Harvard Environmental Law Review*, 9:1(1–41).

Tietenberg, T. H., (1985), *Emissions Trading: An Exercise in Reforming Pollutions Policy*, Resources for the Future, Inc., Washington, DC.

US Congress, Office of Technology Assessment, (1984), 'Acid Rain and Transported Air Pollutants: Implications for Public Policy', Report OTA–0–204.

Utton, Albert E., (1985), 'In Search of An Integrating Principle for Interstate Water Law: Regulation *versus* the Market Place', *Natural Resources Journal*, 25, Oct., 986–1004.

Western Governors' Association, (1993), *Our Lands: New Strategies for Protecting the West*, 600 17th St., Denver, CO 80202.

3. The Moral Psychology of the Environmental Age

Eric T. Freyfogle

Ever since the days when the Western frontier stretched invitingly beyond the far horizon, the American consciousness has valued action over reflection. Collectively we have been a people of motion and bluster, rarely preoccupied by ethical niceties, particularly when dealing with the land. Still, beneath every pattern of conduct is some type of moral psychology, some method of ascribing moral value to the world and dividing right conduct from wrong. With land so plentiful, perhaps it was inevitable that frontier America took for granted the natural world, counting it for little in moral terms. To the nineteenth-century American, the land was little more than setting or backdrop, valued chiefly as an economic asset, protected at most from only the grossest of abuses.

Not the least of the changes brought on by the modern environmental era has been a reassessment of this land-as-backdrop mentality. In some murky manner the land and its component parts – wildlife, plants, water, the soil – are coming to count for something morally. Superficially this change is easy to summarize: We are more concerned about the environment than we used to be, more desirous of conserving resources and wild things, even parts of the non-human natural order that seem to hold no immediate value. But a summary like this hides as much as it reveals. It leaves out the why and the how that lie behind new laws and new terms of discourse. It offers little sense of future direction. Has the green-age moral awakening run its course? Are there instead more jolts and growth spurts that lie ahead? Most pertinently, if in fact we are gradually embracing a new moral order, can we see now what it will look like when finally assembled? Can we sense now the implications it will have for everyday life?

If I read it right, the gradual shift now going on in the human-land link is one of the most profound cultural changes in human history. It is on a par with the shift from the Paleolithic world view to the Neolithic, the shift from polytheism to monotheism, the shift from subsistence living to production for the market. At its most basic level, this ongoing transformation is not principally a matter of technology, economics, or politics, however plainly it implicates these spheres. Instead it is a shift in morality, in what we perceive as valuable and what we view as right and wrong. Before we are through, before we have finally stumbled our way into a new way of imagining our place on the land, we will have been challenged to reconsider and reshape many of our philosophic props: our individualism and utilitarianism; our anthropocentrism and epistemology; ultimately, even our metaphysics and linguistics.

THE RECORD

Back in the early days of environmentalism, in the 1960s and early 1970s, the environmental problems that plagued the land did not seem so difficult. It was a time when people believed in the power of law to bring about change, whether in poverty rates or water pollution. Looking back now, it is easy to smile at the era's naivety, at our inability then to see how deep and resilient were the roots of our prevailing patterns of living and comprehending. Looking back we can also see the considerable difficulty lawmakers had in articulating a new moral order, an order that somehow encompassed the land and promoted its health yet did so without devaluing humans and their aspirations.

The credulous hope and fuzzy moral thinking of this early period is evident in the National Environmental Policy Act of 1969,[1] one of the first federal environmental statutes. In its policy intonations NEPA spoke of 'restoring and maintaining environmental quality'; of 'creat[ing] and maintain[ing] conditions under which man and nature can exist in productive harmony'; of 'the responsibilities of each generation as trustee of the environment for succeeding generations'.[2] The goals sounded impressive, but reflecting on them with the experience of the years, what did they really mean? What did it mean for an environment to possess 'quality', and how did one go about measuring it? What did it mean for humans to interact with nature in 'productive harmony'? If indeed humans stand as trustees for the future, what are our duties, and where do we find a copy of the trust agreement?

NEPA also showed its simple faith in the way that it sought to achieve these lofty goals: by requiring environmental impact assessments before damaging projects were undertaken.[3] What NEPA seemed to say was that our declining ecological plight was not a problem of crabbed values or narrow moral vision. It was the far less troubling problem of incomplete information about ecological impacts. With the right information at the right time, agency heads would stand equipped to make the healthy choices. Handed the right data, they could achieve that blessed natural harmony that Congress so loftily had proclaimed.

The information-based approach that Congress pursued in NEPA was not a new one in 1969. A decade earlier, in the Multiple-Use Sustained-Yield Act of 1960, Congress sought to improve forest-management decisions by pressing officials to consider more land-use options before they set loose the tree-cutting crews.[4] In that Act, Congress told the Forest Service to operate its lands to foster multiple uses, including recreation and wildlife, not just timber production. As it mixed the possible land uses, the Service was asked to pick 'the combination that will best meet the needs of the American people', which was 'not necessarily the combination of uses that will give the greatest dollar return or the greatest unit output'.[5] It was to do this, Congress pronounced, 'without impairment of the productivity of the land'.[6]

As in the case of NEPA, the Multiple-Use Sustained-Yield Act seemed to hold the promise of healthier days ahead. But in the years since 1960 its impact has been modest, perhaps non-existent. Litigants have tried to use the statute to change practices that seem too tilted toward clear-cutting and tree farming, only to be told by courts that the statute is too vague to enforce.[7] How could the courts determine, how could anyone determine, what combination of land uses would 'best meet the needs of the American people'? In practice the Multiple Use Sustained Yield Act did little to slow clear cutting; the values and politics of timber were simply too entrenched, in government and without, to be uprooted by misty legislative oratory.

Like NEPA, the Multiple-Use Act can serve as a helpful mirror of the shifting values of the budding green age. A forest, Congress had come to think by 1960, was more than just lumber in the making. It was still a collection of natural resources, ready and waiting to serve human needs. But it was a richer, more diverse collection of resources than was first understood. In 1960 Congress spoke in terms that were utilitarian and anthropocentric, yet it limited these old ways of thinking and valuing with a telling note of restraint. As it called for the land's non-impairment, Congress suggested that future generations might count for something morally: they might be slowly emerging from the dark to become part of the broadening moral landscape.[8]

Since the 1960s Congress has enacted statute after statute, reflecting the ecological and moral turmoil that has come to characterize the modern age. In the Endangered Species Act of 1973, Congress announced that rare species deserved protection because they possessed 'value to the Nation and its people'.[9] In the Federal Land Policy and Management Act of 1976, it called on the Bureau of Land Management to 'take into account the long-term needs of future generations' and to strive, not just to avoid impairing the land, but to avoid degrading 'the quality of the environment'.[10] About the same time, in particularly awkward style, Congress called on the Forest Service 'to be a leader in assuring that the Nation maintains a natural resource conservation posture that will meet the requirements of our people in perpetuity'.[11]

Although most of what Congress has said over the years has offered little challenge to the old ways of thinking, to the dominance in our calculations of present-day human utility, the statute books here and there offer glimpses of other moral orientations. When Congress finally began to regulate ocean dumping, its first-listed desire was to control dumping 'that would adversely affect human health, welfare, or amenities'.[12]   But Congress was also concerned, independently concerned it seems, about 'the marine environment' and its 'ecological systems'.[13] When Congress tightened the toxic emissions provisions of the Clean Air Act, it was concerned not just about human health but about soils, wildlife and the like.[14] Perhaps most prominently, when Congress enacted the Federal Water Pollution Control Act, its grand aim was to 'restore and maintain the chemical, physical, and biological integrity of the Nation's waters'.[15]

Looking back over the past one-third century of environmental laws, it is evident that Congress has largely stuck close to ideas and understandings familiar to its voters, not so much leading the environmental cause as carried along with it. Try as we might, it is simply not possible to piece together Congress's pronouncements into a coherent moral order, or even into a premeditated vision of ecological well-being. Congress has tried hard to contain pollution, as if pollution were an independent problem rather than a symptom of something deeper seated. It has sought to preserve wild species and wild places, not grasping that the more urgent need is for ecologically healthy landscapes where people can live, not places that people must leave untouched. It has embraced cost–benefit analysis, as if our past mistakes were matters, not of underlying values and visions, but of simple errors in addition and subtraction. Again and again it has spoken of human well-being as the primary if not sole policy goal.

When we shift attention from past to present, it is easy to see why environmental policy these days is approaching a crisis of vision and imagination. In dealing with industrial pollution and wilderness preservation, Congress has addressed the easy issues.   Now it must confront more fundamental problems, ones far harder to handle without calling into question, and perhaps without altering greatly, our comfortable ways of thinking and valuing:

1.   In the area of water quality, Congress must come to grips with nonpoint source pollution, which is caused, not by the discrete actions of big business, but by all of us, more or less in every aspect of our lives.[16]
2.   Congress must return to the issue of threatened and endangered species, this time with the experience-tempered knowledge that conservation plans can succeed only if we find ways for these species to live, not apart from humans in isolated enclaves, but alongside them, in daily life.

3. Congress must revisit the management of wild areas, again with the knowledge that even large areas like Yellowstone Park cannot be managed without considering the larger bioregions of which they are a part, including vast areas where people live and work.
4. Congress must consider the plight of wetlands, which means coming to grips with the decidedly disruptive idea of no-net-loss. No single idea is less consistent with the old ways of thinking than no-net-loss, for what it means ultimately is drawing lines that we stick to forever: not slowing down, not cutting back, not getting what we want in modified form, but living with what we already have.
5. Finally, Congress must consider the issue of atmospheric degradation, which is challenging our old ways of thinking just as much as the wetlands issue. Global warming is an issue that is almost inconceivably complicated, well beyond our reach, which means we have no choice but to set aside our normal arrogance and face up to our ignorance. It is also one of the messy issues that cuts right into daily life, for the sources of greenhouse gases are more or less everywhere. The ill effects of global warming are distant in time, far beyond the normal planning horizon, which means we can address it only by taking a much longer look than is our custom. Finally, global warming involves a byproduct as common as carbon dioxide, which is a pollutant only in a definitional sense that is gravely threatening to our growth-oriented culture: it is a pollutant when there is simply too much of it; it is a pollutant that requires us to take seriously the possibilities of natural limits and appropriate scale; it is a pollutant in the same sense that every product of our lives can be a pollutant.

THE CHALLENGES

Slowly, inexorably, these new environmental issues are disrupting our old ways of sensing the world. As they do so, they are stimulating new moral visions, visions that, to their proponents at least, offer better ways of finding our place in the natural order, visions that offer better guides for identifying living practices that we can sustain.

A useful place to begin surveying these new moral claims is with the noisy challenge being offered to our anthropocentrism, to our long-held assumption that only humans count in moral terms. In the sixteenth century, René Descartes asserted that the painful cries of a tortured animal were the same as noise from a machine's grinding gears: neither machines nor animals had minds or souls, which meant that neither counted for anything morally. Today we have trouble being so sure. The more intently we look, the more difficult it is to justify a sharp moral line between humans and the planet's millions of other species. Why is it that humans count and other species do not? If humans count because they are conscious of the world, then perhaps moral value should also attach to other species that are also conscious. If humans count because they feel pain, or have interests, or set out each day to get what they want, then perhaps other animals that act likewise should also possess value.

In this quest to locate moral value, animal welfare advocates have taken the visible lead.[17] What they urge is an extension of moral value to include certain non-human species. Proponents have no settled answer for how far moral worth should extend. Should it extend to large mammals, or perhaps all mammals? Should it reach beyond that, to birds and fishes and reptiles? Is it more appropriate instead to think that all animal forms have some modicum of moral value, with the value perhaps varying with the level of an organism's sentience or consciousness or ability to pursue goals?

Joining with animal welfare advocates on this issue are a variety of other environmental writers; if they disagree on exactly what we should do, they agree that the time has come for anthropocentrism to loosen its firm grip. Some observers contend that moral value exists, not just in individual non-human organisms, perhaps not even in individual organisms, but at the level of organizational entities such as species or ecosystems.[18] In some way our moral order needs to respect this organizational-level value.

The second challenge being pressed today is to our utilitarian instincts, to our sense that the best way to determine right and wrong when dealing with the land is to look at how an action affects our own pleasure or well-being. Because it lacks moral worth, the land is a mere instrument in utilitarian-type ethical schemes, valuable only in so far as it promotes human well-being. In this moral order, the right way to use the land is the way that produces the most human good. This kind of utilitarianism (using the term popularly rather than technically) has long dominated our thinking about the land, although perhaps never exclusively. The most influential form of utilitarianism today is economic thought, which uses efficiency as its main measure of the good.

In the modern environmental age, the main precepts of utilitarian thought are facing new objections. One concern is with the identity of the individuals whose utility is counted. Past practice (particularly free-market economics) considers only the utility of humans now living – or, even more narrowly, the utility of market consumers with dollars to spend. But what of the many other species that share the planet, either as individual organisms or as collective entities? Should their utility also count for something?[19] If it does, is it possible to devise a logical way to aggregate their utility with ours, making the awkward tradeoffs that will constantly arise? A second concern is the matter of future generations of humans, if not future generations of other species.[20]

If future humans have utilities that ought to enter our calculations, how are we to factor them in, particularly given that, as we look ahead in time, humans not yet born soon vastly outnumber humans now alive? Just as knotty: what are the preferences of these future humans, given that we cannot ask them what they want and given that our acts today will affect their expectations, even their identities?

Related to the issue of future generations is the matter of discounting future gains and losses.[21] In everyday life people unthinkingly engage in discounting: a benefit tomorrow is less valuable than the same one now. Public policy is often determined by aggregating these individual, discounted judgments, particularly when economists do the calculating. But if the planet is to become healthy, can this practice continue? When dealing with the land, perhaps we need to shift to zero discounting, where future costs and benefits count the same as costs and benefits today; otherwise, the future will count for too little.

Perhaps the most potent challenge to utilitarianism comes from those who question whether we even know enough to make all of the necessary calculations of utility and well-being.[22] Can we calculate the harms and benefits of a given action, or even trace and identify them, given nature's complexity and the limits on our knowledge? Consider as an example the grassy Illinois meadow that is plowed up to plant a field of corn. We can calculate the corn that is grown. But what of the manifold other effects that come along with it? Where meadowlarks and bobolinks once nested in the meadow, we now have red-winged blackbirds and crows. Is this a good change or a bad one? Can we calculate the soil erosion from the perennial plowing? Do we know the effects of the silt in the local stream? Do we know what happens when the big-eye chubs in the stream die because they can no longer spot their food in the dirty water? Does anyone know who feeds on these chubs, and what their role might be in maintaining the stream's health?

As ecologists have been telling us now for some time, we can never make one change to nature. Each piece is linked to each other piece, and the ripples of any change spread far and wide. With this level of interconnection, it is hard to decide when a change is good overall, much less measure its overall impact. What are we to do when we lose track of the many ripples, or when we lack the knowledge, the time, or the inclination to look for the ripples in the first place?

Today's third challenge to our prevailing moral psychology cuts at the very heart of the modern democratic, liberal understanding of the world. Particularly since the era still known as the Enlightenment, Western culture has exalted the individual human as the prime measure of value. Whether in philosophy or psychology, law or medicine, value rests discretely in each separate human. Economic theory shares this atomistic focus; what counts there are the preferences of individuals, particularly those with money to spend. Democratic theory does the same, for the democratic political collective, like the free market, is nothing more than an aggregation of individuals.

The problem with this focus on the individual is that it denies basic axioms of the natural world, axioms that environmentalists believe need to form a new point of departure for our understanding of the world. In nature an individual organism cannot live in isolation.[23]   It cannot live without interacting constantly with the surrounding world, taking energy and nutrients, returning wastes, and bumping and pounding against other life forms and inorganic matter. Indeed, the closer we look, the more artificial it seems to talk about the individual organism as a discrete thing, rather than as an inseparable part of something larger. In the natural order, energy and nutrients flow through the system, with life leading to death and on to new life in never-ending cycles. It is the process, the collective, the species, the whole that counts and is the stuff of life, not the individual organism.

This holistic attitude is coming to dominate environmental thinking, overtaking environmental theories that ground moral value at the individual level. The most prominent expression of this holism remains Aldo Leopold's land ethic, so lyrically expressed in the concluding essay of his *A Sand County Almanac*, published in 1949. 'A thing is right', Leopold announced in his oft-quoted line, 'when it tends to preserve the integrity, stability, and beauty of the biotic community. It is wrong when it tends otherwise'.[24] It is the community that has moral value in Leopold's ethic, not the individual member. When deer populations rise, hunting becomes ethical if not even desirable, for an unchecked increase hurts the community as a whole. Today's Endangered Species Act reflects similar logic, valuing a species apart from the individuals that compose it. In the Yellowstone area, to cite another example, the ecosystem is more than the sum of its parts; indeed, the ecosystem's health takes precedence over the health of any individual part.

It is hard to overstate the importance and potential disruptiveness of this new community-minded mode of thought. In the political realm, holism offers a sharp challenge to our dominant philosophies, from liberalism to libertarianism, which aim to enhance private happiness rather than any particular conception of the public good. Environmentalists are accused of being elitists, but what they really are is something even less tolerable to many Americans: they are moralists, out to promote a particular view of the communal good. And like most moralists, they are anxious to form a moral majority – in this case not by forcing people to agree, but by infecting them with a vision of a better way.[25]

At its base, this new community-minded land ethic questions the size and shape of an individual's sphere of personal liberty. As a society, we already have rules that limit individual choice, laws against murder, rape, discrimination and the like. Under the moral psychology now dominant among environmentalists, that personal realm would shrink further. And it would shrink largely for the same reason that it has shrunk over the past century: because we will gradually come to realize that practices long thought innocuous in fact cause grave harm. Acting as landowner, the individual will have fewer options, for a single land parcel will no longer mean much in isolation.[26] Whether driving a car or grilling a steak, individual preferences in the new age will simply weigh much less.

The fourth challenge to our dominant moral vision cuts at our epistemology, the very means that we use to make sense of the world.[27] When debating public policy we want reason to reign, using reason to draw conclusions from our masses of facts and figures. Factual knowledge comes to us empirically, and we are skeptical of factual claims that lack an empirical pedigree. When the Environmental Protection Agency regulates a pesticide, we expect it to offer hard data on the harm. When a species is declared at risk, we want facts and figures to back up any policy move. Like Descartes, we are skeptical people, rejecting what we cannot prove.

The problem here, as environmentalists see it, is that our reliance on empirical data leaves no good way to deal with our yawning ignorance. When we focus solely on the known and make decisions from that base of data, we have no means to factor in the great amount that we do not know. Humans have identified and given names to perhaps no more than 2 percent of the planet's species, and precious little is known about the vast majority of them. Even the modest fruit fly, the subject of untold millions of research dollars, is known only in vague terms.

Environmental writers are sharply critical of the modern urge to rely exclusively on empirical data. As farmer–writer Wendell Berry puts the point, 'the acquisition of knowledge always involves the revelation of ignorance – almost *is* the revelation of ignorance'.[28] While we can amass knowledge voraciously, we must while doing so 'abandon our superstitious beliefs about knowledge: that it is ever sufficient; that it can of itself solve problems; that it is intrinsically good; that it can be used objectively and disinterestedly'.[29] 'In the final analysis', David Ehrenfeld suggests, 'the management of the Earth must be value conscious and value oriented'.[30]

Environmental writers who challenge our focus on empiricism by and large call for greater reliance on other modes of understanding, ones that draw on sentiment and intuition, ones that supplement the factual record with vision and faith.[31] Adam Smith and David Hume are often cited as forebears, but intuition-based thinking hardly began in the eighteenth century. Indeed, it was probably not until then that reason as we know it had sufficient ascendancy for other modes of thought to require a defense.[32] According to many observers, the time has come to revitalize other forms of knowledge, to find ways to incorporate our ignorance with humility, acting more gently and leaving room to correct our inevitable mistakes.[33]   Only in that manner can our decision-making calculus give ignorance the weight it is due.

The environmental challenge to empirical knowledge shows up with increasing frequency these days. In legal settings it often arises as a question of burden of proof. Do we assume that a potent new chemical is harmless unless shown otherwise, or do we assume just the opposite? Do we assume, in dealing with land uses, that the decline of native species is a loss of something morally worthy, a loss to be avoided and mourned, or do we assume that we have lost nothing of value unless someone supplies contrary hard data? In other settings, this issue shows up as a challenge to our pronounced affinity for abstraction, to our tendency to shift from the actual case to the general category with the loss of detail that inevitably accompanies such a shift. When allocating property rights in water, for instance, a water flow here looks much like a water flow there when both are described abstractly in terms of cubic feet per second. When we think abstractly like this, as property theorists are prone to do,[34] we lose track of the peculiarities of each acre and each of nature's component parts. In nature's terms, a water flow here is never the same as a water flow elsewhere, for each supports and helps compose an ecosystem that is unique at least in its details.

This brings us to the final, most fundamental challenge of modern environmentalism. Implicit in the contemporary world view is the sense that humans are distinct from nature. Humans are subjects and nature is an object. This dualism undergirds our anthropocentrism as well as our individualism. It also furnishes a way of sensing our place in the entirety of all creation, a way of thinking about our existence. In this dominant, dualistic order, the individual human can stand back and take stock of all that surrounds him, gazing at a thing that is separate from him and distinct.

This dualistic metaphysic, according to many environmentalists, is the taproot of our planetary decline.[35] The human–nature split that it assumes supplies an ontological base for an ethic of domination. If nature is separate from us, if we are the subject and it is mere object, why cannot we manipulate the land? Why cannot we speak of nature as a bundle of resources? Whether we imagine nature as a complex machine, as Kepler and Newton did, or envision it instead in more organic terms, it is still an object, awaiting our use.

One of the chief aims of ecology, according to its philosophic advocates, is to challenge and ultimately supplant this pernicious dualism.[36] In its place we need a way of thinking that sees humans as part of nature, linked to the rest of the natural order. We need a way of thinking about our place in the world that begins with our connectedness, not our separateness; one that considers the individual human less as a discrete thing and more as a locus or node of forces and interactions.[37]

ASSESSING THE CLAIMS

Taken together, these five challenges could hardly probe more deeply into our accustomed ways of thinking and valuing. Before abandoning the old, however, we need to ask whether these critical strands of thought offer workable alternatives. The truth, it seems, is that they do not, at least not yet and at least not completely. Still, their challenges are strong ones, and they offer useful clues for the paths that plainly lie ahead.

Troubled as we should be with our anthropocentrism, it is far from evident whether and how we might purge ourselves of this ingrained mode of thought.[38] We can act more humbly, respecting more forms of life, but in the end we are probably as inclined as the next species to want to eat and thrive. Deep ecology offers an alternative to this human-centered view, but it is an alternative that is hard to translate into rules for daily conduct.[39] If other species are as valuable as we are, how are we to keep warm and stay alive? When everything is a subject, subject status inevitably loses all of its meaning. When everything has moral value, particularly on equal terms, moral value also comes to mean nothing. At best what deep ecology offers so far is something akin to Albert Schweitzer's reverence for all life – something that is less a guide for crafting rules than a virtuous impulse upon which to grow a more gentle character.

As we consider the many challenges to popular utilitarian thought we have just as much reason to proceed slowly. We can agree, and doubtless should do so, that the line between humans and other species is a thin one. But if we abandon utility and start recognizing value in non-human life forms, either individual organisms or community aggregates, we may soon find ourselves drifting without a rudder. The most practical ethical alternatives are ones that attribute moral worth broadly across the species, tempering this zeal by recognizing gradations in value; that is, other life forms end up with value, but their value is less, often far less, than the value of the individual human. Yet, having recognized this ubiquitous moral value, where do we go from there? How do we step from widespread moral worth to specific rules of conduct, particularly when we have to deal with the confusing maze of differential moral values? The risk is that, lacking guidance that truly binds, we will simply rationalize what we want, drifting step by step into ways of living that are as self-centered as ever.

As we evaluate the assault on our centuries-old commitment to individualism, we have good cause to feel chastised. The natural order, plainly, is far more than just a collection of independent parts, and humans are as interlocked with the natural order as any organism.[40] As Wendell Berry expresses it, 'no matter how sophisticated and complex and powerful our institutions, we are still exactly as dependent on the earth as the earthworms'.[41]

Still, while a stiff pruning is in order we ought to pause before abandoning individualism wholesale. We particularly need to hold on to it when setting the moral duties we owe to one another. Too much talk of community sends shudders down many spines, and rightfully so, for the good of the collective state has been the justification for many twentieth-century genocides. Who is going to play God when it comes time to pick the individual to sacrifice for the community?[42] Like Aldo Leopold, we can strive to enhance the health of our natural communities. But if humans form part of an ecosystem, and if the ecosystem is where all moral value rests, what then is left of our sense of individual dignity – the very sense that has helped lift us up from feudalism and helped free us from so many oppressions?

In the case of the environmental challenge to the popular dominance of empiricism, there is no claim yet that we ought to abandon all of the evidence we derive from our senses. Our goal should be to supplement that knowledge with intuition and sentiment, but to do so carefully and selectively. We can continue greeting with suspicion any knowledge that comes to us from untestable sources, whether revealed religion, mystical imagination, or the imbibed wisdom of daily life. But greeting with suspicion is not the same as rejecting.

In future years non-human nature is likely to serve more and more as a source of instruction for how we should live.[43] The more that we learn of nature's ways, the more accurately we can respect and mimic its processes. We can give sentiment a greater role, but it needs to be the kind of sentiment that has percolated through the thick soil of our experience, the kind of sentiment that is constantly tested against the world to see whether its guidance in fact produces healthy results.

The call for a change in our metaphysics is sufficiently new today that it is hard to get a clear picture of what a full change would really mean, of what it might mean to live in a world no longer populated by discrete beings and things. The most radical alternative to our present dualism presumably is an ontology based on something like the philosophic doctrine of internal relations.[44] Under that doctrine, a living entity (human or non-human) is entirely comprehended by its relationships and interactions with other entities and has no existence apart from its relationships. An idea like this one can be useful to contemplate, but it is hard to conceive of the vast changes that would come if we embraced the idea in daily life. It is hard to imagine a workable ontology based entirely on relationships and flux. Still, there is no escaping the truth that nature's pieces interact constantly. There is no escaping the fact that, when an individual dies, life goes on; when the energy or nutrient flow stops, life comes to an end.

LOOKING AHEAD

In all likelihood today's environmental challenge is not going to prompt us to replace overnight any single pillar of our moral psychology. We will continue to carry with us, as we progress on our pilgrimage, something that resembles our familiar baggage: our tendency to grab for facts and figures, our desire to tote up costs and benefits when setting policy, our preference for the individual human over other life forms.

Yet, if a sudden transformation seems unlikely, changes plainly lie down the road. These changes, I suggest, are likely to be guided and given shape by six basic ideas or understandings.

First, our dealings with the land will be viewed in the future, far more than they are today, as a matter of ethics rather than economics, political process, or technology. Expediency and self-interest will still count for something, just as they do in our dealings with one another. But the basic rules, the guidelines that help maintain the health of the land, will be viewed as issues of right and wrong, not matters of efficiency or popularity. Land abuse will be morally wrong, in much the same way as child abuse and now spouse abuse.

Second, as we set the guidelines for right and wrong living with the land, we are going to need to temper considerably our skeptical empiricism. Temper does not mean replace, and in learning about nature we will need to work harder than ever to see how nature functions and how our actions affect nature's processes. But when the facts run dry we shall need to make a few leaps of faith, erring on the side of protecting the land and its integrity. We cannot keep acting like we can do whatever we want until faced with undeniable proof that we are causing harm.

As we try to grow a land ethic that sinks one of its roots into sentiment or intuition, we are going to face one decidedly troublesome obstacle. Our society strongly resists when the government tells us to be virtuous, when it prescribes a definition of the good life. In a liberal democracy it is the province of each individual to decide what it means to be good. The government's role is more limited, to keep us from causing harm. Only when we see a harm are we willing to let the government act.

In the case of the land, however, much of the harm we cause is invisible, at least to the average person. Even when nature is manifestly altered we have trouble deciding whether the change amounts to damage or whether it is instead a simple matter of putting land to full use. We can respond to this reality through massive public education, helping people to see the signs of natural decline: the missing salamanders, the stunted tree limbs, the salt-crusted soil, and the like. But public education is slow going, and even the best ecologists know only a small part of the story.

In the future our guidelines for dealing with the land must do more than prohibit conduct known to cause harm. We need to use a lesser burden of proof, gathering as many facts as we can but in the end working with solid values as well. One cause for hope here is the strengthening call of the feminist movement. As clearly as any observers, ecofeminists understand the need for a virtue that does more than ban obvious harm.[45] Whether dealing with other people or with the land, the domineering actor is simply too insensitive to the subtle, pernicious harms that are taking place. In the end we need, not just to heed the ecologists when they speak of hidden harms, but to err on the side of caution and mimic nature whenever feasible.

A third principle that will help guide our journey is the idea that land-use rules are properly a matter of community concern, in much the same way that issues of murder and rape are matters for the community, not matters for each person to decide separately. When people get together to discuss and then establish these rules, they will act as citizens, not as individual consumers; they will talk about the community's long-term needs, not their short-term wants.[46] As a community our decision-making processes need to foster this kind of mutual learning and goal setting. It simply will not suffice for policy-makers to look to public opinion polls, to market prices and surveys, or to other sources of data that treat the community as a simple aggregate of individuals. If we fail to see that the community is more than its parts, if we fail to see that people can and will learn from one another, we will never escape what has been aptly termed the tyranny of small decisions, the tyranny of independent, individually made choices that drag everyone down.[47]

One grave challenge on this point of community rules is caused by the difficulty that arises in establishing the community's size. This issue is presented today by the North American Free Trade Agreement and, in Europe, in discussions of national sovereignty over environmental matters. If land-use rules are matters of community concern, who makes up the relevant community? The competing concerns on this issue are as obvious as they are stubborn. Larger community size means distant decision-makers, lack of familiarity, overwhelming information, insensitivity and popular distrust. At the international level it also means limited power and a faint, if not sometimes impalpable, sense of common cause. Smaller community size weakens the tools for addressing global problems. It presents issues of externalities, free riders and competition for economic growth. The most likely answer on this point is for each of us to join multiple, concentric communities, varying in size according to the nature of the environmental issue. All other things equal, smaller and more local will prove better, but nature has an annoying, already familiar way of turning local practices into global decline.

The fourth idea that can guide us stems from our evident need to develop an overall goal for our environmental efforts. From what we know today, that goal will likely be phrased in terms of the functioning of the natural order of which we are a part. It will be some version of Leopold's land ethic, but with people and their aspirations more expressly included in the biotic community. One fashionable phrasing is to speak in terms of sustainability or, more vaguely, sustainable development.[48] Another possibility is to present the goal in terms of ecosystem health. Both definitional approaches have drawn their critics, and no two- or three-word goal is ever going to be more than a slogan. Sustainability sounds too stagnant, too threatening to the human urge to create and improve, and sustainable development sounds oxymoronic.[49] The human health metaphor, some urge, seems too human-centered, too attached to the very individualism or atomism that is a big part of the problem.[50]

Yet, as we get beneath the surface to flesh out the details, it should be possible to develop multiple, workable indices of natural area well-being.[51] Once we have settled on these basic indicators of natural health, we can start gathering and publicizing health data on a regular basis – just as often, and just as much, as we now do with our economic data.[52] For a couple of reasons that have only recently come to the fore, the task of developing these health indicators will be a bit harder than we once thought. The natural order, we now know, is not a static entity, even when it reaches what was once called the climax stage. Change is inevitable even without humans, which means that the nature we seek to mimic is a moving target.[53] Moreover, every species alters its environment, in part tailoring itself to fit its surroundings, in part tailoring the surroundings to fit its needs. If elephants and pandas can rightfully alter their habitats, perhaps humans can rightly do so too.

On the other hand, it is easy to overstate the difficulties presented by these new ecological visions, which to some extent may represent passing fancies within the academy.[54] To say that nature's change is continuous is hardly to say that, in human time frames, all is in flux, or even that in human time frames much of the change is even noticeable. And to say that every species affects its environment is far from saying that all human-caused change is an appropriate part of the natural order; perhaps only a small part of it is. Without question, the realities of change and habitat alteration need to enter into our definitions of community well-being. But we should not let them deter us from developing such definitions and putting them to frequent use.

A fifth guiding idea is that we cannot divorce environmental policy from policies that govern our dealings with one another. Aldo Leopold's land ethic has faced criticism on this point, for Leopold wrote as if our ethic towards the land could be entirely separate from the ethic that governs the interpersonal realm.[55] The philosophic importance of this point is particularly significant when moral value resides at the *community* level in the natural realm but at the *individual* level in the human realm. To knit together these two ethical approaches requires what philosophers term second-order rules. As Bryan

Norton observes, the development of second-order rules, joining ethics and ecology, is 'the great unfinished task of Leopold's land ethic'.[56]

In the international arena, this linkage of issues is often referred to as the matter of equity – between north and south, between developed countries and developing ones. But perhaps a better way to phrase the point is in terms of the inherent unfairness of first-in-time as a method for allocating the planet's limited carrying capacity. If the atmosphere can only accept so much carbon dioxide, why should those who are first to emit gain the perpetual right to continue? If particular types of natural areas need preservation, why should those who are last in line to alter be the ones obliged to refrain? This question is not one of overall wealth -- not one, that is, of equality of result. It has to do instead with equality of opportunity, the opportunity to burden a planet that can only handle so much. When it comes to allocating empty benches in a park, first-in-time might prove fair enough. But when the entitlement being allocated is far more valuable, as it is in the environmental setting, first-in-time is far harder to justify, if not simply impossible.

The sixth and final idea we need to grasp is that, far more than we realize, our languages constrain how we think; they are part of our environmental problem, and part of what needs to change. In describing our dealings with the land, our languages have troubling gaps. We have many words that break nature into parts and treat it as a collection of resources, but few words to portray it as a seamless web. We have many measures to capture nature in quantitative terms; few measures that gauge it qualitatively. We have words that describe nature as separate from us; few words that include us within it.

If the word sustainable does not quite capture the kind of natural order we are seeking, then maybe it is time to make up a new word. If health sounds too human, if harmony sounds too melodious, if balance sounds too static or judicial – then perhaps it is time for a worldwide competition to create words that are more apt.

The debate going on today about wilderness is one illustration of our verbal poverty, and the costs that can accompany it. Ecologists now claim that the human presence on the planet is so pervasive that no spot is entirely unaffected by the human touch. If a tract is not true wilderness – or so the argument seems to go – then why bother to preserve it? Why bother to protect it from further human-caused decline? What our limited language suggests is that there are only two types of land, wilderness and non-wilderness, with only one type deserving of protection.

The problem here is that our current language misses the subtlety, the many gradations between pure wilderness (which may indeed not exist) and a landscape that is as artificial as we can make it. If we choose to limit the term wilderness to areas that are completely unaltered, then we should add new words: a word that covers a natural area only slightly altered, perhaps in invisible ways; a word that covers a natural area (like the Boundary Waters Canoe Area) with plentiful evidence of primitive recreational use but little more; a word that covers natural areas with all native species present except perhaps the largest carnivores and herbivores. By adding these words and others, we will undoubtedly increase our own abilities to see the differences and appreciate them.

CODA: STORIES

In his celebrated essay, 'The Land Ethic', Aldo Leopold called for a continuing evolution in our ethical vision, an evolution that would bring the land into our realm of moral worth. Such a step, Leopold urged, was 'an evolutionary possibility and an ecological necessity'.[57]

Many readers have been heartened and motivated by Leopold's oft-quoted tale of Odysseus and his slave girls. But as with any text held sacred, we need to be careful with literal readings. Leopold suggested that we could extend our ethics to include the land in much the same manner that an earlier generation extended its ethics to include slaves. What once was property, now carried moral worth. As with slaves, so with the land.

The step that we need to take today, however, bears only slight resemblance to the recognition of moral worth in slaves. To treat slaves ethically was to treat them like people, adding them to a known moral category. In dealing with the land, however, the human model is as misleading as it is helpful. The moral step for today's generation is as revolutionary as it is evolutionary.

Instead of Leopold's tale of early Western Greece, perhaps we should draw upon a different tale, one from the ancient East offered by theologian Alan Watts.[58] A king of ancient India, Watts claimed, was disturbed because the land was so rough that it was hard to walk on with bare feet. His solution was to cover the entire land with soft animal skins. But then a Hindu wise man proposed a more gentle approach. Instead of shaping nature, perhaps they might work on the human side. Leave the land alone, the wise man said: put the skins on our feet.

NOTES

1. Now codified at 42 United States Code §§4321–70d (1988). One observer not misled by NEPA was law professor Joseph Sax, who anticipated NEPA's limitations in Joseph Sax, 'The (Unhappy) Truth About NEPA', *Oklahoma Law Review* 26 (1973): 239.
2. 42 United States Code §4331(a), (b) (1988).
3. 42 United States Code §4332(c)(1988).
4. Now codified at 16 United States Code §§528–531 (1988).
5. 16 United States Code §531(b) (1988).

6. 16 United States Code §531(a), (b) (1988).
7. See Sierra Club v. Butz, 3 Environmental Law Reporter 20292 (9th Cir. 1973).
8. Congress would return to the definition of multiple use sixteen years later, when it directed the Bureau of Land Management to follow the same management goal. As it did so, however, Congress made three changes to the old definition, changes that offer clues to the conflicting impulses of the age. Congress now stated clearly that multiple use 'takes into account the long-term needs of future generations'. 43 United States Code §1702(c) (1988). The non-impairment clause, Congress added, would protect not just the land's productivity but 'the quality of the environment'. Ibid. Yet while it made these seeming advances towards greater environmental sensitivity, Congress in an important way cut back on its earlier goal. While the 1960 version called for no impairment, the 1976 act settled for a seemingly much lesser goal, the goal of no 'permanent impairment'. Ibid.
9. 16 United States Code §1531(a)(3) (1988).
10. 43 United States Code §1702(c) (1988).
11. 16 United States Code §1600(6) (1988).
12. 33 United States Code §1401(b) (1988).
13. Ibid.
14. 42 United States Code §§7409(b)(2), 7602(h) (1988).
15. 33 United States Code §1251(a) (1988). The way in which this goal was lowered in actual practice is considered in Barry Boyer, 'Building Legal and Institutional Frameworks for Sustainability', *Buffalo Environmental Law Journal* 1 (Spring 1993): 63, 74 *et seq*.
16. A good discussion is Daniel Mandelker, 'Controlling Nonpoint Source Water Pollution: Can It Be Done?', *Chicago-Kent Law Review* 65 (1989): 479.
17. Among the leading sources are Tom Regan, *The Case for Animal Rights* (Berkeley: University of California Press, 1983); Peter Singer, *Animal Liberation*, rev. ed. (New York: Avon Books, 1990); *In Defense of Animals*, ed. Peter Singer (New York: Basil Blackwell, 1985).
18. The views of many of the leading philosophers of this position are covered in *The Animal Rights/Environmental Ethics Debate: The Environmental Perspective*, ed. Eugene C. Hargrove (Albany: State University of New York Press, 1992).
19. See Peter Singer, *Animal Liberation*, rev. ed. (New York: Avon Books, 1990).
20. See *Responsibilities to Future Generations*, ed. Ernest Partridge (Buffalo: Prometheus Books, 1981).
21. See Herman Daly and John Cobb, *For the Common Good* (Boston: Beacon Press, 1989), pp. 151–8.
22. I consider this issue in *Justice and the Earth: Images for Our Planetary Survival* (New York: The Free Press, 1993), Chapter 7.
23. See Neil Evernden, *The Natural Alien: Humankind and the Environment* (Toronto: University of Toronto Press, 1985), pp. 40, 133; Daniel Botkin, *Discordant Harmonies* (New York: Oxford University Press, 1990), p. 7; Harold Morowitz, 'Biology as a Cosmological Science', in *Nature in Asian Traditions of Thought*, eds J. Baird Callicott and Roger Ames (Albany: State University of New York Press, 1983).
24. Aldo Leopold, *A Sand County Almanac and Sketches Here and There* (New York: Oxford University Press, 1949), pp. 224–5. I consider Leopold's land ethic in detail in 'The Land Ethic and Pilgrim Leopold', *University of Colorado Law Review* 61 (1990), p. 217.
25. See Joseph Sax, *Mountains Without Handrails* (Ann Arbor: University of Michigan Press, 1980), p. 14.
26. I consider this issue in 'Ownership and Ecology', *Case Western Reserve Law Review* (1993), p. 1269.
27. As I do with the term utilitarianism, I use the term epistemology more loosely and broadly than would be appropriate in a scholarly philosophy article. For purposes of simplicity, epistemology as I employ it includes not just how we acquire knowledge – through the senses and/or otherwise – but whether we view that knowledge as complete and how we go about making decisions based on that knowledge. A firm believer in empiricism could, of course, reject all knowledge that cannot be confirmed by the senses yet agree that such knowledge is incomplete, employing then a decision-making process that recognizes our ignorance and somehow accommodates it. My sense, however, is that a decision-making model can work only if the gaps left by our ignorance are somehow filled, rather than left as an indeterminant unknown. As I urge in the text, my sense is that such gaps are best filled by reliance on sentiment and intuition, rather than by way of some formal process that fills the gaps with pure logic. Once we admit sentiment and intuition into the model, we have shifted from pure empiricism into some hybrid of it – which is what I refer to when I talk about the ongoing change in our epistemology.

28. Wendell Berry, *Standing By Words* (San Francisco: North Point Press, 1983), p. 65.
29. Ibid., p. 66.
30. David Ehrenfeld, *The Arrogance of Humanism* (New York: Oxford University Press, 1978), p. 153.
31. Perhaps the most thoughtful proponent of this view is J. Baird Callicott. See his *In Defense of the Land Ethic* (Albany: State University of New York, 1989). Another expression is David L. Hall, 'On Seeking a Change of Environment', in *Nature in Asian Traditions of Thought*, eds J. Baird Callicott and Roger Ames (Albany: State University of New York Press, 1983), p. 99.
32. See John Ralston Saul, *Voltaire's Bastards: The Dictatorship of Reason in the West* (New York: The Free Press, 1992).
33. I consider this issue in *Justice and the Earth: Images for Our Planetary Survival* (New York: The Free Press, 1993), Chapter 7.
34. See Eric T. Freyfogle, 'Ownership and Ecology,' *Case Western Review Law Review* (1993), p. 1269.
35. The most thoughtful analyses are perhaps J. Baird Callicott, 'The Conceptual Foundations of the Land Ethic', in his *In Defense of the Land Ethic* (Albany: State University of New York Press, 1989), p. 75; Neil Evernden, *The Natural Alien: Humankind and the Environment* (Toronto: University of Toronto Press, 1985).
36. See Neil Evernden, *The Natural Alien: Humankind and the Environment* (Toronto: University of Toronto Press, 1985), pp. 75–6.
37. Ibid., pp. 133–7.
38. See Wendell Berry, *Home Economics* (San Francisco: North Point Press, 1987), p. 148.
39. The basic ideas of deep ecology are explained in Bill Devall and George Sessions, *Deep Ecology: Living as if Nature Mattered* (Layton, Utah: Peregrine Smith Books, 1985).
40. An evocative presentation of this idea is contained in Robert Pirsig's novel, *Lila* (New York: Bantam Books, 1991).
41. Wendell Berry, *The Long-Legged House* (New York: Harcourt Brace & World, Inc., 1969), p. 77.
42. See Tom Regan, *The Case for Animal Rights* (Berkeley: University of California Press, 1983), p. 262.
43. See Wendell Berry, 'Nature as Measure', in Wendell Berry, *What Are People For?* (San Francisco: North Point Press, 1990), p. 204.
44. See J. Baird Callicott, 'The Metaphysical Implications of Ecology', in his *In Defense of the Land Ethic* (Albany: State University of New York Press, 1989), pp. 101, 110. Callicott's views are questioned in James Fieser, 'Callicott and the Metaphysical Basis of Ecocentric Morality', *Environmental Ethics* 15 (1993), p. 171.
45. A consideration of the field is offered in Christine Cuomo, 'Unravelling the Problems in Ecofeminism', *Environmental Ethics* 14 (1992), p. 351, which offers a critical assessment of Karen J. Warren, 'The Power and Promise of Ecological Feminism', *Environmental Ethics* 12 (1990), p. 125.
46. The citizen–consumer distinction and its considerable importance is discussed in Mark Sagoff, *The Economy of the Earth* (Cambridge: Cambridge University Press, 1988).
47. See Alison Rieser, 'Ecological Preservation as a Public Property Right: An Emerging Doctrine in Search of a Theory', *Harvard Environmental Law Review* 15 (1991), p. 393.
48. For example, World Commission on Environment and Development, *Our Common Future* (Oxford: Oxford University Press, 1987). An excellent use and expansion of the idea of sustainability is contained in Lester W. Milbrath, *Envisioning a Sustainable Society* (Albany: State University of New York Press, 1989).
49. One critique is Donald Worster, *The Wealth of Nature* (New York: Oxford University Press, 1993), pp. 142–55. Another view is David Orr, *Ecological Literacy* (Albany: State University of New York Press, 1992).
50. Various critical assessments are offered in Robert Costanza, Bryan G. Norton and Benjamin D. Haskell, *Ecosystem Health* (Washington, DC: Island Press, 1992).
51. As we discuss the philosophic basis of our overall environmental goal, we would be wise to downplay the argument on the moral status of an entity such as a biotic community. Whether we value the community instrumentally, or whether we do so in recognition of its intrinsic worth, we are likely to end up with one and the same goal.
52. See Herman Daly and John Cobb, *For the Common Good* (Boston: Beacon Press, 1989), Appendix, for a proposal to revise commonly used economic criteria to include effects on the environment.
53. See Daniel Botkin, *Discordant Harmonies* (New York: Oxford University Press, 1990).

54. See Donald Worster, *The Wealth of Nature* (New York: Oxford University Press, 1993), pp. 142–70; Mark Sagoff, 'Ethics, Ecology, and the Environment: Integrity, Science and Law', *Tennessee Law Review* 56 (1988), p. 77.
55. See Eric T. Freyfogle, 'The Land Ethic and Pilgrim Leopold', *University of Colorado Law Review* 61 (1990), pp. 242–3.
56. See Bryan Norton, review of J. Baird Callicott, *In Defense of the Land Ethic*, in *Environmental Ethics* 13 (1991), p. 186.
57. Aldo Leopold, *A Sand County Almanac and Sketches Here and There* (New York: Oxford University Press, 1949), p. 203.
58. Alan W. Watts, *Nature, Man and Woman* (New York: Vintage Books ed., 1991), p. 51.

PART II

The Law and Economics of Authority in a Federal System

4. Environmental Federalism in Europe and the United States: A Comparative Assessment of Regulation Through the Agency of Member States

James E. Pfander

INTRODUCTION

Since the rise of environmental consciousness in the early 1970s, the European Union and the United States of America have tackled the problem of environmental regulation at the federal or supranational level. In Europe, the Council has largely relied upon its harmonization powers under the Treaty of Rome to issue directives that require Member States to adopt and enforce certain specified standards of environmental protection.[1] Although once a matter of some controversy, the Union's competence to develop environmental measures was bolstered by amendments to the EU Treaty and now seems quite beyond dispute.[2] In the United States, Congress has invoked its considerable powers under the commerce clause to establish a national program of environmental protection characterized by a strong reliance on state enforcement.[3] Recent Supreme Court decisions confirm the breadth of such congressional authority.[4]

Europe and America share more than federal environmental competence; the content of their regulatory initiatives bears some considerable resemblance. Both Europe and America have regulated air and water quality and have done so by imposing direct limits on sources of pollution (by reducing the content of lead in gasoline, for example) and by establishing ambient air and water quality standards that offer a more general test of the adequacy of environmental quality. Similarly, both Europe and America have enacted legislation requiring advance assessments of the environmental impact of certain new projects; indeed, the European directive on impact assessment was quite consciously based upon the first major federal environmental initiative in the United States,[5] the National Environmental Policy Act of 1969.[6]

In addition to similarities in regulatory content, the justifications for central legislative solutions to environmental problems overlap a good deal. Pollution does not respect state borders but often spills over to affect the people of a neighboring state. Measures taken by a single state may thus fail to assure environmental protection. In any case, central rules will tend to prevent the 'race to the bottom' that might otherwise induce states to compete for industrial processes deemed important to local economies by offering lax environmental standards. Concerns about free trade, spillovers and the race to laxity underlie much environmental policy.[7]

But despite some considerable overlap in their regulatory content and justification, environmental initiatives in Europe and America differ quite substantially in terms of regulatory process. In the European Union, the Council typically proceeds by directive – a form of legislation that, in its most specific and concrete form, compels Member States to enact rather clearly specified central environmental standards into the positive law of the Member State. Following the 'transposition' of directives into positive law, the Union places primary reliance on the Member States themselves to assure compliance with environmental standards. When Member States fail to accomplish such transposition within the time limits set in the directive, or when they fail to enforce Union standards in practice, they face the prospect of a proceeding for breach of their obligations under the Treaty.[8] The Commission typically enforces environmental law by suing the Member States themselves rather than by suing polluters directly.

In contrast to the wide-ranging use of directives by the European Union to achieve environmental goals, the Supreme Court of the United States has flatly refused to permit Congress to implement its environmental policy by directing the states to adopt and enforce substantive environmental restrictions. Relying on principles of federalism drawn from the tenth amendment's concern for the coordinate role of the states in the American system of government, the Supreme Court held in *New York v. United States*[9] that Congress could not 'commandeer' the legislative and administrative processes of state governments. Thus, the Court struck down a provision of the Low-Level Radioactive Waste Policy Amendments Act of 1985[10] that was said improperly to 'coerce' New York into enacting appropriate regulations for the disposal of its own low-level radioactive waste.[11]

The divergence in regulatory process between the two systems presents something of a paradox. Most observers accept the fact that the United States has evolved far more completely than Europe from a federation of governments to a federal state.[12] In virtually every measure – common language and culture, extent of national feeling, and size and scope of the national government – the United States appears to be more completely integrated than Europe. Yet the Supreme Court has refused to permit

Congress to use a tool of regulatory federalism that the Europeans accept without question and has done so to protect the states' role in the United States system of government.

The Court's refusal to permit Congress to issue directives to the states appears paradoxical from yet another perspective. In Europe, reliance on the directive has come under attack primarily by those who claim that it does not go far enough to secure the effective enforcement of environmental law.[13] Thus, Union observers have criticized the failure of the Commission adequately to police Member State compliance with directives and have suggested a variety of reforms designed to improve the enforcement of Union law. In contrast to the European attitude, which views it as too weak a tool of law enforcement, most observers in the United States regard the directive as too potent a tool to entrust to Congress.[14]

In this chapter, I offer a comparative assessment of environmental regulation in Europe and the United States that focuses on the use of Member States as agents of central regulatory purpose. The next section begins with a description of environmental regulation in Europe, exploring the legal implications of the widespread use of directives to accomplish environmental goals. The following section offers a similar account of environmental regulation in the United States, culminating in a discussion of the roots of American hostility towards the use of European-style directives. Lack of familiarity may explain a measure of the antipathy. In only the most revealing remark, Professor David Currie argued against the constitutionality of directives on the ground that they were 'contrary to the accepted understanding of a federal union'.[15]

The final section considers the comparative insights that these alternative visions of the directive offer for Europe and the United States. Three points deserve attention. First, its routine acceptance in Europe offers some support for a benign understanding of the directive's potential in the United States. Second, despite the directive's benign potential, differences in the legislative and judicial processes, and in the scope of integration, help explain why observers in the United States regard the directive more suspiciously than their European counterparts. Third, as the European Union continues to evolve towards a more integrated federation, we might expect to find greater interest in judicial protection of Member State autonomy.

EUROPEAN ENVIRONMENTAL REGULATION: DIRECTIVES THAT REQUIRE MEMBER STATES TO ENACT POSITIVE LAW

Although the Treaty of Rome did not confer any special environmental competence on the institutions of the European Union,[16] the Union nonetheless worked out a fairly elaborate body of environmental law.[17] At the last count, some 200 pieces of Union environmental legislation had been agreed[18] and more remain in the pipeline. In adopting such environmental initiatives, the Council of Ministers has almost invariably proceeded by use of the directive – a form of legislation that requires each Member State to enact Union obligations into positive national law.[19] In this section's review of European environmental law, I place special emphasis on the legal implications of the directive.

A. The Origins of European Environmental Regulation

Most observers trace the origins of federal environmental legislation in Europe to the Paris Summit Meeting of the Heads of States in 1972.[20] At that meeting, the Member State leaders endorsed the idea of a common European environmental policy. Since then, the Council has drafted a series of environmental action programs, typically extending for a four- to five-year period, that identify goals and set priorities for environmental legislation.[21] The Council's most recent such program, its fifth, calls for the integration of environmental protection and economic growth in a policy of sustainable development.[22]

Although it has now entered its third decade, the Union's environmental policy was built upon provisions of the Treaty of Rome that provide at best indirect support. The European Union was established in 1957 to achieve a common economic market – to eliminate barriers to the free movement of goods, services, capital and people that were thought detrimental to economic development after the war.[23] Because it predated the rise of environmental consciousness in the early 1970s and focuses on common economic issues, the Treaty understandably contained no specific provision authorizing the Union to legislate in the environmental arena.[24] As a consequence, early environmental initiatives rested upon two relatively general sources of Union authority that were adapted for use in the environment.

The most important early basis for environmental action, Article 100 of the Treaty, authorizes the Council to issue legislation aimed at harmonizing or unifying the laws of Member States that, broadly speaking, affect intra-Union trade.[25] Article 100 thus seeks to implement the hortatory language of the preamble, which defines Union goals to include the 'constant improvement of . . . living and working conditions' and 'the harmonious development of economic activities'.[26] Union institutions have interpreted this language to include an improved quality as well as an improved standard of living. Although once a matter of some controversy,[27] most observers and certainly the Union's institutions themselves have come to accept the Union's power to invoke its harmonization authority in the field of the environment.[28]

In addition to its powers under Article 100, the Union has occasionally invoked Article 235 in support of environmental initiatives.[29] Article 235 provides catch-all authority to the Union, similar in some respects to that given to the Congress of the United States under the necessary and proper clause, and has played an important role in the growth of the legislative competence of the Union.[30] In brief, Article 235 authorizes Union legislation where necessary to achieve a Union objective and where other provisions of the Treaty fail to confer the requisite powers.[31] Given a broad reading of the preamble to encompass quality of life considerations, therefore, Article 235 provides a source of authority in the environmental area beyond that encompassed within the harmonization powers of Article 100. Accordingly, Article 235 has most frequently been invoked to support environmental measures, such as the protection of habitat for endangered species, that bear a relatively attenuated relationship to intra-Union trade.[32]

To the extent that the Union relied on Article 100 of the Treaty to support environmental legislation, it was required to proceed by adopting directives. Article 100 specifies that the Council, acting unanimously upon proposal from the Commission, 'shall . . . issue directives' for the approximation of Member State law.[33] While Article 235 confers broader lawmaking authority, and authorizes the issuance of such other forms of legislation as the regulation,[34] the Council typically invoked Article 100 as the source of its legislative authority,[35] at least in part because of doubts about the propriety of relying on Article 235.[36] The Union's predominant reliance 'upon the directive as the lawmaking instrument for environmental policy'[37] may stem at least as much from the limits of Article 100 as from a preference for the directive as a tool of policy.[38]

B. The Role of Union Institutions in the Making and Enforcement of European Law

The Treaty divides central authority between three Union institutions – the Council of Ministers (which comprises representatives of each of the Member States),[39] the Commission (a body of individuals chosen for four-year terms to perform both legislative and executive functions)[40] and the Court of Justice (a group of 13 judges chosen for six-year terms).[41] The Treaty contemplates that the Commission will initiate legislative proposals, that the Council will enact legislation into law, and that the Court of Justice will pass on the legality of the legislation and on the extent of Member State compliance. The European Parliament, which represents the people of the Member States directly, will apparently play an increasingly important role under the Maastricht Treaty on European Union.[42]

1. The adoption of directives before the Single European Act

On paper, the Treaty divided the legislative powers by vesting the power to propose laws in the Commission and the power to enact laws in the Council.[43] As drafted, such a division of authority located a substantial measure of legislative power in the Commission by giving it some control over the Council's agenda and the kinds of proposals that came before the Council for a vote. In practice, however, the Council long dominated the legislative process by institutionalizing a process of Commission consultation with Council representatives before matters come before the Council for a vote.[44] As a consequence, the legislative process in Europe has been characterized as one that emphasizes intergovernmental bargaining, resembling the negotiation of treaties, rather than one of legislation by representatives of a single governmental entity.[45] 'The legal form is one of decision-making; the practical form is, in fact, consensual bargaining'.[46]

A number of factors have contributed to a legislative output with more bite than one might have predicted from such a process of consensual bargaining between Member States.[47] First, environmental ministers typically represent Member States at the Council level on matters of environmental concern. Such ministers may more willingly accept environmental initiatives than their counterparts in other sectors of the government.[48] Second, the Union legislative process, especially in the environmental field, has grown exceedingly complex and technical. In such a world, Commission experts with a preference for stronger measures may influence the final product, as they translate broad policy goals into specific pieces of legislation.[49] Finally, even in a world of consensual bargaining, Member States may agree to support more a relatively restrictive environmental measure, either because they recognize that it will not enter into force for some years or because they seek to secure gains in other areas.[50]

2. Changes in competence under the Single European Act

Perhaps the most important recent change in European environmental competence was that accomplished with the entry into force in 1987 of the

Single European Act. The Act, which amends the basic EU Treaty, placed environmental policy on a secure footing, with a variety of provisions that confer legislative competence on Union institutions in the environmental field.[51] In particular, Article 100a authorizes the Union to issue environmental legislation for the purpose of perfecting the internal market,[52] thus in a sense ratifying the Union's earlier use of its Article 100 harmonization powers to accomplish environmental goals.[53] In addition, Article 130s authorizes the Council to take action in the environmental field, so long as it complies with the array of general principles in Articles 130r[54] and 130f[5] that define the appropriate scope, and preemptive effect, of such Union action.

Others have explored the implications of these changes in environmental competence at some length. Rather than repeat their observations here, I will briefly summarize the high points of the Union's revised environmental competence. First, Article 100a authorizes the Council to take action by qualified majority, thus abandoning the requirement of unanimity that Article 100 had previously imposed.[56] Second, Article 100a imposes an obligation on the Council not only to consult with the Parliament before taking action but also to exhaust a more formal process of cooperation with Parliament.[57] Thus, Article 100a signals a modest change away from Member State control towards a process that more directly involves popularly elected representatives.[58]   Finally, Article 100a requires that proposals for environmental action take as their base a 'high level of protection', language designed to assure environmental states that the push to complete the internal market would not inevitably reduce the scope of environmental protection.[59]

Contrast these provisions with the somewhat looser, less protective standards that appear in Articles 130r–t. No requirement of parliamentary cooperation appears in such sections,[60] nor do they authorize majority voting as an alternative to unanimity. Nor further do such sections require a high level of protection; indeed, they seem to contemplate a lower level of protection inasmuch as they specifically authorize Member States to maintain more protective standards as a matter of national law.[61] Finally, these sections impose a guideline of subsidiarity, which encourages the Union to act only in cases where the environmental issue can be handled better at the Union than at the Member State level.[62]

Many worried that the Council might attempt to skirt the qualified majority, parliamentary cooperation, and high level of protection rules of Article 100a by relying instead on Articles 130r–t.[63] The Court of Justice's recent decision in *Commission v. Council*[64] would appear to quiet these fears. There, the Court held that the Council had acted improperly in basing the titanium dioxide directive on Articles 130r–t, instead of on Article 100a as the Commission had proposed.[65] Future environmental legislation, virtually all of which bears some relationship to trade matters, may thus necessarily rest on Article 100a, leaving only such matters as habitat directives and common research programs within the ambit of Article 130s.[66]

Entry into force of the Maastricht Treaty, or Treaty on European Union, further cements the Union's environmental competence and broadens the role of Parliament in the legislative process. In addition to Parliament's powers under the cooperation procedure, Maastricht adds a new codecision procedure to Article 100a.[67] Under the terms of the procedure, Parliament may participate in a conciliation committee that will negotiate the final terms of a particular measure between the Council and Parliament.[68] While the unanimity provisions of Articles 130r–t require only consultation with Parliament,[69] the titanium dioxide decision limits the availability of such procedures and enhances the role of the Parliament in the legislative process.

3. The enforcement of Union directives

As noted above, the historically most significant source of legislative competence in the environmental field, Article 100, authorized the Council to issue directives to Member States. According to Article 189 of the Treaty, such directives 'shall be binding, as to the result to be achieved, upon each Member State to which it is addressed, but shall leave to the national authorities the choice of form and methods'. The Treaty thus contemplates that directives will take effect as law upon their transposition into positive law of the Member States.[70] But at the same time the Treaty contemplates effectiveness upon transposition, it imposes a binding obligation on Member States to adopt and enforce appropriate legislation. The Treaty thus empowers the Union, in American terms, to 'commandeer' the Member States into the adoption and enforcement of central environmental measures.

Article 169 of the Treaty attempts to effectuate the Union's power to act through the Member States by authorizing the Commission to bring an enforcement proceeding against a Member State before the Court of Justice.[71] Typically, the Commission follows a three-step process.[72] It first furnishes an informal notice to the Member State, informing the state of its failure to comply with some aspect of the directive and requesting comments. If the comments do not satisfy the Commission, it will deliver a 'reasoned opinion' describing the nature of the Member State's Treaty violations. The great majority of enforcement proceedings terminate in a settlement between the Commission and the state at one of these early stages of the proceeding.[73]

If a settlement does not emerge following the issuance of a reasoned opinion, the Commission will invoke the Article 169 jurisdiction of the Court of Justice.[74] In such a proceeding, the Commission essentially seeks a declaration that the Member State has breached its obligations under the Treaty.[75] Moreover, the Member States owe a duty under Article 171 to take 'all necessary measures to comply with the judgment'.[76] If the Member State fails to do so, the Commission may bring a further Article 169 proceeding to establish the failure to comply.[77]

C. The Scope of Member State Conscription in Europe

The Treaty thus authorizes the Union to rely upon Member States as the administrative vehicles for the enforcement of supranational environmental (and other) law. When the Council passes directives, it does so with a view towards their transposition into the national law of Member States. And when the Court of Justice agrees with the Commission that the state has failed to achieve the required transposition, it enjoys the authority to declare a breach of the Treaty. This section considers how far such conscription of Member States extends in practice.

1. The degree of specificity

The definition of directives in Article 189 of the Treaty may suggest some limitations on the power of the Union to compel Member States to adopt detailed provisions of central environmental law.   Article 189, after all, provides that a directive shall be binding only as to the result to be achieved, 'but shall leave to the national authorities the choice of form and methods'. In contrast to the directive, the Treaty provides that the alternative form of Union legislation – the regulation – 'shall be binding in its entirety and directly applicable in all Member States'. The Treaty thus appears to contemplate a distinction between relatively precise regulations, which take effect upon issuance, and more general directives, which leave Member State legislators and administrators rather more policy-making discretion and take effect only upon transposition into Member State law.

This formal distinction between regulations and directives, however, has eroded over time.[78] The Council has increasingly issued directives that specify rather precise legislative obligations for the Member States – so precise, in fact, that they leave 'Member States little choice as to their implementation under national law'.[79] Such directives, which Rehbinder and Stewart have justly termed 'regulation-type' directives,[80] often contain detailed substantive provisions, including prohibitions, standards, tolerances, as well as similarly detailed procedural rules to govern testing and measurement methods.

While the Union continues to issue what Rehbinder and Stewart term 'typical' directives, those that follow the model contemplated in the Treaty by specifying only the results to be achieved and leaving Member States with some implementation discretion, many directives in the environmental field have a hybrid character. The shellfish and freshwater fish directives provide good examples.[81] In these directives, the Union established standards for the level of pollution in shellfish and freshwater fish waters. While the directive specifies limit values and minimum sampling frequencies and techniques in some detail, it leaves Member States free to designate the waters in which such standards shall apply.[82] A similar measure of discretion accompanies the bathing water directive, which establishes limit values for waters traditionally used by recreational swimmers but leaves the Member States some freedom to define at what point the 'number of swimmers' becomes sufficiently 'large' to trigger the directive's application.[83]

Even such hybrid directives, however, impose rather dramatic constraints on Member State legislative discretion. In *Commission v. Italy*,[84] the Court of Justice held that Italy had violated its obligations under the Treaty by failing to designate any waters to which the shellfish and freshwater fish directives were to apply. In a similar case, the Commission contended that Great Britain had failed to implement the bathing water directive by taking the position that only 27 beaches met the 'large number' of swimmers requirement that triggers application of the directive's water quality standards.[85] Great Britain responded by designating an additional 362 beaches, apparently conceding that its initial designation violated the terms of the directive.[86]

In sum, the Union's reliance on the directive in the environmental field has not limited the specificity of the obligations that the Union may impose on Member States. More significant has been the Union's decision to rely on Member States, rather than legislating into existence Central European institutions (such as a European Environment Agency) with monitoring and enforcement powers.[87] Given that choice, the importance of the distinction between directives and regulations can be easily overstated. In truth, the Union's use of the relatively detailed directive has the potential to achieve results just as far-reaching as those attainable through a regulation, at least in circumstance where Union law envisions more than the mere setting of standards and contemplates Member State creation of new monitoring institutions and procedures.[88] The Council cannot simply regulate such Member State institutions into existence and the directive remains the only practical tool of Union action.

2. The scope of required transposition

As directives have become increasingly detailed, their adoption by the Council requires Member States to take relatively precise legislative steps to comply with their obligations under the Treaty. The obligation of Member States to carry directives into effect through appropriate legislation appears in a variety of provisions in the Treaty, most notably Article 189.[89] As interpreted by the Court of Justice, this obligation of transposition requires Member States to implement directives by enacting laws or adopting administrative regulations 'with unquestionable binding force, or with the specificity, precision and clarity required . . . to satisfy the requirement of legal certainty'.[90]

While the Court frequently includes dicta in its opinions to the effect that the Treaty does not require a verbatim transposition,[91] the obligation of 'legal certainty' in the transposition of relatively detailed environmental directives leaves Member States with little practical discretion. Consider, for example, the Court's handling of the Commission's claim of noncompliance in *Commission v. Germany*.[92] Germany had chosen to implement the air quality directive on sulphur dioxide and suspended particulates[93] by issuing a technical circular that it claimed had the force of law. Germany also contended that, whatever the state of its law, its administrative practice had in fact resulted in the actual observance of all limit values in the directive.[94] What Germany had failed to do was to adopt national laws establishing mandatory air quality standards.[95]

Despite the seemingly technical nature of the Commission's objection, the Court of Justice agreed that Germany had violated its obligations under the Treaty.[96] In part, the Court relied on provisions of German administrative law that gave technical circulars a discretionary, as opposed to legally binding, character.[97] In part, it relied on the failure of the circulars to cover all firms within Germany.[98] At bottom, however, the Court simply held that where a directive establishes a mandatory rule, such as the air quality mandate at issue in the case, Member States must transpose that mandate into their national law.[99] They may not simply take the limit values established in the directive as guidelines for the exercise of existing administrative discretion, even where the exercise of such discretion produces compliance in practice with the requirements of the directive.[100]

The Court's relatively demanding standard of transposition applies not only to the substantive rules in the directive but also to the procedural. In *Commission v. Italy*,[101] the Court found a substantive violation in Italy's failure to enact laws implementing the groundwater directive's[102] affirmative prohibition of the discharge of banned substances. The Court also held that Italy had taken insufficient steps to comply with rules governing the procedures that Member States must follow in authorizing certain kinds of discharges.[103] Finally, the Court held that Italy had failed to comply with so much of the directive as required it to monitor compliance with the conditions in any permits it issued and to keep on hand an inventory of such permits.[104]

Just as it has demanded relatively precise and clear transposition of substantive and procedural elements of directives, the Court of Justice has refused to accept a range of excuses for non-transposition. Thus, the Court has rejected such proffered Member State excuses as national constitutional impediments, chaotic domestic politics, practical and administrative delays and excessive expense.[105] Consider, for example, the Court's decision in *Commission v. Belgium*,[106] a challenge to the failure of Belgium to implement the standards in the directive on the quality of drinking water.[107] Belgium defended primarily on the ground that the expense and complexity of compliance had produced the delay.[108]   The Court began by reminding Belgium that a Member State 'may not rely on practical or administrative difficulties' to justify a failure to implement Community directives.[109] 'The same holds', the Court concluded, 'for financial difficulties', which the Member States must overcome by taking appropriate measures.[110] Appropriate measures in the case amounted to a capital outlay of some 1.5 billion Belgian francs to construct a water treatment plant for the town of Veviers.[111]

To summarize, the Court's transposition learning demonstrates how the issuance of a directive may affect the internal legal order of the Member States. The Treaty relies upon Member States to carry central environmental legislation into effect by adopting and enforcing appropriate national legislation and obviously contemplates that Member States will bear the cost of compliance. Similarly, the Treaty contemplates that central legislative initiatives can dictate the legislative and administrative agenda of Member States. Directives require Member States to adopt legislation or administrative regulations that satisfy the Court's 'legal certainty' test for proper transposition. Relatively detailed directives, such as the air quality and groundwater directives at issue in *Commission v. Germany* and *Commission v. Italy*, impose relatively strict legislative obligations on Member States. Such directives go well beyond Article 189's model of prescribing results that leave Member States a choice as to 'form and methods'; they may compel the Member States to adopt a particular legislative approach to the environmental problems addressed in the directive.[112]

3.   The doctrine of direct effect

While the Member States themselves negotiated the better-defined terms of environmental competence in the Single European Act, the Court of Justice largely bears responsibility for developing the doctrine of direct effect.[113] Under the doctrine, directives that create relatively specific rights for individuals may be asserted by them in national courts even where the Member State has failed to transpose the directive into national law. Direct effect does not apply to all directives; to qualify, the directive must impose a clear and precise obligation on Member States, the obligation must be unconditional, and, it must leave Member States no margin of discretion in implementation.[114] Once such conditions have been satisfied, an individual may assert rights established in a non-implemented directive against the Member State in national courts, invoking a species of estoppel.[115]

Such a regime of direct effect thus gives the directive at least some of the same properties that regulations and Treaty provisions enjoy. But important differences remain.[116] First, direct effect notwithstanding, directives still impose an obligation of transposition on Member States;[117] they thus contemplate implementation of a kind not required of directly applicable regulations and Treaty provisions. Second, the Court of Justice has applied only the most limited form of direct effect to directives. Thus, directives may provide a shield to individuals in defending against claims of illegality under Member State law,[118] and may confer certain affirmative rights on individuals as against Member States.[119] Directives, however, do not 'on their own impose obligations on individuals and a provision of a directive cannot be relied upon as such against individuals'.[120] Thus, the Court has held that a private individual may not enforce the duties that a directive, if fully implemented, would cast on other individuals or firms – thereby rejecting the doctrine of 'horizontal' direct effect for directives.[121]

The doctrine of direct effect has obvious, and somewhat negative, implications for the enforcement of European environmental law. The recognition of 'defensive' direct effect enables firms that face a Member State's more restrictive environmental regulations to escape their effect through an appeal to the terms of an unimplemented directive that harmonizes environmental law at a less restrictive level.[122] The rejection of horizontal direct effect, however, precludes environmental activists from challenging, at least as a matter of European law, a particular firm's emissions as violative of the terms of a directive that has not yet been transposed into Member State law. Nor can environmentalists apparently seek affirmative relief in Member State courts, either in the form of an injunction against Member State approval of a polluting project or in the form of damages for non-implementation, in the wake of a Member State's failure to implement a directive in practice.[123] Such a disparity in effectiveness obviously makes the clear and speedy transposition of environmental directives all the more important.

D. Criticism and Proposals for Change

Although no one in Europe doubts the power of central institutions to conscript Member States, many have questioned the effectiveness of European environmental policy. In part, the criticisms have focused on the substance of the regulations. Many would agree with the sentiments of one well-known observer, who admits that European environmental law has 'not always [been] a model of progressive environmental policy'.[124] Comparative assessments have concluded that while its policy in the field of water pollution measures up quite well, the EU regulates air quality on a less comprehensive basis than the United States.[125]

More recently, criticisms of European environmental law have shifted to the issue of Member State non-compliance. At one time, environmental policy-makers single-mindedly celebrated the number of pieces of such legislation on the books.[126] Simple agreement was counted a major success, in part no doubt because other areas of Union competence, such as transportation, have evaded Union action for years.[127]   Now European observers more widely recognize that the simple passage of central legislation does not ensure the effective enforcement of environmental standards by Member States.[128] With this increased attention on the compliance issue have come proposed changes to improve the quality of environmental enforcement.

In this section, I briefly summarize the nature of the compliance problem in Europe as well as the content of a variety of proposals for change. Interestingly, it appears that Europe has begun to evolve away from complete reliance on Member State conscription as the cornerstone of regulation and enforcement. How far that evolutive process will continue remains something of a mystery. Yet I find it significant that dissatisfaction in Europe with Member States as agents of supranational purpose mirrors in some respects the discontent that led to the ratification of the United States Constitution and the formation of a more national union.

1.   Union enforcement of environmental law

The Union's dependence on Member State enforcement highlights an important weakness of its enforcement scheme. Simply put, the Union has no group of independent environmental inspectors to monitor the extent of compliance with its environmental directives.[129] While the Commission has created a directorate general (DG 11) to deal with environmental issues, among others,[130] it has relatively few resources to commit to enforcement and little authority to conduct field investigations.[131] The Union flirted briefly with the creation of a European Environment Agency with full-blown powers of inspection but the Agency that finally emerged from the Council was limited to research, information-gathering and analysis.[132] Even such a scaled-down research and information Agency took some time to become operational as a result of political wrangling over its siting.[133]

Despite the absence of any central agency with direct enforcement authority, the Union has developed a variety of tools that enable it more effectively to look over the shoulders of the Member States. First, directives typically oblige Member States to send formal letters of compliance to the Commission that specify the nature and content of the legislation or administrative action the state has taken to comply.[134] The failure of the state to offer such evidence of compliance, or the submission of inadequate evidence, provides an obvious source of potential Article 169 enforcement proceedings.[135] The Commission can thus determine whether Member States have formally complied with a directive through the 'reasonably straightforward, and quasi-mechanical process' of monitoring the Member States' communication of compliance measures.[136]

While the mechanical process of reviewing compliance letters enables it to monitor formal compliance, the Commission may have greater difficulty in determining whether the laws communicated by the Member State actually establish a legal regime that complies with the directives. For example, the British government communicated compliance with the bathing water directive by relying upon provisions of the British Control of Pollution Act, neglecting to mention that the Act was not yet in force.[137] Similarly, many Member States implement directives by adopting administrative rulings that may or may not effectively ensure compliance with EU law.[138] Finally, Member States may rely on existing laws in circumstances where the law does not confer adequate enforcement authority.[139] Such examples of non-compliance no doubt violate Article 189, but the Commission may or may not identify and pursue them effectively.

Apart from the problem of determining whether the Member State has adequately transposed EU obligations into law, the Commission faces the troubling problem of measuring the adequacy of Member State implementation in practice.[140] Despite the adoption of Member State law, the actual quality of local drinking water or bathing water may fail to meet Union standards. By the same token, a Member State may approve a new project without first securing the environmental impact assessment required by the relevant directive.[141] In the absence of some mechanism for monitoring the degree of practical compliance, Member States might achieve formal compliance with Union law but tolerate departures from Union standards so routinely as to raise doubts about their practical enforcement of the Treaty obligations.

The Commission has some capacity to deal with the problem of practical non-compliance. For one thing, directives frequently specify reporting obligations that go beyond the simple obligation of communicating the formal transposition of EU law into Member State law. The air quality directives, for example, require Member States to establish stations to sample and report on air quality on a periodic basis.[142] Reports indicative of substandard air quality might lead to Commission enforcement proceedings. In addition, the Commission follows a policy of investigating citizen complaints.[143] Such complaints may produce an enforcement proceeding, if the Commission concludes that a Member State has failed to implement a directive in practice.[144]

Despite the Commission's efforts, however, most assessments of Union environmental enforcement reach rather pessimistic conclusions. Thus, Professor Macrory reports a dramatic increase in the number of enforcement proceedings against Member States, from a low of 16 in 1982 to a high of 217 in 1990.[145] He nonetheless concludes that, absent some substantial changes,[146] the gap between theory and practice will remain.[147] Dr. Ludwig Krämer, the legal advisor to the Commission's directorate general for the environment, has reached the same conclusion, noting disappointing gaps in implementation, particularly as to directives that require Member States to develop implementation plans.[148] Union environmental policy thus appears to suffer from the same 'non-compliance paradox' that plagues the implementation of other aspects of Union law.[149]

2. Proposals for change

Many of the proposals for changing the enforcement of environmental legislation in Europe have already been sketched. Some observers suggest that the Union should strengthen its European Environment Agency, by restoring its omitted enforcement powers.[150] Others note that the Council could improve the level of Commission enforcement by including provisions in directives that require Member States to report periodically on the state of practical implementation – following the model of the air quality reporting requirements.[151] Finally, some observers call upon the Commission to use public relations to place more pressure on Member States to implement environmental directives.[152]

Other proposals for change fall into two categories. In the first category, one finds suggestions that seek to perfect the current model of Member State conscription by improving the prospects that Member States will discharge their transposition obligations more effectively. One finds a reflection of such suggestions in the Treaty on European Union, which amends Article 171 by authorizing the Court of Justice to impose a 'lump sum or penalty payment' on Member States that fail to take the steps necessary to comply with an Article 169 finding that the state has failed to implement a directive. Such penalties may conceivably improve Member State compliance, at least at the formal level. In addition, some have proposed a loosening of the rules that currently preclude individual complainants from seeking judicial review of a decision by the Commission to refrain from instituting an Article 169 proceeding for non-compliance.[153] Finally, some have argued that the Union should do more to offer financial inducements to Member States that face difficulties in implementing certain directives.[154] All such remedies seek to perfect the current system of reliance on Member State enforcement.

A second category of proposed changes includes those that would move beyond the current model of Member State conscription and rely more heavily on direct effect and individual enforcement. Many commentators have urged the Council to issue regulations in the environmental field,[155] thereby bypassing the problems that arise from relying upon Member States to transpose environmental directives into national law.[156] Greater use of regulations would not solve all problems, of course. But while it would do little to overcome the delays Member States have experienced in implementing complex monitoring and rehabilitation programs, use of regulations would at least ensure that environmental standards, binding upon private industry, would take effect immediately in Member States. Depending on Member State rules of standing and justiciability,[157] individuals and citizen groups could enforce such directly applicable rules in Member State courts without awaiting transposition into national law.

In addition to proposals urging reliance on directly applicable legislation, many observers have suggested changes that would better enlist environmental groups into the task of policing implementation of European environmental policy.[158] Environmental activists have played an important role in lobbying the Union and its institutions[159] but have played a less visible role in enforcement.[160] Part of this enforcement gap stems from a shortage of information – citizen groups may not know when Member States fail to achieve environmental standards or propose projects that pose a threat to the environment. Even if groups learn of them, the Member States' systems of administrative or judicial review may not offer the groups effective means to enforce such standards or challenge such disputed projects.[161]

Proposals to make better use of environmental activists naturally focus on these problems. The information-gathering function of the European Environment Agency,[162] coupled with the recently agreed directive on access to information on the environment,[163] may well improve the ability of citizen groups to assist the Commission in monitoring enforcement of environmental law.[164] Others have suggested reforms aimed at enhancing citizen access to the national courts[165] – a reform that finds support in the Union's most recent environmental action program.[166] One proposal calls for the Member States themselves to develop legislation that permits citizen suits along lines recognized in the United States.[167] Another calls upon the Council to issue a directive harmonizing procedural rules to ensure citizen access to the courts to vindicate environmental rights.[168] The Commission recently took the first step toward such harmonization, establishing a working group to study the possibility of promulgating uniform standards for citizen litigation to enforce Union environmental laws.[169]

AMERICAN ENVIRONMENTAL REGULATION: UNDERSTANDING THE BAN ON EUROPEAN-STYLE DIRECTIVES

Our assessment of the Supreme Court's refusal to permit Congress to issue directives to the American states begins with a review the institutions of federal and state lawmaking and enforcement in this country and the modes of intergovernmental cooperation that have arisen here. After sketching the institutions of the Federal government through the eyes of James Madison, this section will review the practical operation of regulatory federalism in the environmental arena and then consider more explicitly the Court's recent decision banning Congress from issuing directives to the states.

A. The Constitutional Plan and the Role of the States

1. The vision of James Madison

In strikingly parallel language, the Constitution vests the legislative power in a Congress comprised of two chambers,[170] the executive power in a President,[171] and the judicial power in one Supreme Court and such inferior courts as Congress chooses to ordain and establish.[172] In addition to creating a tripartite form of national government, the Constitution recognizes, and seeks to guarantee, the states' political role in the government of the Union. Thus, the tenth amendment confirms that the Constitution reserves to the states or the people 'powers not delegated to the United States'.[173] Various provisions oblige the Federal government to respect and ensure the territorial and governmental integrity of the states themselves.[174]

In attempting to determine whether such a compound form of government permits Congress to make use of the states as agents of national purpose, the thoughts of the original federalist, James Madison, deserve special notice. Madison was attempting, in Federalist No. 39, to answer the claim of anti-federalists that the proposed plan effected a complete consolidation or nationalization of governmental authority and thus looked to the eventual disappearance of state governments. His response was surprisingly candid. He began by offering a definition of national and federal governments and then proposed to test the plan against the definition 'to ascertain the real character of the government'.[175] National governments were those that derived their fundamental powers from, operated upon, and were subject to amendment by the people themselves; federal governments were derived from, operated upon, and were subject to amendment by the sovereign states that composed them.

Tested by his proposed standard, Madison determined that the proposed government was 'in strictness neither a national nor a federal constitution; but a composition of both'.[176] In the section that most immediately addresses the Federal government's power to make use of state governments, Madison appears to suggest an affirmative answer. Discussing the operation of the proposed government, Madison begins with a definition. He describes as federal those governments that 'operate . . . on the political bodies composing the confederacy' and as national those that operate on 'the individual citizens, composing the nation, in their individual capacities'.[177] Interestingly, Madison concluded that the government was to operate largely on individuals, but he noted that it contained more 'federal features' than had been generally understood. 'In several cases', Madison noted, 'and particularly in the trial of controversies to which States may be parties, [the states] must be viewed and proceeded against in their collective and political capacities only'.[178] Madison argues, in other words, that the government would act on individuals primarily but would also enjoy some authority to act upon the states themselves.

Completing his analysis, Madison next turned to the idea that we most often associate with federalism, the idea of a national government of enumerated and limited powers that leaves the states a distinct and independent source of sovereignty. Here, Madison argued that the government was national only to the extent of its enumerated objects; it thus left to the states a 'residuary and inviolable sovereignty over all other objects'.[179] Madison was far from contending that the plan barred the general government from acting upon the states within its sphere of authority.[180] Indeed, he noted the Supreme Court's authority to pass upon disputes between states over their territory and sought to justify such authority by noting the Court's impartiality and the necessity of preventing an 'appeal to the sword'.[181]

2. Understanding Madison's vision

Everyone agrees with Madison that the Constitution authorizes the national government to pass laws directly applicable to the citizens of the United States. To cite only the most obvious example, Congress was given general powers of taxation, the President was obliged to execute the tax laws and collect the national revenue, and the federal courts were authorized to hear disputes over the collection of taxes as cases arising under the laws of the United States. But while the congressional powers directly to tax and otherwise regulate the citizenry have been widely accepted, the national government's power to act upon the states in their 'collective and political capacities', as Madison put it, has been far less accepted. Certainly, the Constitution contains nothing like the explicit authorization of directives that appears in Article 189 of the EU Treaty.

While no express answer appears in the document, the Constitution does contain a variety of provisions that appear to contemplate federal reliance on the institutions of state government to achieve national goals. Consider first the system of federal adjudication contemplated in the Constitution.[182] Like the EU Treaty before the Court of First Instance was added, Article III does not mandate inferior federal courts but contemplates only a single mandatory 'Supreme Court' with predominantly appellate jurisdiction. While Congress has the authority to institute lower federal courts, it may refrain from doing so in the expectation that state courts will handle federal judicial business in the first instance.[183]

Two provisions seek to make such state court adjudication responsive to the federal interest. First, the supremacy clause declares the federal Constitution, laws and treaties to be the supreme law of the land and explicitly makes them binding on state judges notwithstanding conflicting provisions of state law.[184] Second, Article III itself confers appellate jurisdiction on the Supreme Court to hear all cases coming from the state courts that implicate such supreme federal law.[185] Thus, Article III envisions original state court adjudication subject to appellate review in the Supreme Court – and thus supports Alexander Hamilton's claim that the courts of the states 'will of course be natural auxiliaries to the execution of the laws of the union'.[186] Such a provision for federal appellate review of state court decisions goes much further to secure federal supremacy than does the preliminary reference procedure of the EU Treaty.

The structure of the federal court system thus offers some support for Madison's claim that the framers contemplated reliance upon the states as agents of federal purpose. Further evidence appears in Article III's declaration that the Supreme Court shall have original jurisdiction 'in [all cases] in which a State shall be a Party'.[187] This striking grant of jurisdiction enables the Court to resolve disputes between the states, such as those over territory, jurisdiction and interstate waters that have occupied much of the Court's original docket.[188] In addition, as I have argued at greater length elsewhere, the jurisdictional grant by its terms authorizes the Court to hear claims to enforce federal obligations against the states in their capacity as such.[189] Indeed, Article III's reference to state–party 'cases' appears to sweep in all cases arising under the Constitution, laws and treaties of the United States.

The grant of original jurisdiction not only confirms that the states as such were to bear obligations to the national government but also suggests that the federal courts were competent to adjudge claims for violation of such obligations and to fashion appropriate remedies. The grant thus resembles the European Court of Justice's Article 169 jurisdiction over actions brought by the Commission to enforce Member State treaty obligations. Madison, then, not surprisingly, emphasized the role of the Supreme Court's original jurisdiction in describing the federal features of the government's operation. His description of the federal features of the plan in Federalist No. 39 specifically includes not one but two references to the Court's original cognizance of claims against the states as states.

What sort of claims did Madison expect the Court to entertain in the exercise of its original jurisdiction? One answer lies in the language of the Constitution itself, which prohibits the states as such from taking a variety of actions that were deemed inconsistent with the national interest. Article I of the Constitution prohibits the states from entering into treaties, alliances and confederations and bars them from impairing the obligation of contract.[190] The fourteenth amendment added the enormously important prohibitions against state deprivations of due process and equal protection of the law.[191] In addition, states were known to have violated the Treaty with Great Britain. The Court's jurisdiction over 'cases' was broad enough to encompass all such violations.[192]

The Constitution thus places duties and restrictions on the states and authorizes the federal courts to police state compliance with such higher law obligations. The Constitution also appears to authorize Congress to impose lawmaking and administrative obligations on the states. Begin with the fact that the supremacy clause not only declares federal law supreme and dictates that federal law will control state law in state court adjudication but also declares that 'the Members of the several State Legislatures, and all executive and judicial Officers . . . of the several States shall be bound by Oath or Affirmation, to support this Constitution'.[193] Such a provision has a dual significance; it not only operates as a directive itself (defining the content of state oaths of office) but also provides the foundation for the efficacy of future directives to state legislative and executive officials.[194]

Couple the suggestive language of the supremacy clause with a variety of provisions that explicitly authorize Congress to impose affirmative obligations on the states. First, the provision in Article I for the apportionment of 'direct taxes' according to the population of the states rests upon the assumption that Congress would enjoy authority to issue a requisition to the states.[195] The purpose of the direct tax provision, indeed, appears to have been to make the requisition power more effective by authorizing the Federal government to go to the people in the event that the states failed to comply.[196]

Second, the Constitution authorizes the Federal government to make use of existing state militias. Article I, section 8 authorizes Congress to 'provide for calling forth the Militia to execute the Laws of the Union, suppress Insurrections and repel Invasions'.[197] In addition, section 8 empowers Congress to provide for organizing, arming and disciplining the militia, 'reserving to the States respectively, the Appointment of the Officers, and the Authority of training the Militia according to the discipline prescribed by Congress'.[198] These powers of Congress to provide for the organization, discipline and calling forth of the militia were complemented by provisions in Article II, section 2, that made the President commander in chief of the militia of the several states 'when called into the actual service of the United States'.[199] The militia provisions thus specifically empower Congress to conscript the states as states into the service of the nation.[200] Together, the two provisions authorize Congress to issue requisitions for money and soldiers to the states, just as it had done under the Articles of Confederation.

Third, the comity provisions of Article IV – the full faith and credit clause and the interstate rendition clause – specifically authorize Congress to make use of state government.[201] Begin with the full faith and credit clause, which consists of two important provisions.[202] In the first sentence, it requires states and particularly state courts to accord full faith and credit to both the legislative acts[203] and judicial proceedings of sibling states.[204] In the second, it authorizes Congress to establish rules governing the admission of such acts and proceedings into evidence and to prescribe the effect thereof.[205] The provision thus establishes a rule directly applicable to state judicial officials and authorizes Congress to make similar binding rules by 'general Laws'.[206]

Article IV, section 2 of the Constitution declares in mandatory terms that the states shall, upon proper demand, return two classes of 'persons'. The first class consisted of fugitives from justice; the Constitution required that such individuals, upon proper demand, 'be delivered up, to be removed to the State having Jurisdiction of the Crime'. The second class consisted of runaway slaves, whom Article IV euphemistically describes as 'held to Service or Labour in one State' and 'escaping into another'.[207] As to runaway slaves, Article IV not only provides for delivery upon claim of the owner but also prohibits the state into which the slave had escaped from discharging the slave from 'such Service or Labour'.[208]

While the fugitive slave provisions were swept away with the Civil War amendments, the rendition of interstate fugitives from justice remains an important part of our national policy. Recently, the Supreme Court acted to assure the effectiveness of such rendition provisions by clarifying the obligations of state officials to comply with rendition requests from sibling states. In *Puerto Rico v. Branstad*,[209] the Court squarely held that federal courts may order state officials to comply with their constitutional and statutory rendition obligations.[210] The decision's significance lies in the Court's explicit repudiation of contrary authority in *Kentucky v. Dennison*,[211] which held that the Federal government 'has no power to impose on a State officer, as such, any duty whatever, and compel him to perform it'.[212] *Dennison*, the *Branstad* Court noted almost casually, had come down at a time of secession and threatened civil war – a time when the practical power of the Federal government was at its lowest ebb since the adoption of the Constitution.[213]

3. Updating Madison's vision

Madison and his colleagues thus envisioned a compound government that would enjoy authority to operate on the people, and to a lesser extent on the states themselves, within its sphere of competence. Like other framers, Madison distrusted the states as loyal agents of national purpose and sought to ensure the general government's ability to bypass them in appropriate situations by taxing and regulating the people directly or by establishing a national army to substitute for reliance upon the state militia. Once a more energetic general government was established, perhaps it could rely more confidently on the cooperation of the states.

One can thus understand the growth in the national government during the twentieth century as the realization of Madison's vision. Barriers to the exercise of congressional power over 'commerce among the several states' – the exceedingly important commerce clause authority of Article I – have been all but swept away. Congress can now regulate many activities once considered purely local on the theory that they affect the national economy.[214] In particular, the Court's decision in *Hodel v. Surface Mining & Reclamation Association, Inc.*,[215] makes it clear that Congress's plenary power over interstate commerce carries with it plenary authority over environmental regulation.

The broadened scope of congressional commerce authority has been accompanied by an enormous increase in the size, complexity and expense of national government.[216] As the national government has grown, so has the acknowledged power of the federal judiciary to enforce federal law against the states. To be sure, the Court still clings to a conception of state sovereign immunity that imposes important limitations on the power of an individual to collect money damages from the state as such.[217] Yet this limitation does not prevent individuals from seeking injunctive relief against state officials.[218] Nor does it prevent other governments, such as the United States or the states themselves, from prosecuting claims against the states.[219] The remedial powers of the federal courts, indeed, have a breathtaking reach when compared to those of the Court of Justice. The federal courts can not only award damages in certain appropriate cases,[220] they can issue injunctions to state officials that compel action on pain of contempt.

Yet the states have not been completely eradicated, or reduced to mere appendages of the Federal government, by this expansion of national authority. State budgets have grown dramatically throughout the century[221] and states retain broad, if not unfettered, control of such matters as criminal, tort, contract and property law, family law, probate, education and insurance. It is in these areas, of course, that citizens have many of their most significant (and numerous) contacts with government. Thus, state and local governments remain the focal point of much political activity as local groups vie to control education policy, streets, sewers, zoning and fire and police protection.

B. The Role of Congress and the States in Environmental Regulation: Acceptable Forms of Regulatory Federalism

Once Congress decides to enter a field of environmental regulation, it may implement its goals by choosing from a number of regulatory approaches or processes. First, and most obviously, it can simply establish a set of federal rules to govern environmentally hazardous activity, direct a set of government officials to police compliance with such rules, and authorize either the federal courts, or some federal agency, to hear claims to enforce its rules. When Congress takes such comprehensive steps, its regulatory scheme may preempt existing state law and foreclose the states from adopting conflicting rules or standards.

In contrast to such completely preemptive federal regulation, Congress may utilize a variety of techniques that preserve state competence. It may, for example, establish a partial set of rules that leaves state law in place or affirmatively delegate lawmaking competence to the states. If dissatisfied with the level of regulation achieved under a regime of state control, as Congress has often been in the environmental field, it can deploy its considerable resources to induce states to establish and enforce environmental standards that meet federal guidelines. First, it can offer the states a financial incentive to adopt the proposed regulatory program.[222] Second, Congress can induce states to adopt a particular set of federal standards by threatening them with a preemptive federal takeover of the regulatory field.[223]

Congress has used each of these regulatory techniques in an effort to achieve its environmental goals. We can find in the environmental arena examples of completely preemptive federal enactments, federal enactments that delegate important decision-making authority to the states, and federal statutes that seek to regulate by imposing relatively exacting obligations on the states. In many cases, as in the Clean Air Act and the Federal Water Pollution Control Act, Congress has deployed a combination of techniques in order to secure state cooperation with its policy goals.

1. Complete preemption

European observers acquainted with the power of Congress to take over the field and regulate to the exclusion of state law may find it surprising just how few times Congress has chosen that course of action in the United States. Virtually every federal environmental initiative preserves a role for state standard setting and state enforcement. While federal statutes and agencies often issue relatively detailed regulations, these regulations typically permit the states to fashion stiffer, more protective environmental standards.[224] Thus, the Clean Air Act,[225] the Clean Water Act,[226] and the Resource Conservation and Recovery Act[227] all establish minimum federal standards that expressly preserve the power of the states to design a more protective environmental program.[228]

Against this pattern of incomplete federal occupation of the environmental field, two exceptions deserve notice. First, Congress has enacted standards for motor vehicle emissions that, almost completely, preempt state law.[229]

Second, Congress has taken similarly preemptive action with respect to certain aspects of its regulatory scheme for toxic substances.[230]

2. Delegation of authority to state decision-makers

Generally speaking, the states may address most pollution problems through the exercise of their police powers. They thus do not require an explicit delegation of authority from Congress to take regulatory action in their respective territories. Nonetheless, many forms of state regulation in the pollution arena would run afoul of the Constitution in the absence of some form of congressional approval. Thus, state regulations that burden interstate commerce would violate the dormant commerce clause,[231] those that conflict with federal standards would violate the supremacy clause[232] as would those that regulate federal instrumentalities.[233] One can thus view a congressional decision to leave state regulatory authority in place as a delegation of authority.

In the environmental field, one finds important examples of delegated state authority in the statutes that authorize the states to regulate federal instrumentalities.[234] The Coastal Zone Management Act seeks to encourage states to adopt land-use and resource management plans to address the environmental implications of development projects in the nation's coastal zones.[235] Congress offered one common incentive, financial and technical assistance, to induce states to develop such programs.[236] In addition, Congress provided that state programs, once approved by the Department of Commerce, could regulate federal activities and projects as well as private-sector activities that require federal permits.[237] Such provisions authorize the states to determine whether such federal activities meet the test of 'consistency' with the approved state program.[238] While Commerce retains the power to override state regulations, the override authority has rarely been invoked.[239] The statute thus confers substantial practical regulatory authority on the states.[240]

3. Cooperative federalism in environmental regulation

In a useful (if somewhat hyperbolic) study of the tools of regulatory federalism, the United States Advisory Commission on Intergovernmental Relations (ACIR)[241] has identified four devices that Congress commonly uses to induce states to comply with federal regulatory initiatives.[242] The simplest and most straightforward device, the attaching of conditions to federal grants-in-aid, enables Congress to use its spending power to induce states to regulate in specified ways. Building on the spending power, Congress has occasionally imposed 'crosscutting' requirements – rules that generally apply to all recipients of federal funds.[243] In addition to such across-the-board requirements, Congress sometimes imposes 'crossover' sanctions – rules that withhold federal funds from certain grant programs to punish state non-compliance with other, more or less unrelated, programs.[244] Finally, ACIR refers to the threat of complete preemption to induce state regulation in accordance with federal standards as 'partial' preemption.[245]

While many observers associate the 'crosscutting' device with the problem of discrimination,[246] Congress has used this approach in a variety of environmental statutes. The best example appears in the provisions of the National Environmental Policy Act of 1969.[247] Section 102 of NEPA requires federal agencies, contemplating proposals for legislation or other 'major Federal actions significantly affecting the quality of the human environment', to prepare an environmental impact statement on the action.[248] Sub-paragraph D makes it clear that NEPA's impact statement requirement extends to any major federal action 'funded through a program of grants to the states'.[249] The Act thus requires state officials to prepare and file impact statements any time they contemplate environmentally significant action with federal grant support – a burden they find relatively onerous.[250]

Crossover sanctions and partial preemption appear in a variety of environmental statutes, perhaps most notably the Clean Air Act.[251] The Clean Air Amendments Act of 1970 dramatically expanded the federal role in the effort to address air pollution in the states. Although the Act declared that each state shall have 'primary responsibility' for assuring air quality within the geographic confines of the states,[252] the Act gave the states relatively little choice in deciding what they would do to carry out such a responsibility.[253]

Congress used a variety of techniques to induce states to implement the EPA's national air quality standards. For one thing, Congress offered to pay anywhere from one-half to two-thirds of the cost of administering approved programs.[254] The provision of such grants, conditioned as they were on submission of a SIP that complied with federal standards, followed a well-worn path. For another, Congress offered the states a partial preemption alternative; the states could either submit a SIP or submit to the federal imposition of a federal plan.[255] In the 1977 amendments, Congress sought to strengthen state compliance in certain non-attainment areas by adding a crossover sanction that requires federal agencies to withhold highway grants if states refuse to comply.[256] Finally, section 176 bars any federal agency from assisting, licensing or permitting any action that fails to conform to an approved SIP, an exemplary crosscut.[257]

Once it developed the SIP device in the Clean Air Act of 1970, Congress extended the pattern of encouraging state adoption and enforcement of federal standards into other areas of environmental law. In the control of water pollution, Congress designated the states as the primary authority for the enforcement of pollution standards.[258] Congress followed a similar pattern in the regulation of surface mining[259] – a partial preemption scheme upheld in the *Hodel* case – and solid waste.[260] Similar, though in some respects less extensive, approaches were adopted in dealing with underground storage tanks and medical waste.[261]

These examples of regulatory federalism undoubtedly rely upon the states as agents of national environmental policy. Like European directives, each of the statutes surveyed here imposes on the states an obligation to take certain specified legislative action in order to participate in the federal program. Thus, section 110 of the Clean Air Act requires each state to enact 'enforceable emission limits' into law,[262] to monitor ambient air quality and provide data to the EPA,[263] to 'prohibit' air pollution sources that threaten the accomplishment of federal goals,[264] and to provide the relevant agencies with adequate funding and personnel to implement and enforce the relevant standards.[265] Similar provisions appear in many other federal environmental statutes.[266]

Such statutes differ from European directives in one important respect, however. In virtually every instance, Congress offers the states a choice. The state can agree to adopt the required laws and establish a regulatory program or it can refuse to do so and let the federal agency handle the administrative chores instead. To be sure, environmental statutes subject the states' choice to important constraints: to avoid becoming agents of national purpose, states must cede regulatory authority in an area of traditional state concern to the Federal government and forgo receipt of federal financial assistance. Yet the preservation of state choice, however constrained, remains enormously important in the United States with implications both for the array of remedies for state non-compliance and for the constitutionality of the conscription.[267]

C. Regulatory Federalism and the Problem of Enforcement

1. Enforcement against the states

Like Europe, the United States faces a two-tier problem in enforcing its environmental laws. In the first place, the federal agency must ensure that the state has taken adequate steps to implement and enforce federal standards. An initial assessment of such implementation takes place when the EPA first approves the state enforcement plan. Obviously, the EPA can simply refrain from approving those plans that fail to transpose federal standards into state law.[268] In addition, the adequacy of the state's implementation and enforcement of its plan remains subject to ongoing EPA oversight. In theory, the EPA might take over enforcement responsibilities if a particular state more or less completely fails to enforce its standards.[269] Alternatively, the EPA might take steps to withhold financial assistance from states that have failed to attain the required ambient air or water quality standards.[270]

None of these enforcement alternatives assures the seamless transposition of federal standards into a state enforcement regime. When the EPA fails to approve a SIP, or approves a SIP in part, it may create a legal twilight zone in which no applicable body of law regulates pollution sources.[271] Such a world closely resembles the situation in Europe when a Member State fails to take action to transpose a directive into national law.[272] In a departure from the European model, the EPA can fill such a gap by supplying its own federal plan,[273] but bureaucratic realities lean strongly against such a procedure. As a consequence, the EPA approval process often delays the entry into effect of binding legal standards.[274]

Practical problems also attend the imposition of other kinds of federal agency sanctions for state non-compliance with federal enforcement standards. States may find the threatened loss of grant money a significant spur to federal compliance but a decision to withhold funds may simply deprive the state of the resources it needs to achieve its enforcement goals.[275] In such cases, the use of a crossover sanction may make more sense; an order imposing a moratorium on highway construction and new sources of air pollution may spur state action at the same time that it actually reduces the incidence of pollution.[276]

As with other sanctions, the federal takeover of a state enforcement program represents a dubious remedy for a state failure to implement federal standards.[277] Serious enforcement efforts require permit and license review, inspections, monitoring, data-generation and litigation; each of these activities requires staff. One observer has estimated, for example, that a federal takeover of strip-mining enforcement in Kentucky would result in federal regulation of 7,000 mining operations and require a staff increase of 300 to 400 persons.[278] Surely a federal agency, such as the Office of Surface Mining, will think twice before issuing a takeover order that would require a staff increase of 40 percent to handle enforcement in a single state.[279] In any case, such a takeover would trigger a breach in federal–state relations that appears fundamentally inconsistent with the model of cooperative federalism that Congress wrote into the environmental statutes.[280]

2. Enforcement against polluters

As noted above, many environmental statutes express a federal policy of state primacy in enforcement.[281] To provide a legal foundation for this role, the federal statute typically requires the state to adopt regulations, emissions standards and monitoring techniques into state law and to provide assurances of adequate enforcement support.[282] Once the state adopts such laws and regulations, it submits them to the relevant federal agency as part of its SIP. Under the Clean Air Act,[283] and other statutes, the EPA approval process constitutes federal rulemaking and thereby establishes an independent federal basis for enforcement.[284] Discharges in violation of a SIP thus violate both state and federal law and subject the polluter in many cases to the prospects of dual sanctions.[285]

Such a regime of dual enforcement presents a variety of intergovernmental problems. The EPA understandably takes the position that it has an independent obligation to ensure the effective enforcement of environmental law. It thus follows a policy of overfiling – filing federal enforcement proceedings, even where state proceedings have been initiated, to assure a resolution that squares with the federal interest. State officials may find it difficult to conclude an enforcement proceeding through settlement in cases where the EPA enjoys overlapping enforcement authority; targets of such state proceedings may regard the federal proceeding as the main event.[286] In addition, targets of such dual enforcement efforts often seek stays of duplicative proceedings or invoke the doctrine of *res judicata* as a bar to overlapping prosecutions.[287]

A final source of enforcement authority appears in the citizen suit provisions of many environmental statutes. Such provisions, based on the famous section 304 of the Clean Air Act,[288] typically authorize any person to institute a civil action to remedy alleged violations of federal environmental standards.[289] The statutes make some attempt to coordinate such private enforcement proceedings with the state and federal enforcement program by requiring private plaintiffs to provide the relevant agencies, and the polluter, with 60 days' notice before instituting suit and by proscribing private suits where governmental enforcement actions have been initiated.[290] Such suits have tended to focus on securing EPA compliance with statutory deadlines, rather than seeking direct enforcement of environmental standards against polluters.

D. Assessing the Federal–State Partnership: The Problem of Adequate Resources

Assessments of the federal–state partnership in pollution control range from those who argue for a complete federal takeover of standard-setting and enforcement responsibility to those who argue for dramatic devolution of responsibility to the states. The argument for a stronger federal role rests in part on history; as Professor David Currie notes in arguing for a broader federal role in air pollution control, 'the states have had their chance, and they muffed it'.[291] Proponents of a stronger federal role also note the continuing hurdles to adequate state enforcement. Thus, in a critique of the application of the cooperative federalism model to surface-mining regulation, Professor Squillace contends that states often lack adequate enforcement resources and too often act to protect local industry.[292] He thus calls for direct federal regulation, using regional offices to ensure consideration of local concerns.[293]

In contrast to these calls for a stronger federal role, many contend that the Federal government should fashion a strategic retreat from environmental regulation. The Advisory Commission on Intergovernmental Relations is only the most devoted and persistent advocate of this view.[294] Its assessment of cooperative federalism, in the environmental field and elsewhere, suggests that the Federal government has moved too far and too fast in the direction of mandating state compliance with federal standards. ACIR thus calls for full funding of federal mandates,[295] an elimination of crossover sanctions,[296] a review of the crosscutting technique,[297] and an approach to partial preemption that leaves far greater discretion in program development, standard setting and enforcement to the states.[298] ACIR's proposal thus seeks in some respects a return to the regulatory model of the 1960s, when the Federal government offered technical and financial assistance but left the states largely alone in the administration of their programs. Its proposal resembles nothing so much as the model of the European directive, with central specification of results to be achieved and Member State control over forms and methods – a model that has largely been superseded in both Europe and America.

Despite these arguments for a dramatically broader, or narrower, federal role, it seems unlikely that the nature of the federal–state relationship will change dramatically in coming years. Most observers have made their peace with a broadened federal role, recognizing that pollution presents problems of nationwide scope that predictably evade state-by-state solutions. Similarly, it seems extraordinarily unlikely that the Federal government will agree to take on the financial and regulatory burdens, not to mention the political challenge, associated with the complete preemption of state environmental competence. Indeed, the federal budget deficit suggests, if anything, that financial necessity will result in the incremental transfer of greater enforcement responsibility to state governments.

One can find evidence that such an incremental transfer has already begun. In 1982, approximately 76 percent of state spending on environmental programs originated in the form of federal grants; by 1986, the figure had fallen to 40 percent.[299] The Clean Air Act expenditures reflect these changes; federal grants accounted for roughly half of state expenditures in the early 1980s and dropped to roughly 40–45 percent by 1990.[300] In the area of enforcement, the evidence of an incremental shift in the direction of real state primacy comes through more clearly. States initiate roughly 70 percent of the enforcement proceedings; the EPA only about 30 percent.[301] By the same token, states performed some 200,000 inspections in fiscal year 1988, roughly 90 percent of the total.[302]

Most observers expect these trends to continue. On the fiscal front, federal grants in aid to the state governments for environmental programs reached a high in 1980 of some $5.4 billion, or about 6 percent of the $91 billion total of grants in all categories for that year.[303] By 1991, the Federal government provided only about $4 billion to support state environmental programs, and this reduced figure represented only 2.7 percent of all grants to the states.[304]

Federal aid to state environmental programs has thus diminished both in absolute terms and as a percentage of total federal grants and forecasters predict a continuing decline.[305] At the same time, state budgets for environmental programs have continued to increase.[306]

The diminishing significance of federal financial support for state environmental programs has been accompanied by an expansion in the scope of the enforcement burden. One source of this enhanced enforcement burden might be termed structural. As the focus of environmental efforts shifts from relatively obvious point sources to less obvious nonpoint sources, the enforcement burdens grow. Similarly, as environmental regulation succeeds with the largest polluters, enforcement and regulatory efforts will tend to shift to smaller, and much more numerous, polluters.[307] A second source of the increasing enforcement burden stems from the passage of new federal legislation. One well-placed source estimates that the new underground storage tank and medical waste provisions[308] brought 43,000 new facilities under the regulatory umbrella in a single state.[309]

This combination of factors will predictably place increasing strain on federal–state relations in the environmental field. Some evidence of this strain shows up in the willingness of states to seek and accept delegated responsibility from the EPA to administer regulatory programs. In the water pollution area,[310] 38 of the 50 states had sought and obtained authority to run the NPDES permit system as of 1990.[311] In the solid waste disposal area,[312] 46 states and territories enjoy authority to administer the permit program for waste disposal facilities. In contrast to this relatively wide participation in the permit programs, only five states have been authorized to administer the program for correcting or rehabilitating existing solid waste sites and only 12 more will seek such authority.[313] One knowledgeable source attributes the dearth of state participation to the costs of such a program.[314]

Without any prospect of substantially increased federal funding, and with the anti-tax sentiments of many state electorates cramping state fiscal resources, it appears evident that some new source of funds must be tapped to underwrite the cost of regulation. Increasingly, it seems, the United States will rely upon the familiar 'polluter pays' principle. The Clean Air Amendments of 1990 authorized air control agencies to collect from regulated sources a permit fee calibrated to recoup the costs of review, monitoring and enforcement[315] – an amount estimated to total $300 to $500 million.[316] Similarly, federal legislation increasingly imposes bond requirements on potential polluters to secure payment of future clean-up costs.[317] One can confidently predict that such fee and bond requirements will become a part of future amendments to other statutes.[318]

E.   The Prohibition on Directives: The Roots of American Hostility Towards State Conscription

As the preceding review makes clear, the United States tolerates a great deal of reliance on state enforcement in the arena of environmental regulation. In regulatory initiatives as wide-ranging as those involving air and water pollution control and the regulation of surface strip mining, states administer standards that have been established by the Federal government and enacted into state law.   Generally speaking, however, states have more or less voluntarily agreed to adopt these standards either to secure a (diminishing) supply of federal grant funds or to protect their authority to regulate important industrial activity from threatened congressional preemption.

But while federal reliance upon state legislative and executive resources has become a routine part of regulatory federalism in the environmental arena, the Supreme Court and most academic commentators have been quite adamant in opposing the power of Congress to issue European-style directives to the states.   In this section, I explore the origins of this hostility as well as arguments against directives that range from those based on the history of the framing and on the political accountability of Congress to states and the people.

1.   The rise and speedy decline of the directive

The EPA almost single-handedly called forth a massive academic and judicial outcry against the use of directives in America.[319] Sometime after the Clean Air Act of 1970 took effect, the EPA promulgated guidelines for state implementation plans that called for important changes in state regulation of automobile emissions in particularly heavily travelled (read dirty) metropolitan areas.[320] Recognizing that it lacked the staff and resources to administer such changes itself, the EPA sought to compel state adoption and enforcement of such requirements as retrofitting emission control devices, dramatic reductions in downtown parking, enhanced access to mass transit, and vehicle inspection.[321]   When states refused to adopt SIPs that included such far-reaching changes, the EPA took the position that it had the authority to impose them by way of a federal plan. Further, the EPA argued that, once the federal plan took effect, the states were obliged to adopt the required regulations on pain of injunctions and civil contempt sanctions.[322]

EPA explained its regulatory approach essentially by arguing that desperate times require desperate measures. Almost no one was persuaded. States filed suit in a variety of federal courts to challenge the EPA's implementation plans and were fairly successful in having them struck down.[323] Although two courts based their decisions on a restrictive interpretation of the EPA's statutory authority, they clearly indicated that such interpretations were essential to avoid decision of the constitutional question whether the Federal government may so conscript the states.[324] When issue was joined before the Supreme Court, the Federal government backed down by taking steps to moot the case and avoid a final judicial pronouncement.[325] Congress also avoided the question, acting in the 1977 amendments to broaden alternative sanctions for state non-compliance and refusing to provide the EPA with explicit authority to seek injunctive support for its issuance of directly binding orders to the states.[326]

While the EPA avoided any authoritative resolution of the question before the Court, its regulatory initiative called forth a variety of critical academic commentary. Most observers agreed that the EPA's attempt to dictate environmental policy to the states unconstitutionally interfered with the states' sovereignty.[327] Most such critiques rest on claims about congressional accountability for the exercise of the disputed power and thus extend Professor Herbert Wechsler's pathbreaking work on the political safeguards inherent in the role of the states in the composition of the national government.[328] Essentially, critics argue that Congress bears no political responsibility for the mandates it imposes through the agency of the states; permitting Congress to use such a device would thus enable it to shift the financial and political costs associated with unpopular programs to state governments and officials.

Apart from fears of congressional irresponsibility, many critics fear that use of federal mandates will displace genuine state political processes and priorities. Thus, Professor Kaden emphasizes the tendency of state directives or mandates to occupy the states' legislative, executive and fiscal capacities.[329] Such legislation bears the stamp of federal coercion and thus lacks any local political content. Kaden contrasts the mandate with more direct forms of congressional regulation, such as those that take over administrative tasks entirely.[330] Such direct forms of regulation do narrow the scope of permitted state action, but the states' 'capacity for political choice within the residual area remains intact'.[331] Similar arguments appear in other critiques.[332]

Finally, a measure of the scholarly dismay at the use of mandates or directives appears to stem from a perception that they represent a new, unprecedented form of federal regulation. The clearest evidence of this attitude appears in the remarks of Professor David Currie, who noted in his critique of the EPA's approach that he could not recall previous statutes that require state officers to engage in regulatory activities.[333] The perception of novelty feeds the argument for a finding that directives violate the autonomy of the states; Currie thus concludes that Congress may not treat the states as 'administrative organs of the Federal government' because 'such a thing is contrary to the accepted understanding of the nature of a federal union'.[334]

2. Formal judicial invalidation of the directive: *New York v. United States*

Justice O'Connor's opinion in *New York v. United States*[335] represents the culmination of the Court's search for some sort of judicially enforceable limit on the scope of Congress's power to regulate in areas traditionally reserved to the states.[336] It comes after what can only be described as the Court's failed attempt to establish substantive limits on Congress's power in *National League of Cities v. Usery*.[337] In *NLC* the Court held that the tenth amendment limits the power of Congress to extend generally applicable fair labor standards to state employees who were performing traditional state functions. After some years of vacillation, the Court reversed itself in *Garcia v. San Antonio Metropolitan Transit Authority*,[338] and held that the tenth amendment imposes no such limitation. If *Garcia* holds up, Congress will decide for itself the substantive scope of its power to subject state functions to general regulatory initiatives.[339] States wishing to remain outside the scope of a federal initiative must persuade Congress to fashion an exception for them.

The decision in *New York v. United States* does not purport to breathe new life into *NLC*; indeed, the Court treats New York's claim as one that fails to present the question.[340] In her opinion for the Court, moreover, Justice O'Connor claims to have made her peace with the breadth of Congress's regulatory authority; the Justice acknowledges that the interstate market in the disposal of low-level radioactive waste comes 'well within Congress' authority under the Commerce Clause'.[341] Having accepted the substantive breadth of the commerce authority, the Justice attempts to fashion a process-based limit on the manner in which Congress may attain its objectives.

Building on the dicta in earlier decisions, O'Connor holds that Congress may not simply '"commandee[r] the legislative processes of the States by directly compelling them to enact and enforce a federal regulatory program"'.[342] The Court thus struck down a provision of the Low-Level Radioactive Waste Policy Amendments Act of 1985 that required the state of New York to 'take title' to waste generated within the state if it failed to make adequate provision for its disposal. For O'Connor, such a provision would commandeer state governments into the service of federal regulatory authority and would thus violate the Constitution's division of authority between Federal and state governments.

Justice O'Connor's opinion does not raise any doubts about the continuing authority of Congress to offer states inducements to adopt particular regulatory schemes. The Justice thus acknowledges the breadth of congressional spending power and notes that conditional spending may well 'influence a State's legislative choices'.[343] Justice O'Connor also notes that the Court has approved 'cooperative federalism', and has thus recognized Congress's power to offer the states the choice of regulating activity in accordance with federal guidelines or submitting to federal preemption.[344]   She distinguishes the spending power and cooperative federalism from the 'take title' provision at issue in *New York* by emphasizing that the approved approaches leave the states free to make an informed choice among regulatory options.   Such regimes of free, if somewhat constrained, state choice differ, according to the Court, from the regime of compulsion involved in the 'take title' provisions of the Low-Level Radioactive Waste Disposal Act.[345]

Justice O'Connor offers two arguments in support of such a process-based limit on congressional power. She bases her first argument in history, arguing that the framers of the Constitution made a conscious choice to authorize Congress to regulate individuals directly and thus deprived Congress of its power to regulate individuals indirectly by issuing directives to the states.[346] Her second argument rests on the asserted need to preserve some measure of state autonomy in the federal system.[347] Viewing the states as comprising a polity separate from the political society of the United States as a whole, O'Connor seeks to assure the accountability of both Congress and the states by keeping clear the lines of responsibility for specific legislative initiatives. Permitting Congress to commandeer state legislative and executive action through the issuance of directives would cloud these lines of accountability and enable Congress to dodge both the political heat for, and the cost of, specific environmental regulations.

O'Connor also shares the concerns of many academic observers with the degradation of state political processes. For O'Connor, the maintenance of viable state political choices represents a cornerstone concern of federalism. Such choices survive when Congress permits a state's citizens to decide whether to participate in permissible federal grant or partial preemption programs; under such regimes, 'state governments remain responsive to the local electorate's preferences [and] state officials remain accountable to the people'.[348] Such responsiveness disappears when Congress compels the state to regulate.

DIRECTIVES AND CONSCRIPTIONS: COMPARATIVE CONCLUSIONS

With this summary of environmental federalism in place, we can revisit the marked difference in European and American attitudes toward the directive. Most European observers view the directive as essentially too weak. Many environmental critics have thus called for greater reliance on the more directly effective regulation as a tool of environmental regulation.[349] In addition, European critics seek to improve Member State enforcement of existing directives. Among other strategies, many support an expanded enforcement and monitoring role for Union institutions, expanded use of the citizen suit, and (assuming entry into effect of Maastricht) broader sanctions for Member State violations of Treaty obligations.[350]

In contrast to the European critique of impotence, observers on this side of the Atlantic tend to view the directive as too potent a tool to trust to Congress. As expressed both in Justice O'Connor's opinion in *New York v. United States* and in the scholarly commentary that anticipated the Court's ban on direct conscription, the concern stems from a desire to preserve a measure of state autonony. In brief, Americans fear that Congress will use the directive to impose unfunded regulatory obligations on the states and thus shift the cost of new programs off the federal budget and onto that of state and local governments. Use of directives will, moreover, drain state political processes of any content as state legislatures face the prospect of adopting federally specified standards into law.

In this concluding section of the chapter, I consider the comparative insights that these alternative visions of the directive offer for Europeans and Americans. Three predominate. First, its widespread acceptance in the European Union offers some support for a benign understanding of the directive's operation in America. Second, despite the directive's benign potential, institutional differences in the legislative and judicial processes help explain why American observers tend to regard the directive as too potent. Third, as the European Union continues to evolve in what Madison would have regarded as a national direction, we should expect to find increased concern among Member States with the directive and perhaps a growing call for judicial protection of the doctrine of subsidiarity.

A. The Arguments for Directives

1. Administrative efficiency

In thinking through the arguments for directives, the leading justification would appear to be regulatory efficiency. In Europe, each of the Member States already had in place a complex and relatively effective administrative state. When the Member States created the European Union, they could thus minimize the cost of administering new, central initiatives by allocating administrative responsibility to Member States. One sees examples of such administrative efficiency in the EC's use of Member States customs officials to collect duties on behalf of the Union.[351] Such reliance enables the EU to carry out its functions without adding staff that would duplicate the work of Member State officials.

The argument for administrative efficiency through the avoidance of duplicative enforcement personnel should appeal to taxpayers in all federal systems, not just in Europe.[352] Not surprisingly, then, we find Congress most likely to rely on states as agents of federal regulation in circumstances where the states already have in place a relatively sophisticated administrative scheme. When Congress began to consider no-fault automobile insurance, for example, early draft statutes relied on existing state insurance regulators.[353] Such reliance seems entirely sensible from an administrative perspective; the Federal government had long since delegated control of the insurance business to the states and had virtually no such administrative machinery in place. Relying on existing state officials makes more sense than hiring new, and perhaps duplicative, federal officials to administer the program. To the extent that the no-fault initiative affected only one aspect of the states' insurance regime, moreover, displacement of state control would have made little administrative sense.

Other examples appear to confirm that the desire to economize on administrative expense explains, at least in part, the desire of Congress to rely on state regulatory personnel. Consider such environmental initiatives as the Coastal Zone Management Act and the Surface Mining and Reclamation Act.[354] To secure relevant environmental protection, both statutes depend heavily on planning and zoning – matters over which state and local governments have traditionally exercised control. Similarly, both the Clean Air and Clean Water Acts – statutes that some describe as the most conscriptive ever passed by Congress – were layered on top of existing state administrative machinery. States had been administering air quality regions and water pollution standards under previous federal statutes and at least some concern with preserving state administrative machinery underlay congressional reluctance to displace them entirely.[355]

Directives seem far less effective, as a general rule, in circumstances where the administrative machinery does not already exist. The EPA experienced great difficulties in securing the creation of a system of permitting for the disposal of solid and hazardous waste under the RCRA.[356] Most states had not established any significant solid waste regulatory machinery, and the EPA was forced to create such a machinery from the ground up, with a series of federal grants to the states. By the same token, European observers note a much graver problem of non-compliance with environmental directives that call for the installation of elaborate new permitting, and monitoring programs.[357] Some have argued for the use of EU grants to assist Member States in implementing new programs.[358]

Viewed from the perspective of the representative citizen, who after all participates as a voter in both the Federal and state governments and pays taxes to both systems, the directive has a certain appeal. Such a citizen must finance two complete governments – one state and one federal – and might well choose a world in which the center implements its policy goals through existing state officials rather than by hiring additional federal personnel.[359] Unfunded federal directives might cause local tax increases to support the additional staff to carry out federal policy but the sum of all such local tax increases might well be less than the cost of fully funding a complete federal program. Surely that seems true in connection with the kind of far-reaching federal directives that have caused the gravest concern – the EPA's transportation control program and the no-fault insurance initiative.

Because the representative citizen plays a political role in both governments, and because legislators in both governments at least in theory respond to citizen concerns, the directive need not necessarily diminish the political accountability of either the state or federal government. After all, no one had difficulty in identifying the EPA as the source of the transportation control plans that triggered public outcry in the early 1970s. Individuals will buttonhole their local officials who will in turn lobby federal agents and members of Congress for a reversal of the policy. Ultimately, of course, the EPA and Congress backed down from their attempt to impose drastic new restrictions on vehicular use in metropolitan areas. While some might decry the failure of the policy, the political systems do not appear to have malfunctioned.

Yet there remains a widespread perception in both Europe and America that the directive obscures the origins of environmental and other central initiatives.[360] Indeed, it may be in Europe where the directive has its greatest tendency to cloud lines of political responsibility. Thus, some Member State politicians may attempt to insulate themselves back home by blaming Brussels for unpopular policies that they may, in fact, support at the Union level.[361] At the same time, the tendency of Brussels to operate behind a veil of secrecy,[362] coupled with the storied 'democracy deficit',[363] may obscure the fact that environmental standards emanate from the center.

2. Regulatory flexibility

In addition to the prospect of administrative efficiency, directives can offer a measure of regulatory flexibility different from that one might achieve through the use of command-and-control regulation administered through the regional offices of national agencies.[364]   Such flexibility seems essential in the European Union, where central legal directives can only enter into effect after they have been translated into the language, culture and legal system of the Member State. One suspects that in the process of translation, European directives attain a measure of local acceptability that central officials might well never achieve. Indeed, as noted above, the process of translation may obscure the central origins of environmental initiatives by clothing them in entirely municipal garb.

The advantages of translation seem far less evident in the United States, which shares a common language and legal culture, yet subtle gains through flexibility may remain. Depending on the degree of discretion left to the states in implementing and enforcing federal standards, local officials can anticipate trouble spots and balance competing interests with perhaps greater flair for local concerns than could a regulator from Washington, DC. By ironing out difficulties and incorporating the federal standards into the existing state and local regulatory environment, states might achieve a better mix of regulations than might otherwise emerge from duplicative government solutions.

I don't wish to push the point too far. Some may regard the existence of local regulatory flexibility as an invitation to let industry off the regulatory hook, rather than as needed play in the joints.[365] Some regulated firms may not cheer the existence of local practices that vary from the national norm.[366] But it remains undoubtedly true that the ultimate effectiveness of an environmental standard depends upon the existence of some relatively firm stake in the enforcement of the measure by those charged with carrying it out.[367] Directives, at least to the extent that they engage local politicians and enforcement personnel in the creative process of lawmaking and enforcement, may help translate a central measure into an effective local law. The problem of distinguishing creativity from laxity will inevitably remain.

3. Retention of Member State control over policy

Perhaps the most striking and confounding aspect of the European experience with directives in the environmental field is the extent to which Member States retain control of their own environmental policy. Consider the situation in Great Britain, where Nigel Haigh has studied in some detail the impact of European environmental directives on British policy.[368] Haigh concludes that British policy has been altered to a surprisingly small degree by the issuance of central directives. What he finds, by and large, are small administrative and occasional legislative adjustments in an environmental policy that has very much a life of its own.

Consider a few examples. Before the EU issued its first water quality directive, Great Britain already had in place a water quality program that focused, not on end-of-pipe emissions but on ambient water quality standards.[369] Once it convinced the Council that water quality directives should respect the British approach and include ambient standards as an alternative to end-of-pipe emission standards,[370] Great Britain could achieve its obligations under the Treaty by adjusting its ambient standards in line with the European values. Like most environmental directives (and most environmental legislation in the United States), the EC's water quality directives established only minimum limit values and did not preclude Great Britain from achieving cleaner water.[371] The directive thus required modest adjustment in ambient standards, and perhaps some changes in monitoring requirements, but left British water policy largely in place.[372]

The air quality directives had a more dramatic impact on British policy, but did not provoke the predictable cries of sovereign outrage.[373] The EU directive on ambient air quality standards for sulphur dioxide and suspended particulates effected a major departure from Great Britain's previous focus on particular sources of smoke and other airborne pollution.[374] While the directive required Member States to adopt and enforce air quality standards, standards that did not appear anywhere in British law, no one in the British Parliament much seemed to mind.[375] As for monitoring, Britain already had in place monitoring stations in many areas of the country.[376] Thus, both in the case of the modest changes required to comply with water quality directives, and the rather more sweeping alterations contemplated by the air quality directive, Great Britain has managed to retain a comfortable level of control over its domestic environmental policy.

Nor has its environmental policy stagnated in keeping with the American critics' prediction that states subject to directives will suffer a form of political anomie. Great Britain recently passed what it regards as a comprehensive and integrated approach to environmental regulation.[377] Though critics have questioned just how integrated an approach it represents,[378] its passage nonetheless demonstrates that British policy continues to evolve creatively, without simply awaiting direction from Brussels. Britain in sum hardly shows signs that its political life has been sapped as a result of its obligation to transpose EU directives into its municipal environmental law. Nor, for all I can tell, have the other developed Member States.[379]

In his discussion of the impact of the air pollution directives, Graham Bennett notes a rather more significant impact on the lesser-developed Member States – Greece, Spain, Portugal and Italy – where EU initiatives have produced a 'comprehensive reordering of existing policies, procedures and administrative arrangements'.[380] Interestingly, Bennett notes the possibility that EU policy may so occupy the attention of such countries as to hinder their development of the more comprehensive structures they need to address environmental concerns.[381] Bennett's work thus suggests that, where Member States lack an established administrative apparatus, directives will not only prove to be less effective tools of policy in terms of likely implementation but will also tend to capture the political process more completely.

In one sense, the relatively limited impact of central directives on well-administered Member States should come as no surprise.[382] As noted earlier,[383] both Europe and the United States typically regulate in the environmental area by establishing minimum standards. Such standards obviously leave a measure of policy-making judgment in the hands of state officials, who can decide both how to achieve the standards and whether to adopt tougher requirements in certain areas. Certainly, the imposition by directive of such minimum standards preserves a much larger share of state regulatory competence than would the adoption of completely preemptive federal regulatory initiatives. Yet American observers tend to shrug off the impact of completely preemptive federal regulations as the necessary price of federal supremacy and to take issue with a form of state conscription that leaves state policy-making more completely intact.[384]

B. Differing Attitudes Towards Directives

If directives offer advantages over central regulation in terms of administrative efficiency and local acceptability, then the divergence in the European and American attitudes may appear all the more puzzling. Part of the American antipathy towards directives may stem from sheer unfamiliarity; their use in such regulatory initiatives as the EPA's air quality control plans caught observers somewhat by surprise. Here, the comparative perspective offers real insights. The European experience (coupled with the framers' attitude towards the federal character of the governmental plan) makes clear that directives are not, as Professor Currie suggested, fundamentally inconsistent with a federal union. Indeed, reliance upon the states as agents of central purpose has an obviously more federal character than reliance upon national regulatory agencies. American hostility runs much deeper than that one might expect from the simple novelty of the device, however, and calls for a closer evaluation of the institutional differences between the systems.

1. Institutional differences in legislative competence

Begin with the important difference in the legislative institutions in Europe and America. In Europe, at least prior to the entry into force of the Single European Act, legislation under Article 100 of the EU Treaty required the unanimous vote of all Member States. In a sense, therefore, European states agreed to their own conscription through the issuance of directives. Such an element of voluntary state participation is lacking in the legislative process in the United States; though the make-up of Congress assures consideration of the interests of the states,[385] and though the states often lobby effectively in Congress, they undoubtedly enjoy less control over central initiatives than their European counterparts.

This institutional difference undoubtedly explains much of the difference in attitude towards the use of directives. American observers, including Justice O'Connor, invariably distinguish the states' coerced, yet still nominally voluntary, participation in a partially preemptive or federally funded program, from their involuntary conscription by way of directive.[386] One can understand the ban on directives in America, therefore, as a way to introduce a measure of state volition into programs of regulatory federalism. We lack any administrable way to secure a binding agreement among the 50 states through the legislative process,[387] so we constrain the process in ways that enable the states to opt in or out after the legislation emerges.

Yet the voluntary–involuntary distinction does not seem wholly explanatory. For one thing, Europe has experienced non-compliance with directives that emerged unanimously from the Council.[388] Such non-compliance may call into question the wisdom of the particular directive. Or it may suggest that internal state political processes do not always work seamlessly; agencies required to implement the directive may not play a role in the bargaining at the Council level that produces agreement on the measure. Similarly, most observers recognize that American states can rarely afford to refuse federal grant programs and must accept the strings that come with them as the price of doing business. Like their European counterparts, American states have had difficulty in complying with the 'voluntarily' assumed burdens of such programs.[389]

The fact that a state's consent does not ensure its compliance with a federal regulation simply underscores the point that the concept of a state's consent remains something of a legal abstraction. European states consent to directives in the same way that American states consent to participate in federal grant programs; they clothe the relevant officials with authority to act in the name of the state. Similar consent underlies the decision of the Member States to enter into, and broaden the competence of, the European Union. Such consents transfer some portion of state sovereignty to the central institutions and the legislation that emerges from them can be seen as the product of such consent. If consent offers the key to the acceptability of directives, therefore, one might locate such a consent in America's decision to form a more perfect union.

The point becomes clearer when one recognizes that the Single European Act abandons the unanimity requirement in favor of a system of qualified majority voting to speed the process of integration. Member State control was further weakened when the Court of Justice agreed with the Commission that the Council could not properly base the titanium dioxide directive on the unanimity provisions of Article 130s in preference to the qualified majority provisions of Article 100a.[390] Despite these important erosions of Member State control, a trend continued in Maastricht, the Union has yet to abandon reliance upon directives as a form of legislation. Although it affords them limited opt-out authority to administer stricter standards, Article 100a of the Treaty requires Member States to transpose at least the minimum standards of an environmental directive into positive law, even where they voted against the measure and thus withheld their consent from its adoption. In short, nothing inherently requires a federal system to couple its use of directives with a unanimity requirement that ensures formal state consent to conscription.

Again, I don't want to push the point too far. European states still exercise a good deal more control over the shape of the final legislative product of the Council than do the American states over that of Congress. Moreover, the construct of consent may tend to ameliorate some of the intergovernmental tensions that might accompany greater congressional reliance upon the directive. Yet Justice O'Connor goes out of her way to emphasize in her opinion in *New York v. United States* that the apparent willingness of New York to participate in congressional solutions to the low-level radioactive waste problem did not operate as consent sufficient to vitiate its tenth amendment claim.[391] It's also worth noting that measures found to lie within the scope of congressional authority under the necessary and proper clause do not require any consent from the states.

2. Differences in the nature of the remedy

Apart from institutional differences in the nature of the legislative process, Europe and America differ rather markedly in the scope of federal judicial power. The Court of Justice enjoys limited authority to entertain preliminary references on matters of Union law from Member States and thus can declare the content of European law.[392] But the Court lacks the power to exercise direct appellate review of decisions of Member State courts. Similarly, the Court of Justice enjoys jurisdiction over claims under Article 169 that a Member State has violated its obligations under the Treaty. But the Court lacks any remedial authority aside from the power to declare the existence of a violation and impose a monetary sanction.[393] Contrast this limited array of judicial tools with the relatively much stronger remedial powers of the federal courts. While the eleventh amendment and the doctrine of sovereign immunity pose some limits on the power of federal courts to award a monetary judgment against state treasuries to compensate an individual claimant,[394] even these limitations can be overcome through a clear congressional statement in legislation adopted under the fourteenth amendment or commerce clause.[395] Moreover, federal courts enjoy wide authority to issue injunctions to state officials.[396] Such injunctive authority has been widely deployed, both to desegregate state schools and other institutions, and to assure state compliance with federal standards imposed under programs of cooperative federalism.[397]

The comparatively stronger array of federal judicial remedies, coupled with the storied willingness of Americans to repair to the courts, threatens state officials with a relatively more potent dose of federal medicine if they fail adequately to implement a congressional directive. In contrast to the relatively civilized declaration of non-compliance that emerges from an Article 169 proceeding in Europe, directives in the United States might threaten state officials with injunctions ordering them to legislate and regulate in specified ways. Such injunctive relief obviously represents a much graver affront to state sensibilities and threatens a graver intrusion into the sphere of state autonomy. Indeed, the first widespread opposition to directives in this country grew out of EPA regulations that threatened state officials with injunctive relief and the prospect of contempt sanctions.[398]

One can thus understand Justice O'Connor's opinion in *New York v. United States* as an attempt to shield the federal courts – the enforcement wing of the Federal government – from the unhappy task of policing state compliance with congressional directives. One can also understand the willingness of O'Connor and others to accept congressional use of its spending power to induce state compliance from a remedial perspective. To the extent such regimes of regulatory federalism merely threaten the state with loss of funds for non-compliance, they threaten state officials less directly with onerous judicial supervision.

Yet, again, remedial differences do not wholly explain the difference in attitude towards directives. For one thing, Justice O'Connor was far from suggesting in her opinion that a directive with a less onerous remedy than the take-title provisions at issue there would have survived constitutional scrutiny. To the contrary, she appears to have laid down a bright line rule against conscription in all circumstances. For another, federal courts have often granted injunctive relief to enforce state compliance with cooperative federalism programs, even where the responsible federal agency enjoys nominal authority to withhold funds.[399] In general, such remedies make more sense than the threat of a grant cut-off because they preserve the intergovernmental relation and ensure a continuing flow of federal funds.

3.   Available alternatives to state conscription

It bears noting, finally, that Europe was designed to function primarily through the agency of Member States. With relatively few exceptions,[400] the Treaty does not confer on the Union institutions powers equivalent to those of Congress to operate directly upon individual citizens, to tax and spend for the general welfare and to regulate commerce by establishing its own agencies staffed with its own personnel. Lacking any tradition of administrative and enforcement competence equivalent to that of the Federal government here, the Union cannot regulate directly, cannot threaten Member States with the partial preemption of their environmental programs and lacks any sizable environmental fund with which to purchase Member State compliance with its decrees.[401] Unlike the United States, therefore, the Union relies upon Member States out of weakness and necessity rather than out of strength.

Perhaps, then, we can best understand the ban on directives in the United States as reflecting this country's relatively more complete integration.

Because Congress can achieve its objectives through mechanisms other than the use of the directive, the Court's decision in *New York v. United States* deprives Congress of only the most straightforward – and most conscriptive – tool. By denying Congress the use of this tool, the Court does not expect to reverse this century's trend towards ever-broadening congressional control of the nation's economic life; Justice O'Connor's opinion purports to leave the substantive scope of the commerce clause intact.[402] Nor does the Court threaten other tools of regulatory federalism that Congress has deployed. One can thus view the decision as largely symbolic, and thus as unlikely to restore a balance of power between Congress and the states.[403]

Symbolism is not all bad, and the governmental structure that emerges from a decision that permits many forms of federal inducement but denies Congress the use of the directive bears some resemblance to structure envisioned by the framers. Although the comments of Madison and Hamilton suggest that the plan enables the Federal government to act through the several states, they may have believed that state governments would continue to resist or simply refuse to enforce such measures as they opposed. In the face of such resistance, Madison and Hamilton may have counseled reliance on the federal courts as an instrument of coercion or upon the option of regulating the citizens directly. The partial preemption scheme approved by Justice O'Connor builds the prospect of such direct regulation into the legislation at the outset. Of course, a judicially policed power of state resistance offers a poor substitute for the robust challenge that Madison anticipated.

In two important respects, however, the decision can be seen as something other than purely symbolic. First, the decision may reflect the fact that a commitment to some measure of state autonomy requires some limits on the scope of the Federal government's power to control state legislative and executive decision-making. Second, the decision may actually contribute to congressional accountability, though perhaps not in exactly the way some commentators have argued. Return to our hypothetical taxpayer, the one who pays taxes to two governments and can understand arguments from administrative efficiency. Many would doubt the ability of Congress to act as an honest broker of the relative cost of achieving its policy goals directly, or through the instrumentality of the states. States have complained for years about the costs of unfunded mandates[404] and only limited relief has been forthcoming. Congress now follows a practice of attaching fiscal notes to its proposed legislation that estimate the cost of compliance the measure will impose on state and local governments.[405] Critics of the fiscal notes, however, complain that Congress does not always heed the implications of such cost estimates and on occasion ignores them entirely.[406] If the directive serves as nothing more than a handy way to shift federal administrative costs off-budget, then our representative citizen (one who supports the directive in theory as a more efficient tool of administration) may doubt its wisdom.[407]

From this perspective, one can perhaps understand why we might wish to permit Congress to issue directives only where it agrees to underwrite the cost of regulation either through grants to the states or through a direct takeover of the regulatory responsibility. Such a regime may force Congress to confront more directly the costs to the states by confronting a real prospect of state non-participation. Such constraints on Congress may give our representative citizen more confidence that the congressional decision to adopt a cooperative scheme offers a chance to economize on the costs of administration.

C. Cautionary Notes for European Integration

So far at least, the Court of Justice has played a largely centralizing role. Thus, while the Court has worked out a variety of doctrines, including direct effect, that tend to broaden the impact of Union legislation, the Court rarely strikes down legislation on the ground that it exceeds the authority conferred upon Union legislative institutions under the Treaty. As a practical matter, therefore, federalism and the doctrine of subsidiarity operates at present in the Union as a political check on the legislative process rather than as a judicially enforceable limit on the breadth of Union legislation.[408] Put in other words, the Court has so far felt little inclination to protect Member States from themselves by striking down legislation to which they have agreed.

As Europe moves towards further integration and expands the role of the Parliament in the legislative process, the American experience with directives may offer a cautionary tale. The Union has already adopted a number of changes that dilute Member State control over the legislative process. The qualified majority provisions of Article 100a, the apparently enhanced power of the Commission to shape the Council legislative agenda, and the codecision role of the Parliament under Maastricht all tend to limit the Member States' ability to block unsatisfactory legislative initiatives. Changes contemplated by the Maastricht Treaty, moreover, would bring added bite to Court of Justice enforcement proceedings under Article 169.

The integrating tendencies of such changes may require the Court to play a more active role in policing the relations between the center and the Member States. Some scholars have already suggested the possible need for such a role and have outlined limits of uncertain scope on central authority.[409] For now, at least, no one has suggested that such a judicial role could or should extend to the limitation or invalidation of the directive as a tool to accomplish Union objectives.

NOTES

1   See infra notes 25–38 and accompanying text.

2   See infra notes 51–66 and accompanying text.

3   See infra notes 241–67 and accompanying text.

4   See infra notes 214–15 and accompanying text.

5   For a description of the European environmental impact assessment directive, linking its development to the model of NEPA in the United States, see Nigel Haigh, *EEC Environmental Policy and Britain* 349–56 (2nd ed. 1987).

6   42 U.S.C. §§ 4321 et seq. For background on the environmental impact statement requirements of NEPA, see Roger W. Findley and Daniel A. Farber, *Cases and Materials on Environmental Law* 103–64 (3rd ed. 1991).

7   On the justifications for environmental regulation at the federal level, see Eckard Rehbinder and Richard Stewart, *Environmental Protection Policy: Legal Integration in the United States and the European Community* 3–13 (1988). In this article, I take for granted that environmental protection requires federal solutions to at least some regulatory problems and focus on the modes or processes by which the central government seeks to achieve its environmental goals.

8   For a discussion of the enforcement of directives, in Europe see infra notes 70–77 and 89–112 and accompanying text.

9   112 S. Ct. 2408, 2428 (1992).

10   Pub. L. 99–240, 42 U.S.C. §§ 2021b *et seq.*

11   See *New York v. United States*, 112 S. Ct. 2408, 2428 (1992). For a more detailed account of the Court's decision, see infra notes 335–48 and accompanying text. See also H. Jefferson Powell, *The Oldest Question of Constitutional Law*, 79 Va. L. Rev. 633 (1993) (criticizing the Court's historical analysis); Saikrishna Bangalore Prakash, *Field Office Federalism* 79 Va. L. Rev. 1957 (1993) (suggesting that while the framers contemplated federal use of state executive and judicial officers, they did not contemplate similar conscription of state legislatures).

12   For illustrative statements to this effect, see Daniel J. Elazar and Ilan Greilsammer, *Federal Democracy: The U.S.A. and Europe Compared: A Political Science Perspective* in 1 *Integration Through Law: Europe and the American Federal Experience* 71, 112 (Mauro Capelletti, Monica Seccombe and Joseph Weiler, eds 1986) [hereinafter *Integration Through Law*]; Samuel Krislov, Claus-Dieter Ehlermann and Joseph Weiler, *The Political Organs and the Decision-Making Process in the United States and the European Community* in 2 *Integration Through Law* 3, 103–8 (emphasizing difference in taxing power of central governments, relatively greater nationalism in Europe than statism in United States, and the 'vast and growing' homogenization of American society); Trevor C. Hartley, *Federalism, Courts and Legal Systems: The Emerging Constitution of the European Community*, 34 Am. J. Comp. L. 229 (1986) (contrasting EU with more mature federal systems of United States and Canada); Eckard Rehbinder and Richard Stewart, supra note 7, at 320–22.

13   See infra notes 129–69 and accompanying text.

14   See infra notes 323–34 and accompanying text.

15   See David P. Currie, *Federal Air Quality Standards and Their Implementation*, 1976 Am. Bar. Found. Res. J. 365, 394.

16   For useful introductions to the European Union, its institutions, and its predominantly economic focus, see George A. Bermann, Roger J. Goebel, William J. Davey and Eleanor M. Fox, *Cases and Materials on European Community Law* (1993); P. Kapteyn and P. van Themaat, *Introduction to the Law of the European Communities* (1989); D. Vaughan, *Law of the European Communities* (1986). Since the entry into force of the Maastricht Treaty on European Union, effective November 1, 1993, what was once known as the European Community now goes by the name the European Union.

17   On the development of European environmental policy, see George A. Bermann, et al., supra note 16, at 1101–23; Ludwig Krämer, *EEC Treaty and Environmental Protection* 1–3 (1990); Graham Bennett, *Air Pollution Control in the European Community: Implementation of the EU Directives in the Twelve Member States* 1–4 (1991); Stanley P. Johnson and Guy Corcelle, *The Environmental Policy of the European Communities* 1–21 (1989); Auke Haagsma, *The European Community's Environmental Policy: A Case-Study in Federalism*, 12 Fordham Int'l L.J. 311 (1989); Richard Macrory, *The Enforcement of Community Environmental Laws: Some Critical Issues*, 29 Common Mkt. L. Rev. 347 (1992).

18   See Richard Macrory, supra note 17, at 348 n.4.
19   On the primacy of the directive as a tool of European environmental policy, see Eckard
       Rehbinder and Richard Stewart, supra note 7, at 33; Nigel Haigh, supra note 5, at 371–7
       (chronological listing of 217 pieces of environmental legislation from 1967 to 1986 includes
       23 regulations and 31 decisions; the balance of Union legislation – 163 pieces – came in the
       form of directives).
20   See Stanley P. Johnson and Guy Corcelle, supra note 17, at 1–2; Eckard Rehbinder and
       Richard Stewart, supra note 7, at 17. A few environmental initiatives preceded the summit,
       including the 1967 directive on the labelling of dangerous substances and the 1970 directive
       on emissions of noise and air pollution from motor vehicles. See Ludwig Krämer, *The Single
       European Act and Environmental Protection: Reflections on Several New Provisions in
       Community Law*, 24 Common Mkt. L. Rev. 659, 660 (1987).
21   See Eckard Rehbinder and Richard Stewart, supra note 7, at 17–18. For summaries of the first
       four action programmes, see Stanley P. Johnson and Guy Corcell, supra note 17, at 11–21.
22   OJ No. C 138 (5.12.93). For a discussion of the fifth action program, see Laurens Jan
       Brinkhorst, *The Road to Maastricht*, 20 Eco. L.Q. 7, 20–21 (1993).
23   On the predominantly economic focus of the Treaty's attempt to secure a common internal
       market, see George A. Bermann, et al., supra note 16, at 317–629; N. Green, T. Hartley and
       J. Usher, *The Legal Foundations of the Single European Market* (1991); D. Wyatt and A
       Dashwood, *The Substantive Law of the EEC* (1992).
24   Thus, the European experience reflects the commonplace idea that environmental concerns
       normally arise after a measure of economic well-being has been secured. See Eckard
       Rehbinder and Richard Stewart, supra note 7, at 18–19.
25   The harmonization authority in Article 100 reflects the idea, familiar to American lawyers, that
       a common economic market cannot tolerate state-to-state variations in the rules governing a
       good's access to the market. Thus, the harmonization powers of Article 100 authorize the
       Union to prescribe uniform, supranational rules in virtually any situation in which disparate
       Member State legislation poses a threat to the internal market. For an overview, see George
       A. Bermann, et al, supra note, at 428–65; P. Kapteyn and P. Van Themaat, supra note 16, at
       467–84.
26   Treaty of Rome, preamble.
27   To the extent that the regulation of pollution has explicit economic overtones, of course, no
       one doubts the Union's environmental competence. Moreover, where environmental
       regulation by Member States poses a threat to the single market, it triggers the Union's
       harmonization powers. Thus, the controversy surrounding the Union's competence before
       1987 tended to focus on its power to develop a comprehensive environmental policy. See
       Eckard Rehbinder and Richard Stewart, supra note 7, at 20–26.
28   . Acceptance by Union institutions can be found in environmental action programs, agreement
       on the terms of environmental directives by the Council and the Commission and in the Court
       of Justice's decisions. Compare *Procurer de la Republique v. Association de Defense des
       Bruleurs D'Huiles Usagees (ADBHU)*, Case 240/83, [1985] ECR 531, ('environmental
       protection . . . is one of the Union's essential objectives'); *with Commission v. Italy*, Case
       92/79, [1980] ECR 1115, (linking directive on sulphur content of fuels to the Council's power
       to eliminate competitive distortions; raising doubts about generality of Council authority). For
       an account of what the Court meant by 'essential' in its *ADBHU* decision, see Auke Haagsma,
       supra note 17, at 324–5 (suggesting that the Court meant to hold that measures seeking to
       achieve environmental goals would justify quantitative restrictions within the meaning of its
       Article 36 jurisprudence).
29   See Eckard Rehbinder and Richard Stewart, supra note 7, at 26–8; Auke Haagsma, supra note
       17, at 321–3.
30   Thus, Article 235 figures as prominently in analyses of the expansion of the Union's legislative
       competence as does the necessary and proper clause in those of congressional authority. See
       C. Sasse and H. Yourow, *The Growth of Legislative Power of the European Communities* in
       1 *Courts and Free Markets* 92 (T. Sandalow and E. Stein eds 1982); Franziska Tschofen,
       *Article 235 of the Treaty Establishing the European Economic Community: Potential Conflicts
       Between the Dynamics of Lawmaking in the Community and National Constitutional
       Principles*, 12 Mich. J. Int'l L. 471 (1991). Joseph Weiler, *The Tranformation of Europe*, 100
       Yale L.J. 2403, 2443–53 (1991).
31   See Treaty of Rome, Art. 235. For a summar of the use of Article 235 in environmental
       legislation, see Eckard Rehbinder and Richard Stewart, supra note 7, at 26–8.

32   See Auke Haagsma, supra note 17, at 326–7; Franziska Tschofen, supra note 30, at 476–7; Ludwig Krämer, supra note 17, at 45.

33   See Treaty of Rome, Art. 100.

34   See Treaty of Rome, Art. 235.

35   See supra note 19.

36   Such doubts have influenced environmental legislation, leading the Council jointly to rely upon Article 100 and Article 235 in some cases. See Eckard Rehbinder and Richard Stewart, supra note 7, at 28. Court of Justice decisions fueled the reluctance to rely upon Article 235, holding in some situations that the Council may not invoke Article 235 in situations where other provisions of the Treaty provide the necessary powers. See generally Franziska Tschofen, supra note 30, at 485–9; Auke Haagsma, supra note 17, at 323–6.

37   Eckard Rehbinder and Richard Stewart, supra note 7, at 33.

38   Some observers miss this point, and appear to assume that the Union prefers on policy grounds to use directives, instead of regulations, to legislate in the environmental field. Such a critique from deliberate choice only makes sense as applied to legislation after the Single European Act enabled the Community to issue regulations under Article 100a. See infra notes 51–69 and accompanying text.

39   For an introduction to the work of the Council, see George A. Bermann, et al., supra note 16, at 50–57; P. Kapteyn and P. Van Themaat, supra note 16, at 103–31. On the process of legislation within the Council, see Samuel Krislov, Claus-Dieter Ehlermann and Joseph Weiler, supra note 12, at 30–59.

40   For an introduction to the Commission, see George A. Bermann, et al., supra note 16, at 57–63; P. Kapteyn and P. Van Themaat, supra note 16, at 103–131.

41   For a general introduction to the Court of Justice, see George A. Bermann, et al., supra note 16, at 69–74; P. Kapteyn and P. Van Themaat, supra note 16, at 145–73. A more detailed account appears in L. Neville Brown, *The Court of Justice of the European Communities* (1989). A Court of First Instance, with limited jurisdiction, was added to Union institutions in 1989. See L. Neville Brown, supra, at 64–9.

42   For accounts of the role of the European Parliament, emphasizing its historically restricted advisory and supervisory function, see George A. Bermann, et al., supra note 16, at 63–8; P. Kapteyn and P. Van Themaat, supra note 16, at 131–45. For a discussion of Parliament's role under the so-called cooperative procedure of the Single European Act, see infra note 57.
     With the entry into force of the Maastricht Treaty, Parliament's role in the legislative process will expand rather significantly. For an account of the Parliament's codecision power under Article 100a(1) of Maastricht, see Laurens Jan Brinkhorst, supra note 27, at 16–17 (describing the 'substantially increased role' of the Parliament under Maastricht's codecision procedure).

43   See generally George A. Bermann, et al., supra note 16, at 51–2; Samuel Krislov, Claus-Deiter Ehlermann and Joseph Weiler, supra note 12, at 30–32.

44   This process of consultation proceeds through a staff of permanent representatives of Member States known as COREPER. On the origins of COREPER, the French acronym for the 'Committee of Permanent Representatives', and the Luxembourg Accord, see George A. Bermann, et al., supra note 16, at 53–5. On the tendency of COREPER effectively to permit the Member States to exercise substantial control over the legislative output, See Samuel Krislov, Claus-Dieter Ehlermann and Joseph Weiler, supra note 12, at 31 (concluding that the Commission's power of initiation, following the advent of COREPER, has been 'sapped of its value'); P. Kapteyn and P. Van Themaat, supra note 16, at 254–9 (Commission may lack practical ability to uphold the Union interest in the legislative process).

45   See G. Federico Mancini, *The Making of a Constitution for Europe*, 26 Common Mkt. L. Rev. 595, 598 (1989). See also Ludwig Krämer, supra note 17, at 27 (Member States regard Union environmental policy 'as an environmental foreign policy rather than a domestic policy').

46   Samuel Krislov, Claus-Dieter Ehlermann and Joseph Weiler, supra note 12, at 32.

47   In their important work on environmental regulation in Europe and the United States, Professors Rehbinder and Stewart begin with a model that distinguishes product regulation from process regulation. See Eckard Rehbinder and Richard Stewart, supra note 7, at 9–13. Recognizing that products move in interstate commerce, Rehbinder and Stewart note that both polluter states and environmental states have incentives to adopt uniform standards. *Id.* at 10–11. By contrast, the more localized effects of process pollution eliminates incentives towards uniformity. *Id.* at 11. 'In the case of process regulation it is difficult to see why there would be any harmonization at all above the lowest common denominator level, since it would never be in the interest of polluter states or importer states to agree to more stringent controls'.

Id. Notwithstanding such a prediction of laxity, Professors Rehbinder and Stewart describe the legislation as relatively protective. *Id.* at 315.

48   See Eckard Rehbinder and Richard Stewart, supra note 7, at 315–16.

49   See Samuel Krislov, Claus-Dieter Ehlermann and Joseph Weiler, supra note 12, at 59.

50   See Samuel Krislov, Claus-Dieter Ehlermann and Joseph Weiler, supra note 12, at 83. Indeed, given the possibility that a provision harmonizing the law of all Member States will displace the more protective provisions of relatively environmental countries, such 'green' Member States as Germany and Denmark may attempt to push towards more progressive legislation.

51   The new environmental sections of the Single European Act have been the subject of much commentary. Useful introductions appear in Ludwig Krämer, supra note 17, at 29–97; Ludwig Krämer, supra note 20; D. Vandermeersch, *The Single European Act and the Environmental Policy of the European Economic Community*, 12 Eur. L. Rev. 407 (1987); Auke Haagsma, supra note 17, at 334–53.

52   Article 100a authorizes the Council, acting upon Commission proposal and in cooperation with the Parliament, to 'adopt measures' for the approximation (or harmonization) of Member State law. Notably, Article 100a provides for voting by a qualified majority and does not limit the Council to the issuance of directives. Finally, Article 100a includes an important opt-out provision for Member States whose interests were ignored in a majority vote, but provides for the Commission to police the application of national provision for disguised restrictions on trade. The opt-out provisions reflects, at least in part, the fears of Germany and Denmark that the push towards an internal market might undermine their internal environmental protections. See Auke Haagsma, supra note 17, at 349–50.

53   See Ludwig Krämer, supra note 17, at 40–41 (drawing the connection between Article 100 and Article 100a, a connection confirmed by the article's numeration).

54   Article 130s specifies a unanimity requirement for Council action on the environment. Article 130r(1) defines the objectives of such action to include such general guidelines as protection of the environment and human health; Article 130r(2) defines such guiding principles as the polluter should pay, pollution should be rectified at the source, and environmental policy should be integrated with other Union policies; Article 130r(3) lists relevant conditions for the Union to consider; and Article 130r(4) enunciates the principle of subsidiarity, which proposes to limit Union competence to matters better handled at the Union level than at the level of the Member States. See Ludwig Krämer, supra note 17, at 51–81.

55   Article 130t specifically authorizes Member States to maintain more stringent measures, so long as they comport with other obligations under the Treaty. See Ludwig Krämer, supra note 17, at 93–7.

56   See Ludwig Krämer, supra note 17, at 32. Article 100a(4) takes some of the sting out of the qualified majority provision by providing Member States with a limited 'opt-out' alternative. See James Flynn, *How Will Article 100a(4) Work? A Comparison with Article 93*, 24 Common Mkt. L. Rev. 689 (1987).

57   Article 149 defines the requirement of cooperation with Parliament. In brief, it requires the Council to lay its legislation before, and explain it to, the Parliament and gives Parliament an opportunity to propose amendments.

58   In practice, it appears that the qualified majority voting provisions will have more effect on Council legislation than the requirement of parliamentary cooperation. See Samuel Krislov, Claus-Dieter Ehlermann and Joseph Weiler, supra note 12, at 57–8 (offering a generally pessimistic assessment of Parliament's role).

59   It seems unlikely, however, that the 'high base of protection' language will provide a standard for the nullification of legislation under Article 100a. The Commission must temper protection, after all, with the political reality that restrictive legislation would trigger Member State rejection. See Ludwig Krämer, supra note 20, at 679.

60   Article 130s thus specifies only consultation with the Parliament, rather than cooperation. See Ludwig Krämer, supra note 17, at 91.

61   See Ludwig Krämer, supra note 20, at 679.

62   It seems unlikely that the guidelines of subsidiarity offers anything more than a flexible standard, designed to guide Union institutions in the making of law rather than the Court of Justice in reviewing the propriety of emerging legislation. See Ludwig Krämer, supra note 17, at 72.

63   See Ludwig Krämer, supra note 17, at 44–5.

64   Case C–300/89, [1991] ECR I–2867.

65   See *Commission v. Council*, Case C–300/89, [1991] ECR I–2867. In so ruling, the Court emphasized that the directive sought to harmonize the rules governing waste from the titanium dioxide industry across Member States. The directive thus had the dual purpose of eliminating obstacles to trade and protecting the environment. Given such a dual purpose, the Court cited its unwillingness to permit the Council to undermine both the parliamentary cooperation provision and the high level of protection provision by basing the directive on Article 130s. *Id.* at I–2900–01.

66   See Han Somsen, *Annotation: Commission v. Council*, 29 Common Mkt. L. Rev. 140, 149–50 (1992).

67   See Laurens Jan Brinkhorst, supra note 27, at 16.

68   *Id.*

69   *Id.* at 19.

70   For general introductions to the problem of transposition, see George A. Bermann, et al., supra note 16, at 166–244; P. Kapteyn and P. Van Themaat, supra note 16, at 310–54; European Institute of Public Administration, *The Implementation of Community Law by the Member States* (1985). For valuable analyses in the environmental field, see Nigel Haigh, supra note 5; Graham Bennett, supra note 17. In addition to effectiveness upon transposition, the Court of Justice has worked out theories of direct effect that produce some effectiveness for directives that Member States fail to transpose. See infra notes 113–23 and accompanying text.

71   See generally George A. Bermann, et al., supra note 16, at 292–316; P. Kapteyn and P. Van Themaat, supra note 16, at 273–81; L. Neville Brown, supra note 41, at 76–85.

72   See L. Neville Brown, supra note 41, at 77–8; Richard Macrory, supra note 17, at 351–2; Rolf Wagenbaur, *The European Community's Policy on Implementation of Environmental Directives*, 14 Fordham Int'l L.J. 455, 462–4 (1990–91).

73   See L. Neville Brown, supra note 41, at 77; Krislov, et al., supra note 12, at 72 (only 0.1 percent of enforcement files opened at the Commission reach the final definitive stage of a Court judgment).

74   In addition to its Article 169 jurisdiction over actions to enforce compliance by Member States, the Court of Justice may entertain matters referred to it by Member State courts under its preliminary reference jurisdiction of Article 177. Article 177 provides for the Court of Justice to issue rulings on the validity or meaning of Union law when a Member State court 'considers that a decision on the question is necessary to enable it to give judgment' in a pending case. For a general account of the preliminary reference procedure, see George A. Bermann, et al., supra note 16, at 245–75. By and large, the preliminary reference procedure has not been a source of important rulings in the environmental arena.

75   The Court of Justice, as initially structured, lacked power to award relief any more dramatic than a declaration; it had no power to impose monetary sanctions on Member States that breach their obligations under the Treaty. The Maastricht Treaty broadens the Court's powers in this respect by authorizing it to impose monetary sanctions against Member States in appropriate cases.

76   See EU Treaty, Art. 171.

77   *Id.*

78   See Eckard Rehbinder and Richard Stewart, supra note 7, at 34–6; David Freestone, *European Environmental Law and Policy*, 18 J.L. and Society 135, 145–7 (1991).

79   Eckard Rehbinder and Richard Stewart, supra note 7, at 35.

80   *Id.*

81   See Nigel Haigh, supra note 5, at 51–60.

82   Some Member States have responded to the freshwater fish directive by designating no such waters, thereby rendering the directive 'effectively inoperative'. *Id.* at 53.

83   The bathing water directive does not authorize the Member States to designate the waters to which the standards in the directive shall apply. *Id.* at 61, 63. Rather, it applies by its terms to waters in which 'bathing is not prohibited and is traditionally practiced by a large number of bathers'. *Id.* at 63.

84   Case 322/86 [1988] ECR 3995.

85   See Nigel Haigh, supra note 5, at 67–8.

86   *Id.* Among the additional 362 beaches designated were those at Blackpool and Southport. The European Court of Justice recently ruled that, in failing to attain the required water quality standards at those beaches, Great Britain violated the bathing water directive. See *Commission v. Great Britain*, Case C–56190 (bathing water) (July 14, 1993) (not yet reported). The Court specifically rejected Great Britain's claim that the time limits for attaining required water

quality ran from the date Great Britain added them to its list of covered beaches, rather than from the date of the directive's entry into force. The Court thus refused to recognize any significant discretion in Member States, ruling instead that the presence of lifeguard stands and changing huts brought the beaches in question within the directive's terms.

87   On the current state of the European Environment Agency, and the decision of the Council to deny the Agency enforcement authority, see infra notes 132–3 and accompanying text.

88   Regulations do not themselves assure Member State compliance, even though they nominally enjoy directly binding effect. Thus, a regulation that required Member States to attain certain pollution standards in, say, bathing waters used by a large number of bathers would not better assure compliance than the bathing water directive that was actually adopted. To comply with such a regulation, Member States would have to adopt monitoring systems to test water quality and take steps to reduce emissions into such waters – precisely the steps required by the directive.

89   For the text of Article 189, see supra notes 77–8 and accompanying text. Other relevant provisions include Article 5s requirement that Member States take 'all appropriate measures . . . to ensure fulfillment of the obligations arising out of this Treaty or resulting from action taken by the institutions of the Union'. See John Temple Lang, *Community Constitutional Law: Article 5 EEC Treaty*, 27 Common Mkt. L. Rev. 645, 647 (1990).

90   *Commission v. Germany*, (Air pollution) Case C–361/88, [1991] ECR 2567, 2602–03.

91   See *Commission v. Italy*, (Groundwater) Case C–360/87, [1991] ECR I–791, I–814; *Commission v. Germany*, (Groundwater) Case C–131/88, [1991] ECR I–825, I–867.

92   (Air Pollution) Case C–361/88, [1991] ECR I–2567.

93   Directive 80/799/EEC (OJ L229 30.8.80). For background, see infra notes 372–5.

94   See *Commission v. Germany*, Case C–361/88, [1991] ECR I–2567, 2579 (argument of Germany).

95   See *id.* at I–2586 (opinion of Advocate General that 'it is not sufficient, for the correct transposition of a directive, that a directive should be observed in fact: it is necessary that the full application of the directive should be equally ensured in law in all circumstances').

96   See *id.* at I–2602–03.

97   See *id.* at I–2600 (under the German legal system, administrative circulars are not generally recognized as rules of law).

98   See *id.* at I–2601–02 (the circulars do not apply to all plants but only to the immediate neighborhood of well-defined plants or buildings).

99   See *id.* at I–2602–03.

100   See *id.* at I–2603–04 (test for adequate implementation turns not on practical compliance but on provisions of national law that establish rules sufficiently clear and precise to inform affected individuals of their rights and duties).

101   (Groundwater) Case C–360/87, [1991] ECR I–791.

102   See *Commission v. Italy*, Case C–360/87, [1991] ECR I–791, I–815–16. The groundwater directive, 80/68/EEC (OJ L20 26.1.80), absolutely prohibits the direct discharge of certain prohibited substances into groundwater and demands the practical elimination of indirect discharge of such substances. For background, see Nigel Haigh, supra note 5, at 79–81. Italy failed to enact laws that established such absolute bans, lumping all substances together in legislation designed generally to limit discharges. Such a failure to establish a bright line rule prohibiting discharges of banned substances was said to violate the Treaty. See also *Commission v. Germany*, Case C–131/88, [1991] ECR I–825, I–868–70 (same; Germany violated the Treaty by failing to enact laws absolutely banning the discharge of prohibited substances into groundwater).

103   See *Commission v. Italy*, at I–817–19. For example, Article 7 of the groundwater directive requires a scientific investigation of the hydrogeological conditions of the area concerned, the possible purifying powers of the soil and subsoil and the risk of pollution from the discharge. Italy's failure to make provision for such an inquiry violated the Treaty. See also *Commission v. Germany*, Case C–131/88, [1991] ECR I–825, I–878–82 (same; Germany violated the Treaty by failing to take adequate procedural steps with respect to issuing authorizations and monitoring compliance with them).

104   *Id.* at I–820–23.

105   See *Commission v. Belgium*, Case 77/69, [1970] ECR 237 (refusing to excuse delays; delays attributed to necessary reliance on constitutionally independent institutions); *Commission v. Italy*, Case 79/72, [1973] ECR 667 (same; delays attributed to premature dissolution of national legislature); *Commission v. Italy*, Case 52/75, [1986] ECR 1359 (same; challenge to time allowed for implementation); *Commission v. Blangueron*, Case C–38/89, [1990] ECR

(same; failure of other Member States to comply).

106 Case C–42/89, [1990] ECR I–2821.

107 See Directive 80/778/EEC (OJ L229 30.8.80). For a description of the origins and content of the directive, see Nigel Haigh, supra note 5, at 42–5.

108 See *Commission v. Belgium*, Case C–42/89, [1990] ECR at I–2832–34.

109 *Id.* at I–2841.

110 *Id.*

111 *Id.* at I–2832.

112 Thus, the air quality directives, which incorporated a policy of mandatory standards, represented a significant change from many Member States' existing regulatory policy. See Nigel Haigh, supra note 5, at 183–6 (discussing impact of air quality directive on sulphur dioxide and suspended particulates).

113 For general introductions to the doctrine of direct effect, see George A. Bermann, et al., supra note 16, at 166–92; P. Kapteyn and P. Van Themaat, supra note 16, at 330–48. For discussions in the context of environmental law, see Eckard Rehbinder and Richard Stewart, supra note 7, at 37–9.

114 See P. Kapteyn and P. Van Themaat, supra note 16, at 333–8.

115 See *id.* at 343.

116 See *id.* at 344–5 (distinguishing between direct effect of directives and other Union legal texts). See also J. Winter, *Direct Applicability and Direct Effect: Two Distinct and Different Concepts in Community Law*, 9 Common Mkt. L. Rev. 425 (1972).

117 The Court of Justice has thus long held that the doctrine of direct effect of directives does not excuse a Member State from its duty to transpose the terms of the directive into Member State law. See *Commission v. France*, Case 167/73, [1974] ECR 359.

118 See *Pubblico Ministero v. Ratti*, Case 148/78, [1979] ECR 1629; *Marshall v. Southampton and Southwest Hampshire Area Health Auth.*, Case 152/84, [1986] ECR 723, 748.

119 See, e.g., *Francovich and Bonifaci v. Italy*, Joined Cases C–6/90 and C–9/90, (Eur. Ct. J. Nov. 19, 1991) (not yet reported) (Member State may be liable in damages to individuals in its own courts for its failure to implement directive that creates specific rights for individuals); *Regina v. Secretary of State, ex parte Factortame Ltd. (Factortame)*, Case C–213/89, [1990] ECR 2433 (courts of Member States may owe duty to suspend operation of national law to the extent it conflicts with Union directives; dismissing as irrelevant fact that Member State law made no provision for such judicial suspension).

120 P. Kapteyn and P. Van Themaat, supra note 16, at 345.

121 See *Marshall v. Southampton and Southwest Hampshire Area Health Auth.*, Case 152/84, [1986] ECR 723. *Compare Defrenne v. SABENA*, Case 43/75, [1976] ECR 455, 475–76 (holding that provision of Treaty imposing obligation of equal pay on Member States enjoyed horizontal direct effect; national courts must thus recognize individual's equal pay claim against the firm for which he/she worked).

122 Such limited direct effect would more dramatically tend to enable firms to escape more restrictive Member State standards if it were not for the fact that EU environmental directives typically establish only minimum standards or limit values and permit Member States to continue to enforce more restrictive requirements. Thus, the drinking water directive allows Member States to maintain stricter standards, See Eckard Rehbinder and Richard Stewart, supra note 7, at 62, as does the directive on the discharge of dangerous substances. See Richard Macrory, *European Community Water Law*, 20 Eco. L.Q. 119, 124 and n.45 (1993). Air pollution directives follow the same pattern, authorizing Member States to apply more restrictive standards in zones needing special environmental protection. See Graham Bennett, supra note 17, at 43 (sulphur dioxide and suspended particulate directive authorizes more stringent Member State standards); *id.* at 86 (same; lead in air directive). As a consequence, one has difficulty arguing that EU environmental legislation preempts or displaces the Member States' authority to fashion more restrictive standards. See Eckard Rehbinder and Richard Stewart, supra note 7, at 40–41.

123 Environmentalists might pursue such claims on the authority of such decisions as *Francovich* (damages for non-implementation) and *Factortame* (injunctive relief against non-implementation). See supra note 119. No less noted an observer than Temple Lang, however, has argued that directives aimed at improving the environment protect the 'general interest' and thus fail the first condition for Member State liability, which requires that the directive confer rights on private parties. See John Temple Lang, *New Legal Effects Resulting From the Failure of States to Fulfill Obligations under European Community Law: The Francovich Judgment*, 16 Fordham Int'l L.J. 1 (1992–93).

Interestingly, however, the Court's transposition jurisprudence in the environmental field has frequently based its requirement of relatively precise transposition on the claim that environmental measures create rights for individuals. Thus, in *Commission v. Germany*, Case C–131/88, [1991] ECR I–825, the Court based its decision that Germany had failed to implement the groundwater directive in part on its conclusion that the directive 'create[s] rights' for individuals. *Id.* at I–867. The creation of such rights, according to the Court, required implementation with sufficient precision to enable individuals 'to be aware of and enforce their rights'. *Id.* at I–868. See also *Commission v. Germany*, Case C–361/88, [1991] ECR I–2567, I–2602 (basing inadequacy of German transposition of air quality directive on inability of individuals 'to know with certainty the full extent of their rights in order to rely on them, where appropriate, before the national courts'). Such decisions may pave the way for the judicial creation of enforcement rights in individuals of a kind that have so far eluded the political process. See infra notes 165–8 and accompanying text.

124   Ludwig Krämer, supra note 17, at 27.

125   See D. Hackett and E. Lewis, *European Economic Community Environmental Requirements* in *The European Community: Products Liability Rules and Environmental Policy* 253–83 (PLI 1990).

126   See Stanley P. Johnson and Guy Corcelle, supra note 17, at 2 (success of Union environmental policy confirmed by the adoption of over 100 legislative acts relating to the environment); Report of the Commission of the European Communities to the United Nations Conference on Environment and Development 30 (1992) (citing passage of 175 legally binding acts as evidence of the significance of European environmental policy).

127   See *id.*

128   See Ludwig Krämer, supra note 17, at 26–7; Richard Macrory, supra note 17; James J. Friedberg, *Closing the Gap Between Word and Deed in European Community Environmental Policy*, 15 Loyola Los Ang. Int'l and Comp. L.J. 275 (1993); Rolf Wagenbaur, supra note 42; Eckard Rehbinder and Richard Stewart, supra note 7, at 251–2, 337–8; Graham Bennett, supra note 17, at 197–200.

129   See Richard Macrory, supra note 17, at 362.

130   DG 11 bears responsibility for environmental issues, nuclear safety, and civil protection; its 150 civil servants draw up proposals for environmental legislation and develop proposed enforcement proceedings. See Stanley P. Johnson and Guy Corcelle, supra note 17, at 6. The EU annual budget for environmental matters amounts to some $36 million, less than 0.001 percent of the EU budget. *Id.*

131   The EC's environmental enforcement unit employed only 10 lawyers as of October 1991. See Richard Macrory, supra note 17, at 336–64 and n.38.

132   See Richard Macrory, supra note 17, at 363; David Freestone, *European Environmental Law and Policy*, supra note 78, at 140; Rolf Wagenbaur, supra note 78, at 471–3. For an overview of the Agency and the political wrangles that attended its birth, see David A. Westbrook, *Environmental Policy in the European Community: Observations on the European Environment Agency*, 15 Harv. Envir'l L. Rev. 257–63 (1991).

133   See David A. Westbrook, supra note 132, at 260 and nn.23–4.

134   Thus, the directives typically specify both a notification date – the date on which the Council formally notifies Member States of the publication of the directive – and a compliance date. See Nigel Haigh, supra note 5, at 34, 39, 42 (setting forth notification and compliance dates for the EU directives on surface water and drinking water). Member States must pass the relevant laws or adopt the relevant administrative rules by the compliance date and inform the Commission of their action by compliance letter. Thus, the United Kingdom complied with the directive on freshwater fish waters by administrative action and issued a letter of compliance advising the Commission of that fact in July 1980, the date set for compliance in the directive. See *id.* at 51, 54–5.

135   Consider, for example, the experience of the British government in implementing the bathing water directive. The government initially designated only 27 waters for bathing – a fact that led to the issuance of a reasoned opinion by the Commission challenging the sufficiency of compliance. In the face of a threatened infringement proceeding under Article 169, the government specified an additional 362 waters. See Nigel Haigh, supra note 4, at 64–7.

136   Richard Macrory, supra note 17, at 352. See also Samuel Krislov, Claus-Dieter Ehlermann and Joseph Weiler, supra note 12, at 73 (the Commission's ASMODEE data base can trace most cases of non-implementation). Certain of this information has entered the public domain. Thus, the Commission's 1990 and 1991 reports to Parliament on the enforcement of Union law provides a relatively clear description of the extent of Member State compliance. The reports

break down Article 169 enforcement proceedings in the environmental area by the nature of the alleged infringement (non-communication, non-conformity, poor application) and further specify the sector of environmental policy (air, water, waste) that formed the subject of the infringement proceedings. Scholars have incorporated such statistics into their assessments of the effectiveness of EU enforcement.

See Richard Macrory, *supra* note 17, at 353, 364–6. In addition to such Commission sources, many scholars have compiled relatively detailed assessments of the extent of Member State compliance with EU environmental law. See, e.g., Nigel Haigh, *supra* note 5 (describing UK compliance with EU environmental directives); Graham Bennett, *supra* note 17 (describing Member State compliance with air pollution directives). *Cf.* James J. Friedberg, *supra* note 128, at 287 (arguing that the absence of any 'official and comprehensive documentation that describes . . . legislative implementation' of EU directives creates an information gap that hampers academic assessments of the effectiveness of EU enforcement efforts).

137   See Nigel Haigh, *supra* note 5, at 64.

138   For example, the British government responded to the directive on air quality and sulphur dioxide by issuing orders to local authorities, directing them to pay heed to the limit values in the directive. See Nigel Haigh, *supra* note 5, at 190. The British government thus refused to adopt any implementing legislation, despite the fact that it lacked any statute setting air quality standards or empowering an agency to set them. *Id.* at 188. France took a similar approach and faced EU enforcement proceedings as a result. See Graham Bennett, *supra* note 17, at 62–3.

139   For example, the Court of Justice recently ruled that Italy and Germany violated their obligation to transpose the directive on groundwater pollution into Member State law where they relied on pre-existing legislative authority. See *supra* notes 93–102 and accompanying text.

140   One can mount a much stronger critique of the availability of information concerning practical non-implementation or wrongful application of Union law. Although the studies of Haigh and Bennett offer some insights, See *supra* note 138, most observers would agree with the claim that the instances of non-application that come to our attention represent only the tip of the iceberg. See Samuel Krislov, Claus-Dieter Ehlermann and Joseph Weiler, *supra* note 12, at 73.

141   For a description of the environmental impact assessment directive, and its reliance on the National Environmental Policy Act of 1969, see Nigel Haigh, *supra* note 5, at 349–54.

142   Thus, both the smoke and sulphur dioxide as well as the nitrogen dioxide directives imposes monitoring requirements as well as requirements of annual reporting to the Commission. See Nigel Haigh, *supra* note 5, at 182–3, 195.

143   As Professor Macrory reports, the Commission adopted its internal complaint procedure in the 1960s, largely to deal with economic and internal market issues. See Richard Macrory, *supra* note 17, at 363. As currently phrased, the complaint policy applies to environmental issues as well and permits any individual, firm or environmental group to lodge complaints of non-compliance with the Commission. *Id.* Interestingly, the pattern of complaints tends to reflect the concerns of local environmental groups; in France, such groups have focused on the enforcement of prohibitions relating to wild animals whereas in Britain they focus on water pollution. *Id.* at 365.

The evidence suggests that the citizen complaint procedure has become a much more important source of Commission enforcement in recent years. Whereas only 11 such complaints were lodged in 1984, that number had grown to 460 by 1989. See David Freestone, *supra* note 78, at 141. Such complaints now represent nearly half of all those received by the Commission in all sectors. See Richard Macrory, *supra* note 17, at 363.

144   See *Commission v. Italy*, Case C–360/87, [1991] ECR I–791, 793 (Commission investigation of Italy's implementation of groundwater directive triggered by complaint).

145   See Richard Macrory, *supra* note 17, at 353.

146   He also reports an increase in the number of proceedings aimed at the states' practical implementation of environmental directives. See *id.* (reporting an increase from zero in 1982 to 62 in 1990).

147   See *id.* at 368–9.

148   See Ludwig Krämer, *supra* note 17, at 27. See also Graham Bennett, *supra* note 17, at 197–8 (identifying implementation problems with air quality directives and noting that the greatest difficulties arise from directives that impose prior approval procedures); Rolf Wagenbaur, *supra* note 42, at 476 (measures should be taken to improve implementation of environmental directives).

149 For the definitive account of the non-compliance paradox, see Samuel Kristov, Claus-Dieter Ehlermann and Joseph Weiler, supra note 12, at 61–88. Historically, the paradox arose from the fact that Member States often failed to implement the directives that emerged from the legislative process, despite the fact that they enjoyed the power to veto proposals at the Council and, therefore, to shape the final contours of the action taken. *Id.* at 61. Non-compliance remains a problem but the regime of majority voting that accompanied the Single European Act makes it somewhat less paradoxical.

150 See Richard Macrory, supra note 17, at 363; Rolf Wagenbaur, supra note 42, at 471–3. See also David A. Westbrook, supra note 132, at 268–71 (arguing that the Agency may leverage its information-gathering authority into a tool of regulation).

151 See Rolf Wagenbaur, supra note 42, at 474–5.

152 The Commission adopted this approach in 1990, releasing for the first time a compilation by country of notices informing Member States of non-compliance with environmental directives. See Richard Macrory, supra note 17, at 365; Rolf Wagenbaur, supra note 42, at 475–6. Wagenbaur supports increased use of the tactic. *Id.*

153 See Richard Macrory, supra note 17, at 367–8.

154 See Rolf Wagenbaur, supra note 42, at 470–71. Although financial responsibility for environmental programs lies with the Member States, Union spending on environmental activities increased from 100 million ECUs ($125 million) in 1987 to 700 million ECUs ($850 million) in 1992. See Laurens Jan Brinkhorst, supra note 22, at 19. The Union underwrites such expenditures from its structural and research and development budget, as well as from the new 'LIFE' fund for the European environment. *Id.* This fund will focus on assistance to threatened areas, particularly in the Mediterranean and North Sea regions, as well as on the protection of habitat for endangered species. *Id.* See also Ludwig Krämer, *The Interdependency of Community and Member State Activity on Nature Protection Within the European Community*, 20 Eco. L.Q. 25, 39 (1993).

Thus far, at least, the EU has done little to condition the expenditure of its structural funds on the attainment of environmental goals by the funded projects. Expenditures from such structural funds support new economic development projects in Member States that often impinge on nature conservation. *Id.* at 44. Moreover, EU Regulation 2052/88 requires EC-financed projects to be administered in harmony with environmental protection, an element of the EC's new emphasis on integrated policy. *Id.* Yet, in practice, Member State expenditure of such funds typically occurs without the input of EU environmental officials. *Id.*

155 As noted above, the Union's environmental competence under the Single European Act extends to the issuance of regulations as well as directives. See supra note 52.

156 See Rolf Wagenbaur, supra note 42, at 468–9; Auke Haagsma, supra note 17, at 353; James J. Friedberg, supra note 128, at 294–5.

157 See infra note 161.

158 See Philippe Sands, *European Community Environmental Law: The Evolution of a Regional Regime of International Environmental Protection*, 100 Yale L.J. 2511, 2521–2 (1991); Philippe Sands, *European Community Environmental Law: Legislation, the European Court of Justice and Common-Interest Groups*, 53 Mod. L. Rev. 685, 689–93 (1990); Ludwig Krämer, supra note 17, at 26; Eckard Rehbinder and Richard Stewart, supra note 7, at 338.

159 See Philippe Sands, *European Community Environmental Law: The Evolution of a Regional Regime on International Environmental Protection*, 100 Yale L.J. 2511, 2521–2 (1991).

160 Perhaps their most visible role has come through the procedure adopted by the Commission to investigate citizen complaints. See Richard Macrory, supra note 17, at 362–5; Philippe Sands, supra note 158, at 2521. In addition, Friends of the Earth in Great Britain recently mounted a challenge to that country's administration of its water quality rules, arguing that the government had granted a variance from rules set out in the directive without first obtaining a derogation from the Union. See Philippe Sands, supra note 158, at 2515 n.30. Nonetheless, citizen groups play a less active role in the enforcement of Union law in Europe than do their counterparts in the United States. See Eckard Rehbinder and Richard Stewart, supra note 7, at 338.

161 In a regulatory world dominated by the issuance of directives, much depends on the willingness of Member States to administer their laws in ways that ensure the effective application of Union law. Yet Member States differ substantially in the role they permit citizens to play in testing the legality of projects that may affect the environment. For the classic discussion of variations in Member State doctrines of standing and in the scope of the judicial or administrative review they permit, see Eckard Rehbinder and Richard Stewart, supra

note 7, at 149–59 (concluding that variations in Member State administrative law preclude uniform application of environmental directives).

162   For an overview of the Agency's information-gathering function, see David A. Westbrook, supra note 132, at 258–60.

163   See Council Directive 90/313/EEC, OJ 1990 L158/56 (June 7, 1990). The directive authorizes any person to seek information relating to the environment from public authorities, without any required showing of interest and upon payment of a charge not exceeding reasonable cost.

164   See Philippe Sands, supra note 158, at 690–91.

165   See Eckard Rehbinder and Richard Stewart, supra note 7, at 338 (proposing development of integrated administrative law to provide judicial access to environmental activists).

166   See Fifth Environmental Action Programme, OJ C 138, at 82 (May 17, 1993) ('[i]ndividuals and public interest groups should have practicable access to the courts in order to ensure that their legitimate interests are protected and that prescribed environmental measures are effectively enforced and illegal practices stopped').

167   See Rolf Wagenbaur, supra note 42, at 467.

168   See Eckard Rehbinder and Richard Stewart, supra note 7, at 338–41. See also Richard B. Stewart, *Antidotes for the 'American Disease'*, 20 Eco. L.Q. 85, 92–3 (1993) (arguing for development of EU law to authorize citizen suits).

169   See Philippe Sands, supra note 158, at 2522. In addition, the Commission has proposed a draft waste liability directive that imposes strict liability of producers of environmentally injurious waste. See Philippe Sands, supra note 158, at 692. The directive not only creates a new cause of action but also prescribes such minimum remedies as damages and injunctive relief. *Id.*

170   Article I of the Constitution establishes the House and Senate, prescribes the members' qualifications for office and sets out in some detail the role the states must play in the election of the members. Article I also defines lawmaking procedure, and the scope of lawmaking competence. In addition to the grant of powers to tax and to regulate 'commerce among the several States' – the two most significant grants of congressional authority – Article I authorizes Congress to make all laws 'necessary and proper' for carrying its objectives into execution.

171   Article II creates the office of the President and obliges him or her faithfully to execute the laws adopted by Congress. Article II gives the President a relatively direct role in the lawmaking process, authorizing him or her to submit draft bills to the legislative branch. It also gives the President veto powers that ensure a presidential role in the final legislative product. In the foreign affairs arena, the President enjoys the authority to initiate treaties with foreign nations subject to ratification by the Senate. Finally Article II sketches the rudiments of the modern administrative state, authorizing the President to appoint executive and judicial officers subject to the Senate's power of advice and consent.

172   Article III provides for the adjudication of the nation's legal business in one Supreme Court and in such inferior courts as Congress may see fit to ordain and establish. Article III extends the jurisdiction of the federal courts to all cases arising under the constitution, laws and treaties of the United States, to cases of admiralty and maritime jurisdiction, and to cases affecting foreign envoys. In addition, Article III provides for federal judicial resolution of certain controversies between diverse citizens, states, foreign nations and their citizens. Congress may regulate the appellate jurisdiction of the Supreme Court and determine the existence and jurisdiction of the lower federal courts.

173   US Const., amend. 10. Like perhaps most provisions that restate the contours of federal-state relations, the tenth amendment has been the subject of conflicting interpretations. Useful summaries of developments since the Court's landmark decision in *National League of Cities v. Usery*, 426 U.S. 833 (1976), appear in Martha Field, *Garcia v. San Antonio Metropolitan Transit Authority: The Demise of a Misguided Doctrine*, 99 Harv. L. Rev. 84 (1985) (recounting Court's decision to abandon the tenth amendment limit on congressional power enunciated in *NLC*); Van Alstyne, *The Second Death of Federalism*, 83 Mich. L. Rev. 1709 (1985). Views about the original conception of the tenth amendment differ. *Compare* Raoul Berger, *Federalism: The Founder's Design* 77–99 (1987) (arguing against interpretation of the tenth amendment as mere truism; discerning an intention to cabin federal government within enumerated powers) *with* C.A. Lofgren, *The Origins of the Tenth Amendment: History, Sovereignty, and the Problems of Constitutional Intention* in *Constitutional Government in America* 331 (R. Collins ed. 1981) (emphasizing the importance of the failure of the tenth amendment to include 'expressly' as a modifier of 'delegated'; arguing that such an omission drains the tenth amendment of much substantive bite).

174   Article I, section 8 authorizes Congress to provide for the use of state militias to suppress insurrections and repel invasions; Article III authorizes the Supreme Court to pass upon territorial disputes between the states; Article IV, section 3 prohibits the creation of new states within the jurisdiction of other states; and Article IV, section 4 provides that the United States shall guarantee to every state a republican form of government and protect each of them from invasion and domestic violence. For an argument that the guarantee clause of Article IV establishes justiciable limits on the power of the Federal government *vis-à-vis* the states, see Deborah Jones Merritt, *The Guarantee Clause and State Autonomy: Federalism for a Third Century*, 88 Colum. L. Rev. 1 (1988).

175   Federalist No. 39, at 253 (Jacob E. Cooke ed. 1961). On the significance of Federalist No. 39, see Martin Diamond, *The Federalist on Federalism: 'Neither a National Nor a Federal Constitution But a Composition of Both'*, 86 Yale L.J. 1273 (1977).

176   Federalist No. 39, at 257. His analysis bears out his conclusion. Madison first observed that the ratification of the Constitution required a majority vote of a convention of the people of each state, not simply a majority vote of the people as a whole. *Id.* at 254. Such a ratification scheme seemed to Madison clearly federal in that it depended on the consent of the states, rather than the people themselves. Some have accused Madison of dissembling here. After all, the preamble describes the act of constituting the government as one undertaken by 'we, the people of the United States' rather than the people of the several states. Yet Madison's fundamental point remains. States, like North Carolina, that chose to remain outside the plan were entitled to do so.

       Next, Madison considered the derivation of the 'ordinary' powers of government. Madison noted that the House of Representatives will derive its representatives from a direct popular vote of the people, according to the plan of apportionment set forth in Article I. In contrast to such a national derivation, Madison pointed out that the Senate's composition was based upon a principle of state equality, with each state electing two members without regard to population. The presidency derived its powers 'from a very compound source' with the states acting through the electoral college as distinct societies but with votes apportioned by population. Ultimate determination was vested in the House of Representatives, which consists of national representatives.

       The principal actors in the legislative process, Congress and the President, were thus drawn in good measure from state institutions. While the Constitution assigned a single vote to each Representative and Senator in the legislative process, adopted a majority voting regime, and thus abandoned the requirement of state unanimity that had characterized the legislative process under the Articles of Confederation, it nonetheless assured the states a relatively direct voice in national politics. This structural guarantee of state political involvement was what Herbert Wechsler later famously described as the 'political safeguards of federalism'. See Herbert Wechsler, *The Political Safeguards of Federalism: The Role of the States in the Composition and Selection of the National Government*, 54 Colum. L. Rev. 543 (1954). For an update, arguing that a variety of factors have contributed to a decline in the states' influence, see Lewis B. Kaden, *Politics, Money, and State Sovereignty: The Judicial Role*, 79 Colum. L. Rev. 847, 857–68 (1979); D. Bruce La Pierre, *The Political Safeguards of Federalism Redux: Intergovernmental Immunity and the States as Agents of the Nation*, 60 Wash. U.L.Q. 779 (1982).

177   Federalist No. 39, at 255.

178   *Id.*

179   *Id.* at 256.

180   Part of the argument, indeed, appears to suggest the contrary. In contrasting them from the plan under consideration, Madison noted that wholly national governments enjoyed the power to control, direct or abolish all local authorities. Under the Constitution, however, municipal or local authorities were no more subject to the general authority 'within their respective spheres' than the general government was subject to local authority within its sphere. See Federalist No. 39, at 256. Madison thus comes close to saying that the national government, within its sphere, can control and direct, if not abolish, the local authorities.

181   *Id.* at 256.

182   See generally Paul M. Bator, Daniel J. Meltzer, Paul J. Mishkin and David L. Shapiro, *Hart and Wechsler's The Federal Courts and the Federal System* 1–64 (3rd ed. 1988); Felix Frankfurter and James Landis, *The Business of the Supreme Court* (1928).

183   For background on the Madisonian compromise, under which Congress was permitted but not obliged to institute lower federal courts, see Charles Warren, *The Making of the Constitution* 325–7 (1928).

184   For accounts linking the supremacy clause to the framers' creation of a system of judicial, rather than legislative, control of state government, see Charles Warren, supra note 183, at 316–24; Akhil Reed Amar, *A Neo-Federalist View of Article III: Separating the Two Tiers of Federal Jurisdiction*, 65 B.U.L. Rev. 105, 224–6 (1985).

185   Article III itself vests the Supreme Court with appellate jurisdiction in 'all other cases', a provision that most scholars read as vesting the Court with jurisdiction to review state court decisions in cases that implicate the Constitution, laws and treaties of the United States – the very texts declared supreme by the supremacy clause. See Lawrence Gene Sager, *The Supreme Court, 1980 Term – Foreword: Constitutional Limitations on Congress' Authority to Regulate the Jurisdiction of the Federal Courts*, 95 Harv. L. Rev. 17, 23–24 (1981); Robert Clinton, *A Mandatory View of Federal Court Jurisdiction: Early Implementation of and Departures from the Constitutional Plan*, 86 Colum. L. Rev. 1515 (1986). For the Court's affirmation of this view, see *Martin v. Hunter's Lessee*, 14 U.S. (1 Wheat.) 304, 342–52 (1816).

186   The Federalist No. 82, at 556.

187   U.S. Const., Art. III, § 2.

188   For an account of the origins and early uses of the Court's jurisdiction over inter-state disputes, see Charles Warren, *The Supreme Court and the Sovereign States* (1924).

189   See James E. Pfander, *Rethinking the Supreme Court's Original Jurisdiction in State-Party Cases* (forthcoming in Cal. L. Rev.).

190   The Constitution also bars the states from emitting bills of credit, coining money, enacting laws that make paper money a valid tender in payment of debts. See U.S. Const., Art. 1, § 10. On the origins of these bans on state fiscal irresponsibility, see Charles Warren, supra note 183, at 5–8, 164–71. For an argument that the framers added 'cases' arising under the Constitution to the jurisdictional language of Article III primarily to assure state compliance with these constitutional limits, see James E. Pfander, supra note 189, at 24–5 and n.186.

191   The civil war amendments worked an enormous reallocation of power from the states to the Federal government. For the argument that this reallocation represented more a perfection of the framers' initial plan than a decisive shift away from an original commitment to state control, see Akhil Reed Amar, *Of Sovereignty and Federalism*, 96 Yale L.J. 1425 (1987).

192   See John J. Gibbons, *The Eleventh Amendment and State Sovereign Immunity: A Reinterpretation*, 83 Colum. L. Rev. 1889, 1895–99 (1983).

193   U.S. Const., Art. VI.

194   Note, for example, the position that Elbridge Gerry, a committed anti-federalist from Massachusetts, took in debates over the power of Congress to call on state officers to execute a federal law: 'Nothing could be plainer than this, that the General Government had a right to require the assistance of the officers of the several State Governments, for they have severally taken an oath to support the Constitution of the United States'. 2nd Cong., 1st Sess., April 25, 1792 *quoted in* Charles Warren, *Federal Criminal Laws and the State Courts*, 38 Harv. L. Rev. 545, 551 (1925).

195   See William Blackstone, 1 *Commentaries on the Laws of England*, app. 238 (H. St. George Tucker ed. 1803) (suggesting that the sum of each state's ratable share of any direct tax would be fixed in advance by Congress); *Hylton v. United States*, 3 U.S. (3 Dall.) 171, (1796) (opinion of Paterson, J.) (direct taxes assume that each state will be assigned a quota); Federalist No. 36, at 226 (Hamilton) (Congress may collect direct taxes or 'have recourse to requisitions in its stead').

196   Consider the remarks of James Madison: 'One remark ought not to be omitted. It is, that every state which chuses to collect its own quota may always prevent a federal collection by keeping a little beforehand in its finances and making its payment at once into the federal treasury'. Letter of James Madison to George Thompson, Jan. 29, 1789 in 11 Madison Papers 433–7. See also Federalist No. 36, at 226 (Hamilton) (emphasis in original) ('The national Legislature can make use of the *system of each State within that State.* The method of laying and collecting this species of [direct] taxes in each State, can, in all its parts, be adopted and employed by the Federal Government'.)

197   Article I, section 8, clause 15. As originally drafted, the provision authorized the use of the militia for the specific purpose of requiring a Member State to 'fulfill its duty under the articles thereof'. Max Farrand, 1 *The Records of the Federal Convention* 61 (1911) [hereinafter Farrand]. The convention decided that such a provision would too much resemble the declaration of war against a Member State, See 1 Farrand 54 (remarks of Madison), and therefore changed the language to speak more generally of the enforcement of laws, repulsion of invasions and suppression of insurrections. See 2 Farrand 382.

198   Article I, section 8, clause 16.

199   Article II, section 2.

200   In a discussion of the militia provisions of the Constitution, Charles Pinckney, a delegate from South Carolina who had served as a general in the Revolutionary War, warmly defended the necessity of authorizing the Federal government to control the militia. As Pinckney explained:

> I am decidedly in opinion [the federal authorities] should have the exclusive right of establishing regulations for [the militia's] Government and Discipline, which the States should be bound to comply with, as well as with their Requisitions for any number of Militia, whose march into another State, the Public safety or benefit should require.

3 Farrand 118. Pinckney thus believed that the Constitution authorized Congress to pass laws regulating the militia and that the states were bound, as states, to carry such laws into effect.

Thus, the implementing statute authorizes the President to call forth the militia 'most convenient to the place of danger or scene of action, . . . and to issue his orders for that purpose, to such officer or officers of the militia as he shall think proper'. 1 Stat. 264, § 1.

This provision specifically authorized the President to issue binding orders to officers holding authority under state law; in particular, it authorized the President to issue orders to the governors of the respective states, who served as the commanding officers of state militias. Later provisions subjected any officer who 'fail[s] to obey the orders of the President' to specified military discipline, including fines and loss of commission. *Id.*, § 5.

For an early decision that presumes the propriety of the power of the President to issue orders binding on the governors, see *Houston v. Moore*, 30 U.S. (5 Wheat.) 1, (1820) (opinion of Justice Washington). But see *id.* (opinion of Justice Johnson) (questioning the President's power to issue binding orders to the governor of the state of Pennsylvania). See also Joseph Story, 2 *Commentaries on the Constitution* § 1207, at 92–3 (1833) (the 'power to call forth the militia may be exercised either by requisitions upon the executive of the states; or by orders directed to such executive').

201   Both provisions descend rather directly from similar provisions that appeared in Article 4 of the Articles of Confederation. Their reincorporation in the Constitution suggests that the framers regarded the new plan as one that continued to operate upon the states as states.

202   The clause provides

> Full Faith and Credit shall be given in each State to the public Acts, Records, and judicial Proceedings of every other State. And the Congress may by general Laws prescribe the manner in which such Acts, Records and Proceedings shall be proved, and the Effect thereof.

U.S. Const., Art. IV.

203   That the clause's reference to 'public Acts' encompasses the work of state legislatures seems clear from the history of the framing. The committee of detail draft of the clause required the states to give effect to 'the acts of the Legislatures, and to the records and judicial proceedings of the Courts'. 2 Farrand 188. Debate on the provision led to its reconsideration by a special committee but no one raised doubts about the propriety of its application to legislative acts. Among other changes, the special committee adopted the final reference to 'public Acts' as an apparent substitute for the more direct reference to legislative acts. See 2 Farrand 485. See generally Walter Wheeler Cook, *The Powers of Congress Under the Full Faith and Credit Clause*, 28 Yale L.J. 421 (1919).

204   Under the law of nations, independent sovereigns often accorded a measure of respect to the judicial proceedings of other nations. Justice Story builds upon that fact in arguing that the full faith and credit clause must have intended to require the states to accord binding effect to the judgments of other states; otherwise, the clause would have been superfluous. See Joseph Story, supra note 200, at §§ 1298–1304. Today, the Court treats the clause in some respects as the framers and Justice Story intended, reading the provision as imposing an obligation on state courts to respect the judgments of sibling states. See, e.g., *Fauntleroy v. Lum*, 210 U.S. 230 (1908) (full faith and credit clause prohibits the recognizing state from refusing to enforce a rendering state judgment said to offend public policy of the recognizing state).

205   The framers' intention to authorize Congress not only to prescribe the rules of evidence for authenticating public acts and records but also to prescribe their 'effect' comes through quite clearly in the records of the convention. When the clause came up for debate, Madison argued for language empowering Congress to prescribe rules for the execution of judgments in other

states. See 2 Farrand 448. Randolph opposed the motion, arguing for a clause limited to evidentiary effect on the ground that nations did not execute judgments of other nations. *Id.* The committee reported a provision that authorized legislative prescription of a rule governing only the execution of judgments. *Id.* at 485. The provision was amended by striking the limiting reference to execution of judgments and thus broadening the power of Congress generally to prescribe the 'effect' of state legislation and judicial proceedings in other states. *Id.* at 488–9.

Many have decried the failure of Congress to exercise the powers conferred upon it through the full faith and credit clause. See Walter Wheeler Cook, supra note 203. As currently codified, the statute merely declares that duly authenticated acts, records and proceedings 'shall have the same full faith and credit' in another state court 'as they have by law or usage in the courts . . . from which they are taken'. 28 U.S.C. § 1738.

206   See Joseph Story, supra note 200, at § 1302–3.

207   On the euphemism, see 4 Elliott Debates 176 (comments of James Iredell).

208   However much one might deprecate the framers' compromise with the 'peculiar institution' of slavery, no one doubts that such provisions cast affirmative obligations on the states as states. When Southern delegates to the Philadelphia convention proposed the addition of fugitive slaves to the clause calling for the interstate rendition of criminals, See 2 Farrand 443 (proposal of Butler and Pinckney of South Carolina to 'require fugitive slaves and servants to be delivered up like criminals') – a provison that had been borrowed from the Articles of Confederation – James Wilson objected. As the delegate from Pennsylvania explained, such a provision 'would oblige the Executive of the State to do it, at the public expence'. 2 Farrand 443. While Wilson thus apparently supported such a public expenditure of state funds to accomplish the national purpose of rendering fugitives from justice, he doubted the propriety of enlisting the states' fiscs in support of the enterprise of slave recaption. Nonetheless, the provision for rendition of slaves was incorporated into Article IV.

209   483 U.S. 219 (1987).

210   See *Puerto Rico v. Branstad*, 483 U.S. 219, 230 (1987).

211   65 U.S. (24 How.) 66 (1861).

212   See *Kentucky v. Dennison*, 65 U.S. (24 How.) 66, 107 (1861).

213   See *Puerto Rico v. Branstad*, 483 U.S. 219, 225 (1987). The decision rejected in *Branstad*, *Kentucky v. Dennison*, 65 U.S. (24 How.) 66 (1861), has been frequently cited to support arguments against the power of the Federal government to conscript the states. See, e.g., D. Bruce LaPierre, supra note 176, at 1045–6.

214   Pathbreaking decisions such as *Wickard v. Filburn*, 317 U.S. 111 (1942) uphold the power of Congress to regulate such apparently local matters as the produce of a family farm on the theory that such production may affect the flow of interstate commerce. Such a broad conception of the commerce clause authorizes Congress to regulate virtually any commercial or productive activity in the United States, so long as the activity has some arguable affect on interstate commerce. It's difficult to conceive of an important environmental initiative that Congress would lack power to undertake under this broad understanding of its commerce clause authority.

215   452 U.S. 264 (1981).

216   Thus, from 1927 to 1990, the total revenues of the Federal government increased from $4.5 billion to $1,155 billion – a factor of 250. During the same period, state and local government revenues grew less dramatically, from $2.1 and $6.3 billion to $632 and $580 billion respectively – a factor of 144. See United States Advisory Commission on Intergovernmental Relations, 2 *Significant Features of Fiscal Federalism* 90 (1992).

217   By its terms, the eleventh amendment bars only suits brought against a state by citizens of another state and aliens. Yet, the Court held in *Hans v. Louisiana*, 134 U.S. 1 (1890), that the states' immunity from suit extended to suits brought by a citizen of the state itself, in an action brought to enforce federal rights. Such an interpretation of the eleventh amendment has been the subject of persistent scholarly attack but has never been overthrown. For a flavor of the debate, see William A. Fletcher, *A Historical Interpretation of the Eleventh Amendment: A Narrow Construction of an Affirmative Grant of Jurisdiction Rather than a Prohibition Against Jurisdiction*, 35 Stan. L. Rev. 1033 (1983); Calvin R. Massey, *State Sovereign Immunity and the Tenth and Eleventh Amendments*, 56 U. Chi. L. Rev. 61 (1989). In its most recent foray, the Court refused to overrule *Hans* by a single vote, essentially on prudential grounds. See *Pennsylvania v. Union Gas Co.*, 491 U.S. 1 (1989).

218   See *Ex Parte Young*, 209 U.S. 123 (1908) (holding that the eleventh amendment does not bar suit to enjoin state official from a violation of the fourteenth amendment).

219   See *United States v. Texas*, 143 U.S. 621 (1892) (United States may sue a state on the Court's original docket); *Rhode Island v. Massachusetts*, 37 U.S. (12 Pet.) 657 (1838) (states may sue sibling states). *But see Monaco v. Mississippi*, 292 U.S. 313 (1934) (eleventh amendment bars suit by foreign nation against a state); *Kansas v. United States*, 204 U.S. 331 (1907) (state may not sue United States without its consent).

220   See *Atascadero State Hosp. v. Scanlon*, 473 U.S. 234 (1985) (Congress may abrogate state immunity from suit for damages in the exercise of its powers under the fourteenth amendment but must do so with an 'unequivocally' clear statement); *Pennsylvania v. Union Gas Co.*, 493 U.S. 1 (1989) (same; commerce clause).

221   For the growth in state and local budgets, see supra note 216. Interestingly, state and local government employment has grown much more rapidly in recent years than has that of the Federal government. Thus, federal employment has increased rather modestly from some 2.5 million employees in 1962 to 3.1 million in 1990. During the same period, state and local employment has grown from 6.8 million to 15.2 million. See ACIR, 2 *Significant Features of Fiscal Federalism* 230 (1992). Much of the growth in state and local payrolls has been financed with federal grant money, such as that to support local education.

222   The Court's most recent teaching on the scope and limits of congressional authority to induce states to legislate by conditioning the expenditure of federal funds came in *South Dakota v. Dole*, 483 U.S. 203 (1987). In the course of an opinion upholding the power of Congress to withhold federal highway funds from states that refuse to raise their drinking ages to 21, the *Dole* Court identified four restrictions on the scope of conditional spending. First, Congress must spend its funds in pursuit of the general welfare, *id.* at 207, – a relatively insignificant restriction given the requirement of substantial deference to the judgment of Congress. *Id.* Second, Congress must act unambiguously, legislating in a way that enables the states 'to exercise their choice knowingly, cognizant of the consequences of participation'. *Id.* Third, Congress must establish conditions that bear some relation to 'the federal interest in particular national projects or programs' – a limitation of which the Court has offered little 'significant elaboration'. *Id.* Finally, Congress may not attach conditions that violate other provisions of the Constitution. *Id.* at 208.

         The decision in *Dole* thus permits Congress to offer states a financial inducement to adopt a specific regulatory initiative. While the Court expressed a willingness to test the proposed regulations against constitutional norms, its decision makes clear that the right of the states themselves to regulatory autonomy does not enjoy protection from federal inducements. Thus, the Court noted that the regulations sought by Congress – state laws proscribing the purchase of liquor by individuals under the age of 21 – would not violate the constitutional rights of the individuals affected. South Dakota could not complain about any diminution in its regulatory autonomy because it was free either to participate or to refuse and forgo federal support. *Id.* at 211.

223   The Supreme Court explained this theory of conditional preemption in *Hodel v. Virginia Surface Mining & Reclamation Association, Inc.*, 451 U.S. 264 (1981), in the course of upholding provisions of the Surface Mining Act of 1977, 30 U.S.C. §§ 1201 et seq., against a tenth amendment challenge. Under the terms of the Act as the Court read it, states in which private firms undertook substantial strip-mining operations were offered a choice: the states could adopt regulations that conformed to minimum federal standards or they could opt out of the program and cede full regulatory authority to the Federal government. See *id.* at 288–9. The Court first demonstrated that the commerce clause empowered Congress to regulate private surface strip mining. See *id.* at 275–83. Such plenary regulatory authority was said to empower Congress completely to preempt state regulation of the field. See *id.* at 290. This greater power of preemptive federal regulation was also said to empower Congress to take the lesser step of allowing the states to maintain a regulatory role – and conditioning that continuing role on the states' adoption of the required federal standards. See *id.* at 290–91.

224   See generally John E. Bonine and Thomas O. McGarity, *The Law of Environmental Protection: Cases, Legislation, Policies* 418 (2nd ed. 1992).

225   Section 110(a)(2) of the Clean Air Act provides that state implementation plans (or SIPS) shall include such enforceable emission limits and other techniques 'as may be necessary' to meet the requirements of the Act. 42 U.S.C. § 110(a)(2). Section 116 specifically states that states may adopt emission and abatement plans no 'less stringent' than federal standards. 42 U.S.C. § 116. Together, the two provisions persuaded the Supreme Court that states retained the power to fashion plans more demanding than federal law requires. See *Union Elec. Co. v. EPA*, 427 U.S. 246, (1976).

226　Section 510 of the Clean Water Act provides that the states retain authority to promulgate effluent and abatement standards no 'less stringent' than federal law requires. 33 U.S.C. § 1370.

227　Section 3009 of the RCRA provides that nothing in the Act prevents the states from imposing solid waste requirements 'more stringent' than those in the Act. 42 U.S.C. § 6929.

228　Environmental federalism in both the United States and Europe thus relies to a large degree on the use of minimum standards. Such a reliance on minimum standards obviously lessens the extent to which federal initiatives displace state programs and ameliorates somewhat the conscriptive effect of central directives. See supra note 122 and accompanying text.

229　Section 209(a) of the Clean Air Act broadly prohibits the states from adopting or attempting to enforce any emission control standard for motor vehicles. See 42 U.S.C. § 7543. Section 209(b) contains the well-known California waiver, which allows the EPA to approve the use in California of different emission control standards. Section 177 authorizes other states to adopt stricter standards, but only if they adopt the California limits. Thus, vehicle manufacturers face only two possible standards, those of the Federal government or those of California. On the interplay between the two provisions, see *Ford Motor Co. v. EPA*, 606 F.2d 1293 (D.C. Cir. 1979). On the application of preemption rules in the context of imported cars, see *Sims v. Florida*, 862 F.2d 1449 (11th Cir. 1989).

230　Thus, the Toxic Substances Control Act of 1976 establishes rules requiring the EPA to screen and regulate potentially toxic substances. See Toxic Substances Control Act, 15 U.S.C. §§ 2601 et seq. Its preemption rules go somewhat further than those of the Clean Air and Clean Water Acts, reflecting a desire to permit some local initiatives but to preclude them when they would disrupt federal choices and the flow of interstate commerce. Thus, section 18 of the Act creates a general rule of non-preemption, and more fully preemptive exceptions in cases where federal testing has commenced or federal rules have been established. See 15 U.S.C. § 2617(a)(2). States can regulate in the face of federal rules only where they persuade the EPA, which the Act regards as a kind of preemption umpire, that the regulation would not 'unduly burden interstate commerce'. 15 U.S.C. § 2617(b). See generally William Rodgers, 3 *Environmental Law: Pesticides and Toxic Substances* 495–9 (1988).

　　　The same interstate commerce imperative operates with less force in the case of pesticide regulation, however. Thus, the Supreme Court recently held that the registration of pesticides under the Federal Insecticide, Fungicide, and Rodenticide Act, 7 U.S.C. §§ 135 et seq., does not prohibit localities from restricting or banning the use of federally registered (and thus arguably federally approved) pesticides. See *Wisconsin Pub. Intervenor v. Mortier*, 111 S. Ct. 2476, 2486 (1991). Such an outcome does not appear particularly surprising; before the decision came down, Professor Rodgers had described as a 'safe bet' the proposition that states would retain authority under FIFRA to enforce laws more stringent than federal minimum standards. See William H. Rodgers, supra, at 321. FIFRA nonetheless contains a preemption provision that seeks to make federal labeling and packaging requirements exclusive. See 7 U.S.C. § 136v(b).

231　On the dormant commerce clause generally, see Laurence Tribe, *American Constitutional Law* 403–41 (2nd ed. 1988). For its application to strike down local statutes that ban out-of-state solid waste, see *Fort Gratiot Sanitary Landfill, Inc. v. Michigan Dept. of Nat. Res.*, 112 S. Ct. 2019 (1992); *Chemical Waste Mgt., Inc. v. Hunt*, 112 S. Ct. 2009 (1992).

232　On the preemption doctrine generally, which bars states from enforcing laws that conflict with federal initiatives, see Laurence Tribe, supra note 231, at 479–511; Ronald D. Rotunda and John E. Nowak, 2 *Treatise on Constitutional Law: Substance and Procedure* §§ 12.1–12.4, at 62–9 (2nd ed. 1992).

233　On the immunity of federal agencies from state taxation and control, see *McCulloch v. Maryland*, 17 U.S. (4 Wheat.) 316 (1819) (barring state from laying a tax on the Bank of the United States), and its progeny.

234　In addition to the Coastal Zone Management Act, treated in the text, see Resource Conservation and Recovery Act, section 6001, 42 U.S.C. § 6961 (making departments, agencies and instrumentalities of the Federal government subject to solid and hazardous waste disposal requirements of Federal, state and local governments). For applications of this non-preemption rule that uphold state regulation of federal facilities, see *Ohio v. United States Dept. of Energy*, 689 F. Supp. 760 (S.D. Ohio 1988); *Maine v. Department of Navy*, 702 F. Supp. 322 (D. Me. 1988). Similar provisions appear in the Clean Air Act, which requires federal departments and agencies to comply with all federal, state and local pollution control requirements. See 42 U.S.C. § 7418.

235   See Coastal Zone Management Act of 1972, 16 U.S.C. §§ 1451–64 (1986). For an overview of the regulatory scheme, see Scott C. Whitney, George R. Johnson, Jr. and Steven Perles, *State Implementation of the Coastal Zone Management Consistency Provisions – Ultra Vires or Unconstitutional*, 12 Harv. Envir'l L. Rev. 67 (1988); Jack Archer and Joan Bondareff, *Implementation of the Federal Consistency Doctrine – Lawful and Constitutional: A Reply to Whitney, Johnson and Perles*, 12 Harv. Envir'l L. Rev. 115 (1988).

236   See 16 U.S.C. § 1455 (1986).

237   See 16 U.S.C. § 1456.

238   On consistency, see Eichenberg and Archer, *The Federal Consistency Doctrine: Coastal Zone Management and 'New Federalism'*, 14 Ecology L.Q. 9 (1987).

239   See 16 U.S.C. § 1456(c). Studies of the provision suggest that the Commerce Department has only rarely invoked its override authority. See Jack Archer and Joan Bondareff, supra note 235, at 144–7.

240   Another important source of delegated state regulatory authority appears in environmental statutes that authorize the states to enforce federal emission standards or limits against private sources of pollution. One example of such delegation appears in the Clean Air and Water Acts, which authorize states to enforce federally-imposed implementation plans that lack any independent basis in state law. Other examples appear in federal statutes that regulate underground storage tanks and medical waste. See Resource Conservation and Recovery Act, 42 U.S.C. §§ 6991–6991i (storage tanks); *id.* §§ 6992–6992k (medical waste). For a general introduction to the statute, see Candace C. Gauthier, *The Enforcement of Federal Underground Storage Tank Regulations*, 20 Envir'l L. 261 (1990).

241   Established through legislation enacted during the Eisenhower administration, ACIR has been a consistent and articulate advocate of preserving the state's role in the federal system.

242   See Advisory Commission on Intergovernmental Relations, *Regulatory Federalism: Policy, Process, Impact and Reform* (1984) [hereinafter ACIR, *Regulatory Federalism*].

243   See ACIR, *Regulatory Federalism* 71–8.

244   *Id.* at 78–82.

245   *Id.* at 82–8.

246   Title VI of the Civil Rights Act of 1964 provides that

>   No person in the United States shall, on the ground of race, color, or national origin, be excluded from participation in, be denied the benefits of, or be subjected to discrimination under any program receiving federal financial assistance.

   42 U.S.C. § 2000d. In subsequent years, Congress extended such crosscutting prohibitions to reach discrimination on the basis of sex, See title IX, Education Amendments Act of 1972, 20 U.S.C. § 1681, and on the basis of disability. See Section 504, Rehabilitation Act of 1973, 29 U.S.C. § 794.

247   See National Environmental Policy Act, 83 Stat. 852, 42 U.S.C. §§ 4321 et seq. For background on NEPA, see Roger W. Findley and Daniel A. Farber, supra note 6, at 103–64. For other examples of crosscutting in the environmental area, see section 508, Federal Water Pollution Control Act Amendments of 1972, 33 U.S.C. § 1368 (barring federal agencies from contracting with polluters); section 306, Clean Air Act, 42 U.S.C. § 7606 (same); sections 307(c)–(d), Coastal Zone Management Act, 16 U.S.C. § 14561(c)–(d) (declaring that federal agencies shall not approve projects inconsistent with state coastal zone management plans).

248   See NEPA, § 102, 42 U.S.C. § 4332.

249   NEPA, § 102(D), 42 U.S.C. § 4332(D). The section goes on to provide that statements may be prepared by state officials, so long as the official has statewide jurisdiction, the official receives appropriate federal guidance, and the federal official independently evaluates the statement.

250   See ACIR, *Regulatory Federalism* 174 (setting forth result of survey of city officials that identifies environmental impact statements as the second most onerous federal requirement).

251   See Clean Air Act, 42 U.S.C. §§ 7401 et seq. The Act reflects evolving congressional dissatisfaction with the willingness or ability of the states to address the problem of air pollution under the less intrusive Air Quality Act of 1967. The 1970 version of the Act requires states to submit plans to achieve air quality standards within the state; amendments to the Act in 1977 and 1990 deepen and extend the federal role. For overviews of the Act's evolution, see William H. Rodgers, Jr., supra note 230, at 172–84; John E. Bonine and Thomas O. McGarity, supra note 224, at 379–82. For a study of the influences of special interests and legislative entrepreneurialism on the Act's evolution, see E. Donald Elliott, Bruce A.

Ackerman, and John C. Millian, *Toward a Theory of Statutory Evolution: The Federalization of Environmental Law*, 1 J.L. Econ. Org. 313 (1985).

252   See Clean Air Act, § 107(a), 42 U.S.C. § 7407(a).

253   The vehicle chosen to achieve this goal was the requirement that each state develop and submit to the EPA a plan to implement and enforce federal air quality standards within their jurisdiction. The EPA was given 30 days to develop such federal standards and the states were given an additional nine months to submit implementation plans (SIPs) that were to include emission limitations, schedules and timetables for compliance. See Clean Air Act, §§ 109–10, 42 U.S.C. §§ 7409–10. Such state plans were subject to approval by the EPA, which was given authority to reject the plan and to substitute an alternative federal implementation plan in its stead.

254   See ACIR, *Regulatory Federalism* 87.

255   See supra note 253.

256   See Clean Air Act, § 179, 42 U.S.C. § 7509.

257   See Clean Air Act, § 176(c), 42 U.S.C. § 7506.

258   See Federal Water Pollution Control Act Amendments of 1972, section 101(b), 33 U.S.C. § 1251(a) (declaring the policy of Congress to 'recognize, preserve, and protect the primary responsibilities and rights of States to prevent, reduce and eliminate pollution'). Subsequent sections call upon the states to submit implementation plans for federal administrative approval. See Clean Water Act, §§ 303, 402, 33 U.S.C. §§ 1313, 1342 (specifying standards for state water pollution control plans; providing for state administration of national water pollution permit program).

259   See Surface Mining Control and Reclamation Act of 1977, section 503, 30 U.S.C. § 1253. The Act provides that any state that wishes to assume exclusive jurisdiction over the regulation of surface coal mining and reclamation operations within its border shall submit a plan to the relevant federal agency. The state's plan must establish that the state has adopted state laws, with appropriate sanctions, that conform to minimum federal standards, that it has established an adequately funded state regulatory agency, and that it can administer the required permit system for surface coal mining and reclamation. *Id.* In addition to the threat of partial preemption, Congress sought to induce state participation with a series of annual grants to cover a significant (but declining) percentage of the states' operating costs. See 42 U.S.C. § 1295(a). As a result, thirty-four states including all states with significant coal reserves, submitted regulatory programs for federal approval. See Mark Squillace, *Cooperative Federalism Under the Surface Mining Control and Reclamation Act: Is This Any Way to Run a Government?*, 87 W. Va. L. Rev. 687, 691 (1985).

260   On the role of the states in solid waste, see Resource Conservation and Recovery Act of 1976, section 1003, 42 U.S.C. § 6902 (declaring policy of establishing a 'viable Federal–State partnership' to carry out the Act's goals for solid waste recovery, transportation, and disposal). On the content of states plans, see RCRA, §§ 3006, 4002, 42 U.S.C. §§ 6926, 6942 (authorizing states to administer plans for issuance and enforcement of permits for the storage, treatment or disposal of hazardous waste; specifying standards for regional solid waste plans). The RCRA represents a relatively detailed federal regulatory initiative that leaves states less room to make and enforce their own policies than some other environmental statutes. See Hubert H. Humphrey III, *The Federal and State Roles in Environmental Enforcement: A Proposal for a More Effective and More Efficient Relationship*, 14 Harv. Envir'l L. Rev. 7, 20 (1990) (describing RCRA as 'significantly' increasing degree of federal involvement). See generally John E. Bonine and Thomas O. McGarity, supra note 224, at 722–6, 775–80.

261   The Hazardous and Solid Waste Amendments of 1984 added a program to regulate underground storage tanks. In many respects, the program resembles other environmental initiatives. Thus, the Act follows the approach of the Superfund legislation in requiring owners of underground tanks to correct petroleum leaks. See 42 U.S.C. § 6991b(h). In addition, the Act calls upon the EPA to develop new regulations to govern new tank performance standards, leak detection, and record keeping. *Id.* § 6991b(c). Finally, the Act authorizes the EPA to approve a state enforcement program, so long as the state adopts standards at least as stringent as those in federal law and the state has adequate enforcement authority. *Id.* § 6991c(a).

       In addition to these standard features, the underground storage tank program includes some innovations. Thus, the Act permits the state to exercise enforcement authority under the Act without enacting any substantive state law, so long as the state has the requisite 'capabilities' and enters into an agreement with the EPA. See 42 U.S.C. § 6991b(h)(7). Such a statute enables the states to enforce federal standards directly, without enacting them into state law.

See Hubert H. Humphrey III, supra note 260, at 26–7.

The Medical Waste Tracking Act, 102 Stat. 2950, 42 U.S.C. §§ 6992–6992K, takes the appointment of the states as agents of federal enforcement one step further. After establishing standards for the transportion and disposal of medical waste and authorizing the EPA to conduct inspections and take enforcement action against violators, the Act includes an express delegation of federal authority to the states. Section 11007 of the Act authorizes the states to conduct inspections and take enforcement actions 'to the same extent' as the EPA. See 42 U.S.C. § 6992f. The Act calls for payment to the federal treasury of any fines collected as a result of such state enforcement proceedings – a feature that one state official describes as a 'substantial disincentive' to such action. See Hubert H. Humphrey III, supra note 260, at 31.

262   See Clean Air Act, § 110(a)(2)(A), 42 U.S.C. § 7410(a)(2)(A).

263   See Clean Air Act, § 110(a)(2)(B), 42 U.S.C. § 7410(a)(2)(B).

264   See Clean Air Act, § 110(a)(2)(D), 42 U.S.C. § 7410(a)(2)(D).

265   See Clean Air Act, § 110(a)(2)(E), 42 U.S.C. § 7410(a)(2)(E).

266   See Clean Water Act, § 402(b), 33 U.S.C. § 1342(b) (authorizing the state to administer a system of permits for water discharges but only if the state adopts laws that apply and ensure compliance with federal standards, that authorize the state to terminate permits for cause, that assure adequate enforcement authority and that provide for monitoring and reports in accordance with federal law); Resource Conservation and Recovery Act, § 4003, 42 U.S.C. § 6943 (requiring state plan to prohibit establishment of new dumps and to provide for necessary regulatory powers); Safe Drinking Water Act, § 1413, 42 U.S.C. § 330g–2 (declaring the state to have primary enforcement responsibility for public water systems, provided the state has adopted required regulations and can conduct such monitoring and inspections as EPA may require); Coastal Zone Management Act, § 306(d), 16 U.S.C. § 1455(d) (state plans must include authority to resolve conflicts between competing land uses, include power to condemn land, provide for public participation, and ensure state-wide coordination).

267   See *Steward Machine Co. v. Davis*, 301 U.S. 548 (1937); *Massachusetts v. Mellon*, 262 U.S. 447, 480–83 (1923).

268   For examples of environmental statutes that authorize the EPA to pass on the sufficiency of the states' transposition of federal standards into state law, see Clean Air Act, § 110(a)(1), 42 U.S.C. § 7410(a)(1); Safe Drinking Water Act, § 1413, 42 U.S.C. § 330g–2(a); Clean Water Act, § 402, 33 U.S.C. § 1342(b); Resource Recovery and Conservation Act, § 4007(a), 42 U.S.C. § 6947(a). The Coastal Zone Management Act confers similar authority on the Secretary of Commerce. See 16 U.S.C. § 1455(d).

269   Section 113(a)(2) of the Clean Air Act authorizes the EPA to enforce state implementation plans directly against polluters after it determines that 'widespread' violations suggest that the state has failed 'to enforce the plan effectively'. 42 U.S.C. § 7413(a)(2). Similar provisions appear in the Clean Water Act, § 309(a)(2), 33 U.S.C. § 1319(a)(2), and the Surface Mining Reclamation and Control Act, which authorizes the Office of Surface Mining to take over enforcement in low compliance states. See 30 U.S.C. § 1271(b).

270   Section 179(b)(1) of the Clean Air Act authorizes the EPA to bar the payment of highway construction funds for the area of the state that has failed to achieve national air quality standards. Section 179(b)(2) authorizes the EPA to limit the construction or modification of major new sources of air pollution in the non-attainment area, a retreat from the 1977 requirement of a moratorium on new source pollution in non-attainment areas. See 42 U.S.C. § 7509(b).

271   On the conditional approval, and partial rejection, of SIPs, see William H. Rodgers, Jr., supra note 230, at 256–64; John E. Bonine and Thomas O. McGarity, supra note 224, at 429–30. As a result of such administrative back-and-forth, a number of sources escaped control. See William V. Luneberg, *The National Quest for Clean Air 1970–78: Some Intergovernmental Problems and Some Proposed Solutions*, 73 N.W. L. Rev. 397, 403 (1978).

272   See supra notes 116–23 and accompanying text.

273   See Clean Air Act, § 110(c)(1), 42 U.S.C. § 7410(c)(1).

274   On the delays in enforcement occasioned by the SIP approval process, see William V. Luneberg, supra note 271, at 400–405.

275   On the authority of the EPA to withhold federal grants as a sanction for state non-compliance, see Clean Air Act, § 129(b), 42 U.S.C. § 7506(b). For the suggestion that such a sanction may cripple the state's air pollution program, see William V. Luneberg, supra note 271, at 449.

276   See William V. Luneberg, supra note 271, at 449. It may also confer some political capital on state environmental agencies that might otherwise lack bargaining power in the state legislative process.

277   See William H. Rodgers, Jr, supra note 230, at 536 (federal regulatory takeover as remote a prospect as EPA action seeking imprisonment of a state governor).

278   See Mark Squillace, supra note 259, at 702.

279   See *id.* Add to this expense the prospect that a state may bid for reinstatement as the primary enforcement agent. A decision returning primary authority to the state might necessitate the layoff of newly hired federal workers.

280   See William H. Rodgers, Jr, supra note 230, at 536 n.2.

281   See supra notes 252–61 and accompanying text.

282   See supra notes 253–60 and accompanying text.

283   See William V. Luneberg, supra note 271, at 407.

284   The authority of the Federal government to enforce approved SIPS under the Clean Air Act appears in section 113. See U.S.C. § 7413.

285   A slightly different situation obtains where the EPA promulgates a federal implementation plan. Such a plan obviously enjoys the force of federal law but has no independent basis in state law. States may nonetheless enforce such federal plans under the authority of federal law. Section 304 of the Clean Air Act authorizes any 'person' to commence a civil action against any person alleged to have violated an emission standard or limitation. See 42 U.S.C. § 7604. Because states are persons within the meaning of this section, they enjoy enforcement authority even in the absence of binding state law. See *Hancock v. Train*, 426 U.S. 167, 195–6 (1976). State invocation of such delegated federal authority may cause problems, however. State courts may take the position that they lack the power to enforce such statutes without some relatively formal state law acceptance of the delegated authority; states may nonetheless commence such actions in federal courts but the state legislature may refrain from appropriating funds to support such enforcement efforts. Similar problems may arise in connection with the enforcement of recent federal statutes that regulate underground storage tanks and medical waste. See Hubert H. Humphrey III, supra note 260, at 30–31, 38.

286   For critiques of the overfiling policy, see Hubert H. Humphrey III, supra note 260, at 13–14.

287   See William H. Rodgers, Jr, supra note 230, at 540–41 (collecting authority).

288   For a collection of the fifteen environmental citizen suit provisions that descended from the Clean Air Act, see *Ruckelshaus v. Sierra Club*, 463 U.S. 680, 682–3 n.1 (1983).

289   See Clean Air Act, § 304(a), 42 U.S.C. § 7604; Clean Water Act, § 505, 33 U.S.C. § 1365(a); Resource Conservation and Recovery Act, § 7002(a), 42 U.S.C. § 6972(a). While the Clean Air Act's section 304 authorizes courts to grant injunctive relief, it does not support the entry of a money judgment. See William H. Rodgers, Jr, supra note 230, at 213.

290   See Clean Air Act, § 304(b), 42 U.S.C. § 7604(b); Clean Water Act, § 505, 33 U.S.C. § 1365(b); Resource Conservation and Recovery Act, § 7002(b), 42 U.S.C. § 6972(b).

291   See David P. Currie, *Air Pollution: Federal Law and Analysis* at 10–1/11 (1981).

292   See Mark Squillace, supra note 259, at 696.

293   See *id.* at 702–7.

294   In another relatively uncompromising critique, Harvey Lieber questions the need for a federal role in water pollution control. See Harvey Lieber, *Federalism and Clean Waters: The 1972 Water Pollution Control Act* (1975). Surveying the water pollution control situation in five states, Lieber concludes that the federal standards adopted in the 1972 statute were clearly justifiable only in Mississippi. *Id.* at 192. Other states, such as New York and Washington were said to present a mixed picture. *Id.* Still others were said to have such highly effective water pollution control regimes (Texas) or such relatively unpolluted waters as to render federal controls unnecessary (Wyoming). *Id.* Lieber's conclusions, at least as to Texas, were called into doubt by a state official's admission that, prior to 1985, 'Texas had poor performance'. See Proceedings, Nineteenth Annual Conference on the Environment, American Bar Association, *Federal Versus State Environmental Protection Standards: Can a National Policy be Implemented Locally?* 24 (1991) [hereinafter ABA Environment Conference] (remarks of B.J. Wynne III, chair, Texas Water Commission).

295   See ACIR, *Regulatory Federalism* 265.

296   See *id.* at 278–9. The report specifically highlights the crossover sanctions that were designed to ensure state compliance with the Clean Air Act, as those it seeks to eliminate. *Id.* at 279.

297   See *id.* at 295.

298   See *id.* at 282–92.

299   See ABA Environment Conference, supra note 294, at 1 (remarks of E. Donald Elliott, General Counsel, EPA).
300   See *id.*
301   See *id.* at 2.
302   *Id.*
303   See United States Advisory Commission on Intergovernmental Relations, 2 *Significant Features of Fiscal Federalism: Revenues and Expenditures* Table 27, at 61 (1992).
304   See *id.*
305   See *id.* (projecting that the Federal government will supply state environmental programs some $4 billion in 1995, or about 1.7 percent of total federal grants).
306   See Hubert H. Humphrey III, supra note 260, at 36 n.175 (noting that states had increased their budgets for air, water and hazardous waste pollution from 1982 to 1986 despite diminishing federal aid).
307   See ABA Environment Conference, supra note 294, at 3 (remarks of E. Donald Elliott).
308   See supra note 261.
309   See Hubert H. Humphrey III, supra note 260, at 32 (estimates based on interviews with enforcement officials in Minnesota).
310   Section 402(b) of the Clean Water Act authorizes the states to develop its own NPDES permit system to regulate the discharge of pollutants into surface waters. See 33 U.S.C. § 1342(b).
311   See ABA Environment Conference, supra note 294, at 20 (remarks of James R. Elder, Director, EPA Office of Water Enforcement and Permits).
312   Section 3006 enables EPA to delegate authority to a state for the issuance of permits to facilities that dispose of solid and hazardous waste. See 42 U.S.C. § 6926(b).
313   See ABA Environment Conference, supra note 294, at 30 (remarks of Nancy Firestone, EPA deputy assistant).
314   See *id.* ('The RCRA 'universe' is potentially three times the size of the Superfund National Priority List. Without adequate resources, states are not necessarily anxious to take on the obligations of corrective action'.)
315   See Clean Air Act, § 502(b), 42 U.S.C. § 7661a(b).
316   See ABA Environment Conference, supra note 294, at 15.
317   For example, bond requirements appear in statutes that regulate the disposal of hazardous waste and the installation of underground storage tanks. See Resource Conservation and Recovery Act, §§ 3004(t), 9003(d), 42 U.S.C. §§ 6924(t), 6991b(d).
318   Apart from fee and bond requirements many environmental reformers place some confidence in the use of market-based regulatory regimes as an alternative to traditional command-and-control regulation. For an overview of the market-based system adopted as part of the Clean Air Act amendments of 1990, see John E. Bonine and Thomas O. McGarity, supra note 294, at 494–513.
319   I say almost single-handedly with proposals to nationalize no-fault insurance in mind. Floated in the early 1970s, such proposals would have required states to adopt federal no-fault automobile insurance standards. See Norman Dorsen, *The National No-Fault Motor Vehicle Insurance Act: A Problem in Federalism*, 49 N.Y.U.L. Rev. 45 (1974). Constitutional doubts about the propriety of such a conscriptive procedure led to changes in the draft, which ultimately failed to emerge from Congress. See Lewis B. Kaden, supra note, at 892 and n.293.
320   The history of EPA's efforts to address vehicular emissions in metropolitan areas has been well told on a number of different occasions. See Richard B. Stewart, *Pyramids of Sacrifice? Problems of Federalism in Mandating State Implementation of National Environmental Policy*, 86 Yale L.J. 1196, 1202–7 (1977); Lewis B. Kaden, supra note 176, at 869–70; D. Bruce La Pierre, supra note 176, at 933–9.
321   See Richard B. Stewart, supra note 320, at 1203–4.
322   EPA took the position that, once a FIP was in place, states were bound to comply with its terms as persons subject to regulation under the statute. If accepted, such a theory subjected the states to the full range of enforcement options set forth in section 113 of the Act. The EPA, however, took the position that it would not seek criminal sanctions for state non-compliance. See D. Bruce La Pierre, supra note 176, at 934 n.587.
323   See *Maryland v. EPA*, 530 F.2d 215 (4th Cir. 1975), *vacated and remanded sub nom., EPA v. Brown*, 431 U.S. 99 (1977); *District of Columbia v. Train*, 521 F.2d 971 (D.C. Cir. 1975), *vacated and remanded sub nom., EPA v. Brown*, 431 U.S. 99 (1977); *Brown v. EPA*, 521 F.2d 827 (9th Cir. 1975), *vacated and remanded*, 431 U.S. 99 (1977). *Cf. Friends of the Earth v. Carey*, 552 F.2d 25 (2d Cir. 1977) (avoiding decision of the question on the ground that New York state had 'voluntarily' agreed to adopt a SIP with the federal requirements). But see

Pennsylvania v. EPA, 500 F.2d 246 (3d Cir. 1974) (upholding constitutionality of EPA's quest for state adoption of the federal plan).

324   See *Maryland v. EPA*, 530 F.2d 215, 226–7 (4th Cir. 1975), *vacated and remanded sub nom.*, *EPA v. Brown*, 431 U.S. 99 (1977); *Brown v. EPA*, 521 F.2d 827, 831 (9th Cir. 1975), *vacated and remanded*, 431 U.S. 99 (1977). *Cf. District of Columbia v. Train*, 521 F.2d 971, 992–3 (D.C. Cir. 1975) (striking down inspection requirement as unconstitutional invasion of state sovereignty), *vacated and remanded sub nom.*, 431 U.S. 99 (1977).

325   See *EPA v. Brown*, 431 U.S. 99 (1977). For an account of the Solicitor-General's strategy to avoid decision of the issue, see Richard B. Stewart, supra note 320, at 1205–6 and nn.48–9.

326   See Richard B. Stewart, supra note 320, at 1207.

327   See Lewis B. Kaden, supra note 176, at 892; D. Bruce La Pierre, supra note 176, at 1034; Deborah Jones Merritt, supra note 174, at 61; David P. Currie, supra note 15, at 394. Cf. Richard B. Stewart, supra note, at 1206–7, 1224–5 (acknowledging that the theoretical prospect of state and local governments reduced to mere appendages of the Federal government would transgress constitutional limits but doubting whether courts should enforce limits on power of Congress to conscript the states).

328   Professor La Pierre, for example, argues for a judicial role in invalidating all unfunded mandates on the ground that they shift the cost of administration to state governments and thus avoid the full payment of regulatory expenses by the national electorate. See D. Bruce La Pierre, supra note, at 1034. See also Deborah Jones Merritt, supra note 174, at 60–1 (EPA mandates make states accountable to Congress rather than state voters; force state budgets to reflect federal rather than local priorities). Professor Kaden was more discriminating; he agreed that the EPA might constitutionally impose bike lane and parking requirements as well as vehicle retrofit requirements on state government but thought that the EPA's imposition of a vehicle inspection program went too far. See Lewis B. Kaden, supra note 176, at 891–2. Professor Stewart characterizes federal imposition of unpopular transportation controls through the agency of the states as 'doubly objectionable' because it forces local officials to implement locally unpopular measures and deflects from federal officials' accountability for federal initiatives. See Richard B. Stewart, supra note 320, at 1241.

329   See Lewis B. Kaden, supra note 176, at 890.

330   *Id.*

331   *Id.*

332   See Deborah Jones Merritt, supra note 174, at 68–9 (arguing that partial preemption differs from direct conscription on the ground that it at least potentially transfers the regulatory burden to the Federal government and offers the states a choice in deciding whether to participate).

333   See David P. Currie, supra note 15, at 391.

334   *Id.*

335   112 S. Ct. 2408 (1992).

336   For a summary of the evolution of the Court's thinking, see H. Jefferson Powell, supra note 11, at 639–52.

337   426 U.S. 833 (1976) overruled by *Garcia v. San Antonio Metro. Transit Auth.*, 469 U.S. 528 (1985).

338   469 U.S. 528 (1985).

339   See *Gregory v. Ashcroft*, 111 S. Ct. 2395 (1991) (holding that the ADEA did not make its intention to bar mandatory retirement of state judges sufficiently clear; suggesting that Congress may only regulate core state functions through a fairly clear statement of an intention to do so).

340   See *New York v. United States*, 112 S. Ct. 2408, 2420 (1992).

341   *Id.* at 2420.

342   *New York v. United States*, 112 S. Ct. 2408, 2420 (1992) (quoting *Hodel v. Virginia Surface Mining & Reclam. Ass'n, Inc.*, 452 U.S. 264, 288 (1981)).

343   *Id.* at 2423.

344   *Id.* at 2424.

345   *Id.* The vice of the Act thus lies not in Congress's decision to regulate low-level radioactive waste or in its decision to involve the states in the administrative scheme but in the false choice Congress gave to the states. As the Court viewed the case, states were offered a choice between taking title to the waste and establishing a disposal arrangement that complies with congressional guidelines. Such a choice, according to the Court, was really 'no choice at all'. *Id.* at 2428. In either case, Congress was directing the states to enact and enforce a federal regulatory program in violation of the Constitution. *Id.*

346   See *id.* at 2421–3. For a cogent critique of O'Connor's historical argument, see H. Jefferson Powell, supra note 11, at 652–64. See also Saikrishna Bangalore Prakash, supra note 11 (agreeing with O'Connor as to the conscription of state legislatures but disagreeing as to the conscription of state executive authority). My own research suggests that O'Connor has overstated the historical argument by neglecting to come to grips with Madison's understanding of the government as compound – as one that operates both on the citizens directly and through the Member States. See supra notes 175–213 and accompanying text. Put in other words, O'Connor fails to recognize that the framers might have empowered the government to act on individuals without disabling it from acting upon the states.

347   Although O'Connor does not elaborate the benefits of preserved state autonomy in detail, she does incorporate other discussions that point to the value of distributing power more widely, the need to preserve the role of states as political checks on the national government, and the importance of states as 'laboratories' of political experimentation, and the enhanced ability of states to draw citizens into the political process. See *New York v. United States*, 112 S. Ct. 2408, 2424 (1992) (citing Deborah Jones Merritt, supra note 174, at 3–10) (offering such a catalog of benefits).

348   *Id.* at 2424. My discussion of the American attitude towards directives assumes that the constitutional text and structure do not definitively answer the question of congressional power. Such an assumption underlies my account's emphasis on the political choice inherent in the Court's decision. Such an emphasis may depart from the Court's view of its decision as driven by higher law considerations but it aids the task of comparison.

349   See supra note 156.

350   See supra notes 165–9.

351   See George A. Bermann, et al., supra note 16, at 966.

352   Note, for example, how prominently the argument from administrative efficiency figures in the framers' assumption that the Federal government could make use of state magistrates for the collection of federal taxes and enforcement of federal law. See Federalist No. 36, at 227 (Hamilton) (answering the claim of anti-federalists that the Constitution would necessitate the hiring of double sets of revenue officers by noting that the Federal government 'would make use of the State officers and State regulations'). See also 1 Farrand 124 (Roger Sherman opposes the mandatory institution of inferior federal courts at the convention on grounds of 'expensiveness . . . when existing State Court would answer the same purpose').

353   See supra note 319.

354   For descriptions of the two regimes, see supra notes 235–40 and 259 and accompanying text.

355   Note in this regard that the chief sponsor of the two statutes, Senator Edmund Muskie of Maine, had served as the chairman of the Advisory Commission on Intergovernmental Relations in 1962.

356   See supra notes 313–14.

357   See supra note 148.

358   See supra note 154.

359   Hamilton makes this point explicitly in discussing the use of state revenue officials to collect federal requisitions in lieu of federal collection of direct taxes.

> As to the suggestion of double taxation, the answer is plain. The wants of the Union are to be supplied in one way or another; if to be done by the authority of the Federal Government, it will not be done by that of the State governments. The quantity of taxes to be paid by the community, must be the same in either case.

Federalist No. 36, at 228.

360   Thus, many academic critics in the United States believe that central directives require the adoption of state and local legislation whose origins the representative citizen will fail to discern. The European experience lends some force to this view but for a variety of reasons the critique from obscured origins appears much less potent in the United States. Consider most importantly the dramatically different assumptions about openness in government; state secrecy simply does not characterize the legislative process here to the same extent as in Europe. See, e.g., David Vogel, *National Styles of Regulation: Environmental Policy in Great Britain and the United States* 826 (1986) (contrasting state secrecy in the UK with wide open public debate in the United States). It thus appears reasonable to conclude that concerned interest groups and newspaper editors could track the federal origins of any directive that imposes particularly burdensome state and local obligations, particularly in view of the fact that opponents of such measures will undoubtedly decry their conscriptive central provenance.

361 See Helen Wallace, William Wallace and Carole Webb, *Policy-Making in the European Union* 29 (1983).

362 On the tendency of the relatively secret process of Union legislation to obscure the origins and purposes of much environmental legislation, see Nigel Haigh, supra note 5, at 4.

363 The deficit stems from the fact that the most representative political institutions, Member State parliaments and the European Parliament, have traditionally played a much less important role in shaping central legislation than have the executive officials of the Commission and the Council. See Eckard Rehbinder and Richard Stewart, supra note 7, at 263–4, 334; Joseph Weiler, supra note 30, at 2466–8.

364 Note that I compare the directive here to central command-and-control regulation; the gains if any in regulatory flexibility through local enforcement may also be attained through the use of other tools of regulatory federalism, such as conditional spending and partial preemption.

365 See supra notes 292–3 and accompanying text.

366 See ABA, *Conference on the Environment*, supra note 294, at 20 (remarks of James Elder) (noting desire of national firms to receive uniform treatment in NPDES permitting program run by the several states).

367 European observers thus note with surprising frequency the importance of political will in the effective implementation of environmental policy. See Ludwig Krämer, supra note 17, at 45; David Freestone, supra note 78, at 148–9 (emphasizing the importance of Member State commitment); Richard Macrory, supra note 122, at 137 (ascribing lack of success of EC policy in some arenas to 'political unwillingness' of Member States).

368 See Nigel Haigh, supra note 5.

369 See *id.* at 20–23, 25–9 (describing Great Britain's commitment to achieving defined water quality objectives by setting emission standards locally and variably, rather than by setting nationally uniform standards). See also Richard Macrory, supra note 122, at 123–6 (discussing the conflict between the EC's emphasis on emission limits and the UK's focus on ambient water quality and noting the compromise that permitted the UK to maintain its ambient focus).

370 On Great Britain's success in seeking EC adoption of water quality standards as an alternative to emission limits, see Nigel High, supra note 5, at 21.

371 See Richard Macrory, supra note 122, at 124–5.

372 See Nigel Haigh, supra note 5, at 76 (describing effect of dangerous substances directive as 'less of a change in practice than a refinement of thought'); *id.* at 67 (describing the bathing water directive as providing a useful yardstick by which to measure coastal water quality).

In contrast to Haigh's account, Professor Macrory ascribes greater significance to the impact of EC initiatives on British water policy. In Macrory's account, Union water law necessitated the creation of the National Rivers Authority, a central water regulatory agency in Great Britain, in the wake of the Thatcher government's decision to privatize water authorities. See Richard Macrory, supra note 122, at 134–5. In general, Macrory concludes that EC law has 'proved a major influence on the current structure of law and administration'. *Id.* at 139.

373 See Nigel Haigh, supra note 5, at 185 (noting that 'a significant turning point in British air pollution control was allowed to pass largely unremarked in Parliament').

374 *Id.* at 171–5 (describing British regulation of air pollution; noting the power of local authorities to issue smoke control orders; noting that such orders represent 'the principal instrument being used to implement' the directive on sulphur dioxide and suspended particulates).

375 *Id.* at 185 (noting that introduction of mandatory air quality standards was a departure from current British practice but noting the absence of concern in Parliament).

376 *Id.* at 192.

377 On the origins and content of Great Britain's Environmental Protection Act of 1990, see John Gibson, *The Integration of Pollution Control*, 18 J.L. & Soc. 18 (1991). Gibson's account suggests that the Act bears some relationship to central EC environmental directives, but also takes account of other factors, both international and domestic. Thus, Gibson notes that in creating a 'red list' of 23 substances whose discharge posed the gravest threat, Great Britain followed the lead of the Second International Conference on the Protection of the North Sea rather than the EC's dangerous substances list of 129 chemicals. *Id.* at 21. By the same token, Gibson reports that Britain's policy of requiring use of the 'best available techniques not entailing excessive costs' derives from the EC framework directive on air pollution but differs by considering factors other than the purely technological. *Id.* at 24. It appears from Gibson's account primarily in the area of access to environmental information that the new Act most closely follows and seeks to implement EC initiatives. *Id.* at 27.

378   *Id.* at 28–9 (noting areas in which the Act fails to consolidate enforcement authority in a single environmental agency and instead divides such authority among central and local agencies with overlapping jurisdiction).

379   Apart from that of Nigel Haigh, few studies of the impact of EC directives on Member State environmental policy appear in the literature. The one exception, Graham Bennett's work on the impact of the air pollution directives, reaches conclusions broadly consistent with those of Haigh. Thus, Bennett reports that the dominant effect in practice on Member State policy was the introduction of binding air quality standards, a conclusion that echoes Haigh. See Graham Bennett, supra note 17, at 109.

380   Graham Bennett, supra note 17, at 199.

381   *Id.* at 200.

382   Recall that because of its interstitial character, federal law 'rarely occupies a legal field completely'. See Hart and Wechsler, supra note 182, at 533. Rather, even in areas where Congress has been active, '[f]ederal legislation has been conceived and drafted on an ad hoc basis to accomplish limited objectives. It builds upon the legal relationships established by the states, altering or supplanting them only so far as necessary for the special purpose'. *Id.*

383   See supra notes 122, 224.

384   See supra notes 330–32 and accompanying text.

385   See supra note 176.

386   See supra notes 343–5 and accompanying text.

387   *Cf. New York v. United States*, 112 S. Ct. 2408, 2435, 2438–41 (1992) (White J., dissenting) (attempting to construct a species of consent by New York to its own conscription through careful analysis of the states' role in the legislative process).

388   See supra note 149 and accompanying text.

389   See Hearing Before the Committee on Governmental Affairs, *Management Deficiencies in Environmental Enforcement: 'Forceless Enforcement'*, S. Hrg. 102–899, 102 Cong., 1st Sess. at 5 (June 13, 1991) (while the EPA's record in enforcement raises questions, state and local enforcement efforts have proven more disappointing; one-half of the over 1000 violators in a two-year period paid no cash penalties) (remarks of Richard Hembra, General Accounting Office).

390   See supra notes 63–6 and accompanying text.

391   See *New York v. United States*, 112 S. Ct. 2408, 2431–2 (1992). Professor Weiler makes much the same point in criticizing the assumption that Member State consent through unanimous voting under Article 235 covers all the problems associated with the Council's failure to respect the enumeration of powers in the Treaty. See Joseph Weiler, supra note 30, at 2452.

392   For a description of the preliminary reference, see supra note 74.

393   See supra notes 74–6 and accompanying text.

394   See supra note 217.

395   See supra note 220.

396   See supra note 218.

397   See, e.g., *Edelman v. Jordan*, 415 U.S. 651 (1974) (upholding the power of federal courts to issue prospective injunctive relief against state officials to compel them to administer a cooperative program of assistance to the Aged, Blind and Disabled in accordance with federal standards).

398   See supra note 322 and accompanying text.

399   See supra note 397.

400   In both the areas of competition policy and dumping, where the Commission investigates and brings actions to challenge anti-competitive practices of private firms or undertakings, the Union has a more directly regulatory function. See George A. Bermann, et al., supra note 16, at 59–60 (competition); *id.* at 995–8 (dumping).

401   The Union does administer a modest fund that provides for grants to support environmentally protective measures in lesser developed Member States. See supra note 154.

402   See supra notes 343–4.

403   Cf. Ronald D. Rotunda and John E. Nowak, supra note 232, at 1993 Supp. at 20 (emphasizing the broad range of regulatory options left to Congress and concluding that *New York* 'is a very limited ruling').

404   See ACIR, *Regulatory Federalism*, supra note, at 265 (recommending that Congress fully fund all expenses directly incurred by state and local governments to implement federal statutory mandates).

405 See Timothy J. Conlan and David R. Beam, *Federal Mandates: The Record of Reform and Future Prospects*, 18 Intergovernmental Perspective 7, 9–10 (1992) (describing the process by which the Congressional Budget Office estimates the cost of new federal initiatives to state and local governments; criticizing cost estimates as conservative and incomplete; noting instances in which estimates were either omitted or much too low).

406 *Id.* at 10 (concluding that the CBO's cost estimates have failed to restrain the growth of legislative mandates).

407 On the increasing importance of scarce resources in United States environmental policy, see supra notes 299–314 and accompanying text.

408 See supra note 62. See also Nicholas Emilious, *Subsidiarity: An Effective Barrier Against 'The Enterprises of Ambition'?*, 17 Eur. L. Rev. 383, 402–3 (1992) (summarizing the arguments against recognizing the justiciability of subsidiarity); Joseph Weiler, supra note 30, at 2463 (concluding that the erosion of the principle of enumeration through the elastic use of Article 235 would likely doom a challenge to the adoption by majority vote of measures that extend the Union's competence to pursue the objective of health); Koen Lenaerts, *Constitutionalism and the Many Faces of Federalism*, 38 Am. J. Comp. L. 205, 220 (1990) ('There simply is no nucleus of sovereignty that the Member States can invoke, as such, against the Union'.).

409 See Nicholas Emilious, supra note 408, at 405 (concluding the Court of Justice may wish to review, at a relatively deferential level, the extent to which central initiatives violate the subsidiarity principle).

5. Which Level of Government Should Be Responsible for Environmental Regulation? The Federalists Versus Calhoun

Perry Shapiro

There is a tension in American public policy between the national interest and state sovereignty. It arose in our early attempts to form a nation and played an important role in the ratification of our Constitution. The tension is reflected in the formation of environmental regulations when the national interest does not coincide with the interests of every state. When there are conflicting interests, what criteria can be used to assign regulatory authority?[1]

A common economic model of federalism postulates interstate externalities, as, for instance, air pollution in an air basin shared by two, or more, states.[2] States, independently pursuing their own narrowly conceived self-interest, adopt inefficiently lax regulatory policies. While the theoretical result is unassailable, I challenge its usually stated implication: the Federal government should be assigned the authority for policies involving interstate externalities. There are serious problems with the extension of the theoretical result to the policy conclusion.

The models which imply the welfare predominance of federal authority describe both state and federal policies as optima of well-behaved social welfare functions. State policies reflect a myopic state preference function which recognizes neither neighboring state preferences nor the effects of its actions on its neighbors. National policies, formed by optimizing a national welfare function, incorporate the preference of citizens of all states and the interstate spillover effects. This formulation does not capture the political environment in which policy alternatives are chosen. The constituencies of both the state and Federal governments are heterogeneous. And regulatory policy, at all levels, represents a political process involving the preferences and opportunities of a heterogeneous population. The existence of a well-behaved social welfare function is unlikely in such an environment. Even though the postulate of social welfare function is unrealistic, nonetheless governments might desire to limit their policy choices to only those on some efficiency frontier. To do so they must know citizen preferences; however, the need to know will limit policy alternatives.

The informational limits on all levels of government restrict their computation of optima. A model, as this one, developed to assign regulatory responsibility, must account for the complexity of the environment within which regulatory decisions are made. The inability of government to know citizen preferences is only one of the barriers to selecting efficient regulatory rules. The rules are formulated in an intensely political environment and they often represent compromises between various interests. In order to capture some regulatory complexities, I have attempted to build a model of interstate competition, cooperation and federal policy in a world of heterogeneous preferences and informational limitations inherent in pursuit of efficient policies. The models link the present complex regulatory environment to the early constitutional debate on state sovereignty versus national interests. If realistic informational constraints are imposed, the model shows that federal policies do not necessarily dominate those achieved through interstate cooperation, even if federal policy were chosen to maximize social welfare. It is unlikely that any level of government only chooses policies that are welfare optima, rather the policies are the results of some political process. A simple majority rule model is used to examine possible political outcomes. The conclusion is a negative one: *there is no assignment of regulatory responsibility that fully dominates any other.*

The chapter proceeds in three parts. The first examines the underlying historical tension between state sovereignty and national interest; the second develops various models of policy choice and the third reports on a numerical example.

STATES' RIGHTS VERSUS NATIONAL INTEREST

Issues of state sovereignty and national interest were central to the formation of the United States of America. While many of the issues are relevant to the assignment of regulatory authority, they are much too complicated to be embodied wholly in the simple model presented here. Nonetheless, there are important lessons to be learned from the deliberations of our intellectual forefathers. The debate over our own Constitution and, in particular, the relationship between states and the national (Federal) government, highlight many of the regulatory difficulties faced in a federation of sovereign states.

One of the features of federation is that independent political entities relinquish a significant degree of their autonomy to a central government. History indicates that there are many people who have recognized the potential gains from cooperative behavior of this nature. In the American case, there was a common interest among the founders of the federation in separating from Great Britain and in the common defense of the American continent against possible threats from England, France and Spain. In the Australian case, there was an apparent emphasis on the benefits from forming a customs union. The military benefits from cooperative behavior seem to have been given little prominence. The Europeans too, both past and present, have given some prominence to the benefits of closer economic and political cooperation, although their interest has varied greatly over time and is not uniformly spread across all nations within Europe. At the present time, while the European Union is forming, it appears that some nations, such as the United Kingdom, would prefer a weak form of cooperation among European nations, and others, such as France and Germany, seek a more centralized structure.

The degree of centralization was one of the most important issues in the American constitutional debate in the eighteenth and early nineteenth centuries. The Federalists, writing under the corporate name of Publius, argued strongly for centralization of power. However, there was a powerful group of Anti-Federalists who presented persuasive and intellectually attractive arguments for a weaker form of union or a group of loosely associated smaller federations. Indeed the Bill of Rights was a compromise struck by the Federalists and Anti-Federalists.

To a large measure, the debate centered on the threat to minority rights posed by a strong centralized government. The Bill of Rights was one manifestation of this concern. Another side, most eloquently presented by John C. Calhoun in the early nineteenth century, argued that minority rights were safeguarded in and protected by the individual states.

While the early concerns were for safety, interstate peace, the trade advantages of customs unions and the maintenance of states' rights, many of the same issues are faced in the search for global environmental policy. Effective policy must naturally encompass the international nature of the problem, and this poses huge difficulties in international relations. But even devising an environmental regulatory policy within one federation, such as the United States, entails many of the same problems as those faced by our founding fathers.

The Federalists, particularly Hamilton, put considerable emphasis on the dangers of interstate competition. To circumvent these dangers the military is a national function as are relations with foreign governments and the regulation of interstate commerce. In *Federalist Papers* 5, John Jay writes of dangers of state sovereignty and the potential of interstate rivalry. His argument for a strong united governing structure is based on the concern that instead of their being 'joined in affection and free from all apprehension of different interest,' envy and jealousy would soon extinguish confidence and affection, and the partial interests of each confederacy, instead of the general interest of all America, would be the only object of their policy and pursuits. Hence like most *bordering* nations, they would always be either involved in disputes and war, or live in constant apprehension of them.[3]

There is little concern in the United States that the federation will fall into interstate chaos and war. But the concern over interstate rivalry remains a salient issue in the formation of environmental policy. There is concern that interstate competition for industry and jobs may lead states to lower their environmental standards. Furthermore, states may be inefficiently lax in enforcing environmental standards when the pollution generated within their borders affects the environmental quality of their neighbors. A Federalist solution, namely, the nationalization of environmental regulation, is one way to deal with the problems caused by interstate competition and environmental externalities. There is a fine body of both theoretical and institutional literature based on the superiority of federal policy.[4]

While not part of the original constitutional debate, John C. Calhoun provides a distinctly different point of view. He was suspicious that a strong central government would offer too little protection for the welfare of minorities. He argued that with a heterogeneous population strong states are necessary to assure the welfare of all.

If the whole community had the same interests so that the interests of each and every portion would be so affected by the action of the government that the laws which oppressed or impoverished one portion would necessarily oppress and impoverish all others . . . then the right of suffrage, of itself would be all-sufficient to counteract the tendency of the government to oppression and abuse of its power and, of course, would form, of itself, a perfect constitutional government.[5]

Calhoun's solution to the problem of the abuse inherent in a monolithic central government was to maintain the power of individual states. The nineteenth-century Nullification Movement was the popular manifestation of Calhoun's concept of the 'concurrent majority'. The idea was simple: for a new statute to become national law it needed approval of all states (presumably the majority of each state); any state could veto that statute and it would only become law if approved by a super majority of states – the non-approving states would then have the right to secede from the union. If Calhoun's idea were adopted, environmental regulation would be the domain of individual states. It would be part of state political process or a result of interstate treaties.

Calhoun's theory is appealing because it recognizes a diversity of interests. The power of the states protects the interest of those not part of the national majority. Calhoun believed that minority rights were protected by giving political power to each geographic partition of the population. Calhoun's ideas were popular, particularly in the South, prior to the Civil War; indeed, James Buchanan's advocacy for the legal right of secession from the European Community,[6] indicates a continued appeal. However geographic partitions are not the only ones possible. The population can be partitioned by commonalty of interests, as were the ethnic millets of the Ottoman Empire. These too would have the effects of giving disproportionate political power to minority groups.

Calhoun was a serious political thinker, perhaps one of the most profound. It is unfortunate that he is associated with the protection of slavery, because his views on the protection of minority interests are important and largely ignored.[7]

While environmental concerns were not part of early federal political thought, the constitutional structure under which it is formed has considerable impact upon the form and effectiveness of environmental regulation. With a strong centralized structure, the regulation will begin with the central government and bear the likeness of the national consensus. With strong state sovereignty, as proposed by Calhoun, environmental policy within a federation will be governed by the degree of cooperation, between the states. Where there is no interstate cooperation, regulation results from a competition between the majority population of the separate states. Interstate cooperation will result in treaties between states that reflect a compromise between the majority interests in the participating states.

A simple model of interstate pollution externalities is proposed to examine the issue of constitutional structure and environmental regulatory outcome. The model is different from most others[8] in that the welfare of the states is not assumed to be represented by the preference function of a representative individual. Instead, each state is populated by citizens with different preferences. The political process yields outcomes that represent the preferences of only one group he majority). In that world the various constitutional regimes result in considerably different welfare outcomes. Indeed, even when there are externalities, interstate cooperation does not ensure unambiguous welfare gains. Even if there are welfare gains from interstate cooperation, it may be necessary to have mechanisms to ensure compliance with the negotiated treaties. In this regard, the central government may need to originate and enforce some environmental regulation, or, at least, to adjudicate interstate disputes.

MODELS OF POLICY CHOICE

Models used to demonstrate the desirability of national regulation have common characteristics. They derive state policy as the optimization of a state objective function, and they begin with the assumption that either all citizens have the same preferences and face the same set of technical constraints or the government knows individual preferences. The modeling effort concludes that states, acting competitively in their own self-interest, will adopt regulations that are inefficiently moderate when there are externalities that negatively affect their neighbors. The observation that externalities produce inefficiencies is used to argue that states should yield their sovereignty over environmental matters to a federation. This conclusion, even if the assumption of a representative citizen is left unchallenged, is itself spurious. Sovereign states can agree to cooperate through treaties over many different issues. Indeed there are, even within the United States, examples of compacts between states, as for instance those that border the Colorado River. What can be the need for federal intervention? It can be justified only if federal policy is superior in some way to that reached through interstate compacts. The successful negotiation of interstate treaties might be very costly, particularly if many states are involved. in which case federally instituted regulation is preferred. All of this is based on the assumption of a common state objective function. Even if there is a common objective function, the resulting policies are efficient only if the population is homogeneous, or the policy-makers' objective is a welfare function that accounts for differences in citizens' preferences.

The model is developed to explore the potential outcome in a federation of states, each with heterogeneous populations. Individuals do not agree on the best policy and policy outcomes reflect the political process used to resolve individual differences. The policy processes explored here are as follows: 1) sovereign states are heterogeneous, state policy choices are made by majority rule and there is no interstate cooperation (interstate anarchy); 2) sovereign states cooperate to establish environmental regulation through treaty; and 3) the Federal government sets environmental policy first in order to achieve a Pareto-efficient outcome and second to maximize the welfare of the majority. None among these sets of policy-making alternatives is unambiguously superior to all the others. It is not surprising, however, that interstate anarchy is clearly inferior to all the rest.

There are two states, 1 and 2, and two types of citizens M (manufacturers) and G (greens). Of the two states, 1 has the larger population, and among its citizens there is a preponderance of Ms. State 2 is smaller than 1 and its majority is G. The population size of each type in each state is denoted by n_{si}, $s = 1,2$ and $i = M,G$. Preferences for clear air A and personal consumption c are represented by a Cobb–Douglas utility function

$$U_{si} = A c_{si}^{\gamma i} \tag{5.1}$$

Individual preference functions vary only by the γ parameter, with $\gamma_M > \gamma_G$, greens have a stronger preference for a clean environment than do manufacturers.

It is common to model the relationship between air quality and consumption as a technology producing pollution as an inevitable byproduct of the production of consumable goods. For this analysis it is more convenient to postulate the air quality–consumption transformation. For each state that transformation function is

$$A_s = a_0 - bC_s \qquad (5.2)$$

where C_s is the total consumption of state s, $C_s = n_{sM}c_{sM} + n_{sG}c_{sG}$ and A_s is the air quality (absence of pollution) produced by s and n_{si} is the number of type i in state s. Air quality is a perfect externality, the amount consumed by each state is the sum of that produced in both. Air quality is

$$A = A_1 + A_2. \qquad (5.3)$$

There is no migration between the states and there is no trade in consumable goods. Each state produces all that is consumed there. The political process is governed by majority rule wherein policy outcomes are determined by popular secret ballot votes. An important feature of this model is that individual types are indistinguishable. Whether a person is an M or a G is known only to themselves, the ballot process maintains their anonymity. Public policy must, therefore, be equitable: as the policy-makers are unable to distinguish a person's type all citizens must be treated equally. By (5.2) public policy that determines the level of the As also sets the level of Cs, and that is necessarily divided evenly among all the citizens of a state. Using lower case c to denote per capita consumption

$$c_{si} = \frac{c_s}{n_s} = c_s \qquad (5.4)$$

for all i and each s, where $n_s = n_{sM} + n_{sG}$.

From the assumptions of majority rule and anonymity, all residents of state 1 will consume the optimum for M types and all residents of state 2 will consume G's optimum. The actual policy outcomes depend on whether regulations are set in an autarkic environment of interstate competition, through interstate cooperative treaty, or through the unilateral actions of the Federal government.

A. Autarky

With state sovereignty and no cooperation, a state will choose local air quality policy to maximize the welfare of its majority without considering the consequences of its policy on its neighboring state. A state can regulate its own production level but not those of its neighbors even though its air quality and that of its neighbors are interdependent, as established in equation (5.3). The regulatory policy chosen by each state can be described as solving the optimization problems

$$\text{State 1: } \text{Max } Ac_1^{\gamma M} \text{ and State 2: } \text{Max } Ac_2^{\gamma G}$$
$$A, c_1 \qquad\qquad\qquad A, c_2$$
$$\text{such that } A = 2a_0 - bn_1c_1 - bn_2c_2. \tag{5.5}$$

The simultaneous solution to the interdependent two-state maximization problems gives the non-cooperative equilibrium.

$$
\begin{bmatrix} c_1^* \\ c_2^* \\ A^* \end{bmatrix} =
\begin{bmatrix}
\dfrac{2a_0\gamma_M}{bn_1(1+\gamma_M+\gamma_G)} \\[2ex]
\dfrac{2a_0\gamma_G}{bn_2(1+\gamma_M+\gamma_G)} \\[2ex]
\dfrac{2a_0}{(1+\gamma_M+\gamma_G)}
\end{bmatrix}. \tag{5.6}
$$

At the non-cooperative equilibrium, because there is no migration, welfare depends on both the type of individual (M or G) and the location. The equilibrium level of utility of each type in each state is

$$U_S^* = A^* c_S^{*\gamma i}. \tag{5.7}$$

B. State Sovereignty and Interstate Cooperation

The majority of each state can improve their welfare if there is interstate cooperation. Whether or not they can negotiate successfully and maintain a treaty is an important question that vexes many attempts at interstate and international treaty agreements. If such an interstate treaty is possible and maintainable it will have certain characteristics. First, the agreement should be efficient (no feasible change in the agreement should make the majority of both states better off) and, second, it should leave the majority of each state at least as well off as they were without cooperation.

Efficiency criterion is met if the equilibrium outcome satisfies the well-known condition for the efficient provision of public goods: the sum of the marginal rates of substitution equals the marginal cost. For this example the criterion is

$$\frac{n_1c_1}{\gamma_1 A} + \frac{n_2c_2}{\gamma_2 A} = \frac{1}{b}. \tag{5.8}$$

The second criterion, for majority rule[9] states is

$$U_{1M} \geq U_{1M}^* \text{ and } U_{2G} \geq U_{2G}^*. \tag{5.9}$$

C.   A Federal Takeover

The predominant theme in the literature on environmental regulation is that policy efficiency is inhibited by narrow state interests. The solution is the intervention of the beneficent national government. The rationale is that the Federal government has the welfare of the entire country as its policy goal. In theoretical terms it will choose only those policies that meet the Samuelson public good efficiency criterion. Calhoun and his nullification followers certainly would have disputed this idea. They would argue that, at best, federal policy represents the welfare of the national majority. Within the context of the models explored here, the two views of national policy are represented by two distinct federal objectives. The first is that the Federal government attempts to choose only Pareto-efficient outcomes within its own informational limitations. The second, which is the Calhoun point of view, is that the Federal government aim is to maximize the welfare of the national majority.

If the Federal government chooses only efficient policies, the criterion is well known, namely, that the national sum of the marginal rates of substitution between air quality and private consumption equals the marginal cost of air quality. The policy outcome would satisfy equation (5.8) as the cooperative solution for the homogeneous states. The exception is that the Federal government would not be bound by the constraint (5.9) that the utilities of the majority groups must be at least as large as they are in the non-cooperative equilibrium. It is reasonable to believe that the Federal government can do at least as well as can the states when they cooperate. But, while the Federal government is not constrained by the limits to the type of arrangements that can be reached through treaties, there are other constraints that act on it. First, the Federal government needs to know citizen preferences in order to formulate efficient policies. Second, while there are not explicit prohibitions on the Federal government against unequal treatment of states, there is considerable political pressure to treat all states equally. This suggests the adoption of national rather than state-specific standards.

If there are but two preference types and the types are known to the Federal government, the use of national standards rather than ones that are state specific, ensures that individuals will truthfully reveal their preferences.[10] The efficient national standard is

$$c = \frac{2a_0\gamma_M\gamma_G}{\gamma_M(n_{1M}+n_{2M}) + \gamma_G(n_{1G}+n_{2G})} \qquad (5.10)$$

From the Calhoun point of view, (5.10) is the best that could be expected from the Federal government. But it is unrealistic to expect the government to act in such an enlightened way. The national government will be motivated by the same political realities as the states are. It is reasonable to suppose that it will act as a conduit for the preferences of the national majority. If the national policy is driven by majority interests, rather than welfare efficiency, the national standard is

$$c = \frac{2a_0\gamma_\mu}{bn(\gamma_M + \gamma_G)},$$ (5.11)

where γ_μ is the preference parameter of the national majority.

A NUMERICAL EXAMPLE

How should environmental regulations be determined, through the competition of autarkic states, through cooperative interstate treaties, or through the regulatory process of the Federal government? If individual preferences are known and the national government policy is set only to achieve efficient outcomes, regulatory authority should be maintained by the Federal government. However, no government body is omniscient, and all are governed by narrow political concerns. A numerical example is used here to explore whether there are policy-making options that clearly dominate all others.

For the numerical example, the following values are used:

γ_M :	1.50	γ_G :	0.75
a_0 :	0.75	b :	1.00
n_{1M} :	0.75	n_{1G} :	0.25
n_{2M} :	0.25	n_{2G} :	0.50

The outcome for the various policy mechanisms is given in Table 5.1.

The rows of the table give the equilibrium levels of utility of each group of citizens, the level of consumption in each state and the air quality under the different policy-making regimes. The first column, labeled 'Autarky', lists the outcomes when states have responsibility for their own environmental policy and there is no interstate cooperation. The values are the ones given in equations (5.6) and (5.7). If the states maintain regulatory responsibility the policy outcome is not uniquely determined if they cooperate. With a majoritarian decision process neither state will join in treaty to cooperate unless the majority population of each state is at least as well off as they were without cooperation the inequality constraint given in (5.10). The two extremes are an agreement that leaves the manufacturers in state 1 indifferent between joining a cooperative effort and not, and one in which the environmentalists in state 2 are just as well off as they were without cooperation. The extreme possibilities are given as 'U_{1M} Min' and 'U_{2G} Min'.

A third alternative is an interstate cooperative solution which sets the state standards midway between the two extremes. This is labeled 'Average'. In this example two possible federal regulatory environments are explored. The first is the one in which the government chooses the efficient policy. The outcome is labeled 'Efficiency'. The second is the one in which the government maximizes the welfare of the national majority. The outcome is labeled 'Majoritarian'.

Table 5.1:   *Outcome for various policy mechanisms*

Values		Interstate Treaty			Federal	
	Autarky	U_{1M}Min	U_{2G}Min	Average	Efficient	Majoritarian
U_{1m}	129.44	129.44	247.49	188.46	138.17	143.65
U_{1G}	24.44	35.68	46.62	41.88	36.72	33.90
U_{2M}	70.46	148.92	37.03	84.50	138.17	143.65
U_{2G}	18.03	38.27	18.03	28.04	36.72	34.90
c_1	9.23	5.57	9.26	7.42	5.85	6.86
c_2	6.15	6.12	2.61	4.35	5.85	6.86
A	4.62	9.84	8.78	9.31	9.76	8.00

In this example non-cooperation is dominated by all the other policy regimes. The welfare of all groups is improved if either enter into a cooperative treaty or the Federal government sets air quality standards. That is the extent of the efficiency gain. This is a simple example, but it makes the point that the efficiency criterion gives no guide to the assignment of regulatory responsibility. Consider the case in which the negotiated outcome is the one in which the standards are the average between the two extremes – the column labeled 'Average'. Were the feds given regulatory responsibility, there would be a welfare improvement for everyone in state 2, but a welfare loss for everyone in state 1, whether or not the national government were majoritarian. Furthermore, if the feds were governed by majority rule, air quality standards would be lower than under a negotiated agreement between the states.

CONCLUSION

The tension over states' rights and the national interest is inherent in any federation. It has played an important role in the United States and it must have an effect on the nature of environmental regulatory authority. Within this environment, what guide can economists give to the assignment of this authority? The simple model of political decision-making with a heterogeneous population provides little help for making that assignment.

The example, while simple, suggests certain lessons about regulation in a federation of semi-autonomous states. The obvious one is that interstate anarchy can always be improved through cooperation. This is a well-known result in models of externalities. Welfare improvements can be achieved through treaties between states without the intervention of the national government.

This example also shows that federal regulatory policy, based on realistic informational requirements, is not an unambiguous improvement over interstate cooperation. And, in fact, the example shows that federal control may lead to lower environmental standards than those achieved through interstate treaty. What, then, is the justification for federal intervention? One possibility is that an interstate treaty may be unenforceable; in particular, if the source of pollution is unidentifiable or if the level of enforcement is unobservable. In those cases, a desirable environmental regulation is possible only at the national level. The Federal government might play a different role: rather than formulating regulatory rules, it can enforce the ones achieved through interstate negotiation.

NOTES

1. A model of state–federal regulatory responsibility is proposed by Lowry.
2. See Petchey (1992).
3. *Federalist Papers* (1961) p. 19.
4. An interesting example is the paper by Jones and Scotchmer (1990). Their concern was devising financial incentives to induce state regulators to efficiently enforce federal environmental regulations.
5. Calhoun (1953) p. 13.
6. Buchanan (1990).
7. Tabarrok and Cowen (1992) try to explicate Calhoun's idea in the model public choice framework.
8. See Oates and Schwab (1988).
9. Of course if the states are homogeneous, the criterion is the same, but the decision is unanimously approved by every citizen of the state.
10. The idea is a simple one. Since all citizens have the same level of air quality, the only thing that is affected by their announced preference type is their consumption. Were the government to choose to give one type a larger consumption than the other, truthful revelation could not be an equilibrium. It would be in each citizen's self-interest to announce his/her preference type as the one that is given the largest consumption. Therefore an equal consumption policy is the

only one for which truthful self-identification is an equilibrium. A more formal proof is as follows.

The government chooses its policy as the solution to the two simultaneous equations

$$n_M \cdot mrs_M(A, c_M) + n_G \cdot mrs_G(A, c_G) = mc(a)$$
$$A = A(c_M + c_G)$$

where n_i is the number of people who reveal themselves to be type i, mrs_i is the marginal rate of substitution of type i and mc is the marginal cost ($1/b$ in the example). The solution to these two equations will define a set of efficient policies. If the policy chosen out of the efficient set gives unequal consumption, for instance $c_M > c_G$, for a fixed value of A, all citizens will announce that they are type M.

If the policy chosen is the equal consumption one then both Ms and Gs will have the same level of consumption as well as the same level of air quality. The individual price of air quality for each citizen is the average marginal cost (mc/n). With equal consumption the marginal rate of substitution for Ms will be smaller than that for Gs, therefore, the Ms's personal price is larger and the Gs's personal price is smaller than their marginal rates of substitution. The equal consumption policy leads to a larger than optimal level of air quality for the Ms and a smaller than optimal one for the Gs. If an M type claims to be a G the policy will be changed to larger values of A and if a G claims to be an M the result is a smaller A. Therefore it is in the private interest of neither type to misrepresent their preferences.

REFERENCES

Buchanan, James M. (1990). 'Europe's Constitutional Opportunity', *Europe's Constitutional Future*, Institute for Economic Affairs , London, 1–20.

Calhoun, John C. (1953). *A Disquisition on Government and Selections from the Discourse*, C. Gordon Post ed., Bobbs-Merrill, Indianapolis and New York.

Hamilton, Alexander, James Madison and John Jay, (1961). *Federalist Papers* with introduction by Clinton Rossiter, Mentor, New York.

Jones, Carol A. and Suzanne Scotchmer (1990). 'The Social Cost of Uniform Regulatory Standards in an Hierarchical Government', *Journal of Environmental Economics and Management* 19: 61–72.

Lowry, William R. (1992). *The Dimensions of Federalism: State Government and Pollution Control Policies*, Duke University Press, Durham and London.

Oates, Wallace E. and Robert M. Schwab (1988). 'Economic Competition Among Jurisdicitions: Efficiency Enhancing or Distortion Inducing?', *Journal of Public Economics,* 35: 333–54.

Petchey, Jeffrey D. (1992). 'An Analysis of Theoretical and Applied Issues in Fiscal Federalism and Local Public Economics', PhD Dissertation, Australian National University, Canberra, Australia.

Tabarrok, Alexander and Tyler Cowen (1992). 'The Public Choice of John C. Calhoun', *Journal of Institutional and Theoretical Economics*, 148: 655–74.

PART III

The Political Economy of Instrument Choice

6. Issues in the Choice of Environmental Policy Instruments

Kathleen Segerson

INTRODUCTION

The design of environmental policy generally involves two components: (i) the determination of goals or objectives, and (ii) the choice of specific policy instruments for use in achieving those goals. For example, in designing air pollution policy, target levels for ambient concentrations of pollutants are set and then alternative means for reducing current emissions to meet those target levels are compared and a choice is made among them.[1]

The determination of environmental goals or objectives can be based on a number of criteria. One of these is economic efficiency. Economists have long advocated setting target levels so that, at the margin, the benefits of additional reductions in pollution equal the costs of achieving those reductions. This ensures the most economically efficient use of the limited resources available to society. Alternatively, target levels can be based on other criteria, such as known or suspected levels of adverse health or ecological effects, or lowest levels achievable at a 'reasonable' cost.

Whether based on economic efficiency or not, once environmental goals have been set, then a choice among alternative policy instruments for achieving those goals must be made. Economists have generally classified the alternative instruments into 'quantity' versus 'price' instruments and 'ex ante' versus 'ex post' instruments. Quantity instruments are traditional regulatory policies that control the quantity of emissions directly, such as emission standards or limits and required installation of certain types of pollution control equipment. Price instruments, often referred to as 'economic incentive' instruments, provide incentives for polluters to control emissions by putting a price on the use of the environment. This could take the form of a tax on emissions or use of a polluting input, a marketable permit system,[2] or a deposit on returnable items.

Both standard regulatory approaches and tax or permit systems are examples of ex ante instruments, which are operative at the time that a polluting activity occurs. In contrast, ex post instruments become operative at the time that

149

damages from that activity occur. In other words, they are tied to the damages rather than the activity itself. The classic example of an *ex post* instrument is the use of legal liability, under which a polluter would be responsible for some or all of the damages that result from his activity. Some liability rules, such as negligence-based rules, are similar to quantity instruments in that liability is imposed only upon failure to meet a given standard (a 'due standard of care'). Under such rules, no payment is made if the firm has 'complied' with or met the due standard. Alternatively, rules based on strict liability principles are similar to price instruments since liability is imposed for damages regardless of the level of care (Cooter, 1984).

Much attention has been given in the theoretical literature to the choice among alternative policy instruments. Both normative and positive approaches have been taken.[3] The normative studies consider which instrument(s) should be chosen, given a particular objective or criterion for choice (usually economic efficiency). The positive studies, on the other hand, have attempted to explain why some instruments have actually been chosen over others. They are based primarily on theories of conflict-resolution and political pressure/influence. Many of the positive studies of instrument choice have attempted to explain why environmental policy in the United States (US) has relied primarily on the use of quantity-type instruments despite the economic advantages of the price-based approaches. Interest in this question is heightened by the fact that price-based policies have been used to a greater extent in Europe, although generally as a means of raising revenue rather than providing strong incentives for pollution control (Hahn, 1989a).

Both the normative and the positive literature on instrument choice have generally focused on decision-making by a single government entity, such as a federal or state government. In practice, however, environmental policy-making involves several levels of government. For example, in the United States both the Federal government and the various state and local governments play a role in setting and implementing environmental quality goals. Similarly, in Europe the European Commission acts as a centralized rule-making body for all the Member States, with the Member States having responsibility for implementation of the directives issued by the central body (Pfander, this volume). Thus, decisions regarding instrument choice are made by different bodies within a federal system, rather than by a single government body, as is usually assumed in the literature.

This chapter discusses some issues that arise in choosing policy instruments in a federal system. We begin with a review of some normative issues that arise in instrument choice. This leads to the conclusion that no single instrument is ideal and that in practice use of a combination of instruments may be more efficient. Positive issues regarding instrument choice are then discussed. While the literature has tended to emphasize the role of political pressure groups, we suggest that the geographical distribution of costs and benefits as well as social/cultural influences are also likely to be important determinants of instrument choice. We then discuss additional instrument choice issues that arise when that choice is made in a federal system. We emphasize the problems of coordinating the different parts of the government involved in the policy-making process. A simple model of the coordination problem is presented and used to identify conditions under which coordination is a particular problem. Throughout we draw on the US experience to illustrate the issues discussed.

NORMATIVE ISSUES IN INSTRUMENT CHOICE

As noted above, there have been numerous studies directed towards the normative analysis of instrument choice. While a comprehensive review of this literature is beyond the scope of this chapter,[4] it will be useful to review briefly some of the basic conclusions that emerge from this literature. We focus on those that are relevant for the discussion in subsequent sections.

A. Abatement Levels and Total Costs

It is well known that, under conditions of perfect certainty, the government can theoretically induce an individual firm to undertake an efficient amount of pollution abatement by imposing any one of the following policies: (1) a per unit emissions tax equal to the marginal cost of abatement at the efficient level; (2) a per unit subsidy for reductions in emissions, with the amount of the subsidy equal to the marginal cost of abatement at the efficient level; (3) a perfectly-enforceable regulation requiring the firm to reduce emissions to the efficient level; or (4) a system of marketable permits, with the total number of permits in the market equal to the efficient level of aggregate emissions (Baumol and Oates, 1988).

While in theory all four policies induce the firm to choose an efficient abatement level, they clearly differ in terms of the total cost to the firm and hence the firm's overall profits. Under the regulation, the firm pays only for the cost of pollution abatement. In contrast, under the tax approach, the firm pays both the cost of abatement and the tax on the remaining emissions. Under the subsidy, the firm pays the costs of abatement but receives a subsidy for each unit abated. Since the amount of the subsidy exceeds the cost of abatement in the range over which abatement occurs, the subsidy results in a net receipt for the firm. The impact of a permit system on the firm's costs will depend upon the firm's initial allocation of permits.

The difference in the impact of alternative instruments on the firm has been cited as one factor influencing the actual choice among instruments (Buchanan and Tullock, 1975). However, it also has implications for the normative choice among instruments. In a perfectly competitive industry, entry and exit ensure that in the long run prices will reflect long-run average costs. If costs are higher under one instrument than another, prices will be higher as well. As a result, demand for the product will be lower and the industry will be smaller. In other words, because of its higher cost, the tax policy will induce more exit from the industry than the regulatory approach. In contrast, the subsidy approach can actually induce entry since it lowers average production costs. The efficient industry size is achieved only when firms pay the full social costs of their activities (so that their entry/exit decisions are based on the total social costs and benefits of their activities), which occurs under the tax policy but not under the regulation or the subsidy approach. Hence, only the tax approach (or an equivalent permit approach) achieves efficiency in the long run (Spulber, 1985).[5] This is one basis for the often-cited belief that economists as a whole prefer emission taxes to regulation as a means of reducing pollution.[6]

The above discussion is based on a comparison of *ex ante* policy instruments. However, similar conclusions hold for *ex post* instruments.[7] For example, it can easily be shown that the efficient amount of abatement by an individual firm could be induced through either a negligence rule or a strict liability rule (Shavell, 1980). However, as with the *ex ante* instruments, the total cost to the firm of alternative liability rules differs as well. For example, the costs under a negligence rule will be similar to those under a regulatory approach, where the firm pays for the cost of meeting the due standard of care but not for any damages that result. However, because firms do not pay for damages under a negligence rule, the equilibrium industry size would exceed the efficient size (Shavell, 1980; Polinsky, 1980). In contrast, under a strict liability rule, the firm would face full social costs, since it would pay for any pollution abatement and for damages.[8]

B. Uncertainty and Other Imperfections

The above results regarding the desirability of alternative instruments assume an idealized world of perfect information. When information is imperfect, additional issues arise in the choice among instruments. For example, Weitzman (1974) has shown that the per firm welfare effects of price and quantity-based instruments are no longer equivalent if there is uncertainty about the marginal cost of abatement at the time that policy parameters are set.[9] In particular, he showed that, with uncertainty about the position of the MCA curve, a quantity instrument would be preferred if the MCA curve is flat relative to the MBA curve, while a price instrument would be preferred if the MCA is relatively steep.

In addition, while in theory a regulation or tax may yield efficient control of an environmental problem, in practice individual policy instruments are generally imperfect. For example, in the context of groundwater contamination from hazardous waste disposal, the design and construction of landfills as well as disposal processes can be regulated. However, in practice these regulations cannot control groundwater contamination perfectly.

There are a number of reasons why instruments that work in theory may be less effective in practice. For example, some actions that affect environmental quality are unobservable (at a reasonable cost) and thus not amenable to regulation (Segerson, 1986). For those actions that are subject to regulation, compliance with the regulation is likely to be imperfect, due at least in part to imperfect monitoring and enforcement (Russell et al., 1986; Wasserman, 1992). In addition, if sites are heterogeneous and the regulations are not tailored to the specific site characteristics, then the regulation will control contamination from that site imperfectly (Shavell, 1984b).

Likewise, the use of liability for damages provides incentives for reductions in contamination but again in practice these incentives are imperfect, since in many cases full payment for damages may not be made (Dewees, 1992). There are a number of reasons why a responsible party may not, in fact, ever be held liable for the full amount of damages. These include (i) limitations on the incentives of victims to bring an action against the party (Shavell, 1982, 1984b); (ii) limitations on the party's assets (ability to pay the judgment) (Shavell, 1984b, 1986); (iii) the difficulty of proving causation (Shavell, 1985); and (iv) imperfections in the legal process (Kolstad et al., 1990). Thus, as with regulation, in practice liability by itself is unlikely to provide fully efficient incentives for pollution control.

C.   Other Criteria

The above analyses of the relative desirability of alternative instruments use economic efficiency as the criterion for ranking policies. However, there are a number of other criteria that can be used for choosing among policy instruments. Bohm and Russell (1985) provide the following list of possible criteria:

1.   static efficiency;
2.   information intensity;
3.   ease of monitoring and enforcement;
4.   flexibility in the face of economic change;
5.   dynamic incentives;

6. political considerations.[10]

When these other criteria are considered, the ranking of alternative policies becomes even more ambiguous (Bohm and Russell, 1985).

For example, both the information intensity of a given instrument and the ease of the associated monitoring and enforcement affect the transactions costs associated with the use of that instrument.[11] If these costs are sufficiently high, they can offset other benefits associated with the use of a particular instrument. An example where transactions costs seemed to have hindered the use of an otherwise desirable environmental policy instruments is marketable permits. Economists have advocated marketable permits as a possible means of achieving economic efficiency along with desired distributional goals, flexibility to adjust to changes in environmental goals over time, and incentives to develop new pollution-abatement technologies (e.g., Montgomery, 1972; Tietenberg, 1980, 1985). Despite their popularity among economists, however, success with the use of permits for trades among polluters has been limited. The United States has experimented with the use of permits over the last decade and their use has recently been expanded in the new Clean Air Act (e.g., Tietenberg, 1989, 1990). While the lead trading program was fairly successful, permit markets for water and air emissions have been less so (Hahn, 1989a; Hahn and Hester, 1989). For trades involving non-uniformly mixed pollutants for which dispersion modeling is required, transactions costs are very high, making trade prohibitively expensive for many small firms. As a result, few trades of this type have occurred (Tietenberg, 1990).[12] Thus, while the permit approach is theoretically attractive relative to other instruments, its relative attractiveness diminishes when the transaction costs associated with the use of this approach are considered.

D.   Multiple Instruments

The fact that no single instrument is perfect as a policy tool suggests the possibility that efficiency might be enhanced through the simultaneous use of multiple instruments.[13] For example, combining the use of regulation and liability can provide more efficient control than the use of either instrument by itself. Such a combination is used in the control of hazardous waste in the U.S., where the generation and disposal of waste is regulated under the Resource Conservation and Recovery Act (RCRA) and cleanup costs and damages from that disposal are subject to liability under the Comprehensive Environmental Response, Compensation and Liability Act (CERCLA).[14] Similarly, externalities from the use of pesticides might be controlled more efficiently by a combination of regulation and taxes or liability than by the use of any one of these alone.[15]

The literature on multiple instruments suggests that in some cases the use of multiple instruments results in complementarity that serves to improve the effectiveness of the individual policies (e.g., Braden and Segerson, 1993; Segerson, 1986; Shavell, 1984b; Kolstad et al., 1990). The components of the package work together towards achieving the environmental goal. In other cases, however, policies can be at odds.[16] The challenge is to design a package that exploits the complementarity while at the same time minimizing conflicting impacts of the individual pieces of the package.

POSITIVE ANALYSIS OF INSTRUMENT CHOICE

In contrast to the normative analyses, the positive studies of instrument choice try to explain why one instrument or combination of instruments was chosen over another in a particular context. Much of the work has focused on why the US has tended to rely on regulation rather than economic incentives as a means of achieving pollution control goals.

A. Political Pressures from Interest Groups

Buchanan and Tullock (1975) argued that the explanation for the predominance of the regulatory approach in the US lies in the different costs (and thus profits) for firms under the alternative instruments. In particular, they argued that, because regulation imposes lower costs on firms than an equivalent emission tax, producers will favor regulation over taxes.[17] This preference would be expected to influence the actual choice among instruments if producers have significant political power.

Both shareholders and employees generally suffer from a reduction in a firm's profits. Thus, both will have a stake in the choice of alternative instruments. Dewees (1983) has emphasized the importance of the impacts on shareholders and employees of existing firms as determinants of the likely political opposition to the use of a given instrument. He argues that the detrimental impact of tax-based approaches on shareholders and employees of existing firms relative to the impact of a regulatory approach explains the predominant use of regulation.

While producers and their shareholders and employees have a stake in the choice of instruments and can exert political pressure for adoption of instruments with the lowest costs to them, 'environmentalists' have a stake in the outcome as well. Hahn (1990) presents a theory of political conflict between producer-oriented interests and the interests of the environmental community as an explanation of instrument choice. He suggests that instrument choice results from a balancing of the interests of firms and environmentalists by regulators or legislators. Recent changes in the orientation of choice (towards more reliance on incentive-based policies) can then be explained by changes in the relative influence of the two groups, as well as the specific features of the individual instruments that have been used.

B. Geographical Distribution

The choice among instruments in a democratic society can also be influenced by the geographical distribution of the impacts of alternative instruments,[18] especially when the improvements in environmental quality take the form of a public good where the benefits are widely dispersed. This is particularly true of global pollution problems such as ozone depletion and global warming, but also holds for regional issues such as acid rain. While the benefits of reducing these pollutants are geographically dispersed, the costs of achieving those reductions are often concentrated in identifiable geographic regions. Representatives of those regions bearing a large share of the cost often view the improvement as a net loss for their region. Thus, they are likely to oppose strongly legislation to implement these improvements.

If the number of adversely affected regions is relatively small, one might expect the votes from other regions to outweigh their negative votes, thereby leading to passage of the legislation. However, the strength of the opposition of representatives from adversely affected regions is likely to be stronger than the support from other representatives when costs are concentrated and benefits are dispersed. While this 'strength of preference' cannot be directly reflected in a one-person/one-vote process, it can be reflected through processes such as 'logrolling' or 'vote trading' (e.g., Buchanan and Tullock, 1962; Stratmann, 1992). With these systems, representatives can leverage their opposition to proposals with strong negative impacts on their regions. Thus, environmental policies with dispersed benefits but costs that are concentrated in particular regions might be defeated even if the proposal results in a net positive gain in a majority of the regions.

An example illustrating the importance of geographical distribution for the choice of policy instruments relates to reductions in sulphur dioxide emissions in the US. For many electric utilities the least-cost method of reducing sulphur dioxide emissions would be switching from high sulphur to low sulphur coal. However, in the US production of high sulphur coal is geographically concentrated. Representatives of the high sulphur production areas were able to block passage of legislation that would have allowed firms to choose the method for meeting the emissions limits, which if passed would have had negative impacts on their regions. Instead, the Clean Air Act that was passed required installation of scrubbers to reduce emissions, an approach that led to higher pollution control costs but did not have the concentrated regional impact of the more efficient approach.[19]

The above discussion suggests that, since different environmental policy instruments have different distributional implications, those who stand to gain or lose from the choice of a particular instrument will try to exert political pressure to influence that choice and the actual choice will reflect those pressures. In the process, the interested groups are likely to engage in rent-seeking activities (such as lobbying activities), which involve large expenditures designed to influence the outcomes of the legislative process and the associated distribution of benefits and costs. While these activities can be very beneficial to those who engage in them, from a social perspective they represent a social loss since no social gain results from these large expenditures (Tullock, 1967; Krueger, 1974). Nonetheless, they can exert a strong influence on the choice of environmental policy instruments.

C. Social/Cultural Influences

The choice among policy instruments, or perhaps even the set of 'feasible' instruments,[20] is also strongly influenced by the social or cultural tenets of the society.[21] By affecting the distribution of costs and benefits, the choice of an instrument establishes entitlements or rights for different groups within society. It establishes who has a right to protection from environmental damages and who has the right to inflict such damages and to what extent (Bromley, 1991). However, the set of acceptable entitlements is influenced by public perceptions regarding the acceptability of certain actions, which is in turn influenced by the culture of the society. In addition, this set can change over time as the society develops.

For example, the culture in the US has historically emphasized individual rights over community obligations. Thus, environmental policies have been based on individual rights. Originally, it was producer-oriented rights that dominated. While there was some early legislation aimed at protecting certain land areas for public use (e.g., establishment of national parks),[22] constraints on the use of private property were limited. Pursuit of individual goals was viewed as both philosophically desirable and consistent with the overall good of society. The overriding concern was with economic growth, which was thought to result from pursuit of individual goals.

Since the 1970s, the emphasis has shifted somewhat towards protection of victim rights, i.e., the right of individuals to be free from environmental harms.[23] This shift reflects both an increased awareness of the environmental effects of production activities and an increased demand for environmental quality. The result has been the cadre of environmental legislation, which either directly constrains the activities of polluters or requires compensation (liability) for damages from or cleanup of contamination from those activities.

However, constraints on individual activities do not necessarily imply that the individual has lost his entitlement. If the individual is compensated for some (or all) of the reduction in income or wealth that results from the constraint, then at least part of the entitlement is retained. In some cases compensation takes the form of subsidies. For example, the government can (and often does) subsidize pollution-abatement costs, as, for example, under cost-sharing programs (e.g., Freeman, 1990). Alternatively, individuals have claimed that regulatory constraints constitute a government 'taking', which according to the Fifth Amendment of the US Constitution requires compensation (e.g., Epstein, 1985).

The takings debate exemplifies the concern with private property rights in the US.[24] There has been a recent movement among conservative landowners to establish that environmental regulations constitute compensable takings, i.e., that the government does not have the right to restrict the use of private property without paying compensation for the resulting reduction in value.[25] To a large extent this movement is a backlash against environmental laws and regulations that are viewed as too protective of environmental interests at the expense of private 'rights' (Kaplan and Cohn, 1992). Interestingly, some courts have found that regulations designed to prevent harms (such as pollution) are not compensable while those designed to provide a public benefit (such as wetlands or open space) require compensation.[26] However, since a harm can be viewed simply as a forgone benefit and vice versa (Fischel, 1985), both 'harm' and 'benefit' must be defined relative to some baseline. Thus, the question of the appropriate baseline remains. Some have advocated that nuisance law or community norms be used to define the baseline (Epstein, 1985; Fischel, 1985). Of course, both of these evolve out of the social structure of the society.

Whether the takings issue is relevant for the design of environmental policy in another country depends on the legal structure of that country, i.e., whether there is legal protection against uncompensated takings, as in the Fifth Amendment of the US Constitution, and on the perceived role of private property in that country, i.e., the societal view regarding who has the right to control land-use (or more generally natural resource-use) decisions. In countries where common property and community control of resources are the norm, the takings issue and its implications for environmental policy design will not arise. However, in countries where private property rights are viewed as an integral part of the social structure, one might expect to see a demand for compensation for the adverse private effects of environmental regulations. The need to pay compensation may in turn affect both the goals that are set for environmental quality and the instruments chosen to meet those goals.

A second example of how social structure affects the set of feasible policy instruments is the use of liability to control environmental damages. Recently, the US has used liability as a legislative instrument for controlling pollution and allocating responsibility for damages. Most notable is CERCLA, which holds responsible parties strictly and jointly and severally liable for cleanup costs from hazardous waste sites and spills of hazardous substances such as oil.[27] Use of liability for environmental damages is consistent with the expanded scope of liability in other areas of US law, such as product liability (e.g., Epstein, 1980; Priest, 1987, 1991) and medical malpractice (e.g., Danzon, 1988, 1991). Acceptability of the use of liability in the environmental context is undoubtedly tied to the general acceptability of liability and use of the legal system as a means of allocating costs among disputing parties. In a society where litigation is not the norm and individuals are not generally held liable for damages resulting from their actions or activities, the use of liability is not likely to be a major component of environmental policy.

When liability is used as a policy instrument, it is likely that the form of the liability rule will vary across countries, depending on the objectives and constraints of each country. While liability under CERCLA is strict and joint and several in the U.S., such a system may put too great a financial burden on producers in other countries. For example, in the Eastern European countries where newly privatized firms are just forming and attracting foreign investment is an important goal, a strict and joint and several rule may be politically infeasible (Boyd, 1993). To the extent that liability is used in those countries, an alternative rule that reduces the burden on polluters, such as a negligence rule, might be more acceptable.

INSTRUMENT CHOICE IN A FEDERAL SYSTEM: THE COORDINATION PROBLEM

The above issues regarding the choice of policy instruments exist regardless of the type of government making those choices. There are, however, some additional issues that arise when environmental policy decisions are made in a federal system, since jurisdiction for environmental policy is spread across levels of government (federal vs. state vs. local).[28] In addition, it can be spread across branches within the Federal or state government (executive vs. legislative vs. judicial) (Arnold, 1979; Ackerman and Hassler, 1981), as well as across agencies within branches (e.g. EPA vs. USDA) or offices within agencies (Hahn, 1990). This distribution of jurisdiction creates coordination problems that do not exist when a single, centralized authority sets all environmental policy.

A. Coordination Across Levels of Government

In a federal system, environmental policies are likely to be made at both the federal and state level, as well as sometimes at the local level (e.g., zoning restrictions). In some cases, both the Federal government and the state governments are controlling the same variables. For example, in the US there are federally-set standards on automobile emissions.[29] In addition, states can set their own standards, although they are constrained to be at least as stringent as the federal standards. Thus, the federal standard effectively sets an upper bound on allowable emissions. The State of California has set automobile emission standards that are more stringent than the federal standards.[30]

Similarly, some states have state-versions of CERCLA, designed to raise money for cleanup of contaminated sites within the state and allocate responsibility for cleanup. For example, the State of New Jersey requires contaminated property to be cleaned up prior to a sale, which goes beyond the requirements of the federal legislation (Dinan and Johnson, 1990). Likewise, the State of Minnesota has its own statute for allocating cleanup responsibility (Ulen et al., 1985).

Alternatively, in some cases the Federal government sets goals and then leaves it to the states to implement policies for achieving those goals (e.g., Freeman, 1990; Portney, 1990). When environmental problems are localized or site-specific, states may have better information about appropriate means of controlling these problems. In addition, they may be better able to oversee implementation and monitor compliance than the Federal government. An example is non-point source pollution in the US. The Clean Water Act requires states to develop and implement plans for reducing nonpoint pollution to achieve federally-specified goals (Freeman, 1990).

When environmental policies are set by individual states within a federation, differences across states can arise. When lack of uniformity relates to product-specification requirements, then producers must meet the regulatory specifications of different states. For example, automobile manufacturers must produce a different car design to meet the California automobile emission standards than they produce for the rest of the country. Of course, this problem is not unique to environmental policies. State differentials exist in other areas of law as well, such as product liability law. In fact, the lack of uniformity in product liability law across states has been blamed for much of the perceived product liability 'crisis' in the US and calls for a uniform federal law have been voiced.[31] To the extent that environmental policy is linked with product liability law, as, for example, when environmental damages stem from use of products such as pesticides or asbestos, these state differentials will affect environmental quality as well.

Alternatively, the lack of uniformity across states can relate to production processes rather than product design or characteristics. For example, different states can have different standards for emissions of both air and water pollutants from stationary sources, waste disposal requirements and land development.[32] If these policy differences create significant cost differentials across states, then in theory firms in states with stringent regulations will be at a competitive disadvantage relative to those in states with less stringent regulations. This could lead firms to seek out low regulation states. A similar argument has been made in the context of differentials across countries.[33] While there is anecdotal evidence of firms moving overseas to escape stringent environmental regulations in the U.S., this phenomenon does not appear to be widespread (e.g., Tobey, 1990). Similarly, there is only very limited evidence of regulation-induced relocations within a country (Bartik, 1988; McConnell and Schwab, 1990).

B.   Coordination Across Branches of Government

In the U.S., environmental policy is influenced by all three branches of the government: (i) the legislative branch, which writes and passes environmental laws; (ii) the executive branch, which writes the regulations implementing those laws; and (iii) the judicial branch, which interprets the laws and the corresponding regulations and oversees enforcement. While each branch looks to the intent of the other in performing its function, there is often considerable leeway in refining the policy at each stage. For example, in the US the courts have played a significant role in determining how laws and regulations passed by the other branches of the government are actually implemented (Ackerman and Hassler, 1981; Melnick, 1983; Anderson, 1993).

An example illustrating the influential role of the courts relates to the 'lender liability' provisions of CERCLA.[34] CERCLA, which was enacted by the legislative branch, included 'owners and operators' in the class of parties potentially liable for the cost of cleaning up contaminated sites.[35] The law includes an exception from liability (the 'security interest exemption') for a party who holds 'indicia of ownership primarily to protect his security interest . . . without participating in the management of the site'. This exemption was designed to limit the liability of lenders who become 'owners' or 'operators' of a site as a result of financial difficulties (in the extreme case, bankruptcy) of the actual owners of the site who used the site as collateral in a loan. Nonetheless, the courts interpreted this exemption quite narrowly in some cases, finding, for example, that a mere 'capacity to influence' the treatment of hazardous waste was enough to void the exemption and invoke liability.[36] In response to what it viewed as an overly broad imposition of liability on lenders through the courts' interpretation of the security interest exemption, the EPA then issued regulations narrowing the class of lenders that could be held liable by requiring 'actual operational participation' in (rather than simply the capacity to influence) hazardous waste management at the site.[37] These regulations were recently invalidated by a federal appeals court.[38]

A second example of interplay between the branches of government is the issue of compensation for regulatory takings. In some cases the courts have ordered compensation for reductions in land values due to environmental regulations, while in other cases they have denied compensation (e.g., Epstein, 1985; Fischel, 1985; Bromley, 1993). Thus, while environmental policies are being set by legislatures and regulatory agencies, the compensation decisions are being made by the courts. To the extent that legislative and regulatory decisions regarding imposition of environmental constraints depend on whether or not compensation must be paid, through its interpretation of the takings clause in the context of environmental regulation the court system has the ability to exert a strong influence on the design of environmental policy.[39]

C. Coordination Across Government Agencies

Even within a given branch of government, there is a need to coordinate policy choice across agencies with some responsibility for factors that affect environmental quality. Often different agencies have different goals or missions, and one agency's policy can be at odds with the other agency's goals.

In some cases, the mission of an agency is not directly related to environmental quality but the decisions it makes in pursuit of its own objectives have environmental quality impacts. For example, the US Department of Agriculture has a myriad of specific programs aimed at controlling agricultural output and raising farmers' incomes (Green, 1990). The best known of these are the price supports for some commodities, such as milk and corn. These policies were not designed with environmental quality in mind. Yet, there has been growing concern that the programs have environmental quality impacts. Specifically, it is felt that these programs increase pollution from the agricultural sector by encouraging production and the use of agricultural chemicals (Just et al., 1991).

Even when two components of the regulatory system have the same overall goal, namely, environmental protection, conflicts can still arise. For example, Hahn (1990) has noted the divergences between the views of the 'program' and 'policy' offices at the US Environmental Protection Agency and the implications of this divergence for environmental policy design. In particular, he notes that the goal of the program office is to produce regulations, while the policy office is concerned with efficiency. This difference has influenced the types of regulatory instruments advocated by the different offices.

A SIMPLE MODEL OF THE COORDINATION PROBLEM

The above discussion points to the myriad ways in which a federal system can require coordination in the design of environmental policy. While the various examples that were discussed differ in many ways, they all share a common feature: decisions that can affect the costs and benefits of environmental quality are made by different bodies that may have different objectives. In this section, a simple model of the coordination problem is presented. The purpose is to provide a simple framework that can be used to identify conditions under which having decisions made by separate bodies rather than by a single 'benevolent dictator' will lead to social inefficiencies. In particular, the model can be used to show that the efficiency of the outcome depends crucially on the timing of decisions (i.e., whether they are simultaneous or sequential) and the nature of the cost and/or benefit functions (i.e., whether they are separable or not).

Assume that environmental quality in a given region is affected by multiple factors, some of which are chosen by one government body and some by another. For example, the Federal government might set environmental goals and priorities while the state governments choose the means of implementing those goals. Alternatively, the Federal government could set emission standards with the states then choosing a level of monitoring and enforcement.

Let x represent the factors chosen by the Federal government and let y represent the factors chosen by the state government.[40] The social benefits from the choice of x and y are given by $B(x, y)$ where x and y are defined so that $B_x > 0$ and $B_y > 0$. We assume that the benefits are the same for both the Federal and the state government.[41] However, the costs associated with the decisions can be separated into those borne by the Federal government, C^F, and those borne by the state government, C^S. We begin with the most general formulation of costs, where the costs of both parties depend upon the decisions of both, i.e., $C^F = C^F(x, y)$ and $C^S = C^S(x, y)$. As will be seen below, the structure of the cost functions will be important in determining whether the decisions by the individual governments are socially efficient.

The socially efficient levels of x and y (x^* and y^*) are those that maximize net social benefits, given by

$$NB(x, y) = B(x, y) - C^F(x, y) - C^S(x, y).$$

The corresponding first-order conditions defining the efficient levels are

$$B_x(x, y) - C^F_x(x, y) - C^S_x(x, y) = 0, \qquad (6.1)$$

$$B_y(x, y) - C^F_y(x, y) - C^S_y(x, y) = 0, \tag{6.2}$$

where subscripts denote partial derivatives. The question of interest is whether the two levels of government will choose the efficient levels of x and y.

Consider first the (perhaps unrealistic) case in which both governments make their decisions simultaneously. We assume that each holds Nash conjectures regarding the behavior of the other, i.e., each assumes that the other will not respond to changes in its decision.[42] Under this assumption, the Federal government chooses the level of x that maximizes its net benefits, $B(x, y) - C^F(x, y)$, given its expectations regarding the state government's choice of x.[43] The first-order condition defining its choice is then

$$B_x(x, y) - C^F_x(x, y) = 0. \tag{6.3}$$

The corresponding condition for the state government, which seeks to maximize its net benefits $B(x, y) - C^S(x, y)$ given its expectations regarding the Federal government's choice of y, is

$$B_y(x, y) - C^S_y(x, y) = 0. \tag{6.4}$$

The Nash equilibrium levels of x and y ($(x^N$ and $y^N)$ are the levels that simultaneously solve (6.3) and (6.4).

Comparing the conditions for social efficiency (equations (6.1) and (6.2)) to the conditions for a Nash equilibrium (equations (6.3) and (6.4)) implies that the Nash equilibrium choices of x and y will be socially efficient if and only if

$$C^S_x = 0 \tag{6.5}$$

and

$$C^F_y = 0. \tag{6.6}$$

In other words, given simultaneous choices by the two levels of government, those choices will be efficient if and only if their costs are separable so that the decision of one party does not affect the marginal cost of the other.[44]

In most cases where both the Federal and state governments are involved in environmental policy-making, the decisions of the two governments will not be simultaneous. Instead, it is likely that the Federal government will move first and the state will then choose its policy in response, i.e., the policies will be determined sequentially.[45] In this case, the state government knows the policy of the Federal government at the time that it must set its own policy. Likewise, in choosing its policy, the Federal government knows that the states will respond to its choice.

If policy decisions are made sequentially, then the state government will choose a level of y to maximize its net benefits given the actual choice of x rather than simply its expectations regarding that choice. The first-order condition is still given by (6.4), with y now being the actual rather than the expected federal policy. This condition defines the state's 'reaction' or response function, $y^S(x)$.

If the Federal government realizes that the state will react according to the function $y^S(x)$, then it will consider this in its choice of y. In particular, it will view its net benefits as $B(x, y^S(x)) - C^F(x, y^S(x))$. In maximizing net benefits, it will thus choose x to satisfy the following first-order condition:

$$B_y - C^F_x + [B_y - C^F_y] \, \partial y^S/\partial x = 0, \qquad (6.7)$$

where the arguments of the functions have been suppressed for notational convenience.

The efficiency of the policy choices when made sequentially can be seen by comparing (6.4) and (6.7) to (6.1) and (6.2). As with the simultaneous choice case, in general the decisions of the two governments will not be efficient. However, unlike the simultaneous case, with sequential choice separability of the cost function is not sufficient to ensure efficiency. Even if the marginal costs for each government are independent of the other's policy choice, the resulting choices will not be efficient.[46] With a separable cost function, (6.7) reduces to

$$B_x - C^F_x + B_y \partial y^S/\partial x = 0 \qquad (6.8)$$

since $C^F_y = 0$. Comparing this to (6.1) implies that even in this case the choice of x will be inefficient.[47] In particular, if $\partial y^S/\partial x < 0$, i.e., if a reduction in the stringency of the federal policy causes the state to adopt a more stringent policy,[48] then the Federal government will choose a level of x that is less than the efficient level. The explanation is the Federal government's ability to push more of the cost of environmental quality onto the states by taking advantage of the states' reaction.[49] Thus, when there are interdependencies between the two governments' marginal costs or marginal benefits and the policy-making process is sequential, the policy choices are not likely to be efficient. In such cases, the fact that choices are made by different government entities is particularly problematic.

The model of the coordination problem presented here is clearly very stylized. Yet it serves to highlight the importance of considering both the interaction between the marginal benefits and marginal costs of the different levels of government and the timing of the policy-making process when evaluating the efficiency of the federal system. For example, the results suggest that, when the benefits or costs are not separable, the federal system is more problematic when decisions are made sequentially than when they are made simultaneously.

SOME OTHER ISSUES

Finally, we simply mention two other issues that relate to the choice among instruments in a federal system.

A. Revenue Redistribution

As noted above, tax-based instruments require that firms make payments to the government. In fact, environmental taxes have been used as a revenue-raising mechanism in some countries (Hahn, 1989a).   In contrast, regulatory approaches do not generate any revenue from complying firms. Likewise, while firms are required to make damage payments under some liability rules (such as strict liability), these payments are made to the victims rather than to the government.[50]

For instruments that generate revenue, some decision regarding use or redistribution of the revenue must be made. In particular, the question of whether the revenue will remain within the jurisdiction from which it was collected arises. This clearly has distributional implications that can affect decisions regarding instrument choice. However, revenue redistribution can also have efficiency implications. If the redistribution is not viewed as lump-sum, i.e., if firms or individuals believe that through their location decisions they can affect the share of the revenue they receive (either directly or indirectly through benefits from the government's use of that revenue), then the redistribution mechanism can lead to inefficient location decisions (Krumm and Wellisch, 1993).[51]

Similarly, if a subsidy-based instrument is chosen, revenue must be raised to finance the subsidy. Issues that are analogous to those for revenue redistribution arise in this context as well.

B. Interjurisdictional Permit Markets

Finally, if a permit approach is used, decisions regarding the initial allocation of permits and the oversight or administration of the market must be made. Since airsheds and watersheds often do not follow jurisdictional lines, the appropriately-defined markets are likely to overlap jurisdictions. If permits are initially sold rather than distributed free of charge, revenue will be raised. This revenue must be redistributed somehow, again raising the same interjurisdictional distributional and efficiency issues discussed above. Even if they are distributed at no cost to existing firms within the permit market, since the permits are of value to firms, the initial distribution will have interjurisdictional implications as well.

CONCLUSION

An important element in the design of environmental policies is the choice of instruments to use in achieving environmental quality goals. The normative literature on instrument choice reveals that, when consideration is given to both the practical difficulties in using particular instruments and the importance of objectives other than static efficiency, then no single policy instrument emerges as an ideal tool for controlling environmental pollution. Instead, each instrument has strengths and weaknesses. Using a combination of instruments, such as regulation coupled with taxes or regulation coupled with liability, can be a more effective approach.

The actual choice of instruments does not necessarily reflect their normative rankings. In practice, the choice is influenced by a number of factors. Positive theories of instrument choice have emphasized the role of pressure from producer and environmental interest groups. We suggest that instrument choice can also be strongly influenced by the geographic distribution of the associated costs and benefits (particularly when costs are geographically concentrated), as well as by social or cultural factors.

Standard models of instrument choice have generally assumed that policy decisions are made by a single government entity. However, in federations such as the US and the European Community, policy-making is multi-layered. For example, in the US both the Federal government and the states play important roles in the policy-making process. In particular, both make decisions that affect environmental quality. In addition, even within the different levels of government, jurisdiction for decisions relating to environmental quality is spread across different branches or agencies. In such a setting, the interactions between the decisions of different government entities create coordination problems that would not exist if decision-making were concentrated within a single government body. Using a very simple model of the coordination problem, we show that the efficiency implications of multi-layered decision-making depends, for example, on the timing of decisions (simultaneous vs. sequential) and the nature of the costs associated with different policy choices. The purpose of the model is simply to illustrate the kinds of issues that can arise when policy-making occurs within a federation. To evaluate more fully the choice of environmental policy instruments in this setting, these issues should be recognized in both the positive and the normative analyses of instrument choice.

NOTES

1. In principle, the choice of goals and instruments should be made simultaneously, since instrument choice can affect the overall cost of achieving a given goal and thus should affect the choice of the goal itself. However, such comprehensive analysis is rare in practice. See Portney (1990) for a discussion of goals vs. means in the context of air pollution policy in the United States.

2. Since a marketable permit system limits the aggregate amount of emissions (or level of ambient quality) to the number of permits issued, it is similar to a quantity instrument (Baumol and Oates, 1988). However, making the permits tradeable creates a price for emissions, namely, the price of purchasing a permit for a unit of emission or the opportunity cost of not selling a permit that the firm holds (Montgomery, 1972). For this reason, permits are usually viewed as economic incentive instruments. Hence, we include them in the category of price instruments.

3. Examples of normative analyses are Bohm and Russell (1985), Weitzman (1974), Adar and Griffin (1976), Fishelson (1976), Kolstad et al. (1990), Segerson (1986) and Shavell (1984a, 1984b). Positive analyses include Buchanan and Tullock (1975), Coelho (1976), Yohe (1976), Dewees (1983) and Hahn (1990).

4. See Baumol and Oates (1988) and Bohm and Russell (1985) for detailed discussions of normative issues related to instrument choice.

5. This requires some restrictions on the form of the damage function. See Spulber (1985) and Baumol and Oates (1988). In addition, the long-run efficiency of the permit approach requires that firms be able to sell their permits if they leave the industry.

6. Another is the amount of information necessary to ensure an efficient allocation of total abatement across firms (e.g., Tietenberg, 1988). Note, however, that the preference for emission taxes over regulation does not necessarily hold when criteria other than static efficiency are used to evaluate policies (e.g., Bohm and Russell, 1985) or when the simplifying assumptions such as perfect information are relaxed (e.g., Weitzman, 1974). See further discussion below.

7. While there are many similarities between the analysis of *ex ante* and *ex post* policies, there are also some important differences. These include their implications for victim incentives and the allocation of risk. See, for example, Segerson (forthcoming) for a comparison.

8. Note, however, that when the marginal benefit of abatement curve is negatively sloped, the damage payment under strict liability is less than the tax payment that would be made under the tax approach, since total damages are less than the marginal damage (marginal benefit of abatement) at the efficient level times the level of emissions.

9. This seminal paper spurred a large body of literature on the comparison of price and quantity instruments in the presence of uncertainty. See, for example, Adar and Griffin (1976) and Fishelson (1976).

10. Included in this last category are distributional considerations (i.e., the resulting distribution of costs and benefits across groups), ethical features of environmental instruments (for example, regarding the morality of certain actions), and the need for economic stabilization.

11. See Shavell (1984a) for a discussion of information costs in the choice between regulation and liability as means of controlling risks.

12. Instead, most of the trades that have occurred have been internal, i.e., trades within a given firm (Tietenberg, 1990). Such trades have lower transactions costs as well as greater certainty about the availability of permits in the future.

13. The need to consider a package of instruments can arise for other reasons as well. Such a need arises when there are multiple dimensions of an environmental problem and a single instrument cannot control all dimensions. For example, use of agricultural chemicals can contaminate both surface water (through runoff) and groundwater (through leaching). Policies designed to reduce soil erosion will generally reduce surface water contamination but will not control groundwater contamination. Similarly, the need for multiple instruments may arise from multiple objectives, such as safety and fuel efficiency in the regulation of automobiles (Hahn, 1986, 1989b). Finally, environmental policy choices are often made in the presence of other policies that create distortions to achieve non-efficiency goals. For example, in the US policies regarding discharge of contaminated waste water from irrigation of agricultural land are made in the presence of distorting policies regarding water price and availability (Weinberg and Kling, 1993). Likewise, policies regarding use of agricultural chemicals are made in the presence of agricultural supply policies such as support prices (Just et al., 1991). In such cases, the entire package of policy instruments affecting environmental quality must be considered when analyzing individual environmental control instruments. See Segerson (1991) for a related discussion.

14. See Dower (1990) for a description of hazardous waste legislation in the U.S.
15. See Grossman (this volume) for a discussion of pesticide regulation in the U.S.
16. For example, Braden and Segerson (1993) show that the ability of a multiple-instrument approach to increase welfare hinges on the nature of the single instruments that are combined as well as on the interactions between pollution-related inputs.
17. In addition, if regulation takes the form of quotas and quotas are limited to existing firms, then the regulation can create a barrier to entry that can actually increase firm profits (Buchanan and Tullock, 1975).
18. See Arnold (1979) for a more general discussion of the importance of geographic distribution in the context of government expenditure decisions.
19. For a detailed discussion of the politics surrounding enactment of the Clean Air Act, see Ackerman and Hassler (1981).
20. Hahn (1990) has recently emphasized the importance of defining the set of feasible instruments or the choice set.
21. While social or cultural considerations are related to political considerations, the two are not necessarily identical. See Clawson (1975, Chapter 9) for a discussion in the context of forest policy.
22. Even the early land policy in the US reflected social or cultural considerations. A primary concern at this time was access to land, reflecting concerns about the lack of access in European countries. For a discussion of the history of federal land policy, see Clawson (1983) and the references cited therein.
23. Similar transitions are evident in other areas of US law as well. One example is product liability law. In the early part of the century, product liability law favored producers since the conditions under which consumers could collect for damages from product-related injuries were very limited. Since the 1970s, however, there has been a move towards more consumer-oriented laws. In particular, there has been a movement away from the privity requirement (requiring a contractual relationship between the injured party and the defendant) and the negligence standard towards the use of strict liability principles in product-liability cases. Some have argued that the shift has gone too far and have called for product-liability reform. See, for example, Epstein (1980) and Priest (1991).
24. See Bromley (1993) for a discussion of property rights in the context of regulatory takings.
25. This movement is exemplified by a number of recent court cases, including the well-publicized *Lucas* case (304 S.C. 376; 404 S.E.2d 895; No. 91–453, slip op. (US Supreme Court, June 29, 1992). See Bromley (1993) and Kaplan and Cohn (1992).
26. See Sax (1971) for a discussion of a 'harm–benefit' approach to determining compensation.
27. See Dower (1990) and Anderson (1993) for descriptions of CERCLA. For other examples of the use of liability in US environmental law, see Opaluch (1984). Liability for pollution damages can also be imposed under common law. See Dewees (1992) and Huber (1988) for related discussions.
28. See Freeman (1990), Portney (1990), Shortle (this volume), and Grossman (this volume) for discussions in the context of US environmental policy.
29. See Crandall et al. (1986) for a description of US regulation of automobile emissions.
30. See Krier and Ursin (1977) for a description of the development of California standards.
31. For a discussion of state differential in the area of product liability, see Miceli, Segerson and Wright (1992).
32. The US has tried to avoid such differences by, for example, requiring that primary standards for ambient air quality be uniform across the country. See, for example, Portney (1990). For a discussion of competition among jurisdictions in choosing policies, see Oates and Schwab (1988, forthcoming).
33. For a discussion of the related literature, see Ulph (this volume).
34. See James (1988) and Toulme and Cloud (1991) for discussions of the case law related to lender liability.
35. Another example of the role of the courts is in defining the terms of the liability that parties face. For example, the treatment of liability under CERCLA as strict and joint and several has come from court interpretation of the legislation rather than language in the legislation itself. See, for example, Anderson (1993).
36. See *United States v. Fleet Factors Corp.*, 724 F. Supp. 955 (S.D. Ga. 1988), 901 F. 2d 1550 (llth Cir. 1990).
37. 57 Fed. Reg. 18344 (1992) (to be codified at 40 C.F.R. Pt. 200).
38. *Chemical Manufacturers Association vs. Environmental Protection Agency*, No. 92–1314. See Schmitt (1994).

39. In fact, some felt that a ruling in favor of compensation in the *Lucas* case (see footnote 25) would bring environmental legislation/regulation to a standstill. See Kaplan and Cohn (1992).
40. Alternatively, x and y could represent the choices of two different branches of the government or two different agencies within a branch. However, we focus on the federal vs. state decisions.
41. Hence, we assume that there are no interjurisdictional environmental externalities (such as transfrontier pollution). In the presence of such externalities, the coordination problem has the additional dimension of internalizing the external costs. While this is a crucial dimension of many environmental problems, we abstract from it here to focus solely on the implications of the interactions between the decisions of the two levels of government. See, however, footnote 44 below.
42. This is a standard assumption in economic models of simultaneous decision-making. See, for example, Varian (1992).
43. This is one possible objective for the government to use in setting policies. Clearly, other objectives are possible as well. (See Mueller (1989) for a discussion of alternative models of government decision-making.) If governments pursue non-efficiency objectives in choosing policies, then obviously the outcomes will not in general be efficient. Since we are interested in how the coordination problem (rather than non-efficiency objectives) affects efficiency, we limit consideration to the case where both the Federal and state governments seek policies that are efficient from their own perspective, i.e., policies that maximize their own net benefits. Since the net benefits of each government are not in general equal to the social net benefits, we are effectively assuming that governments suffer from 'fiscal illusion'. See Fischel and Shapiro (1988) for a discussion of fiscal illusion.
44. Conditions (6.5) and (6.6) would not be sufficient for efficiency if interjurisdictional externalities exist. In this case, the social marginal benefits from the choice of y would not equal the marginal benefits within the state, and as a result the state would not choose an efficient level of y even with a separable cost function. The presence of interjurisdictional externalities is one rationale for having environmental policy decisions made at the federal rather than state or local level. However, since this issue exists regardless of the policy instrument that is used, we do not focus on it here. For a discussion of the implications of interjurisdictional environmental externalities when policies are chosen by local governments, see Oates and Schwab (forthcoming).
45. The opposite is, of course, also possible, i.e., states can take the initiative with the Federal government responding. An example is the regulation of automobile emissions in the U.S., where the State of California took the initiative. See Krier and Ursin (1977).
46. Under separable costs, the state government's decision will be efficient *conditional* on the choice of the Federal government. However, since the Federal government will not make an efficient choice, the resulting choice of the state government will not be efficient either.
47. If both the cost function and the benefit function were separable, i.e., if in addition $B_{xy} = 0$ so that the marginal benefit of y were independent of x, then the choices would be efficient since this would imply $\partial y^s / \partial x = 0$. However, this is unlikely to be the case in practice.
48. Conversely, this implies that the state will react to a stringent federal policy by relaxing its own policy choice.
49. A similar intuition lies behind the results of the tort model with sequential choice. See Shavell (1983).
50. If it is the government that sues the polluter, as under CERCLA, then payment is made to a government trustee. However, the money is not available for general redistribution. See, for example, Anderson (1993).
51. A similar problem can result when oil-rich nations or states (such as Alaska) redistribute some portion of oil revenues to all residents, including new residents.

REFERENCES

Ackerman, Bruce A. and William T. Hassler (1981), *Clean Coal/Dirty Air*, Yale University Press, New Haven and London.

Adar, Z. and J.M. Griffin (1976), 'Uncertainty and the Choice of Pollution Control Instruments', *Journal of Environmental Economics and Management*, 3(3), 178–88.

Anderson, Frederick R. (1993), 'Natural Resource Damages, Superfund, and the Courts', in Raymond J. Kopp and V. Kerry Smith (eds), *Valuing Natural Assets: The Economics of Natural Resource Damage Assessment*, 26–62, Resources for the Future, Washington, DC.

Arnold, R. Douglas (1979), *Congress and the Bureaucracy*, Yale University Press, New Haven and London.

Bartik, Timothy J. (1988), 'The Effects of Environmental Regulation on Business Location in the United States', *Growth Change*, 19(3), 22–44.

Baumol, William J. and Wallace E. Oates (1988), *The Theory of Environmental Policy*, 2nd edn, Cambridge University Press, Cambridge.

Bohm, Peter and Clifford Russell (1985), 'Comparative Analysis of Alternative Policy Instruments', in A.V. Kneese and J.L. Sweeney (eds), *Handbook of Natural Resource and Energy Economics*, Vol. 1, 395–460, North Holland, Amsterdam.

Boyd, James (1993), 'The Allocation of Environmental Liabilities in Central and Eastern Europe', *Resources*, No. 112 (published by Resources for the Future).

Braden, John B. and Kathleen Segerson (1993), 'Information Problems in the Design of Nonpoint-Source Pollution Policy', in Clifford S. Russell and Jason F. Shogren (eds), *Theory, Modeling and Experience in the Management of Nonpoint-Source Pollution*, 1–36, Kluwer Academic Publishers, Boston.

Bromley, Daniel W. (1991), *Environment and Economy: Property Rights and Public Policy*, Basil Blackwell, Cambridge.

Bromley, Daniel W. (1993), 'Regulation Takings: Coherent Concept or Logical Contradiction?', *Vermont Law Review*, 17(3), 647–82.

Buchanan, James M. and Gordon Tullock (1962), *The Calculus of Consent*, University of Michigan Press, Ann Arbor, MI.

Buchanan, James M. and Gordon Tullock (1975), 'Polluters' Profits and Political Response: Direct Controls Versus Taxes', *American Economic Review*, 65(1), 139–47.

Clawson, Marion (1975), *Forests for Whom and for What?*, Resources for the Future, Johns Hopkins University Press, Baltimore and London.

Clawson, Marion (1983), *The Federal Lands Revisited*, Resources for the Future, Washington, DC.

Coelho, Philip R. (1976), 'Polluters' Profits and Political Response: Direct Control Versus Taxes: Comment', *American Economic Review*, 66(5), 976–8.

Cooter, Robert D. (1984), 'Prices and Sanctions', *Columbia Law Review*, 84, 1523–60.

Crandall, Robert W., Howard K. Gruenspecht, Theodore E. Keeler and Lester B. Lave (1986), *Regulating the Automobile*, The Brookings Institution, Washington, DC.

Danzon, Patricia M. (1988), 'Medical Malpractice Liability', in Robert E. Litan and Clifford Winston (eds), *Liability Perspectives and Policy*, 101–27, The Brookings Institution, Washington, DC.

Danzon, Patricia M. (1991), 'Liability for Medical Malpractice', *The Journal of Economic Perspectives*, 5(3), 51–70.

Dewees, Donald (1983), 'Instrument Choice in Environmental Policy', *Economic Inquiry*, 11, 53–71.

Dewees, Donald (1992), 'Tort Law and the Deterrence of Environmental Pollution', in T.H. Tietenberg (ed.), *Innovation in Environmental Policy: Economic and Legal Aspects of Recent Developments in Environmental Enforcement and Liability*, Edward Elgar Publishing, Aldershot, England.

Dinan, Terry and F. Reed Johnson (1990), 'Effects of Hazardous Waste Risks on Property Transfers: Legal Liability vs. Direct Regulation', *Natural Resources Journal*, 30, 521–36.

Dower, Roger C. (1990), 'Hazardous Wastes', in Paul R. Portney (ed.), *Public Policies for Environmental Protection*, 151–94, Resources for the Future, Washington, DC.

Epstein, Richard (1980), *Modern Product Liability Law*, Quorum Books, Westport, CT.

Epstein, Richard (1985), *Takings: Private Property and the Power of Eminent Domain*, Harvard University Press, Cambridge.

Fischel, William (1985), *The Economics of Zoning Laws*, Johns Hopkins Press, Baltimore.

Fischel, William and Perry Shapiro (1988), 'Takings, Insurance, and Michelman: Comments on Economic Interpretations of "Just Compensation' Law", *Journal of Legal Studies*, 17, 269–93.

Fishelson, G. (1976), 'Emission Control Policies Under Uncertainty', *Journal of Environmental Economics and Management*, 3(3), 189–97.

Freeman III, A. Myrick (1990), 'Water Pollution Policy', in Paul R. Portney (ed.), *Public Policies for Environmental Protection*, 97–150, Resources for the Future, Washington, DC.

Green, Robert C. (1990), 'Program Provisions for Program Crops: A Database for 1961–1990', Agriculture and Trade Analysis Division, Economic Research Service, US Department of Agriculture, Staff Report No. AGES 9010, March.

Grossman, Margaret R. (this volume), 'Environmental Federalism in Agriculture: The Case of Pesticide Regulation in the United States'.

Hahn, R.W. (1986), 'Trade-offs in Designing Markets with Multiple Objectives', *Journal of Environmental Economics and Management*, 13(1), 1–12.

Hahn, R.W. (1989a), 'Economic Prescriptions for Environmental Problems: How the Patient Followed the Doctor's Orders', *Journal of Economic Perspectives*, 3(2), 95–114.

Hahn, R.W. (1989b), 'A New Approach to the Design of Regulation in the Presence of Multiple Objectives', *Journal of Environmental Economics and Management*, 17, 195–211.

Hahn, R.W. (1990), 'The Political Economy of Environmental Regulation: Towards a Unifying Framework', *Public Choice*, 65, 21–47.

Hahn, R.W. and G.L. Hester (1989), 'Where Did All the Markets Go? An Analysis of EPA's Emission Trading Program', *Yale Journal of Regulation*, 6, 109–53.

Huber, Peter (1988), 'Environmental Hazards and Liability Law', in Robert E. Litan and Clifford Winston (eds), *Liability Perspectives and Policy*, 129–54, The Brookings Institution, Washington, DC.

James III, Walter D. (1988), 'Financial Institutions and Hazardous Waste Litigation: Limiting the Exposure to Superfund Liability', *Natural Resources Journal*, 28, Spring, 329–55.

Just, R.E., N. Bockstael, R.G. Cummings, J. Miranowski and D. Zilberman (1991), 'Problems Confronting the Joint Formulation of Commercial Agricultural and Resource Policies', in R.E. Just and N. Bockstael (eds), *Commodity and Resource Policies in Agricultural Systems*, Springer-Verlag, Berlin.

Kaplan, David and Bob Cohn (1992), 'Pay Me, or Get Off My Land', *Newsweek*, March 9, 70.

Kolstad, Charles D., Thomas S. Ulen and Gary V. Johnson (1990), 'Ex Post Liability for Harm vs. Ex Ante Safety Regulation: Substitutes or Complements?', *American Economic Review*, 80(4), 888–901.

Krier, James E. and Edmund Ursin (1977), *Pollution and Policy*, University of California Press, Berkeley.

Krueger, Anne O. (1974), 'The Political Economics of the Rent-Seeking Society', *American Economic Review*, 64(3), 291–303.

Krumm, Raimund and Dietmar Wellisch (1993), 'On the Efficiency of Environmental Instruments in a Spatial Economy', Working Paper, Universität Tubingen, Tubingen, Germany.

Magat, Wesley A., Alan J. Krupnick, and Winston Harrington (1986), *Rules in the Making, A Statistical Analysis of Regulatory Agency Behavior*, Resources for the Future, Washington, DC.

McConnell, Virginia D. and Robert M. Schwab (1990), 'The Impact of Environmental Regulation on Industry Location Decisions: The Motor Vehicle Industry', Land Economics, 66(1), 67–81.

Melnick, R. Shep (1983), *Regulation and the Courts: The Case of the Clean Air Act*, The Brookings Institution, Washington, DC.

Miceli, Thomas J., Kathleen Segerson and Arthur W. Wright (1992), 'Measuring the Impacts of Non-Uniform Product Liability Laws on the Cost of US Goods: Phase I', Report to the US Small Business Administration, Office of Advocacy, SBA 5647–OA–90.

Montgomery, David W. (1972), 'Markets in Licenses and Efficient Pollution Control Programs', *Journal of Economic Theory*, 5, December, 395–418.

Mueller, Dennis G. (1989), *Public Choice II: A Revised Edition of Public Choice*, Cambridge University Press, Cambridge.

Oates, Wallace E. and Robert M. Schwab (1988), 'Economic Competition Among Jurisdictions: Efficiency Enhancing or Distortion Inducing?', *Journal of Public Economics*, 35, 333–54.

Oates, Wallace E. and Robert M. Schwab (forthcoming), 'The Theory of Regulatory Federalism: The Case of Environmental Management', forthcoming in *The Economics of Environmental Regulation*.

Opaluch, James J. (1984), 'The Use of Liability Rules in Controlling Hazardous Waste Accidents: Theory and Practice', *Northeast Journal of Agricultural and Resource Economics*, 13, 210–17.

Pfander, James E. (this volume), 'Environmental Federalism in Europe and the United States: A Comparative Assessment of Regulation Through the Agency of Member States'.

Polinsky, A. Mitchell (1980), 'Strict Liability vs. Negligence in a Market Setting', *American Economic Review*, 70(2), 363–67.

Portney, Paul R. (1990), 'Air Pollution Policy', in Paul R. Portney (ed.), *Public Policies for Environmental Protection*, 27–96, Resources for the Future, Washington, DC.

Priest, G. (1987), 'The Current Insurance Crisis and Modern Tort Law', *Yale Law Journal*, 96, 1521–90.

Priest, G. (1991), 'The Modern Expansion of Tort Liability: Its Sources, Its Effects, and Its Reform', *Journal of Economic Perspectives*, 5(3), 31–50.

Russell, Clifford S., Winston Harrington, and William J. Vaughan (1986), *Enforcing Pollution Control Laws*, Resources for the Future, Washington, DC.

Sax, Joseph L. (1971), 'Takings, Private Property and Public Rights', *Yale Law Journal*, 81, 149–86.

Schmitt, Richard B. (1994), 'Appeals Court Invalidates EPA Rules Shielding Lenders from Superfund Law', *Wall Street Journal*, February 10.

Segerson, Kathleen (1986), 'Risk Sharing in the Design of Environmental Policy', *American Journal of Agricultural Economics* 68(5), 1261–65.

Segerson, Kathleen (1991), 'Air Pollution and Agriculture: A Review and Evaluation of Policy Interactions', in R.E. Just and N. Bockstael (eds), *Commodity and Resource Policies in Agricultural Systems*, 349–67, Springer-Verlag, Berlin and Heidelberg.

Segerson, Kathleen (forthcoming), 'Liability and Penalty Structures in Policy Design', in Daniel W. Bromley (ed.), *Handbook of Environmental Economics*, Basil Blackwell, Cambridge.

Shavell, S. (1980), 'Strict Liability Versus Negligence', *Journal of Legal Studies*, 9, 1–25.

Shavell, S. (1982), 'The Social versus Private Incentive to Bring Suit in a Costly Legal System', *Journal of Legal Studies*, 11, 333–9.

Shavell, S. (1983), 'Torts in which Victim and Injurer Act Sequentially', *Journal of Law and Economics*, 26, 589–612.

Shavell, S. (1984a), 'Liability for Harm Versus Regulation of Safety', *Journal of Legal Studies*, 13(2), 357–74.

Shavell, S. (1984b), 'A Model of the Optimal Use of Liability and Safety Regulation', *Rand Journal of Economics*, 15, 271–80.

Shavell, S. (1985), 'Uncertainty Over Causation and the Determination of Civil Liability', *Journal of Law and Economics*, 28, 587–609.

Shavell, S. (1986), 'The Judgment Proof Problem', *International Review of Law and Economics*, 6, 45–58.

Shortle, James S. (this volume), 'Environmental Federalism and the Control of Water Pollution from Agriculture: Is the Current Division of Responsibilities Between National and Local Authorities About Right?'.

Spulber, D. (1985), 'Effluent Regulation and Long-Run Optimality', *Journal of Environmental Economics and Management*, 13, 103–116.

Stratmann, Thomas (1992), 'The Effects of Logrolling on Congressional Voting', *American Economic Review*, 82(5), 1162–72.

Tietenberg, T.H. (1980), 'Transferable Discharge Permits and the Control of Stationary Source Air Pollution: A Survey and Synthesis', *Land Economics*, 56, 391–416.

Tietenberg, T.H. (1985), *Emissions Trading: An Exercise in Reforming Pollution Policy*, Resources for the Future, Washington, DC.

Tietenberg, Tom (1988), *Environmental and Natural Resource Economics*, Scott, Foresman & Company, Glenview, IL.

Tietenberg, T.H. (1989), 'Marketable Permits in the U.S.: A Decade of Experience', in Karl W. Roskamp (ed.), *Public Finance and the Performance of Enterprises*, Wayne State University Press, Detroit, MI.

Tietenberg, T.H. (1990), 'Economic Instruments for Environmental Regulation', *Oxford Review of Economic Policy*, 6(1), 17–33.

Tobey, James A. (1990), 'The Effects of Domestic Environmental Policies on Patterns of World Trade: An Empirical Test', *KYKLOS*, 43(92), 191–209.

Toulme, Nill V. and Douglas E. Cloud (1991), 'The Fleet Factors Case: A Wrong Turn for Lender Liability under Superfund', *Wake Forest Law Review*, 26(1), 127–59.

Tullock, Gordon (1967), 'The Welfare Costs of Tariffs, Monopolies, and Theft', *Western Economic Journal*, 5, 224–32.

Ulen, Thomas S., Mark Hester and Gary V. Johnson (1985), 'Minnesota's Environmental Response and Liability Act: An Economic Justification', *Environmental Law Reporter*, 15, 10109–15.

Ulph, Alistair (this volume), 'Strategic Environmental Policy, International Trade and the Single European Market'.

Varian, Hal R. (1992), *Microeconomic Analysis*, 3rd edn, W.W. Norton & Company, Inc., New York.

Wasserman, Cheryl (1992), 'Federal Enforcement: Theory and Practice', in T.H. Tietenberg (ed.), *Innovation in Environmental Policy: Economic and Legal Aspects of Recent Developments in Environmental Enforcement and Liability*, Edward Elgar Publishing, Aldershot, England.

Weinberg, Marca and Catherine L. Kling (1993), 'The Costs of Piecemeal Agricultural and Environmental Policy Making', Working paper, US Department of Agriculture, Economic Research Service.

Weitzman, Martin (1974), 'Prices vs. Quantities', *Review of Economic Studies*, 41(4), 477–91.

Yohe, Gary W. (1976), 'Polluters' Profits and Political Response: Direct Control Versus Taxes: Comment', *American Economic Review*, 66(5), 981–2.

7. Non-cooperative National Environmental Policies and Capital Mobility

Rüdiger Pethig

INTRODUCTION

The emission of pollutants and its regulation by national environmental policies create international interdependence in a direct way through transfrontier pollution, and in an indirect way through international commodity trade (i.e. trade in final goods) and/or international factor market. This interdependence is particularly obvious in the case of transfrontier pollution (e.g. OECD, 1974; Pethig, 1981) which leads to an inefficient allocation of resources in the absence of cooperation even if the countries involved are not engaged in any international economic interactions. But suppose the impact of domestic emissions of pollutants is purely domestic and the countries are interconnected by commodity trade or international factor mobility. Do we expect that 'institutional international competition' between national environmental policies is efficiency enhancing or distortion inducing?

The interaction between international commodity trade and national environmental policies (with or without transfrontier pollution) has been extensively discussed in the literature (e.g. by Markusen, 1975b; Pethig, 1976; Gronych, 1980; Siebert et al., 1980; Krutilla, 1991; Ulph, 1991; Conrad, 1993; Kennedy, 1993). Essentially, the (in-)efficiency implications of market-related indirect environmental interaction depend on the 'perfectness of competition' in the international markets and on the sophistication of national governments in choosing their environmental policies. As will be elaborated below, governments may either make (strategic) use of or ignore the impact of their environmental policy on trade flows and market-clearing prices in international markets.

The question, whether the interdependence of international factor transactions and national environmental policies is a potential problem of 'ecological dumping' in the course of establishing the internal European market, led to a controversial discussion (Siebert 1991; Rauscher, 1991, 1992a,

175

1992b). Environmentalists worry that if national environmental policies are uncoordinated, international capital will move to countries with low environmental quality standards, and all countries' quality standards will be 'competed down' in order to attract capital in a beggar-my-neighbor style. However, this issue has not yet received very much attention in the theory-oriented literature, in our view. Oates and Schwab (1988) and Long and Siebert (1991) reached the conclusion that with strictly domestic pollution and price-taking firms on the international capital market 'competition among jurisdictions is ... conducive to efficient outcomes' because 'society's and the community's evaluation of the costs and benefits of environmental policy are identical' (Oates and Schwab, 1988, p. 342). Therefore 'the competitive process and the international mobility of capital leads to an efficient allocation of resources' (Long and Siebert, 1991, p. 299). In contrast, Rauscher (1991) shows that in the absence of cooperation it is not in the countries' self-interest to equate marginal pollution damage and marginal abatement costs.

To avoid intermingling of different international effects of national pollution controls the present chapter ignores both transfrontier pollution and international commodity trade to focus exclusively on the interaction of pollution control and international factor mobility on perfectly competitive markets.[1] The principal objective is to investigate interactions of non-cooperative national environmental policies and international capital investments with a special emphasis on the consequences of removing the barriers to international capital transactions.

The efficiency claim of non-cooperative environmental policies in the presence of mobile capital has been established, like the analogous conclusion in the literature on trade and the environment, by assuming

- that all governments have perfect information on domestic pollution damage and abatement costs, and
- that all governments' pollution controls are non-strategic in the sense that they ignore their impact on the market-clearing rate of return on capital in the international capital market.

These assumptions appear to be unsatisfactory since if it is argued that rational and benevolent governments implement the first-best Pigouvian policy of internalizing domestic environmental externalities under perfect information, consistency requires that non-strategic behavior be interpreted as the government's deliberate neglect of international repercussions of its own actions. But unless the country is very small (causing only very small repercussions) deliberate neglect is not rational for a benevolent and omniscient government, since it turns out that Pigouvian taxation is not in the country's self-interest. The repercussions of national environmental policies on international markets for production factors are not insignificant among the larger countries in Europe. Their 'oligopolistic interdependence' is obvious not only in the field of pollution control, but also in various other policy areas, such as monetary and fiscal policy.[2] Therefore, it is necessary to investigate – as Rauscher (1991) does – the non-market interdependence under perfect information *in a consistent way*, i.e. with strategic environmental policy formation.

Though it is important to know what the governments' options are in case of perfect information it is also clear that real-world environmental policies suffer from severe informational constraints. Without perfect information on pollution damage and abatement cost governments usually proceed with politically determined (second-best) emissions standards and/or emissions tax rates – as had been suggested long ago by Baumol and Oates (1971) to avoid the Nirvana status of the Pigouvian approach. Whatever pragmatic rule of pollution control is followed by a country, it will lead to repercussions in international markets which should be well understood in the process of European economic integration which aims at reducing barriers to trade in the markets for capital investments among the Member States of the European Community.

The present chapter addresses these issues in a simple one-sector model applying two different production-emissions technologies: production with integrated abatement technology and production on the basis of pollution-generating capital, but without abatement technology. In the former case, the emission of pollutants can be curbed by using less emission-intensive techniques, e.g., the SO_2 emissions of coal-firing power plants can be reduced by implementing filters. The second production-emissions technology assumes that emissions are strictly proportional to a particular input (here: capital) independent of the level of outputs and other inputs. This assumption appears to be somewhat unrealistic, but it highlights the link between capital mobility and environmental issues in the simplest possible way: any import of (physical) capital is an import of pollution. In each of these two cases the consequences of capital mobility and international capital market liberalization are investigated when, alternatively, non-strategic, strategic or information-constrained environmental policies are pursued.

CAPITAL MOBILITY IN THE CASE OF PRODUCTION WITH INTEGRATED ABATEMENT TECHNOLOGY

A.   The Model

Consider a country that produces a single consumption good with the inputs capital, k, labor, ℓ, and nature's assimilative services that are equal to the total *emission of pollutants, e*. The production function, F, exhibits constant returns to scale, and the per-capita output is given by[3]

$$y = F(k, \ell, e)/\ell = : Y(x, z) \qquad (7.1)$$

where $x := K/\ell$, $z := e/\ell$ and $Y_{xz} > 0$. The economy's aggregate *endowment of labor*, ℓ_0, is constant and so is the *capital endowment*, k_0. Consumers have identical preferences represented by the quasi-concave utility function

$$u = U(c, z), \qquad (7.2)$$

which satisfies $U_{cc} \leq 0$, $U_{zz} \leq 0$ and $U_{zc} \leq 0$. If each consumer has the same working time and receives the same share of capital income and tax revenue (in case an emissions tax is levied), the individual's consumption, c, is

$$c = Y(x, z). \qquad (7.3)$$

Environmental policy may take the form of fixing an emissions standard per capita directly. In what follows, we choose to present the analysis in terms of an *emissions tax policy* which will turn out to highlight the interaction of national pollution controls and the international capital market in a particularly interesting way. Throughout the chapter we assume that firms are price-takers, implying that they set the (per-capita) *emissions tax rate*, t, equal to their marginal abatement cost, $Y_z(x, z)$.

For the purpose of later reference, we briefly recall that in the *closed economy* and under perfect information the emissions standard is efficiently set by maximizing an arbitrary consumer's utility (7.2) subject to (7.1), (7.3) and $\ell_0 \geq \ell$, $k_0 \geq k$. This yields

$$- \frac{U_z(c, z)}{U_c(c, z)} = Y_z(x, z). \qquad (7.4)$$

Obviously, the maximum satisfies $x = x_0 := k_0/\ell_0$, so that equation (7.4) uniquely determines the emissions standard, z. In per-capita terms the left side of (7.4) is the marginal damage of pollution and the right side is the marginal productivity of emissions which equals the marginal per-capita abatement costs in terms of the consumption good. Suppose the government introduces an emission tax with rate t. Then it is profit maximizing for price-taking firms to set $Y_z = t$. Therefore, the efficiency condition (7.4) will be achieved if the government fixes $t = (-U_z/U_c)$ which is known as the *Pigouvian tax*.[4]

On the other hand, if the information about abatement cost and pollution damage is insufficient, government may want to adopt a price-and-standard regime (Baumol and Oates, 1971) where the political process determines 'somehow' an aggregate emissions standard as the environmental policy goal which is then implemented by levying an appropriate emissions tax. The relationship between the standard, z, and the associated emissions tax rate, t, is very simple in the one-sector closed economy: Since $t = Y_z(x, z)$ and $x = x_0$, there is a function $Z : \mathbb{R}_+ \to \mathbb{R}_+$ such that $z = Z(t)$ satisfies $t = Y_z(x_0, z)$. The first derivative of Z is negative, as expected.

B. Non-Strategic Environmental Policy

Suppose now, capital is internationally mobile, environmental information is perfect, and the country under consideration has no impact, or ignores its impact, on the world rental rate of capital, r. As a first step towards the investigation of a two-country model we consider a '*small open country*' that takes the world price of capital as given. To analyze this case we replace the budget constraint (7.3) by

$$c = Y(x, z) - (x - x_0)r. \tag{7.5}$$

If the country imports capital $[x > x_0]$ it pays $(x - x_0)r$ to the 10 foreign capital owners out of its domestic output $Y(x, z)$ and consumes the rest determined by (7.5). Maximization of (7.2) under consideration of (7.1), (7.5) and $\ell \le \ell_0$ results in (7.4)

$$Y_x(x, z) = r. \tag{7.6}$$

As argued above, equation (7.4) means that the environmental externality is perfectly internalized, and equation (7.6) gives us the production efficiency condition that the domestic rate of return on capital be equal to the world price r. It is informative to see what the adjustments in t, x and z are when the world price of capital changes parametrically. The comparative static analysis (Appendix 7A.1) yields the following major conclusions:

1. Result 1
Denote by T *(r),* X*(r), and* Z*(r) the values of* t, x *and* z, *respectively, that are determined as functions of the world price of capital,* r, *through the equations (7.4), (7.5) and (7.6). A small exogenous change of* r *has the following consequences:*

(a) $T_r < 0$, $X_r < 0$ and $Z_r < 0$, *if before the change in r the country's international capital transactions were zero or 'sufficiently' small;*

(b) T_r *ambiguous in sign,* $X_r < 0$ *and* $Z_r < 0$, *if the country exports capital* $(x < x_0)$;

(c) $T_r < 0$, $X_r > 0$ *and* $Z_r > 0$, *if the country's capital imports are 'sufficiently' large;*

(d) *under certain parameter constellations it is feasible that for (and only for) the capital-importing country the sign of* Z_r *is not equal to the sign of* X_r.

Result 1 shows that the small country's optimal response to an increase in the world rate of return on capital is difficult to predict. The only 'unconditional' relationship seems to be that for a capital-exporting country a rise in the world price of capital always leads to increased capital exports and better environmental quality. Note also that $X(r)$ is the country's demand function for capital. One would expect that with an increase in the world rental rate of capital, the capital export [import] would increase [decrease] (i.e. $X_r < 0$). This seems to be the 'regular' reaction, indeed, but Result 1c shows that $X_r > 0$ in case of large capital imports.

Figure 7.1: Capital export and efficient pollution control response

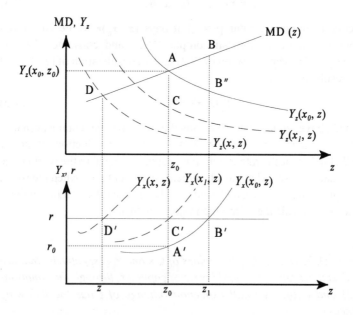

To understand the response $Z_r < 0$ consider Figure 7.1 where the autarky allocation is characterized by (r_0, x_0, z_0) and hence by the points A (upper part of Figure 7.1) and A' (lower part), hence by $r > r_0$. The necessary rise of r_0, $= Y_x(x_0, z_0)$ to r can be accomplished by allowing for various combinations of capital exports and changes in the emissions standard.

(a) Keep x_0 fixed and shift z_0 to $z_1 > z_0$. This implies a move from A' to B' and yields $r = Y_x(x_0, z_1)$ by construction. But the upper part of Figure 7.1 reveals that the difference BB″ between the marginal damage of pollution, $MD(z_1)$, and the marginal abatement cost, $Y_z(x_0, z_1)$ is positive. Hence this strategy is not optimal.

(b) The opposite polar case is to keep z_0 fixed and shift x_0 to $x_1 < x_0$ so that $Y_x(x_1, z_0) = r$ illustrated by the move from A' to C' in Figure 7.1. But the upper part of Figure 7.1 shows that the marginal damage still exceeds the marginal abatement costs: $MD(z_0) - Y_z(x_1, z_0) = AC > 0$.

(c) Consequently, to achieve efficiency the capital imports must be increased beyond $x_1 - x_0$. But by doing so the condition $r = Y_x(x, z)$ can only be maintained if z is simultaneously reduced below z_0. Eventually, one finds $\hat{x} < x_0$ and $\hat{z} < z_0$ satisfying both efficiency conditions, as illustrated by the points D and D' in Figure 7.1.

Observe finally that there are parameter constellations such as that of Result 1a where it is optimal to react to an increase in the capital price by reducing both the emissions tax rate and the level of emissions. This effect appears to be an important feature of capital mobility as the subsequent analysis will show.

We now turn to the two-country model. The country considered so far is called the home country. The foreign country is also characterized by the equations (7.1) and (7.2), but it is notationally distinguished from the home country by starred variables. As before, labor is assumed to be immobile. Perfect capital mobility between both countries is characterized by the condition that capital use in both countries, $k + k^* = \ell_0 x + \ell_0^* x^*$, must not exceed the world endowment with capital, $k_0 + k_0^*$. In formal terms,

$$k_0 + k_0^* \geq \ell_0 x + \ell_0^* x^* \quad \text{or} \quad \sigma_0 \geq \sigma x + x^*, \tag{7.7}$$

where $\sigma_0 := (k_0 + k_0^*)/\ell_0^*$ and $\sigma := \ell_0/\ell_0^*$. If both countries pursue non-strategic environmental policies, it is straightforward that the foreign country, like the home country, is characterized by the equations (7.4), (7.5) and (7.6). Denote by $X(r)$ the home country's per-capita demand for capital when the price of capital is r. The world market for capital clears when total capital endowment equals aggregate capital demand. In view of (7.7) the equilibrium condition can be written as $\sigma_0 = \sigma X(r) + X^*(r)$ which implicitly determines the equilibrium rental rate of capital. In equilibrium, the equations

$$Y_x(x, z) = Y_x^*(x^*, z^*), \tag{7.8}$$

$c = Y(x,z) - (x - x_0) \cdot Y_x(x,z)$ and $c^* = Y^*(x^*, z^*) - (x^* - x_0^*) \cdot Y_x^*(x^*, z^*)$ (7.9)

hold.[5] The relationship between efficiency and equilibrium is summarized as

2. Result 2 (Oates and Schwab, 1988)

In the two-country model, an efficient international allocation of resources is characterized by (7.4) (for both countries) and (7.8). It can be attained by a perfectly competitive capital market and by non-cooperative non-strategic national environmental tax policies with rates

$$t = Y_z = (-U_z/U_c) \text{ and } t^* = Y_z^* = (-U_z^*/U_c^*).$$

C. Strategic Environmental Policy

In this section we wish to show for the two-country model, that the efficient allocation will not be brought about by decentralized non-cooperative action, when the countries take into account the impacts on the international capital market of their own and the other country's environmental policy. The first step is to focus on the interdependence of the countries through their non-cooperative environmental policies as given by (7.7), (7.8) and

$$t = Y_z(x, z) \text{ and } t^* = Y_z^*(x^*, z^*). \tag{7.10}$$

These equations uniquely determine the variables x, x^*, z and z^* for each tuple (t, t^*). In other words, there are four functions X, X^*, Z and Z^* whose derivatives exhibit the following signs (Appendix 7A.2):

$$x = X(t, t^*), \ X^* = X^*(t, t^*), \ z = Z(t, t^*), \ z^* = Z^*(t, t^*). \tag{7.11}$$

Owing to (7.11) the equilibrium rate of return on capital is uniquely determined by the emissions tax rates:

$$r = R(t, t^*) := Y_x[X(t, t^*), Z(t, t^*)] \tag{7.12}$$

with $R_t = Y_{xx} X_t + Y_{xz} Z_t < 0$ and $R_{t^*} = Y_{xx} X_{t^*} + Y_{xz} Z_{t^*} < 0$. We now combine (7.4), (7.8) and the equations (7.11) to define the home country's payoff function as

$$P(t, t^*) := U\{Y[X(t, t^*), Z(t, t^*)] - [X(t, t^*) - x_0] \cdot R(t, t^*), Z(t, t^*)\}. \tag{7.13}$$

The foreign country's payoff function $P^*(t, t^*)$ is determined in a symmetric way. The tuple $(\hat{t}, \hat{t}*)$ constitutes a Cournot–Nash equilibrium, if $P(\hat{t}, \hat{t}*) \geq P(t, \hat{t}*)$, all t, and $P^*(\hat{t}, \hat{t}^*) \geq P^*(\hat{t}, t^*)$, all t^*. To characterize an equilibrium allocation $\hat{x} = X(\hat{t}, \hat{t}^*)$, $\hat{x}^* = X^*(\hat{t}, \hat{t}^*)$, $\hat{z} = Z(\hat{t}, \hat{t}^*)$, and $\hat{z}^* = Z^*(\hat{t}, \hat{t}^*)$ we maximize[6] $P(t, \hat{t}^*)$ with respect to t and $P^*(\hat{t}, t^*)$ with respect to t^*. An interior solution satisfies (Rauscher, 1991)

$$t = Y_z = -\frac{U_z}{U_c} + (x - x_0) \cdot \frac{dr}{dz} \quad \text{and} \quad t^* = Y_z^* = -\frac{U_z^*}{U_c^*} + (x^* - x_0^*) \cdot \frac{dr^*}{dz^*}, \quad (7.14)$$

where

$$\frac{dr}{dz} := \frac{U_t}{Z_t} = \frac{\sigma Y_{yz}(Y_{xx}^* Y_{zz}^* - Y_{xz}^{*2})}{Y_{xx} Y_{zz}^* + \sigma(Y_{xx}^* Y_{zz}^* - Y_{xz}^{*2})} > 0 \text{ and}$$

$$\frac{dr^*}{dz^*} := \frac{R_{t^*}^*}{Z_{t^*}^*} = \frac{Y_{xt}^*(Y_{xx} Y_{zz} - Y_{zx}^2)}{\sigma Y_{xx}^* Y_{zz} + (Y_{xx} Y_{zz} - Y_{zx}^2)} > 0.$$

The equations (7.14) differ from (7.4) because now each unit of emissions has an additional (beneficial or detrimental) effect: it raises domestic capital income from foreign investment $(= (x - x_0) \cdot (dr/dz) > 0)$ in the case that $x < x_0$ or it reduces domestic income by increasing the bill for imported capital in the case of $x > x_0$. An analogous argument applies to the foreign country.

1. Result 3
Suppose, the production-emissions technology is given by (7.1); capital is mobile between both countries; and each country considers its impact on the rental rate of capital as non-negligible.

(a) *The capital-exporting country sets its emissions tax rate at an inefficiently low level and the capital-importing country sets it at an inefficiently high level. In view of (7.11), the capital-exporting (importing) country's emissions level is higher (lower) and its capital export (import) is lower (higher) than in the case of non-strategic behavior.*[7]

(b) *A country's strategic potential of advantageous distortions as measured by the distortive effects* $(x - x_0) \cdot (dr^*/dz^*)$ *and* $(x^* - x_0^*)(dr^*/dz^*)$ *and in equations (7.14) is c.p. the smaller, the smaller is the home country in terms of labor endowment relative to the other country.*

Result 3a does not reflect the popular argument of ecological dumping according to which a country chooses an inefficiently lax environmental policy in order to attract foreign capital. On the contrary, it is advantageous for the capital-exporting country to raise its pollution above the Pigouvian level because relaxing the emissions standard increases the return on its capital working abroad. Conversely, the capital-importing country strengthens its environmental policy in an effort to reduce the bill to be paid on imported capital. As a result, the volume of international capital transaction is less than optimal, whereas the intuitive idea of ecological dumping seems to imply excessive international capital flows into 'pollution havens'.

Result 3b shows that small countries tend to apply Pigouvian emissions tax rates while (very) large countries tend to assume the role of Stackelberg leaders. It is our conjecture that if, in a multi-country setting, all countries are relatively small with respect to the rest of the world, then the corresponding Cournot–Nash equilibrium of strategic environmental policies will be close to the solution where all countries pursue non-strategic Pigouvian policies.

Result 3a is illustrated in Figure 7.2 for the case that in autarky $r_0 < r_0^*$ and $z_0 > z_0^*$. It is also assumed that the marginal damage of pollution $[MD(z) = -U_z/U_c]$ is the same in both countries and depends only on the level of emissions – as is the case when the utility functions are quasi-linear. In Figure 7.2 this initial situation is represented by the points A and A' for the

Figure 7.2: Environmental policy distortions in the Cournot-Nash equilibrium

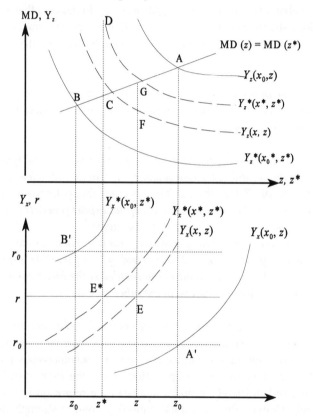

home country and by B and B' for the foreign country. The allocation of the Cournot–Nash equilibrium $(\hat{x}, \hat{x}^*, \hat{z}, \hat{z}^*)$ satisfies $\hat{x} < x_0$, $\hat{x}^* > x_0^*$, $\hat{z} < z_0$ and $\hat{z}^* > z_0^*$. It is characterized by the points E and F for the home country and by E* and D for the foreign country. Observe also that $GF = MD(\hat{z}) - Y_z(\hat{x}, \hat{z}) > 0$ and $DC = Y_z^*(\hat{x}^*, \hat{z}^*) - MD(\hat{z}^*) > 0$ in conformity with (7.14).

Figure 7.2 depicts a situation that is compatible with the Cournot–Nash equilibrium conditions. But it cannot be concluded from this illustration that the equilibrium always satisfies $\hat{z} < \hat{z}_0$ and $z_0^* < \hat{z}^*$ if $(\hat{x}, \hat{x}^*, \hat{z}, \hat{z}^*)$ is the Cournot–Nash equilibrium with $\hat{x} < x_0$, $\hat{x}^* > x_0^*$, $r_0 < r_0^*$. Note, however, that with the help of Figure 7.2 it is possible to establish the following proposition.

2. Result 4

Suppose that $(-U_z/U_c) = MD(z)$ and $(-U_z^*/U_c^*) = MD^*(z^*)$ with $MD_z > 0$ and $MD_z^* > 0$ as in Figure 7.2. Assume also that the home country exports capital in the Cournot–Nash equilibrium $(\hat{x}, \hat{x}^*, \hat{z}, \hat{z}^*)$. Then the home country's emissions tax rate is higher than in the autarkic situation.

To see this, observe first that $Y_z(x_0, \cdot) > Y_z(\hat{x}, \cdot)$ and $Y_z^*(x_0^*, \cdot) < Y_z^*(\hat{x},^*, \cdot)$. Moreover, owing to (7.14) the equilibrium fulfils $MD(\hat{z}) > Y_z(\hat{x}, \hat{z})$ and $MD^*(\hat{z}^*) < Y_z^*(\hat{x}^*, \hat{z}^*)$. In view of $MD_z > 0$, $MD_z^* > 0$ these properties yield the Result 4. Note, however, that the tax rate reduction of the capital-exporting country does not necessarily imply a lower environmental quality. Figure 7.2 illustrates the possibility of an increase in environmental quality.

Unfortunately, it is very difficult to elicit additional properties of the Cournot–Nash equilibrium, because these depend on many second- and third-order effects of production technologies. Rauscher (1991) offers some additional important insights but, in general, neither the slopes of the reaction curves can be determined nor can we exclude multiple equilibria. It is very important to understand better what the strategic distortions of the Cournot–Nash equilibrium are like, in particular how environmental quality differs from that in autarky or from its welfare-maximal level when capital is mobile. Therefore, these issues are taken up again in the next section on the basis of a different production-emissions technology that lends itself more readily to simplifying parameterizations.

D. Information-Constrained Tax or Standard Policies

After having investigated the optimal non-cooperative environmental control under full information we now turn to the price-and-standard approach. Here we do not intend to offer a systematic descriptive or normative analysis of how countries determine their tax rates or emissions standards. Rather we are interested in the repercussions through the international capital market of some simple ad hoc environmental policy strategies either when international capital transactions are liberalized or when the initial situation is already characterized by a perfectly competitive international market).[8]

Consider first the case of a small open economy that reacts as a price-taker to both the emissions tax rate and the world rental rate of capital by setting $t = Y_z(x, z)$ and $r = Y_x(x, z)$. Closer inspection (Appendix 7A.3) yields:

1. Result 5
Suppose the real price of capital increases parametrically.

(a) *If the country keeps its emissions tax rate constant, then its capital exports expands or its capital imports shrink, and its environmental quality improves. The change in welfare is ambiguous.*

(b) *If the country keeps its emissions standard constant by appropriate adjustments of the emissions tax rate, then its capital exports increase or its capital imports diminish as described in Result 5a, but by a smaller amount. This policy is welfare-enhancing if the country invests abroad, but it reduces welfare otherwise.*

In the two-country world, the capital market interdependence is given by (7.11) and (7.12) as shown above. Based on (7.11) it is possible to assess the consequences of different environmental strategies in the process of transition from autarky to full international capital mobility.

2. Result 6
Let the autarkic equilibrium be given by (r_0, t_0, x_0, z_0) in the home country and by $(r_0^*, t_0^*, x_0^*, z_0^*)$ in the foreign country, and let $r_0 > r_0^*$ hold.

(a) *Suppose that after capital market liberalization both countries stick to their emissions tax rates t_0 and t_0^*, respectively. Then*
   – $X(t_0, t_0^*) > x_0$ and $X^*(t_0, t_0^*) < x_0^*$
   – $Z(t_0, t_0^*) > z_0$ and $Z^*(t_0, t_0^*) < z_0^*$;
   – the change in welfare of both countries is ambiguous.

(b) *Suppose that after capital market liberalization both countries stick to their emissions standards z_0 and z_0^*, respectively, by adapting their emissions tax rates appropriately. Denote by t_1 and t_1^* the emissions tax rates at the new equilibrium. Then*
   – $t_1 > t_0$ and $t_1^* < t_0^*$;
   –$X(t_1, t_1^*) > x_0$ and $X^*(t_1, t_1^*) < x_0^*$
   –the home country's welfare increases, and the foreign country's welfare deteriorates.

(c) *Suppose that after capital market liberalization the home country sticks to its emissions tax rate t_0 and the foreign country maintains its emissions standard z_0^*. Then*
   –$X(t_0, t_1^*) > x_0^*$ and $X^*(t_0, t_1^*) < x_0^*$;

$-Z(t_0, t_1^*) > x_0$ *and* $t_1^* < t_0^*$;
- *the home country's change in welfare is ambiguous, and the foreign country's welfare deteriorates.*

To prove the welfare implications of Result 6 we use (7.9) and determine the home country's change in consumption as

$$c - c_0 = \Delta C(x,z) := Y(x,z) - Y(x_0,z_0) - (x-x_0)Y_x(x,z).$$

Clearly, one has $\Delta C(x_0,z) > 0$ for all $z > z_0$ and $\Delta C(x,z_1) > 0$ for all $x > x_0$ and for all $z_1 \geq z_0$. Hence $\Delta C(x_1,z_1) > 0$ whenever $x_1 > x_0$ and $z_1 \geq z_0$. A similar argument applies with respect to the foreign country.

The striking feature of all these policies is that one of the countries or even both may incur a welfare loss after capital market liberalization. The 'risk' of becoming worse off seems to be greater for the capital-exporting country. The

Figure 7.3: Capital market liberalizations with constant emissions standards

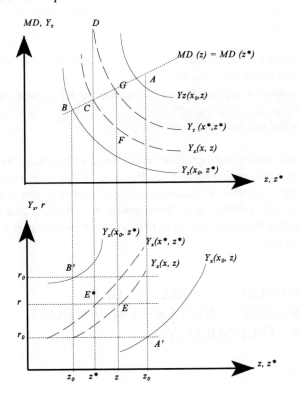

intuition for that is not clear, in particular not for the situation in which both countries stick to their autarkic emissions standards (Result 6b). This case is illustrated in Figure 7.3 where the autarkic situation is given by A_0 and A_0' for the home country and by A_0^* and $A_0^{*\prime}$ for the foreign country (implying $r_0 > r_0^*$ and $t_0 < t_0^*$). The new equilibrium with mobile capital is characterized by the equilibrium price r_1 and by the new tax rates t_1 and t_1^* satisfying $t_1 > t_1^*, t_1 > t_0$ and $t_1^* < t_0^*$.

Suppose finally, capital is already perfectly mobile in the initial situation, each country chooses its emissions tax rate, and the international capital market is in equilibrium. In such a situation, one of the countries may want to change its tax rate. The consequences of that policy can be easily inferred from (7.11) and (7.12):

3. Result 7

Suppose the international capital market is in equilibrium and the foreign country keeps its emissions tax rate constant while the home country increases its own emissions tax rate. Then[9]

(a) *the environmental quality improves in the home country, and it deteriorates in the foreign country;*

(b) *the home country's capital import is reduced or its capital export expanded;*

(c) *the world rental rate on capital decreases.*

These observations conform with intuition: if in a world with perfectly mobile capital a country wants to improve its environment, it has to increase its emissions tax rate. In contrast to the case of a closed economy, this induces capital to leave the country thus deteriorating the foreign country's environmental quality if this country sticks to its initial emissions tax rate (i.e. if it does not 'retaliate')

CAPITAL MOBILITY IN THE CASE OF POLLUTION-GENERATING CAPITAL WITHOUT ABATEMENT TECHNOLOGY

A. The Model

We now consider an alternative production-emissions technology which has been used, e.g., by Gronych (1980) and Long and Siebert (1991):

$$y = F(k, \ell)\ell =: Y(x) \quad \text{and} \quad z = E(x) \quad \text{with} \quad E_{xx} \geq 0. \tag{7.15}$$
$$_{+\ +}\phantom{)\ell =: Y(x) \quad \text{and} \quad}_{+}\phantom{E(x) \quad \text{with} \quad}_{+}$$

As in the previous section, the (home) country produces a single consumption good with the inputs labor, ℓ, and capital, k. Per-capita output, $Y(x)$, and per-capita emissions, $E(x)$, depend on the capital–labor ratio, x, and pollutants are generated and discharged in strict correlation with the use of capital. Input-determined pollutants, often even in fixed relation ($E_{xx} = 0$), are typical for chemical processes, but in many cases the input use does not determine the amount of pollutants *emitted* when emissions can be reduced or avoided by technical devices such as end-of-pipe abatement technologies or integrated emissions reduction technologies.[10] But there is a meaningful (aggregate) interpretation of the technology (7.15) if one considers the variable z as that part of the total natural environment which is destroyed in the process of industrialization or capitalization by turning natural resources such as wild life habitats, forests etc. into industrial sites.

In the closed economy the efficient allocation is easily determined by maximizing (7.2) under consideration of (7.15), $\ell \leq \ell_o$, $k \leq k_0$, and $c \leq Y(x)$. Since emissions cannot be abated, any reduction of the emissions standard (at full employment of labor) requires the reduction of the use of capital. If the damaging effect of pollution is very severe, it may even be optimal not to use the entire capital stock. But idle capital and a rental rate of zero appears to be an unrealistic scenario. Therefore we restrict our attention to those solutions of the constrained maximization problem for which the marginal damage of pollution $(-U_z/U_c)$, is less than the implicit marginal productivity of emissions (Y_x/E_x). This implies, in turn, that the efficient real rental rate (shadow price) of capital is positive:[11]

$$r = Y_x - \left[-\frac{U_z}{U_c} \right] \cdot E_x > 0. \tag{7.16}$$

The efficient allocation is implemented by levying the Pigouvian emissions tax at the (per-capita) rate $t = (-U_z/U_c)$.

B.   Non-Strategic Environmental Policy

Consider first the home country as a 'small open economy'. If this country pursues a non-strategic environmental policy under perfect information, it maximizes (7.2) subject to $\ell \leq \ell_0$, (7.15) and

$$c = Y(x) - (x - x_0) \cdot r \tag{7.17}$$

which yields the condition (7.16), as expected. The comparative statics (Appendix 7A.4) give rise to the following major conclusions.

1. Result 8

Denote by $T(r)$, $X(r)$ *and* $Z(r)$ *the values of* t, x *and* z, *respectively, that are determined as functions of the world price of capital,* r, *through the equations (7.15), (7.16) and (7.17). A small exogenous change of* r *has the following consequences:*

(a)　$T_r < 0$ *and* $X_r < 0$ *(and hence* $Z_r < 0$*)*
　　　(α) *if before the change in* r *the country's international capital transaction is zero or 'sufficiently' small;*
　　　(β) *if the utility function U is quasi-concave (i.e.* $U_{cc} = U_{cz} = 0$*);*
(b)　T_r *ambiguous in sign and* $X_r < 0$ *(and hence* $Z_r < 0$*), if the country exports capital and* U *is not quasi-concave;*
(c)　T_r *and* X_r *(and hence* Z_r*) ambiguous in sign, if the country imports capital and* U *is not quasi-concave.*

The comparison of the Results 1 and 8 shows a few divergences and, on the whole, many similarities. In both cases, the ambiguities are more pronounced for the capital-importing than for the capital-exporting country. With technology (7.15) the directions of change of the tax rate and the emissions standard are hardly more predictable than with (7.1) except in case of quasi-linear preferences. Under technology (7.1) it is not always optimal to change the capital use and total emissions (standards) in the same direction as is trivially the case with technology (7.15).

It is instructive to illustrate Result 8 with the following parametric version of the model (used by Long and Siebert (1991) in a different context):

$$U(c,z) = -\frac{e}{2} \cdot z^2 + c, \quad Y(x) = ax - \frac{1}{2} \cdot x^2, \quad E(x) = x. \quad (7.18)$$

With these simplifications it is straightforward that equation (16) is turned into $r_0 := a - (1 + e) \cdot x_0$ for the closed economy.[12] If capital is mobile and the country under consideration is small, equation (7.18) implies that the representative consumer's utility is $U(c,z) = U(x) = -[(1 + e)/2] \cdot x^2 + (a - r) \cdot c + x_0 r$, and the country chooses its capital-labor ratio in such a way that $r = a - (1 + e) \cdot x$. Subtract $r_0 = a - (1 + e) \cdot x_0$ from the last equation to obtain

$$x - x_0 = \frac{r_0 - r}{1 + e} \quad \text{and} \quad t - t_0 = \frac{(r_0 - r) \cdot e}{1 + e}. \quad (7.19)$$

The equations (7.19) are related to Result 8aβ telling us that efficiency requires the lowering of the tax rate relative to its autarkic level in the capital-exporting country and the increasing of it in the other country. Though Result 8 refers to *marginal* exogenous changes in *r* only and hence relates to the country's adjustments when capital was already mobile in the initial situation, the more restrictive parametric model also allows the assessment of the *non-marginal* impacts of the transition from autarky to international capital mobility.

In the two-country model, capital mobility is given by the constraint (7.7), and the market-clearing rate of return on capital is determined by $\sigma_0 = \sigma X(r) + X^*(r)$ with X and X^* as defined in Result 8. The analog to Result 2 is

2. **Result 9** (Long and Siebert 1991)

In the two-country model, an efficient international allocation of resources is characterized by

$$r = Y_x + \left[\frac{U_z}{U_c}\right] \cdot E_x = Y_x^* + \left[\frac{U_z^*}{U_c^*}\right] \cdot E_x^*. \tag{7.20}$$

It can be attained by a perfectly competitive capital market and by non-cooperative non-strategic national environmental tax policies with rates

$$t = -\frac{U_z}{U_c} \quad and \quad t^* = -\frac{U_z^*}{U_c^*}. \tag{7.21}$$

To obtain more specific information about the efficient allocation (and for later reference in the next section) we employ again the parametric model (7.18). To keep the analysis simple, we also set $\ell_0 = \ell_0^*$ implying $x_0 + x_0^* = x + x^*$ in view of (7.7). Thus it is possible, after some rearrangement of terms, to rewrite equation (7.20) as:

$$\Delta x = \frac{\Delta a + (1 + e^*) \cdot x_0^* - (1 + e) \cdot x_0}{2 + e + e^*} \quad and \quad \Delta t = e \cdot \Delta x, \tag{7.22}$$

where $\Delta a := a - a^*$, $\Delta x := x - x_0$ and $\Delta t := t - t_0 = ex - ex_0$. It is easy to see from (22) that if the countries are identical ($\Delta a = 0$, $e = e^*$, $x_0^* = x_0$) the autarky position with zero capital transactions is efficient. With the help of equation (7.22) the influence of pollution damage on international capital flows can be clarified. If technologies do not differ ($\Delta a = 0$) and the home country is capital-poor ($x_0 < x_0^*$), this country would import capital if emissions were harmless ($e = e^* = 0$). But with harmful pollution the home country may well export capital if the preferences of its citizens are sufficiently greener than those of the other country's citizens.[13]

Table 7.1: Comparative statics

shock → response ↓	$\Delta(a-a^{*})$	Δx_0	Δx_0^{*}	Δe	Δe^{*}
$\Delta z = \Delta x$	+	−	+	−	+
$\Delta t = -\Delta t^{*}$	+	−	+	−	+

Suppose now, the countries are identical initially and then one (and only one) parameter for either country changes. The resultant efficient displacement effects are shown in Table 7.1. It is worth emphasizing that the efficient response is always to move both emissions standards and emissions tax rates into the same direction.

Next we show that the transition from autarky to the efficient international allocation of capital is advantageous for both countries. To see that we consider $P(t, t^{*})$ from (7.26) which is derived below for a different purpose. In (7.26) we replace $X(t, t^{*})$ simply by x, and we set t at its efficient level $t = ex$. This gives us, after some rearrangement of terms, $W(x) := a \cdot x_0 - (1+e) \cdot x_0 \cdot x + [(1+e)/2] \cdot x^2$. On the other hand, in autarky the utility of a domestic citizen is $u_0 := ax_0 - [(1+e)/2] x_0^2$. The difference turns out to be $W(x) - u_0 = [(1+e)/2] \cdot (x - x_0)^2 > 0$ independent of whether the country under consideration is importing or exporting capital.

C. Strategic Environmental Policy

In what follows we want to show that the rule (7.21) is not incentive compatible. As before, we proceed by allowing the countries to fix their tax rates at arbitrary levels to find out whether their self-interest leads them to choose the rate according to rule (7.21). Again, the two countries play a non-cooperative game with emissions tax rates as their strategies. To see the impacts of these policies on the international capital market notice that the capital market equilibrium is characterized by

$$Y_x(x) - tE_x(x) = Y_x^{*}(x^{*}) - t^{*}E_x^{*}(x^{*}). \tag{7.23}$$

The equations (7.7) and (7.23) determine the variables x and x^{*} for each tuple (t, t^{*})

$$x = X(t, t^{*}), \ x^{*} = X^{*}(t, t^{*}) \ \text{and} \ r = R(t, t^{*}) := Y_x[X(t, t^{*})] - tE_x[X(t, t^{*})]. \tag{7.24}$$

If $x = X(t, t^{*})$ is considered in (7.15) and in

$$c = Y(x) - (x - x_0)[Y_x(x) - t \cdot E_x(x)], \tag{7.25}$$

the utility function (7.2) is turned into the home country's payoff function

$$P(t, t^*) = U\{Y[X(t, t^*)] - [X(t, t^*) - x_0] \cdot R(t, t^*), E[X(t, t^*)]\}. \tag{7.26}$$

In a symmetric way, the payoff function $P^*(t, t^*)$ of the foreign country can be derived. The 'best-reply' first-order conditions $P_t(t, t^*) = 0$ and $P_{t^*}^*(t, t^*) = 0$ yield at an interior solution (Appendix 7A.5)

$$t = -\frac{U_z}{U_c} + (x - x_0) \cdot \frac{dr}{dz} \quad \text{and} \quad t^* = -\frac{U_z^*}{U_c^*} + (x^* - x_0^*) \cdot \frac{dr^*}{dz^*} \tag{7.27}$$

where
$$\frac{dr}{dz} := \frac{R_t}{Z_t} = \frac{t^* E_{xx}^* - \sigma Y_{xx}}{E_x} > 0 \quad \text{and} \quad \frac{dr^*}{dz^*} := \frac{R_t^*}{Z_t^*} = \frac{t E_{xx} - \sigma Y_{xx}^*}{E_x^*} > 0.$$

1. Result 10

Suppose, the production-emissions technology (7.15) applies and capital is mobile between two countries each of which considers its impact on the international capital market as non-negligible, then

(a) *the capital-exporting country sets its emissions tax rate at an inefficiently low level and the capital-importing country sets it at an inefficiently high level.[14] In view of (7.24), the capital-exporting [importing] emissions level is higher [lower] and its capital export [import] is lower [higher] than in the case of non-strategic behavior.*

(b) *the strategic potential of advantageous distortions, $(x - x_0) \cdot (dr/dz)$, is c.p. the smaller, the smaller is the home country's labor endowment relative to that of the other country and the greater is the number of countries among which capital is mobile. It tends to zero only if ℓ_0/ℓ_0^* tends to zero and E_{xx}^* or t^* is zero.*

To obtain more specific information on the allocation reached by using environmental policies strategically, we wish to solve the non-cooperative game for the parametric model (7.18). For notational simplicity we assume $\ell_0 = \ell_0^*$ which implies $\sigma = 1$ and $\sigma_0 = x_0 + x_0^*$ (with and σ and σ_0 as defined in (7.7)). To derive the home country's reaction function $t = T(t^*)$ that is implicitly given by the condition $P_t(t, t^*) = 0$ we rewrite (7.24) with the help of (7.18) as

$$X(t, t^*) := \frac{x_0^* + x_0 + \Delta a}{2} - \frac{1}{2} \cdot t + \frac{1}{2} \cdot t^*, \tag{7.28}$$

where $\Delta a := a - a^*$. The payoff function (7.26) is turned into

$$P(t, t^*) := \frac{1 - e}{2} \cdot [X(t, t^*)]^2 - (x_0 - t) \cdot X(t, t^*) - x_0 t + a x_0. \tag{7.29}$$

The derivatives of this function are

$$P_t = \frac{1+e}{2} \cdot X(t, t^*) - \frac{t+x_0}{2}, \text{ and } P_{tt} = -\frac{3+e}{4} < 0, \quad (7.30)$$

$$P_{t^*} = \frac{1-e}{2} \cdot X(t, t^*) + \frac{t-x_0}{2}, \ P_{t^*t^*} = \frac{1-e}{4} \lessgtr 0 \leftrightarrow e \gtrless 1. \quad (7.30a)$$

In view of (7.28) and (7.30a) the home country's best-reply function is

$$T(t^*) := \frac{(1+e)(x_0^* + \Delta a) - (1-e)x_0}{3+e} + \frac{1+e}{3+e} \cdot t^*. \quad (7.31)$$

The foreign country's best-reply function $t^* = T^*(t)$ follows from analogous calculations. The Cournot-Nash equilibrium $\{t = T[T^*(t)], \ t^* = T^*[T(t^*)]\}$ turns out to be

$$t = \frac{(1+e)[(1+e^*)x_0^* + \Delta a] + (2e + ee^* - 1)x_0}{4 + e^* + e},$$
$$t^* = \frac{(1+e^*)[(1+e)x_0 + \Delta a^*] + (2e^* + ee^* - 1)x_0^*}{4 + e^* + e}. \quad (7.32)$$

As before, we use $\Delta x := x - x_0$ and $\Delta t := t - t_0$ with $t_0 = ex_0$ (autarky) to rewrite (7.28) and (7.32):

$$\Delta x = \frac{\Delta a + (1 + e^*)1)x_0^* - (1 + e)x_0}{4 + e + e^*} \text{ and } \Delta t = (1 + e) \cdot \Delta x. \quad (7.33)$$

The comparison of the equations (7.22) and (7.33) gives rise to the following observations (Appendix 7A.6):

2. Result 11

Under perfect information, the lack of international environmental policy coordination has the following effects:

(a) *the direction of change in capital use, emissions standards and emissions tax rates, following exogeneous parameter shifts, is always efficient (as given by Table 7.1);*

(b) *the international capital investment is inefficiently low;*

(c) *the emissions tax rates are inefficiently high in both countries, if and only if $(e - e^*) \in (-2, 2)$, i.e. if the international differences in 'greenness' of preferences are not too large;*

(d) *the welfare of the capital-importing country decreases and that of the other country improves.*

To see the rationale of Result 11d observe first that (7.26) and (7.31) imply

$$\frac{\partial P[T(t^*),t^*]}{\partial t^*} = \frac{(2+e)(x-x_0)+(t-ex)}{(3+e)} \gtreqless 0 \leftrightarrow \gtreqless x_0. \tag{7.34}$$

The corresponding property holds for the foreign country. To determine the point on the best-reply curves where no capital is traded recall that in view of (7.28)

$$X \gtreqless x_0 \text{ and } x^* \lesseqgtr x_0^* \leftrightarrow t \lesseqgtr \Delta a - x_0 + x_0^* + t^*.$$

Suppose, without loss of generality, the Cournot–Nash equilibrium (T_{CN}, t_{CN}^*) satifies $t_{CN} < \Delta a - x_0 + x_0^* + t_{CN}^*$, i.e., the point of intersection of the best-reply curves is located below the line $t = \Delta a - x_0 + x_0^* + t^*$. This situation is drawn in Figure 7.4 where the graphs of the functions $t = T(t^*)$, $t^* = T^*(t)$ and $t = \Delta a - x_0 + x_0^* + t^*$, respectively, are given by CF, GL, and AB. If the line AB intersects CF in point D, as shown in Figure 7.4, the allocation in D is characterized by $x = x_0$ and $t = (-U_z/U_c)$ owing to (7.27). Hence the home country's payoff in D is that of the Pareto-efficient allocation in autarky. Owing to condition (7.34) the home country's payoff decreases along CF in the direction of F so that the payoff in E is less than in D. If AB does not intersect CF the home country's autarkic welfare is even higher than its payoff in point A. Therefore we conclude that the capital-importing countrys welfare decreases.

Figure 7.4: Cournot–Nash equilibrium in the parametric model

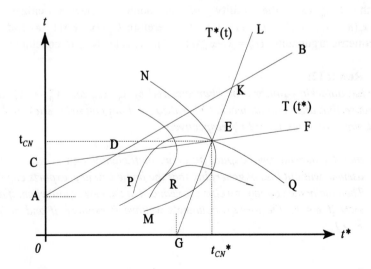

Consider now the situation of the foreign country. Since the slope of AB is steeper than that of GL (tan $\alpha = 1 >$ tan β) these two straight lines always intersect at a point to the left of E such as point K. The foreign country's payoff in K represents its maximum welfare in autarky. But along GL from K towards G the foreign country's welfare increases. Hence its payoff in E is greater than in K.

The payoff indifference curves are difficult to characterize. But if $(e - e^*) \in (-2, 2)$, Result 11c implies that they are shaped as drawn in Figure 7.4, because then the equilibrium tax rates (in point E) are too high as compared with an efficient allocation, such as point R in Figure 7.4.

Result 11 presents us with several surprises: even though the tax rates are too high in both countries, the capital-exporting country pollutes too much and its foreign investment is too small. It appears to be counter-intuitive that the capital-importing country gets worse off after trade liberalization because the technology is such that with its foreign investment it also exports pollution. But apparently, the welfare gain from a cleaner environment is overcompensated by the reduction in welfare from real domestic income.

D.   Information-Constrained Tax Policies

Suppose now, information is imperfect and the countries follow the rule of maintaining their emissions tax rates after capital market liberalization.[15] To fix our ideas let $t = t_0 = ex_0$ and $t^* = t_0^* = e^* x_0^*$ (ad hoc). Then equation (28) is turned into

$$\Delta x = \frac{\Delta a + (1 + e^*) x_0^* - (1 + e) x_0}{2} \tag{7.35}$$

With $t = t_0 = ex_0$ the utility of a home country's citizen is $u = x_0(a - ex_0) - x_0(1 - e)x + (1 - e)x^2/2$. Therefore $U_x = (x - x_0)(1 - e)$ and, via symmetric arguments, $U_x^* = (x - x_0^*)(1 - e^*)$. This leads us to conclude:

1.   Result 12:
Let the autarkic equilibria be characterized by $t_0 = ex_0$ *and* $t_0^* = e^* x_0^*$ *and suppose that after capital market liberalization both countries stick to their emissions tax rates* t_0 *and* t_0^*, *respectively.*

(a)   *then the international capital flows are inefficiently high.*
(b)   *assume without loss of generality that the home country exports capital. Then the home country's welfare is reduced at the new equilibrium, if and only if* $e < 1$; *the foreign country's welfare is reduced if and only if* $e^* > 1$.

It is interesting to observe that in Result 12b the direction of welfare change does not depend on the assumption that both countries stick to their autarkic tax rates. Consequently, if the home country expects to export capital after capital liberalization and suffers heavily from pollution ($e > 1$) it should be advised not to play its Cournot–Nash strategy but rather the strategy $t = ex_0$.

Suppose, as before, that capital is already perfectly mobile in the initial situation, that each country has chosen its emissions tax rate, and that the international capital market is in equilibrium. What happens if one of the countries changes its tax rate?

2. Result 13
Suppose the production-emissions technology is given by (7.15), the international capital market is in equilibrium and the foreign country keeps its emissions tax rate constant while the home country increases its own emissions tax rate. Then

(a) *the environmental quality improves in the home country, and deteriorates in the foreign country;*
(b) *the home country's capital export is reduced or its capital import expanded;*
(c) *the impact on the world rental rate of capital is ambiguous.*

CONCLUDING REMARKS

It has been shown that, in the case of mobile capital, internationally uncoordinated national environmental policies induce allocative distortions when countries are self-interested under perfect information. Long and Siebert (1991, p. 307) may be right 'that the possibility of manipulating environmental policy instruments is an interesting case for the theoretician but not of practical relevance'. However, the existence of strategic potential means that benevolent governments do have an incentive to behave strategically. Whether they have sufficient information to take advantage of this potential or whether their 'environmental policy should not be overloaded with strategic non-environmental targets' (Long and Siebert, 1991, p. 307) are quite different issues.

In the 'strategic' non-cooperative equilibrium at least one country may be worse off after market liberalization than in autarky as demonstrated in the previous section. Hence there is scope for international coordination of national environmental policies which reintroduces the question, of course, how the supranational agency gets all the necessary information on national environmental damages and abatement costs and on the operation of the international capital market to do a better job than the non-cooperating countries.

Our analysis also showed that even if the countries under consideration do not have at their disposal all information necessary for successful strategic manipulation, the countries' interdependence via non-cooperative national environmental policies has important international repercussions. This is true in the case of adjusting environmental policy when capital becomes (more) mobile, but also when one country makes a change in its policy while capital is already perfectly mobile.

All these issues have been scrutinized for two different types of production-emissions technologies. The principal motivation for that double-track procedure was that both technologies capture relevant aspects of the complex reality, and therefore it is important to know how the implications differ. It turned out that the conclusions are fairly robust with respect to the alternative modeling approaches. The phenomenon of 'ecological dumping', if interpreted as advantageous distortive use of environmental policy, is qualitatively the same under both production-emissions technologies. Moreover, regarding the non-cooperative game of strategic environmental policies under perfect information the parametric version of the first model produced much more specific results than the second model.

NOTES

1. Siebert et al. (1980) investigate a neoclassical two-country, two-commodity, two-factor model with both international commodity trade *and* capital transactions.
2. An illuminating example is a recent bill on taxation of firms in Germany. The official reason given for that amendent was to secure the competitiveness of Germany as 'location for industry' (*Standortsicherungsgesetz*) in view of trends of tax legislation in countries that are Germany's major trading partners.
3. The plus or minus sign underneath an argument of a function indicates the sign of the respective partial derivative. Functions are generally represented by upper case letters, and subscripts to functions denote partial derivatives with respect to the argument that is used as subscript.
4. Under perfect information one can also interpret such a policy as being implemented by majority voting – which is known to be Pareto-efficient when all individuals are identical.
5. In view of (7.7) (as an equality) and (7.9) it is easy to check that total consumption equals total production, i.e. $\ell_0 c + \ell_0^* c^* = \ell_0 y + \ell_0^* y^*$.
6. In general, the functions P and P^* are not concave in t and t^*, respectively. Rauscher (1991) shows that if emissions standards are taken as environmental policy instruments (rather than tax rates) concavity can be established if all third-order derivatives of production functions vanish.
7. For more details and economic interpretations see Rauscher (1991).
8. Similar considerations are made in Rauscher (1992a, 226 – 31).
9. All subsequent results are symmetric with respect to reductions rather than increases of the home country's emissions tax rate and with respect to interchanging the role of both countries.
10. An example where abatement devices are not available appears to be CO_2 emissions from burning fossil fuels. But this case is inappropriate for the purpose of the present chapter for two reasons: first, there is no' clear link between CO_2 emissions and international capital investments and, second, the pollution emerging from CO_2 releases is global (warming) while we focus on strictly 'national' pollution in order not to mix different causes of itnernqational environmental interdependence.

11. In formal terms, one maximizes the unconstrained function $V(x) := U[Y(x), E(x)]$ and assumes that $V_x(x) > 0$ for $x = x_0$. Economically speaking, the assumption $V_x(x_0) > 0$ means that the country suffers from an under-supply of capital.
12. As before we assume that $r_0 > 0$ so that the parameters a, e, and x_0 are restricted to the half space $a > (1 + e) \cdot x_0$.
13. More specifically, if the home country is capital-poor $(x_0 < x_0^*)$ and productivities are the same $(\Delta a = 0)$ it will export capital if and only if $(1 + e)/(1 + e^*) > (x_0^*/x_0) > 1$.
14. Long and Siebert (1991) reach this conclusion in a similar model in which environmental protection agencies maximize real domestic income and are free to choose emissions tax rates as a fraction of the (true) marginal damage costs.
15. In view of technology (7.15) the strategy of maintaining the autarkic emissions standards or introducing other standards, as discussed in the previous section, would amount to introducing direct capital market controls.

REFERENCES

Baumol, William J., and Wallace E. Oates (1971), 'The use of standards and prices for the protection of the environment', *Swedish Journal of Economics* 73.

Conrad, Klaus (1993), 'Optimal environmental policy for oligopolistic industries in an open economy', University of Mannheim, Germany, mimeograph.

Gronych, Ralf (1980), *Allokationseffekte und Au enhandelswirkungen der Umweltpolitik*, J.C.B. Mohr (Paul Siebeck), Tübingen.

Kennedy, Peter W. (1993), 'Equilibrium pollution taxes in open economies with imperfect competition', University of Victoria, Canada, mimeograph.

Krugman, Paul R. (1989), 'Industrial organization and international trade', in: Schmalensee, R. and Willig, R.D. (eds), *Handbook of Industrial Organization*, Vol. II, Elsevier, Amsterdam, 1179–1223.

Krutilla, K. (1991), 'Environmental regulation in an open economy', *Journal of Environmental Economics and Management* 20, 127–142.

Long, N.V. and Horst Siebert (1991), 'Institutional competition versus ex-ante harmonization: The case of environmental policy', *Journal of Institutional and Theoretical Economics* 147, 296–312.

Oates, Wallace E., and Robert M. Schwab (1988), 'Economic competition among jurisdictions: Efficiency enhancing or distortion inducing?', *Journal of Public Economics* 35, 333–354.

Markusen, J.R. (1975a), 'Cooperative control of international pollution and common property resources', *Quarterly Journal of Economics* 89, 618–32.

Markusen, J.R. (1975b), 'International externalities and optimal tax structures', *Journal of International Economics* 5, 15–29.

OECD (ed.) (1974), *Problems in Transfrontier Pollution*, Paris.

Pethig, Rüdiger (1976), 'Pollution, welfare and environmental policy in the theory of comparative advantage', *Journal of Environmental Economics and Management* 2, 160–169.

Pethig, Rüdiger (1981), 'Reciprocal transfrontier pollution', in: Siebert, Horst (ed.), *Global Environmental Resources: The Ozone Problem*, Verlag Peter Lang, Frankfurt, 57–93.

Rauscher, Michael (1991), 'National environmental policies and the effects of economic integration', *European Journal of Political Economy* 7, 313–29.

Rauscher, Michael (1992a), 'Economic integration and the environment: Effects on members and non-members', *Environmental and Resource Economics* 2, 221–37.

Rauscher, Michael (1992b), 'Environmental policy and international capital movements', manuscript.

Siebert, Horst, Jürgen Eichberger; Ralf Gronych and Rüdiger Pethig (1980), *Trade and Environment: A Theoretical Enquiry*, Elsevier, Amsterdam et al.

Siebert, Horst (1991) 'Environmental policy and European Integration', in: Siebert, Horst (ed.), *Environmental Scarcity: The International Dimension*, J.C.B. Mohr (Paul Siebeck), Tübingen, 57–70.

Ulph, Alistair (1991), 'The choice of environmental policy instruments and strategic international trade', in: Pethig, Rüdiger (ed.), *Conflicts and Cooperation in Managing Environmental Resources*, Springer-Verlag, Berlin et al., 111–29.

APPENDIX 7A.1 PROOF OF RESULT 1

The variables x and z are determined by the equations

$$S(x, z, r) = Y_z(x, z) \quad \text{and} \quad r = Y_z(x, z), \tag{7A.1a}$$

where $s = S(x, z, r) := -\dfrac{U_z[Y(x,z)-(x-x_0)r, z]}{U_c[Y(x,z)-(x-x_0)r, z]}$. Total differentiation of (7A.1a) yields

$$\begin{bmatrix} U_c Y_{zx} & Y_c(Y_{zz}-S_z) \\ Y_{xx} & Y_{xz} \end{bmatrix} \cdot \begin{bmatrix} dx \\ dz \end{bmatrix} = \begin{bmatrix} (x-x_0)(U_{zc}+sU_{cc})\cdot dr \\ dr \end{bmatrix}, \tag{7A.1b}$$

where $S_z = -[2sU_{zc} + U_{zz} + s^2 U_{cc}]/U_c > 0$. The determinant of the above matrix is

$$D = U_c[Y_{zx}^2 - Y_{xx}U_c(Y_{zz}-S_z)] = V_{xz}^2 - V_{xx}V_{zz},$$

where the function $V: \overset{2}{+} \rightarrow$ is defined by $V(x,z) := U[Y(x,z)-(x-x_0)r, z]$. D is assumed to be negative because $V_{xx}V_{zz} - V_{xz}^2 > 0$ must be satisfied for V to be (locally) concave which is in turn necessary for the equations (7A.1a) to represent a (local) maximum. We solve the equations (7A.1b) to obtain

$$\tfrac{dx}{dr} = [(x-x_0)Y_{xz}(U_{zc}+sU_{cc}) - U_c(Y_{zz}-S_z)]/D, \tag{7A.1c}$$

$$\tfrac{dz}{dr} = [(x-x_0)Y_{xx}(U_{zc}+sU_{cc}) - U_cY_{zx}]/D, \tag{7A.1d}$$

$$\tfrac{dx}{dr} = Y_{zx}\cdot\tfrac{dx}{dr} + Y_{zz}\cdot\tfrac{dx}{dr} = [(x-x_0)(U_{zc}+sU_{cc})(Y_{xz}^2 - Y_{xx}Y_{zz}) + S_z U_c Y_{xx}]/D. \tag{7A.1e}$$

In order to demonstrate that the combined ractions $dz/dr > 0$ and $dx/dr < 0$ may be optimal we observe that (7A.1c) and (7A.1d) imply

$$\tfrac{dz}{dr} > 0 \Leftrightarrow (x-x_0) > \frac{U_c Y_{xx}}{Y_{xx}(U_{zc}+sU_{cc})} =: H > 0,$$

$$\tfrac{dx}{dr} < 0 \Leftrightarrow (x-x_0) < \frac{U_c(Y_{zz}-S_z)}{Y_{xx}(U_{zc}+sU_{cc})} =: K > 0.$$

Since K is greater than H, the interval $[H, K]$ is non-empty. Consequently,

$$\tfrac{dz}{dr} > 0 \quad \text{and} \quad \tfrac{dx}{dr} < 0 \Leftrightarrow (x-x_0) \in [H, K].$$

Suppose now, contrary to the assertion, that $dz/dr < 0$ and $dx/dr > 0$. Then $(x-x_0) < H$ and $(x-x_0) > K$. But $H < K$. Contradiction.

APPENDIX 7A.2 PARTIAL DERIVATIVES IN EQUATION (7.11)

Consider the three equations $Y_x(x, z) = Y_x^*(\sigma_0 - \sigma x, z^*)$, $Y_z(x, z) = t$ and $Y_z^*(\sigma_0 - \sigma x, z^*) = t^*$. Total differentiation yields

$$
\begin{bmatrix}
Y_{zx} & Y_{zz} & 0 \\
-\sigma Y_{zx}^* & 0 & Y_{zz}^* \\
Y_{xx} + \sigma Y_{xx}^* & Y_{xz} & -Y_{xz}^*
\end{bmatrix}
\cdot
\begin{bmatrix}
dx \\
dz \\
dz^*
\end{bmatrix}
=
\begin{bmatrix}
dt \\
dt^* \\
0
\end{bmatrix}
$$

The determinant is $D := Y_{zz}^*(Y_{xx}Y_{zz} - Y_{xz}^2) + \sigma Y_{zz}(Y_{xx}^*Y_{zz}^* - Y_{xz}^{*2}) < 0$. Moreover,

$dx = D^x/D$ with $D^x := -Y_{xz}Y_{zz}^* dt + Y_{xz}^*Y_{zz}dt^*$; $dx^* = -\sigma dx$;

$dz = D^z/D$ with $D^z := -Y_{zx}Y_{zz}^* dt + [Y_{xx}Y_{zz}^* + \sigma(Y_{xx}^*Y_{zz}^* - Y_{xz}^{*2})]dt$;

$dz^* = D^{z*}/D$ with $D^{z*} := -\sigma Y_{zx}^*Y_{zz}dt + (Y_{xx}Y_{zz} - Y_{xz}^2 + \sigma Y_{xx}^*Y_{zz})dt^*$.

APPENDIX 7A.3 PARTIAL DERIVATIVES IN EQUATION (7.11)

The equations $t = Y_z(x, z)$ and $r = Y_x(x, z)$ imply the 'factor demand functions' $z = Z(r, t)$ and $x = X(r, t)$. The partial derivatives of these functions are found by total differentiation of $t = Y_z(x, z)$ and $r = Y_x(x, z)$. Defining $N := Y_{xx}Y_{zz} - Y_{xz}^2 > 0$ one obtains:

$$X_t = -Y_{zx}/N \text{ and } X_r = Y_{zz}/N,$$

$$Z_t = -Y_{xx}/N \text{ and } Z_r = -Y_{zx}/N. \qquad (7A.3a)$$

The policy of Result 5a (policy A) has the effects $\frac{dx}{dr}\big|_A = X_r < 0$ and $\frac{dz}{dr}\big|_A = Z_r < 0$. The effect $Z_r < 0$ is (partially) welfaring improving. Under policy A the impact of dr on real consumption is

$$\frac{dc}{dr}\big|_A = t \cdot Z_r - (x - x_0)$$

which is negative for $x > x_0$ and ambiguous in sign otherwsie. The policy of Result 5b (policy B) requires the choice of dt so that $dz = Z_t dt + Z_r dr = 0$. Hence

$$dx = X_t dt + X_r dr = -\frac{X_t Z_r}{Z_t} \cdot dr + X_r \cdot dr = \frac{1}{Y_{xx}} \cdot dr < 0.$$

The last line can be rewritten as $\frac{dx}{dr}\big|_B = \frac{dx}{dr}\big|_A - X_t Z_r / Z_t$. Hence $\frac{dx}{dr}\big|_B < \frac{dx}{dr}\big|_A$. Under policy B the impact of dr on real consumption is $\frac{dc}{dr}\big|_B = -(x - x_0)$.

APPENDIX 7A.4   PROOF OF RESULT 8

Maximizing (7.2) subject to $\ell \le \ell_0$, (7.15) and (7.17) yields

$$r = Y_x(x) - S(r, x) \cdot E_x(x) \quad \text{with} \quad S(r, x) := -\frac{U_z[Y(x) - (x - x_0)r, \, E(x)]}{U_c[Y(x) - (x - x_0)r, \, E(x)]}. \qquad (7A.4a)$$

Total differentiation of (7A.4a) results in

$$\frac{dx}{dr} = \frac{1 + S_r E_x}{Y_{xx} - S_x E_x - t E_{xx}} \quad \text{with} \qquad (7A.4b)$$

$$S_x = -[(U_{zc} + t U_{cc})(Y_x - r) + (U_{zz} + t U_{cz})E_x]/U_c \quad \text{and}$$

$$S_r = -(x - x_0)(U_{zc} + t U_{cc})/U_c, \qquad (7A.4c)$$

with $S_r > 0$ and $S_r \gtrless 0 \Leftrightarrow x_0 \gtrless x$. Consider (7A.4c) in (7A.4b) to obtain

$$\frac{dx}{dr} = \frac{U_c + (x - x_0)(U_{zc} + t U_{cc})E_x}{(Y_{xx} - t E_{xx})U_c + (U_{zc} + t U_{cc})(Y_x - r)E_x + (U_{zz} + t U_{zc})E_x^2}. \qquad (7A.4b')$$

Total differentiation of $S(r, x)$ leads to

$$\frac{dt}{dr} = S_r + S_x \cdot \frac{dx}{dr} = \frac{S_x + S_r(Y_{xx} - t E_{xx})}{Y_{xx} - S_x E_x - t E_{xx}}. \qquad (7A.4d)$$

APPENDIX 7A.5   DERIVATION OF EQUATION (7.27)

With $P(t, t^*)$ as defined in (7.26) one obtains

$$P_t(t, t^*) = U_c[Y_x X_t - r X_t - (x - x_0)R_t] + U_z Z_t = 0$$

and therefore $-\dfrac{U_z}{U_c} = \dfrac{t Z_x X_t}{Z_t} - (x - x_0)\dfrac{R_t}{Z_t}$, because $Y_x - r = t Z_x$. By definition of R and Z, one has $Z_t = Z_x X_t^c$ and $R_t = (Y_{xx} - t Z_{xx}^t)X_t - Z_x$ and therefore

$$\frac{dr}{dz} = \frac{R_t}{Z_t} = \frac{t^* Z_{xx}^* - o Y_{xx}^*}{Z_x} > 0.$$

APPENDIX 7A.6   PROOF OF RESULT 11

Define $\Delta x := x - x_0$ and consider (7.27) to obtain

$$2\Delta x = \Delta a + x_0^* - x_0 + t^* - t. \tag{7A.6a}$$

With the help of (7.29) the difference $t^* - t$ is transformed to read

$$t^* - t = \frac{(2 - e + e^*)x_0 - (2 - e^* + e)x_0^* - (2 + e + e^*)\Delta a}{4 + e + e^*}.$$ Substitution into (7A.6a) yields

$$\Delta x = \frac{\Delta a + (1 + e^*)x_0^* - (1 + e)x_0}{4 + e + e^*}.$$ Small changes of e and e^* have the effects

$$\frac{d\Delta x}{de} = -\frac{(1 + e^*)x_0^* + (3 + e^*)x_0 + \Delta a}{(4 + e + e^*)^2}, \quad \text{and} \quad \frac{d\Delta x}{de^*} = \frac{(3 + e)x_0^* + (1 + e)x_0 - \Delta a}{(4 + e + e^*)^2}.$$

Define $\Delta t := t - t_0 = t - ex_0$ and consider (7.29) to find, after some rearrangement of terms, that $\Delta t = (1 + e)\Delta x$. Hence

$$\frac{d\Delta t}{de^*} = (1 + e)\frac{d\Delta x}{de^*} \quad \text{and} \quad \frac{d\Delta t}{de} = \Delta x + (1 + e)\frac{d\Delta x}{de}.$$

PART IV

International Trade and Environmental Policy

8. Economic Trade and Environmental Protection

C. Ford Runge

INTRODUCTION: POLLUTION, TRADE AND ENVIRONMENTAL QUALITY

In the 1980s and 1990s air pollution, acid rain and global warming became major items on the international agenda, as environmental issues moved beyond domestic policy.[1] This shift reflects growing recognition of the global impact of economic development and the rising problem of international externalities, as hazards spill over national borders and affect the oceans, air and climate. But just as environmental risks flow through the world's biosphere, so they also flow through the world economy – and threaten to disrupt it. Environmental risks tend to concentrate in those countries with the least regulation. Some regulatory differences exist among countries at the same stage of development, but in the world as a whole the flow of environmental and health risks runs from the North to the developing nations of the South. The mechanism of this flow is trade.

At the same time, growing consumer concerns about environmental quality and pollution in the North are prompting more attention to environmental hazards from imported products, particularly food. As a result, domestic interests and other producers seeking protection from foreign competition are finding a new source of support in the environmental and consumer movements. Import restrictions, when presented as a public health measure, gain a legitimacy that they might not otherwise enjoy.

These events suggest the new realities created by uneven environmental and health regulation and their links to trade. When nations exchange goods and services, they also trade environmental and health risks. These risks are the opposite of services – they are environmental and health *disservices* traded across national borders. This trade in disservices is an emerging source of tension in trade negotiations. The United States and other signatories to the General Agreement on Tariffs and Trade (GATT) are committed to pursuing more open borders in the ongoing Uruguay Round of trade negotiations. But as national health, safety and environmental

209

regulations grow in importance, different national regulatory priorities pose several related problems for trade and development. These differences were especially obvious in negotiations over the North American Free Trade Agreement (NAFTA).

In both NAFTA and GATT negotiations, charges have been made that groups in some countries seek to gain competitive advantage over foreign producers by moving production to sites where environmental regulations are less strict. Alternatively, environmental claims have disguised protectionism, as the environment is used as an excuse to keep out imported products. Producers may also try to export products that threaten the health of consumers in foreign countries. All such actions could do unnecessary harm to *both* environmental quality and world trade, unless new international arrangements are devised to resolve the problems.

THE CHAPTER IN REVIEW

Five main issues dominate the debate over pollution, trade and environment, and will serve as the focus of this chapter. The first is how best to capture the interactions of environmental and trade measures from an analytical and modeling standpoint. The second is the potential environmental impact of trade liberalization, both in the regional context of the North American Free Trade Agreement (NAFTA) and in the global trade talks continuing in the General Agreement on Tariffs and Trade (GATT). The third is the possible use of environmental measures as non-tariff barriers to trade. The fourth is the relationship between trade agreements under NAFTA and GATT and the variety of international environmental agreements (IEAs), such as the Montreal Protocol agreement to protect atmospheric ozone. Finally, a variety of institutional issues present themselves as challenges to policy-makers, and it is with these challenges that the chapter concludes.

ANALYTICAL ISSUES

The analysis of pollution and environmental quality in an international context poses a variety of challenges. The traditional analytical treatment of pollution in a closed economy (absent trade) involves externalities theory in which one agent imposes external costs on others in ways unreflected by market prices. This 'wedge' between market prices and a shadow price reflecting the external effect can be corrected through a Pigouvian tax-cum-subsidy scheme. The complexity of doing so depends in turn on the nature of the external effect.[2] Equivalently, property rights may be redefined and assigned (subject to the costs of these transactions) in such a way that the external effect is made attributable to those who are responsible for it, thus internalizing it (as when two firms are merged). Generalizing from the case of an externality imposed on a few agents, any negative effect imposed on a group of others may be modeled as a public 'bad', so that the theory of public goods and bads applies (Mishan, 1971). In cases of a 'pure' public bad, external costs are imposed in such a way that all agents consume the same amount of the bad (for example, a given level of pollution, such as particulates in the air). The dilemma is that while each agent consumes the same amount, their individual willingness to pay to reduce the negative effect is *not* the same. This stands in contrast to the pure private good (or bad) in which each agent pays the same amount, but the quantity consumed differs depending on individual preferences (see Samuelson, 1954). It is the capacity to misrepresent ones' willingness to pay in the case of public goods or bads which leads to the classic 'free-rider' problem. In the case of pollution, an individual may understate or overstate his or her true willingness to pay for cleanup, since the price mechanism does not reveal true preferences (Sandler, 1992, Chapter 2).

An alternative and analytically convenient formulation is to treat an external effect from the point of view of a producer rather than a consumer, as an input into production (see Antle and Just, 1992). Here, the analytical consequences depend on how pollution affects the production technology of the firm, rather than the consumers' preferences. While the effect of the externality will be valued by the firm at the margin in a (negative) shadow price, this shadow price typically will not correspond to a market price because the market fails to capture its negative impact.

The already complicated situation arising from these market failures is made even more so when the economy is opened to trade. When negative external effects and bads are traded internationally along with goods, or when they enter as negative inputs into international production processes, what has changed analytically is that the effect is 'transboundary' in nature.[3] Its transboundary nature complicates its resolution. A traditional tax-cum-subsidy scheme in a closed economy, for example, presumes that an authority exists which can levy taxes or pay subsidies, or can redefine and reassign property rights. But when one or more nations are involved, and an international authority capable of levying and enforcing such measures is absent, then the national governments must coordinate their actions. This international coordination problem aggravates the tendency of firms or individuals to free ride by shirking responsibility for the external effect or public bad, since costs are borne in part or in whole by foreign individuals and firms, and become the concern of foreign governments. A classic example is the attempt by the US and Canada to develop a coordinated approach to acid rain arising from US emissions of sulphur dioxide (SO_2).[4] There are also important terms of trade effects arising from transboundary externalities, so that the trading interests of nations will be affected by actions taken to regulate them.[5] These terms of trade effects arise from both the costs, and benefits, of internalizing the environmental externality.

Given these complexities, the attempt to integrate externalities theory with the neoclassical theory of international trade is relatively recent.[6] Here we will develop a simple, partial equilibrium approach, following Anderson (1992).[7] Consider a small country facing both market failures and the prospect of trade liberalization, in which its own actions do not affect the rest of the world.[8] The small country produces or consumes a commodity, such as corn, in which an externality results from the failure of the market to account for the impact of corn production or consumption on the natural environment. An example of a production externality might be soil erosion which reduces the productivity of agricultural lands and lowers water quality. An example of a consumption externality might be water pollution from farm chemicals which raises the risk of water-borne disease.[9] The result of the externality is to drive a 'wedge' between private and social costs of production, reflected in the divergence of S and S' in Figure 8.1. These alternative supply curves measure marginal private and social costs, respectively. The demand curve, D, measures marginal private benefits. The price axis refers to the price of corn relative to all other prices in the economy, which remain constant throughout.

In this case, OQ is the level of corn production without either (a) international trade or (b) measures to 'internalize' environmental impacts such as erosion. Production occurs at point e, the intersection of *private* marginal benefits and costs. Net *social* welfare is given as the sum of producer and consumer surplus,[10] minus the social costs of the external effect, or *abe* − *ade*. Now assume that the country shifts from autarky (no trade), to open trade. If OP_0 is the prevailing international (border) price, as in Figure 8.1(a), production would fall to OQ_m, consumption would rise to OC_m and Q_mC_m units of corn would be imported. Net social welfare is now *abfg* − *ahg*, and the welfare gain is *defg*. This gain from trade is both positive and greater than it would have been if no externality had existed in the form of erosion, by the shaded area *degh*. In effect, the country benefits because it imports corn more cheaply than it can produce it, and benefits by reducing soil erosion as well. Imports are 'substitutes' for erosion.

On the other hand, suppose OP_1 is the prevailing international (border) price, as in Figure 8.1(b). The country would thus become a net exporter of C_xQ_x units of corn if it moved to open trade. Net social welfare would be *abik* − *amk*, so the welfare effect of trade liberalization without any

*Figure 8.1: Effects of opening up a small economy to trade in a product
whose production is pollutive*

(a) Importable

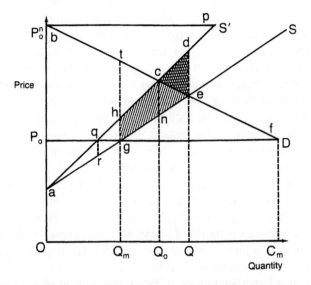

(b) Exportable

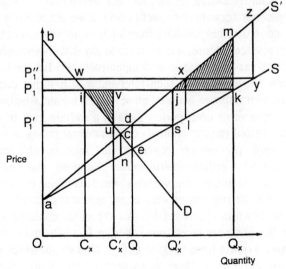

Source: K. Anderson (1992), p. 28. Reprinted with the permission of Harvester Wheatsheaf.

action to internalize the effects of erosion would be *eik – edmk*, which could be a net gain or net loss, depending on the relative magnitude of the *gain* from trade versus the *loss* from increased erosion as production expanded from Q to Q_x.

Several propositions follow from this analysis.   The first is that liberalizing trade in a good with adverse environmental impacts which are left uncontrolled improves a small country's welfare if following liberalization it imports the good; but if it exports it, the negative environmental effects are subtracted from the gains from trade, and the welfare effect is ambiguous. By importing the polluting good, a country lets some other country worry about its polluting properties. By exporting it, it continues to face the social cost of these externalities in the home market.

Now suppose that instead of leaving erosion uncontrolled, the small country *combined* trade reform with an environmental policy intervention sufficient to internalize the externality. Such an intervention could take the form of a tax, charge, or equivalent regulation or change in property rights.[11] *Given* such an environmental policy intervention, the gain from trade liberalization is *qcf* in Figure 8.1(a) and *cij* in Figure 8.1(b), depending on whether corn is imported or exported. In contrast to the situation in which no environmental intervention occurs, *this is a net gain in either the importing or exporting case.*

It is important to note, however, that without environmental intervention, the benefits of liberalization for the exporter would be even greater, by *cde*. Hence, an incentive exists for net exporters to forgo environmental interventions because the benefits from trade are reduced somewhat by the production declines resulting from such environmental policy interventions. In this restricted sense, it is accurate to say that environmental interventions reduce an exporting nation's 'competitiveness'. But the larger loss is in net welfare, in that *without* such interventions, it is not clear that expanded exports will improve net welfare at all. However, whether a small country is an importer *or* an exporter, there is a welfare gain from trade provided that a targeted (nearly optimal) environmental policy is introduced.

A third proposition concerns the relative efficacy of trade and environmental policy instruments.   Suppose that instead of targeted environmental policy interventions aimed at erosion control, it was proposed to use a trade instrument such as an export tax aimed at the same target. This is shown in Figure 8.1(b). An export tax could be used equal to *js* to lower the price producers receive from P_1 to P_1', reducing production and lowering exports form C_xQ_x to $C_x'Q_x'$. This would lower the marginal cost of production to a level equivalent to an environmental intervention, producing a welfare gain of shaded area *jmk*. But the export tax causes consumers to pay $P_1'P_1$ below the opportunity cost of OP_1, leading to a deadweight welfare loss due to excess domestic consumption $C_xC'_x$, equal to the shaded area *iuv*. Hence, using a trade policy instrument reduces environmental degradation as much as an environmental tax set at the same rate, but at higher cost.[12] Trade instruments can thus be used to reduce environmental degradation by a given amount, but they generally will improve welfare less than a more direct intervention at the source of the environmental pollution, and may even worsen welfare.

Moving from the small- to the large-country case, it is possible that the liberalization and/or environmental policies undertaken will affect world prices, so that the price lines in Figures 8.1(a) and 8.1(b) are no longer horizontal. Moreover, the environmental policies and polluting activities of large countries such as the United States or large groups such as the European Community will have global impacts, spilling over and ultimately back into home markets and welfare. Finally, policy changes in large countries may have demonstration or leadership effects on other countries.

In summary, the welfare effects of liberalizing trade are ambiguous if environmental externalities are left uncontrolled; but if they are largely internalized by an appropriately targeted environmental policy, the joint 'liberalization effect' and 'environmental effect' on welfare is positive. Simple welfare analysis thus offers a rudimentary analytical foundation for issues in trade and the environment. At an empirical level, however, there is still very little understanding of the effects of trade liberalization on the environment, and how different commodities and countries will be affected. Trade liberalization is also unlikely to be total or all-inclusive, so that distortions and adverse environmental impacts will remain. This analytical exercise demonstrates an important overriding lesson: environmental externalities influence the welfare outcomes of trade; and trade influences the way in which externalities are borne and resolved. This interdependence requires further analysis, not only at the level of theory, but in terms of recent experience and empirical research.

THE ENVIRONMENTAL IMPACTS OF TRADE

The impacts of trade on environmental quality have been an important focus of opposition to trade liberalization, especially in the context of the North American Free Trade Agreement (NAFTA) and the Uruguay Round of the General Agreement on Tariffs and Trade (GATT). However, most claims about the negative environmental impacts of trade liberalization have been based on limited evidence. In fact, the impacts of trade on the environment vary greatly in degree and by location. In agriculture, for example, there is evidence that reducing subsidies and trade distortions would often help to reduce environmental damages by lowering fertilizer and pesticide use and increasing the efficiency with which soil and water resources are used (Runge, 1991; Harold and Runge, 1993).

In the industrial border region of Mexico,[13] by contrast, limited investment in wastewater treatment and hazardous waste disposal has created serious environmental damages resulting from foreign investments. These damages reflect a failure to address the environmental externalities of larger-scale US/Mexico trade. Yet the NAFTA process has also brought these problems to wider attention, stimulating new environmental investments and the enforcement of stricter standards that would be less likely under a situation of no trade. These investments are part of the trade impacts of NAFTA's environmental 'side agreement'; stricter standards will be overseen by the North American Commission on Environmental Cooperation, an institutional byproduct of trade liberalization. As trade growth raises incomes, demands for a cleaner environment also tend to rise, and new regulatory constraints induce technological innovations which are more environmentally benign.[14]

Five separate impacts of trade growth on the environment may be distinguished. These effects are (1) on allocative efficiency; (2) on scale; (3) on the composition of output; (4) on technology; and (5) on policy. The overall effect of trade on the environment is the sum of these separate impacts, which may be positive or negative, depending on the case examined.

A. Allocative Efficiency

Since Adam Smith (1776) first analyzed the impact of trade on production, it has been observed that greater allocative efficiency results when countries specialize in producing those things for which they have a natural advantage, and then trade with other nations for other products, rather than attempting to produce all of the products in demand at home. Formalized as the theory of comparative advantage, it predicts that countries will utilize their natural and human resources in such a way that abundant resources will be used more in the production of goods and services than scarce resources, which will be conserved. To the extent that these 'factor proportions' rule, trade will promote allocative efficiency by inducing patterns of production which are less wasteful than if every country tried to produce a full range of goods and services itself.

In this sense, more open trade leads to higher levels of economic satisfaction than inward-looking policies closed to trade, and reduces waste of scarce resources. This efficiency in production and exchange means that, for a given endowment of resources, trade will be less wasteful than autarky, the absence of trade. The best empirical evidence of the wastefulness arising from closed economies comes from Eastern Europe and the Former Soviet Union, where 'self-sufficiency' often justified widespread environmental destruction.[15] Less dramatic, but substantial, environmental damage has resulted from the European Community's drive for self-sufficiency in agriculture.[16]

However, the exercise of comparative advantage and more open trade is itself not inconsistent with overexploitation of *globally* scarce resources. If country A is endowed with locally abundant resources S and trades them to country B in return for locally abundant resources W, it may still be true that S or W, while locally abundant, are globally scarce, and would be better conserved than traded. The former Soviet Union, to take a recent example, has offered opportunities to Western game hunters to hunt a variety of globally endangered species,[17] at prices driven low by foreign currency scarcity and internal competition. If these hunting opportunities are traded because of their relative abundance in the Soviet Union, it does not diminish the fact that they deplete globally scarce endangered species. The relative efficiency of comparative advantage and trade is just that: relative.

B. Scale

Granting the allocative efficiency of trade relative to no trade, there is still little question that the scale of economic activity in a world with no trade would probably be much lower, and in this limited sense would impose less wear and tear on the environment. As a mental experiment, such a world would somewhat resemble turning back the clock three or four hundred years, eliminating rail and road transportation based on hydrocarbon fuels, international air travel and transport, and returning largely to locally-based agricultural subsistence. Obviously, it is not possible to turn back the clock; and eliminating trade in the face of today's population levels would probably lead to a global economic and ecological catastrophe, as a population many times that of three or four centuries ago attempted unsuccessfully to revert to local subsistence. The role of increased trade in supporting income growth per capita, and thus supporting higher levels of employment for growing populations is clear. In the US, for example, it is estimated that without the growth in US exports (which doubled between 1985 and 1992), the 1990–93 recession would have been twice as deep, with 100 percent higher levels of unemployment than in fact occurred. Trade growth has been especially notable with developing countries. US export sales to developing countries, according to the US Department of Commerce, rose to $167 billion in 1992, up 14 percent from 1991, largely offsetting weak demand from Japan and the European Community. Exports to developing countries increased in 1992 to 37 percent of total, up from 32 percent in 1990.[18]

As this trade growth increases GDP per capita, does the scale of economic activity do damage to the environment in the same or similar proportions? The question of *scale* can be thought of in the following sense: as growth in GDP per capita occurs (due in part to trade), does pollution increase at the same, decreasing, or an increasing rate, or does it actually decrease? Grossman and Krueger (1991) report evidence that when a cross-section of countries was studied over time, pollution measured by particulates and SO_2 increased at a decreasing rate with GDP per capita up to a threshold of about $5,000 US dollars a year, then decreased, although the total began increasing again at higher income levels. Grossman and Krueger are careful not to impute any clear line of causality in this process, and simply note the apparent association between rising incomes and falling levels of at least these pollutants. The rise in totals at even higher income levels is also unexplained. Clearly, more detailed and disaggregated analysis is necessary. This non-linear relationship between the scale of economic activity and the level of pollution suggests that other forces are at work, influencing how growth due in part to trade affects levels of environmental quality. These include the composition of output, technology and policy decisions (Grossman and Krueger, 1993).

C. Composition of Output

Environmental impacts of trade due to the composition of output can occur when increases in GDP lead to reduced heavy manufactures with large levels of pollution and shifts to higher levels of services with lower levels of pollution. This change in the composition of output may influence total pollution levels, offsetting some of the scale effects of economic growth through trade. The relative growth of the services versus the manufacturing sector in the higher-income nations, coupled with their decreasing per-capita levels of certain pollutants, suggests that shifts in the composition of output may play a role (see Dean, 1991).

D. Technology

A fourth way in which trade may affect the environment is through induced technological innovations. As increased value is given to environmental quality with increases in income, markets for 'green' technologies may develop and grow. These environmental technologies (such as wastewater treatment or materials' recycling) may also be accompanied by changes in traditional technologies (such as shifts towards more energy-efficient and less polluting steel production) which lower the overall level of residuals and hazards from manufacturing processes. Some companies have found that new waste reduction technologies are highly profitable. In 1986, for example, Dow Chemical launched its Waste Reduction Always Pays (WRAP) program, credited with saving millions of dollars. Similar efforts are underway at other companies, including Minnesota Mining and Manufacturing (3–M) and Shell Oil.[19] These experiences suggest that incentives for environmentally beneficial technological innovation may be greater at larger, more integrated manufacturing firms.

E. Policy

All of the environmental effects of trade discussed above, whether arising from allocative efficiency, scale, composition of output, or technology, operate in the context of government policies. Indeed, there is reason to believe that without the increasing stringency of environmental regulation, many of the incentives to alter the character and methods of production so as to reduce waste and pollution would be far weaker. While trade may encourage greater allocative efficiency, the negative scale effects of economic growth on the environment are only offset by composition and technology to a degree largely determined by the regulatory framework. It is the political will to impose such discipline on environmental externalities which ensures that trade liberalization is ultimately welfare-enhancing. In the US, for example, since 1986 the Environmental Protection Agency (EPA) has required a Toxic Release Inventory (TRI), in which plants of 10,000 US manufacturers report annual releases from their facilities into the air, ground and water of some 317 toxic chemicals. These include asbestos, freon, and PCBs, as well as 20 toxic chemical categories such as lead compounds. As this list continues to grow, companies and the public have an increasing basis to 'keep score', utilizing measures such as TRI releases per dollar of sales. Dow Chemical, for example, eliminated practices of injecting hazardous wastes underground before the TRI began, reducing this ratio, while Du Pont Chemical failed to do so.[20] On the one hand, this regulatory framework creates a quantitative basis for reducing emissions. On the other hand, it can create incentives to move production to foreign plants where such oversight is less stringent.

F. Total Effects

The sum of these effects of trade on the environment may be positive or negative, depending on the industry or pollutant involved. Schematically, we can think of trade as inducing allocative efficiency, which in turn leads to economic growth and increased GDP per capital, with attendant negative scale effects. These scale effects may lead to increases in demands for environment protection and policies to accomplish this protection, inducing changing output composition and production technologies which in turn diminish negative externalities (Figure 8.2).

Figure 8.2: Trade/environment linkages

Trade → Allocative efficiency (+) → Growth in GDP/capita
→ Scale effects (–) → Demand for environmental protection
→ Change in policy → Change in composition (+)
→ Change in technology (+).

Note: + denotes positive and – negative environmental impacts.

However, in many cases this chain of events is broken by failures to develop and enforce regulations leading to the internalization of externalities. Where demands for environmental protection are not expressed or heard, as in many poor developing countries, changes in policy leading to changes in composition and technology may not occur.

This was the situation until relatively recently in Mexico. However, one of the most interesting and potentially beneficial consequences of the NAFTA has been to help induce institutional changes both in Mexico and under the trilateral 'side-agreement' to NAFTA. These changes will help to develop more stringent levels of environmental protection and enforcement in Mexico as well as in the US and Canada. This 'environmental conditionality' represents an important new chapter in the evolution of institutional responses to the interaction of trade and environment (see Runge, 1994). We turn now to the opposite side of the trade/environment nexus, the impact of domestic environmental regulations on trade and their role as disguised forms of trade protection.

ENVIRONMENTAL MEASURES AND TRADE BURDENS

When domestic environmental measures lead to claims of *trade* harm, it is generally because a burden has been imposed on individuals or firms seeking to export or import goods or services in the name of domestic (and sometimes global) environmental protection. The question is whether the environmental measure is justified primarily as a form of necessary environmental protection, or is a disguised restriction to trade, in which harmful trade effects loom proportionately larger than beneficial environmental effects.

The issue of whether a government environmental regulation is a non-tariff trade barrier is a question faced domestically in the US by the states under the commerce clause of the US Constitution, and by the 12 Member States in the European Community under the Treaty of Rome. Such questions typically break down into two parts: (1) does the measure create a burden on trade? (2) is the burden justified by the environmental benefits of the regulation? From a legal perspective the apparent burden imposed on trade is a 'gateway concept'. If a burden appears to be present, it opens the way to further inquiry as to its justification, in which its benefits for the environment are weighed against its harm to trade.[21] If 'no burden' is found, then the trade effects of the regulation are not at issue (Figure 8.3).

Figure 8.3: Environment/trade linkages

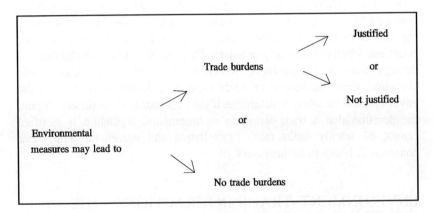

While nearly all environmental regulations impose some differential burdens on commercial transactions, to be trade-related this differential must exist between some foreign and domestic competitors. This differential may be relatively easy to see, as when foreign products are subjected to obviously different standards compared with domestic products. Under Section 337 of the 1930 Trade Act, for example, certain trade cases for foreign violators are heard before the International Trade Commission (ITC), while cases against US firms charged with similar violations are sent to US courts. In general, going before the ITC is regarded as more burdensome to the defendant. Not every differential rule clearly constitutes a burden, however, even though domestic and foreign products are treated differently. Auto safety glass inspected at US auto manufacturers' factories is different from inspections of foreign vehicles' windshields at the border, but the border inspections do not appear to create a differential burden.

Less obvious are standards which appear neutral on their face, but have a differential impact on foreign and domestic products. Provisions of the 1985 Farm Bill sought to apply sanitary processing and inspection standards to chickens from outside the US that were 'the same' as those standards used domestically ('the same' standards were substituted for previous language by members of Congress from Arkansas). The previous language had called for foreign standards 'at least equal to' those used domestically. In a case brought before the federal court for the Southern District of Mississippi, the language calling for 'the same' standard was upheld, despite warnings from the Department of Agriculture that 'such a definitional finding would augur dire foreign trade implications'.[22]

Overall, balancing legal and economic judgments must be made in order to extend the regulation of environmental risk into the international arena. Where trade measures lead to environmental risks, these risks can be remedied through regulations. However many such risks are not subject to regulations in the home market, and may require negotiations with other countries, whether bilaterally or trilaterally as in NAFTA, or multilaterally, through international agreements. Where environmental actions lead to trade distortion, then the burden on trade must be assessed in relation to the environmental benefits, to determine if the trade burden is justified. Again, the decision that a trade-distorting environmental regulation is justified cannot be wholly unilateral. Consultation and agreement with other countries is likely to be necessary.

ENVIRONMENT–TRADE INTERACTIONS: THE MONTREAL PROTOCOL

As the number of international environmental agreements (IEAs) has grown in recent years, new questions have arisen concerning the relationship between these agreements and existing or future trade obligations in GATT.[23] First, there is the question of whether countries are *parties or non-parties* to the treaties, such as the Montreal Protocol affecting chlorofluorocarbon and halon emissions damaging to atmospheric ozone. The Montreal Protocol, signed in 1987 and amended by the London Amendments in 1990, commits the signatory parties to study the feasibility of a ban applied to non-member countries against imports of products made with a process that uses the ozone-depleting chemicals, as well as various other actions affecting trade in these products. In January, 1993, for example, signatories were scheduled to ban the export of these substances to non-parties.[24]   However, fewer than 20 countries were signatories by 1992, whereas over 100 countries are signatories to the GATT Articles. If countries are parties to GATT, with all of the *trade* obligations that this implies, and are also parties to the Montreal Protocol, with all of the *environmental* obligations this implies, then what if these obligations conflict? Alternatively, what if countries which have signed the Montreal Protocol take trade actions to ban imports from countries which have *not* signed the Protocol? Clearly, principles must be established to determine matters of priority and consistency.

In addition to the question of obligations under various treaties to which countries are pledged, there is the question of *extrajurisdictionality*, or whether countries have rights to impose trade measures in response to the environmental policies of other countries. This issue has come to the forefront with the US/Mexico dispute over whether the US can, under GATT, ban imports of tuna caught with fishing methods which kill dolphins in the process, even if these actions are taken outside the territorial jurisdiction of the United States.

A third question, related to the first two, is the legal *standing* of IEAs versus GATT obligations. While the Vienna Convention on the Law of Treaties provides general rules on the relationship of successive treaties, notably that the treaty 'later in time' prevails,[25] the rule applies only where the two treaties address the same subject matter. In the case of a party to both the Montreal Protocol and GATT, for example, the section of the Protocol banning imports of substances produced with ozone-depleting chemicals would prevail over any inconsistent provisions of GATT (assuming the GATT Articles are considered a treaty). While the 'later in time' rule of the Vienna Convention allows subsequent environmental agreements to 'trump' trade obligations, some feel it may make it too easy to override trade rules in the name of these objectives.[26] In cases in which a country is not a party to the IEA, the Vienna Convention (Article 34) states that an IEA that is later in time cannot bind non-party states without their consent, unless the treaty rules becomes customary international law.[27]

In response to this lack of definition and clarity, some leading authorities have proposed a 'waiver' for IEAs, at least temporarily, until better definitions and understanding can be worked out. A waiver limited to say, five years, could include specific current IEAs and provide for future ones as well. In addition to the Montreal Protocol, such a waiver might initially include two other major environmental agreements, the Convention on International Trade in Endangered Species of Wild Flora and Fauna,[28] and the Basel Convention on the Control of Transboundary Movements of Hazardous Wastes and Their Disposal.[29]

In summary, there is currently no consensus on the complicated intermeshing of trade obligations and IEAs. The critical questions include treatment of *parties and non-parties*, the reach of *extraterritorial* actions to protect the environment, the *standing* of IEAs versus GATT obligations, and the issue of a *waiver* for IEAs until some of these questions can be answered more clearly and definitively.

FACING THE INSTITUTIONAL CHALLENGE

As the twentieth century draws to a close, two global trends are converging. The first, and most powerful, is the increasing integration of the world economy, and the resulting interdependence of domestic and international policies affecting trade in goods and services. This trend creates both greater trade frictions, and greater opportunities to develop mutually beneficial trading relationships. It also tests the rules of trade developed under the auspices of the GATT and regional trading arrangements such as the EC and the NAFTA.

The second global trend is the increasing value placed on protection of the environment, and the need for national and international policies of environmental preservation to minimize the bads and disservices that trade can bring. Despite differences in the emphasis given to environment in the North versus the South, there is little doubt that environmental issues will continue to dominate international discussion, including North–South dialogues, in the year ahead, especially given the transformation and diminished security threats posed by East–West relations.

These two global trends are now intertwining in complex ways. These complexities have been the subject of this chapter. Yet despite the many technical issues involved, an important and simple complementarity also exists.[30] In much the same way that international trade rules have evolved in and outside of GATT in response to global economic interdependence, so new international environmental rules are now evolving in response to global environmental interdependence. Out of this mutual evolution an opportunity arises to *link* the objectives of market integration with environmental protection. Curiously, because the gap between environmental standards in the North and South is so great, it is precisely along the North/South axis that the opportunity for such linkage is also greatest.

In the same way that differences in resource endowments create gains from trade between dissimilar nations, so differences in levels of development and environmental protection can create complementaries built on incentives to exchange market access to the North in return for commitments to raise environmental standards in the South. The essential bargain in the making is to link one of the primary objectives of the Uruguay Round of GATT (more open market access) with the objective of raised levels of environmental protection. This is precisely what the negotiations over an environmental side-agreement to NAFTA have reflected: a promise of access to the markets of North America in return for a commitment to environmental improvements and enforcement. What the NAFTA experience suggests most clearly, however, is that trade rules alone are inadequate to the task: *environmental rules* are also required. And where such rules are developed, new *institutions* will be required to monitor and enforce them.

For more than a decade, the US relinquished its role as a leader in international environmental affairs, while continuing aggressively to pursue both regional and multilateral trade agreements. The consequence was to open it to criticism that freer trade was being pursued without regard to its environmental consequences. Restoring balance in the relationship between free trade and a protected environment now requires that the US undertake comparable efforts to create new rules for international environmental policy. In many respects, the opportunity to take the lead in this arena fits naturally with the redefinition of international security resulting from the end of the Cold War.

Both trade and the environment have emerged in the post-Cold War era as issues of primary importance, leading to a new sense of international security, defined in economic and ecological terms.[31] Yet until recently ecological security has often been regarded as competitive with economic prosperity, creating an either/or proposition for policy-makers. While tradeoffs will often be necessary between environmental quality and unrestrained trade, it is increasingly clear that many areas of complementarity exist as well.[32] In order to exploit this complementarity, it will be necessary to develop rules and incentives for environmental protection at both national and international levels which accomplish their objectives with as few burdens for market forces as is feasible; conversely, market expansion must proceed within constraints which protect nations from the negative externalities of economic activity.

In this process, the US will need to take the lead, as reflected in negotiations over an environmental side-agreement to NAFTA. Despite progress in the European Community on both economic and environmental grounds, the unified Europe and new European leadership promoted early in the decade has not emerged.[33] Japan, clearly a powerful force in trade, and a leader in some areas of environmental control technologies, has not yet fully embraced the Uruguay Round goals of market access and the Rio Conference objective of global environmental improvement. By contrast, the North American Free Trade Agreement and its side-agreements, if successful, offer in microcosm precisely the sort of complementarity between trade liberalization and environmental protection possible on a global scale.

There is unlikely to be so lasting a set of institutional issues and challenges for this and future governments than to achieve a new balance between trade and environmental interests, both North and South. In contrast to the balance of destructive forces which has dominated negotiations between nations in the post-war era, this new balance is one of welfare improvements from both economic and environmental sources. To achieve such an equilibrium would reward the welfare of this generation, and generations to come, with continued prosperity and improved environmental quality.

CONCLUSION

In conclusion, five main issues define the trade/environment nexus.

For professional economists, the first issue is an analytical one: how to blend the theory of externalities with international trade theory in a way that allows comparisons of both environmental and trade impacts. Currently, approaches to the problem are evolving from partial equilibrium models towards more general equilibrium approaches. Here we will adopt the simpler, but revealing, partial framework.

The second and most politically charged issue is the concern that trade liberalization, whether in NAFTA or under GATT, will lead to increased levels of environmental damages. There are numerous facets of this concern, which has been expressed strongly by a variety of environmental groups and members of Congress. One is the role of trade in allocating economic activities among countries, some of which are polluting; some of which are not. Overall, trade promotes specialization and efficiency, but may also create incentives to export pollution itself. Many environmental concerns also derive from the fact that as trade expands, 'scale effects' may cause added pollution. Scale effects are the result of increases in the quantity of goods and services moving within countries and across borders, due to the fact that increases in trade lead to greater transportation needs, higher levels of manufacturing output, and general increases in the demand for raw and processed products which can impose greater wear and tear on natural ecosystems. Among these possible scale effects are increasing consumption of non-renewable natural resources including fossil fuels, minerals, and old-growth forests, and increasing levels of air and water pollution. A particularly striking example often cited by environmental groups is the pollution found in the rapidly growing border region between Mexico and the US.[34] It has also been suggested that differences in environmental standards, especially between North and South, will create 'pollution havens' for firms and industries seeking less regulatory oversight, as the composition of goods and services changes. Trade also affects the technologies employed in various countries. Finally, trade may induce policy shifts, either in favor of improved environmental quality, or in the opposite direction.

In contrast to the environmental community's concern over the impacts of more liberal trade, those most directly involved in trade have tended to focus on a third main issue, the potential for protectionism disguised as environmental action. This can occur when a country or trading bloc protects internal markets in the name of environmental health or safety, such as the European Community's decision to ban the import of beef from cattle treated with certain growth hormones. It can also occur when higher levels of environmental standards are used to bar market access to goods and services produced under lower levels of regulation, especially by developing countries. The fundamental issue concerns the ability to distinguish legitimate environmental measures, which may well distort trade, from those which are not only trade distorting but have little basis from an environmental standpoint. Developing such criteria involves complex legal, scientific and institutional issues.

The fourth issue involves the relationship between trade agreements and international environmental agreements (IEAs). In the last decade, a variety of new international agreements have been negotiated in response to global environmental challenges such as ozone depletion, species extinction, protection of Antarctica, and international management of the oceans. The Rio Conference on Environment and Development, held in June, 1992, resulted in a broad new mandate for environmental action, Agenda 21, together with the creation of a new UN Commission on Sustainable Development. Some of these agreements call on their signatories to refrain from trade in certain goods or processes. In the recent NAFTA negotiations, for example, a tri-national commission was created with apparent authority over trade with damaging environmental effects. This commission has authority apart from the GATT, and the existing GATT dispute resolution process. The question is: how are international environmental accords to be balanced with existing or new trade obligations? What body of international law, and which international institutions, should exercise authority over the intersection between multilateral environmental and trade policy?

Finally there are a variety of institutional challenges for policy-makers. The increasingly competitive trade relations between the United States, the

European Community and Japan are one axis along which institutional issues arise. In some respects, the high-income countries of the North are increasingly alike in placing relatively greater value on environmental quality. But these economies are also locked in a high-stakes game of competition for global markets, and their governments face domestic pressures to loosen regulatory oversight. Even given their similarities, differences exist in the North not only in scientific and environmental standards, but in culture and social norms, which will continually confront efforts to harmonize environmental regulations. The gap between the environmental regulations along the North/South axis is even wider, accentuating problems of harmonization and concerns over 'pollution havens' and competitiveness. The NAFTA negotiations reflect these differences in microcosm, with Mexico attempting rapidly to upgrade its environmental regulations in order to satisfy fears in the US and Canada. How global institutions and domestic policies are altered to deal with these problems will determine how effectively trade and environmental issues will be confronted in the years ahead.

NOTES

1.   The material in this section draws on C. Ford Runge, 'Environmental Risk and the World Economy'. *The American Prospect* 1 (Spring, 1990): 114–18, and C. Ford Runge, et al., *Free Trade, Protected Environment: Balancing Trade Liberalization and Environmental Interests*, New York: Council on Foreign Relations, 1994.
2.   Marchand and Russell (1973) and Davis and Whinston (1962), for example, show that if an external effect is not additively separable in its arguments, then a constant Pigouvian tax or subsidy is infeasible: the tax-cum-subsidy must vary at the margin.
3.   M. L. Livingston, H. von Witzke and U. Hausner, 'The Political Economy of International Pollution', Center for International Food and Agricultural Policy, St. Paul, MN, 1993.
4.   V.A. Mohnen, 'The Challenge of Acid Rain', *Scientific American* 259 (August, 1988): 30–38.
5.   Brown, D.K., A.V. Deardorff and R.M. Stern, 'International Labor Standards and Trade: A Theoretical Analysis', University of Michigan, July 23, 1993.
6.   See Krutilla (1991), Merrifield (1988), Antle and Just (1992), and Anderson (1992).
7.   This approach is based in part on K. Anderson. 'The Standard Welfare Economics of Policies Affecting Trade and the Environment', in *The Greening of World Trade Issues*, K. Anderson and R. Blackhurst (eds), Ann Arbor, MI: The University of Michigan Press, 1992, pp. 25–48.
8.   The assumptions underlying the model include the usual ones of partial equilibrium analysis in a trade setting (see J.P. Houck, *The Elements of Agricultural Trade Policies*, New York: Macmillan, 1986), augmented by standard externalities theory. While subject to criticism by advocates of empirical general equilibrium analysis (see M. Hazilla and R.J. Kopp, 'Social Cost of Environmental Quality Regulations: A General Equilibrium Analysis', *Journal of Political Economy* 98:4 (1990): 853–73; and J.D. Merrifield, 'The Impact of Selected Abatement Strategies on Transnational Pollution, the Terms of Trade, and Factor Rewards: A General Equilibrium Approach', *Journal of Environmental Economics and Management* 15 (1988): 259–84), the approach is sufficient for clarifying analytical issues of relevance to public and environmental policy. Among the key underlying assumptions

are that (1) transactions costs prevent spontaneous negotiated 'internalization' of the external effect, ruling out a 'Coasian' solution; that taxes-cum-subsidies are lump sum (non-distorting); that the externality can be accurately measured; that it is a 'product' rather than 'process' externality; that all curves are linear and that the externality begins with the first unit of production; and that the marginal benefit and cost curves fully incorporate feedback effects from the rest of the economy. See K. Anderson, 'The Standard Welfare Economics of Policies Affecting Trade and the Environment', in *The Greening of World Trade Issues*, K. Anderson and R. Blackhurst (eds), Ann Arbor, MI: The University of Michigan Press, 1992, pp. 25–48.

9. John B. Sullivan, Jr, Melissa Gonzales, Gary R. Krieger and C. Ford Runge, 'Health-Related Hazards of Agriculture', in *Hazardous Materials Toxicology: Clinical Principles of Environmental Health*, edited by John B. Sullivan, Jr and Gary R. Krieger, Baltimore: Williams & Wilkins, 1992.

10. The empirical use of consumer and producer surplus measures is itself fraught with difficulty. See R.W. Boadway and N. Bruce, *Welfare Economics*, New York: Basil Blackwell, 1984.

11. See Peter J. Lloyd, 'The Problem of Optimal Environmental Policy Choice', in *The Greening of World Trade Issues*, K. Anderson and R. Blackhurst (eds), Ann Arbor, MI: The University of Michigan Press, 1992, pp. 49–72. The 'equivalence' of these measures is of course not guaranteed in practice as discussed in W.J. Baumol and W.E. Oates, *The Theory of Environmental Policy: Externalities, Public Outlays, and the Quality of Life*, Englewood Cliffs, NJ: Prentice Hall, 1975. The effect of such a policy would be to eliminate the 'wedge' between S' *and* S, so that marginal social costs of production would equal marginal social benefits. In the case of no trade, such intervention would be equivalent to a tax of cn per unit, which would reduce corn production from OQ to OQ_0 in Figure 8.1(a). The welfare benefit from internalizing the externality would be the shaded area cde, due to the reduced erosion resulting from the production fall. From a welfare perspective, we can thus isolate a welfare improvement due to the 'environmental effect', of targeted environmental intervention, assuming no 'liberalization effect'.

12. K. Anderson, 'The Standard Welfare Economics of Policies Affecting Trade and the Environment', in *The Greening of World Trade Issues*, K. Anderson and R. Blackhurst (eds), Ann Arbor, MI: The University of Michigan Press, 1992, pp. 25–48, especially p. 28. What of the behavior of other trading nations in the world? Suppose that a large trading partner of the small country were to liberalize its agricultural trade in corn and/or undertake environmental policies designed to reduce soil erosion as well? In this case, either the 'liberalization effect' and/or the 'environmental effect' on welfare could occur in tandem in both countries. The effect on the small country of either more liberal trade and/or increased environmental intervention (and reduced production) in the large country would be to raise corn prices. If the international price of corn rose from OP, to OP''_1 in Figure 8.1(b), the 'liberalization effect' would rise from cij to cwx, or by $iwxj$ given an environmental intervention which raised the equivalent tax on erosion from js to xl. But if no such environmental policies were taken, gains from the 'liberalization effect' ($ikyw$) would be reduced by the losses from erosion ($mkyz$), which might be a net gain or loss, depending on both the increase in price and, most importantly, how great the divergence was between S and S': in other words, how serious the impact of erosion on welfare.

13. This area is often referred to as the 'maquiladora sector'. A maquiladora is a foreign-owned plant in Mexico subject to duty-free import of raw materials, in which finished products are exported duty free except for value added in Mexico. See Malissa H. McKeith, 'The Environment and Free Trade: Meeting Halfway at the Mexican Border', *Pacific Basin Law Journal* 10:1 (1991): 183–211.

14. C. Ford Runge, 'Induced Agricultural Innovation and Environmental Quality: The Case of Groundwater Regulation', *Land Economics* 63 (3), August 1987. G.M. Grossman and A.B. Krueger, 'Environmental Impacts of a North American Free Trade Agreement', Woodrow Wilson Institute for Public Affairs, Princeton University, October 8, 1991.

15. See James Boyd, 'The Allocation of Environmental Liabilities in Central and Eastern Europe', *Resources. Resources for the Future* 112 (Summer, 1993): 1–6.

16. Monika Hartmann and Alan Matthews, 'Sustainable Agriculture in the European Community: The Role of Policy', Fall, 1991, forthcoming in *Forum for Applied Research and Public Policy* 8, 1993.

17. Mark Schapiro, 'Murder on the Orient: Pricey travel lets US hunters kill rare game', Condé Nast *Traveler* (August, 1993): 23–5. Valentin Ilyachenko, chief of the International Department of Conventions and Licenses in the Russian Ministry of Ecology in Moscow, noted competition such 'that the prices for foreign hunters are actually going down. You can pay the equivalent of a VCR in the West for a Russian brown bear'. He continues, 'we have the same problem with animal trophies as we have with our rare religious icons being sold on the streets of Moscow and St. Petersburg. As the prices for a hunt get lower and lower, we are trading off our natural resources for next to nothing' (p. 24).

18. Steven Greenhouse, 'Surge in Growth in Third World Gives an Economic Lift to US', *New York Times* (August 19, 1993): p. A–1.

19. Faye Rice, 'Who Scores Best on the Environment', *Fortune* (July 26, 1993): 114–22.

20. Rice, p. 115.

21. See Robert Hudec and Daniel Farber, 'Distinguishing Environmental Measures from Trade Barriers', University of Minnesota, Workshop on International Economic Policy, Nov. 17, 1992. The discussion that follows is based largely on this workshop presentation and the discussions of the Study Group on Trade and Environmental at the Council on Foreign Relations, September 14, 1992.

22. *International Trade Reporter*, May 27, 1992. (*Mississippi Poultry Association Inc. v. Madigan*, No. J91–0086(W), DC SMiss 4/23/92.)

23. For an excellent recent overview, see David A. Wirth, 'A Matchmaker's Challenge: Marrying International Law and American Environmental Law', *Virginia Journal of International Law* 32:2 (Winter, 1992): 377–420.

24. The Montreal Protocol on Substances that Deplete the Ozone Layer, *adopted and opened for signature* Sept. 16, 1987, reprinted in 26 I.L.M. 1541 (1987) (entered into force January 1, 1989). See US Congress, Office of Technology Assessment, Chapter 3, pp. 42–6.

25. Vienna Convention on the Law of Treaties, opened for signature May 23, 1969, UN Doc. A/COIF. 39/27, 8 I.L.M. 679, Article 30, 8 I.L.M. at 691. For a general discussion, see Robert F. Housman and D. Zaelke, 'Trade, Environment and Sustainable Development: A Primer', *Hastings International and Comparative Law Review*, 15 (Summer, 1992): 535–612.

26. Housman notes that 'this approach may be broader than actually necessary to insulate the environmental objectives desired. Further, by imperiling free trade this approach may lead to a weakening of the environmental agreements in question'. See Robert Housman, 'The Interaction of International Trade and Environmental Agreements', Center for International Environmental Law, Washington, DC, June 1, 1992, p. 3.

27. John Jackson (1992, p. 1274), in an overview of trade and environmental issues, suggests that even if not customary law, the 'weight' of a large number of countries agreeing to an IEA may affect the likelihood of a GATT complaint by non-parties. 'Sometimes', he writes, 'a sufficiently large number of important trading countries have accepted a later treaty such that those members have felt that the risk of complaint by GATT Contracting Parties who have not accepted the later treaty making is minimal. This is legally a bit messy, but may be pragmatically acceptable'. John H. Jackson, 'World Trade Rules and Environmental Policies: Congruence or Conflict?', *Washington and Lee Law Review* 49:4 (Fall, 1992): 1227–78.

28. The Convention on International Trade in Endangered Species of Wild Flora and Fauna, March 3, 1973, 27 UST. 1087, T.I.A.S. No. 8249, 993 U.N.T.S. 243.

29. The Basel Convention on the Control of Transboundary Movements of Hazardous Wastes and Their Disposal, adopted and opened for signature March 22, 1989, reprinted in UNEP/I.G. 80/3, 28 I.L.M. 649 (1989) (entered into force May, 1992).

30. Robert Repetto, 'Trade and Environmental Policies: Achieving Complementarities and Avoiding Conflicts', World Resources Institute, *Issues and Ideas*, Washington, DC (July, 1993).

31. Jessica Tuchman Mathews, 'Redefining Security', *Foreign Affairs* 68:2 (Spring, 1989): 162–77.

32. A recent suggestion to tie food aid to environmental improvements is Orville L. Freeman, 'Perspectives and Prospects', *Agricultural History*, 66:2 (Spring 1992): 3–11.
33. For an informed and optimistic view of the New Europe, see Axel Krause, *Inside the New Europe*, New York: Harper Collins, 1991.
34. Tim Golden, 'A History of Pollution in Mexico Casts Cloud Over Trade Accord', *New York Times*, August 16, 1993, p. A–1.

REFERENCES

Anderson, K. (1992), 'The Standard Welfare Economics of Policies Affecting Trade and the Environment', in K. Anderson and R. Blackhurst (eds), *The Greening of World Trade Issues*, Ann Arbor, MI: The University of Michigan Press, pp. 25–48.

Antle, J.M. and R.E. Just (1992), 'Conceptual and Empirical Foundations for Agricultural–Environmental Policy Analysis', *Journal of Environmental Quality*, 21: 307–16.

Basel Convention on the Control of Transboundary Movements of Hazardous Wastes and Their Disposal, adopted and opened for signature March 22, 1989, reprinted in UNEP/I.G. 80/3, 28 I.L.M. 649 (1989) (entered into force May, 1992).

Baumol, W.J. and W.E. Oates (1974), *The Theory of Environmental Policy: Externalities, Public Outlays, and the Quality of Life*, Englewood Cliffs, NJ: Prentice Hall.

Boadway, R.W. and N. Bruce (1984), *Welfare Economics*, New York: Basil Blackwell.

Boyd, James (1993), 'The Allocation of Environmental Liabilities in Central and Eastern Europe', *Resources. Resources for the Future*, 112: 1–6.

Brown, D.K., A.V. Deardorff and R.M. Stern (1993), 'International Labor Standards and Trade: A Theoretical Analysis', University of Michigan, July 23, 1993.

Convention on International Trade in Endangered Species of Wild Flora and Fauna, March 3, 1973, 27 UST. 1087, T.I.A.S. No. 8249, 993 U.N.T.S. 243.

Davis, O.A. and A.B. Whinston (1962), 'Externalities, Welfare, and the Theory of Games', *Journal of Political Economy*, 70: 241–62.

Dean, Judith M. (1991), 'Trade and the Environment: A Survey of the Literature', in Patrick Low (ed.), *International Trade and the Environment*, World Bank Discussion Papers.

Freeman, Orville L. (1992), 'Perspectives and Prospects', *Agricultural History*, 66(2): 3–11.

Golden, Tim (1993), 'A History of Pollution in Mexico Casts Cloud Over Trade Accord', *New York Times*, August 16, 1993, p. A–1.

Greenhouse, Steven (1993), 'Surge in Growth in Third World Gives an Economic Lift to US', *New York Times*, August 19, 1993, p. A–1.

Grossman, Gene M. and Alan B. Krueger (1991), 'Environmental Impacts of a North American Free trade Agreement', Woodrow Wilson Institute for Public Affairs, Princeton University, October 8, 1991.

Harold, Courtney and C. Ford Runge (1993), 'GATT and the Environment: Policy Research Needs', *American Journal of Agricultural Economics*, 75: 789–93.

Hartmann, Monika and Alan Matthews (1993), 'Sustainable Agriculture in the European Community: The Role of Policy', fall, 1991, forthcoming in *Forum for Applied Research and Public Policy*, 8, 1993.

Hazilla, M. and R.J. Kopp (1990), 'Social Cost of Environmental Quality Regulations: A General Equilibrium Analysis', *Journal of Political Economy* 98(4): 853–73.

Houck, J.P. (1986), *The Elements of Agricultural Trade Policies*, New York: Macmillan.

Housman, Robert (1992), 'The Interaction of International Trade and Environmental Agreements', Center for International Environmental Law, Washington, DC, June 1, 1992, p. 3.

Housman, Robert F. and D. Zaelke (1992), 'Trade, Environment and Sustainable Development: A Primer', *Hastings International and Comparative Law Review*, 15: 535–612.

Hudec, Robert and Daniel Farber (1992), 'Distinguishing Environmental Measures from Trade Barriers', University of Minnesota, Workshop on International Economic Policy, Nov. 17, 1992.

International Trade Reporter, May 27, 1992 (*Mississippi Poultry Association Inc. v. Madigan*, No. J91–0086(W), DC SMiss 4/23/92).

Jackson, John H. (1992), 'World Trade Rules and Environmental Policies: Congruence or Conflict?', *Washington and Lee Law Review*, 49(4): 1227–78.

Krause, Axel (1991), *Inside the New Europe*, New York: Harper Collins.

Krutilla, K. (1991), 'Environmental Regulation in an Open Economy', *Journal of Environmental Economics and Management*, 20: 127–42.

Livingston, Marie L., Harald von Witzke and Ulrich Hausner (1993), 'The Political Economy of International Pollution', Center for International Food and Agricultural Policy, St. Paul, MN.

Lloyd, Peter J. (1992), 'The Problem of Optimal Environmental Policy Choice', in K. Anderson and R. Blackhurst (eds), *The Greening of World Trade Issues*, Ann Arbor, MI: The University of Michigan Press, pp. 49–72.

Marchand, J.R. and K.P. Russell (1973), 'Externalities, Liability, Separability and Resource Allocation', *American Economic Review*, 63: 611–20.

Mathews, Jessica Tuchman (1989), 'Redefining Security', *Foreign Affairs*, 68(2): 162–77.

McKeith, Malissa H. (1991), 'The Environment and Free Trade: Meeting Halfway at the Mexican Border', *Pacific Basin Law Journal*, 10(1): 183–211.

Merrifield, J.D. (1988), 'The Impact of Selected Abatement Strategies on Transnational Pollution, the Terms of Trade, and Factor Rewards: A General Equilibrium Approach', *Journal of Environmental Economics and Management*, 15: 259–84.

Mishan, E.J. (1971), 'The Postwar Literature on Externalities: An Interpretive Essay,' *Journal of Economic Literature*, 9(1): 1–28.

Mohnen, V.A. (1988), 'The Challenge of Acid Rain', *Scientific American*, 259: 30–38.

Repetto, Robert (1993), 'Trade and Environmental Policies: Achieving Complementarities and Avoiding Conflicts', World Resources Institute, *Issues and Ideas*, Washington, DC.

Rice, Faye (1993), 'Who Scores Best on the Environment', *Fortune* (July 26, 1993): 114–22.

Runge, C. Ford (1987), 'Induced Agricultural Innovation and Environmental Quality: The Case of Groundwater Regulation', *Land Economics*, 63(3).

Runge, C. Ford (1990), 'Environmental Risk and the World Economy', *The American Prospect*, 1: 114–18.

Runge, C. Ford (1994), 'The Environmental Effects of Trade in the Agricultural Sector,' in *The Environmental Effects of Trade*, Paris: OECD (Organisation for Economic Co-operation and Development).

Runge, C. Ford, François Ortalo-Magné and Philip Vande Kamp (1994), *Free Trade, Protected Environment: Balancing Trade Liberalization and Environmental Interests*, New York: Council on Foreign Relations.

Samuelson, P.A. (1954), 'The Pure Theory of Public Expenditure,' *The Review of Economics and Statistics*, 36: 387–89.

Sandler, Todd (1992), *Collective Action: Theory and Applications*, Ann Arbor: The University of Michigan Press, Chapter 2, pp. 19–62.

Schapiro, Mark (1993), 'Murder on the Orient: Pricey travel lets US hunters kill rare game', Condé Nast *Traveler* (August, 1993): 23–5.

Sullivan, John B., Jr, Melissa Gonzales, Gary R. Krieger and C. Ford Runge (1992), 'Health–Related Hazards of Agriculture', in John B. Sullivan, Jr and Gary R. Krieger (eds), *Hazardous Materials Toxicology: Clinical Principles of Environmental Health*, Baltimore: Williams & Wilkins.

US Congress, Office of Technology Assessment, Chapter 3, pp. 42–6. The Montreal Protocol on Substances that Deplete the Ozone Layer, adopted and opened for signature Sept. 16, 1987, reprinted in 26 I.L.M. 1541 (1987) (entered into force January 1, 1989).

Vienna Convention on the Law of Treaties, opened for signature May 23, 1969, UN Doc. A/COIF. 39/27, 8 I.L.M. 679, Article 30, 8 I.L.M. at 691.

Wirth, David A. (1992), 'A Matchmaker's Challenge: Marrying International Law and American Environmental Law', *Virginia Journal of International Law*, 32(2): 377–420.

9. Strategic Environmental Policy, International Trade and the Single European Market

Alistair Ulph[*]

INTRODUCTION

The recent moves to further liberalize trade both at a global level through the Uruguay Round and regionally through NAFTA and the Single European Market have prompted an extensive debate on the implications of such trade liberalizations for the environment, with suggestions from some environmentalists that some forms of trade restrictions may be justified in order to protect the environment (see Anderson and Blackhurst (eds) (1992) and Low (ed.) (1992) for good recent overviews of some aspects of this debate). Many of the contributions from economists to this debate have been framed, explicitly or implicitly, in the context of the conventional competitive model of international trade. But the debate has also prompted some new research which has exploited the literature on strategic international trade with imperfectly competitive markets (see, for example, Helpman and Krugman (1989)) to reassess the links between environmental policy and international trade.

In this chapter I want to summarize some of the findings from this recent literature and draw out some implications for the design of environmental policy within a free-trade area such as the Single European Market (SEM). The structure of the chapter will be as follows. In the next section I will review the conventional analysis of the links between international trade and the environment and implications that have been drawn for environmental policy within the SEM. In the following I will outline the main results from the literature on strategic environmental policy, and finally I will assess what these results might imply for the design of environmental policy in SEM.

[*] Comments by the discussants and other participants are gratefully acknowledged. This chapter forms part of a research programme on environmental policy, international trade and imperfect competition funded by an ESRC grant Y320253038 and an EC grant, for which financial support I am very grateful.

235

TRADE AND THE ENVIRONMENT – THE CONVENTIONAL ANALYSIS

A. The Issues

Environmentalists have expressed a number of concerns about the consequences of more liberalized trading regimes for the environment. At the simplest level there is the concern that the resulting expansion of production, consumption and trade will result in increasing pollution emissions and depletion of natural resources (e.g. Hudson (1992) expressed this concern in terms of the additional amount of energy resources that will be consumed as result of trade liberalization). For example, it has been calculated that the SEM will result in increased emissions of SO_2 of 8–9 percent and of NO_x of 12–14 percent by 2010 in the absence of further policies (Schneider et al. (1989)).

A rather different concern relates particularly to pollution related to processes or production methods (PPM), namely that if countries differ in the severity of policies to protect the environment there will be migration of production activity to countries where policies are most lenient, creating 'pollution havens' or pollution hot-spots. If countries fear that there will be an outward migration of production if they set tougher environmental regulations than other countries they will have an incentive to weaken their environmental regulations (sometimes called 'ecological dumping'). To prevent such ecological dumping it is argued that countries seeking to take a tougher environmental stance need to be able to protect their industries by policies such as subsidies to exports or taxes on imports from countries with weaker environmental policies equal to the difference between the costs of environmental regulations in the two countries (Arden-Clarke (1991)); if that is not allowed (as seems likely under current GATT rulings – see for example, Pearce (1992)) there needs to be harmonization of environmental regulations across countries (sometimes expressed as having 'a level playing field'). Not surprisingly, these policy recommendations often find support from industrialists whose industries are the subject of environmental regulation.

Note the caveat that the problem of ecological dumping is supposed to relate to pollution caused in the process of production. Where pollution is related to the consumption of products, e.g. exhaust gases from vehicles or the disposal of waste, then the same argument suggests that countries will try to protect their producers from imports by setting environmental product standards that are different from, and this may imply tougher than, those of its trading rivals. While this may not be a matter of concern for environmentalists, it represents just as much a distortion of resource allocation as the setting of too lax regulations implied by ecological dumping.

The conventional response to these arguments from economists can be rather baldly summarized as follows. Clearly if there are externalities in the production and consumption process, then a completely *laissez-faire* allocation of resources will not be efficient. In particular it need not be true that trade liberalization will be welfare improving – a country that is led to export (import) more of a good whose production (consumption) pollutes the domestic environment may find that the increase in pollution outweighs the conventional gains from trade (Dean (1992)). But the correct implication is not that trade liberalization should be discouraged, but that governments should impose policies that directly tackle the source of the efficiency, e.g. Pigovian taxes on pollution emissions (e.g. Dean (1992) among others). Provided optimal environmental policies are implemented then the usual arguments about the gains from liberalizing trade go through, even allowing for possible deteriorations in the environment of some countries as a consequence of the expansions of production, consumption and trade (see Anderson (1992) for the formal analysis). Note that it need not be the case that a free-trade equilibrium with optimal environmental policies necessarily leads to more pollution than in autarky. For if countries feel very strongly about the environment then the welfare gains from trade liberalization could be taken, at least in part, in improvements in the environment in all countries (Rauscher (1992), Pearce (1992)).

If optimal environmental policies are not in place, then trade policies such as a tax on exports of a good whose production pollutes the environment, will sometimes achieve some of the effects of environmental policies, but are very much second-best compared to the use of environmental policies. In other cases the use of trade policies can reduce welfare (again see Anderson (1992)), and can be detrimental even in terms of the attempt to protect the environment (see Barbier and Rauscher (1992) for a theoretical analysis in the context of forestry policy and Braga (1992) for a case study of Indonesian forestry policy).

The reason why optimal environmental policies may not be implemented may be explained by the costs of implementing such policies, particularly for poor countries, or by the fact that the political process does not perfectly reflect the preferences of the population for environmental amenity. But, at least in theory, it should not be explained by the ecological dumping argument outlined above. For, as long as pollution is an entirely domestic matter (there is no transboundary pollution or problems of a global commons nature where there are well-known failures of coordination), and as long as trade takes place in competitive markets, then countries have no incentive to engage in ecological dumping (see Long and Siebert (1989)), i.e. they will not distort their environmental policy purely to gain a trade advantage. The reason is simple – if countries take prices as given then they cannot affect their terms of trade by their environmental policy and so should set their environmental policies so as to maximize welfare – i.e. setting marginal damage cost from pollution emissions equal to the marginal cost of abating pollution. Of course this calculation will take account of the fact that the countries are trading; so the optimal level of pollution taxes, say, will be different in a trading equilibrium from those in autarky, simply because the pattern of production and hence the levels of emissions and marginal damage costs will be different in a trading equilibrium than in autarky. But the rule for setting pollution taxes will be the same under autarky and free trade.

In general it will be expected that countries will differ in the severity of their environmental regulations, to reflect genuine differences in either their endowments of environmental resources or their preferences for environmental amenity. And these differences will lead to geographical reallocation of production. But this is just part of the process of countries exploiting their comparative advantage, with countries which are relatively well endowed in environmental resources specializing in the production of goods which make relatively intensive use of the environment (see Dean (1992) and Robertson (1992), among many others, for this argument). Attempts to harmonize regulations or to allow countries to distort trade through export subsidies or countervailing import taxes would interfere with the process of exploiting comparative advantage and produce a less efficient outcome, which may even be inferior from a strictly environmental point of view, from the allocation produced by free trade (combined with optimal environmental policies).

Two sets of arguments have been advanced to suggest that the possibility of production moving to areas of less strict environmental regulation may not be as drastic as some fear. The first set is theoretical. To begin with the process may be self-limiting through a process of 'arbitrage' or factor-price equalization; as production migrates to regions with more abundant environmental resources (lower pollution taxes), this will drive up emissions in those regions and drive down emissions in the regions that lose polluting activities; assuming that governments respond to these changes in pollution, this will lead to tighter regulations (higher pollution taxes) in the laxer regions and conversely in the stricter regions; this process will continue until regulations are harmonized (pollution taxes equalized). Governments may not simply respond passively to changes in pollution but may be concerned about irreversible damage caused by growing pollution and the laxer regions may tighten their policies in advance of future pollution emissions (in other words the calculation of marginal damage costs reflects not just current damages but an option value to prevent irreversible future damage) (see Siebert (1991)). Equally firms may anticipate future tightening of regulations and not find it in their interest to exploit laxer environmental regulations.

The second set of arguments is empirical and suggests that to date the impact of environmental regulation in determining the location of polluting industries has been small. (Surveys of this evidence can be found in Dean (1992) and Pearce (1992).) There are three main kinds of evidence advanced. First it is noted that the costs of meeting environmental regulations form a small part of total costs of production – for example, in the 24 most pollution-intensive industries in the US Tobey (1990) found that environmental regulations accounted for 1.92–2.89 percent of total costs. Second, there have been studies of how the geographical location of polluting industries has changed over time. Low and Yeats (1992) and Lucas, Wheeler and Hettige (1992) show that in the last three decades there has been a migration of polluting industries from developed to developing countries, although in 1988 the OECD countries still accounted for the vast majority (74.3 percent) of industrial pollution (down from 77.7 percent in 1965). There are many factors that could explain this – the natural process of development, changes in other sources of comparative advantage – apart from environmental policy. Lucas et al. show that the growth of toxic-intensity of LDCs accelerated in the 1970s and 1980s, when OECD countries were tightening their environmental policies, which is suggestive of some displacement effect, but also that the policies of the LDCs, in particular the degree of openness of the economies, was also an important contributing factor with the more closed economies experiencing a much faster rise in polluting industries. Finally there are various models which simulate the impacts of environmental policies on production and trade; perhaps of greatest interest are the various models of policies to deal with global warming, since the costs of dealing with global warming are markedly higher than previous pollution problems. As an example, the GREENS model studied the effects of unilateral action by some countries in stabilizing their CO_2 emissions on the competitiveness of those energy-intensive industries; despite very high carbon taxes, the output of those industries declined by only between 1.2 and 4.4 percent while the output of the same industries in regions taking no steps to curb CO_2 emissions rose by less than 1 percent (Oliviera-Martins et al. (1993)). So again the displacement effect of quite large differences in environmental policies appears small.

B. Implications for EC Environmental Policy

I now summarize the implications that are usually drawn from the above analysis of the links between environmental policy and international trade for the design of environmental policy, with particular reference to the Single European Market (see Folmer and Howe (1991), Klepper (1992) and Siebert (1991), on which I have drawn heavily for this section).

The Single European Act (1987) aimed to reduce technical, fiscal and physical barriers to the free movement of goods and factors between the countries of the EC. It also provided, for the first time, a proper legal basis for EC environmental policy, with Article 130r requiring environmental policy of EC policy and Article 130a giving high priority to environmental objectives. The Act incorporated a number of broad principles of environmental policy that had been set out in previous Action Programmes (see Haigh (1990) and Johnson and Corcelle (1989) for detailed accounts of earlier EC environmental policy). For example, Article 130r(2) contains the Prevention Principle and the Polluter Pays Principle while Article 130r(4) sets out the Subsidiarity Principle which says that environmental policy should be taken at the lowest level compatible with dealing with a particular environmental problem, so that pollution problems which occur entirely within the boundaries of a Member State would be the responsibility of its national government.

In terms of product standards the broad approach of the EC has been to try to completely harmonize different national standards. But this is not being done entirely through Community level regulation. If products are not subject to harmonization, then under Article 36, national governments can set national regulations, including limits on the free movement of goods, to protect flora and fauna. Where products are subject to harmonization, Article 100a sets Community-wide maximum standards. However Article 130s allows national governments to set tougher regulations within their sphere of influence. This is subject to two qualifications. First, Article 100a allows for qualified majority voting, and the European Court is still to decide whether a condition for invoking 130s is that the Member State must have voted against the Community regulation. Second, both Articles 36 and 130s may be in conflict with the free movement of goods enshrined in Article 30. The Commission applies the mutual recognition or country of origin principle that if a product is lawfully produced and sold in one Member State it must have access to all Member States. It is left to the European Court to resolve the implicit conflict between the mutual recognition principle and the right of Member States to protect their own environments. The broad principles it has used are that there must be no discrimination between foreign and domestically produced goods or there must be no better policy which could achieve the same environmental objectives but with less discrimination. Thus Italy has been able to restrict the content of phosphates in detergents since this applies to domestic and foreign detergents and there are available detergents which comply with the restriction; but Ireland was not allowed to ban beer in cans since, although aluminum cans are clearly an environmental problem, Ireland had not banned the use of cans for soft drinks. Further examples are discussed in Klepper (1992), who argues that by taking a tough line of rejecting environmental regulations which had the slightest suspicion of being trade-related the European Court has made it unlikely that Member States will try to use environmental regulations to segment markets.

The approach to product standards is thus very much in line with the analysis earlier in this section: where pollution is an entirely domestic concern, national governments should be allowed to set their own levels of environmental regulations, provided that such regulations are not a screen for trade protection; while in the short run there may be differences between Member States, in the long run it is hoped that arbitrage processes will lead to harmonization (Siebert (1991) and Folmer and Howe (1991)).

Similar arguments apply to the case of process and production methods where the freeing up of movement of factors of production raises the concern that Member States may set too lax levels of regulations in order to attract inward investment. Siebert (1991) argues that Member States can be left to set their regulations where marginal damage costs equal marginal abatement costs; in the short run this may lead to different levels of environmental protection, in different Member States reflecting the different scarcity values attached to the environment; while this may lead to relocations of production activity, this is just part of the optimal adjustment to environmental regulation; in the long run the process of locational arbitrage will bring about harmonization of standards. Folmer and Howe (1991) agree that regulations concerning production emissions can be left to the discretion of individual Member States, although they argue that the EC may wish to guarantee that there is a minimum level of environmental quality available to citizens in all Member States; they provide a number of the standard arguments for believing that there is unlikely to be large-scale relocation of production activity.

Obviously transboundary pollution cannot be decentralized to individual Member States to act independently, and if it cannot be resolved by negotiations between the individual parties, then the Single European Act, under the subsidiarity principle, allows for Community action. Siebert (1991) and Folmer and Howe (1991) call for the setting of international diffusion norms for pollution that crosses state boundaries – the analogue of the country of origin principle with states being responsible for pollution which originates within their boundaries but may be exported to other countries; once these norms have been agreed it is then left to individual Member States to decide how to implement them.

This raises the more general question of choice of policy instruments. Siebert (1991) argues that again this should be left to individual states to decide, though noting, along with Folmer and Howe (1991) that the use of instruments such as licenses (for production methods, emissions, or polluters) which are non-tradeable are more likely to be abused as methods of restricting entry than pricing instruments such as emission taxes or tradeable permits.

STRATEGIC ENVIRONMENTAL POLICY AND INTERNATIONAL TRADE

The conventional analysis outlined in the previous section suggested that many of the fears of environmentalists about the effects of trade liberalization such as the creation of the Single European Market are unfounded: with respect to purely domestic pollution, if pollution is related to production there are no reasons to believe that states will engage in ecological dumping and while there may be differences in the severity of environmental regulation this is consistent with differences in environmental scarcity, and if this leads to relocation of production that is an efficient adjustment to resource allocation; in the long run one might expect harmonization of regulations. If pollution is related to consumption, there may be a need to ensure that countries do not use product standards to protect domestic industries, but that requires restrictions on discriminatory use of standards, not necessarily harmonization, though again harmonization may result in the long run. International spillovers are an issue which cannot be resolved by independent action of individual states, but that is true whether trade is liberalized or not. The design of environmental policy within the EC is broadly consistent with this view of the links between environmental policy and international trade.

In this section I wish to re-examine some of these arguments in the light of recent studies of strategic environmental policy and international trade. The particular argument I want to focus on is the question of whether the removal of conventional trade instruments implied by trade liberalization provides incentives for governments to distort their environmental policies from the first-best rule of setting emission targets such that marginal damage costs equals marginal abatement costs. I will begin by considering the case where pollution is related to production, because that is the case for which most analysis has so far been conducted, and also the case where pollution damage is entirely within a country's boundaries, because, as already noted, transboundary pollution provides well-known incentives for countries acting independently not to set optimal policies.

The concern discussed in the previous section is that countries producing pollution-intensive goods may have incentives to protect their domestic industries by setting too lax environmental targets i.e. emission levels where marginal abatement costs are below marginal damage costs, a situation characterized as 'ecological dumping'. The conventional response was that with perfectly competitive markets there would be no incentive for ecological dumping, and attention focused on short-run differences between the targets set by countries with different endowments of environmental resources and the extent to which these would be eliminated in the long run through arbitrage.

However, the assumption of perfectly competitive international markets, while plausible for some markets may not be appropriate for all markets; more importantly it is not a very useful framework in which to analyze the question of ecological dumping for countries which have no incentives to distort their trade using trade instruments, so the question of using environmental policy as a surrogate for missing trade instruments cannot arise. When this assumption is dropped, then scope for strategic environmental trade policy emerges, although as we shall see careful analysis of strategic environmental policy shows that the concerns of environmentalists and the conventional response are too simplistic.

An obvious first step is to analyze the situation where producers act competitively, but countries are sufficiently large that they can influence the terms of trade they face. Rauscher (1994) considers a simple model in which countries produce two commodities, one of which is clean, the other dirty (it uses inputs of an environmental resource in production). Countries impose emission taxes on the use of environmental resources. If countries cannot influence the terms of trade between the clean and dirty commodity, they will set the emission tax equal to marginal damage cost. If countries can influence the terms of trade between the clean and dirty good, then an exporter (importer) of the dirty good will set an emission tax which is higher (lower) than marginal damage cost. The same result is derived in Krutilla (1991). The intuition is straightforward. Exporters of the pollution-intensive good would like to drive up the price of the good in which they have comparative advantage; if they could impose an (optimal) export tariff they would do so; in the absence of such tariffs they will distort their environmental policy to achieve the same outcome. Note that it is importing countries, i.e. those which are relatively poorly endowed with environmental resources, which will cut emission taxes below the first-best rate; countries well-endowed with environmental resources, which might be thought to include poorer countries, far from seeking to become 'pollution havens' would want to set environmental policies which are tougher than would be implied by the first-best rule. The above arguments were made in the context of pollution related to production; if pollution is related to consumption the arguments are reversed: countries which are net exporters will set too lax a pollution tax, those which are net importers will set too tough a pollution tax (Krutilla (1991)).

The above model works within the conventional Heckscher–Ohlin model of international trade with perfect competition at the level of individual producers, although countries have market power. In the past decade, a new set of international trade models have been derived in which producers are modeled as acting in imperfectly competitive markets, and this leads to rather different policy conclusions. The key insight is that with imperfect competition, producers can now earn rents, and this raises the possibility of strategic behavior by either producers or governments to try to shift rents in their favor, essentially by obtaining a larger share of the world market. A number of articles have sought to build on this literature to examine the scope for using environmental policy in a strategic fashion.

A useful starting point is the chapter by Barrett (1994) which uses the familiar Brander and Spencer (1985) framework. Suppose that there are a number of countries which produce a particular commodity (the analysis for the rest of this section will be partial equilibrium – dealing with a single market). In each country there is a single producer (location of producers is taken as fixed), but there are no consumers of this good in these countries. The producers compete in a Cournot fashion (i.e. each producer sets its level of output to maximize profits taking as given the outputs of other producers). Production involves pollution, which can be abated, at a cost. Each government chooses the level of emissions it wants its domestic producer to meet (so governments use emission standards as their policy instrument) and its welfare function consists of producer profits (rents) minus costs of environmental damage. Barrett shows that if governments act non-cooperatively in setting their emission targets, then they will set too high levels of emissions, i.e. marginal abatement cost will be below marginal damage cost. The rationale is exactly that implied in the ecological dumping argument; each government realizes that by allowing its producer to emit more pollution this will reduce the abatement costs it has to face for any given level of output, and so reduce its overall costs of production; *ceteris paribus* this would allow the domestic producer to obtain a larger share of the world market and hence larger profits. Note that when all governments act strategically, then, as long as countries are fairly similar, all governments are worse off than if they had used the first-best rule for environmental policy; for not only will each country have a poorer environment, but the attempt to boost the output of domestic producers at the expense of foreign producers just leads to total output rising and hence total profits falling, with little change in market shares.

While this model predicts that independent national governments will set too lax environmental targets as a surrogate for not being able to use trade instruments such as export subsidies, Barrett makes the important point that the extent of strategic distortion of environmental policy will be less than would be the case if export subsidies could be used; because it is costless to impose export subsidies (assuming they could be financed by lump sum taxation) whereas there is a cost to relaxing environmental targets.

I want now to consider a number of extensions of this basic model. First, note that Kennedy (1993) has derived similar results using emission taxes as the environmental policy instruments; governments will set emissions taxes too low, i.e. below the level of marginal damage costs. How do the two instruments compare? Note first that in the absence of any strategic behavior by governments, with a single producer in each country emission taxes and emission standards would be equivalent. In Ulph (1993) I have shown that the extent of ecological dumping will be greater when governments use emission taxes than emission standards (Copeland (1991) derived closely related results, but in the context of a single country). The rationale is as follows. The purpose of strategic intervention by a government is to try to raise the output of its producer at the expense of lower output by foreign producers. Now, for a given reduction of output by foreign producers, if the domestic producer thinks it is faced with a fixed emission tax it will be encouraged to expand output more than if it is faced with a fixed emission standard, for as its output rises it will have to pay increasing marginal costs of abatement to stay within the emission standard, but a constant tax on extra emissions. Thus for any given reduction in output by foreign producers, domestic producers will get a greater increase in market share when governments use taxes than when they use standards, so strategic intervention is more successful when governments use emission taxes than emission standards. Of course, for the reasons explained above, when all governments act in the same way, welfare will be lower when taxes are used than when standards are used, for there is a greater deterioration in the environment and a greater expansion of output, and hence reduction in profit. Note however that this does not imply that governments will choose to use emission standards. In Ulph (1992b) I showed that the game of choice of policy instruments is a Prisoner's Dilemma, in which, for any given choice of policy instrument by rival governments, it is better for a government to choose emission taxes than emission standards for the reason given above, namely that it will encourage the domestic producer to produce greater output. But the combined effect of this decision by all governments is to make them all worse off than if they had all chosen to use emission standards.

Now as noted earlier, the introduction of imperfect competition gives incentives to both governments and producers strategically to obtain a larger share of the market. In the case of producers, strategic behavior can take the form of investment in capital or R&D designed to lower their operating costs in the subsequent competition for market share. Producers will thus be led to overinvest in capital or R&D (i.e. producers will invest beyond the point where the marginal revenue product of capital or R&D equals the marginal cost of capital or R&D). Note that this strategic behavior by producers is counterproductive for the similar reasons as for governments – in equilibrium all producers overinvest in capital or R&D, which is costly, and this leads to an overall expansion of output which drives down industry profits.

In Ulph (1992a, 1992b and 1993) I have analyzed the implications of such strategic behavior by producers for environmental policy. To begin with, I will assume that governments do not act strategically, so environmental policy is governed by the condition that emissions should be set so that marginal damage cost equals marginal abatement cost (in Ulph 1992a,b I used a slightly different notion of non-strategic behavior by governments – that the target for emissions was specified exogenously, as set, say, by an international agreement; the main results are the same for both definitions). In this sense, there is no ecological dumping. However that still leaves the question of the choice of policy instrument. For exactly the same reasons as given above, the use of emission taxes will induce more strategic behavior by producers than will the use of emission standards, because the return to strategic behavior by producers is greater when taxes are used than when standards are used. Note that even although governments are not engaging in ecological dumping, the level of emissions will be higher when producers act strategically than if producers do not act strategically. These effects are greater when governments use emission taxes rather than emission standards. In terms of welfare, then, the use of emission taxes rather than emission standards will induce a greater reduction in profits, because of the greater incentives for strategic behavior by producers, and greater damage costs because of higher emissions. So welfare is lower when governments choose taxes rather than standards. Nevertheless, for the same reasons as before, the choice of emission taxes will be a dominant strategy for governments.

In Ulph (1993) I considered what happened when both governments and producers act strategically. There are now two effects of relaxing environmental policy. First, there is the direct effect of reducing producers' costs; second, there is the indirect effect that this reduction in cost increases the return to strategic investment by producers, so that there is now a second route by which environmental policy can act on producers' behavior. In terms of the direct effect, since government strategic behavior is essentially a substitute for producer strategic behavior, the fact that producers are acting strategically means there is less need for governments to act strategically. But in terms of the indirect effect, the fact that there is an additional route by which governments can try to help their domestic producers means that there is a stronger incentive for governments to act strategically. In the model I developed in Ulph (1993) it turned out that the direct effect dominated the indirect effect, so that there is rather less ecological dumping when both producers and governments act strategically than when only the government acts strategically.

To summarize, the studies cited so far have shown that there are incentives for governments to weaken their environmental policies by setting emission targets where marginal abatement costs are below marginal damage costs, and the extent of this ecological dumping depends on whether producers are also acting strategically, and on the policy instruments chosen by the government, with the use of emission taxes being a dominant strategy, but leading to an inferior outcome to the case where all governments use standards. However these conclusions have been reached under a rather special set of assumptions and I want now to consider how robust these conclusions are to relaxing these assumptions. There are seven assumptions I wish to vary.

First, it has been assumed that there are no consumers of the product located in the countries which produce the commodity. If there were, then governments would be concerned about the fact that imperfectly competitive markets produce too little output, and would want to encourage producers to expand output. If environmental policy is the only mechanism for doing this, this will reinforce the incentive to slacken environmental regulations (see Copeland (1991), Katsoulacos and Xepapadeas (1992) for discussions in the closed economy context). This may also change the conclusions about taxes and standards; for, as already noted, emission taxes induce higher output than emission standards, and while this is bad for profits it is desirable for consumers; while the choice of emission taxes remains a dominant strategy for governments, with a sufficient share of the world's consumers located in the producing countries, this may produce a superior outcome to the use of emission standards by all governments.

Second, it has been assumed that there is a single producer in each country. If there are several producers, all acting non-cooperatively, then, as Barrett (1994) has shown, this gives a reason for governments to set tougher environmental policies than in the case where there is a single producer, because the optimal outcome from the point of view of a producing country is for its producers to collude and restrict their output; if this does not happen, then government environmental policy may act as a surrogate for bringing about a restriction in output. With a large enough number of firms, the optimal policy may be tougher than the first-best rule of setting emissions where marginal abatement costs equal marginal damage costs. This is similar to the Rauscher (1994) argument discussed earlier that with competitive producers exporters of a pollution-intensive good will want to set environmental policies which are stricter than the first-best.

Third, it has been assumed that producers act in a Cournot fashion, i.e. they use output as the variable they compete with. It is well known from the strategic trade literature that if producers act in a Bertrand fashion – setting prices not output – then that can reverse policy conclusions, and the same is true here. As Barrett (1994) notes, Bertrand competition would lead governments to set environmental policies which are tougher than the first-best rule. The intuition is that in Bertrand competition toughening environmental policy causes the domestic producer to raise its price, but the foreign producer responds by raising its price even further, so each government believes that by toughening environmental policy it will lead to an outcome with higher prices and a larger market share for its own producer. However, while in equilibrium all governments cannot succeed in raising the market shares of their domestic producers, the raising of prices can be beneficial to producers, so in equilibrium producers may make higher profits than if governments had not acted strategically; since there is also a welfare gain from reduced environmental damage, strategic behavior by governments can be beneficial, unlike the case with Cournot competition. Of course this welfare gain is at the expense of consuming countries.

Fourth, it may be thought that the problems of distortion of environmental policy come from the non-cooperative behavior by governments in trying to gain advantage for their domestic producers at the expense of rival producers, and that in a situation like the Single European Market governments may act more cooperatively, so that the problem would not arise. This is only partially correct. If all producing governments colluded in setting their environmental policies, then, reverting to the Cournot model, Barrett (1994) has shown that the governments would want to set environmental policies which are tougher than the first-best rule. The reason is that with no strategic behavior by governments or producers industry output would be higher than that which maximizes total industry profits, so governments would wish to restrict total output, and if environmental policy is the only instrument available for doing that, they will want to set environmental policy to be tougher than it would be in first-best.

Fifth, it has been assumed that all governments with producers located in them are implementing an environmental policy. Suppose that only some governments are trying to cut emissions, perhaps because the pollutant is a global one and only some governments have signed up to an international agreement to cut emissions. This is the situation considered in Ulph (1992b). Of course, if only some governments act to cut emissions, then producers in those countries are going to lose market-share producers in the countries which 'free ride'. But more importantly, I showed that this can change sharply the conclusions drawn earlier about the choice of policy instruments. For if producers are acting strategically, I argued above that the use of emission standards rather than taxes would reduce the extent of strategic behavior by producers, relative to the case where either emission taxes were used, or no environmental policy was implemented. If all producers are affected in the same way, then the use of standards is desirable, because it reduces wasteful overinvestment in capital or R&D and reduces total output, and hence raises industry profits. But if only some producers face a reduced incentive to act strategically, then they will lose market share relative to producers who have not faced a reduced incentive to act strategically. Thus, in addition to the loss of market share due to the fact that some producers are faced with higher costs because their governments are imposing environmental policy on them, there is a second source of loss of market share arising from the change in incentives for strategic behavior induced by the policy instrument being used. Using a calibrated model of a particular industry I showed that the loss of market share due to this change in incentives for strategic behavior would be much larger than the loss of market share due to higher costs of production.

Sixth, the discussion so far has focused on the case where pollution is related to production. But, as the examples in the previous section indicate, much of the concern about the use of environmental policy as a means of protecting local industry is about the use of environmental regulations in the form of product standards. There has not been much analysis of this case in the strategic trade literature. Motta and Thisse (1993) examine the implications of governments setting minimum environmental standards on products, in a context where consumers care about the 'green' quality of products. They show that there can be advantages to a government setting a minimum environmental standard when other governments do not. But the minimum standard they consider is one which the government would set in autarky; they do not consider the question of whether governments would set excessively tough standards as for strategic trade considerations. This is an area where more work would be useful.

Finally, it has been assumed so far that the location of producers does not change as a result of environmental policy. I shall briefly summarize the results of a small number of studies that have addressed this question. Markusen et al. (1993) consider a situation where there are two regions, with one firm based in each region producing products which are imperfect substitutes for each other and whose production causes pollution. Each firm has to decide whether to build a plant in each market to serve local demand, whether to build a plant in its home market and serve the foreign market by exports, or not to produce at all. Assuming a firm chooses to produce, its choice between exporting and building a foreign plant involves trading off higher variable costs if it exports (due to transport costs or other trade costs) and higher fixed costs if it builds a foreign plant. But there is also an important effect in terms of market structure, for if two plants are located in the same market, that will make the market more competitive than if there is only plant located in that market facing competition from imports.

Markusen et al. (1993) then analyze the implications of one region imposing environmental policy. It is not possible to summarize all their conclusions but some broad points are worth making. First, because there are now discrete decisions being taken by producers about plant locations, simple marginal calculations of environmental policy are no longer adequate, for at critical levels of environmental policy, there will be a discrete change in plant locations and welfare will change discontinuously. Second, calculations of optimal environmental policy which ignore these changes in locations could be seriously misleading. Third, while a region which unilaterally imposes environmental policy is likely to drive some plants out of its region, the welfare consequences are much more complex than in the conventional analysis; for example if a foreign firm closes its foreign plant and now serves this market by exporting, that will give the domestic producer a degree of protection, despite being faced by higher operating costs; on the other hand if the domestic firm now decides to build a foreign plant rather than exporting, while environmental policy will make the domestic firm less competitive in its home market, it will become more competitive in the foreign market. Fourth, Markusen et al. analyzed the case where environmental policy operates on variable costs, and raising variable costs will tend to favor a policy of proliferating plants; but environmental policy could also affect fixed costs, and that will tend to favor a policy of reducing plant numbers; the implications for market structure and welfare will clearly differ.

In a related paper, Markusen et al. (1993) analyzed the case where governments in both regions imposed environmental policy but now they assumed there was a single firm which could decide whether or not to locate a plant in each of the two markets (so the issue of market structure is not present); they showed that governments in the two regions may either engage in competition to attract the firm to locate in their region, in which case they will set environmental policy which is too lax, or, if environmental damage costs are high, compete to get the plant to locate elsewhere by setting excessively tough environmental policies ('nimbyism').

In Ulph (1994) I developed a model to analyze a situation where there are several countries, in some of which governments wish to cut emissions of a pollutant; there are two producers, who have to decide whether or not to locate a plant in each market. Because of the assumption that governments who implement environmental policy have to cut emissions by a certain amount, there is no scope for competing between governments in terms of severity of environmental policy; however it is assumed that governments implement environmental policy by means of emissions taxes, and they can decide whether or not to rebate the tax revenues they raise to producers subject to the tax (this captures a feature of the proposed EC carbon/energy tax proposal that for certain sectors exposed to international trade the carbon tax would be waived if the industry took voluntary measures to implement the same reduction in emissions). Some of the findings of this model are as follows. First, it captures some of the aspects of the arbitrage arguments discussed in the previous section to the extent that the emission tax rate is now set endogenously to ensure that the emission target is reached. So the greater the number of plants that locate in a country the higher will be the emission tax in that country. However, contrary to expectations from conventional analysis, having a high emissions tax in a country does not necessarily mean that the price of the good in that country is high, because, as noted above, market structure is endogenous, and a country with high taxes is one with several plants located in it, and hence with a more competitive market structure. Moreover, there can be no presumption that plant location choices will result in completely equal tax rates in all countries, partly because with significant scale economies relative to demand there will not be sufficient plants to bring this about, and partly because equilibrium profits depend also on factors such as the endogenous degree of competitiveness in different markets.

Second, countries may differ in the extent to which their domestic producers are 'footloose'; but having a domestic producer which is not very footloose may be a distinct disadvantage if it allows rival producers to relocate to take advantage of differences in policies, and in particular if foreign firms relocate into the home market, making it more competitive and so driving down domestic profits. Finally, in work that I am currently undertaking these locational choice models are being extended to take account of inter-industry linkages on the demand side. The implication of this is that if producers in one industry are induced by a change in environmental policy to relocate to another country, there could be significant knock-on effects if producers in industries that are linked to the affected industry either upstream or downstream are induced to relocate as well, even if these industries are not affected by environmental policy.

To complete this section, I note two points. First, almost all of the results cited above have been derived from theoretical models, some of which have made very strong simplifying assumptions to ensure tractability of analysis. An important question is how significant these results might be in practice. To date little work has been done to incorporate these kinds of strategic policy considerations into realistic models of international trade. In Ulph (1992b, 1994) I used a calibrated model based on data from the world fertilizer industry to test out some of the theoretical analysis; this confirmed that the strategic factors could be significant, and could be at least as important quantitatively as the kind of effects of environmental policy studied in conventional analysis where environmental policy operates simply by changing costs of production within competitive markets. However, the calibrated model is still far from a realistic description of the particular industry.   Second, all the analysis reported in this section rests on the premise that governments are using environmental policy as a surrogate for trade or industrial policy because such policies have been restricted by trade liberalization.   While this is the framework within which concerns about trade liberalization have ben raised, there may be many policy areas other than environmental policy (e.g. social policy) where governments could act strategically, so the results reported here may be overstating the extent to which environmental policy would actually be distorted to achieve trade objectives.

IMPLICATIONS FOR POLICY

In this section I briefly draw out some of the implications of the results summarized in the previous section for the discussion in the second section of the conventional links between trade liberalization and environmental policy. There are seven points I shall make.

The first, rather obvious point, is that if the concern is with the possibility that governments may wish to distort their environmental policies to achieve trade objectives because conventional trade instruments for achieving these objectives have been outlawed by the process of trade liberalization, then it seems sensible to study the issue in models where governments have a serious rationale for wanting to intervene in trade; models of imperfect competition seem better suited to that purpose than models of perfect competition. The analysis of the previous section does suggest that when models of imperfect competition are studied then the optimistic beliefs of the second section that there was not much need to worry about governments distorting environmental policy to achieve trade objectives, may be misplaced.

A second, rather general, point is that much of the discussion in the conventional analysis seems to centre on questions of harmonization of environmental policies, either *ex ante* or *ex post*, and this misses the serious issue. It is quite possible to build models in the previous section where all countries are assumed to be identical, so that environmental policy in equilibrium is the same in all countries, but yet the policies are distorted in the sense that environmental policy does not satisfy the condition that marginal abatement cost equals marginal damage cost. Of course it is not going to be easy to check whether this condition is satisfied, but it is the relevant condition.

Third, while it is possible to construct plausible models in which governments will indeed have incentives to set environmental policies which are too lax, it is possible to construct equally plausible models in which governments will have incentives to set environmental policies which are too tough. While this may not be of concern to environmentalists, from the point of view of total welfare it is not obvious that one form of distortion is any less serious than the other. This should come as no surprise to those familiar with the literature on strategic international trade. One implication might be that governments are going to find it very difficult to know what form of distortion to environmental policy to implement; it is not clear whether this means they will eschew attempts to use environmental policy for trade reasons, or whether it means they are likely to intervene in quite inappropriate ways.

Fourth, the analysis shows that if producers themselves are acting strategically to manipulate the market for output, then there is an additional route by which environmental policy can have an effect – it not only affects costs of production and hence market equilibrium, but it also affects the level of strategic intervention carried out by producers.

Fifth, the analysis shows that the nature of the policy instruments used by governments can have a significant impact on market equilibrium. Moreover, in some models the choice of instruments which governments might make if they choose independently may not be in their collective best interests. This is reinforced in the light of the previous point, since the form of the policy instrument can affect incentives for strategic behavior by producers. But as with the question of whether governments should set environmental policy too lax or too tough, the question of which set of policy instruments is to be preferred depends very sensitively on the precise models employed.

Sixth, the analysis of the welfare implications of plant location choice when we take seriously the existence of scale economies and imperfect competition which make the location of plants a potential issue of concern to governments, is rather more complex than the discussion in the second section suggested, not least because market structure is now endogenous, and how environmental policy affects the competitiveness of different markets is not straightforward.

Finally, assessing the likelihood of environmental policy affecting plant location by just considering abatement costs as a proportion of total costs is likely to be too simplistic for three reasons. First, what is of relevance is the proportion which differences in abatement costs form in differences in fixed and variable costs between different locations. Second, it is differences in profits in different locations, not just costs, that are going to be important, and these will depend on the endogenous degree of competitiveness of different markets, which I have just argued respond in complex ways to environmental policy. Third, with inter-industry linkages there will be demand-side considerations which can amplify or dampen pressures to relocate triggered by environmental policy in some industries.

I now assess the implications of the above points for the design of environmental policy in a context such as the Single European Market. Clearly, in general terms, the subsidiarity principle must be called into question; national or state governments are going to have incentives to manipulate environmental policies for strategic trade reasons, so there is an a priori case for having some supranational authority such as the Commission overseeing environmental policy. The obvious difficulty is that there is no simple prediction about even the direction in which environmental policy may be distorted, or about which policy instruments should be preferred. The guide to distortion of policy should be in terms of marginal damage costs, which may be difficult for the Commission to verify; one possible approach may be to allow countries to set environmental standards within a range of minimum to maximum, but with the possibility for a country to move outside the range if it can produce evidence that damage cost considerations would warrant that. Some other policy conclusions can be drawn more firmly. Policies such as allowing countries to impose tariffs on imports from countries which have lower environmental targets can certainly not be supported by any of the analysis presented in this chapter.

The most obvious conclusion I would draw is that there is a need to conduct careful empirical research to test whether the welfare losses that might arise from strategic distortions of environmental policy by national governments are likely to be as large as the welfare losses that would arise from a supranational authority imposing limits on the environmental policies of national governments, given its imperfect information about the true damage costs in different countries.

REFERENCES

Anderson, K. (1992), 'The Standard Welfare Economics of Policies Affecting Trade and the Environment', Ch. 2 in Anderson and Blackhurst (eds) (op. cit.).

Anderson, K. and R. Blackhurst (eds) (1992), *The Greening of World Trade*, Harvester Wheatsheaf, Hemel Hempstead.

Arden-Clarke, C. (1991), *The General Agreement on Tariffs and Trade, Environmental Protection and Sustainable Development*, World Wide Fund for Nature, Gland, Switzerland.

Barbier, E. and M. Rauscher (1992), 'Trade, Tropical Deforestation and Policy Interventions', Discussion Paper 15, Beijer Institute.

Barrett, S. (1994), 'Strategic Environmental Policy and International Trade', *Journal of Public Economics*, 54(3): 325–38.

Braga, C. (1992), 'Tropical Forests and Trade Policy: The Case of Indonesia and Brazil', Ch. 11 in Low (ed.) (op. cit.).

Brander, J. and B. Spencer (1985), 'Export Subsidies and International Market Share Rivalry', *Journal of International Economics*, 18: 83–100.

Copeland, B. (1991), 'Taxes Versus Standards to Control Pollution in Imperfectly Competitive Markets', mimeo, University of British Columbia.

Dean, J. (1992), 'Trade and the Environment: A Survey of the Literature', Ch. 2 in Low (ed.) (op. cit.).

Folmer, H. and C. Howe (1991), 'Environmental Problems and Policy in the Single European Market', *Environmental and Resource Economics*, 1(1): 17–42.

Haigh, N. (1990), *EEC Environmental Policy and Britain*, 2nd Edn., Longman, London.

Helpman, E. and P. Krugman (1989), *Trade Policy and Market Structure*, MIT Press, Cambridge, MA.

Hudson, S. (1992), 'Trade, Environment and the Pursuit of Sustainable Development', Ch. 4 in Low (ed.) (op. cit.).

Johnson, S. and G. Corcelle (1989), *The Environmental Policy of the European Communities*, Graham & Trotman, London.

Katsoulacos, Y. and A. Xepapadeas (1992), 'Pigovian Taxes Under Oligopoly', mimeo, Athens University.

Kennedy, P. (1993), 'Equilibrium Pollution Taxes in Open Economies With Imperfect Competition', mimeo, University of Victoria, British Columbia.

Klepper, G. (1992), 'The Political Economy of Trade and the Environment in Western Europe', Ch. 14 in Low (ed.) (op. cit.).

Krutilla, J. (1991), 'Environmental Regulation in an Open Economy', *Journal of Environmental Economics and Management*, 20: 127–42.

Long, N. and H. Siebert (1989), 'Institutional Competition versus Ex-ante Harmonization: the Case of Environmental Policy', Kiel Working Paper No 396.

Low, P. (ed.) (1992), *International Trade and the Environment*, World Bank, Washington.

Low, P. and A. Yeats (1992), 'Do "Dirty" Industries Migrate?', Ch. 6 in Low (ed.) (op. cit.).

Lucas, R., D. Wheeler and H. Hettige (1992), 'Economic Development, Environmental Regulation and the International Migration of Toxic Industrial Pollution: 1960–1988', Ch. 5 in Low (ed.) (op. cit.).

Markusen, J., E. Morey and N. Olewiler (1993), 'Environmental Policy When Market Structure and Plant Locations Are Endogenous', *Journal of Environmental Economics and Management*, 24(1): 69–86.

Motta, M. and J-F. Thisse (1993), 'Minimum Quality Standard as an Environmental Policy: Domestic and International Effects', *Nota Di Lavoro* 20.93, Fondazione Eni Enrico Mattei, Milan.

Oliviera-Martins, J., J-M. Burniaux and J. Martin (1993), 'Trade and the Effectiveness of Unilateral CO2 Abatement Policies: Evidence from GREEN', *Nota Di Lavoro* 47.93, Fondazione Eni Enrico Mattei, Milan.

Pearce, D. (1992), 'Should the GATT be Reformed for Environmental Reasons?', CSERGE Working Paper GEC 92–06.

Rauscher, M. (1992), 'Economic Integration and the Environment: Effect on Members and Non-Members', *Environmental and Resource Economics*, 2: 221–36.

Rauscher, M. (1994), 'On Ecological Dumping', in C. Carraro (ed.) *Oxford Economic Papers*, 46: 822–40.

Robertson, D. (1992), 'Trade and the Environment: Harmonization and Technical Standards', Ch. 17 in Low (ed.) (op. cit.).

Schneider, G. et al. (1989), *Task Force: Environment and the Internal Market*, Commission of the European Communities, Brussels.

Siebert, H. (1991), 'Europe '92. Decentralizing Environmental Policy in the Single Market', *Environmental and Resource Economics*, 1: 271–88.

Tobey, J. (1990), 'The Effects of Domestic Environmental Policies on Patterns of World Trade: an Empirical Test', *Kyklos*, 43: 191–209.

Ulph, A. (1992a), 'The Choice of Environmental Policy Instruments and Strategic International Trade', in R. Pethig (ed.), *Conflicts and Cooperation in Managing Environmental Resources*, Springer-Verlag, Berlin.

Ulph, A. (1992b), 'Environmental Policy and Strategic International Trade', mimeo, University of Southampton.

Ulph, A. (1993), 'Environmental Policy and International Trade When Governments and Producers Act Strategically', mimeo, University of Southampton.

Ulph, A. (1994), 'Environmental Policy, Plant Location and Government Protection', in C. Carraro (ed.), *Trade, Innovation, Environment*, Kluwer, Dordrecht, 123–66.

PART V

Case Studies of Comparative Environmental
Policies

SECTION A

Agricultural Pollution

10. Environmental Regulation in a Confederation: The Case of Pesticide Legislation in the Netherlands

Wim Brussaard

HARMONIZATION OF NATIONAL LEGISLATION IN THE EUROPEAN COMMUNITY/UNION

There exist considerable differences in legislation between the different Member States of the European Union. That was the case in 1958, when six European countries united in the European Economic Community, and with the development of the Community towards the twelve countries that constitute the present European Union, the diversity in legislation has increased ever since. That diversity includes the systems of legislation, the subjects regulated and the contents of laws in the different Member States.

Those differences have been obstructing, and are still obstructing, the realization of the goals of the Community. Therefore the European Treaty has given the Community the responsibility for 'the approximation of the laws of the Member States to the extent required for the proper functioning of the common market' (Art. 3, under h). So harmonization is not a goal in itself, but is related to the objective of integration of the European market.

From the point of view of legislation, the Treaty provides two instruments for the realization of objectives: the regulation and the directive. A regulation has general application; it is binding in its entirety and directly applicable in all Member States (Art. 189). The regulation in fact withdraws a subject from national legislation, and therefore is especially fitting for the realization of the Community's own policy. Most regulations deal with the Common Agricultural Policy. The other instrument, the directive, is binding as to the result to be achieved upon each Member State to which it is addressed, but leaves the national authorities the choice of form and methods (Art. 189). So the directive has more consideration for the differences in legislation between the Member States. Although the national authorities are free to choose for themselves the form and the methods to realize the results dictated by the directive, many directives are so detailed that there is not much freedom left for the national governments.[1]

The directive is the primary instrument for the harmonization of national laws.[2]   The Treaty states that the Council shall, acting unanimously on a proposal from the Commission, issue directives for the approximation of such laws, regulations and administrative provisions of the Member States as directly affect the establishment or functioning of the common market (Art. 100).   On the basis of this general harmonization mandate, in combination with the authority for unforeseen circumstances,[3] a lot of directives have been enacted to harmonize (parts of) the environmental legislation of the Member States. In 1987, by the amendments of the Single European Act,[4] environmental policy was incorporated in the Treaty as an explicit objective of the Community. From then on the environmental measures of the Community had their own juridical basis in a separate title of the Treaty (Art. 130R–T).

According to this title (in the wording of the Treaty till the Maastricht amendments) actions by the Community relating to the environment have the objective to preserve, protect and improve the quality of the environment; to contribute towards protecting human health; and to ensure a prudent and rational utilization of natural resources (Art. 130R, section 1). It is important that the environmental protection requirements shall also be a component of the Community's other policies (Art. 130R, section 2). In preparing its actions the Community shall take account of the environmental conditions in the various regions of the Community (Art. 130R, section 3). But the environmental policy of the Community finds its limitations in the subsidiarity principle: the Community shall only take action to the extent to which the environmental objectives can be attained better at Community level than at the level of the individual Member States (Art. 130R, section 4). Each Member State retains the authority to take stronger measures than the Community, as long as those measures are compatible with the Treaty (Art. 130T). Till the Maastricht Treaty, the environmental actions of the Community as a rule needed unanimity, but the Council could define which decisions are to be taken by a qualified majority (Art. 130S).

Next to the specific harmonization rules in the framework of the environmental policy, the general harmonization mandate, too, is still relevant.   Since the Single European Act of 1987 harmonization measures, which have as their object the establishing, before the end of 1992, of the internal market, can be taken by qualified majority (Art.

100A, section 1). In its proposals concerning environmental protection, the Commission has to take as a base a high level of protection (Art. 100A, section 3). After the adoption of a harmonization measure by a qualified majority, a Member State can still apply national provisions relating to protection of the environment, if the Member State deems that necessary (Art. 100A, section 4). This exception was necessary to meet the wishes of those Member States who did not like the loss of their veto in the unanimity rule.[5]

This EC system for the harmonization of national legislation is not changed by the Maastricht Treaty, the treaty that established the European Union,[6] but some adjustments were inserted in the title on Environment. The requirement that the Community policy on the environment shall aim at a high level of protection is valid now for all environmental measures (Art. 130R, section 2). The reference to the subsidiarity principle has been removed from the title on Environment, but there is inserted a general reference to the subsidiarity principle for areas that do not fall within the exclusive competence of the Community (Art. 3b). An important amendment is that environmental measures no longer need unanimity, but a qualified majority (Art. 130S).

This part has outlined the relationship between European and national regulation, especially in the field of environmental policy. This relationship will be illustrated now by the example of pesticides regulation. First the Dutch pesticides legislation will be set out. The following part will contain a description of the European regulation in this field and its influence on Dutch law.

PESTICIDES LEGISLATION IN THE NETHERLANDS

A. The Development of Pesticides Regulation in the Netherlands

The Netherlands is small and densely populated, and so has a limited area of agricultural land. Nevertheless the Netherlands also is the third-largest exporter of agricultural products in the world after the United States and France. To protect its agricultural products against diseases and pests, and to meet the import requirements of different countries concerning agricultural products, Dutch agriculture is highly dependent on pesticides. As a result, the use of pesticides per hectare is higher than in any other country.[7]

The Dutch have been regulating pesticides for a long time, mainly from the point of view of effectiveness. With the development of environmental legislation, environmental considerations also entered into the pesticides legislation. The first Dutch legislation on pesticides, the 1947 Pesticides and Fertilizers Act (*Wet bestrijdingsmiddelen en meststoffen 1947, Stb. H 123*), was intended to prevent inferior agricultural pesticides from being placed on the market. The act was designed to protect the agricultural sector, so that farmers could be sure that the pesticides they used were effective for the purpose for which they were intended: fighting diseases and pests.

The limited objectives of this act made it impossible to combat effectively the dangers resulting from the toxicity of (otherwise reliable) pesticides. Those dangers threatened not only those who were using pesticides, but also all persons who as merchants or consumers came in contact with toxic substances on agricultural products treated with pesticides. An important consideration too was that this situation could cause problems for export of agricultural products, and could threaten the fertility of agricultural land. Therefore in 1962 a new Pesticides Act (*Bestrijdingsmiddelenwet 1962, Stb. 288*) was passed. This act made it possible for the government to judge the acceptability of pesticides also on the basis of their harmful side-effects for public health.[8]

By about 1970 it became apparent that this was still not sufficient. Extensive pesticide use was becoming a major threat for the environment. It was thought necessary to give greater priority to environmental considerations in the authorization policy for pesticides. Therefore the Pesticides Act was amended in 1975.

The Pesticides Act offers a framework that is elaborated in governmental decrees and ministerial regulations.[9]

B. Objectives and Range of the Pesticides Act

The Pesticides Act regulates trade in and use of pesticides from the point of view of both their effectiveness in achieving the purpose for which they are intended, and the safety and health of humans and of those animals whose protection is desired. The goal of the act is to help protect the environment in which humans, animals and plants live from harmful influences.

The legal concept 'pesticide' includes any substance or mixture of substances, as well as micro-organisms and viruses, intended for use in controlling or repelling animals which may cause injury to plants, preventing or controlling plant diseases, regulating growth of plants, etc. This involves the use of pesticides for agricultural purposes, such as herbicides to control weeds and mildew, insecticides, soil disinfectants and growth regulators. The act is applicable also to the use of pesticides for industrial and domestic purposes, such as wood conservants and disinfectants, cooling-water biocides, rat exterminators, etc. (Art. 1).

The essence of the Pesticides Act is the prohibition against selling, stocking, storing or using any pesticide that has not been authorized pursuant to the act. Responsible for the authorization of pesticides are the Minister of Agriculture, Nature Management and Fisheries in the case of pesticides for agricultural purposes, and the Minister of Welfare, Health and Cultural Affairs in the case of pesticides for industrial and domestic purposes. The decision of each of the two ministers has to be in agreement with the other minister and with the Ministers of Housing, Physical Planning and Environment and of Social Affairs and Employment (Art. 2). The decisions of the ministers are prepared by a committee of experts, the Commission for the Authorization of Pesticides (Art. 20). In preparation is a legal proposal to make the commission independent. In the meantime, since January 1, 1993 the commission has been given a mandate to take decisions on the authorization of pesticides for the ministers.[10]

C. The Authorization of Pesticides

Pesticides can only be authorized by the ministers if three requirements have been fulfilled. In the first place, the percentage of active substances in the pesticide and the composition, color, form, packaging and labeling of the pesticide must comply with general rules issued by the minister. Second, on the basis of prior tests the regulator must be convinced with reasonable certainty that the pesticide is effective for the purpose for which it is intended and that in using the pesticide in conformity with this purpose there will be no harmful side-effects. Harmful side-effects include: damage to public health, negative consequences for the quality of food, and pollution of soil, water and air. The third requirement for the authorization of a pesticide is that the percentage of active substance may not be higher than necessary for the purpose (Art. 3).

If the ministers decide to authorize a pesticide it is given an authorization number. This number must be displayed on the packaging, together with the name of the pesticide and the name and address of the person who has obtained the authorization. The decision of the ministers about the authorization must indicate for what purposes the pesticide may be used. With the authorization the ministers can issue regulations about, for instance, the places where the pesticide may be used, the dosage and the safety intervals that have to be observed, as well as about the composition, color, form and packaging of the pesticide, and the indications on the packing. If the pesticide is extremely toxic, it is possible that the pesticide may only be delivered to certain persons and companies, such as professional exterminators and sanitary departments. The regulations connected to the authorization can be changed and adjusted later on by the ministers (Art. 5).

Authorization of a pesticide must be asked for by the manufacturer, the importer or the dealer (Art. 4). The decision of authorization is registered by the government, with annotation of the name, the active matter and the number of the authorization (Art. 6). The authorization is valid for a maximum period of ten years. After that period the pesticide has to be judged for authorization again. The ministers can allow the pesticide to be used after that period till supplies have run out. Pesticides whose composition and activity are so well known that prior tests are not necessary, can be authorized by the ministers without an application. That authorization is not limited to a certain period of time.

Authorization of a pesticide can be withdrawn by the ministers. This can be done on request of the manufacturer, the importer or the dealer, but also without such a request. Withdrawal of authorization without request is possible if the pesticide has proved to be no longer effective for the purpose for which it is intended, for example because the organism to be combated has become resistant. Also when the pesticide turns out to have such harmful side-effects that it would not have been authorized if those effects had been known at the moment of authorization, the authorization can be withdrawn. A last reason for withdrawal can be that from a point of view of harmful side-effects the authorization is no longer acceptable, for instance because a later authorized pesticide has less harmful side-effects and so is preferable (Art. 7).

If urgently required by the interests of public health or agriculture, the ministers can give a (general) exemption or a dispensation (for individual cases) to sell or use a non-authorized pesticide, or to use an authorized pesticide for purposes other than what it is authorized for (Art. 16a). In this way a quick and adequate reaction is possible in case of a sudden disease or plague.

The Pesticides Act also gives the ministers the authority to issue regulations about the use of objects that have been treated with pesticides. For instance, the ministers can introduce a safety interval for harvesting plants treated with pesticides or cultivating plants on soil treated with pesticides. Those regulations are directed not only to the user of pesticides, but also to the user of the plants and the soil; therefore the user of the pesticide is obligated to inform the user of the plants or the soil about the treatment with the pesticide (Art. 5a).

D. The Pesticides Act in Practice

Research, done in the years 1989–90, has shown that in some respects there can be a considerable difference between the rules and the intention of the act and the way it is applied.[11] For some authorized pesticides the research data about side-effects were missing; in other cases it was possible that the data supplied by the applicant gave an incorrect or incomplete impression of those side-effects. Data other than those supplied by the applicant were only occasionally and not systematically used when deciding upon authorization of a pesticide. Indirect harmful side-effects on the ecosystem were in fact ignored. These conclusions suggest that there can be considerable doubt if actual pesticide practice meets the legal requirement that it must be reasonably certain that no harmful side-effects will be caused by the pesticide.

The research disclosed several other facts as well. The availability of a pesticide that is less harmful for the environment hardly plays a role in the decision about authorization. Once a pesticide is authorized, a new judgment of the authorization after the period of authorization is over hardly ever takes place. The possibility of exemption or dispensation is used in practice to accept forbidden pesticides permanently. In the same way the possibility of allowing a not-any-longer authorized pesticide to be used till the supply has run out is also used for pesticides it is not meant for. Moreover, the decisions of the ministers insufficiently state the reasons for authorizing or not authorizing pesticides.

EUROPEAN REGULATION

A. Directives on Pesticides

The Dutch pesticides legislation as described above is influenced by European regulation in various ways. The Council of the European Communities has adopted several directives concerning pesticides. The reason for these directives was to eliminate barriers to trade between the different Member States of the Community. Directives were issued on the following subjects:

- prohibition of certain active substances in pesticides;[12]
- the maximum levels of pesticide residues in and on fruits and vegetables and cereals;[13]

- the classification, packaging and labelling of pesticides;[14]
- the testing of pesticides according to principles of 'good laboratory practices'.[15]

In 1991 the Council took a very important step by adopting the Directive concerning the placing of plant protection products on the market.[16] The objective of this directive is to harmonize the national statutes about authorization of plant protection products in the Community. As the considerations of the directive state, it is necessary, at the time when plant protection products are authorized, not only to make sure that they are sufficiently effective and have no unacceptable effect on plants or plant products, but also have no unacceptable influence on the environment in general and, in particular, no harmful effect to human or animal health or on groundwater. Therefore the directive orders the Member States to prescribe in their national legislation that plant protection products may not be placed on the market and used in their territory unless they have authorized the product in accordance with the directive (Art. 3, section 1). The directive contains elaborate provisions prescribing how the Member States have to judge the authorization of a plant protection product (Art. 4). Only those products can be authorized whose active substances are included in a Community list of active substances that may be used for plant protection products in the Community (Art. 5 and 6, and Annex I). The directive involves a program for reregistering existing active substances and registering new active substances (Art. 8).[17]

An important element in the directive is the mutual recognition of authorization by the Member States. At the request of the applicant, a Member State has to authorize a plant protection product that has already been authorized in another Member State in accordance with the provisions of the directive. The Member State must refrain from requiring the repetition of tests and analyses already carried out in the other Member State, to the extent that (and this is an important limitation) agricultural, plant health and environmental (including climatic) conditions relevant to the use of the product are comparable in the regions concerned. The applicant must prove that the conditions are comparable (Art. 10, section 1). Whenever a Member State requires, for reasons of non-comparability, a repetition of tests or refuses to authorize a plant protection product that has already been authorized in another Member State, the Commission must be informed. The Commission decides whether comparability exists, taking into account the serious ecological vulnerability problems that may arise in certain Community regions or zones, thereby requiring specific protection measures (Art. 10, sections 2 and 3). It was particularly the Dutch government that insisted on this limitation of the mutual recognition of authorizations in case of non-comparability, to keep the authority to protect the Dutch ground- and drinking water.[18]

The directive had to be implemented by the different Member States within two years after notification. This term ended on July 25, 1993. The bill to amend the Pesticides Act in accordance with the directive was sent to Parliament by the Dutch government on June 1, 1993.[19] This bill contains a lot of amendments of the Pesticides Act, to bring the act in accordance with the requirements of the directive. Important new elements introduced in the act are a prohibition against importing into the Netherlands pesticides that are not authorized, and a system of recognition of authorizations of pesticides by other Member States. The bill also introduces an exception: when the minister has well-founded indications that a pesticide, which according to a European measure has to be authorized, is dangerous for the health of humans and animals or the environment, he can decide to prohibit the delivery and use of that pesticide.

B. Consequences for Dutch Pesticides Law

In the context of this paper it is interesting to ask whether the directive leaves any room for the Dutch and other European governments to pursue their own policy in the authorization of pesticides. According to the decisions of the European Court of Justice, national legislation has to be interpreted in the light of the wording and the objective of a directive, even before the time of implementation has expired.[20] The Directive concerning the placing of plant protection products on the market goes in considerable detail and has to be recognized, by its wording, as a directive intended to harmonize completely the European legislation in this field. The Member States have to ensure timely implementation of the directive. They do not have the freedom to pursue a policy contrary to the directive. Deviation from the directive is only possible as far as the European Treaty permits, or as far as the directive itself leaves room for deviation.

As we have discussed in Part A of this chapter, the Treaty offers here two possibilities. First, Article 130T leaves the Member States the possibility of taking stronger environmental measures than the Community, as long as those measures are compatible with the Treaty. The question will be if stricter criteria for the authorization of pesticides by a Member State will be hindering the principle of free movement of goods in the Community, and so will violate Article 9 of the Treaty. The second possibility is that Member States, after the adoption of a harmonization measure by a qualified majority, can still apply national provisions relating to the protection of the environment, if the Member States deem that necessary (Art. 100A, section 4). As this exception conflicts with decisions of the European Court of Justice in other cases,[21] it is likely that the Court will give a limited interpretation to this article. Several authors argue that the exception is only acceptable when a Member State was overruled in the decision about the harmonization measure, and at the same time the legislation of that Member State offers more protection than prescribed by the measure.[22]

According to decisions of the European Court of Justice, European standards in a directive can have, after the implementation time has expired, effects similar to direct effect in national law, if the rules of the directive are unconditional as regards content and at the same time sufficiently accurate.[23] This can certainly be said of the pesticides Directive. However, till now the European Community has not completed the list of uniform criteria for judging substances (Annex VI of the Directive), nor the list of substances that meet those criteria (Annex I of the Directive). As soon as this has been done, the authorization of plant protection products will be regulated mostly by European law. The list of criteria will show how much room will be left for the Member States to use deviating criteria. For the Dutch government the most important possibility for deviation is embodied in the directive itself: the limitation that mutual recognition of authorizations by the Member States only has to be accepted as far as agricultural, plant health and environmental conditions are comparable. To protect the Dutch ground- and drinking water, the government now has the power to refuse to authorize a pesticide that has already been authorized in another Member State on the ground that the conditions for testing the pesticide in that other Member State are not comparable to the Dutch situation.

CONCLUSION

This contribution has outlined the European system for the harmonization of national laws and the relationship between European and national regulation, especially in the field of environmental policy. In this system, the use of the directive as the primary instrument for harmonizing national legislation leaves the Member States free in the choice of form and methods to achieve the results intended by a directive. As we have seen in this contribution, the European Treaty contains some possibilities for the national authorities to deviate from European regulations, to protect certain national interests.   As the case of pesticide legislation shows, the directive itself can also contain provisions for deviating national decisions.   In that situation the European Commission, and in the last resort the European Court of Justice, have to guard the European unity: they have the authority to decide how far, within the scope of the Treaty and the directive, the possibility of deviation will reach.

NOTES

1.   R.H. Lauwaars in C.W.A. Timmermans, *Europees Gemeenschapsrecht in kort bestek*, Groningen, 1991, p. 81.
2.   See for a thorough discussion of the directive the contribution of James E. Pfander to this book.
3.   Article 235: 'If action by the Community should prove necessary to attain, in the course of the operation of the common market, one of the objectives of the Community and this Treaty has not provided the necessary powers, the Council shall, acting unanimously on a proposal from the Commission and after consulting the Assembly, take the appropriate measures.'
4.   Luxemburg/The Hague, February 17/28, 1986, OJ L 169 (1987).
5.   R.H. Lauwaars in C.W.A. Timmermans, *Europees Gemeenschapsrecht in kort bestek*, Groningen, 1991, p. 224.
6.   Maastricht, February 7, 1992, 31 ILM 247 (1992).
7.   P. Hurst, 'Pesticides Reduction Programs in Denmark, the Netherlands, and Sweden', *International Environmental Affairs*, Vol. 4, No. 3 (Summer 1992), pp. 234–52.
8.   Pesticides Act 1962. Ministry of Housing, Physical Planning and Environment, The Hague, 1984.
9.   H.M.J. Haerkens, 'De Bestrijdingsmiddelenwet 1962', in W. Brussaard (ed.), *Hoofdlijnen van het agrarisch recht*, W.E.J. Tjeenk Willink, Zwolle 1993, pp. 100–105.
10.   'Mandaatregeling College toelating bestrijdingsmiddelen', December 24, 1992, Stcrt. 1992, 252.
11.   E.M. Vogelezang-Stoute in E.J. Matser, *De toelating van bestrijdingsmiddelen, milieu tussen wet en beleid*, Centrum voor Milieurecht, Universiteit van Amsterdam, 1990.
12.   79/117/EEC, OJ L 33/36.
13.   76/895/EEC, OJ L 340/26; 86/362/EEC, OJ L 221/37.
14.   78/631/EEC, OJ L 206/13.
15.   87/18/EEC, OJ L 15/29; 88/320/EEC, OJ L 145/36.
16.   Council of European Communities Directive of July 15, 1991, concerning the placing of plant protection products on the market (91/414/EEC, OJ L 230/1, August 19, 1991).
17.   *See* John D. Conner Jr, Antoinette M. Long and Alain F. Pelfrène, 'Reregistering pesticides in the EC: Responding to Directive 91/414 and forming the European task force', *International Environment Reporter*, September 22, 1991, pp. 695–8.
18.   In large parts of the Netherlands the level of groundwater (also used as source of drinking water) is so high that it is immediately influenced by pesticides.
19.   Tweede Kamer, 1992–1993, 23177, nos 1–2.
20.   *Van Colson en Kamann*, Case 14/83, ECR 1984 (1909).
21.   *Denkavit*, Case 251/78, ECR 1979 (3388/89).
22.   J. Mertens de Wilmars, *Het Hof van Justitie van de EG na de Europese Akte*, SEW, 1986, p. 615. R.H. Lauwaars in C.W.A. Timmersmans, *Europees Gemeenschapsrecht in kort bestek*, Groningen 1991, p. 225.
23.   *Becker*, Case 8/81, ECR 1982 (70).

11. Environmental Federalism in Agriculture: The Case of Pesticide Regulation in the United States

Margaret Rosso Grossman*

INTRODUCTION

Agricultural activities are recognized as a serious source of environmental pollution, and pesticides – insecticides, herbicides, fungicides, rodenticides – contribute significantly to that pollution. Pesticide manufacture and use can lead to serious health and environmental damage. Some of this damage may be acute (caused, for example, by excess exposure); other damage may result from the long-term effects of lower levels of exposure. Many pesticides persist in the environment, and the long-term risks of these toxic chemicals are often difficult to assess. Pesticide residues in foods may also pose hazards. Environmental damage to vegetation, animals and birds, and aquatic life sometimes results from pesticide use (or misuse).

Among other adverse effects, pesticides can contaminate the soil, surface waters, and groundwater. Pesticide pollution of groundwater is perceived as a particularly serious problem because groundwater is a major source of drinking water in the United States. Forty percent of the general population uses public water supplies that are drawn from underground sources; 97 percent of the rural population and 55 percent of livestock also drink groundwater.[1] Groundwater is also an important source of water for irrigation. Groundwater discharges into surface waters and thus affects the quality of waters that sustain fish, wildlife, and aquatic and terrestrial ecosystems.[2]

For many years, the potential for pesticide contamination of groundwater was ignored because of researchers' belief that pesticides would degrade (or be stopped by physical barriers) before reaching aquifers. But many pesticides, including some used frequently, leach into groundwater.[3] In 1989, 30 states were found to have at least some type of pesticide

---

* The author expresses appreciation to The German Marshall Fund of the US for generous financial support. Thanks also to Jeffrey E. Thompson, Research Assistant in Agricultural Law.

contamination in their underground water sources, and over 60 different pesticides were identified in the tested water sources.[4] Overall, an estimated 50 million people in the United States consume water from underground sources that may be contaminated by agricultural chemicals, including pesticides.[5] Moreover, once groundwater is contaminated, cleanup is difficult and expensive.

Several aspects of pesticide pollution are subject to regulatory control. Pesticide manufacture and subsequent access to market can be controlled. Pesticide-use regulation may affect both commercial pesticide applicators and farmers who apply the chemicals. And regulation may affect the way that pesticides are applied, with focus on equipment and handling techniques.[6] The system of federal and state pesticide law described here involves, to some extent, regulation in each of these areas.

The main focus here is US regulation of pesticides under the Federal Insecticide, Fungicide and Rodenticide Act (FIFRA), along with state laws authorized by, or at least not preempted by, FIFRA. But it should be clear at the outset that FIFRA is not the only federal statute that regulates pesticides. Provisions of other laws, too, have implications for regulating pesticide use and protecting the public from harm. For example, the Federal Food, Drug, and Cosmetic Act (FFDCA)[7] authorizes regulations that govern the amount of pesticide residue that may be left on food. The Food and Drug Administration (FDA) administers the Act and monitors the actual pesticide content of commodities. Under FFDCA, the Environmental Protection Agency has authority to set tolerance standards for pesticides in or on raw agricultural commodities, and to establish food additive tolerances for pesticides for processed foods and feeds.[8] The Delaney Clause prohibition of food additives that 'induce cancer when ingested by man or animal'[9] and the Ninth Circuit decision in *Les v. Reilly*[10] are relevant in this context. A proposal for reform of this regulatory system, released by the Clinton administration in September 1993, may lead to amendments in FFDCA and FIFRA provisions. Changes in the pesticide tolerance standard, altered pesticide registration and use provisions, and streamlined cancellation procedures could result.[11]

Another federal effort, the 1991 Pesticides and Ground-Water Strategy (PGWS)[12] describes policies and regulatory approaches the EPA will use to protect the nation's groundwater resources from contamination by pesticides. PGWS focuses on limiting the use of pesticides in areas that are vulnerable to contamination of current and potential drinking water supplies and that contain groundwater that is closely hydrogeologically connected to surface waters. The program relies primarily on source control and reduction policies, implemented through FIFRA labeling requirements, to reduce groundwater contamination. The strategy, however, also emphasizes comprehensive groundwater protection programs (state management plans) developed and implemented by the states.[13] Thus, it describes a new federal–state partnership designed to eliminate unreasonable risks of pesticide groundwater contamination.

Other federal laws also have implications for pesticide use. For example, the Safe Drinking Water Act directs the EPA to protect public water supplies by establishing maximum contaminant levels (MCLs) for certain contaminants, including several pesticides. The Safe Drinking Water Act, in general, does not regulate the sources of contamination in water supplies.[14] The Clean Water Act includes provisions (sections 208 and 319) directed at nonpoint source pollution, of which agricultural pollution (including pollution from pesticides) forms a significant component.[15] These provisions have not been particularly effective, in part because states have not implemented enforceable management plans. The Endangered Species Act[16] requires EPA involvement in determining if pesticide use could affect an endangered or threatened species or its critical habitat; if so, the EPA consults with the Fish and Wildlife Service to determine what measures should be incorporated in the label of the pesticide to provide protection.[17] The Resource Conservation and Recovery Act (RCRA)[18] regulates the collection, transportation, storage, and disposal of hazardous wastes. The definition of hazardous wastes is broad enough to encompass discarded pesticides and pesticide containers.[19] FIFRA does not preempt the provisions of RCRA, and any pesticide that is considered a hazardous waste is subject to RCRA.[20] The practical effect of RCRA, however, is to subject pesticide users and manufacturers only to the disposal requirements because their activities usually are not subject to the other sections of the act.[21] Other environmental protections laws also have provisions that affect pesticide use or disposal.

FEDERAL REGULATION OF PESTICIDES UNDER FIFRA

A. Background

Until enactment of the Insecticide Act of 1910,[22] pesticide regulation was the domain of state law. The Insecticide Act, concerned primarily with protecting pesticide users from ineffective products and deceptive labeling, prohibited the manufacture or transport of any adulterated or misbranded insecticide or fungicide. It did not require federal registration of pesticides or impose significant safety standards.[23] The Act was intended to protect the interests of farmers and cattlemen,[24] and was administered by the US Department of Agriculture (USDA).

Between the world wars, significant technological progress in the chemical industry resulted in development of synthetic organic insecticides. During World War II, these were used to contain diseases spread by insects. After the war, their use in agriculture became common, and production of chemicals increased. Moreover, research led to other agricultural chemicals, potent in effect and targeted to specific pests.[25] Farm organizations, the chemical industry, and government agreed that enhanced federal legislation was needed. The result was the Federal Insecticide, Fungicide and Rodenticide Act (FIFRA) of 1947.[26] As legislative history indicates, it was 'highly desirable that laws governing economic poisons be as nearly uniform as possible consistent with the need for the protection of the public, so that manufacturers may have Nation-wide distribution with a minimum of conflict between the labeling requirements of the various [state] laws'.[27] Thus, FIFRA helped to provide pesticide manufacturers with legal uniformity, avoiding the inconvenience of conflicting state laws. Though the main emphasis of the new law was consumer protection,[28] FIFRA expanded the sphere of federal pesticide regulation to include licensing and labeling requirements, as well as a limited federal role in regulating the manufacture, sale, and use of pesticides. FIFRA also extended regulation to herbicides and rodenticides.[29]

Under FIFRA, the USDA determined whether a pesticide could be registered for sale in the United States. The main factor in this determination was whether 'the composition of the article [was] such as to warrant the proposed claims for it'.[30] The USDA could not refuse registration of a pesticide, even a dangerous chemical, so long as the pesticide did what the maker claimed it would do. Once registered, a hazardous product could be controlled only if it was misbranded or adulterated, and USDA had no authority over persons using a pesticide contrary to its label instructions.[31] In 1964, FIFRA amendments gave USDA the right to refuse to register a new pesticide or to cancel an existing registration if the pesticide would be 'injurious to man, vertebrate animals, or desirable vegetation' when used as directed or in accordance with common practice.[32] But because the Pesticide Registration Division of USDA was understaffed and geared toward facilitating registration, applications were rarely scrutinized fully, and cancellations were few.[33]

In the early 1970s, consumer fears about pesticide residues on food prompted the Federal government to assume a larger role in the management of pesticides.[34] When the Environmental Protection Agency (EPA) was created in 1970, administrative control over FIFRA was transferred from USDA to EPA.[35] Two years later, Congress amended FIFRA, shifting the

focus of pesticide regulation from consumer protection to health and
environmental protection.[36] The current standard for registration reflects that
environmental focus by allowing registration only where the proposed use
of the pesticide will not cause 'unreasonable adverse effects on the
environment'.[37]

After only minor changes between 1972 and 1988,[38] further amendments
in 1988[39] made several significant changes to FIFRA. Most important was
reduction of the time for EPA reregistration of older pesticides, accompanied
by authorization of expenditures for the expedited reregistration
requirement.[40]

B.   Regulation Under FIFRA

1.   Pesticide registration

FIFRA makes it unlawful for any person in any state to 'distribute or sell
to any person any pesticide that is not registered under [FIFRA]'.[41]
Moreover, the establishment where the pesticide is produced must also be
registered.[42]

The Act defines 'pesticide' broadly to include '(1) any substance or
mixture of substances intended for preventing, destroying, repelling, or
mitigating any pest, and (2) any substance or mixture of substances intended
for use as a plant regulator, defoliant, or desiccant'.[43]   Biologically
engineered micro-organisms are also regulated under FIFRA.[44]   Pests may
include '(1) any insect, rodent, nematode, fungus, weed, or (2) any other
form of terrestrial or aquatic plant or animal life or virus, bacteria, or other
micro-organism . . . which the Administrator declares to be a pest'.[45]   The
act specifically excludes humans and 'bacteria, virus, and other
micro-organisms on or in living man or other living animals' from the
definition of pest.[46]

The pesticide registration process requires the applicant to submit a
registration statement that includes extensive information about the pesticide
formula, type of use, proposed label, and data with results of scientific
tests.[47]   The EPA must approve registration of a pesticide if its composition
warrants the claims made for it, its labeling complies with the Act's
requirements, and it works without causing unreasonable adverse effects on
the environment.[48]

FIFRA labeling requirements are articulated in EPA regulations.   These
regulations prohibit false or misleading statements, and require information
including ingredients, warning and precautionary statements, and directions
for proper use.[49]   Labeling information submitted as part of the registration
process cannot be altered without obtaining an amendment to the
registration.[50]

The EPA must also examine the health and environmental effects of the pesticide and determine whether it will perform its intended functions.[51] In making this assessment, the EPA evaluates pesticide data, which it requires from the applicant,[52] to determine whether the pesticide will cause an 'unreasonable adverse effect on the environment',[53] that is, 'any unreasonable risk to man or the environment, taking into account the economic, social, and environmental costs and benefits of the use of any pesticide'.[54] FIFRA broadly defines environment to include 'water, air, land, and all plants and man and other animals living therein, and the interrelationships which exist among these'.[55] Most commentators agree that the EPA must weigh environmental and health costs against economic gains, to determine whether the effects of a pesticide are 'unreasonably adverse' to the environment.[56]

In addition to initial registration procedures, the EPA must analyze for possible reregistration any pesticide with an active ingredient contained in a pesticide first registered before November 1, 1984.[57] The prescribed five-phase process for reregistration is to be completed by 1997,[58] but the process appears to be seriously behind schedule. By July 1993, only eight percent of chemicals had been reregistered,[59] and by September 1993, EPA had only reregistered 250 of 20,000 pesticide products subject to reregistration.[60] The EPA estimates that the reregistration process may not be completed until 2006 because of a projected EPA budget deficit of $20 million.[61] A recent Government Accounting Office report, however, suggests that part of the delay is caused by inefficient management by the Office of Pesticide Programs, which manages the EPA's pesticide program under FIFRA.[62]

2. Pesticide classification

FIFRA has two classifications for pesticides – general use and restricted use.[63] Because pesticides are classified by use instead of by product, a pesticide with several uses may be classified for both general and restricted use. A pesticide is classified for general use if it will not generally cause unreasonable adverse effects on the environment when applied in accordance with its directions or in accordance with widespread and commonly recognized practices. If the pesticide may cause some unreasonable adverse effects on the environment or injury to the applicator, it is classified for restricted use, and limitations are imposed.[64]

Restricted-use pesticides must normally be applied by, or under the direct supervision of, a certified applicator.[65] FIFRA prescribes a federal procedure for certification of pesticide applicators, but allows states to implement their own certification programs for restricted-use applicators.[66]

Because the Act sets forth few federal requirements, state procedures required for certification vary.

A pesticide recordkeeping requirement was added to FIFRA in the 1990 Farm Bill.[67] Under this provision, all certified applicators of restricted-use pesticides must maintain records of their pesticide use that meet relevant state requirements. If the state has no requirements, FIFRA requires the applicator to maintain specific records of the pesticide use for a period of two years. These records must be made available to any federal or state agency that deals with pesticide use or pesticide-related issues and to health-care professionals treating individuals for whom the information would be pertinent.[68] In April 1993, the EPA promulgated final recordkeeping regulations,[69] which specify the types of recordkeeping data required and encourage state–federal cooperative agreements to carry out the requirements of the rules in each state.[70]

3.   Cancellation of registration

The EPA may cancel the registration of any pesticide after five years if the registrant fails to request that the registration be continued.[71] Furthermore, the EPA may issue a notice to cancel a pesticide registration or change its classification if the pesticide or its labeling or other required material does not comply with the law, or when a pesticide is determined to cause unreasonable adverse effects on the environment.[72] When deciding whether to issue a notice of cancellation, the EPA must consider the impact of cancellation on the agricultural economy.[73] Courts, however, have generally given the EPA considerable discretion in initiating cancellation proceedings.[74] The EPA has the burden to show that an unreasonable risk exists, and the registrant may request a full evidentiary hearing on the proceeding.[75] Cancellation is often a long process, though proposed changes to FIFRA would simplify the process.

In particularly hazardous circumstances, the EPA may suspend registration of a pesticide pending cancellation proceedings. FIFRA authorizes two types of pesticide registration suspensions: non-emergency (under which the registrant may request a hearing) and emergency (which requires neither notice to the registrant nor a hearing). Each requires a determination by the EPA that the 'action is necessary to prevent an imminent hazard during the time required for cancellation or change in classification proceedings'.[76] Once implemented, the suspension remains in effect until the EPA issues a final decision on the cancellation proceeding.[77]

4.   Worker protection regulations

Pesticide exposure poses grave risks for agricultural workers, and the EPA is charged with regulating the use of pesticides to protect those who apply pesticides or work in pesticide-treated fields. In 1992 the EPA issued new worker protection regulations that expand the scope and level of protection and require pesticide labels to include data specifically for workers.[78] These regulations apply to workers who are 'handlers' (workers who handle or come into direct contact with pesticides) and persons who do 'hand labor' (tasks that involve the handling of crops treated with pesticides). They apply to virtually any worker who comes into contact with pesticides or their residue, including farmworkers and workers in forests, greenhouses, nurseries, and commercial pesticide-handling establishments.[79]

The worker protection standards recognize that accurate information about pesticides is crucial to worker safety. Thus, each pesticide label must include general safety information, restricted-entry intervals (the minimum time unprotected workers must wait before re-entering treated areas), worker notification statements (posted and oral warnings), and personal protective equipment (for example, special clothing) requirements.[80] Besides required label information, the regulations attempt to increase worker protection in other areas of pesticide use: safety training, application guidelines, personal protective equipment requirements, restricted entry intervals, notice provisions, and mitigation of worker exposure through emergency assistance.[81]

STATE PROGRAMS FOR PESTICIDE REGULATION

A. State Authority Under FIFRA

Despite the comprehensive nature of FIFRA, states retain significant authority to regulate pesticides. The limited federal regulation of pesticides in the Insecticide Act of 1910 left states free to control most aspects of pesticide use, including safety and registration standards, but states actually exercised little of their authority. Only in 1947, with federal enactment of FIFRA, were pesticides regulated comprehensively, and states then tended to rely on federal law to address problems in the pesticide field.

State roles changed significantly with passage of the Federal Environmental Pesticide Control Act of 1972,[82] which amended FIFRA to focus pesticide regulation on health and environmental protection. More importantly for state responsibility, the 1972 Act explicitly provided a role for states in pesticide regulation,[83] and further amendments in 1978 enhanced the state role in the enforcement of pesticide law.[84]

FIFRA now grants states the authority to 'regulate the sale or use of any federally registered pesticide . . . in the State', but states may not permit a sale or use prohibited by FIFRA.[85] The Act has been interpreted broadly to allow states to regulate not only the sale and use of pesticides, but also their registration, suspension and cancellation. Thus, states may impose stricter use requirements without concern of federal preemption. States may not, however, impose labeling or packaging requirements in addition to, or different from, those imposed under FIFRA.[86] FIFRA also grants states the authority to provide registration for additional uses of federally registered pesticides to meet 'special local needs'.[87] Moreover, states are encouraged to establish their own certification programs for applicators of restricted-use pesticides.[88] Although each state certification program is subject to EPA approval, criteria for approval are fairly lenient, and states are allowed wide discretion in implementing the program.[89]

In addition, states may apply for 'primary enforcement responsibility' for pesticide-use violations. After the EPA grants primary enforcement authority, the state is obliged to ensure that the pesticide-use regulations will be enforced.[90] The EPA may also delegate authority to states to issue experimental use permits, which allow registered pesticides to be used temporarily for a new use (or unregistered pesticides to be used temporarily) without compliance with FIFRA registration requirements.[91]

B. State Exercise of Authority

1. Registration

States require registration of both pesticides and dealers. Thus, pesticide manufacturers may have to satisfy multiple pesticide registration procedures before their products can be sold nationally. And although many of the state registration procedures are similar, some are more rigorous than others. For example, Illinois law requires registration of all pesticides distributed or sold within the state, but regulations make it relatively easy for pesticides registered under FIFRA to be registered in Illinois.[92] In contrast, California has been particularly active in regulating pesticide use, imposing standards more stringent than FIFRA.[93] Indeed, California has 26 separate requirements for application for pesticide registration (literally A through Z) and demands submission of extensive data.[94]

States usually require registration of pesticide dealers that sell restricted-use pesticides. Requirements for registration vary, but many states require the dealer to pass an examination that demonstrates knowledge of pesticides and the rules that govern their sale and use.[95] Once registered, a dealer must ensure that sales of restricted-use pesticides are made only to certified applicators. Many states also require dealers to keep records of sales of restricted-use pesticides, including information about the pesticide, quantity sold, date of sale and certain identifying information about the purchaser.[96]

2.   Special local needs

FIFRA authorizes states to allow registration of federally registered pesticides for additional uses if the pesticides meet 'special local needs' and the use in question has not previously been denied, disapproved, or canceled by the EPA.[97] That is, the state may register a pesticide for additional uses, not listed in the federal registration, if the pesticide is federally registered for other uses. States may also register new products if the ingredients in the products are active or inert ingredients found in existing registered pesticides.[98] The key element for the registration exception is the determination by the state that the use of the product is necessary to meet 'special local needs'.[99] The special local need does not necessarily have to be a sudden emergency or a trivial extension of an established use.[100] Disruption of distribution channels, transportation problems, product shortages and other economic obstructions can all create special local needs.[101] The federal EPA may disapprove a special local needs registration[102] or, for cause, suspend a state's authority to issue pesticide registrations.[103]

3.   Applicator certification

FIFRA allows states to develop their own certification plans for restricted-use pesticide applicators. The Act does not prescribe detailed procedures for state plans, though training, proof of competency and reporting are required.[104] The EPA may reject a plan it deems to be inadequate. Nearly every state has an EPA-approved plan for applicators of restricted-use pesticides.[105] Though the state certification plans vary, most distinguish between private and commercial applicators,[106] with more rigorous education and competency testing for commercial applicators.

Many agricultural producers apply pesticides by air because it is often the safest, cheapest and most efficient way to protect their crops.[107] States sometimes use aerial application of pesticides to combat public health threats or economic problems caused by certain pests.[108] Because aerial application often involves a significant risk that the pesticide will drift from the target area, some states have issued specific requirements for aerial pesticide application.[109] These may include, for example, educational requirements, prescribed safety procedures and notification rules.[110]

4.   State enforcement

FIFRA allows states to assume primary enforcement responsibility for pesticide-use violations within their borders. Any state that enters into a cooperative agreement with the EPA has primary enforcement responsibility. Even without a cooperative agreement, the state has primary enforcement responsibility if the EPA determines that the state has adequate pesticide-use laws and regulations, implements adequate enforcement procedures, and keeps records to ensure compliance.[111]

At first, states with primary enforcement authority were slow to penalize violators, sometimes limiting enforcement primarily to inspections and warning letters, instead of fines or license suspensions. Even when fines were assessed they tended to be small, and suspensions were often served during non-productive months to minimize the impact on the violator.[112] In recent years, however, states have renewed their emphasis on enforcing pesticide-use provisions by strengthening civil enforcement statutes and by increasing the size of fines levied.[113]

States authorize different types and amounts of civil and criminal penalties for pesticide-use violations. Some states model their civil sanctions after those used by the EPA, with penalties related to the severity of the infraction and with the number of violations.[114] Other states combine elements from the EPA system with a violation point system, which assigns point values for different types of use infractions, with the fine dependent on the number of points.[115]

Criminal law is implicated in state pesticide enforcement only rarely, for egregious violations.[116] Some states characterize certain violations as felonies, while others restrict criminal charges to misdemeanors.[117]

C.   Special State Programs

Because FIFRA does not preempt the field of pesticide regulation, some states have regulated pesticide use more stringently than FIFRA, or have legislated in pesticide-use areas other than those specifically authorized in FIFRA. Some brief examples (which do not attempt to be comprehensive) indicate the scope and variety of this state legislation.[118]

California has been particularly active in environmental regulation. It enacted worker protection standards before the federal EPA promulgated its first worker protection regulations.[119] Its Birth Defect Prevention Act is intended to prevent pesticide-induced abortions, birth defects and infertility,[120] and allows suspension or cancellation of active pesticide ingredients with significant adverse health effects. The Pesticide Contamination Prevention Act establishes a program designed to prevent further pesticide pollution of groundwater aquifers in California, especially those that may be used for drinking water.[121] This law requires extensive information regarding the water solubility and leaching potential of every pesticide registered for agricultural use in the state, and establishes the Groundwater Protection List of economic poisons that may pollute groundwater even when applied according to label instructions.

Arizona recently enacted special rules to help prevent pesticide contamination of groundwater, with a list of more than 150 pesticide active ingredients that are subject to new reporting and information requirements designed to reduce groundwater contamination.[122]

Kansas law authorizes formation of Pesticide Management Areas, defined geographic areas subject to a pesticide management plan under which application of certain pesticides may be restricted or prohibited.[123] In addition Kansas, like other states, regulates chemigation,[124] 'any process in which pesticides, fertilizers, other chemicals, or animal wastes are added to irrigation water applied to land or crops, or both, through an irrigation-distribution system'.[125] The law requires chemigation permits (issued only after examination), anti-pollution devices, recordkeeping and inspection.

Illinois has enacted a special groundwater protection program that applies to storage and handling of pesticides and fertilizers at agrichemical facilities whose owners or operators agree to participate.[126] The Illinois Environmental Protection Agency and the Illinois Department of Agriculture are to develop a regulatory program designed to prevent groundwater contamination at agrichemical facilities that select this option.[127]

Some states have special laws to regulate commercial lawn-care product application, often with specific notice and safety requirements.[128] For example, New York requires commercial lawn applicators to enter a written contract with property owners and to inform customers about the pesticides to be used and their label warnings.[129] Illinois requires applicators to place visible lawn markers at any usual point of entry onto the treated area, and prohibits lawn-care applicators from releasing wash water or rinsate that contains pesticide residue into the environment.[130]

A few state laws address liability issues raised by use of agricultural chemicals. These laws do not focus on regulation of pesticides themselves, but instead on the agricultural producer's tort liability, under strict liability or negligence standards, to injured persons for contamination caused by the chemicals. Enacted recently in several states, the statutes have been called 'blameless contamination' laws.[131] Although state laws vary in scope and detail, in essence blameless contamination legislation provides that the producer who has used registered pesticides in compliance with label requirements and other applicable law will not be liable for damages associated with the presence of those chemicals in groundwater. Producers who have chemical spills or use pesticides contrary to label directions are not protected by blameless contamination laws.[132]

BETWEEN FIFRA AND STATE LAW: THE QUESTION OF PREEMPTION

As the discussion above indicates, FIFRA does not exclude states from the field of pesticide regulation. States have considerable latitude to enact laws governing, for example, pesticide registration procedures, applicator requirements and recordkeeping rules;[133] to register pesticides for special local needs; and to assume primary responsibility for the enforcement of pesticide-use violations. Section 136v(b) of FIFRA, however, limits state regulatory authority:

> Such State shall not impose or continue in effect any requirements for labeling or packaging in addition to or different from those required under this subchapter.[134]

As the language indicates, this restriction applies only in the area of pesticide labeling and packaging.

In some instances, opponents of state (or even local)[135] pesticide regulation have argued that state laws and regulations in the area of pesticide warnings are precluded by FIFRA, and some litigants have argued that FIFRA precludes damage awards under some state tort law claims. These challenges have raised questions about the extent of state power under constitutional principles, especially under the doctrine of preemption.

Three issues have been problematic. First, does FIFRA preempt all state regulations concerning pesticide warnings that require more than the label warnings prescribed by the federal EPA?[136] Second, does FIFRA preempt state common-law tort actions based on inadequate warnings?[137] Finally, what power do local governments enjoy, under FIFRA and state law, to regulate the use of pesticides?[138]

A.   Federal Preemption In Brief

The preemption doctrine outlines both the power of the Federal government to exclude state governments from an area of legislation and the constitutional inability of states to enter some areas of legislation. The constitutional basis for federal preemption of state law is the Supremacy Clause of the US Constitution. The clause states that '[t]his Constitution, and the Laws of the United States which shall be made in Pursuance thereof . . . shall be the supreme Law of the Land; and the Judges in every State shall be bound thereby'.[139] Concomitantly, the Tenth Amendment to the Constitution protects state sovereignty by providing that 'powers not delegated to the United States by the Constitution, nor prohibited by it to the states, are reserved to the States respectively, or to the people'.[140] The US

Supreme Court has applied these constitutional principles in controversies involving claims of federal preemption or alleged federal intrusion into areas of state sovereignty.

In a recent decision involving local pesticide regulation, the Supreme Court briefly reviewed its preemption doctrine.[141] In essence, in areas where Congress has authority to regulate, congressional intent determines whether federal law preempts state law. In the clearest cases, Congress will express its intention to preempt state law (and the extent of preemption) in the language of the federal statute.[142] Even without explicit preemptive language, Congress may indicate an intent to occupy the entire field of regulation.[143] This occurs when the federal regulation is 'so pervasive as to make reasonable the inference that Congress left no room for the States to supplement it', when the 'federal interest is so dominant that the federal system will be assumed to preclude enforcement of state law on the same subject', or when the goals to be obtained and the obligations imposed implicitly indicate an intent to preclude state authority.[144] Finally, state law may be preempted to the extent that state law actually conflicts with federal law.[145] This occurs when compliance with both laws is physically impossible[146] or when the state law is an obstacle to accomplishment of the full purposes and objectives of Congress.[147]

B. Federal Preemption of State Law under FIFRA

An important component of pesticide registration under FIFRA is EPA approval of pesticide labels. Detailed regulations promulgated under FIFRA require specific warnings and precautionary statements, dictated by the toxicity of the pesticide, to appear on pesticide labels.[148] FIFRA prohibits states from imposing any requirements for labeling or packaging of pesticides in addition to or different from the federal requirements.[149]

1. State warning requirements

In some instances, state law has required pesticide manufacturers to provide product warnings in addition to those included on the federally-approved label. If the state-mandated warnings are considered labels or labeling, FIFRA expressly preempts the state requirement. If the warnings are not labels or labeling, they may not be preempted.[150] Cases challenging warnings required under state law in New York and California have raised the issue of whether state-mandated warnings are preempted by FIFRA.

New York law requires commercial lawn-care applicators to enter a written contract with clients and to provide a list of chemicals to be used (with the EPA-approved label warnings), to provide a cover sheet with further warnings and safety information, and to post signs on the affected property or (for large areas) give notice by publication.[151] Because of costs of compliance and potential exposure to liability, pesticide interests challenged the New York law as preempted by FIFRA. In *New York State Pesticide Coalition, Inc. v. Jorling*,[152] the US Court of Appeals for the Second Circuit held that New York's notification requirements for commercial pesticide applicators did not amount to labels or labeling and thus were not preempted by FIFRA. Beginning from the FIFRA definitions of label and labeling, the court ascertained that the congressional purposes for the labeling requirements were to set minimum standards for pesticide labeling and to ensure that relevant safety information accompanied the product through the stream of commerce to the end user. In contrast, the New York provisions were designed to warn the public at large. They helped further the purpose of FIFRA by using state law to prevent adverse effects of pesticide use on the environment. The court therefore held that the New York warning provisions were not preempted.[153]

The US Court of Appeals for the Ninth Circuit decided a similar case in *Chemical Specialties Manufacturers Ass'n v. Allenby*,[154] which challenged California law requiring warnings posted at the point of sale of carcinogenic or reproductively toxic pesticide products. In essence, the *Allenby* case turned on the question of whether these point-of-sale signs constituted labeling under FIFRA. Applying the Second Circuit's reasoning in *Jorling*, the court stated that because point-of-sale signs were not attached to the pesticide container and did not accompany the product during the period of use, they did not amount to labels or labeling under FIFRA. The court held that FIFRA did not preempt the California law because point-of-sale warnings are not labeling.[155]

Jorling and *Allenby* indicate that states can require manufacturers and applicators to post additional warnings to protect consumers and the general public as long as the warnings do not amount to labeling. Although the determination of what constitutes labeling will probably have to be made on a case-by-case basis, in light of the statutory definition, both *Jorling* and *Allenby* suggest that warnings will not be labeling if they do not physically follow the pesticide from the time of manufacture through its application.

2. State products liability law

State laws requiring pesticide warnings at the point of sale are state regulation of pesticide sale and use, not preempted by FIFRA labeling provisions. The existence of state-imposed warnings raises the question whether these warnings may be used as proof of defective labeling in product liability suits.[156] An even more difficult question is whether state tort claims based on defective labeling are themselves preempted under FIFRA.

Pesticide use or exposure may result in personal injury or even death. Pesticide injury cases can be brought under a number of different theories.[157] Negligence in pesticide use (failure to test, failure to warn) or negligence *per se* (violation of a statutory duty) may be the basis of a suit. Strict tort liability arising from an abnormally dangerous activity (e.g., aerial spray drift, in some states) may also be relevant. Improper pesticide use may constitute a nuisance (a use of property that unreasonably interferes with the enjoyment of other property) or trespass (movement of substances onto the property of another). When the pesticide injury results from a defect in the product itself (and not from improper use), strict products liability in tort may be the appropriate theory of liability. Strict products liability may involve, for example, an allegation of a manufacturing defect (an unwanted and toxic contaminant) or a design defect (unreasonably dangerous combination of ingredients). It may also involve an allegation that warnings provided with the product are defective or insufficient.

a. Federal circuit court decisions   Courts deciding pesticide liability cases have generally agreed that FIFRA does not preempt most state common-law tort actions – those based, for example, on defective manufacture or improper use.[158] When the state tort action is based on the manufacturer's failure to warn, however, difficult questions of preemption arise. Federal courts of appeal have disagreed about whether FIFRA preempts state tort actions based on failure to warn. Moreover, even those courts holding that FIFRA preempts those tort actions have not agreed about whether federal preemption is explicit from the language of FIFRA or implicit.[159]

The plaintiff in *Papas v. Upjohn Co.*[160] had applied pesticides to dogs during his work for a humane society, and thereafter suffered health problems. His complaint was based in part on claims of inadequate labeling. In its first opinion (*Papas I*), the US Court of Appeals for the Eleventh Circuit decided that FIFRA impliedly preempts state common-law tort suits against manufacturers of EPA registered pesticides, but only to the extent that the suits are based on inadequate labeling claims.[161] The US Supreme Court vacated the judgment and remanded it[162] for consideration in light of *Cipollone v. Liggett Group, Inc.*,[163] which evaluated the preemptive effect of federal cigarette advertising statutes.

In *Papas II*, the Eleventh Circuit held that FIFRA expressly preempts state law claims to the extent they are based on the pesticide manufacturer's inadequate labeling or packaging.[164] The court relied on FIFRA section 136v(b), which states that '[states] shall not impose or continue in effect any requirements for labeling or packaging in addition to or different from those required under [FIFRA]'.[165] Reasoning that 'requirements' in section 136v(b) applied both to state statutes and the common law, the court concluded that common-law damages are 'requirements'. An award of damages in tort would, in effect, be a requirement that the chemical manufacturer defendants' labeling include additional or clearer warnings. Thus, state actions for damages, based on pesticide labeling or packaging that fails to meet a standard 'in addition to or different from' FIFRA, are preempted by section 136v(b). Papas's claims for negligence, strict liability and breach of implied warranty were all preempted, to the extent that they required proof that the manufacturers' labeling and packaging caused the injury. State law claims that do not challenge labeling and packaging are not preempted.[166]

In addition, *Papas II* stated that common-law actions challenging the adequacy of warnings on point-of-sale signs, consumer notices, and other informational materials would also be preempted. A manufacturer that has complied with EPA warning requirements on labels and packaging has satisfied its duty to warn.[167]

Arkansas-Platte & Gulf v. Van Waters & Rogers, Inc.[168] was a suit by a landowner who alleged that a chemical manufacturer had failed to warn of environmental risks and hazards to property. In its first opinion in *Arkansas-Platte I*, the Tenth Circuit reasoned that state court damage awards based on failure to warn would be *ad hoc* determinations of the adequacy of EPA labeling standards, hindering the purpose of FIFRA section 136v(b), to ensure uniform pesticide labeling. Thus, the court held that state tort actions based on labeling and failure to warn are impliedly preempted by FIFRA; the court believed that such actions conflict with federal uniform regulation and that Congress intended to occupy the field of pesticide labeling regulation.[169] On appeal to the Supreme Court, this case, like *Papas*, was vacated and remanded for reconsideration in light of *Cipollone*.[170] On remand, the Tenth Circuit adhered to its original opinion, holding that the common-law duty to warn is subject to the same federal preemptive constraints as a state statute.[171]

Worm v. American Cyanamid Co.[172] involved contract claims and failure-to-warn tort claims against a herbicide manufacturer by a farmer whose corn crop was damaged by application of a herbicide. The Fourth Circuit decided that neither the language nor the legislative history of FIFRA indicates an express intent by Congress to occupy the entire field of pesticide regulation.[173] Instead, section 136v(b) only stated the limits of the federal objectives of FIFRA and was 'not an intent to usurp all power, even in the narrow field of pesticide labeling'.[174] Having decided that no express preemption exists, the court continued its analysis to determine whether state common-law tort suits based on labeling claims conflict with FIFRA by frustrating its objectives. Quoting language from *Papas I*, the Fourth Circuit stated that '[a]llowing state common law tort claims based on labeling claims would permit state court juries to do what state legislatures . . . are forbidden to do: impose requirements for labeling pesticides'.[175] Thus, state-imposed duties that would demand labeling requirements inconsistent with FIFRA or its regulations are preempted. Other state standards of care related to product design, manufacture and testing, and state law contract claims and remedies (e.g., rescission of sale) are not labeling and thus not preempted.[176]

Unlike *Papas, Arkansas-Platte,* and *Worm,* the DC Circuit in *Ferebee v. Chevron Chemical Co.*[177] held that no preemption exists. *Ferebee,* the earliest federal circuit court decision on this issue, is the only one holding that FIFRA does not preempt state tort actions for inadequate labeling. *Ferebee* was brought by the estate of a government agricultural worker who contracted pulmonary fibrosis from exposure to paraquat. The DC Circuit held that FIFRA did not 'explicitly preempt' state damage actions, but 'merely precluded states from directly ordering changes in the EPA-approved labels'.[178] On the question of implied preemption, the court found that compliance with both FIFRA and state tort law was not impossible. Moreover, the objectives of state tort law did not conflict with Congress's objectives for FIFRA, because state tort law was meant to compensate injured parties and FIFRA was meant only to regulate pesticides.[179]

b. Other decisions But for *Ferebee,* decisions in federal circuit courts have held that FIFRA preempts (expressly or impliedly) state tort claims based on inadequate labeling or failure to warn. In contrast, federal district courts have been less consistent, with some decisions finding tort claims preempted and others rejecting that view.[180] Even different judges of the same district, the Southern District of Indiana, released conflicting decisions on the issue within a period of less than a year.[181]

Recent cases from the Supreme Courts of Arkansas and Nevada decided whether FIFRA preempts state common-law tort claims alleging failure to warn.[182] In Arkansas, *Ciba-Geigy Corp. v. Alter*[183] involved a farmer whose corn crop was allegedly damaged by herbicide use. Following *Ferebee,* the court concluded that FIFRA did not preempt the claim, either expressly or impliedly. The Nevada case, *Davidson v. Velsicol Chemical Corp.,*[184] focused on the personal injury of homeowners whose property was sprayed with a termiticide. Consonant with *Arkansas-Platte* and *Worm,* the court found no express preemption, but concluded that FIFRA occupied the entire field of pesticide labeling and impliedly preempted the homeowners' claim.

c. FIFRA preemption: questions continue The issue of whether FIFRA preempts state common-law tort actions based on inadequate labeling has not been resolved, as the conflicting decisions in federal courts of appeal and state supreme courts indicate. Two recent US Supreme Court decisions, *Cipollone v. Liggett Group, Inc.*[185] and *Wisconsin Public Intervenor v. Mortier*,[186] are somewhat relevant, though neither decision resolves the issue.

Cipollone v. Liggett Group, Inc. raised the issue of whether federal cigarette advertising laws preempted state law damage claims based on inadequate labeling. The suit, brought by a lung cancer victim who had smoked for 42 years, was an action for damages against cigarette manufacturers, with claims for breach of express warranty, failure to warn about the hazards of smoking, fraudulent misrepresentation of those hazards, design defects and conspiracy to defraud.[187] Cigarette manufacturers defended, in part, on the theory that federal cigarette advertising laws preempted the state claims.

One of the federal cigarette advertising laws at issue, the 1969 Act, barred all 'requirement[s] or prohibition[s], based on smoking and health . . . imposed under State law with respect to the advertising or promotion' of cigarettes.[188] After a review of preemption doctrine, the Court stated that 'we must construe these provisions in light of the presumption against the preemption of state police power regulations'.[189] A plurality of the Court concluded that the language of the statute is broad enough to preempt state common-law actions, as well as state legislative or regulatory enactments. The only claims preempted, however, are those that rely on a state law requirement or prohibition, based on smoking and health, with respect to advertising or promotion of cigarettes. Claims that do not fit within this specific area of preemption may be pursued.[190] Thus, certain of Cipollone's failure to warn and fraudulent misrepresentation claims were preempted, but claims based on express warranty or conspiracy to defraud were not.[191]

The preemptive reach of the 1969 federal cigarette advertising law is similar to FIFRA section 136v(b), which applies to pesticide labeling or packaging requirements, and the Supreme Court remanded two FIFRA cases to federal circuit courts for reconsideration in light of *Cipollone*. On reconsideration after remand, the courts in *Papas* and *Arkansas-Platte* decided that FIFRA explicitly or implicitly preempted state tort law claims based on failure to warn.[192]

Tort cases applying other federal laws with similar preemption provisions have resulted in findings of preemption of state tort claims based on failure to warn or improper labeling. For example, in *King v. Collagen Corp.*[193] the First Circuit relied on *Cipollone* to hold that an express preemption provision in the Medical Device Amendments of 1976[194] preempted any state requirement that establishes new substantive requirements for a device in a regulated area. Thus preemption precluded contract claims based on state law, as well as tort claims arising out of misbranding, misrepresentation and failure to warn.[195] Similarly, in *Moss v. Parks Corp.*[196] the Fourth Circuit held that the preemption provision of the Federal Hazardous Substances Labeling Act, similar in scope to that in FIFRA, preempts common-law tort actions based on failure to warn, when those claims seek more elaborate or different warnings than those mandated by federal laws or regulations. It does not preempt claims based on failure to comply with existing federal regulations.[197]

Wisconsin Public Intervenor v. Mortier[198] was a challenge to a pesticide-use regulation adopted by a small Wisconsin town. In *Mortier*, the Supreme Court held that FIFRA section 136v(a), which permits states to regulate the sale or use of pesticides not prohibited by FIFRA, did not preempt local governments from regulating the use of pesticides. FIFRA did not preempt the town ordinance in question, either 'expressly, implicitly, or by virtue of an actual conflict'.[199] Neither the statutory language nor its legislative history expresses a congressional intention to preempt local pesticide-use regulation. Moreover, to hold that Congress had occupied the field of pesticide regulation to the exclusion of local government would make 136v(b), which prohibits states from imposing their own labeling or packaging requirements, 'pure surplusage'. The Court also stated that the grant of authority in section 136v(a) 'ensure[s] that the States could continue to regulate use and sales even where, such as with regard to the banning of mislabeled products, a narrow pre-emptive overlap might occur'.[200] That is, section 136v(a) does not reveal an intent to preempt the field of pesticide regulation, but rather to leave areas for state regulation consistent with the intention not to preempt.[201] The Court also noted that compliance with FIFRA and the local ordinance is not a physical impossibility.[202]

Both courts and commentators have used the language in *Mortier* to support preemption and no preemption positions. For example, the Fourth Circuit in *Worm* used the 'narrow pre-emptive overlap' language in *Mortier* to support its conclusion that Congress did not intend to preempt the entire field of pesticide regulation, nor did it expressly usurp all power in the narrower area of pesticide labeling.[203] Conversely, some commentary suggests that the analytic approach in *Mortier* implies that preemption extends to cover the entire field of pesticide labeling.[204] Others suggest that the Court's characterization of the pesticide regulatory scheme as not being closed to the states indicates that no preemption exists.[205] Still others suggest that *Mortier* has simply not resolved the issue.[206]

C. State Preemption of Local Law

The Supreme Court decision in *Mortier* focused on regulation of pesticide use in an ordinance enacted by a local governmental body. In holding that local regulation was not preempted, the Court stated that 'FIFRA nowhere expressly supersedes local regulation of pesticide use',[207] and Congress's silence on that issue does not indicate preemption. As the Court noted, local governments are created as political subdivisions for carrying out state powers delegated to them; they are not excluded from the express authorization of power to the states. The Court recognized, however, that states have the authority, indeed the 'absolute discretion', to delegate to local governments the authority to regulate pesticide use or to withhold that authority.[208]

Local governments are created by states, and local governmental power is delegated from the states, either in the state constitution or in state statutes. Thus, though FIFRA does not prevent local units of government from enacting pesticide-use regulations, the states themselves may preempt that regulation.[209] The state's ability to withhold from local governments the power to regulate pesticides depends in part on the status that the state itself has given to the local authority.[210] Local units of government, for example, normally have the status of either a general law government or a home rule government.

General law governments have the power only to regulate in areas that have been delegated to them directly by the state legislature or in the state constitution.   States thus have significant power to exclude general law governments from areas of regulation. They may prohibit local pesticide regulation or expressly permit it. The issue of state–local preemption arises when a state enactment has neither explicitly authorized nor prohibited local government pesticide regulation.[211] Without explicit expression of legislative intent, state courts have to decide if the state legislature implicitly intended to preempt local authority. As with federal–state preemption, the result may depend on whether the state law was intended to occupy the field of regulation.[212] Even if a court finds no state preemption, the state legislature can reverse the court's holding simply by enacting law to make clear that the state intends to regulate the entire pesticide field.[213] This occurred, for example, in California. The California Supreme Court ruled that neither state law nor FIFRA preempted counties from prohibiting certain forms of aerial spraying.[214] Thereafter, the state legislature overruled the decision by enacting a law prohibiting local regulation of pesticides unless that regulation was permitted by specific exception.[215]

Home rule governments (municipalities or counties), which derive their power from state constitutions authorizing home rule status, have nearly exclusive authority over their own municipal affairs.[216] Thus, for home rule units, the preemption issue may be resolved in part by deciding whether the local regulation deals with a matter that is primarily a 'municipal affair' or a matter of 'statewide concern'. When the state legislature expresses its intent to occupy a field of regulation, state law will exclude even home rule units from regulating in that area, but only if the area is one of statewide, rather than local, concern.[217] In some jurisdictions, the state government has more power to preempt regulation by local government, even in arguably local matters.[218]

Thus, the question of state preemption of local regulation turns on the nature of the local government unit, as well as on the nature of the regulation involved. In fact, a relatively small number of the 83,200 units of local government in the United States actually regulate pesticide use. Existing local ordinances control pesticide use by requiring permits, banning specific pesticides, banning or restricting aerial spraying, and requiring specific notice and posting.[219]

CONCLUSION

In the last decades, both the Federal government and the states have assumed active roles in regulating the manufacture and use of pesticides. FIFRA and other federal laws assign the leadership role to the US EPA, but leave significant areas open to state regulation. States have been active participants in the pesticide regulation process, implementing state programs authorized by FIFRA and enacting their own pesticide standards that, where necessary, regulate more stringently than the federal laws. Indeed, in some areas state participation has been critical in addressing localized concerns, because federal regulation has not been particularly speedy or aggressive. Nor have federal programs addressed all of the environmental problems raised by pesticide use; only recently, for example, has the EPA begun to seek effective solutions to the problems of groundwater pesticide pollution.

As the federal EPA continues to implement its strategy for groundwater protection, to proceed with its statutory obligation to reregister pesticides, and to carry out its other duties under FIFRA and related statutes, it is to be hoped that states will continue to seek innovative solutions to pesticide problems within their own borders and to cooperate with the federal EPA to implement FIFRA and other federal statutes. Federal–state cooperation, coupled with creative state (and even local) pesticide programs, can help achieve the appropriate balance between protection of public health and the environment and the continued availability of effective agricultural chemicals.

NOTES

1. Elizabeth G. Nielsen and Linda K. Lee, *The Magnitude and Costs of Groundwater Contamination From Agricultural Chemicals: A National Perspective* 1 (US Dept of Agric., 1987). Figures are from 1980. Between 1950 and 1980, groundwater use increased by 158 percent compared to 107 percent for surface water.
2. US Environmental Protection Agency, *Pesticides and Ground-Water Strategy* 1–2, 5 (21T–1022, Oct. 1991).
3. John W. Mill, Note, *Agricultural Chemical Contamination of Groundwater: An Economic Analysis of Alternative Liability Rules*, 1991 U. Ill. L. Rev. 1135, 1138.
4. Terence J. Centner and Michael E. Wetzstein, *Agricultural Pesticide Contamination of Groundwater: Developing a 'Right-to-Spray Law' for Blameless Contamination*, 14 J. Agric. Tax'n & L. 38, 38 (1992) (citing Batie, Cox and Diebel, *Managing Agricultural Contamination of Groundwater: State Strategies* (National Governors' Association, 1989)).
5. Nielsen and Lee, *supra* note 1, at v. Nearly 19 million people use private wells, which are particularly vulnerable to contamination. Pesticides are not the only source of agricultural contamination. Fertilizer, particularly nitrogen fertilizer, also causes groundwater contamination. *Id*. at 10–17.
6. Glen D. Anderson, Ann E. De Bossu, and Peter J. Kuch, *Control of Agricultural Pollution by Regulation in* Agriculture and Water Quality: International Perspectives 63, 74 (John B. Braden and Stephen B. Lovejoy, eds, 1990).
7. 21 USC §§ 301–392 (1988 and Supp. 1992), especially §§ 342, 346a, 348.
8. *Id*. §§ 346a, 348   (sections 408 and 409 of the FFDCA).
9. *Id*. § 348(c)(3)(A).
10. 968 F.2d 985 (9th Cir. 1992), *cert. denied*, 113 S.Ct. 1361 (1993). *Les v. Reilly* set aside the EPA's decision to provide a *de minimis* exception to the Delaney Clause for carcinogenic additives that posed a lifetime risk of cancer for fewer than one in a million persons. The pesticides at issue in the suit were benomyl, mancozeb, phosmet and trifluralin.
11. John Sheeley and Phil Fraas, *Pesticide and food safety: the Clinton administration proposal*, 11 Agricultural Law Update 1 (Oct. 1993).
12. US EPA, *supra* note 2. The strategy is summarized in 56 Fed. Reg. 56,643–4 (1991). For an overview of the strategy based on a proposal, see Rachel J. Sater, *EPA's Pesticides in Groundwater Strategy: Agency Action in the Face of Congressional Inaction*, 17 Ecology L. Q. 143 (1990).
13. 56 Fed. Reg. 56,643–4 (1991).
14. 42 USC §§ 300f–300j–26 (1988 and Supp. 1992). For a brief discussion of the SDWA, see J. David Aiken, *Protecting the Hidden Resource: The Quiet Crisis in Nebraska Pesticide and Ground Water Protection Policies*, 26 Creighton L.Rev. 639, 644–65 (1993).
15. 33 USC §§ 1251–1387 (1988 and Supp. 1992). Sections 208 and 319 are at *id*. §§ 1288, 1329. For a discussion of these provisions, see George A. Gould, *Agriculture, Nonpoint Source Pollution, and Federal Law*, 23 U.C. Davis L. Rev. 461, 463 (1990).
16. 16 USC §§ 1531–44 (1988 and Supp. 1992).
17. *See* Martha L. Noble, *Pesticide Use and Federal Protection of Wildlife*, 12 J. Agric. Tax'n & L. 160, 165 (1990).
18. 42 USC § 6901–6992k (1988 and Supp. 1992).
19. *Id*. §§ 6903(5), (27). *See* Michael T. Olexa, *Pesticide Use and Impact: FIFRA and Related Regulatory Issues*, 68 N.D. L. Rev. 445, 454 (1992).
20. FIFRA specifically states that 'nothing in this section [referring to the storage, disposal, transportation, and recall of pesticides] shall diminish the authorities or requirements of [RCRA]'. 7 USC § 136q(h).
21. *See* 42 USC §§ 6922–3. Regulations exempt empty containers from RCRA requirements. 40 CFR § 261.7(a)(1), (b)(3). See Olexa, *supra* note 19, at 454–5. The EPA, under the PGWS, plans to establish rules in 1993 for pesticide mixing, loading, storage, and disposal. EPA, *supra* note 2, at 67.
22. Act of April 26, 1910, ch. 191, 36 Stat. 331.
23. Marshall Lee Miller, *Federal Regulation of Pesticides in* Environmental Law Handbook 328, 329 (Government Institutes, Inc., 11ᵗʰ ed. 1991).
24. 2 Frank P. Grad, Treatise on Environmental Law § 8.02 (1987).

25. Michael Shapiro, *Toxic Substances Policy in* Public Policies for Environmental Protection 195, 204 (Paul R. Portney, ed, 1990).

26. Act of June 25, 1947, ch. 125, 61 Stat. 163 (current version at 7 USC § § 136–136y (1988 and Supp. 1993)). The law, by now significantly amended, continues to be called FIFRA. Miller, *supra* note 23, at 329 n.3.

27. H. Rep. No. 313, 80th Cong., 1st Sess. 3 (1947), quoted in 3 William H. Rodgers, Jr, Environmental Law: Pesticides and Toxic Substances 34 n.26 (1988).

28. Cynthia A. Lewis, *Pesticides, in* Law of Environmental Protection § 17.01 (3 Sheldon M. Novick et al. eds, 1994). The statute contained a safety provision declaring a pesticide 'misbranded' if 'when used as directed or in accordance with commonly recognized practice [the pesticide] shall be injurious to living man or other vertebrate animals, or vegetation, except weeds'. Act of June 25, 1947, ch. 125, 61 Stat. 163.

29. 2 Grad, *supra* note 24, § 8.02. FIFRA was further amended in 1959 to encompass nematocides, plant regulators, defoliants, and desiccants. Pub. L. No. 86–139, 72 Stat. 286.

30. Act of June 25, 1947, ch. 125, § 4, 61 Stat. 167.

31. Miller, *supra* note 23, at 329. Until 1964, the USDA could register a pesticide under protest.

32. Act of May 12, 1964, ch. 125, § 3, 78 Stat. 190. Aggrieved applicants for registration (or whose registration was canceled) could obtain administrative review, public hearings, and judicial review. 2 Grad, *supra* note 24, § 8.02.

33. Miller, *supra* note 23, at 330.

34. Gregory J. Mertz, Note, *Dead But Not Forgotten: California's Big Green Initiative And The Need to Restrict State Regulation of Pesticides*, 60 Geo. Wash. L. Rev. 506, 512 (1992).

35. Lewis, *supra* note 28, §17.01. The EPA Administrator is authorized under FIFRA 'to prescribe regulations necessary to carry out the provisions of [the act]'. 7 USC §§ 136(b) and 136w(a)(1). The Secretary of Agriculture still maintains some influence. Before the EPA publishes regulations under the act, the views of the Secretary of Agriculture have to be solicited, §§ 136s(a), 136w(a). The EPA must also cooperate with the USDA in identifying pests to be controlled under the act, § 136w–3(a), and in carrying out provisions or securing the uniformity of regulations under the act, § 136t(b).

36. Federal Environmental Pesticide Control Act (FEPCA), Pub. L. No. 92–516, 86 Stat. 975 (1972).

37. 7 USC § 136a(a). See also § 136(bb) (defining 'unreasonable adverse effects on the environment') and § 136(x) (using that term to define 'protect health and environment').

38. Pub. L. No. 94–140, 89 Stat. 752 (1975) and Pub. L. No. 95–396, 92 Stat. 819 (1978). These amendments are discussed in Rodgers, *supra* note 27, at IX–XVIII, 47–53.

39. Pub. L. No. 100–532, 102 Stat. 2655 (Oct. 25, 1988).

40. 7 USC § 136a–1. *See* Scott Ferguson and Ed Gray, *1988 FIFRA Amendments: A Major Step in Pesticide Regulation*, 19 Envtl. L. Rep. (Envtl. L. Inst.) 10070 (1989). The amendments also changed the disposal process for banned pesticides, Ferguson and Gray, *supra*, at 10079, shifting responsibility for disposal from the EPA to the holders of the pesticides and requiring the holders to notify the EPA of the means of disposal. 7 USC § 136q.

41. 7 USC § 136a(a). Several exemptions to registration exist: transfers of pesticides between registered establishments operated by the same producer for packaging or use as a component; transfer pursuant to an experimental use permit. *Id*. § 136a(b)(1),(2). Other provisions of FIFRA allow pesticides to escape registration (e.g., certain pesticides produced solely for export to foreign countries). *Id*. §§ 136o, 136p, 136w(b).

42. *Id*. § 136e.

43. *Id*. § 136(u). New animal drugs are excluded.

44. Statement of Policy: Microbial Products Subject to FIFRA and TSCA, 51 Fed. Reg. 23,313 (1986). These products are regulated unless specifically exempted, but special EPA data requirements and review procedures exist.

45. 7 USC § 136(t). The administrator may declare any form of plant or animal life that is injurious to health or the environment a pest. *Id*. § 136w(c)(1).

46. *Id*. §§ 136(t), 136w(c)(1).

47. *Id*. § 136a(c)(1). Pesticide registration requires disclosure of valuable, confidential business information. Therefore, FIFRA protects registrants by prohibiting most public disclosures of confidential data. *Id*. § 136h.

48. 7 USC § 136a(c)(5). Although the EPA must approve a pesticide for registration if it meets the statutory criteria, the burden of proving that the pesticide meets the criteria is on the applicant. Rodgers, *supra* note 27, at 105. *See generally* 50 Fed. Reg. 1119, 1120 (1985).
49. 40 CFR § 156.10(a)(1), (5).
50. 7 USC § 136a(f)(1).
51. *See id.* § 136a(a) and (c)(5).
52. *See id.* § 136a(c)(1)(F) and (c)(2). The EPA publishes and updates guidelines that specify the kinds of information required to support pesticide registration, *id.* § 136a(c)(2)(A). The applicant can satisfy the data requirement by generating and submitting new data for each active ingredient in the pesticide, or alternatively, if an ingredient is identical or substantially similar to one that has already been tested, by using data from a previous test. *Id.* § 136a(c)(1)(F).
53. 7 USC § 136a(a) and (c)(5).
54. *Id.* § 136(bb).
55. *Id.* § 136(j).
56. *See, e.g.*, Lewis, *supra* note 28, § 17.02; Miller, *supra* note 23, at 333; and Rodgers, *supra* note 27, at 106.
57. 7 USC § 136a–1(a).
58. *See id.* § 136a–1(b)–(g).
59. 16 Int'l Env't. Rep. (BNA) 688 (22 Sept. 1993).
60. Peter F. Guerrero, Testimony, Pesticides: Registration Delays Jeopardize Success of Proposed Policy Reforms 1 (GAO/T–RCED–94–48, Oct. 1993). See also US GAO, Pesticides: Information Systems Improvements Essential for EPA's Reregistration Efforts (GAO/IMTEC–93–5, Nov. 1992).
61. US GAO, Pesticides: Pesticide Reregistration May Not Be Complete Until 2006 at 7, 10 (GAO/RCED–93–94, May 1993).
62. US GAO, Pesticides: Information Systems, *supra* note 60.
63. 7 USC § 136a(d)(1).
64. *Id.*
65. *Id.* § 136a(d)(1)(C)(i) and (ii). An exception to this requirement exists for some restricted-use pesticides that do not cause 'acute dermal or inhalation toxicity' and that have special EPA-issued application restrictions. Pesticides that fit in this exemption may be applied by anyone in accordance with the label instructions. *Id.* § 136a(d)(1)(C)(ii). Label instructions vary from requiring seasonal permits for application to requiring the user to certify that the label instructions have been read and the pesticide will be applied in accordance with the instructions. See House Comm. on Agric., Fed. Envtl Pesticide Control Act of 1971. H.R. Rep. No. 511, 92nd Cong., 1st Sess. 15 (1971).
66. 7 USC § 136i.
67. Food, Agriculture, Conservation and Trade Act of 1990, Pub. L. 101–624, Title XIV, § 1491, 104 Stat. 3627 (1990), as amended.
68. 7 USC § 136i–1(a)–(c).
69. Recordkeeping Requirements for Certified Applicators of Federally Restricted Use Pesticides, 58 Fed. Reg. 19014 (9 April 1993) (codified at 7 CFR § 110).
70. *Id.* at 19023, 7 CFR § 110.6.
71. 7 USC § 136d(a)(1). Cancellation of a pesticide does not necessarily mean it will no longer be used. The EPA may allow the sale and use of any existing stock of canceled pesticides, *id.*, and may promulgate regulations governing the storage, disposal and transport of canceled pesticides, *id.* § 136q.
72. *Id.* § 136d(b).
73. *Id.* § 136d(b)(2).
74. *E.g.*, Ciba-Geigy v. EPA, 874 F.2d 277 (5th Cir. 1989) (cancellation order for the use of diazinon on golf courses and sod farms). The Fifth Circuit found, though reversing and remanding an EPA order, that the EPA had 'sufficient discretion' to determine that recurring bird kills were an unreasonable environmental effect even though they did not significantly reduce the bird population. The court further held that the requirement that the pesticide 'generally' cause adverse environmental effects did not require a finding that the pesticide caused undesirable consequences most of the time, but only that it created a 'significant probability that such consequences may occur'. *Id.* at 279-80.
75. 7 USC § 136d(b).
76. *Id.* § 136d(c).

77. *Id*. Under proposed changes to FIFRA, cancellation and suspension procedures would be separated. Sheeley and Fraas, *supra* note 11, at 2.

78. Worker Protection Standards for Agricultural Pesticides, 57 Fed. Reg. 38,102 (1992) (codified at 40 CFR §§ 156, 170). *See* Susan A. Schneider, *EPA issues new worker protection regulations*, 9 Agricultural Law Update 1 (Aug. 1992); Charles N. Carnes, *The Proposed Environmental Protection Agency Pesticide Regulations*, 12 J. Agric. Tax'n & L. 170, 170 (1990).

79. 57 Fed. Reg. 38,151–2 (codified at 40 CFR § 170.3).

80. 57 Fed. Reg. 38,147–50 (codified at 40 CFR § 156.200-.212). These regulations apply to information required under the worker protection regulations and do not preempt any other information required under applicable federal or state laws. Carnes, *supra* note 78, at 172.

81. 57 Fed. Reg. 38,151–65 (codified at 40 CFR § 170, subparts B and C). *See* Schneider, *supra* note 78, at 2.

82. Pub. L. No. 92–516, 86 Stat. 973 (1972).

83. *See* 7 USC §§ 136i, 136p, 136u, 136v.

84. *Id*. § 136w.

85. *Id*. § 136v(a).

86. *Id*. § 136v(b).

87. *Id*. § 136v(c).

88. *Id*. § 136i(a)(2).

89. Rodgers, *supra* note 27, at 150–154.

90. 7 USC §§ 136w–1, 136w–2.

91. *Id*. § 136c.

92. 415 ILCS 60/6 (1992 and Supp. 1993); Ill. Admin. Code tit. 8, § 250.30 (1992).

93. *See* Mertz, *supra* note 34, at 518–25.

94. *See* Cal. Food and Agric. Code § 12811 (Deering 1994); Cal. Code Regs. tit. 3, §§ 6170.5, 6172 (Barclay 1994).

95. *See, e.g.*, 415 ILCS 60/13 (1992 and Supp. 1993); Ill. Admin. Code tit. 8, § 250.20 (1992).

96. *See, e.g.*, Ill. Admin. Code tit. 8, § 250.150 (1992); Kan. Admin. Regs. 4–13–30(b) (1993). For brief descriptions of pesticide registration and dealer licensing in Colorado, Iowa, Kansas, Missouri, and South Dakota, see Aiken, *supra* note 14, at 688–90.

97. 7 USC § 136v(c)(1).

98. 40 CFR § 162.152(a), (b).

99. 7 USC § 136v(c)(1).

100. Rodgers, *supra* note 27, at 202.

101. *See* 46 Fed. Reg. 2008, 2010 (1981).

102. 7 USC § 136v(c)(2). EPA cannot disapprove state registration based on 'lack of essentiality of a pesticide or . . . if its composition and use patterns are similar to those of a federally registered pesticide'.

103. *Id*. § 136v(c)(4). Prior to any suspension, the EPA must advise the state of the EPA's intention to suspend and the reasons for the suspension.

104. *Id*. § 136i(a).

105. Approved state plans for private and commercial applicators exist in every state except Colorado (which certifies only commercial applicators) and Nebraska. 58 Fed. Reg. 19014–15 (1993). Nebraska has refused to implement FIFRA certification (and enforcement) programs for several reasons. Aiken, *supra* note 14, at 642.

106. *See, e.g.*, Cal. Code Regs. tit. 3, § 6000 (Barclay 1994) (private and commercial applicators); Ill. Admin. Code tit. 8, §§ 250.80, 250.100 (1992) (private applicators, licensed operators, and commercial applicators).

107. Paul Conlow, *Crop Dusters See Themselves As Vanishing Breed*, N.Y. Times, Nov. 1, 1992, § 13NJ, at 1. Ground-spraying, the most common alternative to aerial application, can cause more crop damage and usually requires more pesticide applications than crop dusting.

108. In 1990, Massachusetts used aerial spraying to eliminate mosquitos that carried the virus eastern equine encephalitis, which posed a threat to human health. Sean A. Murphy, Note, *Aerial Pest Eradication in Massachusetts and California and the Pesticide Malathion*, 19 B.C. Envtl. Aff. L. Rev. 851 (1992). California has used aerial pesticide application to combat the medfly which posed a threat to the state's citrus industry. *Id*. at 852.

109. *See, e.g.*, Cal. Food and Agric. Code §§ 12972, 12986 (Deering 1994). For a discussion of tort liability for aerial pesticide applicators, see William K. Jones, *Strict Liability for Hazardous Enterprise*, 92 Colum. L. Rev. 1705, 1738–9 (1992).

110. *See, e.g.*, Ill. Admin. Code tit. 8, § 250.110(f) (1992) (education about aerial application included as subject for competency testing for licensed applicators); Cal. Food and Agric. Code § 12971 (Deering 1994) (application must prevent substantial drift to nontarget areas); Mass. Regs. Code tit. 333, § 10.03(23)(b) (1987) (notification rules) (cited in Murphy, *supra* note 108, at 862).

111. 7 USC § 136w–1. Co-operative agreements are authorized in *id.* § 136u. The EPA retains enforcement responsibility if states do not assume responsibility. *Id.* § 136w–1(c).

112. Rodgers, *supra* note 27, at 367–8.

113. Sam Brownback, Gregory P. Krissek and Stephen D. Maxwell, *An Overview of Kansas's Regulation of Agricultural Chemicals and Pesticides*, 13 J. Agric. Tax'n & L. 66, 67–8 (1991). Illinois, Indiana, Iowa, Kansas, Missouri, Nebraska, North Dakota, Oklahoma, South Dakota, and Texas have all increased their emphasis on enforcing pesticide violations in the last several years. Oklahoma doubled its amount of assessed fines from 1989 to 1990. These changes have come about largely as a result of societal pressures arising out of fears of pesticide contamination of the environment. *Id.*

114. *See, e.g.*, Kan. Stat. Ann. §§ 2–2438 to –2479 (1993). FIFRA civil sanctions vary from written warnings to fines of $5,000 per violation. 7 USC § 136*l*(a).

115. *See, e.g.*, 415 ILCS 60/24.1 (1992 and Supp. 1993). Illinois assigns a point value of 6 to any pesticide use violation that results in humans experiencing headaches, nausea, eye irritation or other such symptoms that last for at least 3 days, but only 1 point for violations that result in pesticide exposure to humans or animals with no symptoms or damage. Illinois issues a warning at 7 points, a $750 fine at 14 points, and a $10,000 fine for 30 points or more.

116. Rodgers, *supra* note 27, at 368.

117. The Illinois pesticide law characterizes a criminal violation of the statute or regulations as a misdemeanor, with a fine of not less than $5,000. 415 ILCS 60/24 (1992 and Supp. 1993).

118. For further descriptions, especially of programs in California, Wisconsin, Iowa, Arizona, Montana, and Nebraska, see Aiken, *supra* note 14, at 659–67, 669–84.

119. Pesticides and Worker Safety Act, Cal. Food and Agric. Code §§ 12980-85 (Deering 1994).

120. Cal. Food and Agric. Code §§ 13121–32 (Deering 1994).

121. *Id.* §§ 13141–52.

122. Ariz. Comp. Admin. R. and Regs. § R18–6–301 (1992). See Aiken, *supra* note 14, at 663–6 for a description of Arizona programs to regulate nitrogen fertilizers and pesticides.

123. Kan. Stat. Ann. §§ 2–2472 to –2479 (1993). Several other states have similar statutes. *E.g.*, Ariz. Rev. Stat. Ann. § 3–366 (Michie 1994); Iowa Code § 206.21 (1993); and Me. Rev. Stat. Ann. tit. 22, § 1471–M (1993).

124. Chemigation Safety Law, Kan. Stat. Ann. §§ 2–3301 to –3317 (1993). A few other states have specific chemigation acts. *E.g.*, Colo Rev. Stat. § 35–11–101 *et seq.* (1994); Idaho Code § 22–1401 *et seq.* (1994).

125. Brownback, *supra* note 113, at 71. Because chemigation adds pesticides directly to a water system (i.e., an irrigation system), chemigation statutes are intended primarily to reduce the risk of public water supply contamination. *Id.*

126. 415 ILCS 5/14.6(a) (1992 and Supp. 1993). Facilities that meet the requirements for this program will be subject to special storage and handling regulations, *id.* 5/14.4(a), which were to be promulgated by 1 October 1993.

127. *Id.* 5/14.6(b).

128. *See, e.g.*, 415 ILCS 65/1–65/8 (1992 and Supp. 1993); N.Y. Envtl. Conserv. Law § 33–1001 (Consol. 1994).

129. N.Y. Envtl. Conserv. Law § 33–1001(1) (Consol. 1994).

130. 415 ILCS 65/3(2),(3) and 65/5 (1992 and Supp. 1993). Penalties range from $100 for a first offense to $500 for third or subsequent offenses. *Id.* 65/7.

131. Centner and Wetzstein, *supra* note 4; Terence J. Centner, *Blameless Contamination: New State Legislation Regulating Liability for Agricultural Chemicals in Groundwater*, 45 J. Soil & Water Conservation 216 (1990). Centner and Wetzstein discuss laws from Georgia, Idaho, Iowa, Minnesota, and Vermont.

132. Centner and Wetzstein, *supra* note 4, at 40–43.

133. *See, e.g.*, 415 ILCS 60/6 (1992 and Supp. 1993) and Ill. Admin. Code tit. 8, § 250.30 (1992) (registration procedures); *id.* §§ 250.80, 250.90, and 250.100 (applicator requirements); and *id.* § 250.150 (recordkeeping rules).

134. 7 USC § 136v(b).

135. Although the language of § 136v refers to regulation by states, the US Supreme Court has interpreted this to allow regulation by local governments. Wisconsin Public Intervenor v. Mortier, 111 S. Ct. 2476 (1991). For further discussion of *Mortier*, see *infra* text accompanying notes 198–208.
136. *E.g.*, Chemical Specialties Manufacturers Ass'n v. Allenby, 958 F.2d 941 (9th Cir.), *cert. denied*, 113 S. Ct. 80 (1992) (no preemption).
137. *Compare* Papas v. Upjohn Co., 985 F.2d 516 (11th Cir.), *cert. denied*, 114 S. Ct. 300 (1993) (preemption) *with* Ferebee v. Chevron Chemical Co., 736 F.2d 1529 (D.C. Cir.), *cert. denied*, 469 US 1062 (1984) (no preemption).
138. Under FIFRA, *see* Wisconsin Public Intervenor v. Mortier, 111 S. Ct. 2476 (1991). For state law, *compare* Pesticide Public Policy Foundation v. Village of Wauconda, 510 N.E. 2d 858 (Ill. 1987) (preemption) *with* People ex rel. Deukmejian v. County of Mendocino, 683 P.2d 1150 (Ca. 1984) (no preemption).
139. US Const. art. VI, cl. 2.
140. US Const. amend. X.
141. Wisconsin Public Intervenor v. Mortier, 111 S. Ct. 2476, 2481 (1991).
142. Jones v. Rath Packing Co., 430 US 519, 525 (1977).
143. Rice v. Santa Fe Elevator Corp., 331 US 218, 230 (1947).
144. *Id.*, quoted in *Mortier*, 111 S. Ct. at 2481–2.
145. Wisconsin Public Intervenor v. Mortier, 111 S. Ct. 2476, 2482 (1991).
146. Florida Lime and Avocado Growers, Inc. v. Paul, 373 US 132, 142–3 (1963).
147. Silkwood v. Kerr McGee Corp., 464 US 238, 248 (1984); Hines v. Davidowitz, 312 US 52, 67 (1941). For a brief discussion of preemption, in the context of tort law, see Philip H. Corboy and Todd A. Smith, *Federal Preemption of Product Liability Law: Federalism and the Theory of Implied Preemption*, 15 Am. J. Trial Advoc. 435, 444–50 (1992).
148. 40 CFR § 156.10(h). See *supra* text accompanying notes 49–50.
149. 7 USC § 136v(b). The term 'label' refers to written, printed, or graphic matter on, or attached to, a pesticide or its container. *Id.* § 136(p)(1). 'Labeling' includes any label or other matter accompanying the pesticide at any time, or matter to which reference is made on the label or in literature accompanying the pesticide. *Id.* § 136(p)(2).
150. Chemical Specialties Manufacturers Ass'n v. Allenby, 958 F.2d 941, 943 (9th Cir.), *cert. denied*, 113 S. Ct. 80 (1992).
151. New York State Pesticide Coalition, Inc. v. Jorling, 874 F.2d 115, 116–17 (2d Cir. 1989).
152. 874 F.2d 115 (2d Cir. 1989).
153. *Id.* at 119–20.
154. Chemical Specialties Manufacturers Ass'n v. Allenby, 958 F.2d 941 (9th Cir.), *cert. denied*, 113 S. Ct. 80 (1992). *Allenby* also raised an issue under the Federal Hazardous Substances Labeling Act.
155. *Id.* at 945–6. The discussion of *Allenby* focused on express preemption. The court also rejected claims that the California law is impliedly preempted (by its potential effect of forcing manufacturers to amend their pesticide labels) by FIFRA and that the law frustrates the Congressional purpose of FIFRA.
156. The Ninth Circuit opinion in *Allenby* noted that warnings under state law are not admissions of defective labeling. But the court did not have to decide whether the warnings could be used as proof of defective labeling or even if such product liability suits were preempted under FIFRA. *Id.* at 947.
157. These theories are reviewed briefly in John M. Johnson, *An Overview of Pesticide Litigation*, paper presented at the Annual Conference, American Agricultural Law Association, Chicago, Illinois, Sept. 1992.
158. Timothy J. Kuester, Note, *FIFRA as an Affirmative Defense: Pre-emption of Common-Law Tort Claims of Inadequate Labeling*, 40 Kan. L. Rev. 1119–20 and n.9 (1992). *See, e.g.*, Worm v. American Cyanamid Co., 970 F.2d 1301, 1307 (4th Cir. 1992) (allowing claims related to product design, manufacture, and testing).
159. Papas v. Upjohn Co., 985 F.2d 516 (11th Cir.), *cert. denied*, 114 S. Ct. 300 (1993) (*Papas II*); Arkansas-Platte & Gulf v. Van Waters & Rodgers, Inc., 981 F.2d 1177 (10th Cir.), *cert. denied*, 114 S. Ct. 60 (1993) (*Arkansas-Platte II*). *Papas I* had originally left open the question whether express preemption arose under FIFRA, 926 F.2d 1019 (11th Cir. 1991). This decision was then vacated by the Supreme Court, 112 S. Ct. 3020 (1992). In *Arkansas-Platte I*, the Tenth Circuit held that only implied preemption existed and did not decide as to express preemption, 959 F.2d 158, 164 (10th Cir. 1992), *vacated*, 113 S. Ct. 314 (1992). The Tenth Circuit adhered to its earlier opinion in *Arkansas-Platte II*, *supra*.

160. 985 F.2d 516 (11th Cir.), *cert. denied*, 114 S. Ct. 300 (1993).
161. *Papas I*, 926 F.2d 1019, 1026 (11th Cir. 1991).
162. 112 S. Ct. 3020 (1992).
163. 112 S. Ct. 2608 (1992). See *infra* text accompanying notes 187–91.
164. *Papas II*, 985 F.2d 516, 518 (11th Cir. 1993).
165. *Papas II*, 985 F.2d at 519 (quoting 7 USC § 136v(b)).
166. *Papas II*, 985 F.2d at 518–20.
167. *Papas II*, 985 F.2d at 519. See also Chemical Specialties Manufacturers Assoc. v. Allenby, 958 F.2d 941 (9th Cir.), *cert. denied*, 113 S. Ct. 80 (1992), which discusses a related issue – whether warnings under state law are admissions of defective labeling in products liability suits.
168. *Arkansas-Platte II*, 981 F.2d 1177 (10th Cir.), *cert. denied*, 114 S. Ct. 60 (1993). The case (and the latest appeal to the Supreme Court) also involved the question of when the plaintiff's cause of action arose, to determine which version of FIFRA applied.
169. *Arkansas-Platte I*, 959 F.2d 158, 162–4 (10th Cir. 1992).
170. 113 S. Ct. 314 (1992).
171. *Arkansas-Platte II*, 981 F.2d at 1179.
172. 970 F.2d 1301 (4th Cir. 1992).
173. *Id*. at 1305. See also Wisconsin Public Intervenor v. Mortier, 111 S. Ct. 2476, 2485–6 (1991).
174. *Worm*, 970 F.2d at 1306.
175. *Id*. at 1307 (quoting Papas v. Upjohn Co., 926 F.2d 1019, 1026 (11th Cir. 1991), *vacated*, 112 S. Ct. 3020 (1992), *affirming earlier opinion*, 985 F.2d 516 (11th Cir.), *cert. denied*, 114 S. Ct. 300 (1993).
176. *Worm*, 970 F.2d at 1307–8.
177. 736 F.2d 1529 (D.C. Cir.), *cert. denied*, 469 US 1062 (1984). For commentary supporting the finding of no preemption, see Joseph T. Carter, Note, *Papas v. Upjohn Co. – The Possibility That FIFRA Might Preempt State Common-Law Tort Claims Should Be Exterminated*, 45 Ark. L. Rev. 729 (1992).
178. *Ferebee*, 736 F.2d at 1542.
179. *Id*. at 1541–3.
180. Cases holding that FIFRA preempts state tort claims based on failure to warn include Burke v. Dow Chemical Co., 797 F. Supp. 1128 (E.D.N.Y. 1992) (preemption of state claims based on failure to warn only in labeling and packaging); Hurt v. Dow Chemical Co., 759 F. Supp. 556 (E.D. Mo. 1990); Herr v. Carolina Log Buildings, Inc, 771 F. Supp. 958 (S.D. Ind. 1989); Fitzgerald v. Mallinckrodt, Inc., 681 F. Supp. 404 (E.D. Mich. 1987). Cases finding no preemption include Couture v. Dow Chemical, 804 F. Supp. 1298 (D. Mont. 1992); Riden v. ICI Americas, Inc., 763 F. Supp. 1500 (W.D. Mo. 1991); Evenson v. Osmose Wood Preserving, Inc., 760 F. Supp. 1345 (S.D. Ind. 1990); Stewart v. Ortho Consumer Products, 1990 Westlaw 36129 (E.D. La. 1990); Cox v. Velsicol Chemical Corp., 704 F. Supp. 85 (E.D. Pa. 1989); Roberts v. Dow Chemical Co., 702 F. Supp. 195 (N.D. Ill. 1988).
181. *Compare* Herr v. Carolina Log Buildings, Inc, 771 F. Supp. 958 (S.D. Ind. 1989) (preemption) *with* Evenson v. Osmose Wood Preserving, Inc., 760 F. Supp. 1345 (S.D. Ind. 1990) (no preemption).
182. *See* Ciba-Geigy Corp. v. Alter, 834 S.W.2d 136 (Ark. 1992) (no preemption) and Davidson v. Velsicol Chemical Corp., 834 P.2d 931 (Nev. 1992), *cert. denied*, 113 S. Ct. 1944 (1993) (implied preemption). See also Little v. Dow Chemical Co., 148 Misc. 2d 11, 559 N.Y.S.2d 788 (1990) (preemption). For a brief discussion of *Alter* and *Davidson*, see J.W. Looney, *FIFRA preemption of common law tort claims*, 10 Agricultural Law Update 1 (Dec. 1992).
183. 834 S.W.2d 136 (Ark. 1992).
184. 834 P.2d 931 (Nev. 1992), *cert. denied*, 113 S. Ct. 1944 (1993).
185. 112 S. Ct. 2608 (1992).
186. 111 S. Ct. 2476 (1991).
187. 112 S. Ct. 2608, 2613–14 (1992).
188. *Id*. at 2619 (§ 5(b) of the Federal Cigarette Labeling and Advertising Act, 15 USC §§ 1331–40, as amended by the Public Health Cigarette Smoking Act of 1969).
189. *Cipollone*, 112 S. Ct. at 2618. See Justice Scalia's characterization of this statement as 'an extraordinary and unprecedented principle of federal statutory construction', but with a 'blessedly brief' life span. *Id*. at 2632 (Scalia, J., concurring in the judgment in part and dissenting in part).

190. *Id.* at 2621–2. The 1965 cigarette advertising law was also at issue. In its preemption language, the 1965 Act stated that 'No statement relating to smoking and health shall be required in the advertising of [properly labeled] cigarettes'. *Id.* at 2618 (§ 5(b) of the 1965 Federal Cigarette Labeling and Advertising Act). The Court held that the rather narrow provision from the 1965 Act 'pre-empted state and federal rulemaking bodies from mandating particular cautionary statements', but did not preempt state law damage actions based on inadequate labeling. 112 S. Ct. at 2619.

191. 112 S. Ct. at 2625. Several separate opinions in this case indicate lack of clear agreement about the preemptive effect of these federal provisions.

192. Papas v. Upjohn Co., 985 F.2d 516 (11th Cir.), *cert. denied*, 114 S. Ct. 300 (1993); Arkansas-Platte & Gulf v. Van Waters & Rodgers, Inc., 981 F.2d 1177 (10th Cir.), *cert. denied*, 114 S. Ct. 60 (1993).

193. 983 F.2d 1130 (1st Cir.), *cert. denied*, 114 S. Ct. 84 (1993). The plaintiff suffered a reaction to a test dose of Zyderm, a cosmetic medical device (processed cow tissue) injected under the skin.

194. 21 USC § 360k (1988).

195. *King*, 983 F.2d at 1136.

196. 985 F.2d 736 (4th Cir.), *cert. denied*, 113 S. Ct. 2999 (1993). Moss was burned when paint thinner fumes were ignited by the pilot light on a kerosene heater and burst into flames.

197. *Id.* at 740, 741. The preemption provision of the Federal Hazardous Substances Labeling Act in controversy is found at 15 USC § 1261 note (b)(1)(A) (1988): 'No state . . . may establish or continue in effect a cautionary label requirement applicable to such substance or packaging unless such cautionary labeling requirement is identical to the labeling requirement [of this law]'.

198. 111 S. Ct. 2476 (1991).

199. *Mortier*, 111 S. Ct. at 2482.

200. *Id.* at 2486.

201. *See* Worm v. American Cyanamid Co., 970 F.2d 1301, 1306 (4th Cir. 1992).

202. *Mortier*, 111 S. Ct. at 2486–7. For a brief discussion of congressional efforts to overrule *Mortier*, see James Ford Lang, *Federal Preemption of Local Pesticide Use Regulation: The Past, Present and Future of Wisconsin Public Intervenor v. Mortier*, 11 Va. Envtl L.J. 241, 280 (1991–92).

203. Worm v. American Cyanamid Co., 970 F.2d 1301, 1306 (4th Cir. 1992).

204. *E.g.*, Kuester, *supra* note 158, at 1138 ('[T]he Court found that field pre-emption could not be inferred from section 136v(a) because field pre-emption is explicitly stated in section 136v(b).').

205. Corboy and Smith, *supra* note 147, at 472.

206. James L. Moore and J. Greg Dow, *Federal Preemption under FIFRA*, 34 For The Defense 22, 25 (1992).

207. *Mortier*, 111 S. Ct. 2476, 2482 (1991). The Court noted that language in the legislative history of the Act was insufficient to demonstrate congressional intent for preemption. *Id.* at 2483. For a discussion of the role of legislative history in the *Mortier* decision see Timothy A. Quarburg, Note, *Getting the Bugs Out: The Role of Legislative History in Determining the Pre-emptive Effect of FIFRA Upon Local Regulation of Pesticides in Wisconsin Public Intervenor v. Mortier, 111 S. Ct. 2476 (1991)*, 15 Hamline L. Rev. 223 (1992).

208. *Mortier*, 111 S. Ct. at 2483. On remand from the Supreme Court, the Wisconsin Supreme Court could decide whether state law preempted local regulation. Martha L. Noble, *Local Regulation of Pesticide Use*, 13 J. Agric. Tax'n & L. 365, 368 (1992).

209. *Mortier*, 111 S. Ct. at 2483.

210. Pamela Corrie, Note, *An Assessment of the Role of Local Government in Environmental Regulation*, 5 J. Envtl. L. 145, 149 (1986). Another factor is how the courts of the state view preemption. *Id.* at 152. Corrie's note focuses on California law.

211. *Id.* at 150–51. For examples of decisions in cases where the state legislature did not express its intent on the pesticide preemption issue *see* Pesticide Public Policy Foundation v. Village of Wauconda, 510 N.E.2d 858 (Ill. 1987) (preemption of non-home rule unit); People ex. rel Deukmejian v. County of Mendocino, 683 P.2d 1150 (Calif. 1984) (no preemption of county ordinance), overruled by statute; Central Maine Power Co. v. Town of Lebanon, 571 A.2d 1189 (Me. 1990) (no preemption).

212. Corrie, *supra* note 210, at 151.

213. Noble, *Local Regulation, supra* note 208, at 368.

214. People ex rel Deukmejian v. County of Mendocino, 683 P.2d 1150 (Cal. 1984), discussed in Corrie, *supra* note 210, at 176–81.
215. Cal. Food and Agric. Code § 11501.1 (Deering 1994).
216. Corrie, *supra* note 210, at 149–50. The view of local government as a creature of state legislation is called 'Dillon's Rule'. See *id.* at 149.
217. Corrie, *supra* note 210, at 153. See also Central Maine Power Co. v. Town of Lebanon, 571 A.2d 1189 (Me. 1990) (holding that Maine pesticide law did not preempt local setback regulations).
218. *E.g.*, in Illinois. See Corrie, *supra* note 210, at 164.
219. See Lang, *supra* note 202, at 245–7.

12. Environmental Federalism and the Control of Water Pollution from US Agriculture: Is the Current Division of Responsibilities Between National and Local Authorities About Right?

James S. Shortle[*]

Reducing surface- and groundwater pollution from agriculture is a major environmental policy issue in many developed countries (OECD, 1990). In the US, the issue has moved to the forefront of water pollution control policy development now that the Clinton administration and key Congressional committees have made nonpoint pollution control a top priority in the reauthorization of the Clean Water Act.

US water pollution control efforts of the 1970s and 1980s were primarily targeted on industrial and municipal point sources of surface-water pollution. Stringent federal regulatory programs were imposed on these sources while agriculture and other nonpoint sources of water pollution remained largely uncontrolled.[1] There is now substantial agreement among environmental groups, policy analysts and environmental agencies that more must be done to reduce water pollution from nonpoint sources than has been done in the past. Agriculture draws the lion's share of attention in policy debates as a consequence of its status as the leading nonpoint source. Adding to this attention is the high level of societal concern for the impacts of nitrates and pesticides on the safety of drinking water supplies.

The key question in water pollution control policy for agriculture is how to bring about the changes in agricultural production needed to achieve water quality goals. There are two central issues in the analysis of this question. One is the choice of policy instruments for getting farmers to adopt production practices that reduce pollution. Although there are exceptions, the principal

---

[*] I want to thank John Becker, David Abler, Donald Epp, Peter Kuch, Clayton Ogg, Marc Ribaudo and symposium participants for comments and suggestions.

approach to reducing water pollution from agriculture has been moral suasion supplemented to varying degrees by technical and financial assistance. The limited results from this voluntary approach have created a substantial interest in alternative approaches. Among the options that have been proposed are regulation of the use of farm inputs and farming practices, taxes on fertilizers and pesticides and liability for damages (Malik, Larson and Ribaudo, (1992)). The second issue is the proper roles of national and local authorities in the control of pollution from agriculture. Under current law primary responsibility for pollution control in agriculture is held by the states, with the Federal government providing guidelines and technical and financial support for the development of programs. However, frustration over the pace and voluntary structure of state efforts has led to calls for a stronger federal role.

In this chapter I examine the economic merits of the existing division of responsibility for pollution control in agriculture between state and federal authorities. The economic merits of alternative instruments for reducing water pollution from agriculture have been the subject of much attention in recent years. Theoretical issues in the design of pollution controls for agriculture and other nonpoint sources have been addressed by Braden and Segerson (1993), Cabe and Herriges (1992), Griffin and Bromley (1982), Kim et al. (1993), Segerson (1988), Shortle and Dunn (1986), Xepapadeas (1991), and others. A number of less formal but more wide-ranging evaluations have also appeared (e.g., Malik, Larson and Ribaudo, (1992); Abler and Shortle, (1991); Shortle and Dunn (1991)). Empirical work evaluating the cost-effectiveness of alternative instruments and estimating their economic impacts appears regularly in journals on agricultural and environmental economics and in several recent books (eg. Braden and Lovejoy (eds) (1991); Dosi and Graham-Tomasi (eds); Just and Bockstael (eds) (1989); Russell and Shogren (eds) (1993)). On the other hand, the question of the proper roles of different levels of government in the control of agricultural pollution has received little attention in the economic literature.[2] Analysis of this question is especially of interest now because it is at the core of nonpoint pollution policy developments.

I begin with a brief overview of federal and state programs for reducing water pollution from agricultural sources. The purpose is not to catalog existing programs but to identify the major elements and division of responsibilities. The economic logic of the existing division of responsibilities is then examined.

THE STRUCTURE OF WATER POLLUTION CONTROL PROGRAMS FOR AGRICULTURE

Although not a major area of regulatory activity, pollution control in agriculture has not been neglected. Since the late 1970s there have been a number of significant developments in federal and state policy that directly or indirectly address surface- and groundwater pollution from agriculture.[3] In a nutshell, the overall result of these developments is a structure in which the states have primary responsibility for reducing ground- and surface-water pollution from agriculture and considerable flexibility in the choice of ends and means for addressing water quality problems associated with agriculture. The Federal government provides various forms of direct and indirect assistance and sets minimum water quality standards. In addition, there are a number of federal programs that are intended in varying degrees to reduce water pollution from agriculture independently of the states' programs.

A.   Federal Surface-Water Pollution Legislation and Programs

The foundation of surface-water pollution control policy in the US is the Water Pollution Control Act Amendments of 1972. This legislation and subsequent amendments (the Clean Water Act of 1977 and Water Quality Act of 1987) established the basic goals and means of federal policy for rivers and lakes. The legislation assigns the states' responsibility for setting in-stream water quality standards. The standards are subject to periodic review and approval by the US Environmental Protection Agency (EPA), and must provide at a minimum for attaining the key operational goal of 'fishable and swimmable' waters (Freeman (1990)). Industrial and municipal point sources are the focus of the regulatory mechanisms introduced to control water pollution. Specifically, dischargers into rivers and lakes are required to have discharge permits that impose effluent limits. The limits are generally technology based but can be set as needed to achieve water quality goals. The permits are issued and enforced under the National Pollution Discharge Elimination System (NPDES) by the EPA or by states that have received EPA approval. While municipal and industrial sources are the main targets of the NPDES program, some large livestock operations are also required to have permits.

The approach established for the control of agriculture and other nonpoint sources is quite different from the approach taken to point sources. Section 208 of the Water Pollution Control Act Amendments of 1972 required the states to develop and implement area-wide waste treatment plans to control all sources of pollution. As part of the process, the states were directed to identify nonpoint sources of pollution and procedures and methods (Best Management Practices (BMPs)) for their control. Provisions were made for EPA review of the state plans and federal sharing of the planning costs. Nonpoint pollution received greater attention in subsequent legislation but the emphasis on action at the state level with federal oversight and support has not been altered.

Current federal policy towards nonpoint sources is embodied in Section 319 of the Water Quality Act of 1987. This section requires the states to engage in a three-stage process of assessing nonpoint problems, developing nonpoint management plans, and implementing the plans as needed to achieve or maintain in-stream water quality standards on navigable waters that cannot reasonably attain or maintain the standards without nonpoint pollution control.[4] The assessments and management plans are subject to EPA review. Federal grants are authorized to support the process.

Although there are essentially no penalties for states that fail to comply with the provisions of Section 319, all states now have approved assessments and programs and are presumably in the implementation stage (CAST, 1993). Support levels have been modest. Congress appropriated $40 million for FY 1990 and $50 million for 1991. Funds were authorized for 1988 and 1989 but were not appropriated (GAO, 1990). Agricultural programs are a significant part of the management plans developed by most states (EPA, 1992). The programs generally emphasize the three-prong voluntary approach consisting of education, technical assistance, and cost-sharing of BMPs that has dominated public policy towards resource problems in agriculture.

B.   Federal Groundwater Quality Legislation and Programs

The Water Pollution Control Act of 1972 and its descendants pertain only to surface waters. There is no comparable legislation for groundwater. However, there are federally mandated water quality programs that can lead in principle to regulation of agriculture for the purposes of groundwater quality protection. Of particular importance is the Well Head Protection Program established by the 1986 amendments to the Safe Drinking Water Act. The amendments require the states to prepare a wellhead protection program to protect public water wells from contamination from all potential sources. While this program does not call directly for regulation of agriculture, such regulation is an option when developing protection programs. States were required to have approved programs by June 1989. Only 26 have satisfied this mandate (GAO, 1993). As with Section 319, the amendments provided EPA with no power to develop programs for non-participating states or to impose sanctions on them. Unlike Section 319, funds authorized to support the programs have not been appropriated.

The Safe Drinking Water Act may lead to surface- and groundwater pollution control in agriculture in other indirect ways. It requires the EPA to set standards for contaminants in drinking water and requirements for monitoring water supplies and treating contaminated supplies. The states generally have the primary responsibility for enforcement. Moreover, the states can impose more stringent standards than those set by the EPA. Standards have been set for nitrates and a number of pesticides. While this program does not call for direct regulation of agriculture or any other pollution source, it may contribute to pressure for pollution prevention so as to avoid costly treatment.

C. Coastal Zone Management

One of the more significant recent developments in nonpoint pollution policy is the Coastal Zone Act Reauthorization Amendments of 1990. Section 6217 requires participating coastal states to develop Coastal Nonpoint Pollution Control Programs subject to the approval of EPA and the National Oceanic and Atmospheric Administration (NOAA). One important feature of the amendments is that the state programs must be developed and implemented in conformity with national guidelines issued by EPA and NOAA specifying 'management measures' to restore and protect coastal waters. A second feature is that states without approved programs by 1995 will have federal support for their nonpoint source and coastal zone management programs reduced. Hence, unlike the Well Head Protection Program and Section 319 programs, EPA has a stick to encourage compliance of the affected states, albeit small given current funding levels. The plans are to be implemented within three years of approval. Management measures are essentially defined as 'economically achievable' technologies for reducing nonpoint pollution. The US Department of Agriculture (USDA) played a major role in the development of the guidance measures issued for agriculture.

D. Water Quality-Related Federal Legislation and Programs

Some of the most important federal programs that help to reduce water pollution from agriculture are not products of water quality legislation. EPA pesticide regulations and USDA conservation programs fall in this category. The most important EPA activity for agriculture is pesticide regulation under the Federal Insecticide, Fungicide, and Rodenticide Act and the Federal Food, Drug, and Cosmetic Act.[5] The Federal Insecticide, Fungicide and Rodenticide Act requires EPA registration of all pesticides sold for use in the US. The criterion for registration is whether the benefits of use exceed the risks to human health and safety and the environment.[6] The conditions of registration allow the EPA to impose a variety of restrictions on the use of registered chemicals to safeguard the environment, farm workers and consumers. These restrictions include the geographic areas in which a pesticide is used, limits on application rates and treatments per season, formulations, a variety of worker protection measures, and the crops subsequently grown in treated fields. However, EPA is unable to exercise this flexibility in a way that permits it to induce location-specific marginal changes in pesticide use to protect water quality or wildlife (Lichtenberg (1992)). It is at best only a crude instrument for environmental protection. States can impose more stringent regulations on pesticides than those imposed by EPA, including banning an EPA-registered pesticide. A number have done so.

Although not a traditional USDA responsibility, protecting water quality from farming practices has recently become an important part of the agency's mission. A number of long-term USDA technical assistance and cost-sharing programs have been drafted into the effort[7] but the more important developments involve new programs. The 1985 Food Security Act and the 1990 Food, Agriculture, Conservation, and Trade Act initiated several programs that can contribute to reducing pollution from agriculture. The most important of these programs is the Conservation Reserve Program.[8] Under the Conservation Reserve Program farmers enter (voluntarily) into contracts to remove highly erodible and other environmentally sensitive land from production for ten years in exchange for an annual rent plus half the cost of establishing a permanent land cover. The program is primarily a farm income support and supply control measure with soil conservation and water quality benefits. The water quality benefits occur with the reduction in soil erosion and reduced application of chemicals to the land for crop production. Ribaudo estimated the water quality benefits from reduced soil erosion on the 23 million acre enrolment obtained in initial five sign-ups of the Conservation Reserve Program to be between $1.2 and $3 billion with a most likely estimate of $2.05 billion. The benefits of the full 45 million acre enrolment called for by the 1985 version of the Conservation Reserve Program is estimated to be in the range of $2 billion and $5.5 billion with a best estimate of $3.7 billion. As of June 1992, enrolment had increased to 36.5 million acres (USDA, 1993). With targeting to areas with water quality problems, the benefits could be much larger (Miranowski et al.(1989)). In addition to big benefits, the Conservation Reserve Program is a big ticket item. The cumulative annual rental payments between 1987 and 1992 equal nearly $7 billion. The projected total cost of the Conservation Reserve Program is several times this number (GAO, 1992).

EPA and the US Geological Survey (USGS) conduct environmental quality monitoring and assessment programs and research programs to support water pollution protection from agricultural and other sources. USDA also supports research activities that contribute to the management of nonpoint pollution. Prominent among these USDA activities is the Water Quality Initiative. This small-scale five-year program provides education, technical assistance and cost-sharing to farmers in selected project areas around the country. It also funds research and development of pollution control techniques. The program is viewed by some as a test of the effectiveness of the voluntary compliance strategy to reduce pollution in agriculture (Phipps (1991)).[9]

E.   State, Local, and Regional Water Quality Programs

Programs to reduce water pollution from agriculture can be found at several levels below the federal level.   For example, at the lowest level, local governments have used land-use controls to protect groundwater recharge areas in a number of areas (Sobel and Abdalla (1992)).   Arizona, Florida, Nebraska and other states are either using or considering the use of special intrastate water management districts to manage ground- and/or surface-water quality (Apogee Research Inc. (1991); Ribaudo and Woo (1991); Viessman (1988)). There are also a few examples of interstate institutions for water quality management.

Identifying the content of state and local programs to control pollution from agriculture is complicated by the number of states and the variety of legal mechanisms that can be used to implement policy (Ribaudo and Woo (1991)). More difficult than inventorying state programs is determining the difference between what is supposed to happen in principle and what does happen in practice. At this time no studies provide a complete catalog and systematic evaluation of state and local programs. However, a number of recent studies indicate that the state and local governments are acting to control pollution from agriculture and other nonpoint sources (Beccaris (1992); Batie and Diebel (1989); CAST, 1993; Ribaudo and Woo (1991); EPA, 1992; Wise and Johnson (1991)). Of course, states are required to develop and implement plans under Section 319 and other legislation. However, a number of states have initiated efforts that go beyond federal mandates, most notably to protect groundwater quality (CAST, 1993); Phipps (1991)).

During the 1980s the states took the lead in enacting measures to protect groundwater (Batie and Diebel (1989)). Most states now have groundwater protection legislation or are in the process of developing it (Bouwer (1990); Miller and Miller (1992)). Measures taken by states include a variety of types of restrictions on the use of agrichemicals, taxes on agrichemical use, registration fees, applicator and dealer fees, required use of BMPs designed to diminish groundwater contamination, land-use restrictions and liability for damages (Batie and Diebel (1989); Ribaudo and Woo (1991); Wise and Johnson (1991)). One of the best-known groundwater protection laws is California's 'Proposition 65'. Among other things, it requires the Governor of California to publish annually a list of chemicals known to cause cancer or have reproductive toxicity and bans knowingly discharging chemicals on the list into water or on land where it may pass into drinking water. Chemical users bear the burden of proof of safety. Proposition 65 supplemented California's Pesticide Contamination Prevention Act, which was enacted in 1983 explicitly to protect groundwater from pesticides. It provides for listing of pesticides that are suspected leachers and for area-specific restrictions on the use of pesticides that are found in groundwater.

There are a variety of institutional mechanisms that can be used to coordinate water quality management across states (Apogee Research Inc. (1991)). One is independent interstate watershed authorities with powers to manage water quality. Although there are a few examples of intrastate water quality management districts, such as Florida's Water Management Districts, no such entities currently exist for water quality management across state boundaries in the US.[10] Alternatives are interstate compacts or cooperative agreements. Compacts can impose binding measures on the signatories while cooperative agreements are non-binding. Compacts and cooperative agreements that provide for water quality management are not commonplace but there are several important examples. The Delaware River Basin Commission, the Susquehanna River Basin Commission and the Ohio River Sanitation Commission are examples of institutions with water quality management missions that were created by interstate compacts. The Delaware River Basin Commission and the Susquehanna River Basin Commission are the only institutions created by interstate compacts that have powers to control water pollution.   A leading example of a cooperative agreement for water quality management is the Chesapeake Bay Agreement between Maryland, Pennsylvania, Virginia, the District of Columbia, the Chesapeake Bay Commission and the US Environmental Protection Agency.   A major dimension of the state pollution-control activities under the agreement is the control of pollution from agriculture and other nonpoint sources.

F.   New Directions?

A critic need not look long nor hard to find fault with dimensions of existing policies affecting water pollution from agriculture. Two areas in particular command current reform interest. One is the glaring inconsistencies between federal policies for farm commodities, agricultural resource conservation and environmental protection (Reichelderfer (1990)).[11] The second and more immediate area of reform interest is federal nonpoint pollution policy. The vigor with which the states have pursued groundwater protection has defused federal efforts to develop comprehensive groundwater protection legislation. However, there is considerable dissatisfaction with the progress that has been made in managing nonpoint pollution under the provisions of Section 319 and Section 208 before that. Limited funding of nonpoint pollution control programs at the state and federal levels, the reliance of the states on voluntary rather than enforceable instruments, unwillingness of states to identify priority watersheds and the inability of the Federal government to penalize or reward states according to the performance of their nonpoint programs are among the reasons blamed for the modest results (GAO, 1990). A number of proposals for federal policy reform have been offered in recent years.[12] Most proposals call for increased federal funding of nonpoint pollution control efforts. At the modest end of the proposal spectrum are those that call for little more than an increase in federal and state spending on the problem. Proposals from commercial agricultural interests tend to be in this category. There is also considerable interest in reforms that would provide EPA with greater clout over the states and induce the states to make greater use of enforceable instruments. In other words, programs that have 'teeth'. For example, one option is to extend the NPDES requirements to irrigation return flows and small feedlots.[13] Another option is the model provided by the Control Zone Act Reauthorization Amendments. More teeth in this case means providing EPA with greater leverage over the states by linking federal funding to the effectiveness of state programs and mandating minimum enforceable BMPs. While there is little support at this stage for a radical shift in authority for nonpoint pollution control from the states to the Federal government, it is clear that there is much interest in a realignment that constrains state policy choices.

ECONOMIC ISSUES IN THE DIVISION OF RESPONSIBILITIES

The division of responsibilities between state and federal authorities for nonpoint surface-water pollution control and to groundwater protection differs greatly from the division for industrial and municipal point sources. The obvious question to ask, especially given current policy debates, is which approach is better? Should responsibility for nonpoint and groundwater policies be more like point source policies or vice versa? Or is the approach for each about right? Two reasons are generally cited for primacy of the states in the control of nonpoint source pollution (CAST, 1993; EPA, 1988; Greenfield (1985); Malik, Larson and Ribaudo (1992); GAO, 1990). One is that application of uniform technological controls to classes of dischargers of the type applied to point sources is inappropriate for the management of nonpoint pollution given the highly site-specific character of nonpoint pollution problems and remedies. The second reason is that control of nonpoint pollution requires regulation of land use, which is traditionally a prerogative of state and especially local governments. The arguments given for state primacy in groundwater protection are much the same (CAST, 1993).

These reasons help to explain the current approaches taken to nonpoint pollution control and groundwater protection but they do provide a satisfactory justification for the differing approaches to the problems. For example, implicit in the first reason is the presumption that uniform technology-based standards are good policy for point sources and would be good policy for nonpoint sources if the problems were less site specific. Yet, many economists argue that the technology-based approach is poor policy for point sources because it is insensitive to local conditions and greatly increases the costs of pollution control (e.g. Freeman (1990)). This conclusion is only more transparent in the case of nonpoint sources.

In the following paragraphs, I make a case for the current division of responsibilities for water pollution control in agriculture based on fundamental principles from the economic theory of environmental protection and the economic theory of fiscal federalism. The analysis is not intended to defend the specific policies that have been implemented by the states or the Federal government.

A.   The Basic Case for State Primacy

The key benchmark for economic evaluation of pollution-control programs is the difference between the benefits and costs of pollution control. The greater this difference the greater the economic efficiency of the program. To maximize economic efficiency, environmental protection levels in any given location should be increased as long as those who benefit are willing to pay more at the margin than the cost of the improvement. To minimize the costs of control, sources with relatively low incremental control costs should provide relatively more control than sources with relatively high incremental costs. These principles imply that environmental protection levels and the allocation of pollution control between sources should vary between watersheds according to variations in the benefits and costs of water quality protection.

A basic principle of the economic theory of federalism is that economic efficiency in the provision of public goods is generally best served by delegating responsibility for the provision of the good to the lowest level of government that encompasses all of the associated costs and benefits. In the case at hand, the public good is environmental quality. The assumption underlying this principle is that policy choices consistent with the collective preferences of the affected group are more likely when made by decision-makers who represent their interests alone. Federal regulatory policies tend not to be sensitive to local conditions. For example, the Clean Air Act and Safe Drinking Water Act call for EPA to set uniform maximum allowable levels of pollutants. The Federal Water Pollution Control Act sets uniform minimum surface-water quality standards and technology-based maximum effluent standards for industrial and municipal point sources. In contrast, it is generally in the political interests of local authorities to develop policies that are sensitive to local preferences.

Current point source controls constrain the freedom of the state and local authorities to devise policies (in both goals and means) that correspond to local costs and benefits. Economic criticism of the US water pollution policy is centered on the costs imposed by the violation of the principles of optimal pollution control noted above. The technology-based approach leaves little latitude to allocate pollution abatement among alternative sources within the point source category or between the point and nonpoint categories to minimize costs.[14] Both the technology-based standards and the national water quality goals can lead to pollution control levels in which the incremental costs exceed the incremental benefits at particular sites.

The flexibility available to the states under the current policy structure offers the opportunity to avoid the costly inefficiencies of existing point source regulations in the control of groundwater contamination and nonpoint pollution (Freeman (1990)). This flexibility also facilitates policy innovation in an area where the best course is by no means clear. The search for policies that are effective, politically acceptable and economically reasonable has really only just begun and will likely take many years. The current structure of point source regulations is over twenty years but remains controversial. By this standard, debate over nonpoint pollution and groundwater policy should continue well into the next century. The evolution should benefit from information about what works and what doesn't as state and local governments experiment with alternative approaches to the problem. Federal reforms that greatly diminish this flexibility, such as extensive federal guidance specifying BMPs, would be a move in the wrong direction.

B.   Limits of Decentralization

While much can be said in favor of decentralization, there are a number of dimensions of water pollution control that call for federal involvement. For instance, there are problems for which uniformity of outcomes and centralized decision-making are efficient. Federal pesticide regulation is an example. EPA's registration/cancellation tool under the Federal Insecticide, Fungicide, and Rodenticide Act is a crude instrument for addressing the range of societal issues associated with the use of pesticides. State flexibility to tailor pesticide policies to address state environmental problems is desirable for the reasons noted above. However, nation-wide cancellation is an optimal decision when the expected marginal damage to human health and the environment from the use of pesticide is so large that it always exceeds the marginal benefit. EPA pesticide decisions to date appear to fit this characterization fairly well

(Lichtenberg (1992); Cropper et al. (1992)). Centralized responsibility for decisions of this type reduce decision costs and thereby improve the cost-effectiveness of environmental protection.

A number of additional arguments for federal involvement can be advanced. Unlike EPA pesticide regulation, these arguments call more for federal support of nonpoint pollution control efforts and minimum standards than for direct federal regulation.

C. Environmental Spillovers

In cases where pollutants spill over from one jurisdiction to another, optimal policies for upstream jurisdictions should take into account the benefits that are received in downstream jurisdictions. This accounting is unlikely with decentralized approaches for the simple reason that the political fortunes of upstream decision-makers depend on the preferences of upstream but not downstream voters.

Current data on nonpoint pollution problems are inadequate to assess the dimensions of spillover problems. In many cases it is clear that pollution associated with agriculture is exclusively local. Examples are the eutrophication of Lake Okeechobee in Florida, wildlife damages caused by ingestion of selenium in the Kesterson Wildlife Refuge and elsewhere in the San Joaquin Valley of California, and pesticide contamination of groundwater on Long Island. However, spillovers of agricultural pollutants are known to occur and in some cases contribute significantly to downstream problems. A leading example is the Chesapeake Bay, where point and nonpoint sources, including agriculture, in Maryland, Pennsylvania, New York and Virginia have contributed to the significant degradation of the Bay. A number of states contribute to sediments and pesticides flowing down the Mississippi and salts in the lower Colorado. Moreover, even when the physical impacts of pollution occur entirely within a given political boundary, costs may still spill over into other jurisdictions. There is ample evidence in the economic literature that people are concerned about resources that they do not use themselves (Fisher and Raucher (1984)). These non-use values are especially important in the case of unique natural resources. It would not be surprising at all to find that residents of states other than Florida would be willing to pay to protect Lake Okeechobee even if they make no use of it themselves. There is also ample evidence that people care about the quality of others' environment. Indeed, some evidence suggests that the high level of concern for water quality that is found in public opinion surveys is often a concern for the quality of water where others live and work rather than for one's own water (Bord et al. (1993)).

The mix of problems suggests a mix of approaches. In cases where there are no significant environmental spillovers, the case for the decentralized approach remains. In cases where spillovers are significant, a cooperative interstate approach to watershed management is needed. The history of interstate cooperation on water pollution and other problems suggests that federal initiatives are generally needed to bring about cooperative solutions. Use of federal spending to reward states for cooperative efforts and penalize them for non-cooperative behavior is a traditional method of addressing spillovers and would have a role in this case. However, it is also important to develop specialized institutions to coordinate water quality management in watersheds where spillovers are significant. Innovation in this area is needed. Section 319 provides for interstate conferences to address nonpoint problems involving two or more states. The conferences are to be called by the EPA Administrator on request from states that find that their nonpoint problems are caused by sources in other states. To date no such conferences have been called. Formation of compacts and cooperative agreements is encouraged Section 103 of the Clean Water Act. However, with a few exceptions such as the Chesapeake Bay agreement, little has happened along these lines. In so far as environmental spillovers are significant, it would seem that greater federal incentives to form interstate water quality management institutions and exploration of the optimal organization of such institutions are essential.

D.   Fiscal Spillovers and Deadweight Losses

Policies that reduce water pollution from agriculture can provide external benefits beyond those associated with downstream water quality improvements. Specifically, policies that reduce the production of federally subsidized commodities and the use of federally subsidized inputs would reduce deadweight losses associated with the agricultural output and input markets and possibly those associated with tax distortions of labor and capital markets (e.g., Alston and Hurd (1990); Lichtenberg and Zilberman (1986); Weinberg and Kling (1993)). However, while society gains, the benefits will be largely external to the state. As with the downstream benefits from water quality improvements, state decision-makers have little or no incentive to consider these benefits in state policy-making. As in the case of environmental spillovers, these spillovers provide a case for federal grants to states in return for tighter controls on agriculture.

The magnitude of the societal gains from a state's actions will depend on the actions that the state takes, the actions that other states take and federal responses (Shortle and Laughland (1994)). The issues are complex and little research has been done.

E.   Information, Research, and Development

Economically efficient pollution policies require information about the demand for water quality, the linkages between water quality and economic activity, and the costs of changes in economic activity to reduce pollution. Virtually every discussion of nonpoint pollution policy will include some statements about the extreme information intensity of the problem.[15]

The information intensity of nonpoint pollution control is generally an argument in favor of watershed-based approaches and therefore decentralized planning. Watershed specific information may have some value for research and other purposes but the primary value will be for local planning and administration. The costs of obtaining the information should therefore be allocated largely to the specific watershed. If the net benefits of watershed specific plans developed using watershed specific information are no more than the net benefits of centralized plans developed without the benefits of watershed specific information, then the case for decentralized planning, including cooperative plans for problems involving spillovers, is weakened. This would be the case only in the unlikely event that the value of watershed specific information is zero.

In addition to supporting the case for decentralized management plans, information needs also provide support for federal research and development. Some types of information that are needed in nonpoint pollution control planning are non-rival. Examples are the impacts of nitrate or pesticide ingestion on human health, hydrological principles governing the fate and transport of pollutants, and the basic economics of evaluating alternative techniques and the merits of alternative policy approaches. Information of this type is optimally provided at the national level. The numerous EPA, USDA and USGS research and technical assistance programs designed to provide information of this type can be justified on this basis.

F.   Interjurisdictional Competition and Related Issues

Underlying the principle that responsibility for externalities ought to be allocated to the lowest level of government that encompasses the associated costs and benefits is the assumption that public decision-makers act in the public interest and weight costs and benefits to those involved more or less equally. This view corresponds to the traditional 'rational planning' or 'problem-solving' approach to public policy in economics. In this tradition, government serves the public interest and intervenes to correct problems associated with imperfect or missing markets. However, modern theories of public policy and regulation recognize that what governments do in fact is the outcome of the interplay between influential interest groups.[16]

One argument that has been made against decentralized environmental protection generally is that polluters' interests are given excessive weight in local environmental decision-making, but not so much so in federal regulation (e.g. Cumberland (1981)). Although this may be the case in some instances, it is by no means clear that environmental decision-making at the local level is systematically biased towards under-protection nor that federal regulation is systematically closer to optimal than local regulation (Cropper and Oates (1992); Baumol and Oates (1988); Oates and Schwab (1988); Schwab (1988)). Anecdotal evidence from agriculture is not necessarily supportive of the contention that federal intervention is necessary to prevent systematic underprotection of the environment by state and local governments. For example, while the Federal government asserted primacy in surface-water quality policy since the early 1970s, it has done little to regulate nonpoint sources of pollution. On the other hand, states have moved to protect groundwater. Some of the more stringent measures are found in leading agricultural states (e.g. California and Iowa). Pennsylvania's recent Nutrient Management Act is receiving nationwide attention as a bold state effort to combat water pollution from agriculture. Yet, some political observers see the legislation as means by which to prevent stringent regulation of agricultural externalities at the local level. A number of local governments in the state used or were considering the use of land-use controls to address environmental externalities created by agriculture in their jurisdictions. The Nutrient Management Act explicitly preempts these actions.

On balance, recent state initiatives to protect groundwater and political trends would seem to be favorable to the case for state primacy. Agriculture is politically powerful and its clout at the federal and state levels is surely part of the explanation of the delicate treatment of farmers relative to industrial point sources. However, the political power of agriculture is in decline at the same time that the power of environmental interest groups is growing. Inasmuch as some state and local governments do overprotect polluters' interests, federal grants tied to environmental improvements and minimum environmental quality standards can offer safeguards against gross undersupply. Further safeguards can be provided by back-up federal enforcement authority when states fail to act and/or provision for citizen action to force state compliance.

SUMMARY AND CONCLUSIONS

Economic analysis suggests that policies for reducing water pollution from agriculture that are sensitive to local costs and benefits are more likely when policy choices are made at the state and local level. However, a purely decentralized approach is not optimal given pollution spillovers between jurisdictions, fiscal spillovers and the possibility of political failures in which the interests of polluters or environmentalists are overrepresented in pollution policy design. Accordingly, solving water quality problems associated with agriculture should not be the exclusive responsibility of the Federal government or state governments alone. There are important roles for each.

The current structure of nonpoint pollution and groundwater policy seems to have a reasonable balance, with the states having primary responsibility and the Federal government playing a supporting role and providing safeguards in the form of minimum standards. The major weakness in the existing structure is underutilization of formal institutions to coordinate watershed management in the case of spillovers. However, while the outlines of responsibility are more or less appropriate with the one exception just noted, the details need a lot of attention. The voluntary approach to getting farmers to adopt environmentally friendly practices that has dominated state efforts is clearly limited. Coordination between the various federal, state and local programs is needed. Indeed, the number of incentives and regulations that farmers face between USDA, EPA and state agency commodity, environment and conservation programs is quite large and probably well in excess of what is needed to send clear messages about what society deems to be acceptable performance. Integration of ground- and surface-water protection and point and nonpoint programs is also essential for a coherent, cost-effective approach to water quality protection.

NOTES

1.   The relative ease with which point sources of pollution can be identified and controlled made them the logical target of first-generation surface-water pollution control programs. Groundwater quality protection received little attention. Whereas serious degradation of surface-waters was immediately apparent, invisible groundwater resources were long assumed to be unaffected by pollution.

2.   Indeed, questions about proper roles of different levels of government in pollution control have not received much attention generally in the economic literature (Cropper and Oates (1992)).

3.   It is worth noting that there have been a number of market developments during the 1980s that have helped reduce pollution from agriculture. Phipps (1991) provides an excellent overview of how markets have responded to address societal concerns about pesticide contamination of foods, conversion of wetlands and to some extent contamination of groundwater.

4.   The assessments are to (1) identify navigable waters that cannot reasonably attain or maintain water quality standards without nonpoint pollution control, (2) identify nonpoint sources that add significant amounts of pollution to those waters, (3) describe processes for identifying Best Management Practices (BMPs) that address the problems and (4) identify programs for controlling nonpoint problems. Some key features of the requirements for management programs are that they (1) identify BMPs that will be taken to reduce nonpoint pollution, (2)

identify programs to achieve BMP implementation, and (3) provide milestones for program implementation including BMP implementation.
5. Under the authority provided by the Federal Food, Drug, and Cosmetics Act, EPA sets maximum concentrations ('tolerances') of pesticide residues in food. The tolerances are enforced by the Food and Drug Administration through its food inspection program. The tolerances can effectively impose restrictions on the timing and rate of application of pesticides that do not degrade completely by the time the crop reaches the market (Foster and Babcock (1991); Lichtenberg (1992)).
6. See Cropper et al. (1992) for an interesting evaluation of the use of benefits and costs in EPA's registration decisions.
7. These include several cost-sharing programs for conservation and environmental protection practices, technical assistance and education programs.
8. In addition to the Conservation Reserve Program, the 1985 Food Security Act established Conservation Compliance, Sodbuster, and Swampbuster programs. The Conservation Compliance Program makes eligibility for participation in farm income support programs contingent upon development and implementation of approved conservation plans for farmers with highly erodible lands. The Sodbuster Program denies income support benefits to farmers who convert highly erodible land to crop production without an approved conservation plan. The Swampbuster Program denies income support benefits to farmers who convert wetlands to agricultural production unless USDA determines that the conversion would have a minimal impact on the resource. The 1990 Food, Agriculture, Conservation, and Trade Act expanded the Conservation Reserve Program and several new programs to USDA's responsibilities. Among the latter is the Water Quality Incentives, which subsidizes farmers for adopting UDSA approved water quality protection plans.
9. The Water Quality Initiative resembles the earlier Rural Clean Water created by the 1977 Clean Water Act in that it combines education, technical assistance, and cost-sharing of BMPs with research on the effectiveness of technologies and policies for agricultural nonpoint pollution control.
10. The Tennessee River Valley Authority is an independent authority with broad powers of water management but the purpose is to promote regional economic development, not water quality management.
11. USDA commodity policies are generally considered to encourage production patterns that increase soil erosion and agrichemical use. The General Accounting Office (1990) has identified these programs as a major barrier to progress in reducing pollution from agriculture. At the same time, EPA is regulating the use of pesticides and USDA is spending huge amounts on technical assistance and subsidies to farmers to reduce soil erosion, take environmentally sensitive land out of production and adopt farming practices that reduce water pollution. The likely direction of change in USDA policies is towards 'decoupling' of income supports from production decisions 'recoupling' them to conservation and water quality protection measures.
12. Malik, Larson and Ribaudo (1992) provide a concise overview of the types of reforms that have been receiving attention.
13. This approach was taken to dairy waste problems in Florida but the feasibility of the approach is limited to nonpoint sources with certain point source characteristics and possibly then to cases in which the number of nonpoint sources is small (Boggess, Flaig and Fonyo (1993); Malik, Larson and Ribaudo (1992); Phipps (1991)). The EPA (1992) reports huge problems in permitting even the small number of livestock operations currently subject to NPDES requirements.
14. Tradeoffs in pollution control levels can be made between different categories of point sources and between point and nonpoint sources in principal when state in-stream water quality standards are not satisfied by the technology-based standards on point sources.
15. Some useful discussions of the complexities of nonpoint pollution control and their economic implications are found in Abler and Shortle (1991); Braden and Segerson (1993); Malik, Larson and Ribaudo (1992); Cabe and Herriges (1992); and Shortle and Dunn (1986, 1991).
16. At the extreme opposite end of the spectrum from the rational planning view is the view that government is no more than a tool for powerful rent-seeking special interests. A richer perspective recognizes a range of possibilities between these extremes, including the use of

policy favors to powerful special interests in order to gain their acceptance of measures that are in the broader public interest (Rausser and Foster (1990)).

REFERENCES

Abler, D.G. and J.S. Shortle (1991), 'The Political Economy of Water Quality Protection From Agricultural Chemicals', *Northeastern Journal of Agricultural and Resource Economics*, 20:53–60.

Alston, J.M. and B.M. Hurd (1990), 'Some Neglected Costs of Government Spending in Farm Programs', *American Journal of Agricultural Economics*, 72:149–56.

Apogee Research Inc. (1991), 'Watershed Planning and Management: A Background Paper', Prepared for the Water Quality 2000 Steering Committee.

Batie, S.S. and P.P. Diebel (1989), 'Managing Agricultural Contamination of Groundwater: State Strategies', Dept. of Ag. Econ., Virginia Polytechnic and State University, Blacksburg, VA.

Baumol, W.J. and W.E. Oates (1988), *The Theory of Environmental Policy*, Cambridge University Press, Cambridge, MA.

Beccaris, J. (1992), 'The Political Economy of Agricultural Nonpoint Pollution: An Economic Analysis of State and Local Expenditures', MS Thesis, Dept. of Agricultural Economics and Rural Sociology, Pennsylvania State University.

Boggess, G., E.G. Flaig and C.M. Fonyo (1993), 'Florida's Experience With Managing Nonpoint-Source Phosphorus Runoff into Lake Okeechobee', in C.S. Russell and J.F. Shogren (eds), *Theory, Modelling, and Experience in the Management of Nonpoint-Source Pollution*, Kluwer Academic Publisher, Dordrecht, The Netherlands.

Bord, R.J., A. Fisher, R.E. O'Connor and W.J. Wheeler (1993), 'Fresh Water Quality, Quantity, and Availability: American Public Perceptions', Environmental Resources Research Institute, Pennsylvania State University, University Park, PA.

Bouwer, H. (March-April 1990), 'Agricultural Chemicals and Groundwater Quality', *Journal of Soil and Water Conservation*, 45:184–9.

Braden, J.B. and S.J. Lovejoy (eds) (1991), *Agriculture and Water Quality: International Perspectives*, Lynne Rienner Publishers, Boulder, CO.

Braden, J.B. and K. Segerson (1993), 'Information Problems in the Design of Nonpoint Source Pollution Policy', in Clifford S. Russell and Jason F. Shogren (eds), *Theory, Modeling and Experience in the Management of Nonpoint Source Pollution*, Kluwer Academic Publishers, Dordrecht, The Netherlands.

Cabe, R. and J. Herriges (1992), 'The Regulation of Nonpoint-Source Pollution Under Imperfect and Asymmetric Information', *Journal of Environmental Economics and Management*, 22:34–146.

Council on Agricultural Science and Technology (1993), *Water Quality: Agriculture's Role*, CAST, Ames, IA.

Cropper, M.L., W.N. Evans, J.J. Berardi, M.M. DuclaSoares and P.R. Portney (1992), 'The Determinants of Pesticide Regulation: Statistical Analysis of EPA Decision Making', *Journal Of Political Economy*, 100:175–97.

Cropper, M.L. and W.E. Oates (1992), 'Environmental Economics: A Survey', *The Journal of Economic Literature*, 30:675–740.

Cumberland, J.H. (1981), 'Efficiency and Equity in Interregional Environmental Management', *Review of Regulatory Studies*, 10:1–9.

Dosi, C. and T. Graham-Tomasi (eds), *Nonpoint Source Pollution Control: Issues and Analyses*, Kluwer Academic Publishers, Dordrecht, The Netherlands (Forthcoming).

Fisher, A. and R. Raucher (1984), 'Intrinsic Benefits of Improved Water Quality: Conceptual and Empirical Perspectives', in V. K. Smith (ed.), *Advances in Applied Micro-Economics*, JAI Press Inc., Greenwich, CT.

Foster W.E. and B.A. Babcock (1991), 'Producer Welfare Consequences of Regulating Chemical Residues on Agricultural Crops: Maelic Hydrazide and Tobacco', *American Journal of Agricultural Economics*, 73:1224–32.

Freeman, M. (1990), 'Water Pollution Policy', in P. Portney (ed.), *Policies for Environmental Protection*, Resources for the Future, Washington, DC.

Greenfield R. (1985), 'Controlling nonpoint sources of pollution - the federal legal framework and the alternative of nonfederal action', in *Perspectives on Nonpoint Source Pollution*, EPA 440/5–855–001, US EPA.

Griffin, R. and D. Bromley (1982), 'Agricultural Runoff as A Nonpoint Externality', *American Journal of Agricultural Economics*, 64:547–52.

Just, R.E. and N. Bockstael (eds) (1989), *Commodity and Resource Policies in Agricultural Systems*, Springer Verlag, Berlin, Germany.

Kim, C.S., J. Hostetler and G. Amacher (1993), 'The Regulation of Groundwater Quality With Delayed Responses', *Water Resources Research*, 5:1369–77.

Lichtenberg, E. (1992), 'Alternative Approaches to Pesticide Regulation', *Northeastern Journal of Agricultural and Resource Economics*, 21:83–92.

Lichtenberg, E. and D. Zilberman (1986), 'The Welfare Economics of Price Supports in US Agriculture', *American Economic Review*, 76:1135–41.

Malik, A.S., B.A. Larson and M. Ribaudo (1992), *Agricultural Nonpoint Source Pollution and Economic Incentive Policies: Issues in the Reauthorization of the Clean Water Act*, US Department of Agriculture Staff Report No. AGES 9229.

Miller, E.W. and R.M. Miller (1992), *Water Quality and Availability*, ABC–CLIO, Santa Barbara, CA.

Miranowski, J.A., J. Hrubovcak and J. Sutton (1989), 'The Effects of Commodity Programs on Resource Use', in R.E. Just and N.E. Bockstael (eds), *Commodity and Resource Policies in Agriculutral Systems*, Springer Verlag, Berlin, Germany.

Oates, W.E. and R.M. Schwab (1988), 'Economic Competition Among Jurisdictions: Efficiency Enhancing or Distortion Inducing?', *Journal of Public Economics*, 24:29–46.

Organization for Economic Cooperation and Development (1990), *State of the Environment*, OECD, Paris, France.

Phipps, T.T. (1991), 'Commercial Agriculture and The Environment: An Evolutionary Perspective', *Northeastern Journal of Agricultural and Natural Resource Economics*, 20:143–50.

Rausser, G.C. and W.E. Foster (1990), 'Political Preference Functions and Public Policy Reform', *American Journal of Agricultural Economics*, 41:641–52.

Reichelderfer, K. (1990), 'Environmental Protection and Agricultural Support: Are Tradeoffs Really Necessary?', in K. Allen (ed.), *Agricultural Policies in A New Decade*, Resources for the Future Inc., Washington, DC.

Ribaudo, M. (1989), *Water Quality Benefits from the Conservation Reserve Program*. US Department of Agriculture, Agricultural Economic Report No. 606.

Ribaudo, M. and D. Woo (1991), 'Summary of State Water Quality Laws Affecting Agriculture', *Agricultural Resources – Cropland, Water, and Conservation – Situation and Outlook Report*, USDA/ERS/RTD AR–23, pp. 50–54,

Russell, C.S. and J.F. Shogren (eds) (1993), *Theory, Modelling, and Experience in the Management of Nonpoint-Source Pollution*, Kluwer Academic Publishers, Dordrecht, The Netherlands.

Schwab, R.M. (Summer 1988), 'Environmental Federalism', *Resources*, Resources for the Future, Inc., Washington, DC.

Segerson, K. (1988), 'Uncertainty and Incentives for Nonpoint Pollution Control', *J. Environ. Econ. Manage.*, 15:87–98.

Shortle, J.S. and J.W. Dunn (1986), 'The Relative Efficiency of Agricultural Source Water Pollution Control Policies', *American Journal of Agricultural Economics*, 68:668–77.

Shortle, J.S. and J.W. Dunn (1991), 'Economics of Control of Nonpoint Pollution From Agriculture', in N. Hanley (ed.), *Farming and the Countryside: An Economic Analysis of Costs and Benefits*, CAB International, Wallingford, UK.

Shortle, J.S. and A. Laughland (1994), 'Impacts of Taxes to Reduce Agrichemical Use When Farm Policy is Endogenous', *Journal of Agricultural Economics*, 45:2–14.

Sobel, J.B. and C.W. Abdalla (1992), 'Attitudes of Local Government Officials in Pennsylvania Concerning Community Level Groundwater Protection and Management', *Groundwater Policy Education Report 1*, The Pennsylvania State University, University Park, PA.

US Department of Agriculture, Economic Research Service (May 1993), *Agricultural Resources Situation and Outlook Report*, AR–30.

US Environmental Protection Agency (1988), *Nonpoint Sources: Agenda for the Future*, Office of Water Quality.

US Environmental Protection Agency (January 1992), *Managing Nonpoint Source Pollution*, EPA–506/9–90.

US General Accounting Office (October 1990), *Water Pollution – Greater EPA Leadership Needed To Reduce Nonpoint Water Pollution*, GAO/RCED–91–10.

US General Accounting Office (March 1992), *Conservation Reserve Program – Cost Effectiveness Uncertain*, GAO/RECD–93–132.

US General Accounting Office (April 1993), *Drinking Water – Stronger Efforts needed to Protect Areas Around Public Wells From Contamination*, GAO/RCED–93–96.

Viessman, W. (1988), 'Regional Options for Managing and Regulating Nonpoint Pollution', in V. Novotney (ed.), *Political, Institutional, and Fiscal Alternatives to Nonpoint Pollution Abatement Programs*, Bradley Institute for Democracy and Public Values.

Weinberg, M. and C.L. Kling (1993), 'The Costs of Piecemeal Agricultural and Environmental Policy Making', presented at the 1993 Annual Meeting of the American Agricultural Economics Association, Orlando Fl.

Wise, S. and S.R. Johnson (1991), 'A Comparative Analysis of State Regulations for Use of Agricultural Chemicals', in R.E. Just and N. Bockstael (eds), *Commodity and Resource Policies in Agricultural Systems*, Springer Verlag, Berlin, Germany.

Xepapadeas, A. (1991), 'Environmental Policy Under Imperfect Information: Incentives and Moral Hazard', *Journal of Environmental Economics Management*, 20:113–26.

SECTION B

Global Warming

13. Sectoral Differentiation as a Substitute for International Coordination of Carbon Taxes: A Case Study of Sweden

Lars Bergman

INTRODUCTION

Due to the increasing concern for global climate, change measures aimed at curbing the emissions of carbon dioxide are implemented, planned or at least discussed in several countries. However, the effectiveness of national policies in terms of global carbon dioxide emission reduction in general depends on the degree and nature of international coordination of the policies in question. Higher carbon taxes or more stringent regulations in one or a few countries tend to induce international relocations of energy-intensive production. Thus the emission reductions brought about in the 'activist' countries are counteracted by increased emissions in other parts of the world. And as the climate impact of carbon dioxide emissions does not depend on the location of the emission sources, and emission reduction measures are costly, the benefit–cost ratio of unilateral policies might be quite unfavorable.

This aspect of environmental policy is relevant both for a federation of countries such as the EC and a single country such as Norway or Sweden. In fact, Sweden is a suitable 'case' for a discussion of the particular problems associated with unilateral policies against a global environmental problem such as 'global warming'. This is due to the fact that the Swedish economy to a significant degree is specialized in production with relatively high carbon dioxide emissions per unit of output, while most Swedish producers are 'price-takers' on international product markets. Thus, much of the adjustment to a tax on, or direct regulation of, domestic carbon dioxide emissions, is likely to take the form of output reductions in tradeables-producing 'carbon dioxide-intensive' industries rather than substitution of carbon-free inputs for fossil fuels.

In theory the cost of policy-induced structural change in a small open economy need not be very high. Factor prices, and the real exchange rate,

329

are simply adjusted to the levels where capital and labor resources are induced to move from the industries most negatively affected by the carbon tax to the industries where international competitiveness has been most strengthened by the change in factor prices. If this process is sufficiently smooth the cost of the emission reduction is limited to the loss associated with a slightly less efficient sectoral specialization at given world market prices.

But in practice the adjustment process might be quite lengthy; instead of quickly moving into new industries and occupations people may be left unemployed and real capital left idle over an extended period of time. In addition the decline of the emission-intensive industries might mean a loss of subtle sector-specific skills and knowledge being critical for observed pre-policy productivity levels and rates of economic growth. The accumulation of comparable productivity-enhancing skills suitable for other industries and markets may be quite time-consuming and may, in the end, represent a significant cost for the reduction of domestic carbon dioxide emissions.[1]

International coordination of carbon dioxide emission reduction policies is the obvious solution to this problem. But both theory (see, for instance, Barrett (1991), Mäler (1989)) and practical experience suggest that efficient international coordination on a global scale is very hard to attain. Thus it seems most likely that policies aimed at curbing carbon dioxide emissions, at least for some time, will have to be unilaterally designed and implemented by groups of countries such as the EC or even individual countries.

A unilateral policy against carbon dioxide emissions can take the form of a uniform tax on domestic carbon dioxide emissions. But alternative policy designs might be more effective in terms of global emission reductions and/or less costly in terms of GNP losses. One alternative to a uniform tax on the emissions caused by domestic (industrial and household) production activities is to tax the emissions caused by domestic consumption. This amounts to taxing imports in relation to the emissions of carbon dioxide in the process of production and transportation of the goods in question, while exports are exempt from the carbon tax. However, this type of policy would not be compatible with the GATT and in addition the practical difficulties would be substantial.

Another alternative, which can be seen as a simplified variant of the first, is to implement sectorally differentiated carbon taxes. More precisely the tax would be designed to induce carbon dioxide emission reductions primarily in non-tradeables-producing sectors and the household sector. This is the type of policy adopted in Sweden and also proposed for the EC.

Sectoral differentiation of carbon taxation obviously limits the degree of adjustment through output reduction in emission-intensive industries. Thus they are likely to be more effective than uniform taxes in terms of reducing global emissions. At the same time differentiated carbon taxes are economically inefficient in the sense that the marginal costs of emission reduction are not equalized across sectors, and thus the total cost of emission reduction is not minimized.

The purpose of this chapter is to analyze and evaluate different designs of carbon taxes with respect to the overall impact on the economy. The underlying issue is whether unilateral policies against carbon dioxide emissions are reasonably worthwhile for a country, or a group of countries, concerned about the risk for global climate change. The analysis is framed as a case study of Sweden and a specific set of policy designs, and it is based on a numerical general equilibrium type of model of the Swedish economy.

It is obvious that the results of a case study of a particular country and a particular set of policy designs cannot easily be generalized to all countries and all policy designs. However, given the pattern of sectoral specialization in the Swedish economy, Sweden is something like a 'worst case' in terms of the problems associated with unilateral policies against carbon dioxide emissions. In other words the prospects for unilateral policies should be better in a large country such as the US or a federation of countries such as the EC.

CARBON TAXATION IN SWEDEN

Before turning to the actual policy evaluation, a brief presentation of the development of Swedish environmental policy might be useful. The natural point of departure is the fact that environmental protection in a broad sense has a very long history in Sweden.[2] The squirrel was protected already in the fourteenth and fifteenth centuries, and oaks were protected in accordance with laws from 1647 and 1664. A law of national parks was established in 1909. However, it was not until 1967, when the Swedish Environmental Protection Board was established, that 'environmental policy' became a widely recognized concept and an important topic in public debate and policy-making.

As in most other countries, Swedish environmental policy was based on direct regulation, and in the early 1970s subsidies were made to heavily polluting point sources, rather than charges or other economic instruments aimed at creating economic incentives for emission reduction and environmental protection. However, in recent years the situation has gradually changed. Charges on fertilizers and pesticides were introduced in 1984, and since 1986 there is a tax differentiation between leaded and unleaded petrol. The major change came in the early 1990s, following upon several reports of the Commission of Environmental Charges and in conjunction with a major tax reform. Thus as of January 1, 1991 taxes on both carbon and sulphur dioxide emissions are effective, and one year later a tax on nitrogen oxides was introduced. It should be added, however, that the earlier regulations are still in place.

Initially the carbon tax was 0.25 SEK per kg CO_2, corresponding to roughly $US130 per ton carbon, and, with a few important exceptions, it applied to all carbon dioxide emissions from the combustion of fossil fuels. The exceptions were aviation fuels for international traffic and fossil fuels for electricity generation. As long as Sweden's generation of electricity is almost entirely based on hydro and nuclear power, these exceptions are not very important. More important, however, is the fact that the carbon tax had the legal status as an energy tax.

This was important because of a provision stating that the sum of all energy taxes paid by an industrial firm should never exceed a certain fraction of the value of the firm's total sales. At the time that fraction was set at 1.7 percent, which means that this particular provision effectively reduced the energy tax burden of the major energy-intensive industries. Thus for firms already paying the maximum sum of energy taxes the new carbon tax had no impact at all. In other words the carbon tax was in effect differentiated between energy-intensive industries and other sectors of the economy.

The reason for this differentiation is obvious. Due to Sweden's endowments of forests, iron ore and hydro power, the forest and steel industries played key roles in the early phases of industrialization in Sweden. These energy-intensive industries are very export oriented, and they still account for a significant share of Sweden's foreign currency earnings. Concern for these export-oriented energy-intensive industries is obvious in the design of Swedish environmental policy in general and the first version of the carbon tax in particular.

However, as of January 1, 1993 a new energy tax system is effective. There is still a 'pure' energy tax for households, but for industry all energy taxes are replaced by a carbon tax. In the new system there are no limits on the energy tax burden for an individual firm, but the tax rates are differentiated across sectors. Thus the carbon tax rate is 0.32 SEK per kg CO_2, corresponding to roughly $US160 per ton carbon, but only one-fourth of that, i.e. 0.08 SEK per kg CO_2, for industrial firms.

The tax rates were chosen with an eye on the, later abolished, goal to stabilize emissions at the 1988 level. What is more important, perhaps, is that the differentiation between sectors in terms of the carbon tax rates was seen as a temporary arrangement while waiting for an international agreement on coordinated carbon taxation or other measures to curb global carbon dioxide emissions. In other words sectorally differentiated carbon taxes were in effect seen as a substitute for internationally coordinated carbon taxes. In the following the current design of carbon taxes in Sweden will be evaluated by means of a numerical model of the Swedish economy.

MODEL AND DATA

The model is a slightly revised and elaborated version of the one presented in Bergman (1991). A technical description of the model is beyond the scope of this chapter, but a few general remarks are necessary. The first and most important for the interpretation of the results is that the model is a general equilibrium model, a so-called 'computable general equilibrium', or CGE, model. Thus, given a set of assumptions about the economy's resource endowments, world market conditions and the regulatory environment, the model determines relative prices of factors of production and products such that supply equals demand on each factor market and each product market. The magnitude of changes in computed equilibrium prices and sectoral output levels resulting from, say, a constraint on carbon dioxide emissions can give a hint of the adjustment process that would have to take place in the real world, but the model only indicates the final result of the adjustment process.

The base year of the model is 1985, and the main data source is an input–output table of the Swedish economy for that year. In addition extraneous estimates of various elasticities of substitution in production and in consumptions are used. The model is calibrated to replicate the 1985 input-output table. The economy's resources are aggregated into four inelastically supplied domestic resources: labor, capital, hydro and nuclear power production capacity and forest resources. In the production sectors these factors of production, as well as imported fossil fuels, are substitutable inputs. There is only one aggregated household sector. Thus the model does not say anything about the impact of carbon taxation on the distribution of incomes across different types of households.

On the supply side of the product markets there are several production sectors. In Table 13.1 some key base-year data about the production sectors are summarized. In addition to the sectors in the table, there are a public sector and a district heating and water supply sector. It is clear from the table that the sectors forest industry and steel and chemicals are relatively small in terms of value added, but quite big in terms of net exports. In addition these sectors are by far the most CO_2-intensive of the export-oriented sectors. Due to the use of gasoline and oil for residential heating,

Table 13.1: Production sectors and selected 1985 data (value added and net export in 10^9 SEK 1985 and CO_2 in 10^6 tonnes)

Sector	Value added (1)	CO_2 emissions (2)	(2):(1)	Net export
Forest industry	27.1	2.8	0.1033	28.9
Steel and Chemicals	46.1	7.0	0.1518	28.3
Manufacturing	88.4	1.1	0.0124	71.1
Other industries	153.7	1.3	0.0085	19.0
Service and transport	232.4	21.2	0.0912	−8.4

Note: 'Net export' is gross export minus imported inputs used in the sector.

the household sector (not shown in the table) is also rather CO_2-intensive, and the same applies, obviously, to the district heating and water supply sector. However, in terms of carbon tax-induced structural change in the tradeables-producing sector, one should expect the forest industry and the steel and chemicals industries to decline and the manufacturing industry to expand. But as the forest industry, unlike the other industries, to a large extent is based on inelastically supplied sector-specific resources, carbon tax-induced cost increases tend to result in reductions of the price of forest resources rather than output reductions in the forest industry.

In the model it is assumed that the forest industry as well as the steel and chemicals industries are price-takers on international product markets, while the export demand facing the manufacturing industry depends on international relative prices. Thus, *ceteris paribus*, manufacturing industry exports will increase only if the price of manufactured goods is decreased. This means that in the model economy an expansion of manufacturing exports, induced by domestic carbon taxation and a decline in the steel and chemicals industries, will be accompanied by a deterioration of the terms of trade. Although the magnitude of estimates of export-demand elasticities always can be questioned, this mechanism probably reflects an important feature of the Swedish economy.

In addition to equilibrium prices and quantities the model endogenously determines sectoral emissions of carbon dioxide, CO_2, and sulphur dioxide, SO_2. A rather unusual feature of this model is a 'feed-back' mechanism from some environmental quality variables to the economy in a narrow sense. Thus the emissions of SO_2 affect a measure of 'environmental quality', which in turn affects the productivity of the forest industry and thus, in the end, real incomes. There is also a direct link from the measures of environmental quality to the economic welfare of the households. The details of the environment–economy interactions are elaborated in the Appendix.

POLICY OBJECTIVE AND POLICY DESIGNS

The analysis of the policy alternatives has the form of a comparison of a set of projections of the state of the Swedish economy in the year 2000. More precisely each one of a set of 'policy cases' is compared with a 'base case'. The policy cases are based on exactly the same assumptions as the base case, except the assumptions about carbon taxation at home and abroad. Thus the differences between the results in a policy case and the base case are entirely due to the assumptions about carbon taxation. The base case reflects assumptions about technical change, labor force growth, capital accumulation and world market growth between the early 1990s and the year 2000. However it is not intended to be a prediction of the most likely development of the Swedish economy. Rather it is constructed to yield an average 2 percent per annum GDP growth during the rest of the century. Although such a development currently seems quite optimistic, it is rather close to the post-war average rate of economic growth. Thus the results of the model simulations can indicate whether zero or negative carbon dioxide emission growth could be compatible with the average rate of economic growth experienced during the last five decades in Sweden.

Three policy designs and three policy objectives are analyzed. The policy objectives are denoted 60, 50 and 40. The numbers refer to target emission levels, in million tonnes CO_2, at the turn of the century, or rather during the year 2000. The 60 million tonnes per annum level is roughly equal to the emission level observed in 1990, while the other policy objectives thus reflect more or less stringent emission reduction strategies. The policy designs are denoted A, B and C and defined in the following way.

A.   Policy Design A

The target emission levels are attained by means of a uniform tax on all domestic carbon dioxide emissions while no similar measures are implemented in other countries.

B.   Policy Design B

The target emission levels are attained by means of a differentiated tax on all domestic carbon dioxide emissions while no similar measures are

implemented in other countries. The differentiation implies that the tax rate
applicable for industrial firms is one-quarter of the tax rate for non-industrial
firms and households.

C.   Policy Design C

The target emission levels are attained by means of a uniform tax on all
carbon dioxide emissions in Sweden as well as in all other countries.

ECONOMIC AND ENVIRONMENTAL INDICATORS

With three policy designs and three policy objectives there are nine different
cases to evaluate. For this evaluation the following set of economic and
environmental indicators have been selected.

A.   GDP (Gross Domestic Product) in Constant 1985 Prices

This is the standard measure of the aggregated real output of the economy.
To the extent that carbon taxes and emission reductions affect the
productivity of capital, labor and forest resources, that will be reflected in
the GDP indicator. Moreover, as there is always full employment of
available resources in the model economy, changes in the GDP indicator
will only reflect productivity changes.

B.   GNI (Gross National Income) at the 1985 Price Level

This is a measure of the purchasing power of the aggregated factor incomes.
The essential difference between our measure of GNI and GDP is that the
former reflects changes in the terms of trade, while the latter does not.[3]
Thus, to the extent that carbon taxes and emission reductions affect the real
purchasing power of aggregated incomes, that will be reflected in the GNI
indicator.

C.   Sectoral Gross Output Levels

Major changes in sectoral gross output levels imply major reallocations of
resources across production sector. In the real world there are various costs
of adjustment associated with such a reallocation process, but these costs are
not captured by the model. On the assumption that the cost of structural
adjustment is an increasing function of the magnitude of structural change,

this indicator gives a very rough hint of the adjustment costs associated with carbon taxes and emission reductions.

D.   Contribution to Global CO_2 Emissions

If a domestic carbon tax induce output decreases in the price-taking industries, i.e. forest and steel and chemicals, there should be equally big output increases in other parts of the world. But these output increases produce increases in CO_2 emissions. Such policy-induced emission increases in other countries are sometimes called 'leakages'. In the evaluation of the different policy alternatives the sum of purely domestic emissions and the 'leakages' is used as an indicator of Sweden's contribution to global CO_2 emissions. The 'leakages' are calculated on the somewhat arbitrary assumption that sectoral CO_2 emission coefficients are the same at home and in the rest of the world.

NUMERICAL RESULTS

In this section the results of the model simulations are presented. Obviously the numbers should be interpreted with a grain of salt; the model abstracts from important real world phenomena such as unemployment and many other types of adjustment costs, and, as usual, there are significant uncertainties about the magnitude of important parameters. Yet the results are most likely to say something important about the real world, at least until significantly different results are obtained with a more elaborated model or on the basis of better empirical data.

In Table 13.2 the results obtained under policy design A, i.e. a uniform carbon tax, are summarized. In addition to the indicators discussed in the previous section the carbon tax rate is reported. In the model this tax rate is endogenously determined so that the exogenous target emission level is attained. As firms are assumed to minimize their costs, the emission reduction is carried to the point where the marginal cost of emission reduction is equal to the uniform carbon tax rate in each sector. This means that the uniform carbon tax rate is equal to the equilibrium marginal cost of emission reduction. As major output changes in relation to the base case turned out take place in only the forest industry, the steel and chemicals industries and the manufacturing industry, the numbers for the other sectors are not included in the table. Several observations can be made. The first is that the impact of CO_2 emission on full-employment GDP and GNI is quite limited, even when the emissions are reduced by almost 50 percent compared to the base case. Part of the reason for this is that electricity

Table 13.2:   Policy design A: economic and environmental indicators 2000

	Base case	CO_2=60	CO_2=50	CO_2=40
GDP[1]	1244.5	1244.6	1243.6	1241.4
GNI[1]	1239.5	1237.9	1235.3	1230.6
Carbon tax[2]	–	0.25	0.50	0.90
Global CO_2-emissions[3]	78.9	61.6	52.7	44.3
Forest industry[4]	72.4	73.2	75.7	77.8
Steel and Chemicals[4]	187.6	157.3	134.4	103.4
Manufacturing[4]	332.4	342.0	350.1	362.1

Notes
1. In 10^9 SEK in 1985 prices.
2. In 1992 SEK per kg CO_2.
3. In 10^6 tonnes.
4. Gross output in 10^9 SEK in 1985 prices.

production in Sweden is almost entirely based on hydro and nuclear power and thus does not lead to any CO_2 emissions at all. Consequently there is no direct impact on electricity prices of a carbon tax. If the nuclear power plants are to be closed down around 2010 (which the Swedish parliament has decided) and replaced by fossil fuel-based power plants, the macroeconomic impact of constraints on the emissions of CO_2 would significantly increase.

The second observation is that the loss of GNI is around three times as high as the corresponding loss of GDP. This suggests that the carbon tax leads to real income losses through a deterioration of the terms of trade rather than through reduced productivity. The terms of trade losses reflect the restructuring of the export-oriented industry following upon the cost increases in the CO_2-intensive price-taking sectors; in order to attain external balance through expansion of the manufacturing industry, the export prices of this industry have to be reduced. Consequently the terms of trade deteriorate. The third observation follows immediately: the real world costs of reducing CO_2 emissions to a large extent seem to depend upon the costs of the quite significant structural adjustment suggested by the model results, i.e. costs not captured by the model.

The fourth observation is that stabilization of the CO_2 emissions at the 1990 level, i.e. 60 million tonnes per year, would require a 0.25 SEK per kg CO_2 uniform tax at the turn of the century. That is, a tax rate equal to the one introduced in Sweden on January 1, 1991. However, in the model simulation the carbon tax applies to all domestic emissions, whereas in the real world important emission sources were exempt from the tax. It should also be stressed that in order to maintain the emissions at the 1990 level when the economy grows by approximately 2 percent per year, the tax rate would have to be gradually increased over time.

The fifth observation is that the 'leakages', although very roughly estimated, turn out to be rather small. As a result of the policies aimed at reducing Sweden's contribution to global CO_2 emissions to, respectively, 60.0, 50.0 and 40.0 million tonnes per year, emissions at the levels 61.6, 52.7 and 44.3 million tonnes per year, respectively, are realized. Thus, although Sweden is a small open economy and to a large extent specialized in CO_2-intensive export-oriented industries, a purely domestic carbon tax is quite effective in terms of reducing the country's contribution to global CO_2 emissions. The reason for this is simply that a significant share of Sweden's CO_2 emissions originate in non-tradeables' sectors such as transportation and district heating as well as in the household sector.

The final observation is that the output of the CO_2-intensive forest industry increases when the aggregate emissions are constrained. There are two reasons for this counter-intuitive result. The first is the above-mentioned effect that a carbon tax tends to be balanced by a reduction of the price of the inelastically supplied sector-specific forest resources. The second is that reductions of CO_2 emissions through reduced use of fossil fuels also produce reductions of SO_2 emissions (see Tables 13.5–13.7 below), which, in turn, positively affects productivity in the forest industry. This effect also compensates for part of the overall productivity losses due to emission reduction and thus tends to reduce the resulting GDP losses.

Although the cost of CO_2 emission reduction in terms of full-employment GDP or GNI seems to be rather modest, the costs associated with structural change might be significant. One way of reducing the policy induced structural change is, as in the current system of carbon taxes in Sweden, to differentiate the tax rate between industrial and non-industrial emission sources. That is, to adopt policy design B. The results obtained under these conditions are summarized in Table 13.3. As can be seen in the table this policy design is quite effective in terms of reducing the structural change and the terms of trade deterioration associated with the target CO_2 emission reductions. Moreover, although the tax differentiation leads to a less cost-efficient allocation of emission reductions, the overall productivity impact, in terms of increased GDP losses, is quite small. In addition this policy design quite effectively limits the 'leakages'. Thus, quite surprisingly non-uniform carbon taxes turn out to have several nice properties, and policy design B appears to be more attractive than policy design A.

Table 13.3:   Policy design B: economic and environmental indicators 2000

	Base case	CO_2=60	CO_2=50	CO_2=40
GDP[1]	1244.5	1244.1	1242.7	1240.0
GNI[1]	1239.5	1240.1	1239.5	1237.8
Carbon tax[2]	–	0.33	0.67	1.27
Global CO_2-emissions[3]	78.9	60.9	51.5	42.4
Forest industry[4]	72.4	73.1	73.6	74.3
Steel and Chemicals[4]	187.6	170.9	158.9	142.3
Manufacturing[4]	332.4	336.0	339.4	344.9

Notes
1. In 10^9 SEK in 1985 prices.
2. In 1992 SEK per kg CO_2. In accordance with the definition of policy design B the tax rate for industrial sectors is 25 percent of the tax rate in the table.
3. In 10^6 tonnes.
4. Gross output in 10^9 SEK in 1985 prices.

The next step then is to compare unilateral action, in accordance with policy design B, and international coordination of CO_2 emission policies. Clearly this should be done within the frame of a multicountry model. Multicountry modeling, however, is beyond the scope of this chapter. Accordingly the analysis of internationally coordinated policies has to be based on a set of somewhat arbitrary but yet reasonable assumptions. Thus, assuming the same technology at home and abroad, carbon tax-induced changes in relative world prices of tradeables have been computed. Then for each level of target domestic emission reduction the world market price assumptions in the model simulations are adjusted in accordance with the calculated impact of carbon taxes on the relative prices of tradeables.

The results of the model simulation based on these assumptions, 'policy design C', are summarized in Table 13.4. As the internationally coordinated policies are aimed at controlling global emissions, the numbers for Sweden's contribution to the global emissions are not relevant in this case and thus not reported in the table. The most striking feature of the results of policy design C is that they are very similar to those obtained under policy design B. In other words, differentiation of domestic carbon taxes seems to be an almost perfect substitute to internationally coordinated carbon taxes. Obviously better estimates of the relation between carbon taxes and world market prices could change the numbers to some extent, but it is not likely that the general conclusion would have to be changed. In other words, for

Table 13.4: Policy design C: economic and environmental indicators 2000

	Base case	CO_2=60	CO_2=50	CO_2=40
GDP[1]	1244.5	1243.2	1244.4	1240.6
GNI[1]	1239.5	1238.8	1239.7	1236.9
Carbon tax[2]	–	0.26	0.53	0.97
Global CO_2-emissions[3]	78.9	**	**	**
Forest industry[4]	72.4	74.9	73.8	76.5
Steel and Chemicals[4]	187.6	148.8	164.7	129.4
Manufacturing[4]	332.4	341.5	337.6	346.4

Notes
1. In 10^9 SEK in 1985 prices.
2. In 1992 SEK per kg CO_2.
3. In 10^6 tonnes.
4. Gross output in 10^9 SEK in 1985 prices.

a small country with strong preferences for global CO_2 emission reductions unilateral action in accordance with something like policy design B would be effective in terms of the emission objective and need not be considerably more costly than internationally coordinated policies. Needless to say, however, internationally coordinated policies would mean a lot more for the global emissions.

NO REGRET POLICIES?

Reductions of carbon dioxide emissions are generally brought about by a whole set of factor substitutions in industrial and household production. Thus, oil or natural gas is substituted for coal, hydroelectricity or nuclear energy is substituted for fossil fuels in general, capital and labor are substituted for energy, and human capital in the form of new technology is substituted for resource inputs in general. But reductions of the use of fossil fuels tend to reduce the emissions of many pollutants. In particular reductions of the use of coal and oil tend to reduce the emissions of sulphur oxides, i.e. one of the pollutants causing 'acid rain'.

As the environment in Sweden is quite sensitive to 'acid rain' this is a rather important side effect of carbon taxation.[4] Needless to say carbon taxation is not the most efficient way of reducing sulphur dioxide emissions. But the benefits associated with sulphur emission reductions caused by carbon taxes clearly should be taken into consideration in the economic evaluation of the carbon tax. Moreover, if the value of this kind of side effect exceeds the costs of the policy measures in question, carbon taxation is a so-called 'no regret policy'. In other words, it should produce positive net benefits as long as the value of reducing carbon dioxide emissions is non-negative.

The question then is whether any of the policies discussed in the preceding section would be a 'no regret policy'. In order to analyze that issue some measure of the economic benefits due to reduced sulphur emissions has to be brought into the picture. However, such an extension of the analysis opens up a whole set of unresolved issues about the impact of acid rain on the environment and the economic valuation of environmental resources and amenities. Yet some very rough calculations can be done and incorporated in the model.

One aspect of reduced SO_2 emissions is increased productivity in forestry which in the model is a part of the forest industry. This effect is incorporated in the results discussed so far. Another aspect is that reduced SO_2 emission positively affects individual welfare through a healthier environment and improved recreation opportunities. On the basis of a survey of the literature on the environmental effects of coal combustion, Andersson and Åshuvud (1984) estimated the marginal cost of sulphur emissions to approximately 20 SEK per kg (in the 1992 price level), corresponding to 40 SEK per kg SO_2, at the emission levels observed in Sweden in the beginning of the 1980s. It should be mentioned that the tax on sulphur emissions that was implemented in 1991 is 30 SEK per kg of sulphur.

On the basis of these numbers it is possible to put a monetary value on the SO_2 emission reductions produced by carbon taxation and thus construct a measure of 'environmental quality adjusted national income'. What makes such a measure interesting is the possibility that the economic value of SO_2 emission reduction is large enough to compensate for the loss of national income caused by carbon taxation, i.e. the possibility that unilateral carbon taxation in Sweden is a so-called 'no regret policy'.

In Tables 13.5–13.7 model estimates of ENI, environmental quality-adjusted GNI, are reported together with the calculated SO_2 emissions and the previously reported GNI values in the different policy alternatives. In addition the calculated aggregate marginal willingness to pay for SO_2 reductions, MWTP(SO_2), is reported. This number, which is the sum of the MWTP of the aggregated household sector and the forest industry, conceptually corresponds to the estimate by Andersson and Åshuvud. By calibration it was set to 52.5 SEK/kg SO_2 in the base year (1985), i.e. somewhat higher than Andersson and Åshuvud's estimate but somewhat lower than the current tax on sulphur emissions. The base case value,

Table 13.5:   *Policy design A: macroeconomic and environmental indicators*

	Base case	CO_2=60	CO_2=50	CO_2=40
GNI	1239.5	1237.9	1235.9	1230.6
ENI	1230.9	1232.3	1230.9	1227.4
SO_2^1	346	266	228	192
$MWTP(SO_2)^2$	75.2	66.1	62.4	58.6

Notes
1. 10^3 tonnes.
2. SEK per kg SO_2.

Table 13.6.   *Policy design B: macroeconomic and environmental indicators*

	Base case	CO_2=60	CO_2=50	CO_2=40
GNI	1239.5	1240.1	1239.5	1237.8
ENI	1230.9	1233.6	1234.1	1233.5
SO_2^1	346	291	260	226
$MWTP(SO_2)^2$	75.2	68.6	66.0	62.8

Notes
1. 10^3 tonnes.
2. SEK per kg SO_2.

Table 13.7.   *Policy design C: macroeconomic and environmental indicators*

	Base case	CO_2=60	CO_2=50	CO_2=40
GNI	1239.5	1238.8	1239.7	1236.9
ENI	1230.9	1234.2	1234.0	1233.4
SO_2^1	346	269	233	200
$MWTP(SO_2)^2$	75.2	66.9	63.4	60.4

Notes
1. 10^3 tonnes.
2. SEK per kg SO_2.

however, is considerably higher. This is an endogenous result, reflecting the built-in assumption that the marginal valuation of environmental quality increases when the environmental quality deteriorates, and the fact that SO_2 emissions increase between 1985 and 2000 in the base case.

Technical details about the definition of ENI are discussed in the Appendix. Here it is sufficient to stress the incompleteness of our ENI measure and the very preliminary nature of the numbers. Yet it is interesting to note that the environmental quality adjustment of national income amounts to less than one percent of GNI and thus does not significantly affect the aggregate measure of economic growth. The results summarized in the tables speak for themselves. Unilateral carbon taxation in accordance with policy design B seems to be a 'no regret policy' for all the policy objectives investigated; the loss of GNI is more than fully compensated by environmental quality gains. This is also true for the policy objective $CO_2=60$ under policy design A. However, it is also clear that reducing the target CO_2 emissions from 50 to 40 million tonnes per year produces a loss both in terms of GNI and ENI.

CONCLUDING REMARKS

It is a commonly held view that unilateral carbon taxation in a small open economy is both costly and ineffective; the cost of domestic adjustment is high and international 'leakages' are significant. The results of the analysis presented in this chapter suggest that both of these arguments might be wrong. The 'leakages' do not necessarily have to be big, and with a proper sectoral differentiation of carbon tax rates the cost in terms of full-employment national income might be small or even negative. This is particularly the case if side-effects on the emissions of other pollutants are taken into consideration.

These conclusions are based on the model analysis and apply to Sweden, a small open economy which happens to be specialized in carbon dioxide-intensive production. For a large country, as well as for a group of countries within a federation, with some influence on world market prices, the scope for unilateral action should be even wider. Yet even very skilfully designed unilateral policies are inferior to globally coordinated policies.

Finally a word of warning; there is an obvious risk of stretching the model results too far. It still remains to analyze and quantify various types of adjustment costs as well as the impact of carbon taxation on savings and investment decisions and productivity growth. Moreover there is considerable scope for improving our treatment of environmental benefits of emission reductions.

NOTES

1. See also Bovenberg (1993).
2. See Kriström and Wibe (forthcoming) for an account of Swedish environmental policy.
3. Technically the value of exports has been deflated with an export price index in the calculation of GDP, while it has been deflated with an import price index in the calculation of GNI. Thus the GDP measure reflects the amount of goods and services that has been exported, while the GNI measure reflects the amount of imports that can be bought for the exported goods and services.
4. It can be mentioned that almost 90 percent of the sulphur deposition in Sweden originates from foreign sources. As estimates of the 'risk-free' levels of sulphur deposition suggest that quite significant deposition reductions are needed, this means that the problem of acidification in Sweden cannot be solved by domestic emission reductions only.

REFERENCES

Andersson, T. and J. Åshuvud (1984), 'The Environmental Effects of Coal', (in Swedish), *Ekonomisk Debatt*, 2:107–15.

Barrett, S. (1991), 'The Problem of Global Environmental Protection', in Helm, D. (ed.), *Economic Policy Towards the Environment*, Blackwell, Cambridge, MA.

Bergman, L. (1991), 'General Equilibrium Effects of Environmental Policy: A CGE-Modeling Approach', *Environmental and Resource Economics*, 1:43–61.

Bovenberg, A.L. (1993), ' Policy Instruments for Curbing CO_2 Emissions: The Case of The Netherlands', *Environmental and Resource Economics*, 3:233–44.

Kriström, B. and S. Wibe (forthcoming), 'Environmental Policy in Sweden', in Desai, U, *Comparative Environmental Policy and Politics*.

Mäler, K.G. (1989), 'The Acid Rain Game', in Folmer, H. and E. Van Ierland, *Valuation Methods and Policy Making in Environmental Economics*, Elsevier Science Publishers, Amsterdam, The Netherlands.

APPENDIX 13A: MODELING ENVIRONMENT–ECONOMY INTERACTIONS

A.   Physical Measures of Pollution

Environmental damage is generally caused by the current and/or accumulated deposition of various pollutants. Typically this damage is multidimensional in the sense that the deposition of a given pollutant has an impact on a vector of environmental qualities. In general the components of this vector, or aspects of environmental quality, are differently affected as the deposition of a given pollutant increases. In the following it is assumed that at least one aspect of environmental quality is negatively affected by an increase in the current or accumulated deposition of a given pollutant, while no aspect is positively affected. Thus the environmental damage, caused by a given pollutant, say e at time t, is assumed to be an increasing function of the amount of current or accumulated deposition at time t, $D_{e,t}$.

The amount of deposition of a certain pollutant is a function of the emissions of that pollutant within a certain geographical area. For pollutants such as CO_2 that geographical area is the entire globe. The relation between emissions and current or accumulated depositions might be very complex, but here a simple linear relation is assumed. Moreover accumulation is disregarded.

It is assumed that for each type of pollutant there is a level of pollution at which the damage becomes clearly unsustainable or even catastrophical. The corresponding level of deposition is denoted $D_{e,\max}$. It is also assumed that for each type of pollutant there is a level of deposition, $D_{e,\min}$, at which an emission reduction would not produce any noticeable environmental quality improvement. A critical assumption in the following analysis, necessitated by the static nature of the model used, is that there is a range of sustainable levels of D_e between $D_{e,\min}$ and $D_{e,\max}$.

B.   Environmental Quality and Preferences

The key variable in the environment–economy interaction part of the model is an environmental quality index with respect to pollutant e, V_e. This index enters the utility functions of the households and it affects the productivity of resources used in the production sectors. Obviously environmental quality is a public good, i.e. V_e simultaneously enters a number of utility and production functions. The environmental quality index is defined in terms of the aggregate deposition of pollutant e, D_e, in such a way that environmental quality increases when deposition decreases. One way of doing this is to define the environmental quality with respect to pollutant e as the difference between $D_{e,\max}$ and D_e, normalized by the corresponding base-year value. Formally this becomes

$$V_{e,t} = (\frac{D_{e,\max} - D_{e,t}}{D_{e,\max} - D_{e,0}}) \tag{13A.1}$$

which implies that V_e is equal to zero when $D_e=D_{e,\max}$ and attains its maximum value, denoted $V_{e,\max}$, when $D_e=D_{e,\min}$.

Each household, h, is assumed to have preferences over a vector of private goods, x^h, and a vector of environmental quality indices, V. Several assumptions are made about these preferences. One is that if the level of deposition would become equal to $D_{e,\max}$, and thus V_e be equal to zero, the utility of other consumption activities would vanish. In other words it is assumed that the value of the utility function $u(x^h,V)$ is equal to zero whenever one of the environmental quality indices V_e is equal to zero. Another assumption is that there is a positive but diminishing marginal utility of environmental quality. In particular it is assumed that the marginal utility of environmental quality approaches zero as V_e gets close to $V_{e,\max}$.

Given these assumptions about preferences, the utility function of household h can be written

$$U_h = \begin{cases} u_h(x^h)\prod_e (\frac{V_e}{V_{e,\max}})^{\mu_h} & \text{when } V_e \le V_{e,\max} \\ u_h(x^h) & \text{when } V_e > V_{e,\max} \end{cases} \tag{13A.2}$$

On the basis of this utility function it is possible to evaluate environmental policy measures affecting the supply of private goods as well as the level of environmental quality in terms of equivalent variations (EV) or compensating variations (CV). Moreover, on the assumption that all households face the same price vector p and maximize utility subject to a budget constraint, a measure of 'environmental quality adjusted NNP', in the following denoted ENP, can be derived from a first-order linearization of the utility functions around a set of bundles of consumption goods and $V_{e,\max}$.

This measure can be written

$$ENP = p\sum_h x^h + \sum_h \sum_e m_{e,h}(\frac{V_e}{V_{e,\max}} - 1) \tag{13A.3}$$

where $m_{e,h}$ is the marginal willingness to pay for environmental quality related to pollutant e by household h.[1] Thus the last term on the right-hand side represents the adjustment of conventional NNP for the value, in monetary terms, of the environmental damage caused by the emission of pollutants. Obviously ENP and NNP attains the same value only when V_e is equal to $V_{e,max}$.

In order to simplify comparisons between the aggregate real output measure GDP and the aggregate real income measure, the latter is calculated as a gross income measure, GNI, in the model simulations. GNI is equal to NNP plus depreciation of physical capital, and consequently the model variable ENI is equal to ENP plus depreciation of physical capital.

C. Environmental Quality and Productivity

The impact of environmental quality on the supply of private goods operates through the productivity of resources, i.e. capital, labor, energy, raw materials and other inputs, in the production of private goods. It is assumed that deterioration of environmental quality reduces total factor productivity in production. One example of this effect is the negative impact on the total factor productivity in forestry of slower forest growth due to acidification. Another example is the increased need for costly maintenance of bridges and buildings caused by pollution-induced corrosion.

It is assumed that X_j, the output in sector j, is produced by means of a resource input vector R_j and that the productivity of these resources depends on the level of environmental quality. Moreover production leads to emissions of various pollutants, and as any reduction of these emissions at a constant level of output would require additional inputs of resources, the emissions can be regarded as a kind of input in the production process. Thus the production function of sector j can be written

$$X_j = f_j(R_j, E_{e,j}) \prod_e \left(\frac{V_e}{V_{e,max}}\right)^{\rho_j} \tag{13A.4}$$

where $E_{e,j}$ is the emission of pollutant e in sector j.

---

[1] The marginal willingness to pay for environmental quality is defined by the partial derivative with respect to V_e of the expenditure function implied by the utility function (13A.2). By appropriate rescaling this measure can be transformed into a measure of the marginal willingness to pay for deposition reduction.

14. The Implications of Learning About Uncertainty for United States/European Greenhouse Gas Policy

Charles D. Kolstad[*]

INTRODUCTION

The purpose of the conference was to investigate environmental issues that are common to federations, focusing on the EU and the US. In particular, with a hierarchical government and different levels of the hierarchy at which regulatory action can take place, we were concerned with the appropriate level for environmental regulation and how that regulation should be coordinated among levels of the hierarchy. Clearly this question of federal vs. local for environmental regulation is a very appropriate one. When environmental effects are felt in the vicinity of the source, those suffering the environmental damage are best positioned to control the problem. But when environmental effects are not localized, as with carbon dioxide and other precursors of climate change, centralized control may be more appropriate.

Certainly the effects of pollutants leading to climate change (however poorly understood) are not confined to the vicinity of polluters. In fact the climate is probably the purest of public goods with the effects from a single polluter felt worldwide. Consequently, the protection of the climate cannot be left to individual polluters or small jurisdictions. While the EU or US are major emitters of greenhouse gases (i.e., pollutants leading to climate change via the greenhouse effect), the problem cannot be completely solved by unilateral action by either of these unions. Certainly individual member countries of the EU or individual states of the United States cannot take unilateral action that can hope to make any contribution to solving the problem.

[*] Comments from Tom Ulen and Henk Folmer are greatly appreciated. Research supported in part by NSF grant SES 92–09943 and USAID-funded cooperative agreement DHR–5555–A–00–1086.

In fact, unilateral actions by Member States of the US or EU to control greenhouse gases would at best be futile and at worst be disguised policies for some other purpose, such as providing protection to domestic industries. There is a long history of environmental regulations conveniently protecting local industry.

The conclusion of this is that any action on climate change in the EU or US must be taken at the federal level. Because of this, I will focus on the commonalty between the US and the EU in facing the problem of controlling climate change. This is different from many of the papers presented at the conference but I think it is the appropriate tack to take in understanding the control of climate change.

The European Union (EU) has been considering the imposition of a fuel tax. Originally this was to be a carbon tax, but for a variety of political reasons, the tax became a hybrid energy tax, with different rates for fossil fuels and electricity. The US went through a similar though more modest exercise early in 1993. Although a carbon tax was never proposed, a tax based on the thermal content of fuels was offered early in the Clinton administration, only to dwindle to a small motor fuels tax.

Certainly the threat of climate change provided a major impetus to these actions to increase the cost of using energy. Just as surely, however, the uncertainty surrounding the connection between energy consumption and climate change led to the weak action ultimately taken to control emissions of carbon dioxide, a major precursor to climate change. However, one could argue that uncertainty would have the opposite effect. Given that the damage from climate change could potentially be catastrophic, risk aversion would have uncertainty inducing over-precaution with regard to control. Of course the political process is not this far-sighted and is unable to deal with such long-term risks.

If one looks at the political debate, uncertainty is combined with the view that next year or next decade we will know something more about climate change. In essence there are at least three actions that can be taken with regard to climate change control: action, no action and deferred action. This third alternative has received less attention in policy analysis than it deserves. It can be argued that this acknowledged learning about the problem is what is leading to the 'go-slow' on climate control. The view is that if a delay of a decade or two makes little difference to the effects of climate change and if our knowledge of the problem becomes much greater during that period, then it makes sense to delay action. Of course, another valid viewpoint is that irreversible climate change may be brought about by our actions over the next few decades and for that reason we should control the problem now and relax controls later if we learn that we were mistaken.

These views are supported by several analyses in the literature. Manne and Richels (1992) have analyzed the effect of accelerating learning about uncertainty, comparing resolving uncertainty today with doing it in 2020. They find very substantial values associated with accelerated learning. Schlesinger and Jiang (1991) have examined the climatic impacts for the year 2100 of a ten-year delay in controlling CO_2 and conclude the effects are small. Kolstad (1993) has examined the effect of learning about the disutility of climate change in the context of Nordhaus's DICE model and concludes that learning should induce a small bias towards under-control of CO_2 relative to the no-learning case. However, most of these conclusions result from economic models that are less than universally accepted as proper guides to national and international climate change policy.

The purpose of this chapter is to explore a common problem in the EU and the US: the difficulty in unilaterally imposing controls on emissions of greenhouse gases. Our hypothesis is that both bodies are taking the third route of delaying some action until more is known and reducing action that is taken now. This can best be appreciated by examining the effect learning about uncertainty should have on climate change policy. This involves understanding exactly what learning means in the context of climate change and, further, understanding the implications of learning for controlling a stock externality such as carbon dioxide.

In the next sections we will examine the underlying problem of how learning influences regulatory decisions, whether they be by the EU, US or others. We then return to our underlying problem of explaining EU/US reluctance to control greenhouse gases.

UNDERSTANDING LEARNING

At its simplest level, the economic process of 'producing' climate change involves emitting gases like CO_2 today in order to generate welfare today. Obviously CO_2 is emitted to make today's production of goods and services less costly. However, CO_2 and other greenhouse gases have very long residence times in the atmosphere – on the order of many decades. Thus actions today have effects over the long term. Accumulated greenhouse gases have the effect of trapping the heat generated by incoming sunlight, thus warming the earth. This accumulation of gases and warming eventually lead to climate change, causing disutility to future generations. The options available to future generations involve reducing future emissions of CO_2 or mitigating the effects of climate change; reducing the stock of CO_2 is not a decision variable and can only occur over time with natural decay of the atmospheric stock of CO_2.

list of uncertainty

Uncertainty is involved at each step of this process. There is uncertainty over the cost of controlling emissions of CO_2. There is uncertainty over future emissions of CO_2. There is uncertainty over how effective a multi-year program can be to control CO_2. There is uncertainty over how accumulated CO_2 affects climate. There is uncertainty over how climate affects man. There is uncertainty over what mitigating steps man can take to reduce the effects of climate change. There is uncertainty over the effect of climate on non-human biologic systems and the significance of those effects. In fact, the only thing we are certain about is the overwhelming uncertainty in climate change processes.[1]

Before discussing various types of learning, let us focus on the nature of uncertainty that might be involved with climate change. There are three basic types of uncertainty. One is that we are uncertain about the nature of the dynamic system called the climate/economy. We do not know the structural relationships involved in this system and do not know the precise way in which controls affect outcomes. A simple example is our lack of knowledge of the costs of climate control.

Another source of uncertainty occurs when the climate and economy are evolving with a random element. In this case, even if we knew exactly how the economy and climate operate, then because of random shocks we cannot know exactly how these two systems will evolve in the future.

A third type of uncertainty may arise because we are unable to observe what is happening to the economy and climate. Even if the climate and economy are evolving in a deterministic fashion, if we cannot observe the state of the economy or the state of the climate, then we have uncertainty about how to control the problem. Certainly we cannot perfectly observe the state of the climate, not only because our metrics are imperfect (e.g., hurricane frequency) but because the noise in the system makes it difficult to separate what is happening to the climate from what we observe. (For example: temperatures fluctuate widely from year to year; how can we detect an upward trend?)

Thus at the simplest level, think of the problem of determining the right level of emissions, e_t, leading to pollution stock, s_t, using regulations/instruments r_t. One wishes to choose regulations r_t to maximize utility with the evolution of the stock of pollution being influenced by emissions. To complicate things, one is not able to observe utility, emissions or the stock of pollution but rather noisy signals related to these variables.

Thus let the model be

$$\max_{r_t} \int_0^\infty E\{e^{-\rho t}U(e_t,\ s_t,\alpha,\beta)\}dt \tag{14.1}$$

subject to:

$$\mathrm{d}s/\mathrm{d}t = f(s_t,e_t,\alpha,\beta) \tag{14.2a}$$
$$g(r_t,e_t,\alpha,\beta) = 0 \tag{14.2b}$$

where one observes

$$a_t = h(e_t,s_t,\alpha,\beta,\gamma). \tag{14.3}$$

The α, β and γ are random variables that are associated with (respectively), the structure of the system, stochastic shocks to the system, and observational uncertainty. Equation (14.1) above is, of course, just the discounted present value of expected utility, with ρ the discount rate. Equation (14.2a) defines the evolution of the pollution stock s. Equation (14.2b) implicitly defines the economy's response in terms of emissions e, resulting from regulation r. And equation (14.3) defines the variable a that is actually observed – for instance actual global temperature.

The focus of this chapter, however, is not on the uncertainty but on our resolution of that uncertainty through learning. The first thing to clarify is what is meant by learning. This is a more subtle issue than one might expect. For instance, learning need not reduce uncertainty. Suppose one has a random variable with much of its probability mass around the mean but with quite large tails. If learning tells you that the variable is more likely to take on a value in one of the tails, then the posterior distribution on the random variable may very well have a much higher variance than the prior. This is despite the fact that in narrowing the variable down to one of the tails, one has certainly learned.

In the model above, one can hope to reduce the variability of α and γ through learning but β remains uncertain, although one could learn about its distribution. For instance, one can hope to eventually determine the average global temperature change associated with a doubling of CO_2. One might also learn how better to observe climate change. Such learning would reduce the uncertainty in these dimensions. However, to the extent that the economy and climate are subject to random shocks, that randomness can never be reduced.

What does one mean by learning? One way of categorizing learning is into active and passive learning. In active learning, one undertakes actions that can increase knowledge. In the model (14.1–3) above, one can consciously perturb r_t and note how a_t changes, inferring something about the underlying uncertainty of the model. Thus r_t serves two purposes: to control emissions and to yield knowledge about climate–economy interactions.[2] This is analogous to a monopolist facing an unknown demand curve. The monopolist can actively perturb price to learn about the demand curve as well as adjust profit levels (see Balvers and Cosimano, 1990). This view of learning applies equally well whether one is able to perfectly observe the state of the system or not. Perfect observation does not allow one to immediately determine the underlying distributions of the random variables. An alternate way of viewing active learning is as an investment: one can invest in an R&D process which generates information. This is a conceptually similar problem though it requires an expansion of the simple model of (14.1–3).

Passive learning, on the other hand involves the acquisition of learning without taking any action to learn. Such learning falls like manna from heaven and would most likely be associated with the passage of time. Although this might seem like a uselessly simple view of learning, it is in fact the dominant paradigm in economics. Technical change, for instance, is usually characterized as such a process.

These various types of learning may seem somewhat detached from the issue at hand – explaining the EU and US reluctance to act on controlling CO_2 emissions. The point is that the notion of learning is commonplace; but if one wishes to make progress in understanding its effect on regulatory decisions, then a more detailed understanding of the types of learning is required.

LEARNING AND IRREVERSIBILITIES

We now turn to the question of the effect learning has on today's decisions. In other words, in the context of equations (14.1–3), starting from the optimal choice of r in the presence of uncertainty but without learning, r_0, how does the optimal r *with* learning (call it R_0) differ? If $R_0 > r_0$, then learning tends to make regulations tighter; if $R_0 = r_0$, then learning has no effect.

There is quite a literature addressing the effect uncertainty has on sequential decisions. One of the earliest results, due to Simon (1956), is that when uncertainty is normally distributed, when utility is quadratic, and the problem is unconstrained, then the nature of the uncertainty has no bearing on the optimal decision. This is the 'certainty equivalence' result: the expected values of the random variables can be used in calculating the optimal action. If uncertainty has no role, then learning can have no effect on the optimal regulatory action. Malinvaud (1969) extended this result somewhat by relaxing the assumption on quadratic utility (almost any function will do) while tightening the restriction on the type of uncertainty (uncertainty must be 'small').

Around 1970, several articles appeared suggesting that when today's actions constrain tomorrow's opportunities, then the fact that one is learning about uncertainty should move today's decisions towards less of a constraint on tomorrow. Arrow (1968) pointed this out in the case of capital investment where once invested, capital cannot be uninvested. When one is uncertain and learning about that uncertainty, then one should underinvest today relative to the case of no learning. Arrow and Fisher (1974) and Henry (1974) extended this result to the case of environmental irreversibilities, such as building a dam to flood a unique natural environment (e.g., the Grand Canyon). They demonstrated that the simultaneous existence of such an irreversibility along with learning, reduces the otherwise optimal decision as to how much of the environmental asset to exploit. In the environmental economics literature, this value associated with learning has been dubbed the 'quasi-option' value.

And finally, in the early 1980s, Freixas and Laffont (1984) generalized these results somewhat by demonstrating that if utility in two periods is only a function of actions in each period and when today's actions constrain tomorrow's actions, then the faster one is learning, the more one should bias today's actions away from constraining the future.

IRREVERSIBILITIES AND CLIMATE CHANGE

We turn now to a similar issue in the context of global climate change. There are several types of irreversibilities associated with climate change. On the environmental side, the fact that climate change is brought about by the stock of greenhouse gases like CO_2 leads to an irreversibility. Once a ton of CO_2 is injected into the atmosphere, it is there to do its damage until it is removed naturally – people cannot emit negatively, reducing the stock of CO_2.[3] Another irreversibility has to do with the control of emissions of greenhouse gases. Any substantial capital that is sunk into the control of emissions cannot be uninvested if it turns out that climate change is not much of a problem. Just like the atmospheric stock of CO_2, capital only disappears through gradual depreciation.[4]

Thus we have two irreversibilities. The stock nature of CO_2 as a pollutant would suggest that we should under-emit CO_2 today (relative to no learning) if we are in fact resolving uncertainty about the climate. This of course is separate from any risk aversion that might induce us to over-control today to avoid catastrophic environmental effects. On the other hand, the capital irreversibility would suggest that we should under-control CO_2 today if we are learning about the problem.

One of the most widely used models for climate change policy analysis is the DICE model of Nordhaus (1993).[5] His model is a classic Ramsey-type optimal growth model with emissions facilitating output but eventually generating disutility, through a dynamic climate evolution model. In earlier work (Kolstad, 1993), I have reported on adapting the DICE model to a stochastic environment with learning. In that work, uncertainty is in the damages: one is uncertain about whether damages from an x-degree global temperature rise are large or small. If one gradually learns about this uncertainty over time, then the fact that one is learning may influence current decisions regarding emission control. While the climate dynamics are 'hard-wired' into the model (once emitted, CO_2 gradually decays), the irreversibility of emissions control capital can be considered a parameter. The extreme case is emission control capital being infinitely-lived. Figure 14.1 shows optimal 1995 CO_2 control rates (relative to no control) using the stochastic version of Nordhaus's DICE model. The horizontal axis is a passive learning parameter explained more fully in Kolstad (1993). In essence, $\lambda = 0$ is associated with no learning over time and $\lambda = 1$ is associated with very rapid resolution of all uncertainty. Values of λ between zero and one are associated with intermediate rates of learning.

Note from the figure that when emission control capital is fully reversible, then learning has no effect on today's decisions about CO_2 control levels. The apparent climate irreversibility is not an irreversibility at all, at least in terms of influencing today's decisions. The intuition behind this is that any 'error' in emissions today can be corrected tomorrow, before the effects are even felt. Since it is optimal to emit quite a bit of CO_2 over time (even when significantly controlled), this correction mechanism can always be invoked. In other words, an irreversibility only occurs when one *ex post* wishes to emit *negatively* but is constrained by the non-negativity constraint on CO_2 emissions. If the economy were such that zero emissions were more likely, then the irreversibility associated with stock externalities would be expected to be more obvious.

Perhaps an example will make this clearer. Consider an old-growth forest. Suppose we are not quite sure of the optimal ('sustainable') harvest rate. If we think an optimal harvest rate is ten trees a year, then erring and cutting twelve a year for a decade or two can be corrected by cutting eight trees a year for the following few decades. If one erred and cut two hundred trees a year for a few decades, then 'negative cutting' would probably be needed to correct the error. In the first case there is no irreversibility; in the second case there is.

Figure 14.1: 1995 GCH control rates vs. learning rates

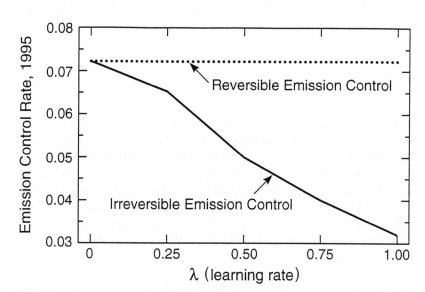

Contrast this situation with that of emission control capital. Here the possibility of wishing to invest negatively in emission control capital is very much more likely. Assume for the moment that emission control capital is infinitely lived. If learning tells us that the problem is much less significant than previously thought, then negative investment may be desirable but not possible. For this reason, Figure 14.1 shows that an irreversibility in capital induces under-control in the presence of learning. The more rapid is the learning, the less the control today, deferring investment in control capital until after learning has occurred.

Unfortunately, the theoretical literature does not have too much to say to help explain this problem. We have what appear to be conflicting irreversibilities. Environmental irreversibilities suggest over-control; control capital irreversibilities suggest under-control. Intuition would say that whichever effect is greater should dominate the result. To investigate this problem further, we have set up a simple three-period model where one can emit in either the first or second period. In the third period we reap damage from climate change. Let e_1 and e_2 be emissions in the first and second period. Furthermore, let s denote the state of nature, a parameter that indicates how severe is the damage from climate change. From the point of view of period 1, s is uncertain. The state of nature determines how severe is the damage from climate change. No learning will mean that the state of nature remains uncertain until the third period. Learning will mean that between periods 1 and 2 the true state of nature is revealed, allowing us to condition second-period emissions on the state of nature. The model can then be written as

$$\max_{e_1, e_2} \quad U[e_1] + \mathfrak{L}\{U[e_2(s)] + V[\rho e_1 + e_2(s), s]\} \tag{14.4}$$

such that $e_1, e_2 \geq 0$

where ρ is the rate of persistence of emissions in the atmosphere (1 − the rate of depreciation). Of course emissions cannot be negative. Utility from emissions (U) is increasing in emissions, reflected the fact that greenhouse gases are emitted because they make it easier to produce goods and services: more emissions, more goods and services. The disutility from emissions (V) occurs in the third period and is a function of the stock of pollution which is the first-period emissions, reduced by atmospheric decay, plus second-period emissions. Furthermore, we represent the irreversibility of the control capital investment by

$$\delta e_1 \leq e_2(s) \tag{14.5}$$

where δ is the rate of persistence of the capital stock. The idea is that whatever control capital is chosen in the first period must be utilized in the second period, less depreciation. The model (14.4–5) is as simple a model as can be developed which embodies the irreversibility associated with the environment and with control capital.

In order to shed some light on problems (14.4–5), we make some assumptions about functional forms and parameter values. In particular, assume utility is logarithmic and that $U(e) = \log(10+e)$, $V(x,s) = a(s)x^2$, $s\varepsilon\{H,L\}$ with $a(H) = 0.1$, $a(L) = 0.01$, prob(H) = 0.2 and prob(L) = 0.8. This is to simulate the two extreme cases where global warming is of high concern (H) in contrast to it being of low concern (L). In essence, there is uncertainty over the extent of damages from climate change.

The two learning situations we are comparing are perfect learning vs. no learning. In the case of no learning, the probabilities remain unchanged for the decisions in both the first and second periods. In the case of perfect learning, uncertainty applies to decisions taken in the first time period but decisions in the second period can be conditioned on the state of the world.

Figure 14.2 shows the results of solving this problem for a variety of different values of δ and ρ. Shown on the vertical axis in the figure is the ratio of first-period emissions with no learning relative to first-period emissions with learning. A ratio of one means that learning had no effect. A ratio greater than one means that the fact that one is learning tends to decrease first-period emissions. Similarly, a ratio less than one means that learning tends to increase first-period emissions.

Figure 14.2: Rate of emissions – Period One

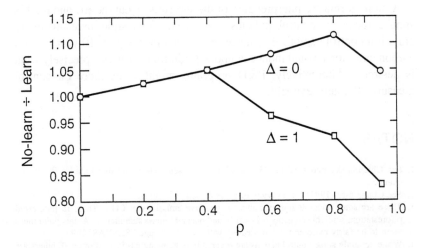

Intuition would suggest that when the environmental irreversibility is strong ($\rho = 1$) and the capital irreversibility is weak ($\delta = 0$), that the ratio should be greater than one. That is in fact what the figure shows. When the environmental irreversibility dominates, then the fact that one is learning tends to depress emissions relative to the no-learning case. The opposite, of a strong capital irreversibility ($\delta = 1$), shows lower emissions for no learning for high values of ρ. This is consistent with intuition, that higher emissions with learning are desirable because of the irreversible nature of control capital investment. In our simple model, the case of small ρ is less interesting. When ρ is small, the persistence of emissions is low which implies low damage and low control levels. At $\rho = 0$, there is no damage from pollution so there is no difference between the learning and no-learning cases.

SUMMARY

This chapter has examined a problem that is common to the EU and the US – the inability to reach agreement on effective CO_2 controls. Although this inability is commonly attributed to a lack of solid knowledge about climate change, we have tried to separate the issue of uncertainty from the issue of learning, which is arguably more significant than uncertainty. We have shown that learning with irreversible emission control capital investment might induce a 'go-slow' approach to CO_2 control and that such an approach might be optimal. This might explain some of the reluctance in the EU and US to adopt policies to control CO_2 emissions.

A more normative interpretation of these results is that the EU and the US should focus on control policies that avoid irreversible investments in emission control capital. For instance, a temporary (e.g. 5–10 year) tax on carbon emissions would induce temporary control measures – precisely what is desired. Alternatively, R&D programs might focus more on control measures that are reversible.

NOTES

1. See Chichilnisky and Heal (1993) for additional discussion of the uncertainties in climate change.
2. See Cunha-e-sa (1991) for a review of types of active learning.
3. There are some technologies available for negative emissions of CO_2. These include rapid reforestation, sunlight screening (of earth!), and ocean biomass stimulation. At this point these seem to be fairly extreme ways of dealing with climate change. See NAS, 1992.
4. While certainly some control actions are reversible (e.g., using gas instead of coal), others are not (e.g., using CO_2 scrubbers).
5. The Global 2100 model of Manne and Richels (1992) and the CETA model of Peck and Teisberg (1993) are two other major models of economy–climate interaction.

REFERENCES

Arrow, Kenneth (1968), 'Optimal Capital Policy and Irreversible Investment', in J.N. Wolfe (ed.), *Value, Capital and Growth*, Aldine, Chicago, IL.
Arrow, K.J. and A.C. Fisher (1974), 'Environmental Preservation, Uncertainty and Irreversibility', *Quarterly Journal of Economics*, 88: 312–19.
Balvers, R. and T. Cosimano (1990), 'Actively Learning about Demand and the Dynamics of Price Adjustment', *The Economic Journal*, 100: 882–98.
Chichilnisky, Graciela and Geoffrey Heal (1993), 'Global Environmental Risks', *Journal of Economic Perspectives*, 7(4): 65–86.
Cunha-e-sa, Maria (1991), 'A Review of Uncertainty and Learning as Applied to Stock Externalities', unpublished manuscript, Dept. of Economics, University of Illinois, Champaign, IL.
Freixas, X. and J.J. Laffont (1984), 'The Irreversibility Effect', in M. Boyer and R. Khilstrom (eds), *Bayesian Models in Economic Theory*, North-Holland, Amsterdam.
Henry, Claude (1974), 'Investment Decisions Under Uncertainty: The Irreversibility Effect', *Amer. Econ. Rev.*, 64: 1006–12.
Kolstad, Charles D. (1993), 'Looking vs. Leaping: The Timing of CO_2 Control in the Face of Uncertainty and Learning', pp. 63–82 in Y. Kaya et al. (eds), *Costs, Impacts and*

Benefits of CO$_2$ Mitigation, Proc. of Conference held at IIASA, Laxenburg, Austria, October 1992.

Malinvaud, E. (1969), 'First Order Certainty Equivalence', *Econometrica*, 37: 706–18.

Manne, Alan S. and Richard G. Richels (1992), *Buying Greenhouse Insurance: The Economic Costs of Carbon Dioxide Emission Limits*, MIT Press, Cambridge, Mass.

National Academy of Sciences (1992), National Research Council, Committee on Science, Engineering and Public Policy, Panel on Policy Implications of Greenhouse Warming, 'Policy Implications of Greenhouse Warming, Mitigation, Adaptation and the Science Base', National Academy Press, Washington, DC.

Nordhaus, William D. (1993), 'Rolling the "DICE": An Optimal Transition Path for Controlling Greenhouse Gases', *Resource and Energy Economics*, 15: 27–50.

Peck, Stephen C. and Thomas J. Teisberg (1993), 'Global Warming Uncertainties and the Value of Information: An Analysis Using CETA', *Resource and Energy Economics*, 15: 71–97.

Schlesinger, Michael E. and Xingjian Jiang (1991), 'Revised Projection of Future Greenhouse Warming', *Nature*, 350: 219–21.

Simon, Herbert (1956), 'Dynamic Programming Under Uncertainty with a Quadratic Criterion Function', *Econometrica*, 24: 74–81.

SECTION C

Tropospheric Ozone Pollution

15. Economic Assessment of Policies for Combating Tropospheric Ozone in Europe and the United States

John B. Braden and Stef Proost[*]

INTRODUCTION

Ozone (O_3) is a curious molecule. High in the stratosphere, it protects living creatures on earth by absorbing harmful ultraviolet radiation. The environmental issue with stratospheric ozone is its depletion by anthropogenic chemicals.[1] But, in the troposphere, the issue is the opposite – too much ozone due to atmospheric reactions of pollutants from combustion and industrial processes. Under certain conditions, ozone concentrations can rise to double or triple the normal background levels. At the elevated levels, ozone can be a major respiratory irritant and a significant health threat for persons with vulnerability. High concentrations of ground-level ozone also impair crops and trees.

Unlike stratospheric ozone depletion, which is a true global problem, excessive tropospheric ozone is regional in scope. The problem transcends local solution because the chemicals that form tropospheric ozone spread with wind currents up to several hundred kilometers, and because there are economies of scale in some of the abatement strategies that can be realized only with widespread adoption.

This chapter provides an economic assessment of tropospheric ozone policies in the United States (US) and the European Union (EU). Table 15.1 provides an overview of the current status of US and European Union (EU) ozone policies. The US has pursued a coordinated national strategy

* We appreciate the helpful comments of three referees and the guidance of Thomas S. Ulen, and we are grateful for the financial support of the following organizations which, however, bear no responsibility for the views expressed: the US Information Agency (University Affiliation Program agreement no. IA-ASPS-G1190234); the Illinois Agricultural Experiment Station, College of Agriculture, University of Illinois; the EC-PRIMES project of the JOULE II research program, Commission of the European Communities Directorate General XII.

of tropospheric ozone reduction for over two decades. While ozone concentrations have not gotten worse during this time, progress is uncertain at best. Europe, on the other hand, in recognition of the member country interrelationships in ozone formation, has only recently begun to consider coordinated action. US policies have emphasized reductions in one category of ozone precursors – the category of volatile organic compounds (VOCs) – while European countries have focused more on the other major category – nitrogen oxides (NO_x). Finally, ozone pollution is tightly linked to transportation choices and industrial development. The different industrial and transportation strategies of the US and Europe provide distinctive starting points for the pursuit of ozone abatement.

In discussing the US and the EC, we use the term 'central' with the national government of the US and the Community government of the EU in mind, and the term 'local' for US states and European nations and their respective subsidiary jurisdictions.

The chapter begins with a technical description of ozone formation and an overview of pollution trends in the US and Europe. Part III turns to a conceptual model of environmental policy in a federal system. The model deals with the issues of multiple sources, transboundary pollution, incentives to cooperate and policy uniformity, and it provides a framework within which to assess the ozone policies being pursued in the US (Part IV) and Europe (Part V). Part VI contains conclusions.

The dominant theme of the chapter concerns policy centralization and, hence, uniformity. Conventional economic reasoning yields a bias towards decentralized policies for regionally distinct problems. This bias must be balanced against insufficient abatement in the presence of transboundary pollution and against some potentially serious institutional barriers, information problems, and economies of scale in solutions. We show that, in many respects, current policies provide various forms of flexibility that help to minimize welfare losses due to centralization, and they also use centralization to overcome the impediments noted above.

TECHNICAL PROBLEM DESCRIPTION

A.   Tropospheric Ozone Formation

In the earth's troposphere, ozone forms from complex reactions of volatile hydrocarbons and nitrogen oxides in the presence of sunlight. Ozone is present throughout the troposphere due to the diffusion of relatively stable and durable organic chemical precursors, such as carbon monoxide (CO) and methane (CH_4). Organic compounds released by vegetative matter are

important sources of ozone (National Research Council 1992, pp. 8–9).
These 'biogenic' sources are largely uncontrollable. There is evidence that
the uncontrollable background levels of tropospheric ozone are increasing

Table 15.1: Comparison of European Union and US policies towards tropospheric ozone pollution

Ozone policy variable	European Union	United States
Ambient standard	Thresholds[a] accepted, but no Community-wide enforceable standard	Primary health threshold enforced nationwide[b]
Emission standards:		
Existing sources	Member state responsibility; no linkage to Community-wide thresholds	State responsibility; linkage to ambient standard through State Implementation Plans
New sources	Community minimum standards; justified by market integration	National minimum standards; justified by commerce powers and cost uniformity
Mobile sources	Community minimum standards for new vehicles; justified by market integration	National minimum standards for new vehicles; justified by commerce powers and increasing returns
Monitoring and enforcement	Member State responsibility; reporting required	State responsibility; reporting required
Precursor emphasis	NO_x–vehicles and combustion	NO_x–vehicles and power plants; VOCs–various sources

Notes
a. The Council of the European Communities in 1992 accepted the World Health Organization's (1987) recommended standards of: 110 micrograms/m³ averaged over eight hours as a health protection threshold; 180 micrograms/m³ averaged over one hour as an information threshold; and 360 micrograms/m³ averaged over one hour as a population warning threshold.
b. The nationwide standard is: 0.12 parts per million (235 micrograms/m³) averaged over one hour not to be exceeded on more than three days in any three year period.

one to two percent each year in North America and Europe (National Research Council 1992, pp. 22–29).[2]

Ozone itself cannot be directly reduced. It can be diminished only by reducing the reactions of the precursor chemicals. The controllable ozone precursors are those resulting from human activities. Because of biogenic emissions, reductions in the anthropogenic fraction produce less than proportional reductions of total emissions, and of ozone.

Table 15.2 panels (a) and (b) summarize the major sources of VOC and NO_x emissions in the US and Europe, respectively. The US and EU data are from different sources, so the criteria used to classify the emissions may not be the same. Transportation fuels are the leading source of VOCs followed by industrial and commercial solvents, and combustion processes excluding transportation. Unspecified 'other' sources are also quite significant, indicating that VOCs are emitted in a great variety of circumstances. NO_x emissions are byproducts mainly of the combustion of fossil fuels in vehicles, industry and power generation. The difference in the mix of NO_x sources in the US and EU reflects earlier adoption of auto emission controls in the US and less reliance on coal and oil for power generation in the EU. The 'other' category is relatively small for NO_x emissions, reflecting the concentration of emissions in a few types of sources.

The chemical reactions causing ozone are highly complex and variable, and the scientific uncertainty about them is great. The ratio of the precursors, not merely their total amounts, seems to be important. According to the National Research Council (1991, p. 7), when the VOC/NO_x ratio is 20 or more, NO_x is the limiting precursor and its abatement is likely to have the greatest effect on ozone formation. When the ratio is 10 or less, however, VOCs are limiting and their reduction offers the greatest potential.[3]

The relationship between ozone levels and concentrations of the precursor chemicals can be represented graphically by the use of iso-ozone lines called isopleths. Figure 15.1 illustrates isopleths generated by smog chamber studies. The axes represent the concentrations of both primary pollutants and the level curves correspond to different ozone levels.[4] Typically the isopleths are negatively sloped, indicating that the precursors are substitutes and are all warped to the origin at the critical VOC/NOx ratio: they are quasi-concave. This means that any linear combination of two $VOC-NO_x$ concentration combinations which are on the same ozone level curve yield a higher ozone level. At ratios of concentrations far away of the critical ratio, the isopleths may even become upward sloping. This means that when the ratio of VOC to NO_x is very small (a VOC-limited environment) reduction of NO_x can actually increase ozone formation. The particular slopes of isopleths create significant challenges for ozone abatement strategies and for economic analysis – a point to which we shall return. Nitrogen oxides tend to 'disappear' (i.e., become chemically non-reactive) more quickly than VOCs. As the precursors move downwind, then, their balance can change and the abatement strategy that will most effectively

Table 15.2. *Sources of VOC and NO$_x$ emissions, 1985, and percentage of total anthropogenic emissions[a]*

(a) United States

Volatile organic compounds		Nitrogen oxides	
Source	% of Total emissions	Source	% of Total emissions
Transportation	40	Transportation	43
Solvent evaporation	32	Power utilities	32
Industrial combustion and processes	12	Industrial processes	20
Other	17	Other	4

(b) European Community

Volative organic compounds		Nitrogen oxides	
Sources	% of Total emissions	Sources	% of Total emissions
Transportation	31	Transportation	54
Solvent evaporation	20	Power utilities	24
Industrial combustion and processes	5	Industrial processes	16
Other	44	Other	5

Sources: EUROSTAT (1991); National Research Council (1991, pp. 258–59) following Placet et al. (1990) and US Environmental Protection Agency (1989).

Figure 15.1: A typical ozone isopleth diagram[a]

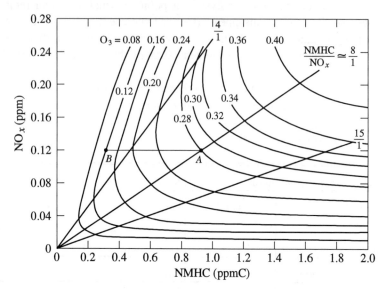

Note: a. NMHC is non-methane hydrocarbons.
Source: Finlayson-Pitts and Pitts (1986).

lower ozone may change as well, from one stressing VOC abatement in a VOC-limited source area to one stressing NO_x reduction in the NO_x-limited zone downwind.

Ozone concentrations are transitory. They vary because of changes in the mix of precursors and in meteorological conditions. High levels are especially associated with the sunny, warm conditions of slow-moving high pressure masses.

B.   Ozone Impacts

There are reasons to be concerned about both the long-term average concentrations and short-term peak concentrations of ozone. Long-term exposure impedes the growth of plants, including important tree and agricultural crops. It may also damage some important commercial materials, such as auto finishes and building façades. Short-term elevated concentrations of ozone are responsible for various types of respiratory distress in humans, including increased propensity to experience asthma attacks, coughing, breathing discomfort and irritation of mucous membranes. Of course, high short-term concentrations also contribute to higher long-term average concentrations.

Based on studies relating impacts to different exposure levels and lengths, the World Health Organization (WHO) (1987) proposed a range of maximum ozone concentrations.[5] Those recommendations are:

- as a health protection threshold (for protection against chronic health effects) – 110 $\mu g/m^3$ averaged over eight hours;
- as a health effect advisory threshold – 180 $\mu g/m^3$ averaged over one hour; and
- as a population warning threshold (for acute health effects) – 360 $\mu g/m^3$ averaged over one hour.

C. Trends in Ozone and Its Precursors

The concentration of tropospheric ozone is a random variable whose value is a function of precursor levels and uncontrollable meteorological conditions. Among the indicators of *peak* ozone levels are:
- second-highest one-hour ozone concentrations;
- concentrations not exceeded by some specified fraction (e.g., 99 or 95 percent) of observations;
- the 'design value' (the fourth-highest daily one-hour maximum concentration in a three-year period;[6] and
- number of days per year on which a particular concentration was exceeded.[7]

For the US, the evidence on peak ozone concentrations during the 1980s hints at improvements but is inconclusive. As an illustration, Figure 15.2 summarizes trends during the 1980s of the distribution for US cities of the second highest daily maximum hourly ozone concentrations.[8] The horizontal line in Figure 15.2 corresponds to the US ambient concentration standard for ozone. The annual distributions reflect readings taken from over 400 monitoring sites; those sites with readings below the line at least two out of every three consecutive years are in compliance with the US standard. What is most evident from the diagram is that the year-to-year fluctuations over this period outweigh any overall trend. The very hot year of 1988, in particular, confounds what otherwise appears to be a very slight downward shift in the distributions.

The number of US air quality regions failing to attain the US ozone standard declined continuously from 96 areas in 1982 to 63 areas in 1987, then increased to 101 in 1988 (a year of especially high temperatures) and 96 in 1989. Based on the years 1989–91, however, only 56 air quality areas violated the NAAQS for ozone (Freas 1993). Clearly, it is difficult to conclude anything about the trend.

Figure 15.2:   *Trends in annual second-highest daily maximum 1-hour ozone concentrations, 431 US monitoring sites, 1980–1991[a]*

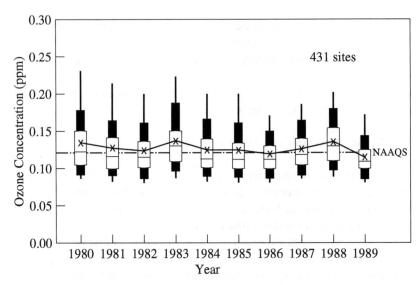

Note: The trends in ambient air quality, presented as boxplots, display the 5th, 10th, 25th, 50th (median), 75th, 90th and 95th percentiles of the data, as well as the composite average. The 5th, 10th and 25th percentiles depict the 'cleaner' sides; the 75th, 90th and 95th depict the 'higher' sites; and the median and average describe the 'typical' sites. For example, 90 percent of the sites would have concentrations equal to or lower than the 90th percentile.

Source: US Environmental Protection Agency (1991).

The US ozone picture is brighter when ambient concentrations are adjusted for exposure rates, expressed as rolling averages, or adjusted for weather conditions. The extreme temperatures in North America during 1988, in particular, and the resulting high ozone readings may have overshadowed an otherwise-downward trend. The South East Coast Air Quality Management District (1989) in California reports that three-year rolling averages of per-capita exposure hours to ozone above 0.12 ppm (235 $\mu g/m^3$) declined nearly continuously after the late 1970s, from 1.6 hours to 0.04 hours per year by the middle 1980s. The three-year rolling average number of days of Chicago ozone readings above 0.12 ppm, normalized for weather variability, also decreased nearly continuously between the late 1970s and the late 1980s, from about 25 days in each three-year period to about 10 (Kolaz and Swinford 1990).

In Europe, only in September 1992 was a harmonized ozone measurement protocol adopted.[9] The protocol will be implemented throughout the Union by 1994. According to Zierock (1989), the (non-comparable) data that are available suggest that ozone concentrations in most member nations regularly exceed 120 $\mu g/m^3$, a long-term health exposure threshold proposed by the World Health Organization (1987). The highest ozone concentrations are found in the middle of Europe – roughly along the Rhine River Valley.

For both the US and the EU, the reports on precursor emissions are more encouraging than those for ozone, but they are widely doubted. The US Environmental Protection Agency (1991) estimates that NO_x emissions declined by approximately five percent in the 1980s while VOC emissions decreased by roughly 19 percent, due mainly to lesser vehicle emissions. The underlying data are widely doubted because they do not correspond very well to observed ambient concentrations of the precursors, and they are based on methods that may systematically underestimate emissions (National Research Council 1992, Chapter 9). As a result, much uncertainty remains about actual emissions in the US and, consequently, the true relationship between emissions and ambient pollutant concentrations.

The European data do not support very definite insights into trends in EU ozone levels or precursor emissions, but they do suggest a general pattern of ozone stabilization over the past decade (Zierock 1989). The trends in precursors indicate absolute decreases in the last decade, particularly for VOCs. Figures 15.5 through 15.7 provide illustrative trends for the Netherlands.

ECONOMICS OF OZONE ABATEMENT

We start by discussing the optimal ozone policy of a central government when this government has perfect policy instruments and has perfect information. This will serve as a benchmark for the discussion of three alternative institutions to implement an ozone policy. These alternatives are complete decentralization, centralized control via maximum uniform ambient concentration standards and finally centralization via maximum uniform emission standards. These alternative institutions have been chosen because they are the archetypes of EC and US ozone policies.

A. The Model

We use a model with two states H and F which together form a federation. The actions of the states are controlled by local governments, and the actions of the federation are controlled by a central government. We use only two local jurisdictions in the model for notational convenience; we in fact implicitly assume that there are many regions. At the start, we will work with only one primary pollutant (i.e., precursor) and only one pollution problem (ozone). The case of two primary pollutants (like VOCs and NO_x for ozone) will be discussed later.

The states emit *pollutants* in amounts q_H and q_F. We will use as reference levels $q_H(o)$ and $q_F(o)$, the amounts discharged prior to any local or central regulation. The emissions are assumed to affect *ambient environmental quality* in H and F through a mechanism we describe as follows.

1. Pollution transport

Pollution is transported and decays during transport, the quantities of the pollutant still effective in H and F equal:

$$t_{HH}q_H + t_{FH}q_F \quad \text{for region } H$$
$$t_{HF}q_H + t_{FF}q_F \quad \text{for region } F \tag{15.1}$$

in this formulation t_{HF} is the share of total emissions coming from region H and active in F. Because of pollutant depreciation we will have for region H (and similarly for region F):

$$t_{HH} + t_{HF} \le 1 \tag{15.2}$$

2. Ambient quality

The emissions generate ambient concentrations z^H and z^F, respectively, for regions H and F, where the concentration z^H (and similarly z^F) is set equal to:

$$z^H = t_{HH}q_H + t_{FH}q_F \tag{15.3}$$

The ambient concentrations $z(o)$ correspond to the reference emission quantities $q(o)$ via (15.3).

The benefits of ozone reduction for each region depend only on its own ambient concentration. The *benefit function* for region H has constant marginal benefits (and similarly for region F):

$$B^H = b^H(z^H(o) - z^H) \tag{15.4}$$

where b^H represents the monetary valuation of the ambient concentrations and is positive.[10]

The *cost function* for each state is only a function of its own emission reduction efforts $(q(o)-q)$:

$$C^H = 0.5 \, c^H [q^H(o) - q^H]^2 \tag{15.5}$$

This cost function represents both the increased abatement costs and the resulting costs to consumers in output markets. We assume that the parameter c in (15.5) is positive, in which case the marginal cost of decreasing emissions is positive, linear and increasing. With a positive value for the parameter b, abatement increases benefits at a constant rate.

3. Governments

The governments have the following objective functions:

$$\text{Central Government:} \quad W = L^H + L^F \tag{15.6}$$

$$\text{Local Government in } H \text{ (similarly for } F \text{):} \\ L^H = B^H - C^H + T^H \tag{15.7}$$

where L stands for local welfare and T^H represents central government transfers or net side payments received from the other region. Thus, we assume that the preferences of local and central governments are 'consistent' in the sense that for matters which only concern the inhabitants of one region, the state government and the central government would make the same decisions if they have the same set of options. We assume moreover that the distribution of welfare will not be addressed through pollution regulation.

B. The Optimal Solution

We assume that the objective function of the central government can serve as a welfare function. An alternative interpretation would be to see the objective functions (15.6) and (15.7) as an expression of the relative power of the local governments in central politics.

First-best results are obtained if the decision-maker has perfect information and perfect control on emissions, q_H and q_F, in both regions. Then, the decision-maker can choose the level of pollution that balances costs and benefits and the mix of abatement activities that minimizes costs. Maximizing (15.6) gives the following first-order conditions for an optimum (superscripts here indicate the first derivative):

$$b\,^{H}t_{HH} + b\,^{F}t_{HF} = c\,^{H}(q_{H}(o) - q_{H}) \qquad (15.8)$$

$$b\,^{H}t_{FH} + b\,^{F}t_{FF} = c\,^{F}(q_{F}(o) - q_{F}) \qquad (15.9)$$

If we assume that government can costlessly redistribute income between states in order to meet distributional goals, we can then disregard the possibility for differential welfare weights on pollution in the different jurisdictions and concentrate on efficiency questions. The optimal emission levels equate the marginal cost of abatement in each region (the right-hand sides in equations 15.8 and 15.9) with the sum of the marginal damage in the region of origin of the emissions plus the marginal damage in the region to which they are transported (the left-hand sides of equations 15.8 and 15.9).

It is important to note that the optimal emission levels and the optimal environmental qualities will typically differ between the two states. There are several reasons for this. Disregarding transboundary effects, the optimal environmental quality could differ if benefits are mainly health-related (see footnote 9) and, *ceteris paribus*, one state is much more densely populated than the other. This gives proportionally higher marginal benefits of pollution abatement and higher optimal abatement. Similarly, if one state is much more industrialized than another and emits more pollutants, we can expect that it is much costlier to achieve the same environmental quality. Purely geographic factors (embedded in the z functions), like the Los Angeles basin that traps pollution, may also lead to differences in the optimal emission levels and environmental qualities.

Over and above the differences in local circumstances, the phenomenon of transboundary transport is another source of difference in the optimal emission levels and environmental qualities. If one region is downwind of the other (e.g. t_{HF} large and $t_{FH} = 0$), then everything else equal, the upwind region (H) should make greater abatement efforts which could be compensated by central government transfers. These optimality conditions are well known and easy to grasp, but they are difficult to implement as we will see when we discuss the different institutional situations.

C.   Extra Complications

Before examining different policy institutions, we first need to acknowledge and relax some limitations of our model. The model ideally would be extended in at least three additional dimensions in order to describe the ozone policy problem more realistically: first, to incorporate two primary pollutants rather than one; second, to introduce the stochastic nature of the ozone pollution; and third, to add the presence of returns to scale in production, making localized abatement policies more costly. These difficulties will be discussed here, but they will not be dealt with in the formal analysis of the alternative institutions to implement an ozone policy in a federal system.

1. Two primary pollutants

Ozone is caused by the interaction of NO_x (indexed n) and hydrocarbons (indexed v). In a more complete model, the ozone level in each region would be a function of the emissions of both pollutants in both regions (for H and similarly for F):

$$z^H = Z^H(t_{HH}^v q_H^v + t_{FH}^v q_F^v, \ t_{HH}^n q_H^n + t_{FH}^n q_F^n) \tag{15.10}$$

As explained earlier, equation (15.10) can be used to define iso-ozone curves. These are generally quasi-concave, but they can have peculiar shapes when the precursors interact in odd ways. For ozone, this happens when the VOC/NO_x ratio is low. The potential for peculiarity in this relationship can complicate the process of identifying an economic optimum.

Maximizing the objective function (equation 15.6) by selecting emissions of pollutants in both regions and taking into account the new definition of Z in equation (15.10) and the cost functions for each pollutant C^{vH} and C^{nH} in both regions, we have the following necessary conditions for the emissions if there is a maximum where both pollutants take on positive values (similar conditions hold for F):

$$b^H z_{1v}^H t_{HH}^v + b^F z_{1v}^F t_{HF}^v = c^{vH}(q_H^v(o) - q_H^v) \tag{15.11}$$

$$b^H z_{1n}^H t_{HH}^n + b^F z_{1n}^F t_{HF}^n = c^{nH}(q_H^n(o) - q_H^n) \tag{15.12}$$

These two conditions for each region equate for each primary pollutant the sum, over the two regions, of the marginal benefits of pollution abatement with the marginal local cost of abatement. This balancing of efforts over two pollutants is not the major problem brought in by using two rather than one primary pollutant. The major problem lies, rather, in the non-convexity introduced into the precursor/ambient relationship and, hence, into the optimization problem. Non-convexity means that the necessary conditions in (15.7) and (15.8) may not identify the best possible outcome. With non-convexity, it can be economically optimal to abate only one of both primary pollutants, but conventional analytical techniques will have a difficult time finding such a solution (Baumol and Oates 1988). The complication of non-convexity is illustrated in Figure 15.3 for the simplest case with one isolated state. The axes represent the local concentrations of both primary pollutants (emissions times transport coefficient). Point O is the initial point. The level curves (Z^0_H, Z^1_H,...) represent the ambient concentration levels in H (Z as defined by (15.10)) and implicitly also the level of benefits in H (the benefits are only a function of Z^H via (15.4)). These level curves have to be confronted with iso-cost functions, e.g. C^1_H, C^2_H, ... The iso-cost functions define the reductions in ambient concentrations of primary pollutants in state H which are achievable for a given total cost level.

The optimization problem, as regards state H, consists then of two parts: first, to identify the points where, for each iso-cost level, one obtains the lowest possible ozone concentration and second, to select the ozone level where the marginal cost of ozone abatement equals the marginal benefit. The first part of the optimization problem is shown in Figure 15.3.[11] The iso-cost curves are expected to be quasi-concave because the marginal costs of abatement for each pollutant taken separately are normally increasing.

Figure 15.3:   Optimal abatement mix and non-convexities

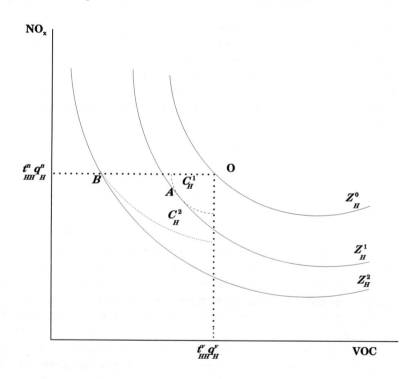

Looking for the lowest iso-ozone curve which is attainable for a given iso-cost level can then easily generate a corner solution (e.g., point B), but it need not be a corner solution (e.g., point A).

Repetto (1987) used the prospect of corner solutions as a possible justification for a difference in emphasis in regional abatement policies for the different precursors, NO_x and VOC. He furthermore argued on empirical grounds that the losses for deviations from the optimal abatement mix are small and, accordingly, that abatement policies should stress NO_x abatement because of its additional role as an acid rain precursor. Mayeres et al. (1993) extended Repetto's analysis by deducting the side benefits for NO_x from the abatement costs for NO_x. Mayeres et al. (1992) performed numerical illustrations including this corrected cost function to show that the loss function can indeed be nearly flat (increasing very slowly) around the optimum abatement mix but that it remains important to know the optimal abatement mix. The reason is that to take a policy of uniform percentage abatement for both pollutants as the benchmark might be far from the optimum and generate accordingly large losses. In other words, a flat loss curve in the neighborhood of the optimum does not release policy analysts from looking for the optimal mix of abatement.

2. Stochastic pollution

The matter of optimal abatement is also rendered more complex by the influence of weather. Ambient air quality is driven not only by emissions but also by wind and sun patterns. Thus, each level of emissions is associated with a distribution of ambient pollution outcomes. A common regulatory response to variable pollution is to set objectives that allow for a threshold and some frequency of exceeding the threshold (Beavis and Walker 1983). The frequency of exceedance is defined in terms of the number of times the threshold is crossed in a particular time interval, such as a month or a year. The threshold reflects a determination that some level is not harmful or, at least, is unavoidable as a practical matter. The allowable variation reflects the fact that outcomes cannot be fully controlled at a reasonable cost.

The threshold/frequency approach to stochastic pollution is subject, in general, to non-convexities (Beavis and Walker 1983). The problem is that the policy options (controlling the average and the variance of the different emission sources) do not comprise a convex set. While the abatement problem will still have an optimal solution (or several solutions that are simultaneously optimal), conventional analytical techniques will not necessarily identify it.

3. Increasing returns to scale in abatement

Another potential source of non-convexity is increasing returns to scale in production. Ozone policies are affected in two ways by increasing returns. First, certain abatement technologies are cheaper if used widely than if used only locally. The obvious example is technology to reduce auto emissions. Automobiles are complex, costly, mass-produced commodities. Automobile pollution control involves many different components, from fuel selection and fuel loading systems, to carburation technology and exhaust processing. It would be more expensive for manufacturers to adapt vehicles to differing emission requirements of many different jurisdictions than to adopt one standard abatement technology for all jurisdictions. The lower vehicle supply costs, to some extent, counterbalance the losses due to over- or under-abatement of vehicle emissions for particular local conditions.

The second manifestation of increasing returns to scale is in industrial agglomeration. Many industries can achieve lower costs when related firms are located in close proximity to one another and to suppliers (Krugman 1992). But, agglomeration may be accompanied by a concentration of the pollutants associated with a particular industry.   For example, this phenomenon certainly seems to fit the ozone problems associated with petrochemical facilities along the Gulf of Mexico and the Rhine River Valley. The costs of concentrated pollution must be balanced against the scale economies of agglomeration.

In both manifestations, economies of scale are yet another source of non-convexity in the optimal abatement problem. Markusen et al. (1993) have shown that pollution abatement policies in the presence of economies of scale in production can have sharply discontinuous consequences for industrial location and pollution levels.

D. The Decentralized Solution

We return now to the simple analytical framework with one pollutant and without non-convexities in order to discuss several archetypal policy institutions for implementing an optimal ozone policy. The first of the archetype institutions which can be used in a federal system is a decentralized policy design. The starting point is that all authority is with the local governments. We will examine mainly the non-cooperative solution which results from a game in which each locality responds naively and selfishly to the actions of the other jurisdiction. This formulation is known as a one-shot Nash–Cournot game.   Later we introduce the possibility of a cooperative solution as a result of a repeated game, of an interconnected game or as the result of a binding agreement between sovereign states.

1.   Nash–Cournot non-cooperative equilibrium

Here we assume that each region takes its own abatement decisions while considering the decisions of the other regions as fixed. This assumption is more easily justified if the ozone ambient concentration is the result of import of pollution from several other regions rather than just one neighboring state. Each region maximizing its own welfare will abate pollution up to the point where the marginal cost equals the marginal benefit within the region itself. This implies two types of inefficiency compared to the optimal solution. The first inefficiency is the absence of emission-abatement specialization between regions: the net cost of pollution abatement (adjusted for transport coefficients) is not equalized between regions.[12] The second inefficiency is the traditional externality problem: each region considers only the damages of pollution at home and not abroad. This means that, other things equal, larger regions, in which more of the pollution causes domestic damages, will have a purely selfish incentive to abate more than small regions, from which more of the pollution crosses the border.

To have a better view on the behavior and the suboptimality of the non-cooperative equilibrium, we will compare each institutional solution against the optimal solution that serves as benchmark. The quantities and values in the full optimum solution described in the previous paragraph are indicated with overline notation.

In this decentralized equilibrium, because of the constant marginal benefits assumption, the optimal choice of emission level for region H (and conversely for F) will not be a function of the level decided by region F:

$$b \,^{H} t_{HH} = c \,^{H}(q_H(o) - q_H) \tag{15.13}$$

$$b \,^{H} t_{FF} = c \,^{F}(q_F(o) - q_F) \tag{15.14}$$

Compared to the full optimum, the emissions will be greater because the jurisdictions do not take into account the benefits of reducing pollution abroad.

In order to make welfare comparisons of alternative institutions for our highly stylized cases (in an already highly stylized model), we adopt the following additional assumptions: identical cost functions ($c^F = c^H = c$) and benefit functions ($b^F = b^H = b$) and identical transport coefficients ($t_{HH} = t_{FF}$ and $t_{HF} = t_{FH}$) for the two regions. The difference in emission levels is then equal to:

$$q^{nc} - \overline{q} = \frac{bt_{HF}}{c} \qquad (15.15)$$

This results from combining (15.8) and (15.13). By using (15.8) and then (15.13) in (15.6) and (15.7), the welfare loss of the decentralized solution $W(nc)$ compared to the benchmark is:

$$\overline{W} - W(nc) = 0.5\frac{(bt_{HF})^2}{c} \qquad (15.16)$$

The difference in emission levels is directly proportional to the marginal benefit of transfrontier pollution and inversely proportional to the slope of the marginal cost function. Steep slopes for the marginal cost function limit the difference in emissions because, starting from the decentralized solution, increasing the emission reduction in order to take into account the damages abroad entails a rapidly increasing marginal cost.

The welfare loss in equation (15.16) corresponds to the 'welfare triangle' shown in Figure 15.4. That loss results when one jurisdiction ignores the foreign benefits realized from its abatement. Similarly, in a more general model with increasing marginal damages, a steep slope for the marginal damage (e.g., pollution rapidly becomes very toxic) implies that the non-cooperative equilibrium will already contain significant abatement efforts and will therefore not be too different from the optimal solution. Consequently, the welfare loss will also be less when the marginal damages are rapidly increasing.

2.   Cooperative solutions

Cooperative solutions can be either implicit, as the equilibrium of a repeated game, or explicit, as the result of a formal agreement between autonomous regions. When, as in the case of ozone, the different regions repeat the ozone game continuously, the different players can observe the actions of the other players and adapt their behavior. Although no formal agreement is made, a strategy where each region chooses a higher abatement level than the Nash–Cournot solution as long as all the others continue to do the same can be an equilibrium if future benefits are not heavily discounted relative to current benefits. The present value of such reciprocated cooperation can exceed the present value of all other strategies. The strategy must be backed up by means of penalizing regions that would defect from cooperation – perhaps with heavy loads of transboundary pollution. Unclear, however, are the mechanics of signaling the initial willingness to participate in de facto cooperation.

Figure 15.4:   Illustration of welfare loss in the decentralized solution

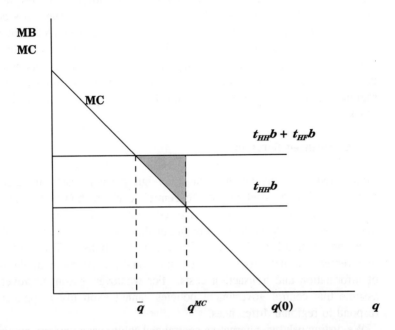

When autonomous regions can make binding agreements, more possibilities are open. These agreements have to be self-enforcing in the sense that each region by joining the agreement should improve its welfare: this means that the larger benefits of pollution abatement should compensate the extra abatement costs incurred by joining the agreement. Barrett (1991) has shown that for a given number of identical regions, the number of signatories will be higher with a lower ratio of the slope of marginal costs over the slope of marginal benefits, but that in this case the benefit of having added cooperation is small. This suggests that the participation will be more limited when environmental treaties are more important (that is, when they have a larger potential for welfare gain).

In some institutional settings, such as the European Union, the central authority can impose a cooperative solution only if all local jurisdictions agree. This unanimity requirement boils down to a participation constraint: the cooperative solution has to be designed in such a way that each of the regions does better with than without the agreement. Without agreement one returns to a Nash–Cournot non-cooperative equilibrium or a fragile repeated game equilibrium. The cost of this participation or unanimity constraint can be reduced if side payments (financial or in-kind) are allowed as an alternative to 'tit-for-tat' exchanges of abatement.[13]   When side payments are not allowed and the costs and benefits vary widely between regions, another way out is the bundling of different issues in one negotiation. If the benefits and costs of these different issues vary across states this enlarges the possibility of making a cooperative agreement through a trade-like arrangement involving reciprocal actions in different policy spheres (Folmer, van Mouche and Ragland 1993). If this bundling is not possible, an agreement to cooperate is extremely unlikely because regions with high abatement costs or low benefits of pollution control would block it.[14]

E.   Centralized Solutions

Centralized solutions begin from sovereign powers vested in a central authority. The possibilities of the central level are however limited by uniformity constraints. A uniformity constraint means, for our purposes, that the imposed (minimum) ambient standard or the imposed (maximum) emission standard applies to all local jurisdictions. The uniformity requirement can have its roots in constitutional provisions or be the result of information and transaction costs. For whatever reason, however, we assume that central government policies cannot explicitly recognize and respond to regional differences.

We distinguish two alternative centralized solutions: a uniform maximum ambient standard and a uniform maximum emission standard. In each case, we assume that the central government is fully informed about the costs and benefits in the different regions and tries to maximize welfare subject to the uniformity constraint. This is a Stackelberg setting where the local governments take the regulation of the central government and the emissions of the other regions as given and where the central government maximizes welfare knowing the likely reactions of the local governments.

For both centralized instruments, we are interested in finding the differences between the centralized polices and the optimal policy (this is the policy of an omniscient central government without the uniformity constraint), and the differences between the uniform centralized policies and decentralized policies. In all cases, we ask whether emissions are higher and what determines the extent of the welfare losses.

There are only a few studies on the welfare effects of centralized environmental regulation in a federal context. When we consider the ambient concentration as a local public good and there is no transboundary effect we can use Oates's (1972) decentralization theorem. He states that the welfare cost of an equilibrium with a centralized uniform level of provision of local public goods compared to an equilibrium where the level of local public goods is adapted to local preferences and costs is always positive in the absence of scale economies in production and in the absence of transboundary effects. In Oates's simplified model, the welfare loss is equal to the sum of the squared differences between the optimal uniformly-imposed level of the public good and the optimal locally decided levels of the public good. This idea can be transplanted to our setting except that we will consider as the regulatory instrument a uniform *maximum* ambient concentration. This makes a great difference because setting a maximum leaves an important role for states. In the case considered by Oates, a uniform maximum level is a much better instrument than a uniform level of local public goods because a maximum equal to the highest locally preferred level achieves a first-best solution. However, if centralized decisions are driven by electoral considerations, the uniform maximum may well be somewhere near the level preferred by the median voter, and probably below the level preferred by the median voter in the locality with the most tolerance for pollution. The welfare losses associated with uniformity would increase as more states are forced below their locally-preferred standard.

Kolstad (1987) discusses the welfare effects of *uniform emission regulations* where two firms each emit a distinctive pollutant. Although the damage of the two pollutants is different, in his model the government is constrained to apply uniform regulation in the sense that only the total amount of emissions can be controlled. The distribution of total emissions over the two polluters is governed by cost minimization (through a system of tradeable permits) and not by the relative damages. This model cannot be transposed to our problem with two polluting regions and transfrontier pollution. The basic difference lies in the behavior of the polluters. Kolstad assumes that firms would engage in emission trading so as to equalize marginal costs, and this assumption allowed him to concentrate on the total quantity of emissions as regulatory control variable. States, however, are not only interested in minimizing pollution-abatement costs but also worry about the damages of pollution in their state. States will thus behave differently from firms. As in Kolstad, we assume that the maximum emission limits imposed on a state are met in a cost-efficient way. This can be accomplished by the local governments using different types of instruments (tradeable permits, emission taxes) to meet the centrally-imposed maximum.

We will consider five stylized cases for which we will study the relative performance of the three institutions (decentralized, centralized maximum ambient concentration and centralized maximum emissions). These cases are: dissimilar states and no transboundary pollution; identical states (this means the same cost and benefit functions) and identical transboundary effects; identical states with one state downwind of the other; identical states and identical transboundary pollution, except that H has lower abatement costs; and finally identical states and identical transboundary but H has higher pollution damages.   The main results for these five cases are summarized in Table 15.3.

1.   No transboundary pollution

In this case the decentralized solution is by definition optimal (see (15.15) and (15.16)).   A regulating central government can make use of this property and set maximum ambient concentrations or maximum emissions above or equal to the maximum of the values obtained in a decentralized equilibrium.   Following Oates's decentralization theorem, the central imposition of uniform values of ambient concentrations or of emission regulations would always entail welfare losses.

2.   Identical regions and reciprocal transboundary coefficients

This case is characterized by the following assumptions:

$$t_{HH} = t_{FF} = t$$
$$t_{FH} = t_{HF}$$
$$b^H = b^F = b$$
$$c^H = c^F = c$$

We know that in this case the pollution abatement is too low in the decentralized equilibrium because the damage in the other region is not considered.   Since, in this particular case, the optimal solution contains identical emission quantities and identical ambient concentrations, the central government can obtain the optimal solution by setting the maximum ambient concentration or the maximum allowable emission rate equal to the optimal values.   Even without perfect information, the central government will know in what direction to go for both local jurisdictions.

3.   Identical regions and one region downwind

This case is particularly relevant for ozone.   The decentralized solution is inefficient because the exporting region H does not take into account the damages in F.   The welfare loss of the decentralized solution in this case equals expression (15.16) because only one region generates transfrontier pollution:

$$(\overline{W_H} - W_H(nc)) + (\overline{W_F} - W_F(nc)) = 0.5 \frac{b^2 t_{HF}^2}{c} \qquad (15.17)$$

Table 15.3: The efficiency of alternative institutions in a federal state

	Decentralized solution (nc)	Maximum emission regulation (q^m)	Maximum ambient concentration regulation (Z^m)	Uniform emission regulation	Uniform emission regulation
no transboundary effects	optimal	optimal	optimal	welfare loss larger with more diversity in benefits and costs	welfare loss larger with more diversity in benefits and costs
identical states identical transfrontier effects	optimal	optimal	optimal	optimal	optimal
identical states region F downwind	welfare loss proportional to transboundary damage	can always do better than nc	more difficult to improve upon nc – downwind state is forced to abate too much		
identical regions identical transfrontier effects region H has lower abatement costs	welfare loss proportional to transboundary damage	can always do better than nc	can always do better than nc		
identical regions identical transfrontier effects region H has higher damages	welfare loss proportional to transboundary damage	can always do better than nc	can always do better than nc		

The central government can always improve upon this allocation by using a *maximum emission regulation*. To see why we can use Figure 15.5. We start in panel 15.5(a) and see that the decentralized equilibrium (point *nc*) contains, for region *F* that does not export pollution, the same emission quantity as the optimal solution (point *Opt*). The idea is then to lower the maximum emission (along the 45° line in Figure 15.5(a)) such as to lower the emissions in the exporting state *H*. This will also pull the emissions in state *F* away from their individually-optimal values, but the cost of this deviation away from the optimum is lower than the gain in welfare by increasing q^H. The maximum emission standard q^m the central government can use satisfies the following equation:

$$b\,^H t_{HH} + \frac{bt_{HF}}{2} = c\,^H(q_H(o) - q_H^m) \tag{15.18}$$

This equation can be compared to the optimal solution (15.8) and the decentralized equilibrium (15.13). The welfare loss of this type of regulation is exactly half the welfare loss in the decentralized solution (15.16).

Improving the *nc* solution by regulating the *maximum ambient concentration* is not always possible. In Figure 15.5(b) the location of point *nc* means that the ambient quality is better in the exporting region *H* than in the importing region *F*. The optimal solution also contains better ambient quality for *H* than for *F*. With the maximum ambient quality instrument Z^m, the central government can achieve all points on the segment *nc,B,A* and *nc,B,A* in Figures 15.5(b) and 15.5(a). Segment *nc,B* is not interesting because it forces the importing state *F* to reduce emissions below its optimum value while leaving unaffected the excessive emissions in the exporting region *H* (horizontal segment *nc,B* in Figure 15.5(a)). It is only on segment *AB* that region *H* is forced to lower its emissions. Points on this segment could be better than the decentralized equilibrium, but they need not be.

In conclusion, regulation of the maximum ambient concentration in this case can either fail to improve upon the decentralized equilibrium or it can improve on the situation with a strategy where the pollution-importing region is forced to reduce its emissions disproportionally.

4.   Identical regions and coefficients, but different costs

Here we assume that region *F* has $\alpha > 1$ larger costs than region *H*. In the decentralized solution, emissions are excessive in both states. Emissions in region *H* are lower than in region *F* because *H* has lower abatement costs. The optimal emissions are lower than in the decentralized solution. In Figure 15.6(a), the point *Opt* is always southwest of the point *nc*.

Figure 15.5:   *Optimal central regulation of maximum emissions (q^m) or*
                  maximum ambient concentrations (Z^m)

           Case: Identical regions and region F downwind of H

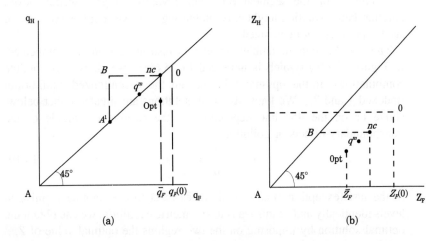

(a)   (b)

Figure 15.6:   *Optimal central regulation of maximum emissions or*
                  maximum ambient concentrations

           Case: Identical regions and lower costs in region H

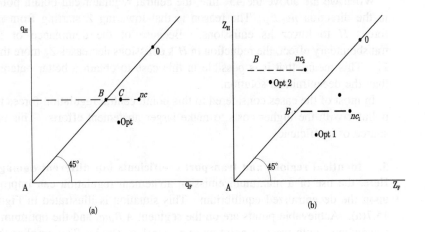

(a)   (b)

The preceding observation is sufficient to conclude that the central government can always improve the decentralized equilibrium via a limit on maximum emissions. The points achievable through this type of regulation are indicated on Figure 15.6(a) by the segment A,B,nc. There exists at least one point C on the segment B,nc which yields a higher welfare level. Another better solution might exist on the segment AB, but the existence of such a point is not guaranteed.

The use of maximum ambient regulatory instrument is more complicated. In Figure 15.6(b) (which is unrelated to 15.6(a)), we show two possible combinations of the optimal solution and the decentralized equilibrium (indexed 1 and 2). We know that both solutions are situated either below, above or on the 45° line depending on the relative magnitude of the transboundary effects of pollution:

$$t + t_{FB}\frac{1}{\alpha} \geq \frac{t}{\alpha} + t_{FB} \tag{15.19}$$

In the last (exceptional) case, both states react to one another's emission levels identically and, if this leads to symmetric equilibria, we can obtain the optimal solution by imposing on the two regions the optimal value of Z.

When we are below the 45° line in Figure 15.6(b), the nc_1 solution can be improved. Regulation of the maximum ambient concentration means that solutions on the segment nc_1,B_1,A can be reached. There exists always a point such as C where region F is forced to lower its emissions and where emissions in region H are not affected. This implies that a better solution can be reached.

When we are above the 45° line, the central regulator can obtain points in the direction nc_2,B_2. The reason is that lowering Z starting from nc_2 forces H to lower its emissions. Because of the dominance of the transboundary effect, the reduction in H's emissions decreases Z_F more than Z_H. This means that it is possible in this case to obtain a better outcome than the decentralized solution.

In most of the cases considered to this point, central regulation forces the polluter with the higher costs to make larger abatement efforts. This is a source of inefficiency.

5.   Identical regions and transport coefficients but different damages
Here, the use of a maximum emission abatement regulation can improve upon the decentralized equilibrium. This situation is illustrated in Figure 15.7(a). Achievable points are on the segment A,B,nc, and the optimum is somewhere south-west of point nc (e.g., *Opt*1 or *Opt*2). This implies that there is at least a point C and may be a point E which do better than nc.

To discuss the effectiveness of a maximum ambient regulation, we need to take into account that the decentralized equilibrium and the optimal solution need not be on the same side of the 45° line. The condition for point *nc* point to be below the 45° line is that the marginal benefit in region *F* equals α (<1), which is the marginal benefit in region *H*), i.e.:

$$t + t_{FH}\alpha > t\alpha + t_{FH} \tag{15.20}$$

The condition to have a lower optimal ambient concentration in state *H* is:

$$(t + t_{FH}\alpha) (1 - \frac{t_{FH}}{t}) > (t\alpha + t_{FH}) (1 - \frac{t_{FH}}{t}) \tag{15.21}$$

In Figure 15.7(b) (which is unrelated to Figure 15.7(a)), we illustrate the two cases. Using similar reasoning as above, one can show that the optimal solution is always southwest of the corresponding *nc* solution (nc_1 or nc_2). In this case, a maximum ambient concentration regulation along the paths nc_1, B, A or the direction nc_2, B' will improve upon the decentralized solution.

Figure 15.7:   *Optimal central regulation of maximum emissions or maximum ambient concentrations*

Case: Identical regions and higher damages in region H

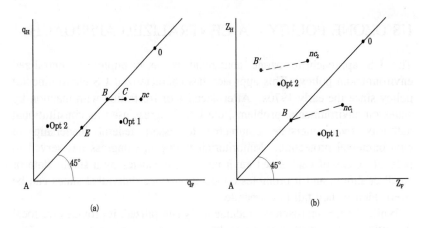

(a)   (b)

6. Extensions

The model used above is highly simplified. We could extend the model by dropping the constant marginal damage assumption. This would make the analysis of central regulation more difficult because each region would then always react when emissions change in the other region. A second extension of interest concerns the use of other regulatory instruments for the central government, such as the control of total emissions by both states, as analyzed by Kolstad (1987). Finally it could be of interest to study the relative gains and losses of the two states for the different institutions and link this to the information needs of the central government (preference revelation issues).

7. A note on information and monitoring

We have neglected up to now the issues of information, monitoring, and enforcement. The issue of information is particularly important to optimize the centralized solutions via maximum emission or maximum ambient concentration regulation and is also at the heart of the uniformity constraint faced by the central government. The monitoring of maximum ambient concentration standards seems to raise more problems than the monitoring of the maximum emission standards in the case of transfrontier pollution. The reason is that the non-respect of the maximum ambient concentration level can be attributed to insufficient local abatement or to an increase of imported emissions.

US OZONE POLICY – A CENTRALIZED APPROACH

The US approach to ozone abatement is an example of centralized environmental policy. This approach has characterized US environmental policy since the early 1970s. After decades of frustration with inaction by states on environmental problems, the US Congress used its constitutional authority over interstate commerce to assert federal leadership in environmental protection. Majoritarian voting in Congress has served to prevent vetoes of centralized environmental mandates by a single state or small coalition, and it promotes cooperation since individual states can be overridden if they fail to cooperate.

While the US approach is fundamentally centralized, it provides for local discretion and variation in some key aspects of implementation. This discretion has the potential to reduce the inefficiencies associated with centralization and uniformity.

In this section, we first review the ozone provisions of the Clean Air Act (CAA), including its amendments since 1970, then we review benefit–cost studies of US ozone-abatement objectives and assess the US approach from the perspective of economic federalism.

A.   Clean Air Act[15]

1.   Ambient standard

The Clean Air Act Amendments of 1970 established National Ambient Air Quality Standards (NAAQS) for conventional air pollutants, including ozone. Each state must formulate a State Implementation Plan (SIP) that establishes policies that will cause air quality to meet or exceed the NAAQS.

The NAAQS allow an '"adequate margin of safety" against adverse health effects' (Portney 1990, p. 20).   The NAAQS for total photochemical oxidants is 0.12 ppm/hr (235 $\mu g/m^3$) not to be exceeded more than three days in a three-year period.   Local governments may declare stricter standards, but the only one to do so is California, with its standard of 0.09 ppm (176 $\mu g/m^3$). The NAAQS for ozone is not attained in many parts of the US, especially Southern California.

The CAA also prohibits significant deterioration of air quality in areas with air that already meets or exceeds the ambient air quality standards. This diminishes the opportunity to create pollution havens in attainment areas and keeps the NAAQS from becoming a lowest common denominator for all regions.

For purposes of determining compliance with the CAA, the US is divided into air quality control regions (AQCRs). Since 1990, air quality regions have been categorized according to their design values. Regions with higher design values have more time to reach the NAAQS, but their SIPs must contain more aggressive abatement measures.   The key provisions are summarized in Table 15.4. The compliance deadlines range from 1993 for regions only marginally above the standard to 2010 for Los Angeles. All but the marginal regions must by 1996 achieve at least a 15 percent reduction of VOC emissions from 1990 levels.

An air quality region can achieve attainment status if it meets the NAAQS, the SIP is approved by the central government, and the region has a 10-year compliance plan.

2.   Emissions

To properly assess US ozone policy, it is important to understand in more detail the regulation of ozone precursor emissions. The emission provisions make it possible to tailor the policy's application to different circumstances.

Table 15.4:   Milestones and SIP requirements for ozone non-attainment areas[1]

Category	Attainment period from 1990	Reasonable further progress	Size of major source (tons per year)	Minimum offsets
Marginal	3 years	none	100 TPY	1.1 to 1
Moderate	6 years	15% in 6 years	100TPY	1.15 to 1
Serious	9 years	15% in 6 years plus 3% per year thereafter	50 TPY	1.2 to 1
Severe	15–17 years	15% in 6 years plus 3% per year thereafter	25 TPY	1.3 to 1 (1.2 to 1 + BACT)
Extreme	20 years	15% in 6 years plus 3% per year thereafter	10 TPY	1.5 to 1 (1.2 to 1 +BACT)
Transport Region	per attainment category	per attainment category	50 TPY	1 to 1

Note: 1. The categories also must meet different technical requirements for abatement in their SIPs, with more costly requirements generally reserved to the worse areas. See the source for details.

Source: Garrett and Winner (1992, p. 10185).

The key distinctions are between new and existing sources and between stationary and mobile sources. All new (or substantially modified) stationary sources, such as industrial facilities and power plants, and all new motor vehicles are subject to standards set by the central government. Called 'New Source Performance Standards' (NSPS), they apply without regard to location. All existing sources, on the other hand, are subject to emission requirements set by local governments as part of their State Implementation Plans. In areas where the nationwide ambient standard is not being met, the local emission standards must equal or exceed the 'Reasonably Available Control Technologies' (RACT) identified through central government research on cost-effective remediation.

Thus, the US approach treats new polluters within an industry the same way, irrespective of location. New sources in different industries can be treated differently, if the costs of abatement warrant it. Existing sources are treated differently by industry type and location.

VOC precursor emission standards generally do not vary with the season, in spite of the pronounced seasonality of high ozone concentrations in all but the more southerly locations. This feature has the effect of shifting the whole distribution of ozone concentrations throughout the year, in addition to truncating the higher tail of the distribution in the most ozone-prone months, as the NAAQS essentially requires.

With industrial and commercial progress, new sources gradually replace the old. So, in the US system, local discretion and variation gradually give way to centrally-prescribed performance standards for emissions. For non-attainment areas, the CAA requires that any new emissions be offset with more than proportionate reductions from existing sources. The offset ratios vary from 1.1 (existing):1 (new) in areas marginally out of compliance to 1.5:1 in the areas with the highest design values. New sources can, and on occasion do, buy ozone reductions from other sources.

The regulations for stationary sources apply to only those sources whose VOC emissions exceed a threshold. The threshold declines from 100 tons/year of VOCs in marginal areas to 10 tons/year in the most polluted areas.

The 1990 Amendments to the CAA recognized the peculiar chemistry of ozone formation by providing that NO_x emissions should be reduced along with VOCs unless the reduction of NO_x would diminish air quality.

3. Division of responsibility

The responsibility for achieving the air quality standards is divided between the central government and local governments. The central government has six areas of responsibility:

1. setting the ambient air quality standards that apply in all localities;
2. conducting basic scientific and economic research on environmental quality and abatement strategies;
3. establishing uniform emission limits for all new stationary-source polluters and motor vehicles;
4. establishing common measurement protocols;
5. providing funds for local environmental control programs; and
6. reviewing and approving the compliance plans developed by local governments.

Local governments have four areas of responsibility:

1. creating detailed action plans ('State Implementation Plans' – SIPs) for meeting the ambient air quality standards;
2. establishing controls on the emissions of existing sources as needed to carry out the SIPs;

3. monitoring emissions and air quality levels with reports to the central government; and
4. enforcing emission standards for polluters.

Clearly, the central and local authorities depend on one another. The central authorities set the basic air quality standards while local authorities monitor air quality levels. The central authorities establish emission limits for new polluters (both mobile and stationary) and conduct cost-effectiveness research on retrofit technologies for existing sources while local authorities, subject to central approval, decide on the limits for existing sources. Central authorities enforce ambient standards while local authorities enforce emission standards.

The interdependence presents classical problems of coordination and incentive compatibility. The central government attracts cooperation from local units by subsidizing the cost of operating local environmental protection authorities, and it discourages non-cooperative behavior through several types of sanctions. If the local area fails to submit an acceptable implementation plan, then the central government can write one instead. If the local area fails to attain the centrally-determined standards by the statutory deadline, the central government can cut off funds that otherwise would be given for highway construction and maintenance, it can raise barriers to new industrial and commercial development, and it can force the area to meet even more stringent abatement requirements. If particular sources are found to be out of compliance, the Act authorizes fines of up to $25,000 per day plus the economic benefit of non-compliance to the sources.

4. Transboundary pollution

There are four major clusters of non-attainment areas in the US: the north-east corridor from Virginia to Maine, with 21 areas; California, with eight; the gulf coast of Texas and Louisiana, with seven; and the Lake Michigan area, with five (OTA 1991, p. 24). Ozone precursor movement is thought to be significant in these areas. State and local officials believe that the transport of pollution from upwind sources is a serious limitation to their ability to achieve ozone reductions (OTA 1991, p. 35).

The CAA provides that local jurisdictions sharing an ozone non-attainment area must develop joint plans for coming into compliance. (Of course, transboundary pollution may also be a problem in attainment areas, but presumably the cost and benefit implications are less serious there.) The central government or local jurisdictions may establish an 'ozone transport region'. Within such a region, at least minimal non-attainment requirements can be applied in attainment areas as well as non-attainment areas, irrespective of whether an individual jurisdiction is upwind or downwind

(Garrett and Winner 1992, p. 10179). One such region, encompassing the area from the District of Columbia and Pennsylvania to Maine, was created in the 1990 CAA amendments.

B. Benefits and Costs of Ozone Reduction in the US

We have mentioned several sources of non-convexity in the case of ozone, including the use of threshold regulation for a stochastic pollutant and the complex relationships between ozone and its precursor chemicals. These difficulties profoundly complicate the identification of a first-best optimum concentration. Most policy discussions are of the second-best benefit–cost type, looking at specific abatement proposals rather than attempting to identify a best concentration.

In anticipation of legislation to amend the Clean Air Act, several studies of ozone policies were commissioned in the late 1980s (OTA 1991; National Research Council 1992). Rather than taking the approach of identifying a level of ozone abatement beyond which the added benefits would exceed the costs, these studies all evaluated a specific level of abatement of one precursor – a 35 percent reduction of VOC emissions below levels of the late 1980s.

1. Benefits

Studies of the benefits of ozone reduction fit into two distinct categories: those that consider health impacts, and those that consider crop impacts. Since US emission limitations tend to reduce both average and peak concentrations, both types of benefits should be realized.

Consider first the health benefits. Krupnick and Portney (1991) place the annual health benefits of a 35 percent reduction in US VOC emissions at between $250 million and $1 billion. The estimates are based on studies of the willingness to pay for relief from the symptoms of acute ozone exposure. Only benefits in non-attainment areas are included. The lower estimate of Krupnick and Portney derives from statistical associations in epidemiological studies; the higher estimate is based on extrapolations from clinical studies.

A different picture emerges from the research of Hall et al. (1992) on the health benefits of ozone reduction in Southern California. This study was completed after the one by Krupnick and Portney, so the authors were able to comment on the differences. As the air quality control region most troubled by ozone pollution, Southern California both warrants a closer look and should exhibit greater benefits of abatement than most other regions. Not surprisingly, Hall and her colleagues arrived at higher estimates of the average willingness to pay for relief from symptoms than Krupnick and

Portney. Furthermore, Hall et al. evaluated symptoms associated with O_3 concentrations as low as 0.08 ppm, rather than stopping at the 0.12 ppm standard. Their basin-wide health benefit estimates for ozone attainment were between \$1.2 and \$5.8 billion, with a 'best' estimate of \$2.7 billion. Curiously, the totals of Hall et al. for Southern California are considerably higher than the *nationwide* estimates of Krupnick and Portney.[16]

A 35 percent reduction in VOC should shift the entire distribution of ozone concentrations. Hence, crop yields also should improve. Adams et al. (1986) found that a 10 percent nationwide reduction in O_3 would have an economic value of \$0.7 billion (1980 dollars) and a 25 percent reduction would add \$1.7 billion. The 35 percent reduction in VOCs proposed in the OTA study would achieve a less than proportional reduction in ozone – probably between 10 and 25 percent – so the crop-loss value translated into 1990 dollars is on the order of \$1 billion to \$2.5 billion. Some of these benefits have already been realized from VOC abatement during the 1980s. But, the study provides an order-of-magnitude sense of the benefits of further abatement.

In conclusion, the available studies indicate that the nationwide acute health and crop productivity benefits of a 35 percent reduction in VOC are in the range of \$1.5 billion to \$5 billion per year. The estimates would increase if it turns out that long-term exposure to ozone can produce chronic health effects and if damages to trees were evaluated.

2.   Costs

Now, we turn to the costs of ozone abatement – more particularly, VOC abatement. The US nationwide total cost estimates for the suggested 35 percent reductions in VOC emissions, again from Krupnick and Portney (1991), range from \$8.8 billion to \$12 billion annually. The cost estimates are based on the most cost-effective abatement technologies for VOCs, excluding limits on driving. Those technologies included further emissions controls for automobiles and trucks as the cheapest means of reducing both VOCs and NO_x. Added controls on stationary sources are somewhat more expensive – a 25 percent reduction in VOCs below 1985 levels can reportedly be obtained for around \$2 billion, about one quarter the cost of a 35 percent reduction. The costs escalate rapidly above the 25 percent level.

Two limitations of the preceding estimates warrant special mention. First, the cost estimates focus on VOC abatement only. More modest reductions of VOCs along with complementary reductions of NO_x might reduce O_3 more cheaply. Second, the cost estimates for VOC reduction are probably more thorough, in the sense of including all relevant economic values, than are the benefit estimates.   Thus, the benefits are more likely to be underestimates than the costs.

Bearing in mind these limitations, for the US as a whole, the estimated costs of a 35 percent reduction in VOC exceed the quantifiable benefits, even when agricultural impacts and the health benefits of sub-NAAQS ozone levels are included. From place to place, however, the balance may be more or less favorable. Areas such as Southern California have already moved far up the cost curve while elsewhere reductions may be possible at more modest cost. Many of the benefits could probably be achieved and most of the costs avoided with a goal of 25 percent reduction rather than the 35 percent goal used in the aforementioned studies, yet in a few areas, more than 35 percent abatement may be justifiable. The fact that the 1990 CAA Amendments put forward only a 15 percent reduction in VOCs as a basic requirement within three years for all non-attainment regions suggests that the questionable economics of a much more ambitious goal were taken seriously. Of course, many of the non-attainment areas will eventually be required to implement reductions greater than 15 percent.

C.   US Ozone Policy and Economic Federalism

Three aspects of the US division of authority over ozone policy are of particular interest: 1) the uniform application of a centrally-determined ambient standard; 2) the division between the central and local governments of competencies over emissions; and 3) the incentive compatibility of measures for coordinating central and local competencies.

1.   Ambient standard
The use of a uniform ambient standard to protect against acute health effects is particularly difficult to justify on economic grounds because ozone problems are, in most respects, regional in scale. Uniformity may be appropriate within a region – indeed, it may be unavoidable – but it is less clear that Phoenix and Philadelphia, or any two cities, should be held to the same standard because it is entirely possible that the local preferences and costs differ from place to place. People and businesses choose to locate in different places, in part, because of differences in the local amenities.

A central tenet of economic federalism is that economic well-being can be enhanced by allowing local jurisdictions to differ to the extent that preferences and costs of production differ. The process of movement and wage adjustment should, over time, bring communities in line – not the same, but each with its own mix of qualities. Of course, not everyone can move. When workers move to get away from an undesirable location, the supply of workers shrinks relative to the demand and wages must increase to attract more workers. And, when too many move in to enjoy a desirable location and supply exceeds demand, employers can pay less. These consequences usually spread to the immobile workers as well and serve as partial compensation, in the case of poor quality, or payment, in the case of good quality. Non-wage forms of compensation, such as better schools or parks, may also evolve. The consequences of these 'general equilibrium' effects is that those who tolerate dirty air should eventually be compensated, and residents of cities where people move to escape bad air should eventually be worse off in other ways. These adaptations must, of course, be understood relative to individual preferences, not to some uniform standard of well-being.

In the case of ozone, meteorological differences, as well as differences in the composition of local industry, certainly cause the cost of abatement to vary from place to place. The same is true for the benefits: when the benefits are mainly health-related, the marginal benefits are related to the population size. This means that the same uniform ambient standard can generate wide differences in benefits among states. By requiring the attainment of a single, nationwide standard, unequal economic burdens are imposed.

The NAAQS were not set on economic grounds – the CAA prohibits it – so it is not surprising to find the potential for inefficiency in the setting of a uniform ambient standard. The prohibition on significant deterioration of air quality in attainment areas also fails a strict efficiency test because it leaves pollution assimilative capacity untapped in some places and it precludes economic developments that might be beneficial out of proportion to their pollution impacts.

Our theoretical analysis of the welfare losses due to uniform standards suggests that the welfare losses are greater when marginal costs and benefits are changing rapidly. No inference is available on the shape of the marginal benefit function for ozone abatement. But, the available studies of precursor abatement costs indicate little slope to the marginal cost functions up to 20 or 25 percent reductions below levels of the late 1980s, and sharply rising costs for greater reductions. Thus, from the cost side, at least, the uniform ambient standard may not have caused large welfare losses in the past. The losses from uniformity are likely to increase in the future, however, as non-attaining ACQRs are forced to take more extreme abatement measures in order to comply.

Of course, the standard has not been met everywhere and this can be explained by high abatement costs and by transboundary pollution. When the import of pollution is important, a single region is bound to have difficulties attaining the ambient standard. In this case, it does not make sense to shift the responsibility for attainment to individual regions. By establishing ozone transport regions, the 1990 CAA amendments took an important step towards more coordination.

In considering the way the ambient standard is being implemented, there is also some comfort in the fact that compliance schedules are longer for dirtier cities facing more stringent abatement. This provides more time for interim measures possibly to forestall the need for more drastic steps, and for technological improvements to reduce the eventual costs.

Having said much about the NAAQS as a uniform standard, we must acknowledge also that it does not really translate into a requirement for uniform air quality. Local governments may choose to pursue air quality better than the NAAQS, as California has, and many parts of the US more than attain it. So, the standard actually truncates one end of the permissible distribution of ambient air quality rather than reducing the distribution to a single point.

2. Emission limitations

The second interesting aspect of the US approach concerns emission limitations. As we noted above, the requirements for new sources and mobile sources are set centrally while the requirements for existing sources are set locally. Those local requirements are informed by central government research on reasonably available control technologies and ozone damages, and they are subject to central review and approval in the SIP process. The local requirements can vary by industry and location. The new source requirements, however, vary only by industry.

The division of authority over emissions reflects two tensions emphasized in our theoretical model: the tension between uniformity and differentiation and the tension between cooperation and non-cooperation in solving transboundary pollution. First, new sources have greater freedom over their selection of technologies than existing sources, so the cost of compliance is more predictable and less likely to vary greatly from place to place, although it will from industry to industry. Under these circumstances, there is less to lose from uniformity within an industry.

Second, for existing sources, the abatement options are more idiosyncratic and the costs are greater than for new sources. Our theoretical argument suggests that uniform standards should occasion larger welfare losses for existing sources than for new sources. The US approach responds by reserving for local jurisdictions the primary authority over existing sources, thereby allowing emissions standards to vary along more margins: location as well as industry. The abatement requirements are more stringent for non-attainment areas where the benefits also are probably greater. In this way, policy variation helps to minimize welfare losses.

Another part of the tension between uniformity and differentiation is the potential for differentiated policies to shrink markets and curtail economies of scale. The existence of widely varying local standards could translate into the need to customize goods and preclude the realization of important economies of scale in design and manufacturing. This is the fundamental argument for market integration, and it is a plausible argument with respect to emission standards for automobiles, RACT requirements for existing sources, and New Source Performance Standards. While the US ozone-emission policies generally provide opportunities for differentiation where uniformity would be most welfare-reducing, one opportunity seems to have been missed. This is the opportunity for seasonal variation in ozone abatement. The requirement of year-round abatement seems unduly rigid and costly for regions where the temperatures and solar incidence are too low much of the year to present serious ozone hazards. The costs might be reduced by requiring some types of abatement only during the more ozone-prone months. For example, with regard to carbon monoxide pollution, the more costly, CO-reducing oxygenated auto fuels are required in non-attaining regions only during certain months of the year.

Growing central control over emission standards in the US can also be understood as a necessary complement to a uniform ambient pollution objective in the presence of transboundary pollution. A more efficient way to solve non-attainment problems in some cases is to require neighboring regions to increase their emission-abatement effort rather than to require a stricter SIP in the non-attaining region. Centralized authority circumvents the strategic roadblocks that frequently impede voluntary agreements to such an end.

3. Coordination

We turn now to the third interesting aspect of federalism in US ozone policy – the matter of policy coordination. Clearly, the centralized, majoritarian US system avoids many obstacles to cooperation among jurisdictions. But, it does not avoid problems of information asymmetry between the central and local authorities. And, until 1990, it had accomplished little with regard to transboundary interdependencies over ozone abatement.

Consider first the information problems. Local governments presumably know more about local preferences and abatement costs. They use this information to negotiate customized abatement plans with the central authority. The central authority, however, has information (air quality models) equal to that of the local government about the relationship between local abatement plans and prospective ambient air quality changes. Furthermore, it can impose substantial penalties on local jurisdictions that fail to prepare or implement acceptable plans. The result is that local jurisdictions can gain nothing by misrepresenting the costs or benefits of compliance. Their incentives are to minimize costs and, if necessary, provide evidence to convince the central authority to improve its air quality models. With regard to transboundary coordination, the 1990 Amendments provide mechanisms to force source regions to modify their SIPs in order to reduce transboundary pollutant fluxes. Attainment areas that would not otherwise be subject to existing-source controls now can be made to comply with those provisions if their emissions end up contributing in non-attainment regions. SIP disapproval and sanctions stand in the way of non-cooperation. This arrangement preserves the flexible characteristics of the SIP approach while also providing leverage to force action by source jurisdictions.

EUROPEAN OZONE POLICY – A DECENTRALIZED APPROACH

The EU is at a different stage in ozone policy formulation than the US. Ozone policy options are still formulated and decided at the level of the Member State (or lower). For this reason, we call the European approach 'decentralized'.

We start by describing current EU regulations and discussing available material about the costs and benefits of ozone abatement. This will be followed by a discussion of the economic federalism dimensions of EU ozone policies.

A.   The Council of the European Union

For understanding EU policy-making on the environment[17] and in particular on ozone, it is important to know that unanimous consent is needed from the Member States for most central environmental regulations or directives. The scope of decisions subject to the unanimity rule was scaled back by the Single European Act of 1987, and the European Commission now has a larger domain of action in which majority rule governs regulations, including environmental regulations, in as far as they have to do with the necessary harmonization to achieve an internal market. So, environmental decisions which have nothing to do with the harmonization still need unanimous consent. The larger domain of action as regards the environment stems from two articles in the Act. One article confers the power to legislate to the extent that these objectives can be better attained at Community level than at the level of the Member States. The second article made protection of the environment an explicit, high-level goal of the EU.

1. Ambient standards

Ozone was among the pollutants recognized in the first European Community environmental action plan of 1973 (Zierock 1989). While the Union has adopted binding regulations on the ambient concentration for several of the pollutants acknowledged in that plan, including NO_x, it has not done so for ozone or VOCs. What does exist is official acknowledgement of common damage thresholds for health and vegetation, and Union-wide protocols for measuring, monitoring, and reporting ozone concentrations (Official Journal of the European Communities 1992). These measures *do not require* abatement actions.

The health threshold has three parts according to the World Health Organization's (1987) recommendations: the 'health protection' component consists of a concentration of 110 micrograms/m^3 averaged over eight hours; the population information threshold is 180 micrograms/m^3 averaged over one hour; and the 'population warning' threshold is 360 micrograms/m^3 averaged over one hour.[18]

2. Emission regulation

The EU has issued several directives on emission limitation of ozone precursors. The most important ones are for automobiles (from 1987 on). Others are expected on the VOC emissions resulting from the storage and distribution of petrol and on the emissions of organic solvents from industrial processes and other processes.

The main ground for the directives on the emission of NO_x and VOC for new automobiles has been the harmonization article requiring harmonization to provide a high level of protection for the environment. From 1992 on, the emission regulations for new automobiles are essentially as stringent as those in the US. In the other sectors, the EU regulations are catching up with US regulations.

In the first environmental regulations under the Single European Act (1987–92), ozone formation and VOC reduction was one of the considerations besides NO_x reduction objectives and CO reduction. Only in the regulations to come (from 1992 onwards) will there be explicit reference to reduction plans for VOC which have been agreed by most EU countries. This agreement has been achieved within the framework of a wider European Protocol on transboundary pollution.

3. Division of responsibility

The European Commission regulates mostly by issuing directives. These directives are not directly and generally enforceable. They set out goals for the Member States to achieve through implementing national legislation.

The main function of the Member States is thus to enforce the directives on emission standards and on the monitoring of ozone.

The application of Community law on environmental matters has been erratic (Smith and Hunter 1992). The European Commission has no real power to enforce implementation. At most, the European Court of Justice can declare an infringement of Treaty obligations by a Member State and require the culprits to pay legal costs.

4. Transboundary pollution

There are as yet no specific legal institutions at the EU level to tackle transboundary problems. Since the Single European Act, however, the European Commission has more legal ground to act on transboundary problems as it is clearly a case where EU action can do better than actions at member countries' level.

In the domain of air pollution, the most important cooperative agreements have been concluded in a wider European framework to which we will turn later.

B. Benefits and Costs of Ozone Abatement

No comprehensive studies exist which compare costs and benefits of ozone abatement. The only relevant study looked at the cost-effectiveness of ozone abatement (Zierock 1989). This study, commanded by the European Commission, proposed a reduction of both precursors. Several atmospheric models are now available which can assess the effects of pollution abatement in Europe on the ozone levels in the Member States.

1. Benefits of ozone abatement

Little work has been done to estimate the benefits of ozone abatement in Europe. While health benefits have been extensively studied in the US, no similar studies are available for Europe. It is doubtful that US estimates could reasonably be transferred to Europe, given differences in revealed preferences (e.g., lesser smoking rates in the US) about respiratory health.

Agricultural damages are probably more comparable. According to Zierock (1989, p. 22), yields of the most sensitive crops are thought to be diminished up to eight percent by elevated ozone levels. Less sensitive crops lose one to three percent of their yields.

2. Costs of ozone abatement in the EU

Zierock (1989, Table 6) presents order of magnitude estimates of precursor abatement costs in EU Member States based on recognized abatement technologies. A graphical summary of those estimates appears in Figure 15.6.

The pattern is roughly the same as the one estimated by the US Congress, Office of Technology Assessment (1991) for the United States. Abatement of both VOCs and NO_x can be obtained most cheaply with further emissions controls for automobiles and trucks. Stationary source controls are more costly. But, the aggregate cost curve (figured by Zierock over total tonnages of *both* VOCs and NO_x) is quite flat up to about a 25 percent reduction (6 megatonnes of the 25 megatonnes of combined emissions for 1980). This level can be achieved for approximately 4×10^9 European Currency Units (ECUs) with the addition of relatively cheap emissions controls on autos, trucks and gasoline dispensing facilities.[19] Beyond 25 percent, however, further reductions require more costly modifications of power plants and solvent uses, both industrial and non-industrial. The estimated total cost of a 40 percent reduction is on the order of 11 billion ECUs. A more disaggregated, and more current study by Mayeres et al. (1993) for Belgium backs up the estimates of Zierock. The costs of Belgian VOC abatement are quite low, up to between 15 and 20 percent abatement. Likewise, the costs of reducing NO_x are low, up to about 25 percent abatement. Beyond these levels, however, much more expensive technologies are required, and marginal and total costs increase rapidly, especially for VOC abatement.

C.   Ozone Policy and Economic Federalism

Regulatory authority over ozone and its precursors remains largely up to EU Member States acting individually. Because of the geography of Europe, the transboundary spread of ozone is important, so a non-cooperative solution would yield large inefficiencies. Before examining the process of cooperation it is useful to examine the positions of the Member States.

The EU Member States have very different interests in tropospheric ozone pollution.   The members are more or less divided into three groups: Germany, France, and the Netherlands are implementing abatement plans domestically and support action by the Community.[20] Belgium, Luxemburg, and Denmark are withholding domestic action pending a Community-wide strategy, the development of which they support. Finally, Greece, Ireland, Italy, Portugal, Spain, and the United Kingdom have declined to support a Community-wide strategy.

The positions taken by the EU members would seem for the most part to conform to a rational assessment of their interests in curtailing ozone. The first group, Germany and France in particular, are industrial enough to have significant problems with ozone and large enough to internalize a large share of those problems within their borders. They may have enough interest to warrant unilateral action so as to limit internal ozone levels. Germany has no ambient standards but has taken a leading role in emission standards. A large enough share of German ozone pollution comes, however, from other nations, both East and West, that many German areas are limited in what they can accomplish without coordinated action. France, in the 1980s, formulated a plan to reduce VOC emissions by 30 percent. Also in the first group, the Netherlands, as a small nation, probably exports and imports much of its ozone and does not fit the internalization story. But, the Dutch have chosen consistently to be leaders on environmental issues within the EU. The Netherlands is the only EU member to have an ambient ozone standard, and it also has a plan to reduce NO_x emissions by 33 percent and VOC emissions by 50 percent by the year 2000.

The second group includes small industrial nations. They may be significant sources of ozone and precursors, but they export a large share of their emissions and import a large fraction of the pollution they experience. Domestic limits on emissions could have only a small effect on ambient conditions. So, progress in reducing ozone in these countries requires a coordinated international effort. By withholding unilateral abatement, these nations can use reductions in their exported pollution as bargaining tools. The Netherlands is the only small member nation with a large stake in ozone abatement that has chosen to act unilaterally rather than to withhold action. There are two possible rationalizations of this attitude. The Netherlands can, through a first move, try to induce other Member States to an implicit cooperative equilibrium. This would however require some conditionality or sanction clause in case the other nations do not follow. A second possible rationalization lies in the possibility that the early adoption of ozone emission standards forces the EU, through the harmonization requirement, to adopt, by a qualified majority, the stricter emission standards.

In the third group are nations with varying reasons for resistance to a Community-wide agreement. Ozone is not a significant problem in Ireland. England exports much of its ozone. Greece and Spain have isolated ozone problems, but they neither import nor export appreciable amounts. Spain and Portugal are setting up monitoring systems, but they view ozone pollution as less important than other problems. Overall, these nations have little to gain from a Community-wide ozone policy except perhaps some side payments. Their bargaining position would be undermined if they were too eager for an EU agreement. In addition to their common stance within the EU on ozone, all but Ireland have declined to sign the Geneva protocols on SO_2.

D. Options for Coordinated Action

EU rules require unanimous consent in order to adopt a tropospheric ozone standard or obligatory Community-wide limits on precursor emissions. This level of agreement has not been achieved except for the emissions of new cars in the framework of the harmonization requirement. The result has been a search for other ways of motivating action.

A partial solution has been found in the 1979 Geneva Convention on Long-range Transboundary Air Pollution, created under United Nations auspices. In 1991, a separate 'Protocol...Concerning the Control of Emissions of Volatile Organic Compounds or their Transboundary Fluxes' (VOC Protocol) was signed by 21 European and North American nations, including all members of the European Community except Ireland and Portugal (United Nations, Economic Commission for Europe 1991; Simpson and Styve 1992). This non-EU framework was successful because it is based on the agreement of different member countries acting individually and cannot be blocked by a unanimity rule. (Ireland and Portugal could have blocked an EU initiative.)

The new provision calls upon large, highly industrialized nations to curtail VOC emissions by 30 percent before the year 2000, and smaller or less industrial nations to prevent increases.[21] In both cases, the base emissions levels are those realized in the 1984–90 period. Each signatory nation must designate its preferred option.

The VOC Protocol has become the focal point of European ozone policy. It was followed by the 1992 agreement on thresholds and monitoring, noted above, and it served as the principal motive to issue new directives on VOC emissions in petrol distribution and solvent use. Modeling studies performed as part of the European Co-operative Programme for Monitoring and Evaluation of the Long Range Transmission of Air Pollutants indicate that attainment of the Protocol, accompanied by no change in NO_x levels and constant emissions for non-signatories, would reduce mean ozone levels by four to eight percent in north-western Europe and one to four percent elsewhere (Simpson and Styve 1992). But, peak ozone occurrences would be reduced more significantly – 40 to 60 percent for episodic concentrations over 150 micrograms/m^3.

While the signing of the VOC reduction protocol is an achievement and will probably generate ozone reductions, the proposed strategy of equal proportionate reduction is not necessarily cost-effective, and neither is the policy of uniform emission standards. This means there is still a long way to go in ozone policies in Europe, both in achieving ozone reductions and in accomplishing the reductions at low cost.

CONCLUSIONS

The problem of tropospheric ozone pollution is complicated by the diversity of the sources, the complexity of the chemistry, and the multiplicity of affected jurisdictions. Not surprisingly, in view of these complications, ozone has proved to be one of the least tractable air pollution problems.

The US has aggressively pursued ozone abatement as a nationwide priority for over two decades. Majority decision-making has enabled the US to overcome local differences about environmental goals and to pursue a centralized strategy for ozone abatement. The result is a set of policies that, on the surface, appear quite blunt. They include uniform minimum air quality goals, to be achieved at any cost, and emissions limits that are increasingly uniform. Not only is it centralized, but the US approach relies on regulations rather than incentives.

The difficulty with centralized policies is that they can sacrifice efficiency by forcing homogeneity on heterogeneous local jurisdictions and polluters. In the case of ozone, the weaknesses of a centralized approach have been addressed through subtle but potentially important flexibilities in US regulations. Those regulations provide several margins along which local jurisdictions can seek locally cost-effective ways of achieving the centrally-imposed ambient standard. They also use economic criteria to set emission limitations for new sources. The potential inefficiencies of emission quotas are moderated by the availability in the US of emission offset trading in local markets, and in any case they may not be too serious since the costs of abatement are small enough, up to approximately 20 percent abatement beyond levels of the late 1980s.

The major sources of inefficiencies which remain in the US system are the uniformity of the ambient concentration standard and the progress that continues to be required in adapting regional responsibility for abatement to the transfrontier dimension of ozone. This is an important ingredient in many of the remaining non-attainment regions.

The European Union is at a much earlier stage than the US in the development of a strategy for combating ozone. The unanimity requirement for EU decision-making over many issues has been a stumbling block for 20 years. The member nations have quite different interests in ozone pollution, so unanimity over a comprehensive strategy has been impossible to achieve, except on selected component policies, such as catalytic converters for automobiles, that involve significant local benefits or that can be justified in terms of product harmonization (to achieve economies of scale).

The Geneva protocols over transboundary pollution have provided a forum for limited, voluntary agreements among European nations on a more comprehensive approach. This non-EU framework can not be blocked by a unanimity rule. Those agreements contain cost-inefficient uniform percentage reductions and lack enforcement mechanisms.

We see manifested in ozone policies two different types of federations: one with significant centralized power; the other with more limited central power. Action has been swift and decisive in one, slower and more cautious in the other; more uniform in one, more differentiated in the other; more aggressive against transboundary polluters in one, more protective of them in the other. Yet, we also see points of convergence of their ozone policies. Their parallel interests in cost-effectiveness have led both to provide some measure of local and industrial differentiation, and their parallel, competitive interest in market harmonization and economies of scale have caused both to adopt uniform emission control requirements for automobiles, the largest source of emissions.

NOTES

1. The diminution of stratospheric ozone in recent decades has been a source of worldwide concern. Several types of industrial chemicals, particularly chlorofluorocarbons, are thought to have caused the depletion. In recent protocols nations voluntarily agreed to phase out the chemicals most destructive of stratospheric ozone.
2. According to the National Research Council (1991, p. 22): 'the additional tropospheric ozone is believed to have counteracted only a small fraction of the stratospheric loss, even if the trends observed over Europe [a 10 percent increase of the O_3 concentration throughout the troposphere column over a decade] are representative of the entire northern midlatitude region'. Furthermore, tropospheric ozone accumulation increases the near-surface trapping of solar radiation and may contribute to a warming of the surface of the earth. These potential cumulative effects of tropospheric ozone, both positive and negative, are at this point speculative and outside the scope of this chapter.
3. As an illustration of the scientific uncertainty, Zierock (1989) reports critical precursor ratios of 3 and 13.
4. The graphical relationship between precursor concentrations and ambient ozone levels for specific conditions of temperature and solar radiation. Changes in climatic factors have the effect of shifting the ozone isopleths.
5. Zierock (1989, Table 1) provides a good summary of the WHO recommendations.
6. The seemingly arbitrary choice of a *fourth* highest value over *three* years reflects the structure of US standards for ambient ozone. This is discussed further in the next section.
7. See National Research Council (1991, Chapter 2) for a discussion of ozone concentration measures and their relation to environmental standards.
8. Many different summary measures of ozone concentration have been proposed. Peak ozone measures tend to focus on one-hour readings. A common indicator of peak ozone is second-highest daily one-hour reading realized in a year. Another indicator, known as the 'design value', is the fourth-highest daily maximum one-hour reading within a three-year period. And, a third indicator is the number of days in a year when the one-hour ozone standard was exceeded.
9. Council directive of September 21, 1992.
10. b^H can be given more structure by assuming the population is homogeneous in the different regions and across regions so that the total benefit of a region becomes a product of its population P^H and benefit per inhabitant v:

$$P^H = P^H_V (z^H) \tag{15n.1}$$

11. The graph can be elaborated to discuss other cases. Isopleths which are partly positively sloped can be introduced. Confrontation with iso-cost curves can then generate an optimal policy with either increased emissions (and cost savings) or decreased emissions of one pollutant. One could also try to represent transboundary pollution. The local concentrations would then be defined as the weighted sum of emissions in H and F and the iso-cost functions would be a compilation of the cost functions in both states and of the associated ozone reduction benefits in the other state.

12. The possibility of trade in emissions could be envisaged (Markusen 1975).

13. For an empirical illustration in the case of global warming where the efficiency loss is very small see Eyckmans et al. (1993).

14. For a discussion of the role of the participation constraint see Eyckmans, Proost and Schokkaert (1993).

15. For a broader treatment of US air quality policy, see Portney (1990).

16. Curiously, Krupnick and Portney also offered an estimate of $300 million in annual benefits for ozone reduction in the South Coast area – more than their lower-bound estimate for nationwide benefits.

17. A useful overview of the Eurpoean Community Environmental legal system can be found in Smith and Hunter (1992).

18. The WHO recognizes that damages are associated with a continuum of ozone concentrations and are not zero below the recognized threshold (Zierock 1989, p. 13). The threshold has been accepted by the EC as a reasonable policy guideline.

19. For purposes of rough comparison, one ECU was worth approximately one US dollar in 1990, near the publication dates of the OTA (1991) and Zierock (1989) studies.

20. This section draws heavily on Zierock (1989).

21. An intermediate option also is allowed for nations whose emissions contribute to localized ozone problems in other countries. These nations may elect the thirty percent reduction in the areas with transboundary consequences while also electing a national goal of no overall increase. Of course, this implies that VOC emissions could increase in some regions to offset the reductions in the transboundary source areas.

REFERENCES

Adams, R.M., S.A. Hamilton and B.A. McCarl, 1986, 'The Benefits of Pollution Control: The Case of Ozone and US Agriculture', *American Journal of Agricultural Economics* 68: 886–93.

Barrett, S., 1991, 'The Paradox of International Environmental Agreements', Discussion paper, London Business School.

Baumol, W.J. and W.E. Oates, 1988, *The Theory of Environmental Policy*, 2nd Ed. Cambridge University Press, Cambridge, England.

Beavis, B. and M. Walker, 1983, 'Achieving Environmental Standards with Stochastic Discharges', *Journal of Environmental Economics and Management* 10: 103–11.

Braden, J.B. and D.W. Bromley, 1981, 'The Economics of Cooperation over Collective Bads', *Journal of Environmental Economics and Management* 8: 134–50.

Chock, D.P., 1988, 'A Need for a More Robust Ozone Air Quality Standard', Paper 88–121.5, Proceedings of the 81st Annual Meeting and Exhibition of the Air Pollution Control Association, Dallas, TX.

Dodge, M.C., 1977a, 'Combined Use of Modeling Techniques and Smog Chamber Data to Derive Ozone-Precursor Relationships', in *Proceedings of the International Conference on Photochemical Oxidant Pollution and Its Control*, Vol. II, Dimitriades, Ed., EPA–600/3–77–001b, pp. 881–9.

Easterbrook, G., 1993, 'Winning the War on Smog', *Newsweek*, August 23, p. 29.

EUROSTAT, 1991, *Environmental Statistics*, European Communities, Luxembourg.

Eyckmans, J., S. Proost and E. Schokkaert, 1993, 'Tax Instruments and Participation Constraints in Greenhouse Negotiations', Paper presented to the European Association of Environmental and Resource Economists Annual Meeting, Fontainebleau, France, July.

Finlayson-Pitts, B.J. and J.N. Pitts, 1986, *Atmospheric Chemistry: Fundamentals and Experimental Techniques*, New York, John Wiley & Sons.

Folmer, H., P. van Mouche and S. Ragland, 1993, 'Interconnected Games and International Environmental Problems', *Environmental and Resource Economics* 3(4): 313–36.

Freas, W., 1993, US Environmental Protection Agency, Research Triangle Park, NC, Personal communication, August 20.

Garrett, T.L. and B.D. Winner, 1992, 'A Clean Air Act Primer: Parts I, II, and III', *Environmental Law Reporter* 22: 10159–89, 10235–61 and 10301–29.

Hall, J.V., A.M. Winer, M.T. Kleinman, F.W. Lurmann, V. Brajer and S.D. Colome, 1992, 'Valuing the Health Benefits of Clean Air, *Science* 255 (February 14): 812–17.

Kolaz, D.J. and R.L. Swinford, 1990, 'How to remove the influence of meteorology from the Chicago area ozone trend', Paper 90–97.5, 83rd Annual meeting and exposition of the Air and Waste Management Association, Pittsburgh, PA.

Kolstad, C.D., 1987, 'Uniformity versus Differentiation in Regulating Externalities', *Journal of Environmental Economics and Management* 14: 386–99.

Krugman, P., 1992, *Geography and Trade*, University Press of Leuven, Leuven, Belgium, and MIT Press, Cambridge, MA.

Krupnick, A.J., 1993, 'Vehicle Emissions, Urban Smog, and Clean Air Policy', in R.J. Gilbert, ed., *The Environment of Oil*, Amsterdam, Kluwer Academic Publishers, pp. 143–77.

Krupnick, A.J. and P.R. Portney, 1991, 'Controlling Urban Air Pollution: A Benefit–Cost Assessment', *Science* 252 (April 26): 522–8.

Lieu, S. and B.R. Wallerstein, 1993, 'The Applicability of Economic Assessment in Policy Formation', Paper presented at the 1993 Western Economic Association Meeting, Lake Tahoe, NV.

Maler, Karl-Goran, 1990, 'International Environmental Problems', *Oxford Review of Economic Policy* 6: 80–108.

Markusen, J.R., 1975, 'Cooperative Control of International Pollution and Common Property Resources', *Quarterly Journal of Economics* 89: 618–32.

Markusen, J.R., E.R. Morey and N.D. Olewiler, 1993, 'Environmental Policy when Market Structure and Plant Locations are Endogenous', *Journal of Environmental Economics and Management* 24: 69–86.

Mayeres, I., S. Proost and D. Miltz, 1992, 'Photochemical air pollution: the policy dilemma of non-convexities', Unpublished manuscript, Center for Economic Studies, Catholic University of Leuven, Belgium.

Mayeres, I., S. Proost and D. Miltz, 1993, 'The Geneva Hydrocarbon Protocol: Economic Insights from a Belgian Perspective', *Environmental and Resource Economics* 3: 1–23.

National Research Council, 1991, *Rethinking the Ozone Problem in Urban and Regional Air Pollution*, National Academy Press, Washington, DC.

Oates, W., 1972, *Fiscal Federalism*, Harcourt Brace Jovanovich, New York.

Oates, W. and C. Schwab, 1988, 'Economic Competition among Jurisdictions: Efficiency Enhancing or Distortion inducing?', *Journal of Public Economics* 35: 333–54.

Official Journal of the European Communities, 1992, Council Directive 92/72/EEC of September 21, 1992 on Air Pollution by Ozone, No. L 297/1–7.

Placet, M., R.E. Battye, F.C. Fehsenfeld and G.W. Bassett, 1990, 'Emissions Involved in Acidic Deposition Processes', *State-of-Science/Technology Report 1*, National Acid Precipitation Assessment Program, US Government Printing Office, Washington, DC.

Portney, P.R., 1990, 'Air Pollution Policy', in P.R. Portney et al., eds, *Public Policies for Environmental Protection*, Washington, DC, Resources for the Future, Inc., pp. 27–96.

Repetto, R., 1987, 'The Policy Implications of Non-Convex Environmental Damages: A Smog Control Case Study', *Journal of Environmental Economics and Management* 14: 13–29.

Rijksinstituut voor Volksgezondheid en Milieuhygiene (RIVM), 1991, *Nationale milieuverkenning 1990–2010*, Samson H.D. Tjeenk bv, Alphen aan den Rijn, the Netherlands.

Scott, A.T., 1976, 'Transfrontier Pollution: Are New Institutions Necessary?', in *Economics of Transfrontier Pollution*, Organization for Economic Cooperation and Development, Paris.

Simpson, D. and H. Styve, 1992, 'The Effects of the VOC Protocol on Ozone Concentrations in Europe', Norwegian Meteorological Institute, Oslo, EMEP MSC–W Note 4/92.

Smith T.T., Jr. and R.D. Hunter, 1992, 'The European Community Legal System', *Environmental Law Reporter*, 22 (No. 2, February): 10106–35.

South East Coast Air Quality Management District, 1989, '1989 Air Quality Management Plan', South East Air Quality Management District and Southern California Association of Governments, El Monte.

United Nations, Economic Commission for Europe, 1991, 'Project de Protocole de la Convention sur la Pollution Atmospherique Transfrontière à Longue Distance de 1979 Relatif à la Lutte Contre Les Emissions de Composes Organiques Volatils ou Leurs Flux Transfrontières', Geneva.

US Congress, Office of Technology Assessment, 1991, *Catching Our Breath: Next Steps for Reducing Urban Ozone*, Washington, DC, US Government Printing Office, OTA–0–412.

US Environmental Protection Agency, 1989, *NEDS Source Classification Codes and Emissions Factor Listing*, Washington, DC.

US Environmental Protection Agency, 1991, *National Air Quality and Emissions Trends Report, 1989*, Office of Air Quality Planning and Standards, Research Triangle Park, NC, EPA/450/4–91–003.

Weitzman, M.L., 1974, 'Prices vs. Quantities', *Review of Economic Studies* 41: 477–91.

World Health Organization, 1987, *Air Quality Guidelines*, WHO Regional Publications, European Series, No. 23, Copenhagen.

Zierock, K.-H., 1989, *Photochemical Oxidants: Summary of Studies Relevant to an Abatement Policy*, Office for Official Publications of the European Communities, Luxembourg, CD–NA–11929–EN–C.

SECTION D

Environmental Dimensions of National and International
Security

16. European Environmental Security: Threats and Solutions

Kent Hughes Butts

INTRODUCTION

This chapter argues that environmental variables, now broadly defined, are creating political instability in regions that are strategically important to the security of the European Community. It examines methods used by the United States to address environmental security problems that could be applied to Europe, and recommends that the North Atlantic Treaty Organization (NATO), formerly dedicated to repelling the East Bloc and Soviet military threat, take advantage of these methods and its expanded Strategic Concept to promote solutions to environmental problems in areas strategically important to Europe. This will promote political stability and reduce potential security threats to the continent, while strengthening military-to-military contacts.

The Cold War era is well past and today's international environment is characterized by regional conflict and economic competition. In this new milieu, policy-makers have come to understand that old issues, once subjugated either by totalitarian governments or by a need to focus on the much greater threat of thermonuclear war, have resurfaced and demonstrated their capacity to promote regional instability. In 1993, the US Secretary of Defense defined the four dangers that threaten international security as: Regional Dangers, Nuclear Dangers, Dangers to Democracy and Economic Dangers. Because the environment is a major variable in all of these dangers, it is now considered to be a relevant issue to those who craft international security policy. The field of environmental security is increasingly recognized for its contributions to explaining and offering solutions to regional conflicts that threaten international stability.

The European Community must concern itself with the multiple environmental problems of regions strategically important to its security, either directly, by posing health risks, or indirectly, by promoting political instability. For example, Chernobyl was an unfortunate accident that could well be repeated. Were it not for favorable weather conditions at the time, much greater contamination of agricultural products and direct threats to human health could have resulted. The Former Soviet Union (FSU) retains numerous nuclear, biological and chemical weapons and processing sites that cannot be considered environmentally safe or properly managed. As the recent Tomsk nuclear accident indicates, other such incidents must be considered probable.

Further, environmental degradation, land erosion, inadequate water, overpopulation and scarcity and degradation of resources are issues that threaten political stability in the FSU, Eastern Europe, Africa and the Middle East. The Gulf War had its roots in competition over a scarce resource for which there is a global imbalance of supply and demand. Water resource management in the arid Middle East has the potential to promote conflict among such militarily powerful adversaries as Iraq, Turkey and Syria. Perhaps more telling is the potential for instability caused by localized environmental problems that cause populations to lose confidence in the leadership of their governments and their ability to provide for their needs. When this occurs in regions strategically important to Europe, European security is directly threatened.

THE RISING IMPORTANCE OF ENVIRONMENTAL SECURITY

The meaning of environmental security differs between organizations and groups falling into issues related to physical damage of the environment by military forces, and international environmental problems that can lead to political instability and regional conflict. There are those who believe, for instance, that the military itself, by its very function, degrades the environment and often perceive the military to be violators of environmental security. Thus, maneuver damage from heavy tanks and other military operations that cause erosion and pollute the soil, or the production of weapons with the resultant discharge of effluent into water systems (Rocky Mountain Arsenal for example) typify the type of environmental security threat that this group of critics decry. Others approach environmental security from the perspective of its contribution to international conflict or political instability. This group concerns itself less with the military as an agent of environmental damage and more with the ramifications of widespread environmental degradation. Thus, cross-border pollution such as the discharge from high sulphur coal-burning power plants that gives rise to acid rain in other countries, over-grazing that results in migration, or the competition for scarce and strategically important resources are all legitimate topics for analysis by international security scholars.

However, the practitioners of environmental security have moved forward with workable definitions and have designed agenda to accomplish policy objectives.   In her statement before the United States Congress, the Department of Defense Deputy Under-Secretary of Defense for Environmental Security, Sherri Wasserman Goodman, captured a widely accepted definition of environmental security when she defined DOD's role as, 'Ensuring responsible environmental performance in defense operations and assisting to deter or mitigate impacts of adverse environmental actions leading to international instability'.[1]

It is the second part of this definition, the contribution of environmental issues to political instability and conflict, that has the greatest relevance to European security.   In what has become a watershed for the discussion of environmental security issues, Jessica Tuchman Matthews, in her article in *Foreign Affairs* pointed out that natural resource, demographics and environmental variables have a major impact upon economic performance and therefore have the potential for creating political instability.[2]   To understand the relationship between environmental degradation and political instability it is helpful to look at the social science literature concerning systems theory.

Applying systems theory to studies of state politics helps to explain the dimensions of environmental security.   If society is thought of as a 'system or pattern of human interaction, enforced and reinforced by cultural, political, economic, social and physical supports', studies of variables which support the leadership or power center of such a system contribute to one's understanding of the state.[3]   Social theorists such as David Easton came to value the applications of systems theory to society.   When the social structures and institutional entities of society are recognized and viewed as functional elements in systems, a framework is created that enlarges our explanatory and predictive capabilities.[4]

If a state system is properly maintained, communication extends to the full spatial reaches of the state and feedback or communication from the periphery to the core is assured.   Such two-way communications (feedback loop) serves to both reinforce a sense of community and belonging throughout the system and alert leadership elements when members of society perceive that the resources of the state are not being properly managed.   The system receives two types of inputs – demands and support. If the system is functioning in equilibrium, resources will be managed in such a manner that demands will be met and popular support for the system will be sustained.   If a system receives feedback on environmental conditions and demands, then it engenders appropriate responses to satisfy those demands and by so doing earns legitimacy (ensures support) from the members of the system.[5]   Thus, the physical resources necessary to sustain the political system are a critical system support. Equilibrium in the system is attained when the requisites or functions necessary for the system's survival are performed in an optimum manner.   When environmental problems erode this resource base, equilibrium is prevented and governmental legitimacy is threatened. Many authors have found the systems approach useful when analyzing environmental security. In his article 'Redefining Security in International Security', Richard Ullman considered a threat to national security as any event with the potential to drastically affect the quality of life for the population of a state or which might narrow the scope of policy options to the state's leadership.[6] In *Foreign Policy*, Norman Myers also applied systems theory to environmental issues in countries that are of strategic importance to the United States. He found a direct correlation between environmental degradation and retarded economic performance and a commensurate wave of stresses being placed on the state's political systems.[7] Similarly, Thomas Homer-Dixon et al., reported evidence suggesting a correlation between scarcities in renewable resources – where scarcity was caused by overconsumption, population growth and an alteration in the pattern of distribution for the resource – and conflict.[8]

In the United States the recognition of this linkage between environmental instability and conflict has given rise to a growing body of policy that addresses environmental security issues. In 1991, the National Security Strategy of the United States incorporated the environment for the first time, pointing out that the management of natural resources in a sustainable fashion that provides for the needs of future generations represents a national security interest of the United States. Further, that because of the transboundary nature of global environmental problems and the stresses from regional and national environmental degradation, the environment is already contributing to political conflict.[9] Congress, led by then Senator Al Gore and Senator Sam Nunn, Chairman of the powerful Senate Armed Forces Committee, created the Strategic Environmental Research and Development Program that dedicated millions of dollars of DOD funds to the solution of the overwhelming environmental problems facing the United States and the world. The rationale for diverting DOD, intelligence and research assets to the solution of environmental problems was based on the concept that ethnic and regional conflicts among the many independent states having access to sophisticated conventional weapons and the potential to develop weapons of mass destruction 'could well be exacerbated by environmental problems'.[10]

European security increasingly turns upon events in the developing world which, because of ethnic tension and overpopulation, is particularly vulnerable to disruptions caused by environmental factors. Many developing countries have artificial political borders established by colonial fiat or political expediency in prior times. Africa's borders, for example, were delineated by the Berlin Conference in the last century and often encompass multiple culturally-distinct ethnic groups. In South Africa there are over nine Black national groups of over one million people that speak different languages. When environmental problems threaten the governments of such countries, their inability to meet systemic demands for food, shelter and employment is often seen by ethnic groups not represented proportionately in the existing government as evidence of discrimination and an improper allocation of resources. This sows the seeds for political instability.

In the Cold War era, totalitarian or single-party states were often able to maintain order and governance among these various national groups through the use of force. The current emphasis on democracy and efforts by both the European Community and the United States to promote democratic reform around the world has brought a reduction in the number of totalitarian or single-party states and the establishment of numerous new democratic governments. Lacking the ability to use force to suppress popular demands, these governments are likely to be much more vulnerable to perceived benefit inequities and the ramifications of environmental degradation. This situation is magnified by the fact that population growth in the developing world quite often exceeds 3 percent per year and in some countries reaches a level of 4 percent per year, which doubles the population of the country in less than 20 years. When these governments fail, the resulting conflict or emigration often threatens the security interests of Europe and the United States.

The US Department of Defense has not been alone in recognizing the threat to security posed by environmental issues. NATO has also integrated the environment into its strategic concept. In November 1991, the heads of state and government of the Alliance met in Rome to develop a new Strategic Concept. The strategic framework that underpins this concept articulated the security challenges and risks facing NATO. Recognizing that the threat has changed, the Alliance stated that risks to its security from aggression are substantially reduced and that economic, social, environmental and ethnic difficulties, which promote instability, are now significant threats to Alliance security.[11] The concept broadened the Alliance mission from focusing exclusively upon the Warsaw Pact threat; NATO's missions now include dialogue and cooperation with Eastern countries, the promotion of democracy and political stability and the mitigation of environmental problems that threaten these missions.[12]

Thus, both NATO and the US Department of Defense have institutionally recognized the importance of environmental matters to political stability and the mitigation of regional conflict. Such recognition is important given the substantial environmentally related threats faced by Europe today.

THREATS TO EUROPEAN ENVIRONMENTAL SECURITY

The principal threat to European security traditionally has been state-sponsored military aggression. NATO was organized to deter, and defend against, Soviet and East Bloc attack. The countries of Central and Eastern Europe are no longer occupied by Soviet forces and they have drastically reduced the size of their own military forces. In the Former Soviet Union (FSU), military forces are being reduced and a nuclear weapons dismantling program has been instituted. Cooperation agreements between the United States and the FSU are well developed and several of the former East Bloc countries have expressed an interest in joining NATO. Today, the primary threat to Europe comes from a breakdown of civil order, political instability and economic failure, all of which have an environmental dimension.

While environmental factors are rarely a primary cause of the fall of a government, they frequently exacerbate existing problems or are a catalytic factor. Environmental problems can overload a political system preventing it from meeting popular expectations. Chief among them is the demand for economic development.

When economic development ceases or when the economy struggles, governmental legitimacy is threatened. This is the case in the Ukraine, where the once-heralded Ukrainian government came to power on the popular belief that breaking with the Soviet Union would offer a rapid improvement in the standard of living. Mineral rich, industrialized and blessed with a strong agricultural sector, the Ukraine was expected to flourish. However, in the two years since independence there has been a steady decline in Ukrainian production, hyperinflation of 50 percent a month, bread-lines and increased poverty. In fact, the Ukraine's economic decline has been more dramatic than economic decline in Russia. As a result, Prime Minister Leonid Kuchma has been forced to resign, work stoppages are called to protest governmental decisions and the collapse of government and reunification with Russia are now real possibilities, as only 47 percent of the population would now back independence from Russia.[13]

Factors that reduce the ability of a government to satisfy the needs of its people, often economic needs, reduce the conditions necessary for peace and threaten stability in regions important to European security. Environmental factors impair the quality of life at every level of socioeconomic development. At the very basic subsistence level, eroded overgrazed soils, depleted aquifers and destroyed habitats and ecosystems threaten the livelihood and ability of agrarian populations to feed themselves. A failure at this level results in massive migration or starvation. Such is the case in the Horn of Africa. At the rudimentary industrial level, polluted water and high concentrations of sulphur dioxide and other particulate matter in the air shorten the lives of the population, increase the cost of maintaining a workforce and impair productivity at the most critical phase of a country's development. This is a chronic problem in the Former Soviet Union. Cleaning up industrial effluent and toxic and hazardous waste sites, necessary to improve the health of the population, would divert valuable resources needed to promote short-term economic development. In the most-developed nations, auto emissions and fossil fuel power plant discharge give rise to global warming, acid rain, chemical smog and the reduced ability of estuary ecosystems to support the life necessary to sustain fisheries. Addressing these issues is costly, controversial and often reduces the profitability of domestic industry, which may flee, transferring valuable jobs to countries with less stringent environmental laws. These environmental problems are promoting instability in countries critical to European interests, such as democratic reform.

Newly formed democratic regimes taking over from long-term totalitarian governments are under pressure to demonstrate their competence and the superiority of democratic forms of government. Their ability to succeed is greatly impaired when widespread respiratory disease, chronic infant mortality and an inability to provide safe drinking water for an increasingly educated and environmentally aware population, interfere with the country's industrial development program. These governments are often faced with political borders that fail to circumscribe culturally homogeneous populations. Multiple nationalities and ethnic groups within the same border complicate the governance process and make it even more important for the government to demonstrate its ability to equitably distribute scarce resources. Many environmental factors impede efficient political system management, such as increased population, uncontrolled migration, resource scarcity or degradation, public health problems and uncontrolled pollution. These factors are major contributors to instability in critical regions that are strategically important to the security of Europe. When nations in these regions fail to manage successfully their environmental problems, European security is put at risk.

Because of its resource wealth, insular nature and geographic separation from countries that threaten its national security, the United States has been, to some degree, protected from threats experienced by the European continent. Europe has no such barrier between itself and the culturally distinct neighbors to the east which have traditionally provided a threat to the security of Europe. These countries and those regions from which Europe obtains its strategic mineral resources and important trade, are vital to European security interests, but are today threatened by difficult environmental problems.

The control of nuclear weapons, other weapons of mass destruction and their waste in the FSU has been greatly complicated by the dissolution of the former superpower. The fact that the Ukraine, Belarus and Khazakstan, for example, retain nuclear capability and the potential for nuclear accidents of regional proportion, must be considered disturbing to European states. Concern for environmental problems associated with managing the downsizing of the Soviet nuclear arsenal is shared by Europe's allies and US Senators Richard Lugar and Sam Nunn sponsored legislation providing $800 million for this purpose.[14] Twenty-five million dollars in FY93 funding has been allocated to Belarus for the remediation of nuclear problems on former Soviet military bases.[15]

In addition to nuclear weapons, Eastern Europe and the Former Soviet Union continue to produce nuclear power with outdated and unsafe nuclear reactors. Sixteen large Soviet-produced, graphite reactors, similar, if not identical to the nuclear reactor which malfunctioned at Chernobyl still operate in the former Soviet territories.[16] Traditional weather patterns and seasonal wind directions place Europe at risk from accidents that might occur at these plants. Thus far, efforts to provide alternative sources of power to the countries dependent upon these reactors have proved unworkable.

Beyond these threats, Europe suffers from the continued environmental problems associated with Cold War weapons production and the economy of the Former Soviet Union. The Soviets' almost total disregard for environmental responsibility has created a nightmare of environmental problems that span the length and depth of the Former Soviet Union. In the north and south, waters have been heavily polluted either by the dumping of nuclear reactor or other industrial waste products.   Such cavalier treatment of water resources has polluted fisheries and threatened the livelihood and environmental health of the European fishing industry.[17] Unfortunately, the Former Soviet Union lacks the resources necessary to mitigate these problems.

Natural resource management is an environmental issue very important to stability. Energy production in the Former Soviet Union is critical to efforts to modernize the economy and sustain newly established democratic regimes. Yet energy production has fallen. Coal production is not meeting established goals and is increasingly recognized for its health risks by the populace and coalminers, who are now demanding greater attention to environmental health problems. Petroleum production has fallen consistently since the late 1980s due to a combination of such environmental difficulties as a lack of water resources, drought and electrical power disruptions, which plague oil production in Western Siberia.[18] The accident at Chernobyl drew popular attention to the risks associated with Soviet graphite reactors and created powerful opposition to efforts to expand nuclear power production. Recognizing the importance of the energy variable to regional political stability, the United States Overseas Private Investment Corporation has agreed to support Texaco's proposed $80 million restoration of Western Siberian oilfields by providing Russia with $2.8 million in loan guarantees and insurance.[19] Such intervention will be required frequently if the former Soviet states are to overcome their substantial environmental problems.

Environmental problems, such as resource scarcity and population, threaten European security in many ways. Many of the regions upon which the European Community depends for resources and trade are already threatened by instability. They are the Former Soviet Union and Eastern Europe, the Middle East and Southern Africa and Maghreb. The Middle East and Former Soviet Union are strategically important to Europe. Over 80 percent of the world's petroleum reserves are located in the politically troubled Middle East. The FSU, a major oil producer, exports over 2 million barrels of oil per day. Europe depends upon oil imports for most of its petroleum needs, importing over 7 million barrels of oil per day.[20] Europe is virtually 100 percent dependent upon foreign imports for the four most strategic minerals: chrome, cobalt, manganese and platinum. Southern Africa alone accounts for over 50 percent of the reserves of these minerals; and, in conjunction with the FSU controls 90 percent, 63 percent, 91 percent and 99 percent, respectively, of their reserves.[21] The Maghreb of North Africa is also a source of petroleum for Europe and has historic colonial ties that make it a sensitive area for Europeans and a source of many of the foreign workers that are flowing to Europe. These regions are struggling with high rates of population growth, newly elected democratic regimes, long-simmering ethnic conflict, the new threat of political Islam and weak economies. Environmental factors greatly complicate the regional governments' ability to manage these threats and therefore are putting European security at risk. (See Figure 16.1.)

A.   Population and Migration

Europe is threatened by the high population growth in the developing world and migration trends which reflect the freedom of human resource mobility after the breakdown of controls during the Cold War era. Population growth puts pressure on the social infrastructure of a country and increases demands on the government which can only be met through increasing resources and economic growth. Thomas Malthus pointed out that increases in population bred pressures on government that led to wars and recognized that the population growth in Europe was increasing geometrically while the food production natural resources were increasing arithmetically. Europe was

Figure 16.1:   Regions critical to European security

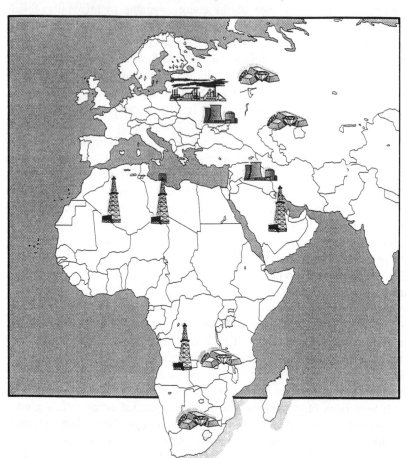

saved from chronic resource scarcity by the opening of the new world which served as an outlet for excess population and a source of additional resources. Today, no such escape valve exists. Populations can double in as little as 35 years when annual population growth rates exceed 2 percent, which is the case in much of the developing world. Cultural norms, often based on agricultural needs, have sustained high population growth rates. At the same time, life-extending technologies, better nutrition and access to medicine have greatly reduced death rates. In the developing world, population growth is now increasing exponentially and the states' economies and natural resource bases cannot keep pace. This environmental problem threatens the ability of governments to meet the needs of their populations and promotes domestic instability and outward migration pressures, frequently to the more-developed countries of industrialized Europe.

Examining three countries of the Maghreb with particularly close ties to Europe – Algeria, Morocco and Tunisia – makes clear the problems of the burgeoning population of the developing countries. The population of these three countries is some 60 million. Their annual population growth rate is approximately 2 percent. Thus, within 40 years their population will exceed 120 million people.[22] Unemployment among these three countries averages approximately 17 percent.[23] To these countries, Europe represents the new frontier that the Americas provided to Europe 400 years ago. The average per-capita gross domestic product (GDP) for the Organization for Economic Cooperation and Development (OECD) countries averages $17,097. The average GDP per capita for Algeria, Morocco and Tunisia is less than $1,200. This explains the fact that as of 1992 there were 5.5 million immigrants from the Maghreb in Europe.[24] Algeria, Morocco and Tunisia, alone, account for some 46 percent of all non-European community foreign employees.[25]

Trends and migration pressures indicate that Europe will serve increasingly as a target for East–West and South–North migrations. (See Figure 16.2.) Through the early 1980s, barriers in communication and transportation and the political controls of the Cold War era reduced the migration of workers and asylum-seekers to the industrialized world. Since then, economic conditions have deteriorated, a world recession has occurred, sophisticated transport systems have become commonplace in the developing world and political barriers to migration have fallen away. As a result, Europe has experienced increases in those seeking asylum from approximately 70,000 in 1983 to a 1990 total of some 442,000. Not counting East Germans and ethnic Germans from the East, Germany accepted over 190,000 asylum applications in 1990, an increase of approximately 60 percent from the previous year alone.[26]

While many immigrants seeking asylum can speak to the issues of ethnic conflict, war and oppression in the countries from which they emigrate, much of the conflict has its roots in a scarcity of resources that precludes the government from satisfying the needs of all ethnic groups within its borders. This failure and subsequent loss of legitimacy provides a fertile ground for radical philosophy, such as political Islam and oppression. In Algeria, for example, the Islamic Salvation Front (ISF) received the majority of the votes in the recent election. It was their success in the election and inability of the government to deal with the demands of its population that forced a military coup in January 1992.[27]

Figure 16.2:   Population and immigration pressures

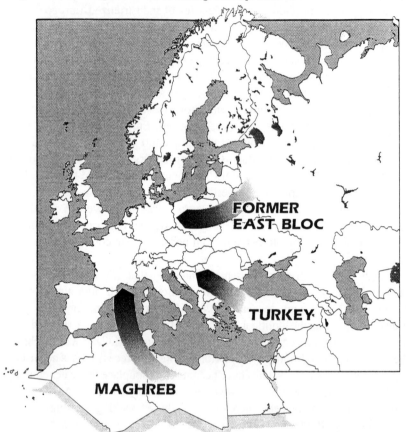

An even greater threat to Europe comes from continued East–West migration from the FSU and Eastern Europe. The harsh realities of life in the East Bloc gave rise to large-scale migrations to Western Europe throughout the 1950s and early 1960s. The construction of the Berlin Wall and the enforcement of the Iron Curtain reduced outflows from the Warsaw Pact countries to approximately 100,000 people per year. The fall of the Iron Curtain brought a wave of new immigrants and, in 1989, some 1.3 million people fled Eastern Europe and the Former Soviet Union for Western Europe. Continued political instability and economic failure in the new republics of the former East Bloc are giving rise to conflicts throughout the FSU. Approximately 600,000 people are thought to be 'internally displaced' in the FSU. The continued shaking out of economic and political organizational structures and political borders can be counted upon to threaten Western Europe for years to come.[28]

Recognizing the threat to their social and economic stability, Western European countries have attempted to emplace more demanding control over the flows of immigrants from East and Central Europe. The Berlin Conference of October 1991 created new measures for controlling immigration and laid a plan for obtaining agreements from supplying countries to aid in stemming the migration flow. However, Europe must develop greater efforts to promote economic and environmental improvement in the emigrant countries if it is to be successful in stemming the flow of illegal immigrants.[29] In addition, if the continued political turmoil in the Middle East and spread of political radical Islam continues, Europe will have the potential of internal security threats posed by the large number of Moslem immigrants whose presence in Europe continues to grow.

The magnitude of the immigration problem and the need for Europe to take definitive action becomes clear when one recognizes that there are already 10 million immigrants in the European Community, a total approximately equal to Belgium's population. OECD estimates for the next 30 years call for an additional 30 million immigrants to arrive in Europe. With the 1990 foreign populations of Germany at 8.2 percent, France at 6.4 percent, Belgium at 9.1 percent and Britain at 3.3 percent, it is likely that the additional immigrants would exacerbate the growing trend in xenophobic, violent behavior towards immigrants and popularity of racist and anti-foreigner propaganda on the part of opposition political parties.[30] With an estimated 17 million people out of work in Europe and a European unemployment rate of an unusually high 11 percent, opposition to increased immigration is certain to promote widespread debate.[31]

The average world population growth is approximately 1.7 percent per year. This adds approximately 100 million people per year to the world's population. Between the years 1990 and 2030 it is estimated that global population will increase by some 3.7 billion, 90 percent of which will be in the developing world.[32] Thus, in the countries of the Middle East, upon which Europe depends for much of its energy needs and in Southern Africa which supplies most of Europe's strategic minerals, rapidly increasing populations create spiraling poverty by causing increasing environmental decline. Burgeoning populations in these areas have no choice but to till marginal soils and steep slopes, to hack away the remaining tropical rain forests and over-graze narrow flood plains. The end result will be an even greater decline in the ability of these areas to provide for their food and water needs and irresistible pressures to migrate and seek a reallocation of scarce resources by way of violent conflict. These population and migration pressures threaten European security interests and have their roots in environmental problems their governments cannot solve.

B.   The Economic Threat

Economic growth can, of course, sustain burgeoning populations and arrest environmental decline and, thus, promote longevity in newly formed democratic regimes.   However, in the areas of strategic importance to Western Europe, it is unlikely that this will occur, leaving them vulnerable to the environmental threat. The growth in real per-capita income for sub-Sahara Africa in 1991 was −1 percent. In the Middle East and North Africa, it was −4.6 percent and in Eastern Europe, real per-capita income fell 14.2 percent.[33]   Poverty is correspondingly high with 7.1 percent of the population in Eastern Europe, 33.1 percent of the population in the Middle East and North Africa, and 47.8 percent of those living in sub-Sahara Africa living in absolute poverty with an annual per-capita income of less than $370 per year.[34]

In the most important area to European security, the Former Soviet Union, instability resulting from economic collapse is a growing possibility. The FSU's real GDP growth in 1992 was −18.5 percent.[35] Real national income growth for 13 of the 15 FSU countries was negative for 1991, while consumer prices escalated at a rate of least 70 percent during 1990 and 1991 for all FSU countries with some seeing consumer prices increase by nearly 125 percent.[36] This runaway inflation and falling productivity does little to support the new democratic regimes struggling to demonstrate their legitimacy to a population that expected radical improvements in lifestyle and economies under Western-oriented economic and democratic systems.

The chances for any near-to medium-term improvement in the economic stability of the FSU are slim indeed. The republics generally lack legal, economic and fiscal legislation and regulations and the political organizational power to enforce them. Lacking this framework, regional administrations have increasingly ignored central authority economic directives and potential foreign investors have lost confidence. Mineral traders seeking to export FSU minerals describe the situation as chaotic, with a decreasing amount of sales made by official organizations and most business done through a system of bribery and corruption with plant production managers and newly created entrepreneurial middlemen.[37] Traditionally dependent upon mineral exports for its foreign exchange, the FSU is witnessing significant falls in its most critical mineral exports. From their 1980s peaks, crude steel production for 1991 had fallen 19 percent; gold production had fallen 29 percent; cobalt production had fallen 64 percent and the extremely critical category of oil exports was down 50 percent.   Industrial output for 1991 fell by nearly 2 percent, while agricultural output fell by over 4 percent.[38]

Auguring against any rapid improvement in these dismal production figures is the high debt of the FSU. Soviet Union debt doubled to approximately $67 billion during the 5 years prior to its collapse and its credit-worthiness was tarnished by a liquidity crisis that precluded the payment of some $4.5 billion in short-term debt in 1990.[39] The FSU has yet to recover from the loss of the Council for Mutual Economic Assistance (COMECON) drop of export-market prices in the global economy and the move to convertible currency, all of which occurred in 1991. Russia, which owes 85 percent of this approximately $68 billion debt, recently watched as its parliament overrode President Yeltsin's austere budget to create a new budget deficit of some $22 billion, twice what President Yeltsin had proposed and equal to one-quarter of the country's GNP. This decision by a Russian parliament, led by old Communist hardliners, caused the IMF to delay providing an additional $1.5 billion in funding.[40]

Part of Russia's problem is that it has attempted to move to a market economy without establishing a legal foundation for taxation, property loss or privatization. Regional administrators have therefore been forced to use informal and illegal methods to establish economic policy.[41] As a result, 'Russia is experiencing hyper inflation, collapse of government, disastrous capital flight and economic chaos'.[42] The byproduct of this collapsing economy is sabre rattling and a growing disenchantment with the liberal central government leadership by the Russian military, which blames the failing economy and exponential inflation for the lack of success in bringing new recruits into the Army.[43] In addition, the failure of the central government to meet the demands of the political system is leading increasingly to a Soviet-style breakup of the Russian Federation. Maverick provinces such as Chechenya, Tataria and Bashkiria are claiming increased autonomy or declaring their independence, while Nizhny Novgorod and other provinces are pursuing aggressive economic plans in contravention of Russian federal statutes.[44] Add to this the fact that Russia is helping to fight a civil war in Tajikistan that threatens to further strain its economic resources and promote additional ethnic conflict. Some Russian experts fear that the great danger in this economic collapse is the potential threat to nuclear power stations or chemical factories should internal civil war within Russia or the FSU occur.[45]

C. The FSU Environmental Threat

In addition to the threat of instability plaguing the FSU, two other areas also seriously affect European security. These are the presence of weapons of mass destruction and the potential for environmental degradation from nuclear, chemical and biological waste and further nuclear-related accidents.

Russia recently admitted to producing 45,000 nuclear warheads and now has on hand a 1,200 metric ton inventory of bomb-grade uranium. Since the breakup of the FSU, Russia has been unable to gain control of many of its nuclear weapons, which remain in the hands of the governments of Belarus, the Ukraine and Kazakstan. The Russians have negotiated and are continuing to negotiate to gain control of these nuclear weapons and recently reached an agreement in principle for the Ukraine to turn over these weapons to Russia.[46] Because of the internal chaos and breakdown in control over its former republics and the overwhelming need for foreign currency, often through the sale of weapons, the possibility of nuclear arms falling into the wrong hands is genuine.[47] Indeed, the head of the American Central Intelligence Agency, Mr R. James Woolsey, testified before Congress that, 'Russia has yet to create an effective system for controlling exports of sensitive military equipment and technologies related to the development of nuclear, chemical, or biological weapons'.[48] These weapons and their waste are a primary environmental health threat.

Even more likely is the possibility of further environmental damage to Europe because of nuclear accidents in the Former Soviet Union. The Chernobyl disaster of 1986, which resulted in the death of over 250 people and contaminated livestock thousands of miles away in Britain, was but the most publicized of many FSU nuclear accidents. Since 1986, at least four other major accidents have further threatened European confidence in Soviet management. The most recent was the chemical explosion at the Siberian Research Complex in Tomsk. Two hundred separate safety problems or accidents occurred in 1992 alone.[49] The FSU has 45 nuclear power reactors in operation and 15 of them are RBMK models similar to the one involved in the Chernobyl accident. These graphite core reactors are highly unstable because an accident causing the loss of water increases the nuclear chain reaction.[50] Lacking the estimated \$5 billion required for upgrading the most important FSU reactors, the Russian government has stated its plan to operate the plants for their full 30-year life and is also moving forward with a plan to build an additional 30 nuclear plants.[51]

Radioactive contamination is the leading environmental problem in the Former Soviet Union, well ahead of water and air pollution. In addition to the potential for an accident at a nuclear power plant, the FSU has many former nuclear research facilities and nuclear waste storage sites at which a devastating environmental accident could occur at any time. The plutonium-producing plant at Chelyabinsk has experienced a series of accidents and experts fear that poorly constructed nuclear dumps could easily leak and further contaminate the area. The 1957 accident at Chelyabinsk spread radioactive contamination over approximately 8,000 square miles of the country.[52] With the proper wind conditions, Europe is indeed vulnerable to fallout from accidents occurring at these nuclear sites.

The Former Soviet Union has been extremely cavalier in its approach to the disposal of nuclear materials. Well known is its disposal of nuclear reactors in its northern seas from the Pacific Ocean to the Baltic. The effects on the Soviet population of improper handling and storage of nuclear materials are pronounced. Sizeable portions of the population have birth defects and other forms of impaired health because of exposure to radiation. Industrial waste has poured untreated into virtually all the major Soviet rivers and industrial cities have a sulphur dioxide emission rate that is often four times greater than that in the European Community.[53] Such pollution threatens not only the economic viability and human resource base of the FSU but also Europe. In many of the former republics and regions of the Russian Federation, little expertise is available to help manage these environmental problems and increasingly the civilian governments are unable to exert control or manage the state resources. Visitors to the Former Soviet Union and those who conduct business there frequently speak of the relative efficiency of the military. Under such conditions the potential for further instability and a direct environmental threat to Europe from Soviet environmental problems is pronounced.

SOLUTIONS

The evolution of environmental security has brought with it new opportunities and concepts for dealing creatively with today's global problems. Narrowly defined approaches to problem solving, ossified during the four-decade Cold War, have been broadened to include important linkages between variables upon which political stability depends. Environmental factors are now broadly defined and recognized for their importance to national security; failing to address environmental problems can undermine a government's legitimacy and promote instability. Yet, many newly formed democratic regimes are struggling with weak economies and newly established political infrastructures and lack the resources necessary to address environmental problems effectively. The resulting instability threatens European security. These environmental problems should be addressed by Europe's strongest central organization – the military.

Early optimism concerning the rise of a politically unified European Community has been replaced by frustration and a sense of opportunity lost. During the Cold War, Europe was often led by the United States and galvanized by the common threat of the Soviet empire. With both these factors significantly diminished, European countries have, as has the United

States, turned their attention to domestic problems exacerbated by the weak global economy and have allowed centrifugal forces to undermine the grand vision of a monetarily and politically unified EC. Germany's rigid fiscal policies, necessitated by the costly reunification effort, led to the unravelling of the monetary union as weaker countries were forced to pursue unilateral monetary policies. The economic integration that was to pave the way towards European unity has been delayed and with it a common economic policy with which to address European security issues.

Less successful yet are efforts to achieve political integration and the united leadership required to create a common European foreign policy. Lacking the visionary leadership of a Schuman and the unifying fear of communism, nationalism and competing domestic priorities have overcome the glacial inertia towards political union. Denmark's willingness to agree to the Maastricht Treaty under exemptions for important defense and monetary policies elucidates the weakness of European political unity. Much like the 1994 South African elections, Maastricht 1996 will only be a meeting to develop a plan for political union.[54]

While efforts to achieve economic and political union may be problematic, NATO remains a viable security organization with a history of foreign policy success, a functioning organizational infrastructure, the leadership and resources of the United States and an expanded strategy. NATO's priority on protecting the security and freedom of member countries has not changed, but it has a more relevant strategic concept. The 1991 Rome Declaration of Peace and Cooperation formalized efforts to broaden NATO's purpose from deterring the East Bloc military threat to include promoting stability. This new concept has many new missions, from out-of-area peacekeeping to environmental assistance.[55] Although many individual countries are slow to support political and economic union, NATO, as the Council on Foreign Relations discovered during a research trip to Europe, is enjoying widespread support.

> Everyone, including French and Russian representatives, acknowledges the need for NATO. France is moving to rejoin the Alliance's military committees. Central European nations seek membership. East European representatives are even more outspoken than their West German counterparts in advocating the importance of NATO's survival.[56]

Thus, unlike other organizations, NATO need not create new organizational frameworks or mount costly and time-consuming efforts at consensus building and leadership development to be effective. NATO is politically acceptable to key regional actors, its members have expanded out-of-area operations into places such as Somalia and it can address security issues immediately. How should this be achieved?

A. The US Model

While the United States is a member of the Alliance and NATO, its environmental program has been developed separately, concentrating largely on domestic issues. US participation in NATO thus far has focused primarily on deterring the Communist threat and on attempting to develop new missions and a force structure that meets both European needs and the post-Cold War domestic pressure to downsize the military. Yet, it has the potential to participate in and lead NATO environmental outreach efforts. Therefore, in developing an environmental program for NATO, it is instructive to examine the DOD approach which is making a substantial contribution to environmental security. DOD is the largest agency of the US Government, with a budget of approximately $264 billion per year. DOD bases and training areas occupy some 25 million acres of the United States and DOD manages over 1,000 installations.[57]   Half of DOD's environmental security mission is to ensure that DOD operates in a responsible environmental manner that maintains the support of the American people.

Given the length of the Cold War and the importance of DOD facilities in developing weapon systems and munitions to deter Soviet aggression, the Department of Defense should be expected to have a great quantity of industrially-related environmental problems yet to remediate. This is the case. Estimates of the cost of cleaning up DOD installations run from $30 billion to $400 billion. The Defense Environmental Restoration Program has spent $6.5 billion to the end of FY93 on remediating toxic and hazardous waste related to DOD activities and on the cleanup of formerly owned defense bases. For FY94 alone, DOD is requesting $2.3 billion from Congress to continue its cleanup efforts.[58]   Because DOD often must develop new technologies to cleanup specific toxic and hazardous waste sites and has approximately 18,000 potential hazardous waste sites, DOD funding for cleanup is expected to remain over $2 billion a year into the foreseeable future. Because of the dollar values involved and the political importance to individual members of Congress, toxic and hazardous waste cleanup and DOD cleanup of bases designated for closure by the Base Realignment and Closure Committee have top priority at DOD and require the close attention of its environmental leadership.

To ensure that DOD does not create new forms of toxic and hazardous waste and that it is executing its daily operations missions in accordance with state, local and federal environmental laws, the Department of Defense is spending $2.5 billion in FY94 on compliance.[59]   Because DOD installations comprise small cities, forests, deserts and wetlands that are part of estuarian environments, achieving compliance is a complex and difficult task. To help, DOD has entered into cooperative agreements with the Environmental Protection Agency, state and regional regulators and environmental groups to develop synergies that allow it to bring the greatest expertise to bear on achieving compliance, which sometimes runs counter to maintaining operation readiness. For example, at larger US bases such as Camp Le June and Ft. Bragg, the red cockaded woodpecker, an endangered species, has been found to inhabit important training and artillery impact ranges for some of the military's most important units. In situations such as this, the military must modify training and seek workable solutions with environmental groups that help to monitor wildlife. DOD spends some $30 million yearly to identify and protect natural and cultural resources such as flora, fauna, historic and archaeological sites and artifacts.[60] Thus, DOD is one of the largest land managers in the United States and is arguably a positive force for environmental conservation because development on DOD lands is limited and much land is preserved in its natural state to serve as multi-use and training land.

Recognizing the important contribution that DOD can make to conservation, the US Congress in 1991 appropriated some $10 million to promote the stewardship of DOD in natural and cultural resource areas. Under the Legacy Program, multiple government and non-government partners work with the Department of Defense on hundreds of separate efforts to inventory, protect and manage scarce biological resources. In other projects, the Department of Defense is working closely with the leaders of western tribal Indian councils to preserve archaeological sites that have been deemed priceless. Thus, Congress is helping DOD to make a contribution to the aesthetic side of environmental preservation. While it is difficult to set a dollar value on the maintenance of an endangered species or the restoration of an historical, archaeological site, DOD and Congress recognize the importance of these efforts and increasingly use DOD resources to satisfy the demands of the American people for such preservation.

Because DOD remains a major contractor for defense systems and maintains many industrial munitions plants involved in the production of weapons systems and munitions, it has moved aggressively to establish a pollution-prevention program so that it can minimize the amount of funding spent to clean up toxic and hazardous wastes in the future. The program has been successful and DOD has been able to reduce by 55 percent the amount of hazardous waste it produces annually. Given the fact that hazardous waste disposal costs for industry have gone up 600 percent between 1987 and 1991, such a reduction is an obvious way for DOD to contain its environmental costs.[61]

A primary component of the pollution-prevention program is the engineering solution: determining how weapons systems are designed, constructed, utilized and maintained and eliminating characteristics of a weapon system that produce toxic or hazardous waste. Such engineering solutions require cooperation between the Department of Defense and industry. In addition, as the result of the 1984 Montreal Protocol and Title IX of the Clean Air Act Amendments of 1990 and recent presidential emphasis, DOD is moving aggressively to phase out ozone-depleting substances from its inventory.[62] While many of these substances have recently developed substitutes, many important uses of the substances are related to critical defense weapon system components for which there is currently no substitute. DOD is working closely with industry and investing millions of dollars in research and development programs to meet the requirements of these agreements and legislation and is also making a strong effort in the area of environmental technology.

Working closely with EPA and other knowledgeable organizations, DOD is prioritizing its environmental technology requests of R&D laboratories to ensure that they are dedicated to high priority uses. DOD is also reenergizing its focus on the strategic environmental research and development program originally proposed by Senators Nunn and Gore. For FY94 DOD has requested $325 million from Congress to execute its environmental technology program.[63] As previously mentioned, DOD has many toxic and hazardous waste sites that are unique to the defense sector and must develop technology to remediate these sites. The technology that is being developed could be exported to other countries and used to facilitate environmental cleanup in some of the more problematic Euro-Asian hazardous waste sites.

The US Army Corps of Engineers is a DOD asset and a major command of the US Army. It has a larger, non-military function, performing work for other agencies of the US Government on a reimbursable basis. The Corps is known best for its work in constructing military and civil works projects both in the international arena and in the United States. However, environmental protection is a primary mission of the Corps. As America became less interested in domestic water resource development schemes and its priority shifted to environmental stewardship, the Corps of Engineers has been called upon to perform an increasing amount of environmental service to the United States and its overseas allies. The Corps is heavily involved in toxic and hazardous waste remediation efforts in the United States and has served as a major contractor at the Hanford, Washington, nuclear waste area and other superfund sites. For a number of years the Corps of Engineers has been one of the primary agents of the Environmental Protection Agency's superfund remediation work, generally accounting for over 40 percent of superfund cleanup in a given year.[64] Because the Corps has operations in virtually all states and national organization, technology and cleanup procedures developed to clean up such diverse sources of pollution as nuclear, chemical, nerve agent and carcinogenic industrial wastes in one state are easily transferred to similar sites in other states.

The Corps of Engineers makes many contributions to environmental security beyond its toxic and hazardous waste cleanup role. It is responsible for the nation's waterways, harbor and river transport artery maintenance, water resource schemes such as dams and also manages some 12 million acres of US land. To help it perform its tasks properly, the Corps of Engineers has developed several labs such as the Construction Engineer Research Laboratory (CERL) in Illinois and the Waterways Experimentation Station (WES) in Mississippi. Both labs have made major contributions to environmental systems management. CERL has been a leader in the development of geographic information systems for environmental management, designing computer systems that allow training areas to be digitized and complex training requirements balanced against environmental constraints. The WES is well known for developing computerized water-flow management programs that have allowed civilian agencies to better manage water flows from critical estuaries such as the Chesapeake Bay.

In addition to these activities, under the Water Resources Development Acts of 1986, 1988 and 1990, the Corps of Engineers was assigned the responsibility for wetland permitting.[65] Because wetlands provide a primary feedstock for commercial and sport fishing, are valuable for recharging groundwater, provide nesting areas for threatened and endangered species and serve as stops on waterfowl flyways, the Corps' management of the wetlands allows it to make a major contribution to the nation's environmental security.

Under section 404 of the Water Resources Development Act of 1990, the Corps of Engineers has been given regulatory supervision over the remaining 93 million acres of US wetlands and considers approximately 15,000 individual permit applications per year.[66] As part of its wetlands management role, the Corps has established a wetlands research and development program and in 1991 began a $22 million three-year study targeted at restoring and developing wetlands and improving their management in combination with other organizations and research and development agencies. The Corps is also a leader in several major efforts to restore wetlands in the Kissimmee River of Florida and Everglades National Park. In these projects, the Corps is working closely with the state of Florida in a joint effort as well as with the Fish and Wildlife Service and the Environmental Protection Agency. The Corps of Engineers Wetland

Projects also support international agreements such as the North American Waterfowl management plan of the United States and Canada.[67]

These domestic contributions of the Department of Defense are significant and offer models upon which NATO might develop programs for addressing critical environmental problems both within the Alliance and out of area in regions strategically important to European security. The militaries in Europe receive the same criticism for land use and abuse as do DOD forces in the United States. To the degree that European militaries are able to accomplish their cleanup, compliance, conservation and pollution-prevention missions in a successful manner, they will garner public support, more easily maintain access to training areas and maintain control of their operational programs. Recognizing this, some defense organizations are changing their behavior. In Britain, the Ministry of Defence (MOD) has environmental stewardship of some 242,000 hectares throughout Britain. To overcome criticism that MOD management limits public access, the Ministry has institutionalized environmental compliance as a method of doing business and gaining public support. It is closely monitoring the impact of exercises, appointing conservation officers for its units, replanting trees and even using horsemen to patrol areas where the use of four-wheel drive vehicles might otherwise erode the delicate flora.[68]

Although still evolving, the US environmental security mission is an excellent role model for other militaries to follow in their effort to meet increasingly stringent environmental standards while maintaining their operational readiness. In addition to internal environmental security missions, the military can make a great contribution to the second tenet of DOD's definition of environmental security: mitigating impacts of adverse environmental actions that lead to international instability. Secretary of Defense Les Aspin has articulated four threats to the national security of the United States and in each of these DOD can make a contribution. These threats are regional dangers, nuclear dangers, dangers to democracy and economic dangers.

One of the primary tools for addressing international environmental security is the US Security Assistance Program, once largely utilized to develop military capabilities among allies. The Security Assistance Program is now being used creatively to help nations develop the economic health and environmental infrastructure necessary to maintain stability. Since 1991, Congress has provided $30 million for DOD efforts to promote biodiversity and conservation efforts and democratic awareness on the part of foreign militaries. This makes good sense. The military in the developing world is often the best organized and efficient element of the government and present in all areas of the country, to include distant frontiers and areas composed of minority ethnic groups. Encouraging the military to accomplish civic action and environmental projects in areas populated by disenfranchised minority groups promotes nation-building and demonstrates the concern of the government for its divergent population base.

The chief cause of political instability is poverty. The United States is increasingly aware that its Security Assistance Program nation-building projects help governments address the needs of the civilian population, reducing the conditions of poverty and promoting legitimacy in the eyes of the people. Thus, the DOD Security Assistance Program has helped host country militaries to rebuild water supply systems, construct hospitals, drill wells, build sanitary landfills, roads and airstrips for previously isolated sections of the country. Such projects contribute to the economic and health and overall environmental well-being of a nation and identify the military with non-traditional roles and as making a positive contribution to the needs of the people.

This work recognizes the contribution of military environmental security projects to reducing poverty and promoting economic sustainability. For example, in Africa, DOD established its coastal security program which provides patrol boats, law of the sea education, training in boarding procedures and communication systems to fledgling naval units of host government militaries along the African littoral. With these assets the countries have been able to patrol their exclusive economic zones and limit poaching and the rapacious over-fishing of foreign trawler fleets. Such a program reduces the likelihood that valuable local fisheries, critical to the well-being of the health and economy of a nation, are depleted beyond their carrying capacity and allows the government to obtain royalties from foreign fleets.[69]

DOD expanded upon the concept of the Coastal Security Program to establish biodiversity in a conservation program that encourages the military to conserve its wildlife resources. The focus of the program has been on anti-poaching and habitat maintenance projects such as developing bridges and roads in game parks, putting in small dams to maintain wetlands and fisheries and developing the local military capacity for protecting terrestrial wildlife against the all too prevalent poachers. This program has many advantages. It maintains military-to-military contact and helps sustain natural resources that are important both to domestic hunters and fishermen and to the tourist industry, which brings hundreds of millions of dollars into Africa every year. Assistance programs in these areas stand against the forces of poverty and contribute to the political stability of the governments that receive the assistance.

Another area of international importance within the DOD organization is the Center for Global Environmental Excellence located in the Construction Engineer Research Laboratory. The purpose of this center is to 'provide a proactive ability to spatially evaluate the environmental risks and sensitivities of actions (or inaction) and policies worldwide using a format similar to an environmental assessment or impact statement based on emerging technological capabilities'.[70] Because of the DOD global mission and presidential executive orders of 1978 making the United States responsible for its environmental actions overseas, the center can make a major contribution to DOD's ability to execute its environmental security mission. Identifying potential environmental problems and mitigating them is more cost effective than attempting to wrestle with the potential political instability that can result. The Center accomplishes this with computer models that help plan environmental stewardship on a global basis. The format combines spacial analysis of geographic information systems with advanced and emerging remote-sensing technology. By digitizing large quantities of existing environmental data, it can offer information to help manage such diverse environmental variables as treaty negotiations, water-use planning, mineral resource prospecting and development, vegetative resource health and disease control, insect control planning, disaster planning and land-use management. This geographic information system has the capability of doing environmental sensitivity analysis that would allow governments to better manage their environmental efforts and more efficiently allocate resources to critical environmental problems in a timely fashion.[71]

Other DOD-related programs include initiatives from the civilian leadership of the United States. For example, Senators Nunn and Lugar proposed legislation that provided $800 million to assist the Former Soviet Union's nuclear environmental disarmament program. The legislation has been broadened every year so that it does not focus exclusively on dismantling weapons, but allows for environmental cleanup, such as the $25 million allocated to Belarus to clean up nuclear-related waste on a Former Soviet military base.[72] The Corps of Engineers has been actively involved in helping its Soviet counterpart design facilities in which disassembled nuclear weapons could be safely stored. Because of the limited development of Soviet technology in this area and the superior experience of the Corps of Engineers in constructing facilities for storing sensitive radioactive waste, this project is providing technology transfer and making a significant improvement in nuclear security for the Former Soviet Union and its European neighbors.

Vice-President Gore was the force behind the establishment of the environmental task force that combined intelligence collection assets of the DOD and the Central Intelligence Agency to address problems. Data from the intelligence agencies has been provided to high-level civilian academics whose mission is to develop ways of using the data for global environmental improvement. The potential benefits of this program are now being realized.

Recently civilian academics have been able to monitor undersea volcanic eruptions by using data collected from naval intelligence assets. The Navy's underwater sound surveillance system (SOSUS) was designed at a cost of $15 billion to track enemy ships and submarines. It is a network that surrounds the globe with underwater listening devices tied directly to US Navy shore stations through 30,000 miles of undersea cable.[73] The Navy now filters out high frequency signals and pipes the low frequency signals required directly to scientists at the National Oceanic and Atmospheric Administration Pacific Marine Environmental Laboratory in Newport, California. Monitoring undersea disruptions will aid in predicting platetechtonic shifts, earthquakes and tsunamis. Dr D. James Baker, the agency's administrator, pointing out the revolutionary impact that this information will have on the earth sciences, stated, 'we want to understand the environment', and that the new information, 'gives us a window on the ocean that we can't get in any other way – almost a global picture of what is happening'.[74] Given the potential for these systems to provide critical environmental data on such topics as soil contamination, marine data on overfishing and poaching, climatic change and disaster prediction, this task force has the potential of further demonstrating the unique contributions of military assets to the realm of environmental security.

The Department of Defense definition of its environmental security mission includes ensuring that its military operations and training are conducted in compliance with environmental laws and deterring or mitigating the environmental causes of political instability and conflict in the international arena. The contributions that the Department of Defense have made in these areas are not balanced. There has clearly been a greater emphasis placed on the former aspect of its mission, that of ensuring DOD compliance and stewardship. Only now is the international conflict and instability component of environmental security beginning to receive the substantial DOD resources available. Nevertheless, the DOD environmental security program offers an excellent model on which to pattern NATO environmental security activities.

B.   A NATO Approach

Now that NATO is no longer needed to protect Western Europe against the Soviet Union, it could be very useful in providing the sense of security within which the new democratic republics of Central and Eastern Europe can thrive.[75]

Jean Kirkpatrick

As recognized in the New Strategic Concept, NATO is in the particularly fortuitous situation of having extensive membership and capabilities well suited for executing these new security functions, which the EC, WEU and CSCE cannot duplicate; NATO is in the best position to address Europe's environmental security problems. Because the United States is a member and quite often takes a major leadership role in NATO policy and activities, the environmental management skills and capabilities developed through the DOD program are available to NATO. Bringing these substantial capabilities to bear on NATO's cooperation and dialogue concept would be relatively easy to achieve. First, because the use of the military for non-traditional contributions to national security is a favorite theme of the new Clinton administration, the use of DOD assets to support a NATO environmental security program should have US support. In addition, US environmental elements are already at work in Europe assisting cooperation partners. The Corps of Engineers, for example, has performed work in Poland and the FSU on major environmental threats such as nuclear disarmament and waste storage. Moreover, Mr Gary Vest, the Principal Assistant Deputy Under-Secretary of Defense for Environmental Security, is a co-chair of pilot studies for the NATO Committee on the Challenges of a Modern Society and is already providing new concepts for NATO's participation in environmental security measures. By drawing upon the US program and assuming an environmental security assistance mission, NATO could demonstrate its relevance at a time when many question its very existence. It would also establish greater contacts with the former East Bloc militaries, which are already demonstrating that they are losing faith in the new democratic regimes and help reduce the threats to governmental legitimacy and stability caused by chronic, often untreated, environmental problems. It would also reinforce the idea of civil primacy in the civil–military relations.

For its part, NATO has established the institutional framework for international environmental security projects and activities. In its redrafting of the Alliance Strategic Concept, the North Atlantic Council stated that,

> Risks to Allied security are less likely to result from calculated aggression against territory of the Allies, but rather from the adverse consequences of instabilities that may arise from serious economic, social and political difficulties, including ethnic rivalries and the territorial disputes, which are faced by many countries in Central and Eastern Europe. . . .They could . . . lead to crises inimical to European stability and even to armed conflicts.[76]

In discussing the concept's broad approach to security and protecting peace in the new Europe, the Alliance points out the 'opportunities for achieving Alliance objectives through political means' are substantially greater in the new security environment and that security and stability have political, economic, social and environmental elements as well as the indispensable defense dimension.[77]

Efforts to achieve NATO objectives include the use of dialogue and cooperation with the purpose of decreasing the risks of conflict by reducing misunderstandings; fostering confidence-building measures; and establishing regular military contacts with Eastern and Central Europe utilizing the framework of the London Declaration.[78]

In addition, such creative uses of NATO are reinforced by the Charter of Paris for a New Europe, which encourages the Alliance to 'develop broader and productive patterns of bilateral and multilateral cooperation in all relevant fields of European security, with the aim, interalia, of preventing crises or, should they arise, ensuring their effective management'.[79] Thus, NATO has the institutional framework and strategic concept upon which to build an environmental security assistance program towards countries whose environmental problems pose a threat to political stability and European security.

Individually, some member countries have established environmental directives that encourage such international cooperation. Germany, for example, recognizes that its Federal Armed Forces have multiple capabilities with which to mitigate environmental damage or enhance environmental protection. Under Article XXXV of the Basic Law, administrative assistance and disaster relief can be provided and under other directives technical support may also be provided for environmental purposes. Indeed, the Federal Armed Forces in their own regulation encourage 'providing technical and logistical equipment, specialized knowledge and methods developed and used for the defense mission . . . for the purpose of protecting the environment'.[80] The German technical concept for environmental protection also states that 'environmental problems can only be solved by international cooperation and this applies to the Federal Armed Forces as well'.[81] Thus, the United States, Britain and Germany, the most powerful military members of NATO, have committed their armed forces to promoting environmental stewardship and international environmental outreach.

NATO has begun nascent efforts in international environmental cooperation. In the mid-1970s, representatives from NATO's Naval Forces formed a working group to exchange information about environmental protection and national regulations and to standardize procedures for dumping waste at sea.[82] However, it is the NATO Committee on the Challenges of Modern Society (CCMS) that has been the leader on environmental issues through its pilot studies on critical environmental issues. Created in 1969 to provide a social dimension to the Alliance, the

CCMS programs have assumed greater significance as NATO's military dimension has waned. The 1992 NATO Work Plan for Dialogue, Partnership and Cooperation emphasizes NATO's Third Dimension, scientific and environmental programs and highlights the CCMS role in developing institutional relationships with cooperation partners – the countries of East and Central Europe and the Former Soviet Union. The CCMS has a record of success promoting environmental technology development and transfer and cooperation between the United States and Europe and between NATO and its cooperation partners. One of the important pilot projects that has been initiated by the CCMS under the framework of the North Atlantic Cooperation Council (NACC) is the 'Cross-Border Environmental Problems Emanating from Defense Related Installations and Activities Studies'. These studies address radioactive contamination in the Barents, Kara, Laptev and Baltic Seas as a result of decommissioned nuclear vessels and the drainage of polluted rivers into these marine areas.[83] Participating in this study are the Czech Republic, Estonia, Hungary, Latvia, Lithuania, Poland, Russia, the Slovak Republic, Kyrgystan and the Ukraine as well as eight NATO member countries.[84]

In late February 1993, the CCMS for the first time met in formal session with the members of the NACC. At this meeting the NATO Assistant Secretary-General for Scientific and Environmental Affairs stressed the importance of the Alliance's scientific and environmental programs to its new objectives and emphasized NATO's commitment to addressing important environmental issues, such as defense-related and natural disaster problems in critical regions. During this meeting, cooperation partners requested assistance with environmental problems concerning water pollution, soil and air contamination. All member countries in attendance agreed that international cooperative action was the only method to successfully address most European cross-border environmental pollution problems.[85] NATO military elements have the technical expertise and organizational capabilities to help the Cooperation Partner militaries address these issues.

CCMS has initiated other pilot projects aimed at furthering important international environmental contact with critical regions. Its work has produced a NATO environmental mission statement demonstrating the commitment of NATO commanders to environmental stewardship and an environmental principles statement for NATO commanders. Other important issues addressed by the CCMS pilot studies include the role of the military in executing the Montreal Protocol.[86] However, much of CCMS effort has been dedicated to building consensus among the NATO military forces and impressing upon its commanders that environmental stewardship is a mission that should be part of the military's daily activities. That is to say, the

CCMS focus has been more internal than international. Clearly, the CCMS and NATO have the potential to do much more in addressing environmental security out of area rather than focusing primarily upon the externalities of their own military operations.

In order to address the environmental problems of the FSU, Central and Eastern Europe, NATO and other allied military organizations, such as the US European Command (EUCOM), should develop a strategy for using the military component to execute NATO's strategic concept of promoting regional stability in environmentally troubled areas. The institutional recognition of the need and importance of executing such a strategy has been articulated in the written frameworks of the DOD, NATO, NACC and many member countries. The Cooperation Partners of East and Central Europe, themselves, are requesting such assistance. NATO should capitalize on their interest by using the dialogue and cooperation tenets of the new Strategic Concept to promote environmental assistance towards these and other strategically important areas with an environmental security assistance program similar to the US Security Assistance Program. The objective of this environmental security assistance program should be to mitigate environmental problems that have the potential to erode economic and health factors, undermine governmental legitimacy and promote instability and further involve host nation militaries in the solution of their country's environmental security issues.

The NATO environmental security assistance program should not operate in a vacuum. It should seek synergy by working in close cooperation with other North Atlantic Cooperation Council (NACC) and bilateral and international programs, such as those of the International Atomic Energy Agency and the Helsinki Commission, whose missions are to promote stability and environmental improvement in critical regions. For instance, the US Agency for International Development (USAID) spent nearly $500 million in FY91 on its environmental programs, concentrating on education, training, economic policies and infrastructure.[87] A NATO environmental security assistance program could capitalize on new USAID-built roads to distant regions of a given country to provide environmental assistance in the newly opened area, or assist USAID in broadening training programs to include the host government military. Moreover, the NATO environmental security assistance program should focus on those countries receiving priority from the NAC civilian, policy-making arm so that environmental assistance teams support the overall Alliance security strategy.

NATO militaries have diverse technical assets, including engineers, public health, sanitation, environmental and industrial and WMD waste cleanup specialists, which can be formed into assistance teams. These resources can make significant contributions in such diverse areas as developing food distribution systems; providing medical and health care; upgrading waste water, sewage, transportation and other public utilities necessary to sustain the economy, education and training, disaster relief and emergency management. Environmental assistance teams can perform environmental mitigation operations themselves, conduct joint mitigation and improvement exercises with host government militaries and train host government militaries to conduct environmental mitigation programs. (See Figure 16.3.)

The environmental programs of other agencies would also benefit from a NATO environmental security assistance program. The Organization for Economic Cooperation and Development (OECD) has many environmental programs dedicated to Eastern Europe and the Former Soviet Union, funded for several hundred million dollars. The Poland, Hungary, Assistance for Economic Restructuring (PHARE) Program is also well funded and includes multiple environmental improvement objectives. The UN Environmental Program and the United Nation's Development Program both target developing countries and, as previously mentioned, the US Congress has multiple individual environmental initiatives, such as the Nunn–Lugar proposal, for Eastern Europe and the FSU.[88]

Figure 16.3: NATO support for environmental security

These are but a few of the many programs whose objectives and initiatives could be coordinated and supported by the NATO environmental security assistance program. In fact, NATO could serve as a clearing house for environmental proposals to be funded by outside donors. This clearinghouse function would establish priorities, bring order to the current, uncoordinated and unfocused efforts of multiple donor agencies and governments, avoid waste and duplication of effort and allow the concentration of resources against the environmental problems most likely to threaten European security interests.

The program's objectives could also be tied to the goals of multilateral lending institution programs in order to gain their financial support, or support for multilateral initiatives to the developing countries assisted by the teams. Developing countries, whether in Eastern Europe, the FSU, the Middle East or Africa, frequently have one thing in common concerning environmental problems. They lack the administrative resources to properly evaluate, chronicle and address their environmental issues. Simply put, the environmental problems dwarf the bureaucratic resources available. The NATO program can address this problem by helping to develop host country militaries into environmental security resources, which can execute environmental projects, such as building primary water treatment facilities, dams and irrigation schemes, or providing emergency management assistance, such as monitoring radiation from potential nuclear disasters in the FSU and evacuating the populace caught in its path, or assisting in the cleanup of toxic and hazardous waste at former East Bloc military bases. NATO teams could also train the host government military to properly evaluate environmental problems and prepare grant requests from multilateral organizations whose mission it is to aid in the solution of such problems.

Under this environmental security assistance team concept, military training teams could be sent to target countries with country-specific tailored programs that could include:

- establishing geographic information systems for local or national environmental planning;
- creating environmental security cells at national or regional level to promote cooperation between civilian and military environmental resources;
- establishing lecture programs on critical environmental issues such as the legal and financial requirements to solve environmental problems;
- oversight of environmental infrastructure construction;
- assessment and remediation plan development;
- environmental threat monitoring;

- water resource management;
- natural resource conservation practices;
- disaster relief planning and training;
- environmental health education training;
- energy conservation program development;
- restoration of military facilities.[89]

The environmental security assistance program concept is mutually beneficial. Those countries to which its teams are deployed would benefit from having additional resources to assist them in their efforts to bring environmental problems under control. Further, their indigenous military forces would be trained to perform non-traditional military missions that promote nation-building and help to develop governmental legitimacy. NATO for its part, would further demonstrate its relevance in the post-Cold War security environment and take advantage of the good will of European and Cooperation Partners to further promote the concept of European unity and the value of US military participation in European security endeavors.

As the $2 billion already spent on the seemingly endless quagmire of Somalia demonstrates, precluding conflict is much more cost effective than the ad hoc commitment of combat forces. The commitment of NATO Environmental Security Assistance teams can help mitigate the causes of future conflict and preclude NATO out-of-area combat missions, which could split the Alliance. It is a visionary concept whose time has come.

NOTES

1. Sherri Wasserman Goodman, Deputy Under-Secretary of Defense (Environmental Security), 'Statement before the United States Senate Committee on Armed Services', Subcommittee on Military Readiness and Defense Infrastructure, June 9, 1993, p. 2.
2. Jessica Tuchman Matthews, 'Redefining Security', *Foreign Affairs*, Spring 1989, pp. 162–78. Another early and important effort to broaden the definition of national security to include environmental challenges was Michael Renner, *National Security: The Economic and Environmental Dimensions*, Washington: World Watch Institute, May 1989.
3. W.A. Douglas Jackson and Marwyn S. Samuels, *Politics and Geographic Relationships*, Englewood Cliffs, New Jersey: Prentiss-Hall, 1971, p. 5.
4. David Easton, *A Framework for Political Analysis*, Englewood Cliffs, New Jersey: Prentiss-Hall, 1965. See also, Karl W. Deutsch, 'The Growth of Nations: Some Recurrent Patterns of Political and Social Integration', *World Politics*, January 1953, pp. 168–95 and Gabriel Almond, 'A Developmental Approach to Political Systems', *World Politics*, Vol. XV, No. 2, January 1965, pp. 183–214.
5. Ibid., p. 128.
6. Richard H. Ullman, 'Redefining Security', *International Security*, Vol. 8, No. 1, Summer 1983, pp. 129–53.
7. Norman Myers, 'Environment and Security', *Foreign Policy*, Spring 1989, pp. 23–41.
8. Thomas F. Homer-Dixon, Jeffrey H. Boutwell and George W. Rathjens, 'Environmental Change and Violent Conflict', *Scientific American*, February 1993, pp. 38–45. See also, Thomas F. Homer-Dixon, 'On The Threshold: Environmental Changes As Causes of Acute Conflict', *International Security*, Vol. 16, No. 2, Fall 1991, pp. 76–116. Not all authors believe that there is a correlation between environment and conflict. See, for example,

Daniel Deudney, 'The Case Against Linking Environmental Degradation and National Security', *Millennium: Journal of International Studies*, Vol. 19, No. 3, 1990, pp. 461–76.

9.   *National Security Strategy of the United States*, Washington: US Government Printing Office, August 1991, p. 22.

10.   Sam Nunn, 'Strategic Environmental Research Program', Senate floor speech, June 28, 1990.

11.   NATO, 'The Alliance's New Strategic Concept', November 7, 1991, NATO Press Service, Press Communique S–1 (91) 85, p. 3.

12.   Ibid., p. 6.

13.   Vladimir Shlapentokh, 'The Ukraine Migraine: How the Escalating Feud With Russia Could Lead to Something Worse', *The Washington Post*, September 5, 1993, p. C–2. See also, Alexander Tkachenko, 'Ukrainean Premier Steps Down', *The Washington Post*, September 10, 1993, p. A–32 and Steven Erlangen, 'Ukraine Questions the Pricetag of Independence', *The New York Times*, September 8, 1993, p. A–8.

14.   Don Oberdorfer, 'Bush Offers $175 Million For Non-Nuclear Ukraine', *The Washington Post*, December 10, 1992, p. A–12.

15.   Rachel Fleishman, Special Assistant for International Security, Office of the Deputy Under-Secretary of Defense for Environmental Security, Interview, Washington, DC, September 2, 1993.

16.   Commission of the European Communities, 'EC Assistance to the Soviet Union and the Countries of Central and Eastern Europe in Nuclear Safety', News Release, IP (91) 526, June 1991. See also, George Rodrigue, 'Under a Cloud: Soviet Nuclear Program Left Legacy of Ills, Anger', *The Dallas Morning News*, August 10, 1993, p. 1.

17.   Victoria Pope and Julie Corwin, 'Radiation in Russia', *US News and World Report*, August 9, 1993, p. 40. See also, George Rodrigue, 'A Ravaged Land: Pollution Woes Intensify During Post-Soviet Era', *The Dallas Morning News*, August 8, 1993, p. 1.

18.   Jean-Christophe Fueg, 'Soviet Oil Production Begins to Falter', *World Oil*, August 1989, p. 83. See also, various issues of Energy Information Agency, *International Oil and Gas Exploration and Development Activities*, Quarterly Reports.

19.   Stephen A. Holmes, 'Russia–US Sign Space, Energy Deal', *The New York Times*, September 3, 1993, p. A–6.

20.   Directorate of Intelligence, Central Intelligence Agency, *Handbook of International Economic Statistics – 1992*, Washington: US Government Printing Office, 1992, p. 128.

21.   US Bureau of Mines, *Mineral Commodity Summaries, 1993*, Washington: US Government Printing Office, 1993.

22.   US Department of Commerce, *Statistical Abstract of the United States 1992: The National Data Book*, Washington: US Government Printing Office, 1992, p. 820.

23.   William T. Johnson, *NATO's New Front Line: The Growing Importance of the Southern Tier*, Carlisle Barracks, PA: Strategic Studies Institute, 1992, p. 8.

24.   The Economist, *The Economist Book of Vital World Statistics*, New York: Times Books (Random House) 1990, pp. 34–35. See also, 'EC's Matutes Discusses Ties With Maghreb', *Foreign Broadcast Information Service (FBIS)*–WEU–92–048, March 11, 1992, p. 6.

25.   'Eurostat, Composition of Extra EC Foreign Residents', (IP 90 492) Luxemburg, Brussels, June 19, 1990.

26.   US Committee for Refugees, *World Refugees Studies, 1991*, Washington: USCR, 1991, pp. 7–13. For an in-depth perspective on migration and European security see Lawrence Freedman and John Saunders, *Population Change and European Security*, New York: Brassey's, 1991.

27.   Remy Leveau, *Algeria: Adversaries in Search of Uncertain Compromises*, Chaillot Papers, Paris: Institute for Security Studies, 1992.

28.   US Committee for Refugees, 1991, p. 9.

29.   Organization for Economic Cooperation and Development, *Trends and International Migration*, Paris: OECD, 1992, p. 33.

30.   'EC: Immigration from Eastern Europe Studied', *FBIS*–WEU–93–114–A, June 16, 1993, p. 5.

31.   Perhaps the European country struggling most with immigrant-related social stability problems is Germany. In the last year, non-violent ultra-right-wing offenses, such as distributing Nazi propaganda, have doubled to approximately 7,000 and over 2,500 violent acts have been perpetrated against foreigners in the past year. See, for example, Rick Atkinson, 'Germany Unable To Stem Flood of Attacks on Foreigners', *The Washington Post*, August 28, 1993, p. A–15 and 'Push Comes to Shove: Western Europe is Ailing, Angry and Afraid of the Future', *US News and World Report*, June 14, 1993, pp 53–64.

32. World Bank, *World Development Report 1992: Development and the Environment*, New York: Oxford University Press, 1992, p. 7.
33. Ibid., p. 32.
34. Ibid., p. 30.
35. International Monetary Fund, *World Economic Outlook: May 1993*, Washington: International Monetary Fund, May 1993, p. 14.
36. Directorate of Intelligence, *Handbook of International Economic Statistics* – 1992, pp. 56–7.
37. George J. Coakley, Chief, Division of International Minerals, US Bureau of Mines, Interview, Washington, DC, September 2, 1993.
38. Directorate of Intelligence, p. 62.
39. The World Bank, *The World Debt Tables, 1992–93: External Finance For Developing Countries, Vol. 1, Analysis and Summary Tables*, Washington: The World Bank, 1993, p. 29. See also, Louis Uchitelle, 'New Man, Old Burden: Moscow Owes $68 Billion', *The New York Times*, December 16, 1992, p. A–14.
40. Lee Hockstader, 'Russian Parliament Rejects Budget Cuts, $22 Billion Deficit Could Risk Loss of Aid', *The Washington Post*, August 28, 1993, p. A–18 and 'The Case of Aiding Russia', *The Washington Post*, September 9, 1993, p. A–20.
41. Peggy McInerny, 'Regional Economic Development Thwarted', Kennan Institute for Advanced Russian Studies: Meeting Report, Vol. 10, No. 13, 1993.
42. McInerny, 'Collapse of a Civilization, Not an Economy', Kennan Institute for Advanced Russian Studies: Meeting Report, Vol. 10, No. 11, 1993.
43. Roland Evans and Robert Novak, 'Yeltsin's Challenge', *The Washington Post*, April 26, 1993, p. A–19.
44. Serge Schmemann, 'Russia's Peril: Soviet Type Breakup', *The New York Times*, March 15, 1993, p. A–6.
45. 'The Commonwealth and the Military', Vol. IX, No. 9, 1992. See also, McInerny, 'Caucuses, Ethnic Conflict and Economic Decline', The Kennan Institute for Advanced Russian Studies: Meeting Report, Vol. 10, No. 14, 1993 and Steve Le Vine, 'Brutal Tajik Civil War Shakes All Central Asia, Communists Rule Again After 20,000 Die', *The Washington Post*, February 5, 1993, p. A–1.
46. William J. Broad, 'Russian Says Soviet Atom Arsenal was Larger Than West Estimated', *The New York Times*, September 26, 1993, p. 1 and Elaine Sciolino, 'US Will Draw Up Strategy to Aid Ex-Soviet States', *The New York Times*, February 8, 1993, p. A–1.
47. Fred Hiatt, 'US May Buy Soviet Uranium', *The Washington Post*, November 24, 1992, p. A–17.
48. R. Jeffrey Smith, 'CIA Chief Says Russia's Controls on Spread of Arms Remains Weak', *The Washington Post*, February 25, 1993, p. A–18. See also, Jim Hoagland, 'Lots of Russian Nukes For Sale', *The Washington Post*, February 23, 1993, p. A–18.
49. Pope and Corwin, 'Radiation in Russia', p. 40. See also, Commission of the European Communities, 'Chernobyl Four Years On', (Statement by Mr Cardoso E. Cunha and Mr Ripa Di Meana), press release, IP (90) 342, April 26, 1990 and, Commission of the European Communities, *Nuclear Safety: The European Community Following the Chernobyl Accident*, Brussels, Directorate-General for Information, 1989. Other relevant sources are, Michael Dobbs, 'After the Soviet Union's Collapse Are Its Nuclear Safeguards Next?', *The Washington Post*, September 7, 1993, p. A–12 and Rick Maze, 'Nuclear-Arms-Control Fears Take Center Stage', *Army Times*, March 15, 1993, p. 30.
50. Ibid.
51. Pope and Corwin, p. 40.
52. Michael Dobbs, 'In the Former Soviet Union, Paying the Nuclear Price', *The Washington Post*, September 7, 1993, p. A–1. See also, George Rodrigue, 'Suffering for the Past', *The Dallas Morning News*, August 11, 1993, p. 1.
53. Robert J. Samuelson, 'Of Deutschmarks', *The Washington Post*, February 2, 1993, p. A–21.
54. Dan Zanini, Senior Army Fellow, 'Council on Foreign Relations Trip Report from its May 1993 Visit to NATO', Washington, DC, August 1993.
55. 'Rome Declaration on Peace and Cooperation', November 8, 1991, NATO Press Service, Press Communique S–1 (91) 86.
56. Dan Zanini, Trip Report, p. 4.
57. William H. Parker III, 'Environment Moves to Front Burner', *Defense 90*, March/April 1990, pp. 21–32.
58. Sherri Wasserman Goodman, 1993, p. 4.
59. Ibid., p. 9.
60. Ibid., p. 8.

61. Ibid., p. 10.
62. Ibid., p. 11.
63. Ibid., p. 12.
64. Henry J. Hatch, 'Chief of Engineers Charge', Address to the 45th Meeting, Environmental Advisory Board, Ft. Worth, Texas, April 12, 1989, p. 5.
65. Patrick J. Kelly, 'The Greening of the Corps: A Balanced Approach in Protecting Wetlands', *Military Engineer*, March–April 1991, pp. 31–4.
66. Ibid., p. 32.
67. Ibid., p. 33.
68. Ann Hills, 'A Green Ministry', *Geographical Magazine*, May 1991, pp. 16–20.
69. Scott Fisher, 'Biodiversity Country Projects', Washington, Office of the Assistant Secretary of Defense, International Security Affairs, Africa Region, March 1992, p. 1.
70. Corps of Engineer's Research Lab, Environmental Sustainment Laboratory, 'Center of Global Environmental Excellence', Champaign, IL, 1992.
71. Robert Lozar, Director, Environmental Sustainment Laboratory, Corps of Engineers' Research Laboratory, Interview, Washington, DC, September 1, 1993.
72. Rachel Fleishman, Interview, September 2, 1993.
73. William J. Broad, 'Long Secret Navy Devices Allow Monitoring of Ocean Eruption', *The New York Times*, August 20, 1993, p. A–1.
74. Ibid.
75. Jean Kirkpatrick, 'Despite Optimism After Communists Fall, Europe Has Not United', *Sunday Patriot News*, December 5, 1993, p. B–15.
76. NATO, 'The Alliance's New Strategic Concept', 1991, p. 3.
77. Ibid., p. 6.
78. Ibid., p. 7.
79. Ibid., p. 8.
80. Federal Ministry of Defense (Germany), *The Technical Concept*, 'Environmental Protection in the Federal Armed Forces', Bonn: Federal Ministry of Defense, 1990, p. 42.
81. Ibid., p. 46.
82. Ibid.
83. Wendy Grieder, US National CCMS Coordinator, US Environmental Protection Agency, 'Memorandum: Status of the NATO/CCMS Program', May 10, 1993 and 'NATO Works with Cooperation Partners on Environmental Problems', *NATO Review*, April 1993, p. 34, see also, Jean-Marie Cadiou, 'The Environmental Legacy of the Cold War', *NATO Review*, October, 1993, pp. 33–5.
84. Ibid.
85. Ibid.
86. NATO, 'Interim Report of CCMS Pilot Study on Defense Environmental Expectations', (ASG/SEA 93) 85, February 17, 1993, Brussels, NATO, March 25, 1993. See also, Gary D. Vest and Robert Coles, co-chairs Executive Board and Sub-Groups I, II and III of the pilot study, 'Meeting Minutes', NATO School (SHAPE), August 25–27, 1993.
87. US Army Corps of Engineers, 'Peacetime Engagement and National Assistance in Eastern Europe and the Soviet Republics' (draft working paper), Washington, DC, November 21, 1991.
88. Randy Ridley, 'DNA is Key To Nunn–Lugar', *Defense News*, November 8–14, 1993, p. 24 and Kurt Tarnoff, *The Environment As a Foreign Policy Issue*, Washington: Congressional Research Service, The Library of Congress, November 25, 1991, p. CRS–13.
89. Odelia Funke, 'Environmental Dimensions of Security: The Former Soviet Bloc Nations', Paper prepared for The International Studies Association Meeting, Atlanta, GA, March 31 – April 4, 1992, pp. 17–18. See also, Government Accounting Office, *Former Soviet Union: Assistance by the United States and Other Donors*, Washington: US Government Printing Office (GAO/NSIAD–93–101), December 1992.

17. Environmental Security: Geopolitics, Ecology and the New World Order

Simon Dalby

ENVIRONMENTAL (IN)SECURITY

In the February 1994 issue of *The Atlantic Monthly* magazine, under the alarming title of 'The Coming Anarchy', Robert Kaplan (1994) paints a depressing picture of the twenty-first century. He argues that in many parts of the world the political organization of the nation state will come apart. Brutal warfare, of the sort seen recently in Somalia and Liberia, is likely to become endemic in many parts of the planet. Indeed crime and warfare may become indistinguishable. Overpopulation will reduce many cities to overcrowded chaos in what will soon no longer be possible to call the 'developing' world. Many of these people will be immigrants from an increasingly devastated and eroded rural environment. Deforestation will continue in the futile search for croplands and cash until there are no forests left to cut. Disease will spread uncontrolled through the rising urban populations. Shortage of resources and pressure of numbers will lead to political breakdown, chaos in many places and the rule of military Mafiosi.

Depressing as this picture is, Kaplan is not alone in his concern about environmental degradation and resource shortages as a key ingredient to political insecurity in the immediate future. Since the end of the Cold War numerous discussions of the themes of the interrelationships of environment and political conflict have appeared in the academic and policy journals, as well as in think-tank publications and the popular press. It was also a theme at the Rio summit in 1992 (Doran, 1993). This discussion of 'environmental security', as the discourse is now often known, raises very many questions about how both security and environment are understood (Myers, 1993; Prins (ed.), 1993). These questions go to the heart of governance in the post-Cold War order. The possible answers point to many difficult and disturbing contradictions in contemporary political thinking.

Environment issues are obviously linked to many 'North–South' issues. International economic development, as practiced for the last few decades, has failed much of the world's population. In the 1980s, when the 'debt crisis' aggravated matters, the global pattern of 'development' led to the annual net transfer of billions of dollars from poor to rich states (George, 1991). In many current cases the export of resources, to pay the interest on dubiously negotiated and acquired debts, is simultaneously removing potential wealth, and degrading the environments that could produce wealth in the future for forthcoming generations. The 'structural adjustment' policies of international financial agencies have aggravated the condition of poor people in numerous places. The processes of economic change they induced have rendered women particularly insecure (Mackenzie, 1993). Viewed in a comprehensive manner, such issues clearly suggest that if security is to be provided for all, then dealing with international insecurity will also require rethinking of international economic arrangements (Middleton, O'Keefe and Moyo, 1993).

This chapter tackles the conceptual and political difficulties raised by this discourse of environmental security. First it briefly reviews the debate about expanding and reformulating notions of national and international security in the 1980s, arguments that are the precursors of the contemporary literature on environmental security. But the new interpretations of security have faced an uphill struggle for acceptance in policy-making circles, and among established political elites, in many states. Traditional Cold War interpretations of security in geopolitical terms have often been very persistent. Indeed, as the bulk of this chapter argues, the most dangerous contradictions in current thinking may be precisely where new ideas of environmental dangers are uncritically linked to older geopolitical conceptions of security. The implications of these debates for environmental governance are profound; the chapter closes with some reflections on these themes, relating both to policy matters and to the larger conceptual issues involved.

RETHINKING SECURITY

National security, the highest expressed value of many states through the period of the Cold War, has traditionally defined threats as coming from external military organizations, or internally, from within the state in terms of subversion or the failure of law and order. The normal rationale for territorially defined states is to provide a political unit that protects citizens from both internal and international threats to their physical safety. It also protects their property, while preserving and promoting the supposedly commonly held values of the community encompassed by the state. Military responses were paramount in security thinking through the Cold

War period (Buzan, 1991). But through the 1980s, while the superpower confrontation was again the focal point of international politics, many critical voices were raised. They argued both that nuclear weapon-based security was impossible, given the exceptional dangers posed by the destructive capabilities of the weapons, and also that conventional conceptions of security were far too narrowly focused.

Some authors argued that security needed to be expanded and rethought to encompass much larger concerns and include not just the welfare of the state apparatus, but the overall well-being of citizens. Threats, to which the provision of security is the response, could be more widely interpreted to include hazards not directly attributable to foreign military activity. Richard Ullman (1983, p. 133) suggested that

> A more useful (although certainly not conventional) definition might be: a threat to national security is an action or sequence of events that (1) threatens drastically and over a relatively brief span of time to degrade the quality of life for inhabitants of a state, or, (2) threatens significantly to narrow the range of policy choices available to the government of a state or to private, non governmental entities (persons, groups, corporations) within the state.

The 1973 oil crisis had somewhat changed the traditional Western understanding of security as limited to military, espionage and sometimes economic matters. Security of fuel supply rapidly became a matter for consideration in security discussions. But in many of these expansions of the ambit of security the geopolitical and military focus remained paramount. Concern over fuel supplies easily articulated with traditional concerns for trade route vulnerabilities in wartime, and with the military exigencies of ensuring supply lines (Haglund, 1986). Other resource availability questions followed, but discussions of ecological matters were not central to security concerns. Important bilateral resource and pollution issues such as water supply and acid rain have not traditionally been explicitly included in security discussions.

Other researchers and political leaders, in particular through the work of the Independent Commission on Disarmament and Security Issues (1982), have promoted the understanding of security as 'common security'. This approach emphasizes the interconnectedness of the fate of citizens in one state with those of other states in an interdependent state system armed with modern weapons. In addition, non-Anglo-Saxon understandings of security, including the Third World concerns with domestic instability, ethnic conflict and development difficulties have worked to broaden the ambit of security concerns in academic discussions (Job (ed.), 1992). These considerations have also extended security thinking to matters of human rights and questions of the rights of indigenous peoples, and to other matters (Klare and Thomas (eds), 1991). More strictly military interpretations have also tackled matters of the destructiveness of nuclear war, and the possibilities of rethinking military strategies in quite drastic ways, not least to limit the devastation to all concerned in contemporary military conflicts (Booth (ed.), 1991). Following some hints in the direction of linking environment and security in the 'Brundtland Report' (World Commission on Environment and Development, 1987), academic analyses have investigated the relationships between international politics and environmental issues (Rowlands and Greene (eds), 1991; Kakonen (ed.), 1992; Lipschutz and Conca (eds), 1993). Peace researchers have also investigated these matters from a number of perspectives (Finger, 1992; Brock, 1992a).

Increasingly, and in particular in the US since the end of the Cold War, interdependence in economic affairs and a growing recognition of the common fate of humanity in the face of global environmental degradation have extended perceptions of the political limits of security (Mische, 1989; 1992; Mathews, 1989). The armaments of Cold War, the nuclear forces and heavily armed conventional forces of superpower confrontation, are useless to deal with rising sea levels, droughts in crop-growing areas, and refugees displaced because of environmental degradation. Indeed some authors point to the role of military buildups in eroding national security by accumulating the ability to destroy but not improving the ability to defend (Renner, 1989). But these reformulations stretch the conventional views of what properly constitutes security and the role of states to very considerable lengths. These new ideas have influenced some policy-making in Europe and the US, and have undoubtedly shaped the rhetoric of many politicians anxious to court the 'green' vote. But despite some limited success in matters such as international agreements on measures to protect the ozone layer (Benedick, 1991), they face an uphill struggle to influence the course of foreign policy-making on matters that have entrenched economic constituencies.

THE PERSISTENCE OF GEOPOLITICS

Traditional realist and geopolitical interpretations of national and international security have been very persistent despite the rapid changes in the world polity in the last five years (George, 1993; Gusterson, 1993). This 'persistence of geopolitics' has immediate political consequences in terms of the continuation of the strategic and military interpretations of international politics after the Cold War; interpretations that may not run in parallel with the aspirations of those who argue for the extension of conventional understandings of security to encompass various 'green' themes. If the resistance to drastic restructuring of the US military in the early tenure of the Clinton administration is anything to go by, it suggests that the power of the military to define the terms of political strategy is very considerable (Borosage, 1993–94). The persistence of geopolitical thinking also acts as a powerful constraint on how the global political economy operates.

Geopolitics is a term with many meanings; its use here refers simultaneously to the traditional interpretations of it in terms of the struggle for world power, and the arguments that geographical factors are important in that struggle (Parker, 1985). But it is also related to the assumptions in contemporary security thinking that assume that geographical space has to be divided up, surveyed, monitored and patrolled to control political and military developments in the interests of states (Rifkin, 1991). Beyond this geopolitics is also a practice of statecraft that uses popularly understood geographical terms to define the world of foreign policy options in specific ways (O'Tuathail and Agnew, 1992). The argument in what follows deliberately conflates these meanings, because they are usually intimately (but uncritically) linked in discussions of security and foreign policy in Western states. Security is usually understood in spatial terms at a variety of scales (Dalby, 1990).

On reflection, the persistence of geopolitical thinking in Western powers is not all that surprising. The political events of the last five years have widely been interpreted as a victory for NATO policies of geopolitical confrontation with communism. Interpretations suggest the triumph of liberal democracy and 'the end of history' in Francis Fukuyama's (1992) provocative phrase. These interpretations ignore the alternative interpretations of the end of the Cold War which emphasize that the key to explaining those events was a drastic reconsideration of security policy in Moscow (Dalby, 1993). This argument suggests that the Gorbachev administration decided to abandon reliance on military power to offer security and reformulate security as a political option requiring an appreciation of the economic and ecological dangers of cold war-type militarism (MccGwire, 1991). This in turn led to their agreements on nuclear forces and the dismantling of their alliances in Eastern Europe. The subsequent implosion of Soviet power has obscured these developments and provided powerful justification to arguments that the events of the late 1980s were proof of the superiority of capitalism and liberal democracy. The military victory by the American-led coalition in the Gulf war in 1991 only added to this interpretation of events. Such 'triumphalism', by according 'victory' or 'vindication' to the US and NATO, works to obscure many of the political and economic difficulties that result from the uncontrolled expansion of the Western model of development.

The persistence of the focus on geopolitics concentrates attention on external matters rather than internal changes as the response to changing international circumstances. It also operates to construct boundaries in ways that both grants them permanence and minimizes responsibilities towards societies within those boundaries. Matters of economic interaction are relegated in importance as military determinations define roles and responsibilities. Geopolitical specifications of boundaries are also tied to discourses of moral certitude, where the power doing the defining of the political situation can, by using territorial boundaries pronounce on legitimate and illegitimate policy actions (Campbell, 1993).

Concentrating on 'external' events also acts to reduce 'domestic' responsibility for actions that happen 'abroad'. They also operate to assign blame to foreigners, and sometimes to justify the use of violence and war as legitimate policies. 'Internal' matters are often defined as being irrelevant to the policy options available. This is one of the clearest lessons of the Gulf War. The United States will remain vulnerable to, or indeed increase substantially its vulnerability to, political developments in the Gulf if it does not move to conserve oil consumption. Given the expected decline in non-OPEC oil sources towards the end of the 1990s this is particularly important. 'If the United States wants to be serious about reducing the degree of its political vulnerability to domestic and international upheaval in the Middle East, then it must raise taxes on gasoline, motor fuels, petroleum products or carbon emissions' (Inman, Nye, Perry and Smith, 1992, pp. 67–8). Constructing the Gulf solely in terms of a geopolitical arena of importance because of its supplies of petroleum ignores the 'demand' side of the energy equation. As Amory and Hunter Lovins (1982) long ago pointed out, the easiest option for US foreign policy in the Gulf is energy-efficient automobiles and roof insulation in North American buildings.

Classical geopolitical theorizing was also, in part, about maintaining Western supremacy over global politics (Parker, 1985). This chapter also argues that in its various manifestations contemporary geopolitical discourse operates to construct 'security' and geopolitical 'order' in ways that act to perpetuate this domination. This extends to contemporary discussions of environmental matters in a number of important ways. These limitations are clear in the discussions of global environmental security; and have important implications for policy in both the 'North' and the 'South'. If these matters are to be discussed in terms of security it is also vital to investigate the sources of environmental conflict in the underdeveloped world, rather than accept the often ethnocentrically tainted conventional interpretations about environment and economic growth.

Many recent critical writings have suggested that much of the 'Northern' discourse on global environmental problems ignores these issues and consequently misses much of importance in policy formulation (Centre for Science and Environment, 1992). The critics have also pointed to the inequities of the global political economy in which 'Northern' states are responsible for producing the majority of greenhouse gas emissions (Agarwal and Narain, 1991), not to mention acid rain, radioactive and toxic wastes and chlorofluorocarbons (CFCs). At the Rio 'Earth Summit ' these themes were clear in the stances of some 'Southern' representatives who were obviously reluctant to sign up for global policies to solve a problem predominantly caused by 'Northern' states who were better able to pay for the perceived cleanup costs.

This persistence of geopolitics in the face of numerous calls for rethinking security in fairly drastic terms leads to a number of political and interpretative dilemmas in discussions about environmental security. Reformulated notions of security are always in danger of co-optation by the more conventional interpretations (Dalby, 1992a). The political and policy options resulting from different interpretations of 'security' are often dramatically different. The following section outlines six loosely defined, and overlapping, dilemmas, to try to clarify what is at stake in these debates. Clarifying these matters provides insight into the complexity of contemporary environmental governance, and suggests that thinking in terms of security may well be much less than helpful.

DILEMMAS OF ENVIRONMENTAL SECURITY

Environmental themes in international politics were one of the foci of the UNCED conference in Rio de Janeiro in June 1992. But the absence of very substantive widespread agreements on many issues at the conference suggests that widespread political tensions exist over matters of environment (Middleton, O'Keefe and Moyo, 1993). These are, in many ways, clearest when viewed through the 'lenses' of security analysis. They relate to matters of the global consequence of industrialization; questions of 'development' of agriculture and renewable resources in many underdeveloped states; matters of how power and control supposedly provide security; ethnocentric and developmentalist perspectives on the relationship of environment to development; the attribution of the status of a 'global problem' to many issues that have more specific causes; and finally, to matters of the militarization of environmental issues and the role of the military in 'environmental security'.

A.   Industrial Development vs. Environmental Security

The United States-led coalition that defeated the Iraqi forces in 1991 in the Gulf was clearly there for more than simply concerns about the sovereignty of Kuwait. The war was also, if indirectly, about the availability of oil supplies for the world's industrial states. Concerns about the damage done by oil spills and the pollution from oil-well fires alerted Western publics to the damage that technological warfare can do to the environment. The much bigger ecological question raised during the war was what exactly was being secured by the coalition's military actions. The American way of life was referred to on a number of occasions in the public discussions of the war's rationale.

But it is precisely the Western world's oil consumption that is the largest contributor to anthropogenic greenhouse gas emissions. These gases are what are causing climate changes, which in turn are probably going to imperil agricultural productivity, rainfall patterns and related water supplies, and weather conditions generally (Mintzer (ed.), 1992). If what is secured is the Western world's pattern of fossil fuel consumption, which indirectly causes climate changes, then this form of 'security' seems dubious indeed (Dalby, 1992a). If the climate changes aggravate refugee problems and promote migration on ever larger scales, insecurity will become the condition for many more people (Weiner, 1992–93; Woehlcke, 1992). What then is being secured?

Understanding security in geopolitical terms as relating to the supply of fuel and resources to modern economies offers one form of security, at least in the short term. But it promises long-term difficulties in terms of global environmental change with all the political instabilities that are likely to ensue. The alternative is to focus on the impact of fossil fuel consumption and argue that the environmental integrity of the biosphere is what should be 'secured'. A very different series of policy options then come into play. Conservation of energy and recycling resources then look like the way to proceed.   Slowing fossil fuel consumption by reducing its use and developing renewable alternatives are more appropriate policies, which, as noted above, have the added benefit of reducing the perceived necessity for Western military interventions in the Middle East, or elsewhere, to protect fuel and resource supplies.

The differences between these two foci of concern for security are very considerable. The much celebrated Brundtland Report on *Our Common Future* (World Commission, 1987), fudged the issue, arguing that economic growth was essential to generating the necessary wealth to solve environmental problems (see Visvanathan, 1991). But the dilemmas of development and security are not limited to this, possibly the most obvious, concern.

B. Enclosing the Commons

In January 1994, in apparent confirmation of Kaplan's (1994) concerns about war and environmental degradation, peasants rose in rebellion in southern Mexico to protest against the economic conditions brought about by years of 'economic development' in the Chiapas region. Development that had brought poverty and the marginalization of numerous people was directly linked, they argued, to plans for an expansion of trading links with the rest of North America. Questions of the ownership of land were also raised in a manner that resonates with other arguments from around the world about the enclosure of common land, and the control of forests and other ecosystems, that provide subsistence necessities to peoples on the margins, at best, of a cash economy (*The Ecologist*, 1993).

Numerous critical articles about development have pointed to the ecological costs of policies of modernization which operate to exploit resources in underdeveloped parts of the world in the name of progress and development (Barbosa, 1993). The poor and indigenous people of many areas have lost access to forests and other resources that supply survival foods and medicines (Shiva, 1988). In resisting the encroachment of modern agriculture or forestry practices, the poor and dispossessed often become the target of security forces that see their opposition as a challenge to the development of the modern state that, according to conventional security thinking, is essential to the provision of security for the state's population. But if the practices of enclosing land and dividing up ecosystems into privately worked plots undermines the integrity of those ecosystems, as it has so obviously done in the Amazon and elsewhere (Hecht and Cockburn, 1990), then the question of what exactly modernity is securing once again is obvious.

In the case of the tropical rain forests this is particularly the case to Northern commentators, not just because indigenous peoples are victims of the near genocidal results, but also because the rain forests are so biologically diverse. Fear of the continued massive loss of genetic diversity, potential food plants and medicines alerts activists to campaign for the preservation of forest lands. But it has also become very clear in the case of the Amazon, as elsewhere, that doing so requires rethinking 'development' and the political order that it supports in quite drastic ways (Guimaraes, 1991). Once again the question of what is rendered secure has to be asked. Is the object that is secured the ecological integrity of valuable environments, or the political order that benefits in the short run from their destruction? Environmentalists fear the latter, but hope for the former. The priorities of many development agencies and their military supporters in many underdeveloped states are often very different.

C. Security as Power and Control

Understanding security in geopolitical terms is closely related to the construction of political order in terms of carefully demarcated spaces, surveillance of these spaces and the threat to use violence to maintain the spatial order of modernity. At the small scale these patterns are clear in terms of property and ownership of sections of geographical space. At the larger scale they are essential to the operation of political order in terms of territorial states (Dalby, 1992b). The possibilities of political organization are limited by these geopolitical specifications of the possibilities of community within nation states, and at the smaller scale, within the administrative regions of the state. Domination and control, and the ability to police those spaces with the use of violence if necessary, are taken for granted in conventional analyses of security and the role of the modern state.

But these assumptions about security are vulnerable to critique from two directions. Viewed through feminist lenses these ideas of security suggest that particular 'masculinist' notions of force and violence are in play denying the possibilities for political arrangements not based so explicitly on force. Security provided by force and spatial demarcations of political realms, has, so the feminist critique argues, rendered numerous people insecure (Peterson, 1992; Tickner, 1992). During the Cold War security was widely presented as protection and safety, but the threat of nuclear destruction undermined the assertions of safety. In the process it called into question even the possibility of the technological provision of security.

At the smaller scale personal safety is not secured by these arrangements in many societies. Questions of livelihood and environmental sustainability in underdeveloped states, many of which are facing the financial constraints of 'structural adjustments', are not easily understood in the terms of Cold War security discourses. Neither can global climate change be controlled or dealt with by these ways of thinking and acting. Rethinking power and security by looking at it through feminist 'lenses' suggests focusing on structural inequities, and the social relationships of both domination and cooperation, as a better approach to understanding the social dynamics of conflict, and the processes of environmental degradation (Seager, 1993; Mies and Shiva, 1993). Getting away from competition and the dynamics of polarization and focusing on diplomacy, cooperation and the construction of communities across spatial boundaries offers a very different view of security.

So too does an attempt to formulate the principles of security if one looks to ecology for models. Security, understood as protecting the integrity of biological systems suggests a language of recycling, adaptation, built-in redundancy, constant change, mutualism and cooperation (Dalby, 1992b). This is a far cry from conventional matters of security doctrine which draw from metaphors of physics rather than ecology. But looked at in these terms conventional notions of security seem anathema to advocates of environmental security, understood in the sense of protecting ecological integrity by appropriate social arrangements.

D. Ethnocentrism and Global Managerialism

Aggravating the geopolitical difficulties of clearly seeing the links between conventional notions of security and environmental problems are the persistent problems of ethnocentrism. A particular problem results from the presuppositions, in many policy discussions about global environmental issues, that environmental issues are basically similar the world over (Broad and Cavanagh, 1993). 'Developmentalist' reasoning often suggests that the underdeveloped states are merely at an earlier stage of development than the states of the 'North'. The, at best highly questionable, assumptions that pollution is a price of economic progress, and that pollution controls are an added cost to production, are often drawn on to argue that environmental protection is a luxury that the rich can afford but the poor states of the world cannot. Thus the environment is understood as an externality to economic activity. While this model of environmental matters might have had some veracity in industrialized states in the 1970s, it manages to obscure many important factors involved in the relations between development, conflict and environment. Not least among these is the important role that export-oriented forestry and agriculture in some parts of the Third World play in degrading soils, introducing pesticide hazards and displacing subsistence agricultural populations (Faber, 1993).

The literature challenging conventional 'Northern' (and some 'Southern' elite) understandings of development, security and progress is vast and fast growing (Amin, 1990; George, 1991; Lummis, 1991). A summary of this debate is beyond the scope of this chapter (see Sachs (ed.) 1992, 1993). But a number of themes are particularly germane to the discussion of environmental security. Some of the worst environmental disasters in underdeveloped states are not a result of pollution *per se*, but of damage to renewable resources due to logging and inappropriate agricultural practices, many of which are adopted as short-term survival strategies by displaced people. The destruction of ecosystems due to damming rivers, mining, logging and monoculture plantation-style farming, are of greater concern than industrial pollution in many developing countries (Shiva, 1988). Environmental degradation is occurring as a direct consequence of the type of development being practiced. These points are also overlooked by many advocates of development in the underdeveloped states, convinced that modernity beckons if only their 'backwardness' can be overcome. The argument that pollution is a temporary, unfortunate, byproduct of the process of development misses the point that the resource base, and hence the livelihood of many of the poorest people in these states, is the direct casualty of conventional development strategies. Renewable resources, land, water, forests and soil form the immediate survival necessities for the rural poor in much of the underdeveloped world; they are being destroyed at alarming rates. As recent research makes abundantly clear, environmentally induced conflicts in developing states are very often linked directly to the destruction or expropriation of these resources (Homer-Dixon, 1993).

Misunderstanding these problems, and misunderstanding the inter-connection between modes of development and the potential for political conflict that can spill over state boundaries, may operate to maintain the political *status quo* in the short run, but it does little to alleviate the suffering of the poorest people of the planet. Neither does it get at the roots of biodiversity loss, tropical deforestation or soil erosion; all matters of long-term concern for the 'security' of populations in the developing states. In parallel to these conceptual difficulties conventional scientific discourse on global environmental issues also often obscures the necessity to reform the global economy as a step in preserving the natural fecundity of the planet (Taylor and Buttel, 1992).

E.   The Responsibility for 'Global' Security

Constructions of 'the North' and 'the South' are conflations of enormously diverse political and economic systems which usually obscure much more than they reveal. Important also is the geopolitical construction of such entities as separate. The boundary-making practices of these constructions suggest an impermeability and hence a lack of responsibility for what occurs on the other side of this boundary (Campbell, 1992, 1993). They also suggest that what happens internally has little impact on external developments, a powerful ideological understanding that obscures the impacts of the global political economy across international boundaries. Thus the resource flows of timber, minerals and agricultural products, which form important components of the resource base of Northern states, are often not seen as being related to environmental destruction. This is particularly true when such activities are seen as essential to the processes of economic development.

Some themes, like global atmospheric change and ozone depletion, in the literature on environmental security are clearly global in nature, in that they are physical changes to the ecosphere in its totality. While these phenomena are clearly global in scope it is important to note that their impacts may vary quite widely. Ozone depletion tends to be more serious at higher latitudes. The predictions for global climate change also suggest that the largest changes here will also come in the higher latitudes, although sea-level changes in particular may impact tropical states; Bangladesh being only the most obvious candidate. In terms of numbers of species the largest current biodiversity losses are occurring in the tropical rain forests. Some residents of these states argue that these forests, and their biological fecundity, are the sole possession of their peoples, rather than the common heritage of humanity. Thus they invoke the traditional language of national security and sovereignty to construct environmentalist policies as a threat (deLemos, 1990). Other phenomena which are included in environmental security discussions in general, such as decertification, or conflicts over specific water supplies, are often much more localized in their occurrence and limited in their potential for international, if not intranational political conflict. They are nonetheless of major importance to many people in many different states.

It is also important to note that the causes of environmental changes are in many cases driven by Northern industrial activities. Given the claim that these matters are defined as global problems by those in the North it is not surprising that many in the South object to being asked to pay the price for 'fixing' the problems. Recent research suggests that in the event of substantial global climate change due to carbon dioxide increases in the atmosphere, the underdeveloped parts of the world are likely to have greatest difficulty maintaining crop production (Rosenzweig and Parry, 1994). It is not surprising that many advocates of the poor in the Third World argue that the rich states in the North should foot the bill, and that distinctions should be made between luxury consumption in the North and subsistence needs of peasant farmers in the South (Agarwal and Narain, 1991; McCully, 1991). It is also crucial to bear in mind, at least in the case of CFCs and the ozone issue, that these substances are produced by a small number of corporations in particular factories in particular states. Suggesting that the causes of this particular problem are in some sense global is to obscure the specific responsibilities of Northern states and corporations operating in their territories (Shiva, 1993).

F.   Militarism and the Environment

Considerations of environmental security have often suggested a role for the military in the preservation of environmental systems. More specifically some suggestions have been made that the military become 'super park wardens', enforcing bans on hunting and using sophisticated remote-sensing equipment and intelligence technology to police ecological reserves (Butts, 1992). These proposals are a logical outgrowth of the proposals to 'convert' the post-Cold War military of many states into more contemporarily useful institutions. However the critics of park-style conservation approaches to environmental problems are quick to point out that these approaches to environmental protection are rarely adequate either to protect 'nature' or deal with the social problems that endanger the ecosystems that are supposedly being protected. Indeed the problems of park-style proposals and the ideas of debt for nature 'swaps', that have been in vogue in recent years, is precisely that they fail to deal with the poverty and lack of resources that many in the underdeveloped world face.   Imposing conservation efforts without local consent and support is unlikely to be successful in the long run because of the failure to tackle the poverty that leads to environmental degradation (Byers, 1992). With the support of local communities, who have an economic interest in maintaining specific ecosystems, the need for a military-type approach or 'imposed conservation' is often eliminated.

Other criticisms of this approach argue that it makes little sense to use an institution that has such an appalling environmental record to protect the environment (Renner, 1989, 1991). The legacy of Cold War military environmental destruction is part of what some writers on environmental security see as the problem of environmental security. The environmental legacy of Cold War nuclear test ranges, weapons-making facilities and abandoned toxic wastes at military facilities in many states is an important aspect of the issue (Ehrlich and Birks, 1990; Davis, 1993; Feshbach and Friendly, 1992). Given the military's normal exclusion from environmental regulations in many states, under some variation of the theme of sovereign immunity, surely, so the argument goes, this is the very last organization that should be in the environmental protection business (Finger, 1991a).

An extension of this argument suggests that the institutional ethos and structure of many military organizations makes them unsuitable candidates for doing environmental jobs. Institutions concerned with secrecy and centralized control are not appropriate social organizations for dealing with environmental issues (Deudney, 1992). The question then is whether, in the process of extending the ambit of threats requiring a military response, one isn't militarizing society rather than dealing more directly with social difficulties. As Lothar Brock (1992b, p. 98) writes 'Defining environmental issues in terms of security risks is in itself a risky operation. . . . we may end up contributing more to the militarization of environmental politics than to the demilitarization of security politics'.

All this suggests that the military of the future ought to be limited to doing its traditional tasks of narrowly defined defense, while environmental agencies are given responsibility for environmental monitoring, cleanups and regulation. Decentralization and sensitivity to local conditions are also important. Subsidiarity, to use the European phrase for tackling problems at the appropriate scale, is clearly important. Openness and democratic oversight are also important factors in environmental politics. In her analysis of innovative arrangements for managing common property resources, Elinor Ostrom (1990) makes it clear that these work best where stakeholders are openly involved in the processes of monitoring and decision-making. The legitimacy crisis faced by nuclear power in many states can easily be traced, in part, to its traditional penchant for secrecy. The lesson to be learned here is that environmental matters are profoundly political, not technical matters that can be dealt with by unaccountable 'experts'.

ENVIRONMENT OR SECURITY?

Security implies safety and predictability for some human group, organization or state. Because it refers to widely held personal and political aspirations the term retains considerable ideological force in policy debate. Indeed it is precisely this attribute that has led a number of authors from widely differing political persuasions to advocate linking it with environmental matters. In its dominant formulation as national security, the concept has historically had considerable political efficacy in justifying military preparations, espionage and many of the less savory activities of states. But the ideological power of the theme of security also lies in its ability to obscure the specificity of security. Where national security has been the highest expressed value of state, it has often worked to cloak the operation of security for a political elite, a security which has often rendered the rest of the population insecure in various ways (Job (ed.), 1992). In the case of underdeveloped states whose governments have been run by the military, or dominated by military considerations, 'security' has all too often been used as the rationale for internal repression and violent policies to eradicate political opposition (Ball, 1991).

In the same way environmental security may often refer to security for some and obscure specifically who is rendered insecure. In so far as environmental security is understood in fairly conventional terms to refer to international conflict triggered by some environmental change or disaster, then the question of specifically who suffers is easily occluded in the considerations of the military dimensions of the situation. Ethnocentric assumptions about the world, combined with the geopolitical premises of conventional security thinking, thus offer a dangerous policy framework for future environmental policies if they are couched in the jargon of environmental security. This policy framework will not deal with the most pressing problems of the early twenty-first century, in the sense of alleviating them and easing the plight of the victims of current environmental degradation. The danger here lies in the possibility that these policies might succeed in maintaining the political *status quo* in ways that isolate Northern publics from the already increasing violence in the developing states that concerns Kaplan (1994) in his recent *Atlantic Monthly* article, but which does nothing to facilitate the improvement, or the long-term sustainability, of the ecological bases of these places. Such strategies may shore up the legitimacy of state structures in the short run, but may very well aggravate environmental matters in the longer run (Finger, 1991b).

In combination these trends pose the troubling possibilities of Northern states acting to impose their will on the international community in the name of environmental survival. Already a number of writers have advocated converting the role of NATO to deal with a wide range of security threats including environmental matters (Springer, 1991). Manfred Worner, NATO's Secretary General, is on record as arguing that

> [W]e are increasingly broadening our security notion to include both new military threats and the non-military challenges that come to us from the Third World. The immense conflict potential that is building up in Third World countries, characterized by growing wealth differentials, an exploding demography, climate shifts and the prospect of environmental disaster, combined with the resource conflicts of the future, cannot be left out of our security calculations, no matter how we translate our broader analysis in operational aspects in the longer term. (Worner, 1991, 103–4)

But Worner is clear that the management of the threats to global security will clearly come from the West and Japan. They will provide the wealth and supervise the management of problems in the twenty-first century, hopefully in increasing concert with the powers of Eastern Europe. Because the NATO states and Japan between them generate more than half the world's wealth:

> That places a tremendous responsibility upon them for managing their own mutual relationships harmoniously as a precondition for managing the larger affairs of our world. The secret of security in the future is that it is increasingly indivisible and that we all share the responsibilities for its management. (Worner, 1991, 104–5)

The ideological force of such arguments in the face of 'environmental threats' could be very considerable. After all who could possibly be 'against' protecting the earth. But if such 'global managerialism' were to run into opposition from Southern states the possibilities of military intervention and political coercion, all in the name of environmental security, are not too hard to imagine.

ENVIRONMENTAL GOVERNANCE

There are then considerable political difficulties in extending security to encompass ecological matters without drastically reformulating the term. Military threats are relatively easy to understand, and very easy to mobilize populations against. They are countered by specific (mainly military) institutions which usually have clear priority in national government spending in times of national crisis or war. Environmental threats are usually less direct than traditional military threats. Their diffuseness, their incremental evolution, and their potential for unforeseen synergistic effects, lead to many difficulties in dealing directly with environmental matters in the terms of national security (Prins (ed.), 1993). But the questions raised by discussions of environmental security challenge conventional modes of governance even more profoundly.

Government priorities with short-term economic performance often override long-term ecological considerations. At least in the liberal democracies, policy debate is often limited to discussing things that can be formulated in monetary quantities. Policy decisions in domestic affairs deal with discrete linear decisions tied to budgetary allocations and defined performance criteria. Conventional 'realist' thinking in international affairs operates in terms of narrowly construed interests, balances of power, relative positioning of states in the world order and a focus on GNP growth to ensure that the resources for military preparation are available. Environmental issues cannot be tackled like either financial policy decision-making or realism in foreign affairs (Prins, 1990). Ecology is about interconnections and circular causation, indirect effects and long time scales. As a result, the political mechanisms that have traditionally dealt with decision-making in the state system are often not adequate. Conventional geopolitical reasoning is not appropriate for dealing with environmental issues on the global scale. For ecological issues multilateral negotiations to support and strengthen unilateral initiatives, hopefully based on principles of enlightened self-interest, or perhaps more specifically, in Gwyn Prins's (1990) term 'selfish altruism', where long-term sustainability is preferred over short-term gratification, are more appropriate. But these patterns of thinking have not been dominant in post-Cold War international politics.

It has often been harder for states to mobilize populations around concerns for population growth or pollution, or short-term energy consumption reductions, which require a less focused and more diffuse series of economic and social changes, since these are not so immediately threatening to individuals. In addition, the causes of ecological disruption are often domestic, making them a matter of internal political struggle, rather than presenting the threat in terms of an external 'enemy' against whom it is easy to mobilize. Nonetheless this difficulty seemed to be lessening in the late 1980s and early 1990s; the concern for environmental issues being reinforced by a new wave of international concern and the emergence of a green consumer movement. Indeed it seemed that in the early 1990s public opinion was often well ahead of government action and attention to these themes.

But this combination of heightened concern over very complex matters ironically leads to the danger of thinking about many environmental issues in terms of security issues. Precisely because environmental threats are more diffuse but action to deal with them is demanded, the temptation may well lie in focusing on specific aspects of environmental dangers that can be 'blamed' on some group, state or group of states in the traditional patterns of geopolitical reasoning. 'Their' deforestation endangers 'our' atmosphere. 'Their' CFC plants are threatening the ozone layer, therefore 'their' production must be stopped. 'Their' environmental policies are producing refugees which threaten 'our' society and which 'we' have to deal with, therefore political changes must be made 'there'. These patterns of geopolitical reasoning ignore the cross-boundary linkages and the complexity of environmental interconnections, but are politically potent precisely because of their oversimplifications.

Manfred Worner's comments raise similar important questions about the role of environmental governance on the part of both the United States and the European Union. But they do so on the largest scale and in ways that only partly refer to the more frequently discussed matters of internal environmental policies. Obviously the possibilities for reorienting the economy of Europe on more sustainable lines are important for global greenhouse emissions and other pollution problems (Bremer (ed.), 1992). While the European Union offers considerable potential in dealing with cross-border environmental management questions, larger issues of its relations with the rest of the world may be much more important for questions of 'environmental security'. What is at stake in Manfred Worner's discussion is simply whether the most powerful states will operate to protect their own 'turf' from the consequences of environmental degradation in ways that are little concerned with the larger global scale of environmental problems. If the philosophy of global managerialism, or control of the planet's resources and environments by the rich and powerful, albeit dressed up in the ideological garb of ecological universalism, is advocated, then questions of human rights and democracy globally may very well be sacrificed (Hildyard, 1993). Isolationist policies that operate on the assumption that what happens in distant parts of the world is of little concern to the citizens of developed states, is as Kaplan (1994) implies, but never quite says, a very dangerous gamble.

The geopolitical premises of policy that emphasize modern conceptions of political identity often lack a sense of responsibility for 'the Other', people and societies that are apparently not directly connected in any way to 'our' society (Levinas and Burggraeve, 1992). But the environmental insecurities of our time suggest that these geopolitical specifications of reality obscure the important interlinkages between people the world over. The challenge to governance posed by the discussions of environmental security suggest that conventional notions of security, sovereignty and limited territorially-bound responsibility lie in the way of tackling many of the most pressing problems of global politics. Solutions are not obvious; none of the more thoughtful writers on environmental security offer many. What they do offer is a clear recognition that the environmental predicament we collectively face requires the suspension of assumptions that business as usual offers adequate conceptual and political tools to tackle global problems.

REFERENCES

Agarwal, A. and S. Narain (1991), *Global Warming in an Unequal World: A Case of Environmental Colonialism*, Centre for Science and Environment, New Delhi.

Amin, S. (1990), *Maldevelopment: Anatomy of a Global Failure*, Zed, London.

Ball, N. (1991), 'Militarized States in the Third World', in M.T. Klare and D.C. Thomas (eds), *World Security: Trends and Challenges at Century's End*, St. Martin's, New York, pp. 197–224.

Barbosa, L.C. (1993), 'The World System and the Destruction of the Brazilian Amazon Rain Forest', *Review*, 16(2): 215–40.

Benedick, R.E. (1991), *Ozone Diplomacy: New Directions in Safeguarding the Planet*, Harvard University Press, Cambridge, Mass.

Booth, K. (ed.) (1991), *New Thinking About Strategy and International Security*, Harper & Collins, London.

Borosage, R.L. (1993–94), 'Inventing the Threat: Clinton's Defense Budget', *World Policy Journal*, 10(4): 7–15.

Bremer, B. (ed.) (1992), *Europe by Nature: Starting Points for Sustainable Development*, Conspectus Europae, Amsterdam.

Broad, R. and J. Cavanagh (1993), 'Beyond the Myths of Rio: A New American Agenda for the Environment', *World Policy Journal*, 10(1): 65–72.

Brock, L. (1992a), 'Peace through Parks: The Environment on the Peace Research Agenda', *Journal of Peace Research*, 28(4): 407–23.

Brock, L. (1992b), 'Security Through Defending the Environment: An Illusion?', in E. Boulding (ed.), *New Agendas for Peace Research: Conflict and Security Reexamined*, Lynne Rienner, Boulder, CO, pp. 79–102.

Butts, K. (1992), 'Why the Military is Good for the Environment', paper presented at the International Studies Association annual meeting, Atlanta, April.

Buzan, B. (1991), *People States and Fear: An Agenda for International Security Studies in the Post-Cold War Era*, Lynne Rienner, Boulder.

Byers, B.A. (1992), 'Can Armies Save Parks? Armed Forces and the Conservation of Biological Diversity', paper presented at the International Studies Association annual meeting, Atlanta, April.

Campbell, D. (1992), *Writing Security: United States Foreign Policy and the Politics of Identity*, University of Minnesota Press, Minneapolis.

Campbell, D. (1993), *Politics Without Principle: Sovereignty, Ethics, and the Narratives of the Gulf War*, Lynne Rienner, Boulder.

Centre for Science and Environment (1992), 'The Centre for Science and Environment Statement on Global Environmental Democracy', *Alternatives: Social Transformation and Humane Governance*, 17(2): 261–79.

Dalby, S. (1990), *Creating the Second Cold War*, Pinter, London and Guilford, New York.

Dalby, S. (1992a), 'Security, Modernity, Ecology: The Dilemmas of Post-Cold War Security Discourse', *Alternatives: Social Transformation and Humane Governance*, 17(1): 95–134.

Dalby, S. (1992b), 'Ecopolitical Discourse: "Environmental Security", and Political Geography', *Progress in Human Geography*, 16(4): 503–22.

Dalby, S. (1993), 'Post Cold War Security in the New Europe', in John O'Loughlin and Herman van der Wusten (eds), *The New Political Geography of Eastern Europe*, Pinter, London, pp. 71–85.

Davis, M. (1993), 'Dead West: Ecocide in Marlboro Country', *New Left Review*, 200: 49–73.

deLemos, H.M. (1990), 'Amazonia: In Defence of Brazil's Sovereignty', *The Fletcher Forum of World Affairs*, 14(2): 301–12.

Deudney, D. (1992), 'The Mirage of Ecowar: The Weak Relationship Among Global Environmental Change, National Security and Interstate Violence', in I.H. Rowlands and M. Greene (eds), *Global Environmental Change and International Relations*, Macmillan, London.

Doran, P. (1993), 'The Earth Summit (UNCED): Ecology as Spectacle', *Paradigms*, 7(1): 55–65.

The Ecologist (1993), *Whose Common Future? Reclaiming the Commons*, New Society, Philadelphia.

Ehrlich, A.H. and J.W. Birks (1990), *Hidden Dangers: Environmental Consequences of Preparing for War*, Sierra Club Books, San Francisco.

Faber, D. (1993), *Environment Under Fire: Imperialism and the Ecological Crisis in Central America*, Monthly Review Press, New York.

Feshbach, Murray and Alfred Friendly (1992), *Ecocide in the USSR: Health and Nature under Siege*, Basic, New York.

Finger, M. (1991a), *Unintended Consequences of the Cold War: Global Environmental Degradation and the Military*, Syracuse University Program on the Analysis and

Resolution of Conflicts, New Views of International Security, Syracuse, Occasional Paper 10.

Finger, M. (1991b), 'The Military, The Nation State and the Environment', *The Ecologist*, 21(5): 220–25.

Finger, M. (1992), 'New Horizons for Peace Research: The Global Environment', in J. Kakonen (ed.), *Perspectives on Environmental Conflict and International Relations*, Pinter, London.

Fukuyama, F. (1992), *The End of History and the Last Man*, Random House, New York.

George, J. (1993), 'Of Incarceration and Closure: Neo-Realism and the New/Old World Order', *Millennium: Journal of International Studies*, 22(2): 197–234.

George, S. (1991), *The Debt Boomerang: How Third World Debt Harms Us All*, Westview, Boulder.

Guimaraes, R.P. (1991), *The Ecopolitics of Development in the Third World: Politics and Environment in Brazil*, Lynne Rienner, Boulder.

Gusterson, H. (1993), 'Realism and the International Order After the Cold War', *Social Research*, 60(2): 279–300.

Haglund, D. (1986), 'The New Geopolitics of Minerals', *Political Geography Quarterly*, 5(3): 221–40.

Hecht, S. and A. Cockburn (1990), *The Fate of the Forest: Developers, Destroyers and Defenders of the Amazon*, Penguin, Harmondsworth.

Hildyard, N. (1993), 'Foxes in Charge of the Chickens', in W. Sachs (ed.), *Global Ecology: A New Arena of Political Conflict*, Zed, London, pp. 22–35.

Homer-Dixon, T. (1991), 'On the Threshold: Environmental Changes as Causes of Acute Conflict', *International Security*, 16(1): 76–116.

Homer-Dixon, T. (1993), 'Across the Threshold: Empirical Evidence on Environmental Scarcities as Causes of Violent Conflict', paper presented to a conference on Environmental Change and Security, University of British Columbia, April.

Independent Commission on Disarmament and Security Issues (1982), *Common Security: A Programme For Disarmament*, Pan, London.

Inman, B.R., J.S. Nye, W.J. Perry and R.K. Smith (1992), 'Lessons from the Gulf War', *The Washington Quarterly*, 15(1): 57–73.

Job, B. (ed.) (1992), *The Insecurity Dilemma: National Security of Third World States*, Lynne Rienner, Boulder.

Kakonen, J. (ed.) (1992), *Perspectives on Environmental Conflict and International Relations*, Pinter, London.

Kaplan, Robert D. (1994), 'The Coming Anarchy', *The Atlantic Monthly*, 273(2): 44–76.

Klare, M.T. and D.C. Thomas (eds) (1991), *World Security: Trends and Challenges at Century's End*, St Martin's, New York.

Levinas, E. and R. Burggraeve (1992), 'Exteriority as the Source of Civilisation', in B. Bremer (ed.), *Europe by Nature: Starting Points for Sustainable Development*, Conspectus Europae, Amsterdam, pp. 205–21.

Lipschutz, R.D. and K. Conca (eds) (1993), *The State and Social Power in Global Environmental Politics*, Columbia University Press, New York.

Lovins, A. and L.H. Lovins (1982), *Brittle Power: Energy Strategy for National Security*, Brick House, Andover, Mass.

Lummis, C.D. (1991), 'Development Against Democracy', *Alternatives: Social Transformation and Humane Governance*, 16(1): 31–66.

Mackenzie, F. (1993), 'Exploring the Connections: Structural Adjustment, Gender and the Environment', *Geoforum*, 24(1): 71–87.

Mathews, J.T. (1989), 'Redefining Security', *Foreign Affairs*, 68(2): 162–77.

McCully, P. (1991), 'How WRI is Attempting to Shift the Blame for Global Warming', *The Ecologist*, 21(4): 157–65.

MccGwire, M. (1991), *Perestroika and Soviet National Security*, Brookings Institution, Washington.

Middleton, N., P. O'Keefe and S. Moyo (1993), *Tears of the Crocodile: From Rio to Reality in the Developing World*, Pluto, London.

Mies, M. and V. Shiva (1993), *Ecofeminism*, Zed, London.

Mintzer, I.M. (ed.) (1992), *Confronting Climate Change: Risks, Implications and Responses*, Cambridge University Press, Cambridge.

Mische, P.M. (1989), 'Ecological Security and the Need to Reconceptualise Sovereignty', *Alternatives: Social Transformation and Humane Governance*, 14(4): 389–427.

Mische, P. (1992), 'Security Through Defending the Environment: Citizens Say Yes', in E. Boulding (ed.), *New Agendas for Peace Research: Conflict and Security Reexamined*, Lynne Rienner, Boulder, pp. 103–19.

Myers, N. (1993), *Ultimate Security: The Environmental Basis of Political Stability*, Norton, New York.

Ostrom, E. (1990), *Governing the Commons: The Evolution of Institutions for Collective Action*, Cambridge University Press, Cambridge.

O'Tuathail, G. and J. Agnew (1992), 'Geopolitics and Discourse: Practical Geopolitical Reasoning in American Foreign Policy', *Political Geography*. 11(2): 190–204.

Parker, G. (1985), *Western Geopolitical Thought in the Twentieth Century*, Croom Helm, London.

Peterson, V.S. (1992), 'Security and Sovereign States: What is at Stake in Taking Feminism Seriously', in V.S. Peterson (ed.), *Gendered States: Feminist (Re)visions of International Relations Theory*, Lynne Rienner, Boulder, pp. 31–64.

Prins, G. (1990), 'Politics and the Environment', *International Affairs*, 66(4): 711–30.

Prins, G. (ed.) (1993), *Threats Without Enemies: Facing Environmental Security*, Earthscan, London

Renner, M. (1989), *National Security: The Economic and Environmental Dimensions*, Worldwatch Institute, Washington, Worldwatch Paper 89.

Renner, M. (1991), 'Assessing the Military's War on the Environment', in L. Brown, et al., *State of the World 1991*, Norton, New York.

Rifkin, J. (1991), *Biospheric Politics: A New Consciousness for a New Century*, Crown, New York.

Rosenzweig, C. and M.L. Parry (1994), 'Potential Impact of Climate Change on World Food Supply', *Nature*, 36: 133–8.

Rowlands, I. and M. Greene (eds) (1992), *Global Environmental Change and International Relations*, Macmillan, London.

Sachs, W. (ed.) (1992), *The Development Dictionary*, Zed, London.

Sachs, W. (ed.) (1993), *Global Ecology: A New Arena of Political Conflict*, Zed, London.

Seager, J. (1993), *Earth Follies: Coming to Feminist Terms with the Global Environmental Crisis*, Routledge, London.

Shiva, V. (1988), *Staying Alive: Women, Ecology and Development*, Zed, London.

Shiva, V. (1993), 'The Greening of Global Reach', in W. Sachs (ed.), *Global Ecology: A New Arena of Political Conflict*, Zed, London, pp. 149–56.

Springer, A.L. (1991), 'Protecting the Environment: A New Focus for the Atlantic Alliance', *Proceedings of the Academy of Political Science*, 38(1): 128–39.

Taylor, P.J. and F.H. Buttel (1992), 'How do we Know we have Global Environmental Problems? Science and the Globalization of Environmental Discourse', *Geoforum*, 23(3): 405–16.

Tickner J.A. (1992), *Gender and International Relations: Feminist Perspectives on Achieving Global Security*, Columbia University Press, New York.

Ullman, R.H. (1983), 'Redefining Security', *International Security*, 8(1): 129–53.

Visvanathan, S. (1991), 'Mrs. Brundtland's Disenchanted Cosmos', *Alternatives: Social Transformation and Humane Governance*, 16(3): 377–84.

Weiner, M. (1992–93), 'Security, Stability and International Migration', *International Security*, 17(3): 91–126.

Woehlcke, M. (1992), 'Environmental refugees', *Aussenpolitik*, 4(3): 287–96.

World Commission on Environment and Development (1987), *Our Common Future*, Oxford University Press, Oxford.

Worner, M. (1991), 'Global Security: The Challenge to NATO', in E. Grove (ed.), *Global Security: North American, European and Japanese Interdependence in the 1990s*, Brassey's, London, pp. 100–105.

Index